NEWGAMES

STRATEGIC COMPETITION IN THE PC REVOLUTION

TECHNOLOGY AND STRATEGY SERIES

Series Editors: John McGee and Howard Thomas

Forthcoming titles

BOGNER
The World Pharmaceutical Industry

BULL & THOMAS
Entrepreneurship

THOMAS, LEGGE & LOCKETT
The Frontiers and Challenges of Strategic Management

THOMAS & MCGEE
Creating Strategic Advantage

Other titles of interest

DAEMS & THOMAS
Strategic Groups, Strategic Moves, and Performance

DENNING
Making Strategic Planning Work in Practice

DOZ
Strategic Management in Multinational Companies

FREEDMAN
Strategic Planning in Major Multinational Companies

LLOYD
Entrepreneurship

MCNAMEE
Developing Strategies for Competitive Advantage

Related journals - specimen copy available on request

European Management Journal
International Business Review
Long Range Planning
Scandinavian Journal of Management

NEWGAMES

STRATEGIC COMPETITION IN THE PC REVOLUTION

John Steffens

Pergamon Press

Oxford · New York · Seoul · Tokyo

U.K.	Pergamon Press Ltd, Headington Hill Hall, Oxford, OX3 0BW, England
U.S.A.	Pergamon Press, Inc., 660 White Plains Road, Tarrytown, New York 10591-5153, U.S.A.
KOREA	Pergamon Press Korea, K.P.O. Box 315, Seoul 110-603, Korea
JAPAN	Pergamon Press Japan, Tsunashima Building Annex, 3-20-12 Yushima, Bunkyo-ku, Tokyo 113, Japan

First edition 1994

British Library Cataloguing in Publication Data

A catalogue record for this book is available from the
British Library

Library of Congress Catologing in Publication Data

Steffens, John.
Newgames : strategic competion in the PC revolution / by John Steffens.
p. cm. -- (Technology and strategy series)
Includes bibliographical references and index.
1. Microcomputers I. Title. II. Series.
QA76.5.S718   1993
338.4' 700416--dc20   93-43104

ISBN 0 08 040791 9

Printed and bound in Great Britain by Butler and Tanner Ltd, Frome

Dedicated with love and thanks
to my Mother and friends,
whose names are known to themselves.

FOREWORD

John Sculley

Chairman of the Board,
Apple Computer Inc.

Back in the late 1970s, when the personal computer industry was just beginning, Apple Computer introduced the Apple II. It had 4k of standard memory and customers used their own TV set as a monitor. At that time, there were 200,000 personal computers in the world, and if people wanted to use them, most had to go through some kind of basic — and usually painstaking — instruction.

Today, over 200,000 personal computers are manufactured in a single week. More importantly, personal computers play a central role in our lives, and have become indispensable in the educational environment. Although the pace and magnitude of change in the industry since 1980 has been nothing short of revolutionary, it is really only emblematic of a larger — macro-economic — shift that is transforming the world economy.

We are on the verge of a transition from one world economic order to another — a fundamental shift that has the potential of bringing about one of the most exciting periods in human history. For most of this century, the industrialised countries succeeded by taking natural resources out of the ground — oil, crops, and coal — adding manufacturing know-how to those resources and turning them into products. Then, they developed services around these new products.

In a very short time we have seen a dramatic change in that economic system. Today we are no longer in the Industrial Age. We are in an information-intensive, global-dynamic economy. The resources are no longer just those that come out of the ground. The resources today come out of our minds. They are ideas and information.

Although it was a combination of products and services that spawned the information revolution, the most significant of these was the personal computer. In tracing the evolution and production of the first and subsequent personal computers, Dr. Steffens examines the conditions that were necessary to transform the early personal computer from a toy for hobbyists into a force that has fundamentally changed the way the world conducts its business. His discussion of the concept he calls, "Newgames" helps to explain how it is by rethinking the basic rules of the game that organizations will succeed in the Information Age.

The irreversible trend toward more information intensive industries has huge implications in terms of the kinds of jobs that will be available for people around the world, and will have an enormous impact on the role of information technology in the world. The successful organizations will be those that realise that the high-performance work organization will quickly replace the low-skilled, low-wage industrial-based organizations of the past. The successful communities will be those that mobilize and manage their own natural and human resources.

A high-performance work organization is one that moves information swiftly and easily through its organization for decision and action. It is one that recognises that information is the currency of modern life, and understands that the value a nation's workforce adds to the world economy is measured by the skills of that workforce. Therefore, high-performance work hinges on the quality of the skills of the workforce, and on how adept a workforce is at problem solving, identifying issues, and communicating.

In addition to a careful examination of these trends, Dr. Steffens also sheds light on what is — perhaps — the single most significant technological development of the decade: That is, the convergence of industries.

As he points out, the once separate industries — telecommunications, computing, and consumer electronics — are beginning to converge, based upon their common use of digital technology, creating one of the largest "mega-industries" in the world, and some tremendous sources of new opportunity.

Already, we are using products that reflect this trend. For example, when you check your bank account balance over the telephone, you are at the crossroad of personal computing and telecommunications. Or when you order a movie over cable TV you are at the intersection of consumer electronics and media and publishing.

On reviewing Dr. Steffens' observations of this development, I was struck by the huge opportunities that are now ripe for harvest: Opportunities to apply innovative user interface technology to the challenge of navigating through the oceans of digital information which are quickly becoming available to all of us; and opportunities to apply knowledge of networking technology to the problems of accessing pervasive networks, particularly in the context of mobile computing, where you take your computing environment with you wherever you go.

The success or failure of all these products will be determined by how well individuals and institutions use these new technologies and services in innovative ways. To that same point, one of the central messages of Dr. Steffens' book is that the practice of mapping new technology on top of old processes usually produces dismal results. Indeed, just as the failure to adapt to the new ground rules can have disastrous consequences for business organizations, the thoughtful application of a "newgames" strategy has the potential to bring about the kinds of productivity gains that were originally anticipated with the advent of the personal computer. It is only through fundamentally transforming the way people think, work, learn and communicate that we will see the productivity promise through personal computing become a reality.

So, it is with added enthusiasm that I look forward to recommending Dr. Steffens' book to my colleagues both inside and outside of the information industry. All of us need to revisit how when appropriately directed, personal computing will continue to help us to: do the things we used to do, better; to do what we dreamed of doing, easily; and to do things we never imagined....

PREFACE
TECHNOLOGY & STRATEGY SERIES

John McGee

Howard Thomas

Technology and technical change has always posed problems in the analysis of markets and of competition. Technical change is concerned with changes in the state of scientific knowledge and with the way in which that knowledge can be brought to bear in markets by firms.

However, the analysis of markets and of industries has been marked by a predominance of static modes of analysis — what is the nature of the market structure, how does this affect the commercial policies of firms and what implications does the present structure have for the performance of firms and the efficiency of markets? This has proved a taxing enough agenda for industrial economists trying to understand the implications for efficiency as well as for strategic management researchers attempting to explain the relative success of firms. Technical change, however, generally requires investment and always requires some form of change within firms with consequences for the way in which competition evolves. Industry analysis, which might be thought of as a sort of meeting ground for economists and strategy researchers, requires a frame of reference which is more truly dynamic in character. In other words the framework of industry analysis should contain within it a way of explaining the paths by which an industry can change and the mechanisms by which the alternative paths might be triggered. By contrast the existing frameworks enable us to interpret industry structures in terms of their implications for efficient resource allocation and for competition on the implicit assumption of no change in the attendant underlying conditions, specifically the state of technical knowledge.

Of course economists have not been unconscious of this challenge. For many economists the notion of long run marginal cost is essentially a dynamic one where expected future technical change does not only affect the future course of prices but is also a crucial factor in determining the current price. The simplest and most direct incorporation of dynamics has been through models where technical change is treated as exogenous to the system and its implications explored. A more complex view allows for technical change to be treated endogenously, that is that technical change is induced or retarded by economic variables which are themselves determined within the economic model. Thus, the level of prices will itself have an effect on stimulating the rate of technical change in a way hypothesized and tested within the model under consideration.

For strategy researchers even these endogenous models of technical change are insufficient. For the strategist the questions of interest concern the major decisions taken within the firm that condition the resource structure and behaviour of the firm and further effect the competitive dynamics in the market. For a strategy researcher it is essential to know how technical change is incorporated into the strategic thinking of the firm, how it is translated into investment decisions and into the value chain of the firm (and of the industry), and thereafter how it affects competitive dynamics. Traditionally the strategy literature treats technology as an implementation issue. The firm determines its strategy and this, in turn, defines how technology will be used. This ignores two problems — how does technology enter the strategy formulation process, and how are technological capabilities fostered and managed so as to create the basis for competitive advantage? To make progress along these dimensions requires addressing several points: (1) what is the relationship between technology and the economic conditions within which strategy is formulated, (2) what characteristics of technology and innovative activity affect the choice of and implementation of strategies, (3) how might technological issues be incorporated into strategic thinking and planning, and (4) how does technology affect the underlying capability of firms and how is this translated into competitive advantage? These issues are the agenda of this Technology and Strategy Series published by Pergamon Press.

The first book in this series focuses on the successive waves of change and transformations in the personal computer industry since its inception in the early 1970s. This industry is a classic case of exogenous technical change causing waves of technical innovation and strategic change. The industry begins as a "hobbyist" industry slowly developing its markets until incursions by the major computer players such as IBM fundamentally change the underlying economics and transform the market into a mass market. The fundamental theme of the book is the nature and significance of "newgame" strategies, that is the need to fundamentally transform the value chain or business system of the suppliers in order for the next stage of the industry's cycle to take place. The nature of the newgames at each new stage is closely related to the way in which the underlying technological conditions have developed. Indeed as time goes on there is a shift from an upstream-dominated industry dominated by suppliers with protected technologies to a downstream, market driven industry in which technology is widely diffused but still a driving force behind product specifications and user behaviour. The players also shift in parallel, the hardware orientation giving way to a software focus and the change in the centre of gravity from IBM to

Microsoft is particularly well described. As the industry conditions change we see not simply a diminution of the supply driven, monopolistic effect of closely held technology. More powerfully than this we see that technology still has a systematic effect on the industry dynamics even though it is more widely held and especially because its effects are mediated through software rather than through hardware. The personal computer industry boundaries are becoming fuzzier in response to these changes and we see in the final chapters how technology may continue to be intimately linked to the strategic development of the major players.

CONTENTS

AUTHOR'S PREFACE

John Steffens

Oxford, England

"The land of literature is a fairy land to those who view it at a distance,
but, like all other landscapes, the charm fades on a nearer approach,
and the thorns and briars become visible." [1]

"No one can draw more out of things, books included, than he already knows.
A man has no ears for that to which experience has given him no access." [2]

During the 1980s and 1990s, technological change has become an all pervading phenomenon which is characterised by the idea that the industrialised world has entered the age of the information technology[3] revolution, the world of the microcosm.[4] Although the term revolution is open to contest,[5] quite clearly, the pace and impact of technological evolution is unprecedented in the known history of mankind.

One of the most significant beacons of such change has been the personal computer.[6] Moreover, whilst it has become a pervasive product finding its way into every corner of our lives, some of its most powerful implications have taken place in the business environment. It is this focus upon the story of how developments in the technology and performance of personal computers have created an entirely new industry, companies, markets and customers, that forms the basis of this book.

However, this is not just another book about personal computers and what they do to our business lives. A number of factors differentiate its substance, making it relevant to many other industries impacted by the world of microelectronics.[7] Firstly, it is based upon an academic research study which I originally conducted as part of a doctoral thesis; secondly, the research was an investigation into the overall evolution and relationship of personal computer technology, the industry and its business markets; and thirdly, the research produced a broader conceptual paradigm for thinking about the pattern of industry and market evolution encountered with personal computers, which I have entitled — *Newgames*.

The setting for this book is therefore about the strategic development of the United States personal computer industry. It traces the pattern of evolution from its origins to the present and provides a study of the complex relationships between technological change, strategic behaviour and the structural evolution of the industry and its markets. Clearly, technological change is significantly altering, if not totally destroying, the conventional boundaries and conditions of competition for an ever increasing number of industries and markets. Companies competing in such environments are faced with the need to better understand the forces for change and to allocate their resources appropriately and in time to ensure their survival in the future. My experience as both a consultant and educationalist has convinced me that a key issue for management is the increasing occurrence of entry by existing or new companies into newly emerging and established markets. Whilst entry in itself is hardly a new phenomenon, the increasing pace of technological change, together with the growing trend towards various forms of internationalisation of industries and segmentation of markets suggests that many managers are now facing an increasing level of complexity in their business environments. As a result, it appears to me that management need a new framework through which to consider such phenomena. This book attempts to provide such a framework. It is therefore written for practitioners who need to develop strategies for a business either planning to create, enter, or already competing in a newgame environment and for scholars wishing to better understand the issues. It is also directed at those who are interested in industry and market evolution, particularly the case of the personal computer.

The computer industry[8] was chosen as the focus for the research, due to my previous experience and interest in the area, with particular emphasis being placed upon the emergence of the personal computer industry in the United States and the hardware[9] companies serving its respective markets at home and overseas. The period covers its early evolution during the 1970s up to the early 1990s. Focus was placed upon the relationship between drivers of the process for technological change and their subsequent impact upon the process of evolution in the structure of the industry and its markets.

By adopting an in-depth longitudinal study of a specific industry for a finite period of time, it has been possible to gather primary data to examine these issues. In addition, sources of secondary data have supported and complemented the research data base and have been used to present the findings from the earliest to the present day situation. The study thus provides a rich descriptive analysis of the impact of technological change upon market performance brought about by the heterogeneity of competitive strategies pursued over time.

The book itself is divided into nine chapters, with an Epilogue, which is followed by a set of Notes on each chapter, a technical glossary, then a bibliography and finally an index. The reader is advised that the Notes provide further details in the form of references or comment, which it was felt should be left outside the body of the text in order to preserve the flow of the reading. Where the Notes provide a short bibliographical reference, the reader is advised to turn to the Bibliography for further details of the source. Similarly, given the high number of technical terms that unavoidably had to be included in a work of this nature, the reader is requested to first check in the Notes to obtain the name of the term, from which they may proceed to look up the definition in the Technical Glossary, which is located further towards the end of the book. However, for reasons of space and tidyness, technical terms are only referenced in the Notes section of the chapter in which they first occur in this book.

Furthermore, a number of diagrams in this book have been reproduced from various sources with the permission of the copyright holders. These tables and figures come from a number of reputable organisations involved in industry and market research. The data has been used to illustrate market sizes, competitors' shares and major industry participants along with various other measures. In some cases the data has been chosen to reflect the assessments of market characteristics as it was believed to be at the time of the analysis, which refers to the particular period under discussion in the relevant part of the book. Subsequent data might well show an increase or decrease on some of the figures originally calculated, equally, other sources may have shown a somewhat different set of characteristics. This variation of data from different time-periods and sources is a fact of the industry and its markets. Therefore the reader is advised that all this data was provided in good faith by the organisations concerned, but that neither these organisations nor the author or publisher can in any way be held responsible for any errors or differences of data that might be identified by comparison with other sources. The reader is therefore asked to consider the data shown in this book as representing approximations which provide a suitable backdrop for discussion of general patterns of competitive behaviour, performance and market development. They should not be interpreted as being anything other than one set of data findings which may be openly considered and contrasted to comparable sources of data, with no prejudice for or against any particular source.

In terms of structure, the book is divided into four major sections. The first provides a background to the study and the basic nature of the technology surrounding the personal computer. In Chapter One, the conceptual development of the "Newgames Framework" is described in some detail, since this framework is then used throughout the remainder of the book to analyse and observe the process of competitive behaviour and its impact on the evolution of the industry and major markets. Chapter Two then provides a broad introduction to the nature of the technology that is central to the personal computer, insofar as it is important to understand the ideas put forward later in the book. Naturally, readers requiring a more thorough examination of the technology are referred to other more specialised and technical works. In addition, the chapter describes the development of the technology in the context of the evolution of the electronics industry during the 1960s and 1970s, that led to one of the conditions necessary for the development of the first microcomputer,[10] which was the forerunner of today's personal computer.

Having provided a background to the conceptual framework and technology involved, the second part of the book traces the evolution of the personal computer industry from its earliest stages up to the mid-1980s. Using the language of the newgames framework, the period is divided into four stages, namely, catalytic, embryonic, take-off and the period referred to as the entry of the giants and legitimisation. These are covered in Chapters Three to Five. In each stage, the newgames framework analyses the patterns of change both in the core technology, competitors' strategies in terms of their value chains and aspects of customer behaviour. These are then translated into a description of their impact upon the broad structure of the industry and its markets, with much of the material in this part of the book being based upon information gathered for the original doctoral thesis.

The next part of the book, picks up the story from the mid-1980s and effectively continues to apply the newgames framework to the patterns of evolution of the personal computer industry and its markets up to mid-1993. In Chapter Six it is seen that the industry moves through three subsequent stages, namely, consolidation, maturation and saturation. During these stages, further newgame strategies emerge that lead to significant changes in the structure of the personal computer industry and the relative performance of its major competitors. Furthermore, personal computers are seen to become the dominant type of product in the computer industry, creating major changes in the structure of the overall industry. The phenomenon of "downsizing"[11] is also reported upon and reflects the ultimate predicted pattern of evolution of the personal computer newgame. Chapter Seven then looks at the patterns of evolution in the worldwide personal computer industry and its markets during the late 1980s and early 1990s. Here it is seen that the markets have evolved as three major and quite distinctive regions. It also addresses the issue of considering to what extent these three regions are moving towards formation of a global industry and market-place.

The last section of the book, is divided into two separate but interconnected parts. Chapter Eight provides a summary of the book by identifying the major drivers to change in the evolution of the personal computer industry and its markets. It also reflects upon some of the lessons that emerge from the study about the nature of newgames and strategic behaviour as well as drawing together the pattern of current developments in the industry and its markets. It is then followed by Chapter Nine, in which the reader is provided with some ideas of how the industry and its markets may evolve in the 1990s and what implications such scenarios may have for competitors in this environment. In particular, it explores some of the trends developing on the base of digital technology,[12] which are leading towards increasing convergence between the computer, telecommunications[13] and consumer electronics[14] industries. Finally, the book closes with an Epilogue.

ACKNOWLEDGEMENTS

Many people helped me to complete this book and the doctoral thesis on which it is based. Thanks are due to all, but only some can be acknowledged here in person. In addition to the large number of people whom I interviewed during my research, there are, I feel, many other writers whose thoughts and ideas I shared by reading their materials. Most of these people I have never met, but I should like to acknowledge their contribution in stimulating my thinking and introducing me to fresh ideas. Included also, are the various students with whom I have discussed competitive strategy and marketing in high technology industries and who were willing to make constructive comment and criticism about some of my ideas. Often their observations have helped me focus my thoughts more sharply and I hope have resulted in a clearer style of writing in this book.

Amongst those people whom I wish to specifically name, my first thanks go to Dr. John McGee, who supervised me whilst I wrote my thesis and subsequently during the writing of this book. Also thanks to Professor Michael Yoshino at Harvard Business School, who focused my initial research on the fascinating issues to be explored in the evolving personal computer industry, as well as laying many of his personal resources at my disposal during my research at Harvard.

Extensive assistance was given in the early development of my ideas by Professor John Stopford and Agha Ghazanfar, both of whose encouragement and discussion were invaluable. Jeremy Smithers, also made important contributions and did much to stimulate my interest in the field of office automation. At the London Business School, Nick Grattan and Pat Rowham of the Computer staff provided special assistance and advice in the original computational work, whilst Pat Mulcay of the Library Information staff has been a constant source of help in tracing references and abstracts. Special thanks are also due to Helen Pettit, Eve Rodgers and Bobbie O'Neill, for their patience and assistance in typing the manuscript from my notes for this book, whilst Debbie Watson helped with the production of various diagrams. Tessa Webster is owed considerable thanks for her assistance in compiling the technical glossary and in checking the bibliography. Appreciation and thanks also go to Wendy Cocks, who was responsible for compiling and producing the index to this book.

Also, thanks are due to my friends who supported and encouraged me over the years of this work and who always made me feel I would get there in the end. Whether they, or I, are more surprised that this work is finally completed, I am not sure. However, I know I would not have got here without their support and encouragement. In particular, I should like to thank Laura Cousins, who not only has been a good friend and professional colleague, but has also been willing to listen with patience to my various ideas and provided a source of sympathetic and constructive feedback.

Certainly, this book would not have been possible if it had not been for the time and co-operation given by the large number of senior executives who agreed to be interviewed as part of the original study. My appreciation extends to all of them for their time and interest in the research. In addition, I should like to thank the various research executives at International Data Corporation, especially Jack Hart and Bruce Stephen in the United States and Simon Pierce in Europe, together with members of Dataquest Inc. and Infocorp, who provided me with vast amounts of information to compliment my own research endeavour. There are also many industry observers from the media, consultancies and market research companies, as well as colleagues at both the London Business School and Harvard Business School who provided valuable observations and comments to whom thanks are due.

Generous funding for my doctoral research were provided by both the Centre for Business Strategy at the London Business School and the English-Speaking Union, and I would like to thank all those who made these funds available. Additionally, I should like to thank both Dr. John McGee and Dr. Howard Thomas, as the series editors of which this book forms a part, for choosing this book to be included in their series. My thanks also go to Sammye Haigh, David Sharp and Peter Lister and their staff at Pergamon Press for helping to make this book a reality, together with Jane Macmillan and Bridget Hall of Pergamon's marketing department for helping to bring it to the market. In addition, I should like to thank all those who have taken the time to promote this book in their various ways to as wide a readership as possible. I also owe a large debt of gratitude to all the individuals and organisations who have kindly given permission for use of copyright materials. These are acknowledged individually under each relevant diagram in the body of the work. However, whilst every effort was made to trace the copyright holders, in those cases where it was not possible, the author and publisher will be pleased to make the necessary arrangements at the first opportunity.

Finally, I should like to thank the following persons, together with their respective staff who took the time to read through the manuscript to this book prior to its publication and were kind enough to provide reviews for its jacket cover. They include:

Peter Bonfield,
Chairman and Chief Executive,
ICL Plc;

Robert Corrigan,
IBM Vice President, President,
IBM Personal Computer Co;
Michael Dell,
Chairman and Chief Executive,
Dell Computer Corporation;
Dr. Tadahiro Sekimoto,
President,
NEC Corporation;
Enrico Pesatori,
Vice President and General Manager,
Personal Computer Business Unit,
Digital Equipment Corporation;
and again
Bruce Stephen,
Director of PC Hardware and Pricing Programs,
International Data Corporation.

My warmest thanks also go to John Sculley, Chairman of Apple Computer, Inc. and his staff responsible for agreeing to read through the manuscript and provide the Foreword to this work.

Whilst I am deeply grateful for the contributions of all those mentioned above, the views expressed in this work are, of course, my own and if there are any errors of observation I apologise to those concerned. No harm has been intended. Naturally, there may exist differences of opinion, but I hope that these will serve to stimulate discussion and interest in both the Newgames concept and the story of the PC Revolution.

John Steffens
Oxford, England,
October 1993.

LIST OF FIGURES

LIST OF TABLES

Chapter One

CONCEPTUAL FRAMEWORKS

*"When a thought is too weak to be expressed simply,
it should be rejected."*[1]

INTRODUCTION

The past decade has witnessed a significant increase in the scale and pace of change in the structure and nature of various industrial and commercial markets. Changes in technology, legislation and political conditions have dramatically altered economic conditions of competition. As a direct result of these changes many companies have been forced to either create new strategies or alternatively to accept decline and subsequent failure of their businesses.

Whilst the basis of these events is essentially a reflection of the dynamic pattern of business cycles, there are other forces at work. These forces are by no means completely novel. However, their impact and intensity, together with their increasing frequency have created an unprecedented situation.

The forces include:
— rapid change in core technologies,[2]
— a shift towards deregulation by national governments,
— privatisation of state-owned industries,
— embracing of market based economic policy by previously centralised economic systems, and
— significant shifts in consumer patterns of behaviour.

Nowhere is the technological change seen more clearly than in the evolving information technology industries. In particular the core technology of microelectronics. Microelectronics products and components have diffused into a wide variety of markets and types of customers, ranging from military to industrial and commercial applications. However, perhaps the most

I

significant area of their use has been in computers[3] and telecommunications,[4] which together represent the platform of the information technology revolution.

Developments in the core technology of computers have led to dramatic changes in product price and performance. Yet in many ways an even more significant change has taken place within the industry and its markets. As the technology has moved forward, the basic concept of the computer itself has changed. With each new conceptual phase, new competitors have entered the market and changed the rules of the game. Thus a process of industry and market evolution has taken place which has developed new forms of competition, which has led to fundamental changes in the structure of the industry and its markets. The name given to this phenomenon is *Newgames*, whose conceptual framework is explained more fully later in this chapter.

In order to investigate this phenomenon, an analysis of the evolution of the personal computer industry and its markets was undertaken, since this provided a perfect example of all the aspects inherent in a newgame environment.[5] Focus was placed upon the relationship between drivers of the process for change and their subsequent impact upon and interaction with the structure of the industry and its markets of which they form a part. Central to the research was investigation of the relationship between technological change, competitive behaviour in the industry and the evolution of customer behaviour in given market segments. In order to investigate these issues, four research questions were formulated to provide a path for enquiry into the newgame phenomenon as it evolved within the personal computer industry and its markets. These questions were:

(1) What factors differentiate entrants to an industry and its markets? This allowed a categorisation of the different types of company that entered the industry and its markets.

(2) What types of strategy do entrants pursue at different stages of the industry's evolution? This allowed an investigation of the way in which entrants' value chains[6] evolved over time and how they formed new types of strategic groups.[7]

(3) What impact do various strategies have upon the performance of the industry and its markets? This allowed an investigation of the strategies of suppliers, competitors (both entrants and incumbents) and distributors and to see how they interacted to influence the pattern of industry and market evolution.

(4) What is the pattern of interaction between competitors' strategies and the behaviour of customers? This allowed an investigation of the relationship between competitors and their customers and their resulting patterns of market segmentation.

Naturally, in researching these questions, the scope of investigation was deliberately wide, so as to capture the broad relationship between the various players. However, it must be stressed that in order to keep the research as a manageable proposition, the key focus of the investigation was upon the fortunes of the personal computer hardware companies and the impact of technological change upon their competitive strategies. Therefore, whilst the various other players such as suppliers, software developers,[8] distribution channels and customers in the newgame environment form an important part of the overall study, their relevance is always in relation to the hardware companies. Similarly, the main attention is given to the evolution of the business user segment for personal computers, since this has come to form the major share of the overall market.

In order to study these issues systematically, the strategic behaviour of the major personal computer hardware companies, both winners and losers, was studied over the period of 1975 to mid-1993. The research methodology involved both primary and secondary data collection and interviews with some 150 executives, industry analysts and observers.

The results to these investigations, whilst exhibiting certain unique characteristics, also provide a background for developing more general insights into the nature of competitive conditions in newgame environments. In particular, the analytical framework provides a rich overview of the relationship between technological change and competitive behaviour, together with their interaction and impact upon the industry and market structures and patterns of evolution. The foundation of the framework is based upon ideas and concepts previously developed from the fields of industrial organisation, competitive strategy, marketing and technological innovation. By drawing these ideas together, a simple hybrid model of the nature of newgames has been developed which is able to provide a better understanding of the patterns of interaction that take place between the various key elements within a newgame situation.

The resulting picture that emerges enhances our perception of the process by which companies may succeed or fail in newgame environments. Given the increasing complexity of such environments and their more regular occurrence, it is to be hoped that the newgame framework will provide a basis for further in-depth investigation of other industries and markets.

Within this chapter, the background to the ideas used in development of the newgame framework is first of all described,[9] before moving on to present the basic conceptual framework surrounding the nature of newgames. Finally, a number of examples are given which present a broad picture of the range of environments within which newgames have occurred, as well as highlighting the various causes of the phenomenon.

THE COMPETITIVE STRATEGY MODEL

The basis for the analytical framework of the newgame environment is to be found in the contemporary version of the competitive strategy model, which has been derived from ideas developed in the field of industrial organisation in particular, by Bain[10] and Scherer,[11] as well as from the literature surrounding the theory of the firm.[12] The objective of the framework was to try and capture the key drivers for change in the evolution of an industry and its markets.[13] For this reason, the newgame model was based upon the interrelationship between changes in structure and changes in process. The model itself is a hybrid and is thus based on ideas from various fields of academic research. It has evolved against a background of efforts to develop a greater integration of ideas between the field of strategic management[14] and the areas of industrial organisation,[15] technological change[16] and marketing.[17]

At the heart of the framework is Porter's model of competitive strategy[18] which focuses attention upon the analysis of the firm and its relationship to suppliers, potential and existing competitors and buyers. Fig. 1.1 illustrates the extension of Porter's original five force model to a six force model, which divides the buyers between distributors and purchasers/end-users.[19] This has been to ensure that the analyst and manager appreciate that the relationship between competitors and distributors versus competitors and end-customers needs different treatment. As such Porter's model captures a number of structural relationships, however, it is essentially a supply side model and one which is relatively static in nature. For this reason, concepts from the marketing field were incorporated into the model, so as to reflect the changes in market structure and most importantly, to also appreciate the process of changes in buyer and user behaviour.

However, a key weakness of the Porter model has been its lack of attention to the role of technological change which he relegates to an exogenous variable.[20] Since technological change is considered to be one of the major drivers to change originating within firms entering or already competing within the newgame environment, then clearly an alternative

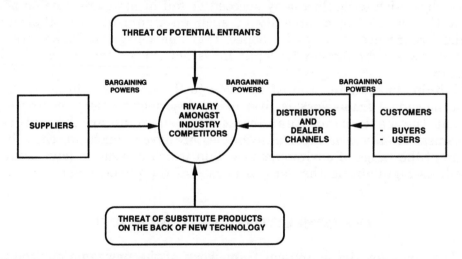

Source: Adapted with the permission of The Free Press, a division of Macmillan, Inc. from COMPETITIVE STATEGY: Techniques for Analyzing Industries and Competitors by Michael Porter. Copyright © 1980 by the Free Press.

Fig. 1.1. Six forces driving industry competition.

treatment of technological change was necessary. It was for this reason that Joseph Schumpeter's ideas,[21] concerning the "Process of Creative Destruction" were incorporated into the framework, since they provide a description of the dynamic process of imperfect competition driven by changes in the basic conditions, including technological innovation and/or the degree of regulation. Fortunately, there is a convenient marriage between Shumpeter's and Porter's ideas about sources of competition, for just as Schumpeter emphasised new technologies or sources of supply as the seedbed of cost and quality advantages, so too does Porter emphasise the importance of differentiation and low cost leadership.[22] The question of what choice and combination of resources will provide the best competitive advantage in a given set of industry and market conditions is of course the domain of the strategic management literature, whose basic ideas are also incorporated into the model and for a review of which, the reader is recommended to refer to McGee and Thomas.[23]

However, central to the concept of newgame environments is the idea of changing industry and market boundaries. Here the competitive strategy model was found to be wanting, since its main focus is upon the firm and not upon the industry or its markets. In order to effectively bridge this gap, the concept of strategic groups was therefore used to provide a better understanding of how strategies of various competitors, both entrants and incumbents impacted the evolution of the industry and its markets.

STRATEGIC GROUP ANALYSIS

Although the concept of strategic groups appears as a supply side concept, it is in fact based upon the observed similarity between the behaviour of firms,[24] in other words their strategies. The term "strategic groups" was first used by Michael Hunt,[25] who argued that each potential entrant to an industry faced a different set of problems depending upon the target group chosen. He then attempted to isolate "barriers to entry to each strategic group" in a descriptive vein. However, it was Porter[26] who developed the accepted definition of a strategic group in terms of the similarity of competitive behaviour:

"A strategic group is the group of firms in an industry following the same or a similar strategy along the strategic dimensions. An industry could have only one strategic group if all the firms followed essentially the same strategy. At the other extreme, each firm could be a different strategic group. Usually, however, there are a small number of strategic groups which capture the essential strategic differences among firms in the industry".[27]

This view of the world presents a departure from the traditional industrial organisation view of the world,[28] which tended to treat all firms as similar, except in terms of size. The strategic groups concept therefore provides a kind of contingency approach,[29] which captures the reality of the fact that managers within companies are faced with a choice of strategies, which are dependent upon the resources and competencies available to them, as well as what might be considered the most expedient or politically acceptable. Development of the literature on the topic of strategic groups has been well documented elsewhere, in particular by McGee and Thomas,[30,31] where the respective authors have provided exhaustive reviews of the main studies in the field. Readers are therefore, referred to these sources and to the more recent studies of Cool and Schendel,[32] Fiegenbaum,[33] Fiegenbaum and Thomas,[34] Mascarenhas[35] and McGee and Segal-Horn.[36] Here it is simply necessary to appreciate how the concept of strategic groups adds to the competitive strategy model and its additions described above.

When using the concept of strategic groups, an industry is not just seen as an arena within which companies compete with one another and whose strategies merely reflect differences of size. Instead, the industry is treated as being made up of a group or groups of competitors, whose group membership is defined by their particular strategies, which are in turn a reflection of their asset structures. As an industry evolves, one would expect to see a growth in the number of strategic groups, which would reflect on the variety of asset configurations of the different types of competitors. In time, as the industry matured, it might be that the number of strategic groups declined, reflecting an increased level of concentration, which would itself be a symbol of the convergence of the different types of strategies and hence asset configurations.

Whilst a number of strategic groups exist in an industry, entrants might therefore choose to compete in one of the groups, whose level of competition was less intense. This is an important proposition, since it opens the opportunity for entrants to pursue a path of sequential entry,[37] that entails initially competing in one group and gradually building a set of assets suitable to transfer to another and more profitable group. Associated with the idea of strategic groups is the concept of mobility barriers and although often compared to entry barriers,[38,39] mobility barriers exist around a group of competitors already in a marketplace and are associated with the investments that they have made to establish their competitive position. In effect they therefore result from the strategies pursued by members of a particular strategic group. Thus the particular asset configurations chosen by managers within companies belonging to a particular strategic group will be a reflection of their chosen strategies. The greater these assets become, the higher will be the mobility barriers. At the same time, organisational inertia, bureaucracy and culture[40] may well act as a barrier upon the ability of a particular firm to reconfigure its assets in such a manner that it would be able to pursue a strategy that would make it a member of an alternative strategic group. McGee and Thomas[41] identify three broad categories of mobility barriers that are illustrated in Table 1.1. Market related strategies to create differentiation are clearly decision variables for the firm representing examples of strategic choice, since they require an initial investment cost that will take some time to take effect and establish competition on equal terms.[42] Indeed,

Table 1.1. Sources of mobility barriers.

DIFFERENTIATION *	ECONOMIES OF SCALE*	ECONOMIES OF SCOPE
Product line	Economies of scale:	Ownership
User technologies	production marketing administration	Organization structure
Market segmentation		Control systems
Distribution channels	Manufacturing processes	Management skills
Brand names	R&D capability	Boundaries of:
Geographic coverage	Marketing and	firms diversification vertical integration
Selling systems	Distribution systems	Firm size
		Relationships with influence groups

* Note some of the differentiation characteristics and economies of scale characteristics are interchangeable.

Source: Based upon original table in *Strategic Management Research*, John McGee and Howard Thomas, edited by John McGee and Howard Thomas, p.150. © 1986, John Wiley and Sons, Ltd. Reprinted by permission of John Wiley and Sons, Ltd.

ex ante, the investment decision carries with it the risk that the outcome may not achieve appropriate market positioning and, furthermore, buyers may not respond to an imitative product in the same way as to the leader's initial offering. Industry supply characteristics include the more conventional scale effects of industrial economics. However, McGee and Thomas stress the more interesting alternative of investments in supply side assets for the firm. Effective R&D capability and/or marketing and distribution networks are not easily defined and therefore not easily determined by an imitative competitor, especially in the short-term. Such factors play an important part in the pattern that emerges in analysis of the newgame environment. Lastly, there exist economies of scope that to a large extent may reflect underlying core competencies[43] and managerial abilities of the firm.

The value of the strategic group concept to the newgame framework, lies in its ability to view the pattern of industry evolution as being based upon changes in the membership and configuration of different strategic groups. In effect, within the newgame framework, the value chain of a competitor is treated as a proxy for that particular company's strategy. Thus a strategic group is tantamount to a group of competitors with similar value chains, which are themselves reflections of particular configurations of assets, strategic resources[44] and/or core competencies. Given that newgames are especially concerned with analysis of strategies that reconfigure existing or create totally new value chains within the industry, then it therefore follows that by tracking the patterns of strategic group memberships[45] and changes in the asset configurations of different groups, one is provided with a rich descriptive measure of how the overall structure of the industry changes through time. In particular, it takes the somewhat static model of Porter's modified version of six forces for change together with the value chain and places them into a dynamic environment. In the same way, the concept of newgames emphasises the changing nature of the various industry and market forces that then impact the composition of the value chains of companies within various strategic groups. Indeed, some of these strategic groups may exist outside the core industry and therefore involve entry from multiple businesses, which reflect the trend towards increasing diversification.[46] In particular, it will be seen that the newgame environment is concerned with strategic group membership that crosses conventional industry boundaries and indeed, involves the dissolution or destruction of such boundaries. In such complex environments, a company may find itself belonging to a strategic group which effectively transfers from one industry sector to another and in so doing, changes the nature of the industry structure. By focusing upon strategic groups within the evolution of a newgame environment, one therefore begins to capture the dynamics of change within the various elements of the competitive environment in a way that is not possible by conventional industry analysis. In this respect, the use of the concept of strategic groups provides a bridge between the firm as the major unit of analysis and its impact upon determining the patterns of change in the industry and its markets at different stages of the newgame environment's evolution. We now therefore proceed to look specifically at the concept of the newgame and its underlying principles and assumptions.

THE NEWGAMES CONCEPT

Newgames are complex business environments and are best conceived of in terms of an holistic system. As such, they incorporate fundamental changes in the conditions of competition and in the way we organise our businesses. They also involve the creation of new concepts and new ways of thinking about the world around us, whether we be competitors or customers. In order to make sense of this complex environment it is necessary to break it down into its constituent parts that can then be analysed in more detail. However, at all times, it must be remembered that each constituent part is also linked to other parts of the overall business system. Furthermore, it is best regarded as an open system and therefore may be affected by factors outside the immediate environment, as well as encountering complex and often volatile feedback effects within the more immediate environment.

The definition of a newgame states that:

Newgame environments result from the successful implementation of a newgame strategy, which itself represents a new combination of asset structures fundamentally different from previously existing arrangements. Newgames involve new concepts and new ways of thinking about the world around us, whether we be competitors or customers. The opportunity for newgame strategies may emerge from step-changes in political, 'egal, economic, ecological, social or technological conditions or by a unique and creative restructuring of a company's assets (strategic resources). Newgame environments pass through distinctive stages of evolution, wherein the critical factors for success, both for entrants and incumbents, change significantly, reflecting major shifts in the value chains of industry members. The pattern moving from an emphasis upon the technological or operational elements of the chain towards a more complex integrated approach with increasing value being generated through marketing and downstream activities.

Thus, as shown in the definition above, the essence of a newgame concerns the creation of a new set of competitive conditions, which successfully overturn the existing set of conditions and hence change the rules of the business game in a specific industry and its markets.

Using the ideas of the competitive strategy model and strategic groups, newgames can be viewed from a number of alternative, yet complementary perspectives. These include issues in two key areas. Firstly, those concerned with the overall nature of newgame environments and secondly, those concerned with newgame strategies. To make sense of these issues, this section will proceed to describe the basic model of newgame environments, highlighting their basic nature and characteristics and then considering the nature of newgame strategies and comparing these with those of non-newgame strategies. The next three sections will then proceed to develop further details concerning the impact of newgames upon the value chain, evolutionary patterns of newgame environments and the nature of market and marketing barriers. Finally, some examples of newgames are provided at the end of the chapter.

Newgame Environments

Included in the newgame environment are virtually all elements of the business environment, although the focus is upon an industry and its markets. Perhaps the best approach to conceptualise the newgame environment is to consider it as a complex open system. Fig. 1.2 illustrates the causes and development of a newgame environment and is referred to in the following commentary. On the edges of this system exist various macro scale forces that can create opportunities for change. These include political, legal, economic, ecological and social policies or values that are often in a state of change, sometimes taking place quite rapidly in a short period of time. As such they represent the exogenous environmental factors for driving change that surround the industry and its markets.

Another factor for driving change which may be exogenous or endogenous to the industry is technological change. In this context, technological change involves step-changes in technology representing innovation in product components, finished products design or production processes.

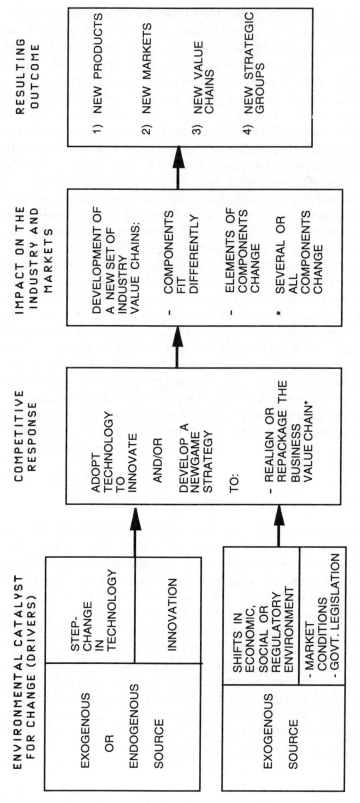

Fig. 1.2. The causes and development of newgame environments.

* Such strategic reconfiguration of a company's assets may sometimes take place due to intellectual insight and inspiration in the absence of an environmental catalyst.

When a step-change or major displacement of the previously existing balance of forces occurs, then the opportunity is created to set in motion the metamorphosis of a newgame environment. The catalyst to create the embryonic first stages of a newgame environment are found within a relatively rare resource, namely, human entrepreneurism. Whether based around an individual or a team, the entrepreneurism generates a 'Vision' of a new product, a new production process, a new market or a new way of doing business. Such entrepreneurism may occur in a start-up venture or within a large established corporation, where it is referred to as intrapreneurism.[47] In those instances where the 'Vision' is implemented, we witness the emergence of a "Newgame Strategy", which in itself is the next stage of evolution in the Newgame Environment.

Hence the external forces will usually create the opportunity for entrepreneurism to provide a competitive response in the form of adopting innovative products and/or to develop a newgame strategy to generate an innovative method of operation or production. In all cases, the result is either the creation of a new type of business value chain or a realignment and repackaging of the existing form of business value chain. If the newgame strategy succeeds then the impact on the industry and its markets results in the development of a new and more successful business value chain that either reflects a different mix to the existing components or a change in the content of the value chain, either partially or completely. The resulting outcome is a new type of product, new markets, a new dominant industry value chain and the formation of new strategic groups. It is important to appreciate that the key characteristics of a Newgame Environment that distinguish it from simply being a new product/market are therefore that it creates a totally new set of value chains for the emerging industry and its markets, together with new sets of strategic groups.

Given these factors, it naturally follows that the impact of newgame strategies upon the industry and its markets is central to the pattern of evolution of the newgame environment and is a function of the nature of the newly formed value chain. However, before considering these issues in more detail, it is necessary to understand the nature of newgame strategies and how they compare to other classes of strategy.

Newgame Strategies

In the previous section, newgame strategies were seen to be a key factor for causing the creation of newgame environments. This section will therefore proceed to describe the characteristics of newgame strategies, to see how they occur in relation to oldgame strategies in terms of a product/market matrix and by comparing them in terms of (thinking) approach and perspectives to strategies found in other environments, namely samegame and endgame environments.

The Industry-Market Environment Matrix

Figures 1.3(a) to (d) plot a series of situations that help to explain the evolution of newgame environments. Each figure depicts a matrix made up of four boxes, known as the Industry–Market Environment Matrix. Within each quadrant there may occur strategic groups of companies which are lettered in each of the illustrative figures. The key to the figures clarifies the types of value chain in terms of whether they are endgame, samegame or newgame strategies. Furthermore, the newgame strategic groups also represent companies creating, developing or pursuing newgame value chains.

Quadrant one reflects an oldgame industry environment with its established markets and contains a set of oldgame strategic groups. The oldgame environment may either be in a declining endgame situation or a stable samegame situation. For the purpose of this illustration, in Fig. 1.3(a) the strategic groups in quadrant one are initially treated as pursuing samegame strategies. It is also assumed that they are surrounded by substantial industry entry barriers, which have deterred direct entry into the industry, even by established outside companies from other industries. Normal business expansion takes place by companies moving downwards into quadrant three as shown in Fig. 1.3(b) and exploiting new markets with the same product-technology as used within the core sector above.

Assuming that a step-change in core technology or a deregulation of the industry were to occur, then the incumbent companies could expand by moving into quadrant two and developing a newgame industry to serve the existing core markets. This case is not illustrated, since in practice it rarely happens. Instead, it is more usually an entrepreneur or company outside the core industry that develops a new product, which acts as a substitute for existing products in the core industry and its markets. Initially, the new product, which is the result of a newgame strategy occurs in quadrant four at time T+1, which is the situation illustrated in Fig. 1.3(c), where it serves an otherwise new or undeveloped market. Both the product and the value chain in this quadrant are different to those in quadrant one, which is the preserve of the samegame environment.

Issues concerning the pattern of evolution of a newgame environment are dealt with in more depth later in this chapter. For the moment the reader should note that if the initial newgame strategy successfully develops a newgame environment, then in time, competitors from the new strategic groups within quadrant four will move into quadrant two at time T+2, where they will directly challenge the incumbents with their samegame strategies in quadrant one, which is illustrated in Fig. 1.3(d). What is important to note is that the newgame strategies pursued in quadrant two are different from the samegame strategies inside quadrant one in terms of both the product solution (concept) and the underlying organisational value chains.

Hence the tactics of the newgame strategy player does not represent a head-on frontal attack upon the established samegame strategy player from outside the industry, but rather it offers an alternative choice to customers in the market, which draws them away from the incumbent competitors. The reason for this change of preference is based upon the ability of the newgame players to provide a value chain that creates a product or service perception amongst the customers, both new and old,

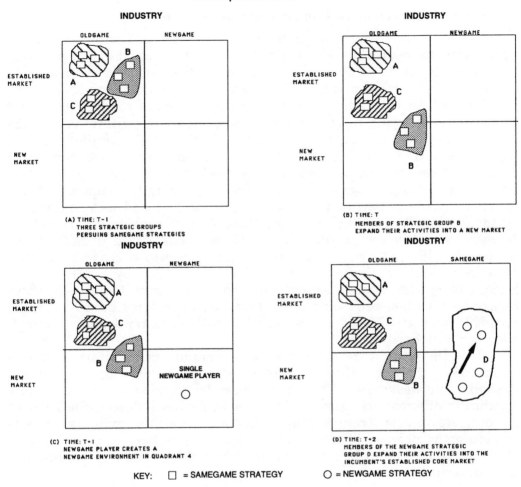

Fig. 1.3. Evolution of newgame to oldgame and samegame environments.

which provides better value than the previous solutions. The essence of the seduction is based upon the idea of a new concept. A concept that provides a better solution, whether it be in terms of the product or the production process to other strategies in terms of the thinking process behind their inception or development, as well as the more basic tactical dimensions. The result of the newgame strategy if it is successful, leads to changes in the structure of the two parts that now form the industry, namely the oldgame and newgame elements. A tension exists between these two elements that demands a victor. The process of evolution of the newgame and oldgame environments now formed in Fig. 1.3(d) is explored shortly by means of analysing the impact of the newgame strategy upon the value chains of the various strategic groups. However, before moving onto this topic it is necessary to consider the nature of the newgame strategy itself.

Newgame and Oldgame Approaches to Competition

For the most part, strategic behaviour is concerned with playing the samegame to maximise one's position relative to the competition. Alternatively in an endgame environment, strategy is concerned with optimising one's position within the constraints of a declining competitive environment. In both situations, the strategic rules of conduct are based on the ideas of trying to gain a competitive advantage within an existing industry and set of market structures. The task is therefore one of optimising within given constraints and is usually conducted through a deductive form of analysis, employing somewhat mechanistic systems and frameworks for supporting a "vertical" style of thinking.[48] Companies choose between a broad or narrow range of products/markets and seek to compete, by identifying and trying to attain those factors considered critical for success, on a low cost and/or differentiated basis. More usually, those companies with sufficient resources will either occupy a broad leadership position or seek to challenge the leadership position by emulating the leader's functional capabilities and value chain structure. Conversely, those companies with limited resources will focus upon a selected group of market segments and avoid head-on competition with industry leaders through adopting a niche strategy.[49]

Newgame strategies do not seek to emulate competitors' resource structures, but rather, they attempt to convert the existing incumbent's strengths into weaknesses. This they achieve by introducing and developing a radically different structure of value chain for the industry. Such moves not only create new strategic groups, but may also raise mobility barriers to reduce the degrees of freedom available to members of other specific strategic groups in such a way as to reduce their levels of profitability and performance.

Newgame Strategic Thinking in Practice

It would be misleading to suggest that in practice entrepreneurs or managers involve themselves in the type of rationalisation exercises outlined above. In practice, the start-up type of company may well find the entrepreneur identifying latent market opportunities based on 'hunches' and experience. As a classical "project champion", within larger organisations, the intrapreneur or team have a faith or belief that the intended new product will find a market "niche". Very often, such a product may initially be brought to the market with a premium price and aimed at innovative customers who accept the product, even though its performance may be somewhat limited or even unreliable. However, if the initial 'vision' is in tune with the needs of the time, then other competitors will follow the initial newgame strategy with incremental or even substantial improvements that refine the cost structure, together with improving the product quality and performance.

At present, what is important to understand is that whilst the initial drivers to change have their roots in external trends or step changes drawn from the overall environment, a subsequent and further key contributing factor to the development of a newgame strategy is based upon the way in which people perceive and think about such changes. Thus in one respect, the analyst may rightly conclude that newgame strategies deliberately seek to change the rules of the game, rather than focusing mainly upon issues of positioning relative to existing competition. By such means, if successful, a newgame strategy offers the greatest potential for creating a competitive advantage, although the scale of success will, of course, be dependent upon how dramatically the underlying industry cost structure and value chain is altered by the new entrant, and the scale of response in terms of market demand. In practice, what the analyst is describing is a process by which the individual or team of entrepreneurs and/or managers have broken out of conventional oldgame thinking. They have seen an opportunity to develop a technology, to respond to a change in legislation or to some other exogenous trend or step-change, in such a way that it is inherently new and very different to the current approach and thinking.

Characteristics of Newgame and Oldgame Strategies

In Table 1.2 some of the major characteristics of newgame and oldgame strategies are compared in terms of their approach and impact upon the competitive environment. These are considered under the following headings:

Table 1.2. Newgame strategies versus other strategies.

COMPARISON FACTORS	NEWGAME STRATEGIES	SAMEGAME AND ENDGAME STRATEGIES
1) INTELLECTUAL APPROACH	- INDUCTIVE - CREATIVE - LATERAL THINKING - VISION AND IMAGINATION	- DEDUCTIVE - MECHANISTIC - VERTICAL THINKING

2) STRATEGIC AIMS	- CHANGE THE GAMEPLAN
	- CREATE NEW KEY
	  FACTORS FOR SUCCESS
		- SEEK COMPETITIVE ADVANTAGE
		  WITHIN THE EXISTING GAME

3) STRATEGIC TACTICS	- CUSTOMER FUNCTIONALITY - CREATE NEW WANTS - REPACKAGE/REDEFINE VALUE CHAIN	- LOW COST - DIFFERENTIATION - BROAD VS FOCUS - POSITIONING

4) STRATEGIC FOCUS	- LIMIT COMPETITORS
	  DEGREES OF FREEDOM
	- POINTS OF LEVERAGE
	  ALONG VALUE CHAIN
	- MARKET BARRIERS
	  (PHYSICAL + PSYCHOLOGICAL)
	- NEW STRATEGIC GROUPS
		- IDENTITY
		- MARKET RESEARCH
		- TECHNOLOGY
		- TARGETING

5) IMPACT ON INDUSTRY	- CHANGE THE UNDERLYING
	  VALUE CHAIN
		- CHANGE THE MAKEUP
		  OF STRATEGIC GROUPS

6) IMPACT ON MARKETS	- CREATE TOTALLY NEW
	  MARKETS AND USER DEMANDS
		- EXPAND MARKETS AND
		  AND SEGMENTATION

7) IMPACT ON COMPETITION	- MAJOR: FORCING CHANGE TO
	  NEWGAME CONDITIONS AND
	  CREATING NEW COMPETITIVE
	  ADVANTAGE
		- VARIABLE: DEPENDING ON
		  ON DEGREE OF COMPETITIVE
		  ADVANTAGE

Intellectual Approach

The newgame strategy is based upon inductive reasoning and is creative in nature, being based upon a vision and imagination generated by lateral thinking. In contrast, the oldgame strategies tend to be deductive in their reasoning, highly mechanistic in their development and based upon vertical thinking. It may well be that some correlation exists between the culture of a company and its ability to develop newgame strategies. For example, those organisations whose technical research and development, together with their marketing research activities, are highly ritualised in terms of bureaucratic reporting and control procedures, appear less likely to develop newgame strategies than a more flexible, open style of cultural organisation. Hence newgame strategies are not just a function of the opportunity and originator of an idea, but are also likely to be dependent on a variety of factors concerned with the organisation structure, its culture and styles of management and leadership.

Strategic Aims

These are very much concerned with trying to create a new gameplan or to change the existing gameplan and generate a new set of key factors for success. Newgame strategists tend to be of the breed that ask the question "why not?", rather than "why?" Their aims are driven by an optimism and positivism so often lacking in oldgame decision makers. As previously mentioned, the 'vision' of the newgame strategist is a major driving force, with points of detail being a secondary issue which must be faced at a later stage. In some respects, the newgame strategist is the high-risk strategist. Failure is rarely considered as an option, although in practice, success of a newgame strategy is far from guaranteed. Indeed, many potential newgame environments may never come into existence, simply because the implementation process necessary to convert a 'vision' or 'idea' into reality was never followed through effectively.

In terms of creating competitive advantage, the newgame strategist should be more involved with developing flexible and adaptable sources of competitive advantage, since if successful, newgame competitive rivalry, especially in its earlier stages, will be undertaken in a highly volatile and unstable environment. Hence an aim of creating a sustainable competitive advantage may be somewhat unrealistic, however desirable. In contrast, the oldgame strategist seeks competitive advantage within the existing environment and often talks about sustainable competitive advantage, which may be a valid aim in this relatively more stable environment. Here the thinking is marginal and rarely holistic in nature. A large number of people within the organisation tend to focus upon issues in their specific function or area of responsibility. There is generally an acceptance of the 'status quo'. In its most rigid form, there is hardly any competition, such as might be found in a monopoly or state-owned enterprise, or the competition may be cosmetic, as in conditions representing a cartel, (whether overt or covert), when regulatory constraints discourage the practice or obscure the need for creative competition entirely. Indeed, one might argue that the reason why deregulation so often causes the creation of a newgame environment is precisely because the regulated environment hides enormous frustration in terms of unsatisfied demand from potential customers and lack of opportunity for competitive entrants.

Strategic Tactics

From the above, it follows that newgame strategies are bound to adopt tactics which are intended to repackage or redefine ways of doing business. There tends therefore to be a strong belief in creating something entirely new for the customer. However, this should not be misread as a synonym for customer or market orientation, especially when one remembers the high incidence of failures amongst newgame strategies.

The fact that an entrepreneur or intrapreneur believes there is a market for a new 'vision' or 'idea', does not mean that the same 'vision' or 'idea' has a high potential demand (latent or otherwise)! Due to some of the classical problems of market research surrounding a new product/market, in practice, the basis of most newgames are still product–technology or service–operations driven, albeit they may be linked to a strong 'gut-feel' or 'hunch' about the market potential. However, the skill or talent for identifying latent product/markets, which subsequently grow into a newgame environment is very real, although rare. In such instances where it does succeed, it is based upon a strong conviction in the reality of an opportunity to create new patterns of demand in existing or as yet undeveloped markets. These are based upon the ability to look beyond the present solutions, products or services and envisage alternatives as yet not fully understood by either the innovator or potential customers.

In contrast, the oldgame tactics are concerned with a much more narrow vision of the future. Given the strategic aims are based upon developing and creating sustainable competitive advantages within the existing environment, the tactics tend to be based around choosing to compete in the conventional arena as a broad or narrow based player. The more intense the competition in a given market the more important are issues of positioning and general marketing (which are themselves relatively poorly understood or executed by the majority of companies). Cost leadership and/or product differentiation or differentiation in one or more elements of the value chain are the generic bases for developing competitive advantage. Naturally, if a company is imaginative enough to create major differentiation along its value chain then it has broken the confines of its oldgame strategy and is entering a newgame environment. However, this is a question of degree and tends to be the exception for most established companies.

Strategic Focus

This refers to those areas of business activity upon which the strategist will direct both the strategic aims and tactics of a given company. For a newgame strategist, the focus is upon identifying and establishing points of leverage along elements of the value chain. These will change as the newgame environment develops through its various stages of evolution. For example, in the initial stages of a newgame environment a player may simply concentrate upon creating a new product technology which focuses key resources and effort solely on the product development area. A subsequent entrant, say an established company, may choose to focus more on creating new and increased value in their distribution or marketing activities. At a later stage, an entrant (or by now existing player), may attempt to change the newgame rules by large adjustments in the scale of resources and levels of investment in high technology for production, information handling, marketing or service activities.

Although not necessarily clearly identified, a newgame strategy, particularly in a more developed stage of a newgame environment, or as a departure from a samegame environment when implemented with sufficient resources, may limit the competitors' degrees of freedom. For example, this could result from high levels of investment in existing plant and machinery or distribution channels by competitors, when a newgame strategist decides to invest in and implement a new form of distribution channel. In such circumstances, the competitors may be reluctant or unable to afford to invest for the short term in the newgame type of resources. A further strategic focus of the successful newgame strategy is upon a shrewd assessment of the psychological as well as the physical barriers to market entry. (These points are discussed later in the chapter.) Hence, the orbit of initial newgame activity is more usually outside the core oldgame business environment and the strategic focus is frequently upon developing the company outside established strategic groups, as described in the previous section.[50]

Oldgame strategies focus upon issues identified through market research (formal or informal), which tend to highlight the identity of a company and its products in the existing environment. Hence, significant resources in a mature samegame environment are often directed towards promotional activities that are concerned with 'image' building and enhancing at both the corporate and product levels. Specific targeting and establishment of yet more segments as a source for potential differentiation become a major focus of activity. However, most of such activity tends to be at the margin. That is not to say that the returns may not be viable, but in the extreme form such strategies are seeking to create demand in ever more marginal levels of segmentation, as seen for example by the competitive behaviour in the cosmetics industry or in some of the typical impulse purchase markets.

In order to investigate the impact of newgames upon the industry, the market and conditions of competition, the next three sections will consider each in turn, under the headings of the impact upon the value chain, patterns of evolution and the market and marketing barriers.

THE VALUE CHAIN IMPACT

As previously stated, the key characteristic of a Newgame Environment that distinguishes it from simply a new product/market is that it creates a totally new set of value chains for the emerging industry and its markets, together with new strategic groups. The impact of a newgame strategy upon an industry value chain is best understood by analysing the formation of a newgame environment in terms of the creation of such new strategic groups. Porter emphasises that:

> "Every firm is a collection of activities that are performed to design, produce, market, deliver and support its product. All these activities can be represented using a value chain.... A firm's value chain and the way it performs individual activities are a reflection of its history, its strategy, its approach to implementing its strategy and the underlying economics of the activities themselves".[51]

He also emphasises that the relevant unit for construction of the value chain is at the level of the firm, since an industry or sector wide value chain would be too broad and fail to capture the essential differences between companies' value chains, which form the basis of their respective sources of competitive advantage. In reality a number of the dominant competitors share a similar shape of value chain that is treated in aggregate as a representation of the industry as a whole. Furthermore, it is also important to remember that when considering the value chain, it is value as perceived by the buyer and not cost that is being measured when assessing the competitive position of a firm.

The starting point for seeking competitive advantage, whether by means of an oldgame or newgame strategy, therefore involves defining and understanding the value chains of competing firms in various strategic groups. In practice this is not an easy task for the analyst, since value is highly subjective and is essentially a perception of the end customer. The value chain itself should help us to determine where the value is generated within the company, which may be anywhere along the elements of research, development, production processes, marketing, distribution or after-sales service. Whether the company owns and controls each of these elements of the value chain is also an important issue. However, ownership may not be essential for achieving value, since close cooperation with a supplier on an exclusive arrangement could yield a proprietary value. Whilst the researcher, academic, consultant or business planner may adopt a formal analysis, it must be remembered that for many competitors, the practical evaluation of such concepts is clearly not present in their activities or decision-making. Instead, a mental picture of the structure of the industry and its markets, based on historical experience most usually forms the guidelines and framework within which they make their strategic decisions. Indeed, this general lack of attention to the value chain may well be a contributing factor to why so many companies fail to appreciate the implications of shifts in value chains over time. This in itself is usually a reflection of limited investment in good quality behavioural customer market research, for without this, it is virtually impossible to determine the reasons why customers value a particular company's product or service. Furthermore, although value activities along the generic value chain (e.g. research, marketing or distribution) provide the building blocks for competitive advantage, it is the unique combination of linkages among these activities which actually creates the overall relative advantage. Identification and recognition of how to create an improved set of linkages, and/or the establishment of a new set of value activities, form the central components of a newgame strategy, which in practice is often done more by intuition, rather than by formal analysis.

If the newgame strategy (however it is derived) is able to provide a greater value to markets than the existing set of competitors' value chains, then it will grow, be imitated and eventually displace the existing oldgame value chains. The pattern and pace of the resulting industry and market evolution can therefore follow a number of alternatives. Hence both the pattern and pace of evolution emanating from a successful newgame strategy is therefore likely to be governed by the scale of difference between the value offered by the newgame competitor, relative to the values offered by the oldgame competitors. Therefore, it follows that the greater the value difference, the more dramatic will be the impact upon the oldgame industry and its market structures. Furthermore, once a newgame set of value chains begin to crystallise, there still exists the opportunity for a subsequent entrant (with a suitable asset structure) to generate significant additional value along any of the major elements in the value chain. The result of this type of subsequent newgame strategy is to once again create a process of displacement and substitution in the structure of competitors' value chains. The opportunity to create significant further value to satisfy the customers' demands within the newgame environment accounts for the generic stage-wise pattern of evolution that will most frequently develop in such an environment. Whilst the impact on the various competitors' value chains represents the most obvious measure of change, it is also important to recognise that such changes lead to the changes brought about in the structure and membership of strategic groups. In this respect strategic groups become a proxy for the value chains of their member companies.

These ideas and the illustration of the impact of a newgame strategy upon the industry competitors' value chains and strategic groups are presented visually in Figs. 1.4(a) to (f). The variables in the matrices resemble the diagrams shown earlier in the series of Figs. 1.3(a) to (d). However, in this instance they focus upon the chronological pattern of change within the strategic groups themselves.

Let us assume therefore that at time T-1 the industry consists of nine companies competing in the samegame environment of quadrant one. The competitors are divided into three strategic groups, namely, A, B and C. The value chain for each strategic group differs only in their relative efficiency reflecting variation in their cost structures and degree of differentiation, which in itself could for example be due to differences in their degrees of vertical integration. Each of these companies pursues a samegame strategy within their particular strategic group.

At some time during time T, a new entrant appears in quadrant four pursuing a newgame strategy whose value chain (in its embryonic form) is radically different to any of the value chains present amongst the strategic groups A, B or C in quadrant one. Assuming that the newgame competitor is successful in establishing a new market from the new value created by its chain of activities, then other start-up companies or entrants from other industry sectors will enter quadrant four. Their value chains will reflect those of the initial entrant and so form a new strategic group D. At this stage, the value chains of competitors in strategic group D are still highly unstable and evolving rapidly.

At time T+1 competitors from strategic group C recognising the opportunities in the newgame environment change the form of their existing samegame value chain to one similar, but not identical to that of the dominant newgame value chain in group D. They then move to compete in quadrant two, thus forming a second new strategic group. At the same time, members of strategic group D, whose value chain has now stabilised, also move upwards so that they compete in both quadrants two and four. Thus quadrant two now supports two stable strategic groups whose value chains are both variants of a newgame strategy. In this illustration, by way of example the reason that strategic group C remains separate from group D is that members of strategic group C are assumed to incorporate certain elements in their value chain, such as an established distribution channel, that is not yet available to or developed by members of strategic group D.

During time T+2 the members of strategic group B move into quadrant four with newly established business units that are based upon a significantly different newgame strategy from either of strategic groups

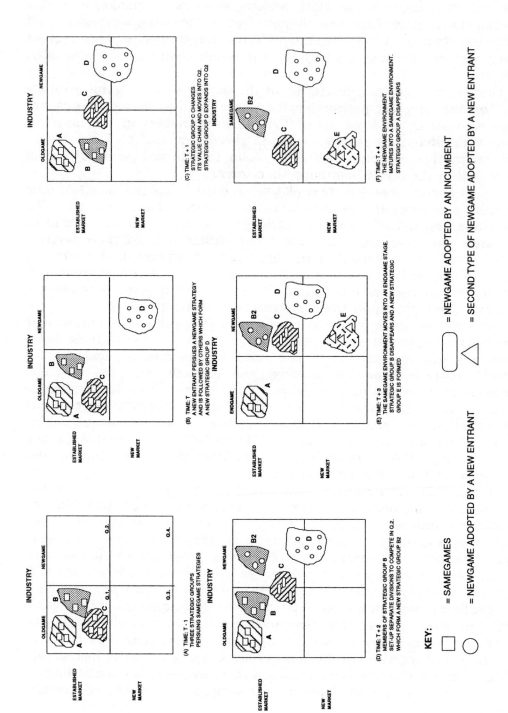

Fig. I.4. Evolution of strategic group business-matrices.

C or D. However, this raises an important point, namely that companies in strategic group B, may still continue their operations in quadrant one, following their established samegame strategy and value chains. At the same time, through diversification, they may set up a new business area within the overall group, but one which is structured with a new value chain. Hence, for the illustration, members of strategic group B are assumed to create a new strategic group B2, which is made up of subsidiaries or divisions that are still part of the same companies as in strategic group B, but are structured with new value chains and represent new business ventures within the respective companies.

This suggests therefore, that it is more useful to consider the strategic group in a given industry quadrant as representing the value chains (strategies) of business units. In some cases the business unit may represent the entire company, whilst in other cases it may represent a specific area of business. Furthermore, it should also be noted that here we are talking about different business areas that reflect some form of related business diversification. For example, IBM was in mainframe computers,[52] but then decided to diversify its activities firstly into the newgame of minicomputers[53] and then subsequently into the newgame of personal computers. In such a situation, it would be unrealistic and misleading to suggest that IBM consisted of a single strategic group which followed the same value chain in its mainframe business as in its minicomputer and personal computer businesses. Hence, it makes more sense in this context to depict IBM as having three value chains and belonging to three strategic groups. In the case of IBM's personal computer value chain, this value chain represented a new configuration for both itself and the industry. Such a move represented a challenge by an incumbent samegame strategic group to leap-frog the previous newgame strategic groups. Thus in the hypothetical example of Fig. 1.4., if the strategy of strategic group B2 is successful, then a second wave of the newgame is created and members of strategic groups C and D will be forced to respond by adapting their value chains to the new form developed by strategic group B2, or maybe even to develop new business units that would represent new strategic groups.

Such a process of moves and counter moves may continue for a considerable period of time. At each stage a successful strategy based upon an innovative and more competitive value chain will force incumbents (both from the samegame and newgame environments) to reassess their competitive positions. Their choice will be between trying to imitate the latest newgame strategy and hence re-configure their value chain accordingly. Alternatively, they may choose to develop a leap-frog approach and destabilise the newgame environment by creating a more radical newgame strategy and supporting value chain. Naturally, this second option presupposes that the company is able to create a sufficient competitive advantage by means of technological or organisational innovation.

In the illustration, by the time of T+3, those companies that failed to adapt to either the first or second wave of the newgame will find themselves in a declining endgame situation. It must be emphasised that these companies represent the incumbents from the initial samegame environment that failed to respond or adapt to the development of a stable newgame environment. As such, they represent the remnants of an outdated concept or solution and as such are thus doomed to decline, with limited chances for survival in the longer term. By now, their industry structure and its inherent value chains are no longer able to offer value to the customers' demands in the newgame environment. As such they represent the victims in the destruction of an obsolete pattern of business. However it is through such destruction that the creative process emerges to form a newgame industry, within which further newgames, such as those of the new strategic group E are formed.

Under certain conditions, an "oldgame" may continue to co-exist alongside a "newgame" for a considerable period of time. Only under those circumstances where the newgame products are a direct substitute in the same set of markets as the oldgame products, will rapid entropy of the oldgame take place. However, as illustrated in many case studies, once a newgame environment becomes established, its market boundaries will often begin to encroach upon those of the oldgame competitors by means of "sequential entry", ultimately forcing them out of the business, as illustrated by the disappearance of strategic group A by time T+4. Ultimately, at time T+4 when technological innovation has been exhausted or the impact of deregulation has worked its way through the system, then the newgame strategic groups stabilise and the environment takes on the form of a samegame, with companies once again competing by means of limited incremental improvements in cost structures or limited product–market improvements. However, the length of time for such a process to evolve will be dependent on the scale of value improvements offered by the newgame for the customer, over the existing oldgame. Naturally enough, such differences will be a function of the particular catalyst to change, the strategic group structures and market conditions. Once the resulting conditions take on the style of another samegame environment, then competition will again be based upon samegame strategies and will continue until such time as a further newgame is created, most probably from outside the industry when the cycle will then start all over again.

Clearly, the important lessons for any company to recognise are that the process of evolution just described will change the structure and membership of the strategic groups within the samegame environment. In addition, this matrix illustrates that competitors may belong to more than one strategic group within the same industry, when samegame and newgame environments are existing side by side. Hence the need to recognise that in such circumstances, we have to consider the nature of the value chains within any given company at the level of its business unit strategy and not just at the overall corporate level. In other words, it is not appropriate to analyse the strategic group at the level of the firm, but instead, at the level of the business unit. How this will affect individual companies will be a function of time, the historical pattern of strategic group membership, the intended point of entry (new strategic group) chosen and the asset structure of the particular company. Certainly, an established group of companies may be forced to abandon their traditional core strategic group, or at least shift their main focus of investment to alternate strategic groups, represented by their newly formed business units. In addition, it also follows that the most effective form of newgame strategy will restrict the degrees of freedom surrounding existing strategic groups, hence raising their mobility costs over those existing prior to the creation of the newgame environment. Or alternatively, a newgame strategy may be based upon a key factor for success (either industry or market related), which effectively blockades further entrants, for example, the holding of a unique set of technology patents by a newgame entrant, as illustrated by the case of the Xerox Corporation during the 1960s.

More usually, it is the uniqueness of the combination of value activities within the linkages of a newgame strategy value chain, that take time to imitate and hence offer a significant and sustainable competitive advantage, at least in relation to the oldgame competitors. Over the different phases of the evolution of the newgame environment, it is to be expected that additional strategic groups will emerge as a result of successful entry by start-up and incumbent firms. Thus entrants to a newgame environment (whether they be start-up or existing companies) will need to consider, the scale of both their existing and potential mobility barriers surrounding their respective present and targeted strategic groups. However, as well as industry related strategic group mobility barriers, consideration must also be given to the market related barriers facing competitors in their respective strategic groups and these will be considered after the next section. However, firstly we turn to look at how newgame environments evolve over time and how they relate to samegame and endgame environments.

NEWGAME EVOLUTION

Newgame environments form one of three categories of business evolution, the other two being oldgames, consisting either of samegame or endgame[54] environments. Each environment reflects a unique set of characteristics concerning the structure of the industry and its markets, together with associated patterns of strategic behaviour and pace of evolution or decay. However, it should not be assumed that the pattern is a stagewise growth model. Rather, in reality a variety of patterns may link newgames, samegames and endgames. Thus in some situations a newgame may be created in isolation, mature into a samegame and decline through an endgame. In other cases, an existing samegame may be challenged by a related newgame and in time, the newgame may destroy the samegame industry, which would go into decline as an endgame, whilst the newgame matured into a samegame, as previously illustrated in Fig. 1.4. The classical industry life-cycle divides the evolutionary pattern into five stages, namely, embryonic, growth, shake-out, stability and decline.

If one superimposes the three stages of the business environment's evolution on top of this model, one sees the result in Fig. 1.5. Clearly, the newgame environment is concerned with the earlier stages of this model and it is upon this section that we shall now focus.

The focus of the study of a newgame environment concerns the pattern of evolution that takes place within the newgame stage of the industry life-cycle. It is also concerned with the pattern of evolution that takes place in the early stages of product diffusion into the marketplace. Two models are proposed for reflecting upon the creation and evolution of newgame environments.

The first model is illustrated in Fig. 1.6 and highlights the underlying pattern of development of the value chains within strategic groups as the newgame industry moves towards a more stable state. At stage one, the strategic behaviour of firms in a potentially related industry leads to the creation of an embryonic value chain resulting from the first newgame strategy. In stage two, companies from the core samegame industry follow the early entrants into the newgame environment. This leads to further development and a crystallisation of the underlying value chains and rapid growth for the industry. When either an incumbent to the newgame industry or a new entrant then develop a second newgame strategy, then as shown in stage three, it redefines the evolving value chain structure. The same changes take place in stage four where further newgame strategies are introduced, thus once again altering the critical factors for success. By stage five, the core strategic groups of the newgame industry have developed relatively stable value chains and the strategic focus moves from differentiation and innovation in the technology towards creating differentiation in the marketing and distribution elements of the value chain in response to the increasing range of segmentation that has developed in the industry's markets. Any new entrants at this stage, tend to pursue niche samegame strategies as the industry matures from a newgame into a samegame environment.

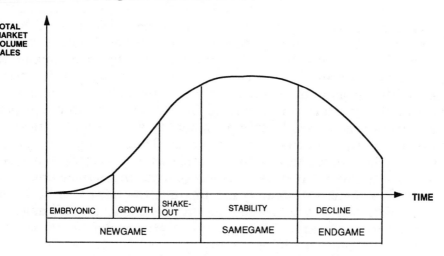

Fig. 1.5. The business environment life-cycle.

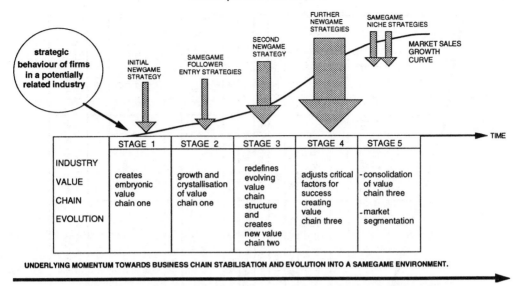

Fig. 1.6. Creation and evolution of newgame environments.

Life cycle models are notoriously prone to prove exceptions rather than the rule, however, their most useful purpose is to provide a clear picture of the major patterns that evolve over time. Hence, although newgames in general may develop in a variety of patterns, nevertheless certain consistent patterns can be identified as characteristic of each stage of their evolution. Fig. 1.7 illustrates that a newgame environment can be divided into seven stages of evolution, after which time it becomes a samegame environment or commences a further round of newgame evolution.

The basis of the seven stages are divided between catalyst, embryonic, take-off, growth, entry of the giants and legitimisation, consolidation and finally maturation and saturation. These name labels are primarily a reflection of the configuration and dynamics of the value chains of the dominant companies at each stage of evolution and the characteristics of the markets in which they compete. Fig. 1.7 traces the changes that take place in a number of factors within a technology based newgame environment which are listed in the left hand column. The characteristics of each variable are then entered into the contents of each box below the relevant stage of evolution.

Study of these characteristics suggest a number of patterns may be expected to emerge during the evolution of a newgame environment. At the catalyst stage, exogenous forces as discussed earlier in this chapter will be forming the potential conditions for the opportunity to be created that will lead to the implementation of an entrepreneurial driven newgame strategy, however, no formal industry structure will exist at this stage.

In the embryonic stage of the newgame industry's formation the structure of the industry is highly fragmented as crude value chains are formed by the first few entrants, industry barriers are low and the first strategic groups are forming, although in practice these may simply consist

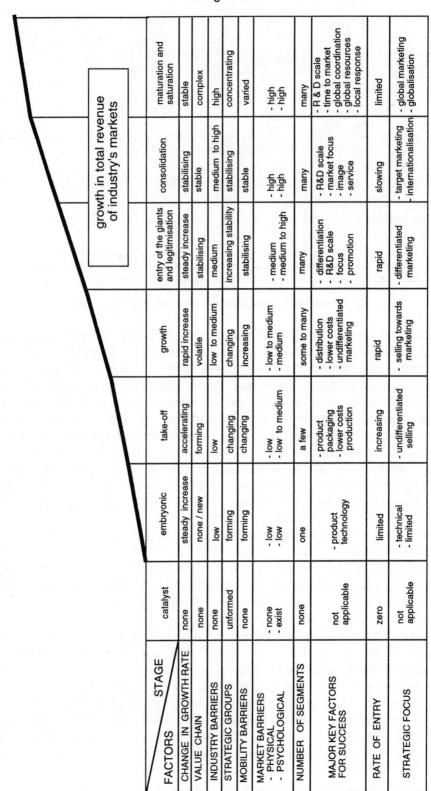

FACTORS \ STAGE	catalyst	embryonic	take-off	growth	entry of the giants and legitimisation	consolidation	maturation and saturation
CHANGE IN GROWTH RATE	none	steady increase	accelerating	rapid increase	steady increase	stabilising	stable
VALUE CHAIN	none	none / new	forming	volatile	stabilising	stable	complex
INDUSTRY BARRIERS	none	low	low	low to medium	medium	medium to high	high
STRATEGIC GROUPS	unformed	forming	changing	changing	increasing stability	stabilising	concentrating
MOBILITY BARRIERS	none	forming	changing	increasing	stabilising	stable	varied
MARKET BARRIERS - PHYSICAL - PSYCHOLOGICAL	- none - exist	- low - low	- low - low to medium	- low to medium - medium	- medium - medium to high	- high - high	- high - high
NUMBER OF SEGMENTS	none	one	a few	some to many	many	many	many
MAJOR KEY FACTORS FOR SUCCESS	not applicable	- product technology	- product packaging - lower costs production	- distribution - lower costs - undifferentiated marketing	- differentiation - R&D scale - focus - promotion	- R&D scale - market focus - image - service	- R & D scale - time to market - global coordination - global resources - local response
RATE OF ENTRY	zero	limited	increasing	rapid	rapid	slowing	limited
STRATEGIC FOCUS	not applicable	- technical - limited	- undifferentiated selling	- selling towards marketing	- differentiated marketing	- target marketing - internationalisation	- global marketing - globalisation

growth in total revenue of industry's markets

Fig. I.7. Seven stages of newgame environment evolution.

of individual companies. The market consists of a single segment with low barriers. The key factors for success are primarily based upon the product–technology which caters for the early technically orientated innovators in the marketplace. The strategic focus of competitors is therefore technical and limited in scope.

Providing that the newgame concept has generated sufficient demand, then the market expands and attracts more entrants, although most of these are still relatively small firms or start-up companies. At this point the newgame industry will move into its take-off stage with growth of revenues accelerating into double-digit figures. Strategic groups will now start to form different value chain structures, with the focus of attention shifting towards creating more efficiencies in production so as to gain the advantage of lower costs. The rate of entry into the industry also increases as psychological market barriers begin to emerge and a few segments begin to develop in the market. This then encourages more resources to be placed into the selling effort.

After the take-off stage the industry moves into its fourth stage of evolution, namely the growth stage. It is usually at this stage that the industry begins to show the characteristics of an industry in its own right, with well established channels of supply and distribution forming around the core competitors. Revenue growth moves into figures in excess of 50 to 60 per cent per annum, thus attracting a vast number of entrants, some of which now come from established large company backgrounds. Given the resources available to such entrants, industry barriers begin to rise quite rapidly and at least two forms of strategic groups emerge, consisting either of small companies and start-ups against the more established larger companies. The latter create new types of value chain and raise the costs of physical market barriers through the development of more sophisticated channels of distribution. Segmentation of the market continues to increase and undifferentiated marketing begins to be adopted by some of the competitors. The key factors for success continue to involve development of lower costs in production, but in addition, distribution and marketing begin to play an increasingly important role. The strategic focus thus begins to shift from basic selling of products towards a marketing approach that starts to take more account of the issues surrounding pricing, distribution and promotional activities.

Following the growth stage with a large number of entrants and rapid expansion of the market, it is inevitable that the critical mass of the industry and its associated markets will reach a legitimisation stage. This represents the establishment of the industry on its own terms, with well developed suppliers, competition, distribution channels and customer markets. At the same time, the rate of market growth will begin to slow. A number of larger well established entrants are expected to enter the industry at this stage, frequently coming from other related industry sectors. Hence, this stage is also referred to as the "Entry of the Giants". Such types of entrant may also pursue newgame strategies that create new types of value chains and a battle will now ensue, between the established earlier entrants and the new wave of larger competitors. There is no guarantee that the larger entrants will necessarily win. What does seem apparent however, is that the industry is now moving from an entrepreneurial type of culture into a professional enterprise type of culture and that those companies that fail to make the transition are unlikely to succeed for the reasons explained in Chandler's[55] exposition on the subject.

During the subsequent consolidation stage the overall market continues to grow but much more slowly than in the growth stage, albeit that in certain segments growth may be well below or above the industry average. Furthermore, initially some substantial new market segments may develop. At the same time, the value chains of various strategic groups become more stable and the industry barriers and mobility barriers become higher. It is during this consolidation stage, that the competitors in the industry begin to mature as organisations. Thus Chandler's[56] pattern of development towards managerial enterprises begins to gather pace. By now a large number of segments will have developed in the marketplace and both physical and psychological market barriers have reached a high level.

Gradually, the core markets move into maturation, the rate of entry slows and the newgame reaches its final stage, gradually taking on the hallmarks of saturation. The key factors for success now become more complex and vary considerably, thus creating a greater distinction between the strategic groups and their underlying value chain structures. Although lower costs remain an important factor for success, the strategic focus shifts to target marketing. This move stimulates greater emphasis upon establishing product differentiation that is fuelled by larger investments in research and development in an effort to leap-frog existing competitors' technology. For those companies with limited resources niche strategies become the dominant pattern of competition. The emphasis upon product differentiation amongst a large range of competing products forces a number of competitors to adopt greater focus upon promotional activities that build positive images for both the companies and their products in specific target markets. Later in this stage, as competition intensifies, price wars become more common and margins put pressure upon suppliers, competitors and distribution channels. Only the strong survive and a large number of smaller or weaker competitors are forced out of the business raising the level of concentration. The industry is now of a significant scale in terms of its total resources and will include a number of large players whose management is increasingly forced to develop improvements in the linkage of their value chains to extract the best standards of quality and lowest cost structures. These factors force the strategic focus of such companies into establishing a strong position beyond their regional markets on an international scale, not only in terms of developing other geographical markets, but also for improving the efficiency and sources of competitive advantage inherent in their respective value chains.

Naturally, throughout all these different stages of the newgame's evolution, there will have been some degree of international competition. However, it is more likely that international competition will become increasingly important during the consolidation, together with the maturation and saturation stages, as competitors look to overseas markets to maintain their growth. In so doing, further newgame strategies are likely to emerge, since the major competitors seeking a world-wide scale of operation will be forced to dramatically reconfigure their value chains in order to optimise their range of resources and hence gain competitive advantages.[57] In today's world, internationalisation on a world-wide scale usually involves developing various elements of the value chain in the three major regions[58] of the global economy, namely, North America, Europe and the Pacific Rim (especially in Japan). Details of this process are discussed in Chapter Seven. For the present, the general patterns of the newgame evolution will be described. The growth rate of the overall market is now relatively slow, but again it may vary from segment to segment, not only in terms of customer application, but also geographically. The value chains of strategic groups move towards an international composition, demanding greater management effort on issues concerning co-ordination and control of resources as well as in planning and implementation. Barriers to the industry are now high for broad scale global players, as are mobility barriers around the dominant strategic groups, so that entry into the industry is very low. The world-wide industry gradually moves towards increasing concentration by series of corporate failures and cross-border mergers and/or acquisitions.

In the marketplace, physical barriers are high, especially since they involve greater resources to develop and maintain a world-wide distribution system. Psychological barriers are also high, since cultural factors have to be overcome and companies have to invest resources to establish their name in areas where they are not well known. The number of segments becomes very large representing a mix of geographical and user characteristics. In some cases these segments will gradually reduce, if competitors are able to create products that are homogeneous in nature and appeal to customers on a world-wide basis.

The key factors for success in this stage of the newgame environment have now become very complex. Companies competing at the international level may be forced to form strategic alliances in order to gain access to the necessary resources of technology and distribution. The emphasis in the value chain has shifted away from technological elements more towards marketing and service, whilst the approach to the market is far more costly and necessitates sophisticated marketing techniques. However, it must be stressed that technology still remains a major driving force for competition in the industry as a whole and indeed, control of core technologies in this type of marketplace will be a critical advantage to any competitor. Due to the enormous costs involved in maintaining a presence in core technology, some competitors may decide to abandon this part of their value chain and rely instead upon branding and marketing products from other manufacturers. The pressure to shift down the value chain at this stage is due to the fact that management needs to seek excellence in every aspect of the value chain. For some, this is an impossible task, whilst for others the development of standards and relatively little perceivable differentiation in the nature of the product itself to the customer, forces them to place greater effort into creating differentiation further down the value chain. Thus pre-sales service, promotional activities, training, after-sales-support and maintenance all become vitally important in a competitor's strategic efforts to persuade a customer to perceive its products and service as being of better value than the competition. As the industry moves further towards handling products that may be perceived more and more as commodity items, then competitors will be forced to invest an increasing share of their resources in offering additional items that attempt to differentiate their products and emphasise the need for target marketing. Ultimately, unless a further newgame strategy emerges to boost the industry onto another level of the life cycle, the newgame environment will mature during its international saturation stage into a samegame environment. In some cases, the international form of competition may mature into a global business environment, as is suggested in stage seven of Fig. 1.7.

In summary, this section has suggested that newgame environments form part of three stages of business environment evolution, along with samegames and endgames. As such, newgame environments pass through seven possible stages of evolution as they move from their pre-formation catalyst stage through various stages of growth to consolidation and saturation, during which a process of internationalisation and/or globalisation is likely to take place. During each stage, the industry, its competitors, strategic groups and markets experience fundamental changes in structure and behaviour. Each stage therefore necessitates a reappraisal by competitors as to their strategies and will usually require a reconfiguration of their value chains, if they are to be able to maintain a competitive position.

So far, the newgame framework has analysed the forces for creation of and the general characteristics of newgame environments and strategies. It has also shown the impact of newgame strategies on value chains and the composition of strategic groups as well as providing a general model of the characteristics of evolution of newgame environments. In effect, these issues have in large part concentrated upon supply side factors. However, the newgame environment is an holistic framework that attempts to bring together all aspects of the business environment and so finally, we need to consider how markets evolve and in particular to pay attention to the way in which newgame markets conceal a variety of subtle barriers to entry.

MARKET AND MARKETING BARRIERS

Market Barriers

The concept of market barriers refers to the obstacles which a potential entrant needs to overcome in order to gain user and/or buyer acceptance and hence sales of a given product. As such, market barriers are demand side characteristics which represent and reflect the pattern of demand (both overt and latent) of consumers. Market barriers are segment specific. Thus for any overall market, specific sets of market barriers will surround individual segments. Some of the characteristics may be common to all segments, whilst other characteristics may only be present in certain segments. A second proposition concerning market barriers is that they will change over time. Indeed, the concept of market barriers changing over time fits perfectly with the "adoption" categories described in the literature by Rogers[59] about diffusion of innovations. Roger's main focus was to consider a person's "innovativeness" as,

" . . . the degree to which an individual is relatively earlier in adopting new ideas than the other members of his social system".[60]

However, market barriers are not simply a function of pace or timing of adoption, since they refer to two different aspects of any given market segment, which may be divided between psychological and physical barriers, both of which may change over time.

Physical and Psychological Market Barriers

Physical market barriers refer to structural features of a market segment, examples include the scale of investment required to establish a network of distribution outlets, a large direct sales force or a major promotional campaign budget. These are usually overt in nature. Psychological market barriers refer to behavioural features of both buyers and/or end users towards adopting a particular product or service. Examples include loyalty to a supplier based upon length of association and establishment of trust, or lack of awareness through ignorance about a particular product's features. In international markets, the psychological barriers may involve a lack of knowledge about the foreign entrant company, or aversion to buying "foreign-goods" and possible concerns about security of supply.

By recognising these features as representing market segment barriers, an important linkage is established at a conceptual level between supply side and demand side conditions, which provides a common focus upon the strategic behaviour and performance of a company, both within its given strategic group and the market segments within which it is active. It should also be noted that market barriers may reflect generic features of a particular market segment at any given point in time, as well as company or product specific features. Thus not only do the height of market barriers vary around different market segments over time, but they will also vary in relation to strategic groups or particular companies. This is illustrated in Fig. 1.8 which shows that physical market barriers exist as the outer boundary and need to be overcome by all competitors seeking entry to the particular market segment. However, when a company enters a particular market segment, its performance will not only be dependent upon its specific strategy and strategic group membership, but will also

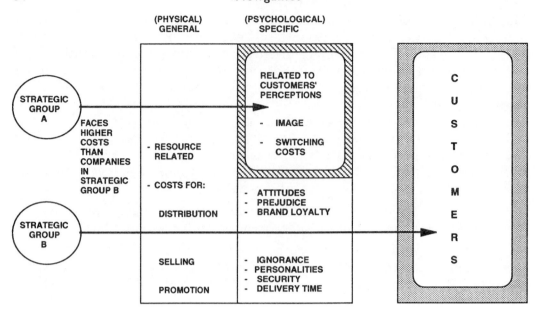

Fig. 1.8. Generic and specific marketing barriers.

be dependent upon its perceived position by the customer segment. Hence, companies from strategic groups A and B may both overcome the overt general physical barriers, yet only companies from strategic group B are able to overcome the latent or less obvious psychological barriers in order to enjoy successful penetration of the given customer group, even though both sets of companies might pursue similar strategies. Conceptually, this idea is based upon the literature of communications and decision sciences in the marketing field, where detailed attention has been given to decision-making and purchasing behaviour.[61]

The phenomenon is of central importance to using the newgame framework of analysis, since it provides a powerful explanation of variation in strategic performance over time. Furthermore, its implications are important to management, since it emphasises their need to appreciate that newgame environments require a subtle understanding of the latent characteristics of customer demand when developing both entry strategies and maintenance strategies within newgame environments. Such appreciation is not derived solely by means of dry market research data reflecting levels of demand in terms of volume, prices, distribution channels, etc. Useful as some of this analysis may be, the essential focus of attention needs to be upon the minds of the consumers and the subjective values that they draw about particular products or services. These issues are best understood by exploring the psychological behaviour of consumers in terms of their objective functions in addition to the more conventional measure of customer needs.

Objective Functions versus Customer Needs

Some examples of the contrast in strategic focus between "objective functions" and merely satisfying customers' existing needs are illustrated in Table 1.3. Newgames clearly upset the status quo and change the rules of the game, both of which require an understanding of the latent market and how best to restrict the response of the competition. Indeed, successful newgame strategies require a high degree of skill in human organisation and leadership, but in addition they require a high degree of long-term vision and imagination.[62]

This idea is in sympathy with the observations of Christopher Lorenz,[63] who points to the fact that many managers are heavily influenced by market research, so much so, that they use it as a decision substitute, instead of for decision support. Referring to comments by Stephen King, a director of J. Walter Thompson, Lorenz highlights that:

Table 1.3. "Objective Functions" versus "Customer Needs".

EXTERNAL CATALYSTS FOR CHANGE	INITIAL NEWGAME AGENTS	OBJECTIVE FUNCTION	EXISTING APPROACH
DEREGULATION CLIMATE	LAKER U.S. AIR PEOPLE'S EXPRESS	LOW-COST NO-FRILLS AIR-TRAVEL	EXPENSIVE FULL-SERVICE
REPACKAGING & REALIGNING BUSINESS CHAIN	MACDONALDS	FAST CONVENIENT CONSISTENT LOW COST MEAL SERVICE	LOW COST VARIABLE STANDARD SNACK RESTAURANT
SEMICONDUCTOR AND SOFTWARE TECHNOLOGY	APPLE TRS COMMODORE	PERSONAL USER-FRIENDLY COMPUTING	CENTRALISED DATA PROCESSING
PRODUCTION TECHNOLOGY REPACKAGING	SWATCH	LOW COST FASHION ACCESSORY TIMEPIECE	DURABLE REPLACEABLE TIMEKEEPING
PRODUCTION TECHNOLOGY REALIGN BUSINESS CHAIN	CD DISCS/ PLAYERS	HIGH QUALITY DURABLE MUSIC MEDIA INTELLIGENT MACHINES	REASONABLE QUALITY FLEXIBLE MUSIC MEDIA INTELLIGENT MACHINES
SEMICONDUCTOR AND DISPLAY	HP TI	HAND-HELD PORTABLE RELIABLE FAST PERSONAL	DESK-TOP SLOW ELECTRO-MECHANICAL CALCULATORS OR HAND HELD LIMITED ACCURACY SLIDE RULES

"Obsessive reliance on market research, and a mistaken belief in it as the provider of direct answers, completely stifles any attempt to create that 'meaningful distinction' which is at the heart of competitiveness in today's crowded marketplace".[64]

As Lorenz suggests, the fundamental point is that most market research techniques (which often are central supports to samegame strategies), merely measure what the consumers themselves know they want or prefer. Such information may be perfectly valid when a company is seeking incremental improvements to its products. However, to create a newgame strategy, a company is unlikely to gain much useful information by asking potential consumers to predict their feelings about a product that may not, as yet, have been developed and which may be unfamiliar. Instead, it needs to look beyond consumers' currently expressed needs to understand their underlying behaviour patterns and then to lead the market by creating and stimulating a new want, which had previously been a subconscious or even unknown desire.

The Newgame Strategic Framework: A Marketing Approach

As previously mentioned, the newgame strategic framework is hybrid in nature. This is because it combines the contemporary competitive strategy model with that of the marketing model by linking analysis of the customer and marketplace with that of the various elements of the value chain, strategic groups and the industrial organisation model. However, the emphasis of the newgame approach is strongly marketing orientated, since it adopts the maxim that strategic success in a newgame environment is based upon developing newgame strategies that best satisfy customers' objective functions. Within the hybrid framework, which is illustrated in Fig. 1.9 the focus involves identifying the wants (both current and potential) of customers and/or users in a chosen set of target markets, having first of all segmented the market structure and analysed the existing and potential competition in each segment. The next step involves considering the leverage relationship the company has with its various industry suppliers along the value chain, especially in terms of costs and control in relation to those of its competitors in the given target segments. The strategic aim here is to reduce costs to the industry average in these segments or, better still, to become a cost leader.[65] If neither of these conditions can be met, the company will need to base its strategic tactics upon achieving a differentiated position at one or more points along the value chain.[66] By creating cost leadership or a differentiated position or both, the company would implement a strategic mix[67] that was intended to gain a competitive advantage over existing and potential competitors within the chosen market segments. If neither a cost leadership or differentiated position could be developed or sustained, on a broad market basis, then it would have to be achieved by the company focusing its business activities on a smaller number of segments, or by shortening its value chain in which it was active, i.e. reduce its degree of vertical and/

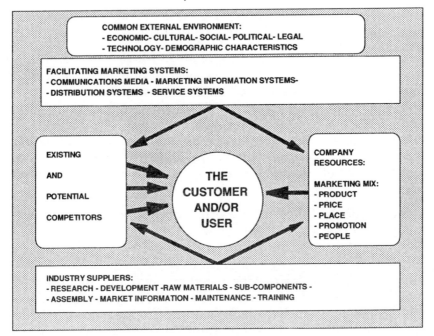

Fig. 1.9. Strategic environment and competitive forces.

or horizontal integration. Alternatively, it might need to exit the business.

Assuming the company chooses to compete, it would develop a marketing mix within the strategic mix, which would make use of the various marketing facilitators illustrated in Fig. 1.9. Naturally, its strategic aim would be to develop a strong competitive advantage in these areas, all of which help to project the company as being in a relatively strong position, compared to its competitors in the chosen market segments. Here, however, the strategic tactics would be focused upon "positioning" both the company and its products in order to maximise its leverage relative to the competition with both existing and potential buyers and users. The middle and lower stratas of Fig. 1.9 therefore represent an amalgam of the classical concepts developed from both industry supply and market demand side frameworks. Overarching the entire set of areas and activities exists the macro scale environment encompassing the range of factors impacting the company, competition and their respective markets.

In summary, this verbal description, as represented diagramatically in Fig. 1.9, suggests a "watershed" in the convergence of ideas between the major schools of thought drawn from the previously identified fields. This is not to suggest the absence of a need or existing effort to refine and develop our understanding of details within this framework. Problems of analytical consistency, together with major practical problems in formulation, still more so in implementation, still abound. Indeed, it would seem reasonable and honest to argue that for many companies the practical reality of their strategic behaviour is still trying to catch up with the ideas and concepts developed in both the industrial organisation and marketing literature of over thirty years ago. This "theory gap" is clearly recognised in Thomas Bonoma's comments, when he states,

> "...the academic and trade stimulus, which seemed strong on strategic marketing but uncomfortably silent regarding *specific* guidelines for how the strategies were to be made to work".[68]

He proceeds to also identify the "competitive gap" when he states,

> "...marketing, supposedly the science of buyers *and* sellers, seemed to concentrate myopically on the buyers and gave passing attention at best to how the sellers might become more efficient at their marketing practices".[69]

A point similarly taken up by other academics, who argued forcibly that although the marketing concept was born out of the need to *compete* more effectively, the message too often conveyed was "know thy customer" to the exclusion of "know thy competitor".[70]

Taking these various criticisms together, contemporary theory has only just begun more recently to merge the industry side and market side approaches together into a hybrid framework. Furthermore, both sides still appear highly mechanistic in their approach and analytical frameworks. In addition, the emphasis upon strategic formulation has tended to neglect the more essential factors of concern to the practising manager involving problems of implementation.

Although the implementation issue applies equally to both newgame and oldgame strategies, the newgame paradigm clearly addresses the need for an holistic approach. Hence newgame strategies focus on both supply and demand side structures, but they also use a creative and lateral style of thinking, the content of which both addresses the "objective functions" of buyers and users. Such strategies recognise the importance of market barriers, yet at the same time seek to limit competitors' degrees of freedom and adjust the key factors for success by fundamentally changing the rules of the game, by means of structural alteration to the value chain system.

Since the success of newgame strategies (in common with all strategies) is also dependent upon the implementation process, it is important to acknowledge that the ability of any company to succeed will be a function of certain internal management and organisational factors. These involve the company's ability to identify and link together:

(1) the external opportunities for change,
(2) the "objective functions" of the marketplace,
(3) the market barriers (both physical and psychological),
(4) the key factors for success in the current business system, and
(5) the competitive advantages and functional competence of existing competitors.

All of these factors are tied up in the approach adopted in this book to the study of *Newgames and Strategic Competition in the PC Revolution*.

In summary, newgame strategies can be understood as being different from oldgame strategies in a variety of dimensions. Most importantly they reflect a fundamental distinction in terms of intellectual approach, aims and focus. These in turn create a much more significant impact upon the prevailing conditions of competition (when successfully implemented) than oldgame strategies. Successful implementation of newgame strategies will be dependent not only on the criteria of strategic 'vision', but also on the practicalities and challenges involved in developing and sustaining a flexible and adaptive form of organisation. Indeed, the currently popular concept of "re-engineering"[71] awakens management to the idea of sometimes destroying old processes completely, in order to gain more efficient ways of working in organisations. In a similar context, it would appear that the "learning organisation"[72] may well be an important step towards coping with newgame environments. Indeed, combining these concepts and others forms the basis of this author's own newgame organisational model, which is referred to as "The Intelligent Organisation".[73]

EXAMPLES OF NEWGAMES

In order to complete the overview of newgames, the final section of this introductory chapter presents some examples of Newgame Environments, which should provide the reader with tangible situations and draws attention to the increasing frequency and importance of such events in the modern business world.

The newgame framework suggested that conditions for changing the value chains of competitors within an existing business system or for creating a new business system may initially be caused by factors which are either exogenous or endogenous to the firm. Endogenous factors may include political, legal, economic, ecological, social or technological events. Examples of each are given in Table 1.4.

Geopolitical Newgames

The changes that were set in motion during the late 1980s in the former Soviet Union, together with the Central and East European bloc countries all reflect a monumental example of a geopolitical newgame. The vision of "perestroika" and its architect, Mikhail Gorbachev provided the catalyst to change the communist political, economic and social systems. Whilst the aftermath of the first wave of changes are still having their effect, the current and future impact of these forces is and will dramatically alter the structure of virtually every industry sector within these countries. The shift from supply side led centrally planned economic systems of production to some form of intended market driven economies represents a most dramatic change in the value chains of companies operating within this environment. It is to be expected that the vast majority of companies, both large and small will not survive the process. However, the optimist may argue that the oldgame has to be swept away in its entirety if a newgame environment is to be born successfully. Clearly, the immediate

Table 1.4. Examples of the creation of newgame environments.

STAGE OF CORE INDUSTRY	CATALYST FOR CHANGE	SOURCE OF CHANGE	KEY ASPECTS OF OLD VALUE CHAIN IMPACTED BY THE NEWGAME STRATEGIES						NEWGAME CREATED
			CORE TECH	PROD	MNFT ASSEM	MKT	DIST	SVCE	
Data processing - maturing	Technology	Semiconductors industry	*	*		*	*	*	Personal computers
Potato crisps - mature	Technology	Redefine product	*	*	*				Potato snacks
Reprographics - mature	Technology	Xerography	*	*	*				Photocopiers
Watches - mature	Technology	Quartz Digital	*	*	*	*	*	*	Quartz watches Digital watches
Computer software - maturing	Technology	Personal computers		*	*	*	*	*	Shrink-wrapped software
Motorbikes - mature	Strategic marketing and design	Redefine product			*	*	*	*	Smaller, lower-powered bikes
U.S. airlines - mature	Regulatory change	Redefine service				*	*	*	Cheaper "No-frills" service
Electro-mechanical calculators - mature	Electronics technology	Microchips LED displays	*	*	*	*	*	*	Handheld electronic calculators
Refillable ink pens - mature	Technology	Create substitute product	*	*	*	*	*	*	Disposable pens
Banking - mature	-Technology - Regulatory change	Redefine services		*		*	*	*	Broader financial services

outlook is bleak. However, if newgame strategies are allowed to succeed and sufficient resources and Western investment are made available, then in time newgame industries will arise from the ashes of these lands.

Legal Newgames

In recent years, a number of industry sectors in the United States, Europe and parts of the Asia/Pacific region have experienced the impact of deregulation upon their business environments. Such legal changes represent a powerful force for creating newgame environments, since it allows the entry of new competitors pursuing newgame strategies. In some cases, the entrants are large established companies from other countries that had previously been excluded from the home market, as in the case of the telecommunications industry. Similarly, deregulation of financial services in the United Kingdom during the early 1980s led to the convergence of industry sectors that had previously been prohibited from conducting business directly in other related sectors. In this instance, after deregulation, competitors in the clearing banks found themselves open to competition from building societies and similarly clearing banks started competing in the general house mortgage market. Insurance companies, pension funds, merchant banks and brokers all found that the industry had suddenly expanded overnight to encompass a wide range of new markets, however, they also included some substantial established new competitors from these other sectors.

Other situations have witnessed the emergence of a number of new start-up ventures as in the Carter administration's deregulation of civil airlines in the United States, which led to a new set of competitive conditions, generating a different set of factors for success and major shifts in the underlying value chains of competitors in the airline business. Yet after the creation of a newgame environment brought about by the entry of smaller, low cost, no frills carriers, the industry experienced a second wave of newgame strategies instigated by some of the larger carriers, which gained competitive advantage by developing various elements of their value chains to take advantage of their computer reservations systems, access to terminal gates at major airports and restructuring their routes to a hub-and-spoke system. All of these factors led to their achieving significant control of sales and distribution channels, which furthermore contributed value to their operations. As a direct result of the subsequent competitive advantage gained by such carriers, most of the smaller carriers were then wiped out either via acquisition or liquidation. The industry structure that emerged was then dominated by the larger megacarriers. At the same time, it should also be noted that a number of the traditional established incumbents failed to effectively cope with the change and were also either acquired or forced into liquidation, although a few sought to survive under the protection of Chapter 11.[74] Such developments have further impacted policy within the European Community and its Single Market, by forcing governments to support the consolidation of national carriers and in some cases with limited cross-border arrangements in order to ensure that Europe as a whole is able to maintain its own megacarriers to compete in a global newgame environment and not simply a European newgame environment.

Economic Newgames

Economic forces for generating newgame environments tend by their very nature to be intrinsically connected to political or legal forces. At a macro scale they could involve changes in a government's economic policy towards a particular industry sector, which could introduce grants or loans to enable new entrants into the market. Such a situation might be developed to encourage foreign inward investment that could encourage the establishment of research and development operations or production facilities in a country that had previously only provided an export market. For example, the level of quotas on Japanese cars imported into the United States encouraged certain Japanese car manufacturers to change their strategy to invest directly in the United States. In so doing, the Japanese started to compete with a modified value chain that altered their competitive position with the indigenous United States manufacturers. Various aspects of Japanese management of their value chain have influenced their operations and the degree of competition in the United States, forcing United States competitors in turn to adjust their operations in order to remain competitive.

A further example of economic forces for change involves the growing number of industries whose target market has moved from being national or regional into global. Such changes reflect major adjustments in trading patterns and have forced competitors to reconfigure their value chains in terms of location and content in order to move towards development of global newgame strategies.

Ecological Newgames

Growing concern from environmental lobbies and consumer groups have made issues relating to protection of the environment a political issue. In some cases this has forced legislation upon companies concerning control and treatment of pollutants. At another level, it has provided an opportunity for some companies to reappraise certain aspects of their operations in the light of the "green movement". In some consumer goods, new brands have been produced to cater for the environmentally conscious market segment, such as in detergents, clothing or food. Other companies have realised the public relations value of being seen to be environmentally concerned, so that companies in industries ranging across oil exploration, airlines, pharmaceuticals, chemicals and road transport are all promoting their efforts to protect the environment. Whether such efforts are having as great an effect on the problem as sometimes claimed, and whether the motivation for such behaviour is philanthropic or commercial can be difficult to determine. However, what is clear is that ecological forces are increasingly encouraging companies in all sorts of industries to re-evaluate their operations and products with a "greener" perspective. In some instances the impact is marginal and could not be considered as an example of a newgame. However, in other cases, such as environmentally friendly detergents and some food-stuffs, an initial wave of change can be seen to be developing. Naturally, such changes are closely linked to social forces.

Social Newgames

Perhaps the most subtle of the exogenous forces that can provide the basic conditions for the evolution of a newgame are social in nature. Generally they develop over a reasonably long period of time, however, when combined with other forces, such as ecological or technological, they can interact to form a powerful and relatively speedy process of change.

In this context, examples of social change include the shift in values towards ecologically sound products. Already a significant number of consumers in developed economies are demanding either directly in the market, or indirectly through government legislation to see higher standards adopted in this area. This is a trend that is likely to continue, thus forcing companies to adopt "greener" strategies. Another example of social change can be seen in the increased levels of computer literacy[75] resulting from education in schools, colleges and the workplace in response to the rapid diffusion of personal computers in our society. Increased awareness about the potential role of computers in our society has led to the creation of a vast range of computer related businesses that became possible only because society changed and accepted the apparent need for such products in our lives.

Technological Newgames

The most frequent and possibly the most powerful force for change in our modern societies is technology. Sometimes this may be exogenous to an industry, whilst on other occasions it is endogenous, being developed by a company within the industry. Examples abound of technology change forcing the creation of a newgame. In some instances the technology is inherent within the components of a product, whilst at other times it involves the production process, be this in a manufacturing or service business.

As already outlined in the newgame framework, step changes in core technology often tend to occur outside the industry amongst suppliers of alternative technology to the conventional suppliers, as in the case of microelectronics, which in a relatively short period of time diffused into a vast number of industry sectors to substitute or complement and thus improve upon previous mechanical, electrical or hydraulic systems. Virtually all the cases of substitute technologies during the industrial period of the last hundred and fifty years have led to some form of newgame. Examples are too numerous to mention, but a few of the more recent are provided in Table 1.4.

Very rarely do any of these forces act in pure isolation. They are often connected, so that political forces are often manifest in legal forces, whilst social forces are closely linked to ecological forces and technological and economic forces also go hand in hand. What is important to remember in each of the examples given of newgame environments in Table 1.4 is the fact that these forces, powerful as they are, merely provided the opportunity for change. The catalyst to change, the substance that melded these respective forces together to form the basis of a newgame environment was entrepreneurism. The "vision" and ideas of the entrepreneur or intrapreneur that responded to the opportunities materialised in the form of a newgame strategy in some form or other. Success of such a strategy is the hallmark of a newgame environment. The following chapters will explore these issues and others in more depth as they analyse the behaviour and competition in the evolution of the newgame involving the personal computer industry—or more succinctly— *Newgames: Strategic Competition in the PC Revolution.*

Chapter Two

PERSONAL COMPUTER TECHNOLOGY

"When the world's first microprocessor, the Intel 4004, appeared in 1971 it had not come about as a conscious effort on Intel's part to develop a computer on a chip but more as a result of their desire to produce a flexible set of component parts for a range of programmable calculators. The origins of today's microcomputers therefore lie in the history of calculating and recording techniques. This is not the whole story, however, for part of the microcomputer's uniqueness lies in its small size, and this we owe to the development of microelectronics, which play an equally important part in its evolution."[1]

INTRODUCTION

The origins of the personal computer can be traced back to events both within and outside the computer industry, some historical and some more recent. This chapter describes the early ideas that subsequently led to the development of the modern computer and then proceeds to present an overview of the basic technology within personal computers. Finally, a summary of the development of the field of microelectronics and the subsequent invention of the microprocessor[2] is provided, which essentially made the personal computer a technical reality.

EARLY HISTORICAL PROGRESS

The Path of Inventions to the Computer

Earliest computation technology can indeed be traced back to the ancient world. In its earliest stages, development in computation was principally one of techniques, including the abacus, logarithms and the slide rule. Mechanical calculating machines were first seen with the demonstration of Blaise Pascal's working model in 1643, which was followed by a more sophisticated machine developed by Gottfried Liebniz. During the seventeenth and early eighteenth century, other significant developments in mechanical calculator design followed, which included the hand crank drive mechanism as well as the employment of punched metal plates (forerunners to punched cards) to store information to control Joseph Jaquard's weaving machine.[3]

Perhaps one of the most famous names in the early history of computers is that of Charles Babbage, who conceived the idea of his "Difference Engine"[4] and the later "Analytical Engine".[5] Unfortunately neither conception was ever made operational. Another major advance in computer technology during the mid-nineteenth century was the development of the algebra of logic by George Boole. This was to be the basis of switching theory[6] developed by Claude Shannon in the following century, which ultimately was applied to the design of electronic computers. Development of punched cards and the machines to process them was stimulated in the late nineteenth century by the needs of the U.S. Census Bureau, which led to the development of a commercial tabulator[7] by its inventor, Herman Hollerith. His company, the Tabulating Machine Company was to be the forerunner of IBM. Thus throughout the latter half of the nineteenth century and well into the twentieth century, mechanically based calculators continued to be developed, incorporating improvements in speed and efficiency.[8] The Comptometer[9] was invented by Dorr Felt (1884) in the USA as a key-operated adding machine, whilst William Seward Burroughs developed a 90-key machine with a nine decimal digit capacity in 1892. By the second quarter of the twentieth century the theoretical principles of basic computing had become established. What was now necessary was an alternative to mechanical technology that could convert the numerical formulae at a more efficient speed. The technology was to be provided by the growing field of electrical engineering, that was to form the seedbed for the subsequent development of the electronics industry.

The Earliest Computers

There are a number of contenders for "The inventor of the computer", including Vannevar Bush at MIT in the 1930s, as well as the German, Conrad Zuse during the same period. However, it was not until the 1940s that the first true electronic computer appeared. This was the ABC (Atanasoff Berry Computer), built by John Atanasoff. The ABC did not become recognised as such until after a long and involved court case that ended in 1972. Until that time the ENIAC (Electronic Numerical Integrator And Calculator), designed and built by Eckert and Mauchly, was credited with being the first electronic computer, which had been completed in late 1945 at the University of Pennsylvania. However, the size of this early machine was considerable, occupying 1500 square feet of floor space, weighing over 30 tons and consuming over 150kW of power. Several years later, in 1949, the EDSAC (Electronic Delay Storage Automatic Calculator), developed by Maurice Wilkes in Cambridge, became operational. A further limitation on all of these early machines was that they were also extremely difficult to program.[10,11] This problem was largely solved by John Von Neumann, the mathematician, whose ideas overcame the problem of reprogramming a computer. His contributions ranged from setting forth, in detail, the logical design of the computer, to introducing the concept of instruction modification and to working out the details of the computer's electronic circuitry.

During this period of development in the late forties, electronic computers were used only in research and by the government. However, in 1951, Univac 1 was delivered to the USA Census Bureau and became the first commercial computer. 1951 also saw the completion of Whirlwind 1, at MIT, representing the first real-time computer. During the next thirty years, the power and scope of application of computers was to continue to expand at an accelerating pace, ultimately leading to the development of the personal computer. Yet although by 1951 the fundamentals of computing had become well established, the process by which personal computers were to become a reality and develop into the now familiar item was very much determined by developments that took place outside the computer industry itself, namely, in the field of microelectronics, which developed during the period of the 1950s and 1960s. Before considering these developments, it is important to first appreciate the basic technology that is involved in the personal computer, so that the role of different technologies and their relative importance can better be understood.

THE PERSONAL COMPUTER DEFINED

The Elements of a Personal Computer

No single standard definition exists for a personal computer, since its performance and applications are continually changing with advances in technology. In the embryonic stage of the industry's development they were defined as:

> ". . . The basic, inexpensive microcomputer systems designed for the hobbyist for his own use in his own home".[12]

However, by the early 1980s personal computers were to be found in offices, factories and other locations, operating a wide range of applications. By the early 1990s the communications facilities on personal computers could be interlinked through a local area network[13] to a wide variety of other computers and peripherals.[14] Furthermore, the personal computer's shape, size, power and reliability has continued to evolve so rapidly, that a variety of new forms of personal computer have entered the market, including the portable,[15] laptop[16] and handheld[17] versions.

Whatever the type of computer, it is misleading to think of a personal computer as a single machine. Computers are actually systems[18] comprising of several parts, each with a particular task. The four major elements common to most units are:

(i)   Central Processing Unit (CPU).[19]
(ii) System's Internal Memory.[20]
(iii) Input facilities.[21]
(iv) Output facilities.[22]

Such elements of the computer are referred to as hardware because in a sense they are solid, hard objects. They are shown schematically in Fig. 2.1, whilst their descriptions are provided in the following section. However, to make a computer work, one also requires software,[23] which consists of programs that are responsible for controlling the tasks performed by the hardware. Since these are stored in an electronic format, they are invisible to the user and can be changed around to suit a given application. They are therefore maleable and non-rigid, hence the name software. Together computer hardware and software form a computer system.[24] Because personal computers are systems, it has allowed competition to enter and take place at a variety of levels and technological innovation has therefore occurred in all four elements, creating a continual feedback effect, which has provided new opportunities for competition. Since competition has been largely based upon improvements or innovations in the technology price/performance ratio, the personal computer has evolved into an increasingly wider range of applications as improvements have taken place in each of the elements. To understand how these elements interact with one another, it is necessary to consider their respective functions and capabilities.

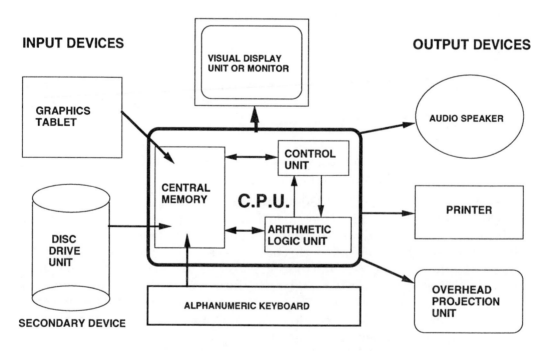

Fig. 2.1. Computer system hardware.

The Central Processing Unit (CPU)

The "brain" of a computer is the CPU, which controls all system operations including the manipulation of all external equipment (printers,[25] disks,[26] tapes, etc.). Design of the CPU and its associated capabilities has always been a core area for product differentiation, since this will determine the resulting potential power and performance of the overall computer. As a general overview it may be considered to consist of the following components:[27]

*   Arithmetic[28] and Logic Unit.[29]
*   Control.[30]
*   Address Handling.[31]
*   A Multiplicity of Registers.[32]

Together these elements form the microprocessor which is at the heart of a personal computer. Consisting of a silicon chip[33] its functions are to control a computer, carry out calculations and to direct data between input devices, output devices and memory. Essentially, a microprocessor is an integrated circuit[34] package that contains a complete electronic circuit or family of circuits that make up the CPU.

System's Internal Memory

Besides the microprocessor, a computer needs some way of storing the information entered into it and uses two types of internal memory. The first is volatile and is known as RAM, or Random Access Memory[35] and allows the user to store temporary data, whilst the second is non-volatile and known as ROM, or Read Only Memory,[36] in which the user cannot store data. RAMs are categorised as static or dynamic.[37] Both types of RAM lose their contents when the computer's power supply is cut off. Hence, from the earliest single board microcomputer onwards, there existed a need for secondary or back-up memory, which could hold data permanently and load it back into RAM when needed. ROM chips contain permanent data, which stores the computer's operating system,[38] and are programmed by the computer manufacturer. Whilst they do not lose their information when the power supply is cut, they can only be "read from", that is, their contents can be examined but not altered.

Input and Output Devices

Since a computer has to be able to communicate with other electronic devices, various forms of product and circuitry are used to transfer information either to or from the computer and are known as input/output devices. Data may thus be input through a mouse,[39] keyboard, microphone, etc., which may be linked to some form of permanent memory storage devices,[40] which initially consisted of cassette tape recorders, but nowadays come from high capacity disk drives.[41] Whilst information is being processed it is displayed on visual display units, VDUs[42] (e.g. television sets or screen monitors).[43] Then, the results can be displayed in a form of hard-copy permanent media, which initially consisted of a low quality printer, but which nowadays may include high quality laser printers,[44] plotting devices or special overhead slide projectors. Such devices are referred to as computer peripherals, which are connected to a personal computer through standard interfaces.[45] The interfaces themselves consist of a combination of plugs, sockets and cables, as well as appropriate software, whose function is to control the transfer of data between the computer and the relevant peripheral.

How Personal Computers Work

Hardware

Hardware Components

Personal computers are distinguished by a number of factors. These may include their configuration (stand-alone[46] or multi-task/multi-user[47]), their microprocessor technology, the size of the data word they can handle, or by their compatibility with other devices. The operation of personal computers, of whatever type, is broadly the same. Differences in operation, from one personal computer to another, are determined by variations in the systems design, basic technology, storage capacity[48] and other specifications that determine the machine's overall performance. Personal computers are designed mainly from standard components and the complete system will be used in a variety of configurations, according to the particular set of peripherals selected by the user. However, both the interactions between components and the data flows between the CPU and its associated units are complex and represent an important area for product differentiation in terms of the skills available in the design team of any single personal computer company.

Transmission

A bridge between the internal components of a computer and the interface to peripherals is provided by three standard information "highways": the data, address and control buses.[49] On most personal computers, data passes between the computer and its peripheral devices in the form of 8-bit[50] bytes.[51] The rate at which the data is transferred is measured in signals per second, known as the baud rate.[52] The lower the baud rate, the slower the data transmission time, but the likelihood of transmission errors is correspondingly lower. Parallel transmission[53] is the fastest method and is therefore employed inside the personal computer, where speed of transfer is of prime importance, whereas serial transmission[54] is most frequently used where the communication links are comparatively long, e.g. from the computer to a printer.

Successful data transfers demand very strict control of the transmitter, receiver and data lines. The data bus provides a highway for many components and a highly regulated system of traffic flow is essential to avoid data crashes, so that most internal data flows are controlled by the CPU. An important feature in the design of the personal computer therefore results from the types and nature of interfaces, both between personal computer internal components and with external peripherals, thus dictating the types of interconnections which are, and are not, permissible. Neither system designers, nor computer users, can be expected to check the detailed specification of interconnection arrangements necessary whenever two devices are required to work together; thus certain standards have been evolved by the industry.[55]

Standards and Differentiation

The importance of standard buses and interfaces must be emphasised. Personal computer systems are not static, but are continually evolving and they therefore need to accept upgrades in configuration to accept product advances and expansion in the needs of the user. The use of a standard bus makes it possible to upgrade processor power and facilities, by plugging on additional printed circuit boards[56] into the personal computer's chassis.[57]

As already explained, input and output involve the various processes and equipment for getting information into and out of the computer. These facilities of a personal computer comprise input/output[58] ports and interface circuits,[59] many of which could be bought by the personal computer company "off-the-shelf". However, a variety of computer applications require specially designed interfaces, which not only necessitate skills in design and technical production, but also offer a microcomputer company the opportunity to develop the unique aspects of performance within the product. Thus, the personal computer company is always faced with a choice between how many "standard" components to use in a particular machine versus how many "specialised" components. The latter being designed to provide differentiation and unique product features.

Peripherals

Around the core computer there exist a number of related units known as peripherals. These are devices that perform an input or output action (sometimes both) and although not part of the core microcomputer, peripherals have formed an important part in the development of personal computer systems. Because a microprocessor itself is of no value unless information can be entered and retrieved, then the minimal configuration for a personal computer usually consists of a keyboard and some form of visual output device. However, on its own, such a configuration would be useless, since it demands that the user keys in the whole application program[60] and data, every time the computer is switched on.[61] Thus some form of off-line[62] storage for programs and data are an essential part of the system. Initially, cassette tape players and recorders were adopted to connect with the early microcomputers as a low cost storage device. Not surprisingly, their limited capacity and slow access speed were unsuitable for business applications, which stimulated demand for floppy disk[63] and subsequently hard disk storage.[64] Output data was initially available on TV sets and paper-tape read-out printers.[65] However, once again, demand for higher quality resolution and print quality led to video monitors and various improved types of printer being adapted and then developed to work with business personal computers. Initially printers were of fairly low quality using dot matrix technology,[66] but subsequently, other technologies such as ink-jet[67] and laser have been developed that provide high quality output at lower prices.

It should be noted that in practice the distinction between processors and peripherals is extremely fluid and has depended on the level of integration, which itself has been based on the nature of the machine and the design preferences of the personal computer company. Fig. 2.2 illustrates some of the variations of the basic elements. Indeed, as the microprocessor technology has evolved from 4-bits to 8-bits then through to 16-bit and 32-bit machines,[68] the system configuration has also changed to reflect an environment in which the microcomputer operates with its user. Thus personal computers have evolved from simply being stand-alone units to networked[69] units with high communication powers.

Given the wide variety of components and elements available when designing a personal computer system, hardware manufacturers therefore have to decide what level of integration to adopt in their system design and what importance to attach to ergonomic factors, which although probably increasing costs, may significantly influence buyers' buying behaviour. A number of the personal computers developed in the early

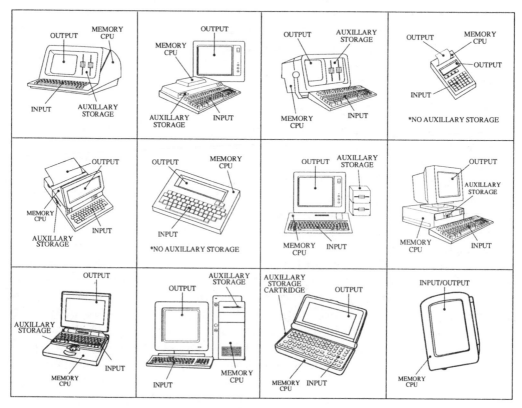

Fig. 2.2. Variations in the configuration of personal computers.

stages of the industry's development adopted a fairly high level of integration, often placing keyboard, output and auxiliary storage in the same box as the CPU and memory. Over time, however, user needs have tended to put emphasis on a modular systems approach, which in turn opens up more opportunities for third party peripheral manufacturers. In addition, it should also be remembered that for most personal computer companies, the major components and peripherals are usually supplied by outside companies anyway.

Software

In addition to the hardware, computers need to operate various forms of software, without which the computer is next to useless. Software is typically divided into three main categories, which are described in this section and consist of:
*   Operating systems.
*   Languages.[70]
*   Application programs.

An overall computer system consists of a number of parts, all of which must match exactly for it to work. Between the user and the hardware is a whole hierarchy of software, each of which plays a role in enabling the user to communicate with the computer.

Operating Systems

At the centre is the operating system, which represents the lowest level of software in most computer systems. It schedules the microcomputer's use and relieves users of the task of writing code that deals directly with system hardware resources, including peripherals such as disks, printers and display units. An operating system is usually designed initially for one hardware family, although it is technically possible to subsequently modify the operating system to other hardware systems.

In the early stages of the personal computer industry's evolution, no standard operating system existed for the industry, which created a "Catch 22" situation. This arose, because the software houses[71] were not encouraged to write programs for a new machine unless "the user base"[72] provided them with a sufficiently large market to make it worth the investment in software development. However, in 1974 an operating system CP/M-80[73] was developed and licensed to other companies, so that it rapidly became the standard operating system for the industry. The introduction of 16-bit based microcomputers opened up a competitive battle for acceptance of the standard operating system for 16-bit machines. The battle was won by the combined resources of IBM and Microsoft, which developed the MS-DOS[74] version for IBM's first personal computer as PC-DOS.[75] However, besides MS-DOS, a number of other operating systems have evolved, the most successful of which has been Apple Computer's Macintosh proprietary operating system, whilst other operating systems such as Unix[76] and UCSD-p[77] have slowly developed niche markets for technical and scientific personal computer applications. In the late 1980s a new IBM operating system emerged in the form of OS/2.[78] Each of these developments has reflected new generations of computer system and highlights the fact that technological competition is not only conducted in the hardware elements of the system, but also in its software.

Applications Programs

However, whilst operating systems control the computer's functions, in order for the machine to be useful, it needs a set of commands that enable it to perform specific types of task or application. Such commands form the application program. Application packages[79] solve users' problems, and as such include several categories. They may be used for word processing, data management, communications, accounting, spreadsheets,[80] games, education and utilities.[81]

To a large extent, the relationship between personal computer hardware and application software is so close, that analysis of either in isolation would fail to capture the dynamics and forces driving the development and diffusion of personal computers. Essentially, applications programs and their level of sophistication (i.e. their degree of usefulness to an operator or end-user) are dependent upon the power of the microprocessor, CPU and peripherals, especially Random Access Memory storage. The important features to recognise in this relationship are that as developments have taken place in hardware, these have in turn created the opportunity for more sophisticated application programs to be written. These in turn have experienced varying degrees of success in the marketplace (depending on the quality of the software package itself). In those cases where the software has been a 'winner', demand for such programs has been extremely strong. As more and more users gain experience on such programs, then realisation of their particular needs and the potential productivity gains which such software can provide become more apparent. As a result of this increased awareness, the users then expect further developments in applications software, particularly in integration of different types of package, for example, word processing and graphics programs or graphics programs and spreadsheet programs.

However, more complex programs require a greater amount of processing power, which has been achieved with each increase in the power of the microprocessor from 8-bit to 16-bit and then to 32-bit units. Linked to increases in Random Access Memory it has been possible for such developments to take place. Thus a form of virtuous circle has taken place, whereby developments in applications software[82] are linked back to developments in processing power and Random Access Memory capacity. The details of this inter-relationship are described in various parts of this book. However, before moving forward to consider the technological development of the personal computer and its impact upon the evolution of the industry and its markets, let us briefly return to consider the events that led to the creation of the first microprocessor in the form of the evolution of microelectronics technology.

DEVELOPMENT OF MICROELECTRONICS

As with much of modern industrial technology, the work of Michael Faraday and others laid the basis for development of establishing electrical power. Their discoveries subsequently led to the development of electrically based devices such as the vacuum tube valve.[83] Following from the application of valves to the first electronic based computers, further developments in electronics and semiconductor[84] technology have led to rapid advances in the performance, miniaturisation and lowering of costs in computer technology.

The early computers employed large quantities of valves, but these were bulky, caused tremendous heat problems and were never a reliable electronic device. Companies working in the communications field also realised these limitations and Bell Laboratories played an important role in developing the device that became known as the germanium point-contact transistor,[85] which was announced on 23rd December 1947.[86]

Until 1954, work in the early years of transistor development was concentrated on perfecting the germanium transistor, since in practice it was difficult to manufacture. However, in the process of research, a method of growing single crystal silicon was developed, again at Bell Laboratories. Since silicon (which comes from sand) was a more abundant material than germanium and could be made to produce transistors capable of working reliably at high temperatures, silicon became the main material for their production. The use of silicon also led to the introduction of the planar process,[87] which allowed transistors to be made in a batch-production process and hence at significantly lower costs.

Texas Instruments (TI), which was still then a young firm, started building on the research work at Bell Laboratories and commenced commercial production of the first silicon transistor in 1954. Since that time, technological developments have contributed to a high rate of growth in the semiconductor industry, which is illustrated in Figs 2.3 and 2.4. This growth encouraged roughly three periods of peak entry by new competitors during 1952 – 1953; 1959 – 1963 and 1968 – 1972. However, the number of entrants has declined severely since 1972 with Japanese companies now holding a significant share of the global market.

TI's lead in this development lasted three years and catapulted it to the top of the industry by 1957. In the late 1950s, both Fairchild Semiconductor and Motorola entered the semiconductor industry and rose to success on:

". . . the wave of new technology using silicon and relying on the oxide masking, diffusion, planar and epitaxial techniques".[88,89]

All of which had begun in the early 1960s.

However, whilst TI adapted successfully to the changing technologies, other companies did not do so well. Thus both Transitron (the second largest transistor firm in the late 1950s) and Hughes were forced to drop out of the ten top transistor firms by the mid-1960s. The increasing complexity

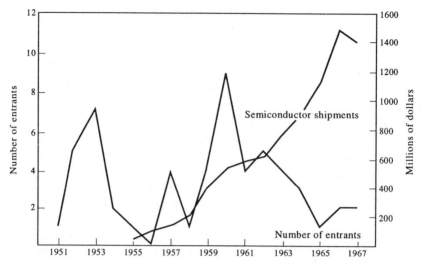

Source: Robert W. Wilson, Peter K. Ashton and Thomas P. Egan, *Innovation, Competition and Government Policy in the Semiconductor Industry.* A Charles River Associates Research Study, 1980, p.14.

Original work based upon the following sources: A sample of ninety semiconductor firms for which entry dates could be found were obtained from the following sources: Golding (1971, pp. 154-171, 242-244); Tilton (1971, pp. 52-53, 79); Braun and McDonald (1978, pp. 61-62, 67); Industrial Technology Hearing (30 October 1978, p.91).

Semiconductor production figures for 1955 through 1959 are from Tilton (1971, p.90). Figures include captive production. Data from 1960 to 1967 from U.S. Department of Commerce, 1979, *Report on the Semiconductor Industry,* Washington D.C.: U.S. Government Printing Office, September, p.39.

Reproduced by Permission of Charles River Associates, Incorporated, © 1980.

Fig. 2.3. Entry into the semiconductor industry compared with growth in semiconductor production: 1951 - 1967.

and sheer numbers of components in electronic products being developed during the late 1950s was causing technical manufacturing problems for many companies. Interconnecting large numbers of discrete components was a laborious and time-consuming process. Efforts to overcome such problems led to the introduction of the integrated circuit, the first patent for which was filed in February 1957. Both TI and Fairchild were producing integrated circuits in commercial quantities by late 1961.

The 1960s witnessed new waves of technology in semi-conductor technology, where competition took the character of a race, with sizeable rewards going to firms that gain a technological lead. As Robert Noyce has commented:

"A year's advantage in introducing a new product or new process can give a company a 25 per cent cost advantage over competing companies; conversely, a year's lag puts a company at a significant disadvantage with respect to its competitors".[90]

Such races have tended to occur within specific product fields, the main ones of the period are illustrated in Fig. 2.5. The major product areas where such battles took place were in early bipolar logic,[91] custom

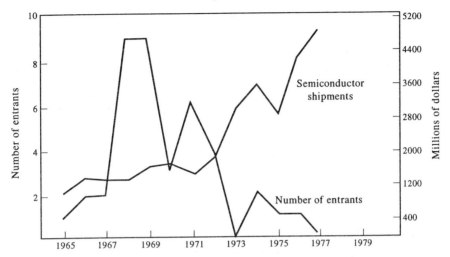

Source: Robert W. Wilson, Peter K. Ashton and Thomas P. Egan, *Innovation, Competition and Government Policy in the Semiconductor Industry*. A Charles River Associates Research Study, 1980, p.15.

Original work based upon the following sources: A sample of ninety semiconductor firms for which entry dates could be found were obtained from the following sources: Golding (1971, pp. 154-171, 242-244); Tilton (1971, pp. 52-53, 79); Braun and McDonald (1978, pp. 61-62, 67); Industrial Technology Hearing (30 October 1978, p.91).

Semiconductor Shipments from U.S. Department of Commerce, 1979, *Report on the Semiconductor Industry*, Washington D.C.: U.S. Government Printing Office, September, p.39.

Reproduced by Permission of Charles River Associates, Incorporated, © 1980.

Fig. 2.4. Entry into the semiconductor industry compared with growth in semiconductor production: 1964 - 1977.

LSI(large scale integration),[92] LSI memories, customised circuits[93] and microprocessors. The first large demand for digital integrated circuits were developed in the late 1960s, when a variety of bi-polar families of integrated circuit products were developed. TI emerged in the early 1970s as the eventual winner in terms of widest usage, market acceptance and growth.

Whilst the bi-polar logic war was in full heat, semiconductor firms were also making plans and investing in research in what they believed was to be the next generation of digital integrated circuits, namely, custom LSI. Whereas bi-polar logic was dominated by standard off-the-shelf parts, a custom circuit is manufactured by a semiconductor firm that works closely with the customer to design and build a circuit optimised for the customer's specific design. The rationale behind the belief that custom circuits would be in greater demand than standard circuits lay in the idea that innovative customers would seek differentiation of their products at the integrated circuit level. This had been possible with standard integrated circuits by clever interconnections.

Since most of the logic needed in an LSI area could be packed into a few integrated circuits, scope for performance differentiation was hence much reduced. Both TI and Fairchild believed the best approach to LSI was to standardise all aspects of the circuit design, except the final-mask. However, developments in metal-oxide technology (MOS)[94] led to an

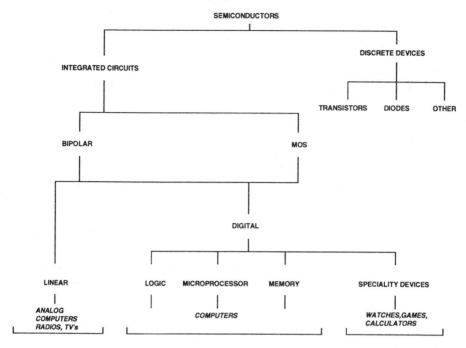

NOTE: Type in italics, denotes types of end-use.

Source: Robert W. Wilson, Peter K. Ashton and Thomas P. Egan, *Innovation, Competition and Government Policy in the Semiconductor Industry*. A Charles River Associates Research Study, 1980, p.20.
Reproduced by permission of Charles River Associates, Incorporated, © 1980.

Fig. 2.5. Family tree of semiconductor technology and end uses.

alternative technology race, which was pioneered by GME (a Fairchild spin-off), that was taken over by Philco-Ford in 1966. Other small firms such as AMI, General Instrument and North American Rockwell also entered during the late 1960s. Although early forecasts for MOS technology were favourable, demand did not take off until 1970. AMI emerged as the MOS leader in 1969,[95] whilst the TI and Fairchild approaches had faded into oblivion.[96]

Even allowing for the fact that enormous sums were invested in both technologies, the TI and Fairchild experiences both illustrate an important point, namely, that even in a booming industry, most innovations prove unsuccessful.[97]

Semiconductor integrated-circuit memories had been produced since the mid-1960s; however, the race to produce a low-cost, high performance memory did not begin in earnest until 1968. The opportunity for growth was perceived as being in the substitution of magnetic cores[98] then used in computers by semiconductor memories. The cost of fabricating conventional bi-polar integrated circuits had fallen sharply and MOS technology was beginning to show considerable potential as a magnetic core replacement and at a cost lower than bi-polar — but which was still more expensive than magnetic core storage.

In 1968, several new companies were formed to develop semiconductor memory products, hoping to take advantage of this technological and market opportunity. These included Intel and Mostek that ultimately were to become the sales and technology leaders. Although some of the established incumbents were also developing semiconductor memory products, none appeared to make sufficiently major commitments to exclude new entrants at this stage.

By early 1970, at least eighteen companies were involved in some form of semiconductor memory. In 1970, the first major breakthrough occurred with the introduction of the first 1K[99] Random Access Memory. The pioneer in breaking the technological barrier to the 1K RAM was Intel, with the development of polysilicon[100] MOS technology. However, Advanced

Table 2.1. Leading United States semiconductor manufacturers: 1955-1975.

1955 Transistors	1960 Semi-Conductors	1965 Semi-Conductors	1975 Integrated Circuits
Hughes	Texas Instruments	Texas Instruments	Texas Instruments
Transitron	Transitron	Motorola	Fairchild
Philco	Philco	Fairchild	National Semiconductor
Sylvania	Gen. Electric	Gen. Electric	Intel
Texas Instruments	RCA	Gen. Electric	Motorola
General Electric	Motorola	RCA	Rockwell
RCA	Clevite	Sprague	Gen. Instrument
Westinghouse	Fairchild	Philco-Ford	RCA
Motorola	Hughes	Transitron	Signetics (Philips)
Clevite	Sylvania	Raytheon	American Microsystems

Source: I.M. Macintosh, "Large Scale Integration Aspects," IEEE Spectrum, June 1978, p.54.
Reproduced by permission of the Institute of Electrical and Electronic Engineers, Inc.
© 1978 IEEE.

Memory Systems was the first to market a 1K RAM, with Intel following three months later. Although Intel's device was not reputed to be as fast as the Advanced Memory System's unit, it was easier to use[101] and was supported by a much more aggressive advertising and promotional campaign that overcame the then financially troubled Advanced Memory Systems lead in 1K-RAM sales.[102] In 1973 the second round began with 4K MOS memories being introduced by Intel, TI and Mostek, each vying for dominance. Other firms, including Advanced Memory Systems and National, held back, waiting for an industry standard to emerge.[103]

Intel chose to modify its new 4K memory to be compatible with TI products; however, TI proved unable to meet supply commitments, supposedly due to production problems. At the same time, Mostek's design was gaining favour over the designs of TI and Intel.[104] Thus, by 1974, Mostek's 4K RAM memory had emerged as the standard for most of the industry, which signalled the time for entry by National, Motorola, American Microsystems and others.[105] Table 2.1 illustrates the leading U.S. companies that were active in the respective technological developments of the semiconductor industry during this entire period from 1955 to 1975.

The developments in semiconductor technology just described all laid the prerequisites for the birth of the microprocessor, which, along with continued improvements in memory technology, were to drive the development of the personal computer.

THE BIRTH OF THE MICROPROCESSOR

The catalyst that led to the development of the microprocessor came in 1969, when Busicom, a Japanese manufacturer of calculators, approached Intel to develop a chip set for a new range of programmable printer – calculators. Although Busicom specified a dozen chips (a typical amount for calculators in production at the time), Intel is reported to have believed they could increase the number of MOS transistors on each chip from the normal 600 – 1000 to 2000, by using their new silicon gate technology.[106] The chip set became known as the MCS-4, the 4-bit CPU having about 2200 transistors on it. Initially, Busicom held all sales rights on the chips, but after negotiation, Intel gained the right to sell the devices for non-calculator applications. Marketing by Intel of the 4004 CPU began in November 1971. Thus the first microprocessor was not originally designed with personal computers in mind, as the quote in the introduction to this chapter points out very clearly.

Computer Terminals Corporation (CTC), (which subsequently became Datapoint) contracted Intel and TI to develop chips for a new terminal. Although neither design was used, Intel continued to develop the device, with the result that in April 1972, the first 8-bit microprocessor was announced by Intel.

"This [the 8008][107] was a more general purpose device than the 4004, having an instruction set similar to a minicomputer's interrupt capability and the capacity to address directly 16K bytes of programmable memory."[108]

Other firms were slow in entering the microprocessor area. According to one source, only Rockwell International and National introduced their own 4-bit designs within that first year after Intel's announcement.[109] However, once the microprocessor showed signs of gaining customer acceptance, other firms began development of their own designs. Meanwhile, Intel began deliveries of an 8-bit microprocessor, the 8080, which incorporated the instruction set of the 8008 and yet was supposed to be twenty times faster.[110] One source estimated that Intel's 4-bit and 8-bit microprocessor held 99 per cent of sales in March 1973,[111] which partly accounts for why the 8080 became the first de facto industry standard.

However, in 1974, a serious competitor entered the microprocessor market in the form of Motorola, which introduced its 8-bit, 6800 microprocessor.[112] The 6800 also offered four support chips as well as a development system, a move that was to influence subsequent entrants and spawn ranges of peripheral devices such as cathode ray tubes (CRT)[113] controller chips[114] and direct memory access chips (DMA).[115]

During the following year of 1975, a mass entry of competitors took place in the microprocessor arena, which forced firms to cut their prices. Motorola was the first to cut prices in the 8-bit area; in September 1975, it reduced distributor-level prices on the 6800 by as much as 60 per cent. In October, Intel followed with price cuts of 50 per cent on small quantity orders of the 8080 and peripheral devices. Soon, other suppliers followed the trend.[116] Intel continued to hold a market lead during 1976 and introduced the 8085, which offered additional features to the 8080. Motorola increased its market share from 15 to 20 per cent, whilst most noteworthy amongst new product entrants was Zilog, whose improvements of the Intel 8080 in the Z80 microprocessor led it to gain rapid market acceptance.

Such fierce competition and the experience curve continued to drive down microprocessor prices. During the third quarter of 1975, the price of the Intel 8080A was $110, by the first quarter of 1976 it was down to $40 and a year later this figure had halved to $20.[117] By early 1976, the microprocessor market was well established. According to two sources,[118,119]

"... 19 microprocessors were available or announced by July 1974; by 1975 the number was 40 and by 1976 it had grown to 54".

The pace of technological change in semiconductor technology is perhaps best expressed in the now famous industry quotation, known as "Moore's Law". In 1965, Gordon Moore of Fairchild predicted that function density, that is the number of functions that can be performed by the integrated circuit, would double every year. Moore's Law held true for more than fifteen years. This relationship is illustrated in Fig. 2.6.

Thus, increasing functional density and the experience curve effect generating improved yields have both combined to generate cost declines and improved performance that have characterised the semiconductor market. These are factors that have both led to the creation of the earliest

Table 2.2. Summary of the major ideas and inventions leading to the development of microcomputers.

EARLY COMPUTATION

500 B.C.	- ABACUS
1614	- LOGARITHMS
1621	- SLIDE RULE
1643	- PASCALINE CALCULATOR
1822	- DIFFERENCE ENGINE
1834	- ANALYTICAL ENGINE
1890	- HOLLERITH ANALYSER

EARLY ELECTRONIC COMPUTERS

1936	- ZI
1943	- COLOSSUS
1944	- ASCC
1945	- ENIAC
1946	- VON NEUMANN COMPUTER THEORY
1948	- MANCHESTER MARK 1
1949	- EDSAC
1951	- UNIVAC

SEMICONDUCTOR TECHNOLOGY ORIGINS

1948	- GERMANIUM TRANSISTOR
1954	- SILICON TRANSISTOR
1958	- INTEGRATED CIRCUIT
1962	- MOS FIELD-EFFECT TRANSISTOR

MICROELECTRONICS DEVELOPMENTS

1971	- FIRST MICROPROCESSOR(4004)
1972	- FIRST 8-BIT MICROPROCESSOR (8008)
1974	- FIRST NMOS MICROPROCESSOR
1974	- FIRST + 5 VOLT MICROPROCESSOR (6800)
1974	- FIRST CMOS MICROPROCESSOR (1802)
1974	- FIRST 16-BIT MICROPROCESSOR (PAGE)
1976	- FIRST 8-BIT MICROCOMPUTER (8048)
1978	- 16-BIT MICROPROCESSORS (8086, Z8000, 68000)
1980	- FIRST 32-BIT MICROPROCESSOR (iAPX 432)
1984/85	- 32-BIT MICROPROCESSORS (68020, Z80000,)

Source: From J. A. McCrindle, *Microcomputer Handbook*, Collins Professional and Technical Books, 1985, Chapter One, J. A. McCrindle, 'The Origins of Today's Microcomputers', p.20.
Reproduced by Permission of Blackwell Scientific Publications Limited., © 1985.

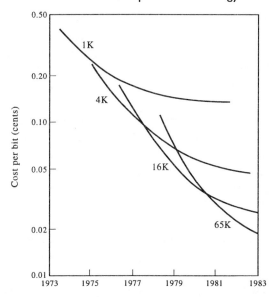

COST PER BIT of computer memory has declined as is shown here for successive generations of random-access memory circuits capable of handling from 1,024 (1K) to 65,536 (65K) bits of memory. Increasing complexity of successive circuits was primarily responsible for cost reduction, but less complex circuits also continue to decline in cost.

Source: Robert W. Wilson, Peter K. Ashton and Thomas P. Egan, *Innovation, Competition and Government Policy in the Semiconductor Industry.* A Charles River Associates Research Study, 1980, p.27.
Original work based upon the following source: From *Microelectronics*, Robert N. Noyce. Copyright 1977 by Scientific American, Inc. All rights reserved.
Reproduced by Permission of Charles River Associates, Incorporated, © 1980.

Fig. 2.6. Estimated decrease in computer-memory cost: 1973 - 1983.

personal computers and have been a major driving force in the evolution of the personal computer industry. Table 2.2 therefore illustrates the development stages in both computing techniques and electronics, which lay the foundations and underpinned subsequent development of the personal computer.

SUMMARY

In summary, this chapter has described the basic nature of the personal computer and the foundations of the personal computer industry, as they relate to technological change. Although historical in the nature of its content, understanding such developments is extremely important, since competitive behaviour amongst the semiconductor manufacturers is driven by technological innovation. These companies then look to their customers in the personal computer industry to carry their component technologies to the commercial marketplace. Thus the strategic behaviour and performance of semiconductor companies such as Intel, Motorola, NEC and others are a major force in developing the type of performance that can be expected from personal computers.

In conclusion and from an historical perspective, the initial events leading to the development of the first microprocessor suggest that:

(i)   There was a long gestation period during which the theoretical ideas for computing were developed, but the limitations of mechanical technology blocked their practical implementation.

(ii)   The basis of the personal computer resulted from the evolution of microelectronics technology during the 1950s and 1960s. This was based upon a continual improvement in the price/performance ratio of processors, reflecting faster processing speeds[120] at lower unit costs, together with increasing miniaturisation.

(iii)   The original technology development did not focus or aim at a conscious objective to produce a microprocessor. Instead it resulted from a semiconductor manufacturer attempting to solve a technical component problem for programmable calculators.

(iv)   The core microprocessor technology was developed outside the computer (core) industry.

(v)   Competition amongst the semiconductor manufacturers involved heavy investment in research and development that required the creation of high volume markets to recover returns. However, these markets also experienced heavy price discounting by the lead technology company.

(vi)   A year's advantage in introducing a new product or process could provide a 25% cost advantage over competitors. Hence, there has been a heavy emphasis by the semiconductor manufacturers to establish innovative leads with new families of microprocessors.

(vii)   The competitive battles have been based upon improving the price – performance ratio of microprocessors in the following:
         —   greater chip-set capacity;
         —   larger address-sizes;[121]
         —   faster speeds of processing;
         —   lower power requirements.

(viii)   These features drove the semiconductor manufacturers to aggressively develop the personal computer market with rapid introduction of "new families" of microprocessor or "derivations" which in turn forced a high pace of new product introduction amongst the personal computer manufacturers.

At a general level, these events highlight the degree of uncertainty and hence risk associated with a company which is locked into a specific "technological trajectory".[122] In addition, it can be seen that even in a high growth industry, large scale investment in "competing technologies" does not necessarily lead to commercially successful innovations. Furthermore, step-changes in price performance technology have led to new waves of entrants into the semiconductor industry. With each new wave, new strategic groups have formed and new markets have developed. Yet in

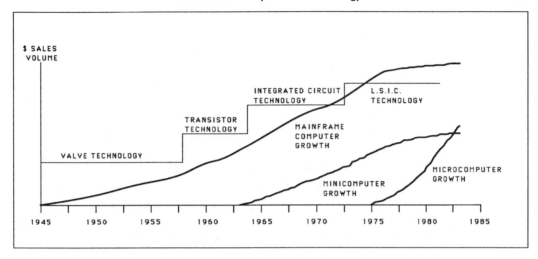

Fig. 2.7. Step changes in the "core" technology and its impact on the evolution of the computer industry.

many instances the new markets have themselves represented new industries, made up of new competitors applying the technological components to new uses. From an historical perspective, Fig. 2.7 illustrates how the step-changes in the core technology have led to the development of new types of computers, commencing with the earlier mainframes and working through to microcomputers.

However, although microprocessors formed the core technology of the early personal computers, these developments in technology were necessary, but not sufficient conditions for the evolution of personal computers. Indeed, the development of the embryonic market for personal computers did not emanate from semiconductor manufacturers, nor the major computer companies. Instead, it was largely driven by entrepreneurial and market forces. Therefore the next chapter will analyse just how the early stages of the personal computer market evolved, by looking not only at technological developments, but also at the way in which entrepreneurial and social conditions in the latent market led to the emergence of a catalytic stage of the personal computer industry and its initial market.

TECHNOLOGY NOTES

Levels of Technology Integration

The least integrated hobby computer was the basic microprocessor board (MPU), which was often referred to as the single board computer. The typical MPU board consisted of the MPU itself, system controller, system clock, some form of external data interface, decoders, PROM[123] monitor, at least 256 bytes of RAM and connectors. Most MPU boards were sold in quantity by industrial manufacturers to the OEM[124] market, whilst those that were sold in units were for evaluation purposes. Examples were the

Intel SBC 80/10 and SBC 80/20.

Hobbyist MPU boards were usually intended for use with an existing mainframe. An example was the Cromemco ZPU, which was based on the Zilog Z-80 microprocessor and could be used with Altair, Imsai, Processor Technology and other computers with the "hobbyist standard" bus.

It is important to note the distinction between a single-board computer and a single-board system. The latter included integral input – output (I/O) capability, requiring only a power supply for operation. Some single-board systems even included the power supply, e.g. the Intersil "Intercept Jr", which used batteries. Since the primary function of the single-board system was to familiarise the user with the MPU's instruction set (in contrast to MPU boards, which were primarily for hardware component evaluation), they were usually supplied with extensive programming documentation. The price of single-board systems varied depending on the interface capability, memory, expandability and provided I/O. Since the requirements of keypad/LED (Light Emitting Diode[125]) I/O were relatively unsophisticated, it was not unusual for single-board systems to cost less than many single-board computers. For example, the price of the KIM-1 single-board system from MOS Technology was approximately one-third the price of the initial Apple Computer, which required external peripherals.

Systems were defined as an MPU board packaged within a cabinet and offered with a power supply. The system manufacturer could elect to offer his product without integral I/O, leaving the choice of I/O peripherals to the user, thus avoiding the expense of a control panel. Examples of boxed systems without control panels were the "Poly-88" from Polymorphic Systems and the various MPU models of the Digital Group. Alternatively, the system manufacturer could include the control panel in his finished product. This class of product was best represented by the MITS Altair and IMS Imsai offerings, which were the most popular type of system forming the basis of the hobbyist computer market in 1976.

The boxed systems with a control panel appealed to the user in several ways. Firstly, it allowed immediate use, since programs could be entered through the panel switches and the results displayed on the front panel LEDs. Secondly, it had the psychological attraction of actually "looking like a computer". Finally, the front panel display represented a powerful diagnostic aid. However, market research conducted at the time suggested that,

> "... the importance of the control panel diminishes with the user's sophistication and access to peripherals, other features taking precedence. However, the control panel would appear to be of great importance to first-time hobbyists".[126]

Evidently the popularity of this type of system suggests that its general attributes were congruent to the needs of the market at the time.

A few boxed systems made use of an alphanumeric keyboard and cathode ray tube (CRT) display, thus replacing the toggle switches[127] and

LED. Their minimum configuration prices were higher than those of otherwise comparable hobby systems, which together with their reduced flexibility made them a somewhat less attractive option for the hobbyist.

Levels of Assembly

The hobby microcomputer kit involved assembly at the component level. The individual boards had to be soldered and in some cases, even interboard connections had to be hand-wired. As a result, there was considerable variation in what kit manufacturers required of their purchasers. The typical kit consisted of five basic groups: front panel, power supply, motherboard (or backplane)[128]/chassis group, MPU board and a memory board. Since the degree of experience in kit assembly amongst purchasers was varied, the satisfaction of customers was equally wide. Many aspects of the kits left the purchaser frustrated and on occasions dissatisfied with the product.

One way to overcome such problems was to purchase the kit in an assembled form. However, fewer purchases were made in this category, largely for reasons of the average 40 per cent differential that existed in the selling price between kit and assembled form of the same system. In addition to the cost factor, kits also fulfilled the hobbyist's desire to "understand the workings of the computer" as well as make it work. A similar buying pattern was typical of hi-fi and radio kits. Furthermore, the experienced kit hobbyist often had the desire to customise his unit. The assembled kit found its market amongst purchasers who had identified an immediate application for the system and did not wish to take the time or risk involved in getting the machine operational. Such applications frequently involved BASIC language capability and therefore necessitated a greater initial outlay for more software, memory and peripherals than were provided in the basic kit package. One point that should be emphasised is that the assembled kit did not mean "ready for operation". This point was misunderstood by many purchasers, who assumed that the collective purchase of a mainframe, CRT, additional memory, cassette drives, etc. was sufficient to obtain an integrated and pre-assembled system. However, this was not necessarily the case and pointed to the potential for a supplier which was prepared to develop a truly integrated system of this nature.

In addition to the hobby kit manufacturers, a number of companies supplied third party memory expansion units and peripherals for this market. The central requirement of all hobby computer kit peripherals was that they should be inexpensive. This meant that even the lowest-priced commercial equipment was priced beyond the means of the average hobbyist. As a result, hobbyists developed their own "alternative" systems, ranging from "CRTs" built from surplus keyboards and modified television sets, to "mass memories" consisting of audio tape decks. The most important types of peripheral included the alphanumeric keyboard terminals (KBTs); stand-alone printers; cassettes and floppy disk drives.

Alphanumeric keyboard terminals could consist of the keyboard alone, keyboard with LEDs, keyboard with CRT or modified TV, or a keyboard with printer. At the low end, the price of the basic keyboard could be $20 rising to $1000 for a reconditioned keyboard/printer from companies such as Olivetti and National Teletypewriter Corp. Stand-alone printers for hobbyists were generally slow matrix units with short line widths. The MP-40 from Micro Peripherals Inc., printed the ASCII 64-character set at a speed of 75 lines of 45 characters per line per minute at a price of $425 assembled with power supply. Southwest Technical Products' PR-40 had identical function/speed characteristics, but was available in kit form for $250. Program storage for use by hobbyists was generally placed on standard tape cassettes, using consumer-type audio units.

In November 1975, hobbyists met in Kansas City to agree on a standard encoding technique. The technique agreed upon was a variant of the phase-encoded Manchester method and was subsequently referred to as the "Kansas City" or "Computer Users' Tape System (CUTS)" standard. The adoption of this standard is an interesting illustration of the collective power of end-users that already existed within the emerging market and their leverage over suppliers to begin to conform to an industry standard. However, cassette storage suffered from severe problems of slow speed and access, which led to demand for a faster and higher capacity permanent storage device. In 1975, MITS offered a floppy disk system for the Altair. Its supplier, Pertec, purchased the company (Icom) responsible for packaging the Pertec drive with formatter[129] and operating system. The MITS price for a floppy formatter and drive was $1,980, whilst the cost of a competitive product, the Icom "Frugal Floppy" and formatter was $1,195 plus interface card.[130] One of the cheapest floppies was the "Baby 1" from STM Systems, which had an unformatted capacity of 100K bytes, about one third of the Icom drive, but sold for $750 with formatter and power supply.

Chapter Three

THE EARLY STAGES

"Inventors and men of genius have almost always been regarded as fools at the beginning (and very often at the end) of their careers."[1]

INTRODUCTION

Applying the newgame framework outlined in Chapter One, the remaining chapters of this book will seek to identify and explain the patterns and relationships between technological change, strategic behaviour by companies and their respective impacts upon the industry and markets of this newgame environment surrounding the personal computer.[2]

It was shown in the previous chapter how developments in the field of electronics led to the invention of the microprocessor that forms the core technology driver of the microcomputer. Following from these developments, this chapter will trace the early period of evolution of the newgame environment, which consists of the catalyst, embryonic and take-off stages. The chapter itself is divided into two halves. The first half deals with the catalyst and embryonic stages of development and highlights the basic conditions that led to the creation of the newgame environment for microcomputers. It then proceeds to consider the nature of the technology drivers and how these were incorporated into the development of the industry structure. This is followed by an analysis of the pattern of market evolution, with attention being directed towards defining the changes in size, growth rates and trends leading to the early patterns of segmentation. The user profiles, distribution networks and promotional activities are also considered in terms of their evolutionary patterns. Finally, the pattern of strategic moves made by the major competitors are explored, with attention being drawn to the changing sources of competitive advantage and their reflection in the structure of competitors' value chains that led to the resulting pattern of competitive performance.

The second half of the chapter deals with the Take-Off stage for the industry, during which three new entrants, namely, Tandy, Commodore and Apple Computer changed the structure of the industry and its markets. After initial exploration of the nature of the new entrants and the strategic groups that they and other competitors formed within the industry, the market conditions and patterns of emerging market segmentation are considered. Overall, the market is seen to evolve into three discrete segments, which are made up of a hobbyist, educational and small business market with some competitors pursuing broad based strategies across all three segments, whilst others follow a focused niche strategy. Development of the distribution channel and its increased role in the value chain of leading competitors is also addressed. Finally, the chapter reviews the performance of the new entrants and the pattern of change which takes place in the industry and its markets at these early stages of the newgame environment's evolution.

THE CATALYST STAGE

The catalyst stage of the microcomputer industry and its initial market represents a period that has been described as one of "crystallisation" and has the following characteristics:

> " Before a market materialises, it exists as a latent market. A latent market consists of people who share a similar need or want for something that does not yet exist. For example, people want a means of more rapid calculations than can be achieved by mental calculation or by using a paper and pencil. Until recently, this need was imperfectly satisfied through abacuses, slide rules and large desk calculators".[3]

In the case of microcomputers, the catalyst for commencement of the microcomputer industry lay in the combination of three key factors. Firstly, as was shown in the previous chapter, there were the significant reductions in cost and improvements in the performance of semiconductor technology, which were brought about by competitive forces operating in an already existing, but rapidly growing related industry. However, by itself, this was not sufficient to create the opportunity for a newgame environment. The additional factors included a strong latent demand as described above for microcomputing amongst a core group of electronics/computer hobby enthusiasts. In addition, on the supply side, there existed a creative and entrepreneurial set of individuals who built the earliest microcomputers.

Thus the "Catalyst Stage" represented a pre-market period in which there was no existing industry to serve the potential market for microcomputers. The latent demand for microcomputers resided in a group of non-commercial enthusiasts of computer science and technology that had developed during the 1960s. These enthusiasts were to form the first microcomputer market and were known as hobbyists. Their interest in computers had been generated from their experience in college of timesharing terminals[4] and courses in computer programming.[5] In addition, some students had built experimental kits with the low-cost integrated circuits introduced by Texas Instruments. As a result two distinct groups of hobbyists emerged, one interested in software development and programming and the other in building electronic hardware kits. To support their activities, they established associations and clubs, whose membership was frequently linked together by common-interest electronics magazines.

Nevertheless, although there existed a latent market for personal computing, in 1970 although the price of computer component technology continued to decline at a rapid pace, the cheapest computers still cost in excess of $10,000, which was well beyond the reach of almost any hobbyist. Furthermore, at this time virtually no established computer company showed any interest in developing machines for individual users. Instead, companies producing large mainframe computers and the medium range minicomputers felt that their solutions and concepts of computing satisfied the existing marketplaces very effectively. This point is illustrated in Fig. 3.1 where the potential market for microcomputers is shown as a low power and performance segment addressing the needs of individuals. This was a segment outside the frame of reference and experience of the larger computer companies, thus they chose to ignore it. Had this not been the case, then the evolution of the personal computer newgame environment would probably have looked quite different.

As it was, the stimulus to launching the first microcomputer was focused by the desire amongst two of the major electronic magazines to

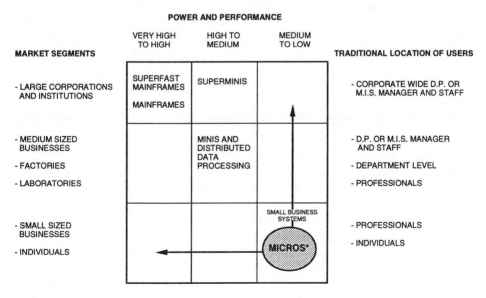

* In 1975 microcomputers entered the bottom right box. In time improvements in their performance would lead to their expansion in the direction of the arrows.

Fig. 3.1. Computer power and performance for market segments in the 1970s.

be the first to offer a basic computer kit as part of a reader promotion campaign. By early 1974, competing microprocessors had been developed by Intel, Motorola and Texas Instruments and were applied to a variety of basic kits, however, none of them managed to generate sufficient support or demand to create a real market for microcomputers. Then in July 1974 an offer accompanied an article in Radio-Electronics magazine which promoted the Mark 8, which was a printed circuit board and book of experiments. This event generated greater interest in the field as other hobbyists published books of experiments, which were accompanied by a minimum of hardware kit.

By late 1974, although it was extremely limited in its performance, supposedly over 1000 Mark 8 machines had been sold. Its success and linkage to Radio-Electronics magazine prompted the rival magazine, Popular Electronics to look for a more powerful machine with which to take the lead in stimulating reader interest. Such a machine was found as the "brainchild" of Ed Roberts, who conceived of a hobbyist kit computer called the Altair. What made the Altair different to the Mark 8 and its predecessors was that although basic in its design and performance, it was nevertheless a real computer, which technically could do much more than simple experiments and might be expanded by additional circuit boards to perform a number of the tasks on a simpler scale than much larger computers. Thus the Altair was clearly differentiated from its rivals in terms of its technically higher performance. Furthermore, its maker and inventor was an entrepreneur who chose to develop his company into a vehicle for expanding sales of the machine to the emerging embryonic market for microcomputers. In this respect, the latent demand amongst those electronic hobbyists who were wanting a central processing unit capable of driving peripherals and reading computer programming languages[6] was at last partially satisfied. The Altair was initially perceived

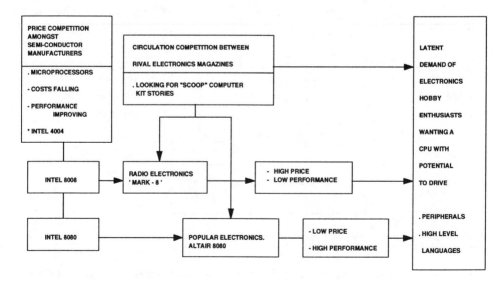

Fig. 3.2. The catalyst stage of the personal computer industry.

to give sufficient value to a number of hobbyists to stimulate the first real wave of demand for a microcomputer. These factors and the pattern of events during the catalyst stage of the personal computer newgame environment are summarised in pictorial form within Fig. 3.2.

In summary, the catalyst stage resulted from various factors. First of all were the innovations in the core technology of microprocessors which were developed by companies within the semiconductor industry. These provided the opportunity for hobbyists interested in computer software and electronic kits to develop basic low cost, but low performance experimental machines. In addition, the competitive rivalry between two electronics magazines stimulated the interest of individuals in the development of the first microcomputer. After which, early forms of competition were to emerge and move the newgame environment into its embryonic stage of development.

Before considering the embryonic stage of the industry and its market, some points about the nature of the basic technology involved in the earliest microcomputers need to be presented in order to appreciate both the nature and limitations of these early machines and hence their impact upon the newgame environment.

Early Product Technology

Each stage of the newgame environment reflects differences in various aspects of the technology, the industry and its markets. Since technology represents a major driving force to change within the newgame environment, it is important to understand both its nature and pattern of change between each stage of evolution. Naturally within the newgame environment the price and performance of the technology determines the capabilities of the personal computer. Furthermore, how companies perform is partly determined by their capabilities in technological development, whilst the products that they produce effect how the market will respond in terms of its growth patterns. Thus as the technology improves, both in terms of lower prices and improved performance, opportunities are created for new products to be launched which usually change the competitive position of companies as well as opening up new market segments.

In the case of the early evolution of the personal computer industry, as the catalyst stage gave way to the embryonic stage, the technology in both the microprocessor and associated parts of the early Altair microcomputer met the minimal definition of a computer, nothing more and nothing less. It lacked any permanent storage, its memory board[7] could hold only about one paragraph of information and its input involved flipping tiny switches, whilst its output involved interpreting the pattern of flashing lights. Lastly, until paper tape readers and a form of BASIC[8] language (a high-level programming language)[9] became available, Altair owners had to "speak" to their machines in the highly technical machine code.[10]

However, whilst limited in its basic initial configuration, the Altair was nevertheless a distinct departure from the previous kits which had been produced for hobbyists. The product was based upon an Intel 8080 microprocessor which was about ten times faster than its predecessor, the Intel 8008. Most importantly, the MITS Altair had been designed with a system which would potentially allow the machine to interface with a variety of input and output peripherals, which was a feature not available on the earlier kits. On price, the machine was $395 in kit form and $621 pre-assembled, which compared to $1,000 for its predecessor, the Mark-8 machine. Thus in terms of product/price performance, the MITS Altair had a distinct competitive advantage. Here at last was a machine that could perform like a real computer and offered value to the latent market of hobbyists.

For the sophisticated hobbyist, the MITS Altair provided the potential to connect a number of peripherals and develop application programs. However, for this it needed to operate BASIC, which required sixteen times the amount of memory available on the initial Altair machine. Thus, the early Altair machine was forced to undergo rapid enhancements both to its memory capacity, interface boards,[11] software capabilities and range of peripherals. Most important amongst the peripherals was the requirement that the data be stored in a permanent form that would not be destroyed as soon as the machine was switched off. To solve all of these technical challenges within a short space of time would be expecting too much of the capabilities of a single small company like MITS with its limited scale of resources.

However, the limitations of MITS and the Altair created an opportunity for a number of additional new competitors to develop and produce a wide variety of components for linking to the microprocessor as well as a range of peripherals and software. Since even the lowest priced peripherals for commercial computers were beyond the purchasing power of the average hobbyist, "alternative" systems were developed, ranging from display terminals built from modified television sets to "mass memories" consisting of audio tape decks. Other competitors began to produce and sell single board based systems[12] using newly developed microprocessors from Motorola, Texas Instruments and the newly formed Zilog company. By early 1976 this competition had driven down the cost of microprocessors, whilst performance had been improved, thus expanding the demand amongst the hobbyist users. Thus once again the pattern which emerges is one where the opportunity to meet the need for technology improvements led to new entrants offering their products, which forced down prices and increased the size of the market.

During this embryonic stage the hardware limitations severely constrained the software available. During 1975 the applications programs were essentially written for microprocessors with access to 4 or 8 Kb[13] of temporary or Random Access Memory (RAM), which limited the computer's capacity to handle powerful software programs. Demand for increased RAM was evident and thus suppliers addressed the opportunity for offering lower priced units with increased storage capacity. Indeed, this pattern of increasing the power and performance of various component technologies and also lowering their prices due to the learning curve and experience curve effects has been a major driving force for the evolution of the microcomputer. However, it must be appreciated that the technology of this first generation of microcomputers was extremely limited. The reliability of the machines suffered from the effects of poor quality control in assembly and components' procurement. However, these limitations provided the opportunity for new companies to enter the competition and led to the development of the creation of a distinctive microcomputer industry that was to separate from the general microprocessor industry.

THE EMBRYONIC STAGE

Industry Forces

The major forces shaping the evolution of the microcomputer industry during its embryonic stage were:

(a) the declining costs in semiconductors (specifically microprocessors), which brought about learning curve and scale effects in the semiconductor industry;

(b) the latent demand for low-priced microcomputers amongst end-users;

(c) the innovative activities of individual entrepreneurs both within the user market and amongst component and peripheral suppliers.

As the growth in supply and demand accelerated, a fragmented industry structure began to emerge to serve a home/hobby market. Competition was on a price and performance basis, making technological innovation at the level of the microprocessor and components the most crucial factor for generating a temporary, yet usually unsustainable, competitive advantage.

By the embryonic stage of the microcomputer industry there already had emerged distinctive suppliers, competing firms and users, examples of which are illustrated in Fig. 3.3. However, the key potential linkages in the industry of both a vertical and horizontal nature did not occur at this stage except by way of negotiated agreements. The competing firms were small, local start-up operations, with national distribution mainly via mail order. These firms were drawn largely from suppliers of computer components or peripherals, whilst a few were created by customers who had a technical knowledge of computer kits and electronics. The nature of these companies is considered next.

Types of Competing Firms

Suppliers to the early microcomputer companies consisted of two groups: those that produced the microprocessor unit (MPU), memory and other integrated circuits, and those that produced other components. Historically, microprocessor and integrated circuit suppliers had sold integrated circuits as independent components and had not been involved in selling systems or even sub-systems. As a result of the growth in demand for single board computers amongst hobbyists, certain integrated circuit manufacturers such

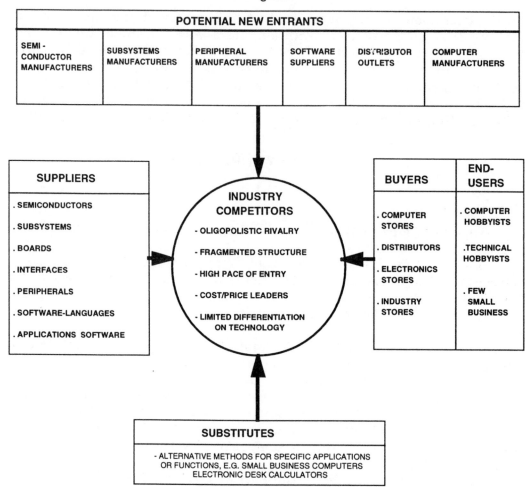

Fig. 3.3. Elements of the major forces driving the microcomputer business environment in early 1977.

as Intel, MOS Technology and Intersil adapted their single board microcomputers to attract further growth in demand from this emerging market sector.

The second group of electronic component suppliers consisted of companies who manufactured a wide range of products for use in the electronics based industries. Their products included keyboards, electronic components, knobs, switches, wire and cable, and printed circuit board substrata.[14] Companies within this group rarely supplied directly to the end-user, but instead distributed directly to product manufacturers including the hobby computer kit manufacturers.

The earliest microcomputer manufacturers were small companies, which included MITS, IMSAI, Sphere and Intelligent Systems Corp. As well as serving the hobby market, these types of company were also developing configurations and systems software for non-hobbyist end-users. Examples of the major entrants during the period 1975 to early 1977 are illustrated in Table 3.1.[15] In Table 3.1 it can be seen that entrants consisted of new start-up companies and small established companies which diversified from their core businesses, usually in electronics components or computer peripherals. Thus there was virtually no "unrelated" product diversification[16] into the market. Nor was there any entry by large established companies such as the mainframe or minicomputer manufacturers. In addition, only one notable instance occurred of a semiconductor manufacturer integrating forward, which occurred when the relatively small MOS-Technology introduced a low cost hobbyist computer. Given the limited maturity of the distribution channels emerging at this stage, it is not surprising to see that there was a total absence of backward vertical integration. Furthermore, there were no foreign entrants to the market undertaking geographic expansion.

In addition to the microcomputer computer companies there were the manufacturers of mass storage[17] peripherals (cassette[18] and floppy disk drives), terminals, paper-tape readers[19] and punches,[20] stand-alone printers, plotters[21] and special peripherals (e.g. voice[22] and optical character encoders/decoders[23]). With a few exceptions, established peripheral and subsystem suppliers did not sell directly to hobbyists. Lastly, there existed suppliers whose products included software (primary applications packages), instruments manufacturers, supplies (paper and magnetic media)[24] and books. Sales of these products to hobbyists was primarily through the emerging retail computer and established electronic stores.

With the exception of companies such as MITS, IMSAI and a few others specialising in hobby microcomputers, the majority of the suppliers and manufacturers described above were initially only involved in the microcomputer business as a minor part of their activities. Furthermore, the market was still small scale, although its size and growth were starting to develop at an accelerating pace.

Table 3.1. Notable entrants into the personal computer industry: 1975 - mid-1977.

NAME OF FIRM	DATE OF ENTRY	NATURE OF PARENT (1)	NATURE OF ENTRY MOVE (2)	CORE BUSINESS ACTIVITY	VERT.INT.
MITS ALTAIR	Jan-75	DOMINANT	RELATED	HAND HELD CALCS	
IMS IMSAI	Nov-75	DOMINANT	RELATED	COMP SYSTEMS	
SOUTH WEST TECH	Nov-75	RELATED	RELATED	AUDIO COMP KITS	
PROCESSOR TECH	Jun-76	SINGLE	RELATED	4K MEM BOARDS	FORWARD
POLYMORPHIC	Jun-76	SINGLE	RELATED	COMP BOARDS	FORWARD
DIGITAL GROUP	1976	SINGLE	RELATED	ALTAIR-BOARDS	FORWARD
TELETYPE	1976	DOMINANT	RELATED	TELEX MACHINES	
CROMEMCO	Feb-77	SINGLE	RELATED	COMP BOARDS	FORWARD
MOS-TECH	Aug-76	SINGLE	RELATED	SEMICONDUCTORS	FORWARD
VECTOR GRAPHIC	Feb-77	SINGLE	RELATED	MEMORY BOARDS	FORWARD

1) Nature of Parent: This refers to the nature of the parent company, just prior to entry into the microcomputer industry. Category details are shown in the chapter notes (15).
2) Nature of Entry Move: This reflects the nature of the entry move in relation to the company's business prior to entry into the microcomputer industry. Category details are shown in the chapter notes (15).

Source: Based upon data collected from various articles and reports.

Evolution of the Embryonic Market

Size, Growth and Trend Forecasts

By the end of 1974, there seemed little doubt that a potential market for home-based microcomputers existed. But the microcomputer was still viewed as a stand-alone machine that was principally the preserve of the hobbyist and enthusiast and not part of the mainstream computer industry. Rather microcomputers were seen as a minor adjunct to the rapidly expanding microprocessor industry. It must be remembered at this stage in time, microprocessors were finding a numerous range of applications as they were placed into various industrial and commercial products which could be improved by electronic based control systems and were often linked to various sensing devices. Examples included a variety of white goods products such as washing machines, dishwashers and refrigerators; transport and engine monitoring devices; avionics and medical equipment as well as a wide variety of scientific and engineering equipment. The diffusion of the microprocessor was rapid and widely spread. Therefore, the early microprocessor boards and microcomputers built by hobbyists represented a small part of the market for semiconductor manufacturers and the possibility of the microcomputer developing as a full industry in its own right was still a matter of conjecture at the time.

When considering some of the data at this time, a number of features stand out to characterise the hobby computer market in the period 1975 and 1976. Firstly, the market was unique, so that parallels with existing consumer electronics and office products markets, including amateur Citizen Band radio, Hi-Fi equipment, pocket calculators, wordprocessors[25] or office copiers, were not really valid. Secondly, the market was essentially undefined, since products, users and applications were difficult to classify, continually changing and unquantified. A further issue was that whilst the core microprocessor technology was developing rapidly, at the same time it was usually incompatible with other previous models, which necessitated the development of new systems and software. In addition market boundaries were fluid with commercial and industrial systems being used by the hobby/home market. Finally, the channels of distribution were undefined and in a state of flux. Since the market was immature it lacked stable manufacturers or stable patterns of pricing policy which meant that market forecasts varied greatly in their predictions. Indeed one of the problems facing research into the hobby computer market in its early stages of development was the fact that very little data exists, because the market was so new. Thus forecasts for the period 1975 and 1976 to the early 1980s were extremely wide in their range of estimates as illustrated in Fig. 3.4. This variation in future market potential caused great uncertainty at the time for early competitors.

According to one market research report, during 1976, some 17,458 computers of all types were purchased for use in the home of which 72 per cent were supplied by hobby computer manufacturers. The two largest suppliers MITS and IMSAI accounted for 45 per cent of the total. However,

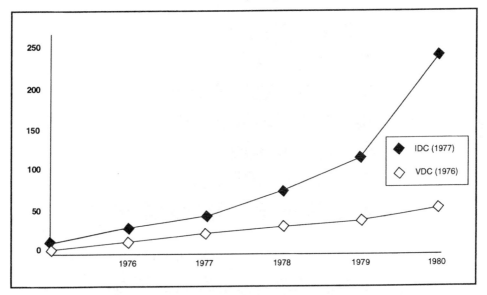

Sources: Adapted from Venture Development Corporation (VDC), *The Personal Computer Industry*, 1976, and International Data Corporation (IDC) Reports, 1977.
Reproduced by permission of Venture Development Corporation, © 1976 and International Data Corporation, © 1977.

Fig. 3.4. Projected forecasts in personal computer sales: 1975 - 1980.

more than one quarter of the computers produced by MITS and IMSAI did not reach the home. They were instead sold to commercial, educational and industrial users, indicating the growing demand for the microcomputer from these sectors.[26] At this time, the average amount spent by hobbyists on software was estimated to be about five per cent of their system base, equivalent to only $33 per year. The percentage of applications used by owners of microcomputers in the hobby sector is illustrated in Fig. 3.5, in which games were shown to be by far the most popular specialised application for hobby computers.

By mid-1977, the market for the personal microcomputer grew to an installed base[27] of approximately 100,000 units, thus signalling the development of a substantial market. Although the majority of sales were made to computer hobbyists, this group was not as heterogeneous as say, stamp collectors or corporate businesses. All that was generally known about them was the fact that they had some form of previous exposure to computers, either as a result of job contact or educational experience. Yet apart from this one common characteristic, they were, en masse, an unknown quantity. Effectively, no segmentation existed in the market at this time, except along demographic lines which reflected the high density areas of purchase in terms of geographic location and occupation. In 1976 distribution of hobbyists was centred around major population centres, the largest concentration being on the West Coast, with others in the New England and Atlantic Seaboard States.[28] This in turn reflected the centres of electronics based engineering companies, since 40 per cent of all computer

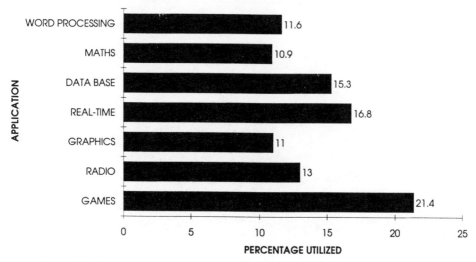

Source: The Personal Computer Industry, Venture Development Corporation, 1976.
Reproduced by permission of Venture Development Corporation, © 1976.

Fig. 3.5. Relative usage of micro systems in 1976.

hobbyists were also directly employed as programmers or electrical engineers, with the remaining 60 per cent comprising of students or teachers using computers as educational aids. A significant finding of the study conducted by Venture Development Corporation was that 57.3 per cent of this population were non-owners,[29] suggesting that at the time a large potential demand for microcomputers existed within this group.

Segmentation

During most of 1975, MITS held a virtual monopoly in the market. There was no segmentation and barriers to entry were low. Entry into the industry was dependent upon being able to provide hobbyists with a microprocessor and central processing unit which could either out-perform the Intel 8080, or was priced more competitively, or both. Thus competitors differentiated their products on the basis of price and technical performance with little apparent sensitivity to market segments. However, this pattern began to change during the latter part of 1976.

By this time the hobby computer market showed signs of developing in three directions. Firstly, there was the core hobbyist segment, a technical/ engineering group whose interests lay in experimenting with hardware designs and developing applications programs. In addition, other hobbyists began to emerge who seemed more interested in the potential to use the computer as a tool, especially for writing programs in BASIC and for designing games programs in this media. The second segment lay in the consumer home market, where it was believed that, with falling hardware prices and improvements in technological performance, there would be a high demand amongst consumers (particularly in the younger age groups) for microcomputers to run games and educational programs. Lastly, the third segment which was initially pursued by a new entrant and the strongest competitor to MITS, namely IMSAI, was the small business market. However, many industry analysts and competitors at this time felt that the targeting of this segment by IMSAI and to a lesser degree, MITS, was premature. This opinion was based on the belief that neither the hardware nor software technology, nor the level of marketing and support services were adequate or sufficiently low-priced to attract customers in this segment.

User Profiles

Although competition was emerging against the industry founder and leading company, MITS, it should be pointed out that there was still a high level of cooperation between individuals to try and solve many of the technical problems. Most of the earliest microcomputer companies largely shared the same background and experience as many of their customers and in the entrepreneurial environment, most founders of such companies were open to suggestions and ideas from their customers.

Active computer clubs also provided a focus and forum for regular debate and discussion amongst users. In this manner, the component suppliers and microcomputer companies were easily made aware of their customers' wants and needs through such forums. However, due to weaknesses in management organisation, such as poor quality control or delays in component supply, the companies were not always able to deliver their promised products. This failure to supply inspired a number of frustrated customers to regard the challenge as an opportunity to go out and start their own company to produce a component that would not only satisfy their own needs, but also those of their colleagues. By early 1976, people were thus beginning to realise that not only might such activities be interesting in their own right, but they might also be profitable. The market was becoming commercially orientated. The culture of the market is well described by Chuck Peddle, a semiconductor designer and a subsequent driving personality in the personal computer industry.

> "They [the hobbyists][30] made the business happen.... They bought computers when they didn't work, when there was no software for them. They created a market, and then they turned around and wrote the programs that brought other people in."[31]

Thus it can be seen that the core "early adopters"[32] of microcomputers included in their midst many of the original innovators. Although these users were to set in motion the development of the personal computer industry and its associated markets, their characteristics as described above were clearly distinct from those users in the market segments which were subsequently to evolve, namely the consumer and business users.

Distribution Channels

Initially, the major proportion of sales for single board computers to hobbyists were made through distributors known as electronic stores, which had traditionally sold electronic components and kits for audio systems and electronic measuring devices. Within the specific category of electronic stores three broad categories existed, namely broad-line stores, private label stores and surplus stores. The broad-line stores included companies such as Radio Shack, Allied and Olsen, all of which were franchised and carried a wide inventory of products bearing both their franchiser's labels and those of other companies. A large part of their inventory included consumer goods such as portable radios, hi-fi equipment and pocket calculators. The private label stores such as Heath were also franchised. However, their stock was somewhat less consumer-orientated than that of the broad-line stores. Finally, a number of independent surplus stores existed that carried hobby products including keyboards, power supplies, other miscellaneous components and subsystems. Such stores tended to promote themselves via advertisements in the computer hobbyist magazines.

However, these traditional electronic stores soon found a new type of distribution channel developing in the microcomputer market as an increasing proportion of single board computer products purchased by hobbyists were instead sold through the emerging computer stores. These retail computer stores were a new phenomenon that had not really existed prior to 1975. However, by 1976, at least one hundred such stores were believed to exist which consisted of three categories. The categories consisted of franchised stores, distributorships and independent stores. These types of store were to form the basis of the distribution network that was to evolve in support of the demand for microcomputers.

Franchised stores were started by MITS. However, their exclusivity restriction encouraged others to enter the market as "non-exclusive", both in territory and products. In late 1976, the first Computerland pilot store was opened offering products from some of the major competitors to MITS, namely, IMSAI, Processor Technology, Polymorphic, Southwest Technology and Cromemco. This competition hit hard at the MITS Altair computing centres.

Distributorships were non-exclusive and initially operated on a regional basis. These pooled their orders to obtain quantity discounts, trade software, share advertising costs and generally co-operated in most other respects. Apparently, the initial relationship between companies such as MITS and distributors was highly informal. As a result, in 1975 many observers felt that their operations were uncommercial in nature and that therefore retailing computers was not a viable undertaking. However, not withstanding such scepticism, the first Byte shop distributorship was opened in December of that year and by November of the following year, there were at least 20 Byte Shops in operation.

Independent stores represented the largest single class of store. Most were formed as new, individual ventures, although some were expansions of existing operations, such as electronic stores. Independent stores were variable in their size and capabilities, ranging from less than $5000 to over $100,000 in monthly revenues. In addition, the ratio of commercial sales to hobby sales varied considerably.

With computer stores opening all over the country, counter-top sales replaced mail order, although the latter was to return to the industry a few years later. The shift from direct mail to retail stores represented the raising of a potential entry barrier for microcomputer suppliers. Under mail order conditions, advertising and availability of product for despatch were the key requirements. Although with mail order, dissatisfied customers could return their goods, this could be a lengthy process. Over-the-counter sales meant suppliers had to adjust their market strategies to take account of three changes. Firstly, they had moved into a more exposed position against competitors' products, since both dealers and buyers had the option to compare products before purchase. Secondly, dealers demanded a profit margin through discount purchase and hence pressure was brought on the manufacturers' margins, which in time might lead to aggressive pricing. Lastly, the supplier now needed to spend more on promoting and packaging his product to encourage dealer support. This represented a further development in the evolution of the value chain, although in practice, the ability for a company with a technical background to recognise the need to shift resources into this area of the business was often lacking and in consequence resulted in many cases of decreased performance.

Promotional Activity

Electronics magazines provided the first promotional channel for microcomputers. Publications such as Popular Electronics carried small adverts for manufacturers' machines, with coupons for information requests or direct orders through the mail. However, buying by mail was not to prove an effective channel of distribution until later in the industry's evolution, for the reasons stated in the previous section. In particular, the claims of misrepresentation concerning certain product announcements created scepticism and frustration amongst the user community.

Whilst advertising for mail order represented the earliest form of promotion, clubs and exhibitions provided the forums for the early microcomputer world. Hobbyists could participate amongst fellow enthusiasts and obtain "inside" news and information about products and innovations. The first significant computer trade show was really a one-company event based on MITS and the Altair machine. However, other shows soon followed, including the New Jersey Computer Festival (May 1976) which represented both an exhibition and conference. In June 1976, The Mid West Area Computer Club Conference drew 4,000 people. Then, in August 1976 the first national show took place in Atlantic City with the Personal Computing Festival.

Whilst mail order, computer clubs, trade shows and conferences were extremely important vehicles for promoting the early microcomputer suppliers, initially they were relatively unsophisticated in a commercial sense and extremely limited in scale. What they did do was to provide a useful yet informal platform for promotional activity to a market whose wants and needs were more concerned with technical features and price rather than in image. Hence, little competitive advantage was exercised in the area during this stage of evolution and indeed few of the competitors had the necessary knowledge, contacts or resources to differentiate their products along this dimension. However, this pattern is not surprising, given that the newgame hypothesis suggests that competitive advantage is usually to be found upstream in the early stages of the newgame environment life cycle.

Having looked at the nature of the embryonic market in terms of its size, structure, customer type, distribution channels and promotional activities, we shall now turn to consider the strategies and performance of the major competitors during this period.

Competitive Behaviour in the Embryonic Stage

It was suggested in Chapter One that step-changes in technology can create opportunities for innovative behaviour since they provide a means to establish new value chains. The first of these value chains represents a newgame strategy which reflects a new way of doing business. Such a strategy was adopted by MITS with its Altair microcomputer. In this instance the newgame strategy was successful and the new product (the microcomputer) therefore established a completely new market which consisted of the hobbyists. This then led to the development of the microcomputer industry with companies competing with similar types of value chain to the initial entrant.

Since changes in competitive advantage manifest themselves in the form of new strategies, for the newgame environment to continue to evolve, not all of the competing companies can follow the same strategy. Instead, some of the subsequent entrants will need to develop newgame strategies of their own based upon alternative value chains. An example of a second newgame strategy is illustrated later in this section with the case of IMSAI, when the competitive process was driven by the creation of a different value chain from that of the earlier competitors. This pattern of strategic moves may be represented as a series of attempts to secure competitive advantage resulting from new ways of configuring their strategic resources, which represent adjustments in the respective companies' value chains. If successful, these moves will not only alter the relative performance of the competitors, but will also lead to a change in the structure of the industry, including the creation of strategic groups as well as increasing the entry costs for subsequent competitors.[33] This section illustrates how this pattern developed during the embryonic stage of the newgame environment for microcomputers.

Essentially, the competition developed in distinctive phases. The first phase was in the form of strategies directed at competing at both the component and later the central processing board level. To understand how these strategies developed Fig. 3.6 illustrates the areas in which the early competitors chose to compete on product technology. As the first entrant, MITS managed to gain a temporary competitive advantage over previous single board microprocessor suppliers by purchasing its Intel

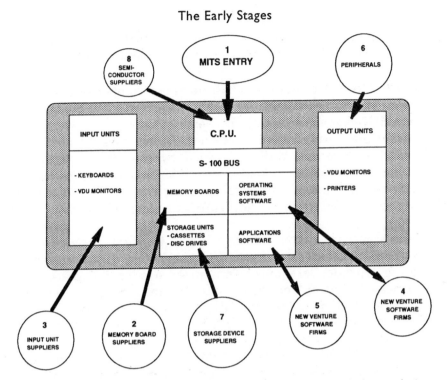

Note: The various numbers attached to the labels of the different types of entrant depict the approximate sequence in which they occurred within the embryonic stage of evolution.

**Fig. 3.6. Competitive moves around the MITS microcomputer:
1975 - 1976.**

microprocessors significantly more cheaply than at normal market prices. Secondly, the design of the computer's internal S-100 bus-system allowed the Altair to potentially interface with a range of peripherals which had previously not been possible with other microprocessors. Hence, an initial competitive advantage was established by MITS on the basis of a low procurement cost of the core technology and innovative design of its bus-system. However, the pricing policy of MITS was such that it was barely able to make break-even on its central processing unit, hence it was unable to extract monopoly profits from the core product. As a result, the major contribution to the profit margin needed to come from the memory and other expansion boards,[34] peripherals and software.

However, it was precisely at this level that MITS was most exposed to competition. In this respect, the MITS S-100 bus-system behaved as a two-edged sword, for it permitted other firms to enter by providing compatible expansion memory boards which offered a better price/performance ratio than MITS. Hence, although MITS initially held a competitive advantage in the core microprocessor technology, it was unable to protect itself against other component suppliers, since the value chain for MITS was imitated by most of the early entrants that followed MITS into creating the embryonic stage of the industry. Furthermore, MITS was also vulnerable to peripheral suppliers, where the company had no competitive advantage and found itself overpriced relative to the competition, who had the advantage of experience curve effects and volume scale production.

In an effort to differentiate itself from these competitors, MITS sought to gain a competitive advantage by "Bundling"[35] its BASIC software with its non-competitive memory boards. However, this was not successful, since users merely "copied" the software onto paper-tape reels. Hence, a potential competitive advantage was quickly eroded by the weakness of copyright regulations and the technical ease with which the copy could be made from a master. Unfortunately, this form of early piracy was a phenomenon which has remained a problem for software developers right up to the present day.

Thus the structure of the industry during the first 10 months consisted of MITS as the sole supplier of a boxed single-board system, surrounded by a growing number of competing suppliers of components, whose competition was based on technical performance and price. Technological innovation was taking place mainly around expansion boards and peripherals, the purchase of which allowed the hobbyist user to develop the basic computer to a level that would actually have some value and applications. Against this background, MITS was trying to develop a wide range of such accessories, but was unable to deliver a suitably high level of quality or reliability in its offerings to maintain control of the market. As the market moved to demand assembled units more than kits, standards of reliability in the product and delivery became even more important.

The next phase of competition began in November 1975, when MITS lost its monopolist position for supplying single-board CPU's as two new entrants, Southwest and IMSAI joined the market. Southwest Technology had originally started by producing memory boards for the Altair. On competing at the CPU level, it used a lower priced yet higher performance microprocessor, thus representing a technology-based innovation to differentiate its product. The other entrant IMSAI, had diversified from its systems business and although using the same microprocessor as MITS, differentiated its product by marketing on an aggressive sales basis to the small business segment, thus representing a market niche strategy. This represented a shift in the location of advantage down the value chain and was a harbinger of future competitive behaviour in the industry. IMSAI generated two competitive advantages in its entry strategy. The first was to "focus" upon the potential market segment of small businesses. This was achieved by targeted selling and promotional activity, which attempted to redefine the nature of the microcomputer from being a hobbyist's tool or pastime into a product suitable for use by the business person. The second advantage gained by IMSAI resulted from its not insisting upon exclusivity arrangements with its dealers (an arrangement made by MITS), which had led to some reported dissatisfaction amongst franchised dealers.

In response to these new competitors, MITS introduced a second product in 1976 based on the Motorola microprocessor used by Southwest Technology. However, it was unable to negotiate a more favourable cost of supply than its competitors and ran into a number of technical problems with the project. Throughout 1976, additional entrants adopted the S-100 bus, which meant that their products could use interface and memory boards developed for the MITS Altair. Hence, the good but non-patented design of the S-100 bus exposed MITS to more rapid competition in the component and peripheral level than might otherwise have been the case. The floodgates were now open and new start-up companies began to rapidly emerge, eager to take a share of the rapidly expanding market. For example, Vector Graphic undertook strategies that differentiated its position through developing a close relationship with the distribution channels. Although MITS itself had started to sell Altair machines into the small business sector through the Altair Centre franchise shops, IMSAI stepped up the scale of investment in this part of the value chain. This development created a wider range of possible sources of competitive advantage, thus providing the opportunity for a greater diversity of strategic behaviour, which in turn would lead to the creation of strategic groups within the evolving industry. In particular, IMSAI's identification of the small business market provided opportunities for firms to differentiate and hence gain competitive advantage along marketing dimensions other than solely on a technical price/performance basis.

The competitive advantage for MITS gained by its low cost of microprocessor procurement was thus virtually removed within 18 months of its entry, along with its technical S-100 bus system innovation. The company's only remaining distinctive advantage now lay in the size of its installed base and the general awareness of its name as "the pioneer" amongst users. However, with so many new first time buyers still entering the market and an industry-standard bus emerging, new entrants found little evidence of switching costs and easily attracted a number of the MITS customers.

As a result of IMSAI's success, by late 1976 the potential for development of the small business market segment was becoming apparent. This stimulated interest amongst software and peripheral suppliers to consider focusing their products on what was expected to prove an even greater size of market than the hobbyist market. Thus, competitors' value chains began to evolve towards gaining competitive advantage through the power and impact of marketing activities as well as technical price and performance characteristics. This was especially the case for promotional and distribution activities aimed at the "early adopters" in the small business segment. However, in practice, the weaknesses in most of the firms in the areas of product quality control, delivered technical performance (as opposed to planned) and poor organisation management meant that only a few firms were able to develop any significant technical or marketing advantage at this stage.

Although MITS maintained market leadership during 1976, it was nevertheless rapidly losing its position. The potential erosion of the MITS leadership position is further highlighted if one considers the fact that the first IMSAI computer was sold in December 1975, eleven months after

MITS sold its first Altair. Therefore, MITS had achieved much of its market leadership by being the "first-entrant/first-mover". By early 1977, the pace of growth of the microcomputer industry was high and encouraged further rapid entry by new start-up companies. MITS now came under competitive pressure from MOS-Tech, the semiconductor company, which was making a direct frontal attack on the market by forward vertical integration. However, with the exception of MOS-Tech, the majority of entrants were unable to offer any significant product differentiation over the MITS Altair. But for MITS its inability to regain a competitive edge meant that its leadership position was under threat.

However, the competition moves described in this section help to account for the way in which links within the industry value chain developed during the period. In particular, it emphasises the distinction between the various strategies of the competitors. The strategies are illustrated in Fig. 3.7. Four categories have been identified, which included two groups of companies making Flanking Attacks, one group based upon differentiated marketing, the other based upon technological differentiation. The other two groups of companies made direct Frontal Attacks. One group consisted of the semiconductor manufacturers involved in forward integration, whilst the other consisted of distributors making backward integration moves. In some instances these consisted of new start-up companies, whilst in others, they were established companies. For the reasons described in this section, competitive advantages were based upon

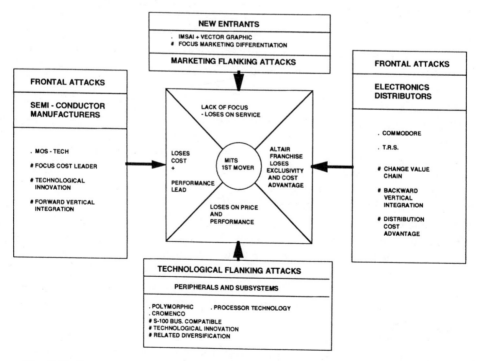

Fig. 3.7. Actual and potential areas of entry into the personal computer industry: 1976 - 1977.

cost leadership factors, versus those involving "value" based factors such as reliability, quality and ease of access. Managerial and logistics weaknesses remained a problem for most of the competitors at this stage of evolution. This was due largely to the absence of any significant entry barriers, which meant that such companies were still essentially underfunded and often relatively poorly managed concerns. They were able to survive largely because of the speed of market expansion and the absence of any major competitor which could exercise significant market power. The market leaders, namely, MITS and IMSAI were both flawed by a failure to achieve success in their subsequent product development. Like many of the competitors at the time they encountered operational problems that may have reflected too much emphasis on technical issues and a lack of commercial orientation. Thus the industry and its core market (hobbyists) was nearing a watershed, which would need a new type of entrant to generate change in the strategic direction of competition and to release the latent demand in further potential market segments. It is to this type of change that we now turn in considering the take-off stage.

THE TAKE-OFF STAGE

Industry Forces

During 1977, three companies entered the market for microcomputers using different asset structures. One of the firms was a new venture, Apple Computer, whilst the remaining two, Tandy Radio Shack and Commodore, were both established, medium-sized companies. By taking advantage of the continued technological advances within components, all three companies developed their own style of newgame strategies. Their strategies centred upon repackaging the basic product and reconfiguring the elements and structure of their respective business value chains. The impact of their strategies shifted the industry from its "embryonic" stage to its "take-off" stage, which was characterised by creation of a set of distinct strategic groups, failure and exit by certain incumbents, together with expansion and segmentation of the marketplace and a further wave of entrants.

In early 1977, the personal computer industry was characterised by its fragmented nature, the two principal reasons being:

(1) low overall entry barriers;

(2) absence of economies of scale and experience curves.

As seen in the embryonic stage described in the previous sections, three types of company were manufacturing and/or assembling personal computers. These included the small start-ups, together with the small and medium sized companies that had diversified from their core business in electronic components and/or peripherals. With only a few exceptions, virtually all held limited bargaining power over their semiconductor suppliers. Distribution channels were independent of all but the two leading competitors and some carried products of the integrated circuit manufacturers and miscellaneous producers (e.g. instruments, tools, supplies and books for hobbyists). Overcoming fragmentation offered a very significant challenge to any company which could enter at this time of low entry costs, with little risk of effective retaliation from small and relatively weak incumbent competitors. By now the microcomputer markets had expanded into two major overlapping segments, namely home-users and hobbyists.

> "Of the 17,458 computers of all types purchased in 1976 for use in the home, 12,520 (72 percent) were supplied by so-called hobby computer manufacturers, of which the two largest suppliers (MITS and IMS) accounted for 63 per cent".[36]

These figures were based on a market size of $36 million, which was forecast to grow to $179 million by 1981, at an average annual compound rate of increase of 37 per cent.[37] Neither of these markets was perceived by the major computer manufacturers as representing related business opportunities. Although some signs suggested microcomputers might penetrate the small business markets, at the time they were still considered unsuitable for serious business applications. Therefore, the new wave of entrants in 1977 came from sources closer to the hobbyist and microcomputer marketplaces.

New Entrants and New Strategic Groups

The three major entrants in 1977, Apple Computer, Tandy Radio Shack (TRS) and Commodore each practised a form of entry strategy that was distinctly different from the incumbents. The three entrants took advantage of technological changes in four areas of component supply.

The first was in the core microprocessors, of which two new ones had been introduced in 1976, with volume shipments commencing in 1977. The Intel 8085 offered additional features to the 8080, whilst the Zilog Z-80 contained improvements in architecture over the 8080 and incorporated all the 8080 instructions in its extensive instruction set. The performance and the low price of the Z-80 microprocessor made it an attractive core component for use by many of the major personal computer manufacturers. The alternative 8-bit microprocessor was the MOS 6502 which was manufactured by a Commodore subsidiary and used both by Commodore and Apple. Thus, three families of microprocessors emerged as the core technology to the new generation of microcomputers, which in turn restricted the opportunity for technological differentiation at this level.

The second key change in technology concerned operating systems software. This arose due to the fact that the adoption of a limited range of microprocessors provided an opportunity for standardisation in operating systems, since application software developers saw the economic advantage of writing for a single operating system, which would run on virtually most personal computers. In fact, the operating system that eventually qualified as a standard for 8-bit machines, CP/M-80, had originally appeared before the Altair itself. CP/M (Control Program/Monitor) was designed and developed by a computer science professor, Gary Kildall, during 1973 to 1976. Kildall set up Digital Research to sell CP/M in 1976. Yet the novelty of an effective operating system meant a lack of initial market knowledge for pricing policy. Thus, in 1976, CP/M had been sold as a licence to an early microcomputer company for only $90. Within a year, a licence for CP/M cost tens of thousands of dollars, when in 1977, IMSAI purchased CP/M. It was such a good operating system for its time that it became the industry standard. Not until IBM introduced its personal computer in 1981 with a different operating system, did Digital Research face any serious competition. Only Commodore and Apple chose to adopt their own proprietary systems and even these machines could run CP/M by using appropriate expansion interface boards.

The third key technology change was of an evolutionary nature and occurred in storage systems. The early machines and initial entries of Apple, Commodore and TRS all used cassette drives for off-line storage. During 1976, disk drives existed and were used heavily on mainframes and minicomputers, but to mount a disk drive on a microcomputer was too expensive, since they typically cost around $3500. However, a number of microcomputer companies and individual designers recognised that if the microcomputer was ever to become a serious business machine, it would require a low-cost drive system with software and a controller board.[38] Shugart (a major disk drive manufacturing company) appeared attractive in its offer of 5 1/4 inch drives; however, the use of 8 inch drives by IBM had established certain standards for the devices. No standards existed for the smaller disk drives, so that, in consequence, there was no guarantee that disks written on one brand of machine would be readable on another. The then recently started microcomputer company, North Star, had selected the Shugart drive and sold it for $800, whilst Morrow developed an 8 inch drive for $1000 during 1977.

Lastly, due to the forces driving product technology in the semiconductor industry, the price/performance ratio of random access memory (RAM) and read only memory (ROM) continued to improve, as costs per bit fell from 1.3 cents in 1977 to 0.5 cents by 1979. Furthermore, during 1978, 32K RAMs started to become commonplace and hence by early 1979 the standard configurations of the microcomputer had shifted from assembled kits to fully integrated systems.[39]

Most importantly, when taken together these technological developments created a new class of machine. This reflected a move to standardise on three families of microprocessors and the emergence of a dominant disk operating system, which was CP/M-80. The standardisation on microprocessor operating systems meant that applications software was now able to be developed for more than one single machine. In theory, any program written to run on CP/M-80 using a particular manufacturer's microcomputer could run on another manufacturer's machine, providing that it used the CP/M-80 operating system.

Two additional features created the potential for more powerful and hence useful types of applications software to be written. The first was the introduction of disk-storage devices[40] to replace cassette-tape devices. This meant that data could be accessed much more rapidly and that larger storage capacity was possible. The second involved increased capacity in random access memory which allowed larger sizes of data and application program to be processed by the microprocessor. Wordprocessing and accounting packages now became a reality which stimulated growth of demand in the emerging small-business segment.

These changes represented a distinct departure from most of the earlier suppliers, including MITS, Processor Technology, Southwest Technical Products, Polymorphic, Cromemco and Compucolor, many of which had initially been major subsystem assemblers. They provided equipment with a resident program language, (usually BASIC), and left most software development to the purchaser/user. Whilst the incumbents continued to offer component systems for assembly, the new entrants provided integrated computer packages,[41] including Commodore (PET Model 2001), Apple Computer (Apple II), APF (Pe Cos One) and Tandy Radio Shack (TRS-80). Component systems, such as those offered by MITS, offered the user flexibility, provision for expansion and opportunities to attach a wide range of peripherals — albeit with limited software and low reliability. However, expansion potential and flexibility were key considerations for the hobbyist buyer.

In late 1977, basic prices for hobbyist equipment with this flexibility were in the $2000 – $3000 range, which provided a machine based on an 8-bit microprocessor (such as the Intel 8080 or newly introduced competitive microprocessor, the Zilog Z-80). In addition, a typical configuration would include 16K of Random Access Memory (RAM), an

Table 3.2. Personal computer equipment comparison of systems.

INTEGRATED SYSTEM	COMPONENT SYSTEM
PRICE: $600	PRICE: $2800
RADIO SHACK MODEL TRS-80	IMSAI MODEL 8080
Z-80 MPU 4K ROM 4K RAM DISPLAY (64 char. T.V.) KEYBOARD CASSETTE RECORDER 4K BASIC	8080 MPU 4K ROM 16K RAM 80 character CRT KEYBOARD CASSETTE RECORDER (2) 8K BASIC (Level II) Built in expansion provided (22 Cards) 28 amp power supply Commercial grade construction Machine Programming Option

Source: Adapted from Arthur D. Little, *The Personal Computer Industry,* 7 September 1978, p.3. Reproduced by permission of Decision Resources, Inc., © 1978.

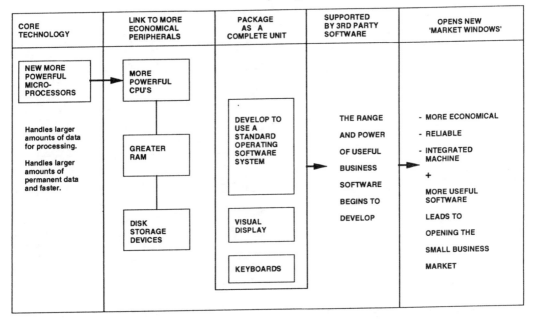

Fig. 3.8. The link between core technology and development in market applications.

80-character cathode ray display terminal with alphanumeric keyboard and Level II BASIC software. By integrating several components into one unit or offering them as a single package, the new entrants were able to reduce the basic price of equivalent computer hobbyist equipment to the $600 – $800 range. However, such cost savings also meant a decrease in equipment flexibility and capability, as illustrated in Table 3.2. However, the lower prices and ease of usage were to open new market segments, where the growth in demand offered the opportunity to achieve volume-based economies of scale. By introducing the technology in a "friendlier" package, companies such as Commodore, TRS and Apple were creating a new product package at prices which could appeal to a set of new market segments. This pattern is illustrated in Fig. 3.8.

Since the new generation of personal computers was to appeal to a wider market than just hobbyists, greater resources were allocated to elements farther along the value chain, as illustrated in Fig. 3.9. To reduce unit costs, greater automation occurred in production. Commodore even controlled its own semiconductor company to produce its low cost microprocessors. Tandy (with no previous manufacturing experience) exploited its competitive advantage of a major chain of electronics stores and brought its experience of mass merchandising to the marketplace. Whilst Apple was a new start-up venture, it was nevertheless quick to learn and encouraged extensive third-party software development due to its machine's expansion capabilities, at the same time as looking to improve standards of documentation and service support.

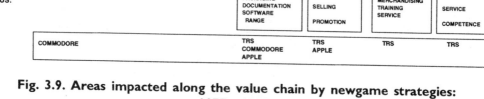

Fig. 3.9. Areas impacted along the value chain by newgame strategies: 1977 - 1978.

Newgame Strategies and Industry Changes

The previous section suggested that changes in technology affected the strategies pursued by entrants and incumbents. It also suggested that the newgame entry strategies of Tandy, Commodore and Apple incorporated significant changes in the asset structures of their value chains, relative to those of the existing incumbents. This section will illustrate how these changes were to feed through to the changes in industry and market structure. The starting point for the analysis is the existing dominant pattern of value chains and how they were impacted by the value chains of the new entrants.

Changes in Value Chain Structures

During the first part of 1977, the industry leader and major competitors consisted of the first wave of entrants which had initially focused on the hobbyist market segment and were then starting to try and develop the small business segment. During the next two years, entrants to the industry forged stronger links along the value chain by forward and backward integration, which is illustrated in Fig. 3.10.

Evidence of the shift in resource focus came in the nature of the product, the size and scale of the personal computer suppliers, the nature of marketing activities and the distribution channels. Tandy, Commodore and Heath (which had continued to focus upon the hobbyist segment) were all established medium sized companies, with electronic products and markets already serving the existing hobbyist segment. They therefore had the advantage of lower manufacturing costs (learning and experience curve effects) and more professional management. Commodore also controlled its

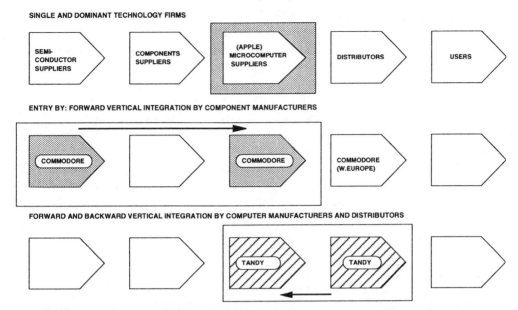

Fig. 3.10. Value chain linkages within the personal computer industry during 1979.

own semiconductor microprocessor manufacturing facilities due to its acquisition of MOS Technology. However, these features also represented a larger scale of overheads and the potential of less commitment and far less organisational flexibility. The major effect of these developments upon the prevailing competitors' value chains was to reduce the average costs of assembly and permit cross-component purchasing with other products in their range.

The new entrants also changed the cost structure of marketing and distribution activities. Tandy had years of experience in marketing and merchandising a wide range of electrical and electronic consumer products through its own chain of 800 nationwide Radio Shack stores. Commodore, although smaller, had control of an extensive chain of specialist business equipment outlets. Both companies therefore immediately increased the scale of resources available and subsequently necessary for effective promotional advertising, selling, training and distribution. Although each feature represents additional overheads to a new entrant, for Tandy and Commodore their personal computers represented an additional product to cover costs, which minimised the marginal costs. Both the new companies, Apple Computer and to a less extent, Vector Graphic, also used their investment in advertising and promotional dollars very skilfully, with much emphasis being placed upon the potential business user of personal computers.

Albeit that competitors still required to seek cost advantages in supply costs, the dominant pattern of value chains for the industry changed to place increasing importance upon assembly, marketing and distribution activities. Competence in achieving lower than average unit costs in production and assembly involved investment in capital equipment, management and skilled operators. Costs associated with regional and national advertising and promotional campaigns in business publications, as well as cooperative advertising with dealers, further raised marketing costs. Extensive distribution channels, such as those of Tandy and Commodore, represented enormous capital investment, which none of the smaller entrants or incumbents could rapidly imitate. Linked to effective promotional activity, such outlets provided a distinctive competitive advantage as was demonstrated by their rapid success after entry.

McGee addresses the nature of competitive advantage and competitive strategy within the small firm, and compares their characteristics to larger firms[42] where he presents a broad dichotomy between "simple" and "complex" businesses as a focus to help in understanding the problems faced by small firms.

> "A 'simple' business is one where competitive advantage arises from doing one thing better than anyone else — e.g. having access to low cost raw materials (e.g. high purity Australian iron ore) or low cost labour, or a specific product designed by the owner manager. Complex businesses have typically higher value added. Superior performance depends on doing a number of things well and being able to co-ordinate and manage complex interactions between the different elements in the cost structure."[43]

McGee's viewpoint is empirically supported by the findings within this research. In particular, the initial entrants established competitive advantage by doing one or a few aspects well (e.g. design or access to cheap microprocessors), whereas later entrants needed to manage a more complex range of functions along the value chain. Indeed, many of the early simple businesses in the personal computer industry failed to transform their asset structures to the more complex form of business organisation, which came to dominate the later stages of the newgame environment.

Underlying McGee's general propositions is the idea that, within "innovatory" environments:

> "... growth [*within the small firm*][44] requires new product-market choices, development of new specific assets, and major changes in management process ...".[45]

By analysing the value chains of the major entrants and incumbents, together with their market focus, it is intended to demonstrate the pattern described by McGee, and outlined in the conceptual framework of newgame environments. The most effective measure of such changes is to look at the pattern of strategic groups which began to form within the industry during this period.

Strategic Groups

By late 1977, the industry structure was showing signs of change as a result of the entry strategies pursued by Tandy, Commodore and Apple.

The core hobbyist market still remained loyal to MITS and IMSAI, but many new users, especially those who were professionals, purchased the integrated, lower-priced and more reliable second generation machines.[46]

The competitors consisted of the first generation incumbents and the second generation entrants. Low entry barriers to the technology and the rapidly expanding number of distribution outlets encouraged further entrants, most of which were start-up companies. Although most suppliers were active in the hobbyist market, the small business market attracted many entrants, so that competitors offered a similar product to both segments. Table 3.3 illustrates the key suppliers in late 1977.

During the following twelve months the membership of the strategic groups changed. Firstly, the industry leader, MITS, was sold to Pertec, the disk and tape drive manufacturer. The acquisition was a failure due to major differences in culture between the two companies and the departure of the founder of MITS, Ed Roberts. In consequence, during 1978, Pertec was unable to match the competition of the new entrants. In addition, the second place competitor, IMSAI, which had focused upon the business hobbyist user segment, suffered severe internal management problems. As a result of these factors, it lost considerable funds and damaged its image with its launch in 1978 of a technically unsatisfactory second generation product. Hence, both the leading incumbents were no match for the competitive competence of Tandy and Commodore. By the end of 1978, leadership of the industry had changed hands. The three new entrants Tandy, Commodore, Apple Computer, along with two incumbents, Cromemco and Ohio Scientific, accounted for more than 70 per cent of the total market, with Tandy holding 40 per cent.

Table 3.3. Key personal computer suppliers in late 1977.

COMPANY	EQUIPMENT	MARKET SEGMENTS		
		HOBBYIST	CONSUMER	SMALL BUSINESS
VIDEO BRAIN COMPUTER	VIDEOBRAIN		X	
RADIO SHACK (TANDY)	TRS-80	XX		X
COMMODORE	PET 2001	XX		X
MITS (PERTEC)	ALTAIR	XX		XX
IMSAI	8080	XX		XX
CROMEMCO	Z-2	X		X
SOUTHWEST TECH.		X		X
APPLE COMPUTER	APPLE II	XX		X
APF	PECOS ONE	X		X
INTELLIGENT SYSTEMS	COMPUCOLOR II	X		X
HEATH (SCHLUMBERGER)	H8, H11	X		X
OHIO SCIENTIFIC		X		X
POLYMORPHIC	SYSTEM 8813	X		X
PROCESSOR TECHNOLOGY		X		X
XITAN	ALPHA 2	X		
VECTOR GRAPHIC	VECTOR 1			X

KEY: XX = More prominent supplier in sector.
     X = Participating in the sector.

Source: Arthur D. Little, *The Personal Computer Industry*, 7 September 1978, p.2.
Reproduced by permission of Decision Resources, Inc., © 1978.

The strategic group patterns which emerged during 1978 are illustrated in Fig. 3.11. Tandy rapidly became the industry leader and based its competitive advantage upon its large-scale distribution network which was perfectly suited to the hobbyist and emerging small business market. It was also highly experienced in merchandising and held the benefit of an established brand name. Commodore also enjoyed an extensive and established distribution network which was mainly centred upon the West European market where there was relatively little local competition. Furthermore, Commodore also controlled the development and manufacture of its own semiconductors which allowed it a shorter product development cycle. Although a new start-up venture, Apple Computer quickly attracted a significant following of software developers for its Apple II machine, which offered considerable flexibility due to its high capacity for expansion boards. Hence a large number of third-party software applications began to be developed for the Apple II, especially in the educational and games markets. The fourth strategic group consisted of the early entrants to the industry which were now the incumbents. Faced with inefficiencies in production and a limited market focus, their value chains failed to adapt to the new structures introduced by Tandy and the other new competitors. Thus they ended up in a declining market segment. Finally, the new entrants such as Cromemco and Vector Graphic concentrated on developing their niche markets for scientific/engineering or small business applications. Members of this group built their competitive advantage upon high quality of product and service for a particular market segment.

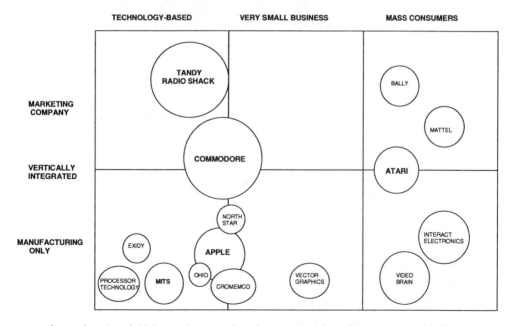

Source: Based on field data and reports from International Data Corporation and A. D. Little, Inc.

Fig. 3.11. Strategic groups in the personal computer industry around 1979.

Overall, the stability of the strategic groups was such that Tandy, Commodore and Apple were gradually moving closer together and would eventually become direct competitors with similar value chains. The early entrants' strategic group were far less stable and in overall decline, whilst members of the niche strategic group were relatively stable and initially not under direct competition from Tandy, Commodore or Apple.

However, by mid-1979 the strategic groups had changed again, since IMSAI and two less prominent participants, Polymorphic and Xitan had gone out of business, whilst others, including the established electronic kits manufacturer, Heath, had not experienced the success they had anticipated. Key factors which accounted for failures during this period were attributed to the following:

(i) inability to compete in hardware performance in the technology-based market segment;

(ii) inability to shift successfully from the hobbyist to the very small business segment.

For those companies that had targeted the mass consumer market, such as Video Brain, the projected rapid growth in sales simply did not materialise during 1978. Thus, such companies suffered from low sales revenue and lower margins than the competitors in the small business segment.

By 1979, the industry had attracted more than 35 entrants, most of which were actively pursuing the small business market. Because demand was strong, weak competitors were also able to continue operations, even with poor operating margins or excessive operating expenses. The new entrants came from three backgrounds. As Tables 3.4 and 3.5 show, Tandy Radio Shack came from a background in merchandising electronic components, electronic hobby kits and Hi-Fi equipment. Commodore was a vertically integrated office products supplier, with control of its own

Table 3.4. Entry patterns during the take-off stage.

NAME OF FIRM	ENTRY DATE	NATURE OF ENTRY MOVE	PAST ACTIVITY	STRATEGIC MOVE
ALTOS	1977	NEW VENTURE	NONE	FOCUS ON SMALL BUSINESS
APPLE	1977	NEW VENTURE	NONE	GENERAL PURPOSE MICROCOMPUTER
COMMODORE	1977	RELATED EXPANSION	OFFICE PRODUCTS CALCULATORS	GENERAL PURPOSE MICROCOMPUTER (W.EUROPE)
SMOKE SIGNAL	1977	RELATED EXPANSION	MICROCOMPUTER COMPONENTS	SMALL BUSINESS MICROCOMPUTER
TANDY RADIO SHACK	1977	NEW VENTURE	MASS MERCHANDISING RADIO, HI-FI KITS	GENERAL PURPOSE MICROCOMPUTER
VECTOR GRAPHIC	1977	RELATED EXPANSION	MEMORY-BOARDS	SMALL BUSINESS MICROCOMPUTER

Table 3.5. Characteristics of entrants during the take-off stage.

NAME OF FIRM	PARENT COMPANY	VERTICAL INTEGRATION	HORIZONTAL INTEGRATION	SPECIALISATION	SCALE
ALTOS	NONE	NIL	NIL	HIGH	SMALL
APPLE	NONE	NIL	NIL	HIGH	SMALL
COMMODORE	OFFICE PRODUCTS RETAIL AND MANUFACTURING	S-M-D (1)	EXPANSION INTO MICROS. PREVIOUSLY IN ELECTRONIC CALCULATORS	MEDIUM	MEDIUM
SMOKE SIGNAL	NONE	NIL	NIL	HIGH	SMALL
TANDY RADIO SHACK	CONSUMER ELECTRONICS MERCHANDISING	M-D (2)	NEW MOVE INTO OWN MANUFACTURE	LOW	MEDIUM
VECTOR GRAPHIC	NONE	NIL	NIL	HIGH	SMALL

Key:
(1) S-M-D = Supplier, Manufacturing and Distribution.
(2) M-D = Manufacturing and Distribution.

semiconductor technology as well as an extensive distribution network. Entry by both companies represented expansion in their product range into related products.

The move was more significant for Tandy, in that its traditional operations were based upon marketing other manufacturers' products under the Radio Shack brand name. The establishment of its own manufacturing/ assembly facilities therefore involved greater uncertainty than Commodore, which had experience as a vertically integrated company. In this sense, Tandy and Commodore undertook market-related diversification. The other group of entrants, (excluding the new start-up ventures) made technology-related diversifications. Most of these firms were already active in the manufacture of microcomputer components or peripherals and therefore had the skills necessary for designing and manufacturing personal computers. Apple Computer, North Star and Vector Graphic were all in this category. There was very little "unrelated" product diversification into the market at this stage and indeed, although many of the entrants were relatively new companies, few were specifically established to produce a personal computer as their first product.

A further feature of entrants at this time was the absence of any of the larger established data processing (e.g. IBM, DEC) or office products/ systems companies (e.g. Wang, Xerox). Such companies still believed they had no synergistic rationale for entering the market at this time. Instead, they chose to compete in the small business segment by offering more expensive minicomputer-based desktop systems.

In summary, the embryonic stage of the industry was characterised by a competitive core of MITS and IMSAI, whose strategic behaviour was in most respects similar to the other small, single-technology firms which entered the industry at the time. It is thus difficult to identify any clear strategic groupings set within a fragmented and relatively unlinked industry value chain. However, with the entry of Tandy and Commodore the industry now supported two medium sized international companies with established vertically integrated value chains. Their emphasis upon marketing and distribution channel activities within the value chain forced other competitors, both entrants and incumbents to either imitate and develop similar capabilities or alternatively to be trapped in their limited market position. Over time therefore the industry witnessed the formation of five early strategic groups, which reflected differences in their members' respective value chains, their strategies and subsequent performance. Therefore, the next issue to consider relates to the developments that took place in the structure of the market as a result of changes in the nature of strategies introduced by these companies.

Market Conditions

Earlier in this chapter, it was shown that in the embryonic stage, most of the market consisted of hobbyist users, many of whom purchased their microcomputers in kit form. By late 1976, two new market segments were beginning to emerge, namely, the general consumer and the small business user. However, it is important to recognise that these segments were initially more a distinction of location and application, than of a totally different type of buyer. In other words, many of the early "consumers" and "small business" users were in fact hobbyists using their microcomputers in the home (for games or programming functions) or for limited business applications.

For the microcomputer to penetrate both the general consumer and small business markets, then not only would the product itself need to improve (both in terms of price and performance), but the functional competence of the technology-based hobby computer firms would also need to shift, in order to overcome the new set of market barriers. New entrants also needed to overcome the entry barriers, but some were better placed to succeed, due to their competitive advantages reflected in a different set of value chains from those of most of the incumbents.

In 1977, U.S. consumption of personal computer systems priced below $15,000 (mainframes and associated peripherals) totalled 23,000 – 25,000 units valued at $60 – $70 million.[47] During 1978, U.S. consumption had increased to approximately 240,000 units valued at about $170 million. The dramatic growth between 1977 and 1978 could be chiefly attributed to the introduction of a new generation of low-priced personal computers in mid- to late 1977.

The Radio Shack TRS-80, announced in August 1977, reduced the basic entry price of a personal computer from just over $2000 to $599. Around the same time, Apple Computer announced their Apple II personal computer ($1200), whilst Commodore Business Machines announced the PET personal computer ($800). Other manufacturers followed in 1978, bringing many basic personal computers to within a $500 to $1500 price band. However, during the following two years (1977 – 1979) among the leading personal computer models, there only occurred one price reduction. Radio Shack reduced the price of their 16K RAM based TRS-80 from $1038 to $899 and their 4K RAM model from $599 to $499, in 1979, to coincide with

Table 3.6. Price changes for selected personal computers.

EQUIPMENT MODEL	MANUFACTURER	INTRODUCED	RETAIL LIST PRICE U.S.$
TRS-80	RADIO SHACK	Aug-77	1038 (Aug-77) 1038 (Aug-78) 899 (Aug-79)
SORCERER	EXIDY	Jun-78	..... (Aug-77) 1355 (Aug-78) 1350 (Aug-79)
APPLE II	APPLE COMPUTER	Jul-78	1545 (Aug-77) 1345 (Aug-78) 1345 (Aug-79)
PET	COMMODORE	Jun-77	995 (Aug-77) 995 (Aug-78) 998 (Aug-79)

NOTE: (1) Includes the following equipment:
Z-80 or 6502 8 bit microprocessor unit
Keyboard
Black and white TV monitor
Cassette recorder for Mass Memory Storage
16 Bytes RAM user memory
8K basic software

Source: Arthur D. Little, Inc., *The Personal Computer Industry*, 12 October 1979, p.2. Reproduced by permission of Decision Resources, Inc., © 1979.

the announcement of their TRS-80 Model II machine. As illustrated in Table 3.6, prices of Apple and Commodore machines showed little decrease during this period. Given the strong demand and high market growth rates, suppliers were able to sustain prices of their products for given performance characteristics.

Even in 1978, only one supplier had dedicated its product exclusively to the consumer market segment — Video Brain, with a price of $500. So long as suppliers experienced strong demand, prices could be expected to remain stable. However, the process of market segmentation that was starting to develop meant competition was more based upon improvements in performance, rather than price reductions, at least in the small business segment. The hobbyist segment showed slight price declines during this period, whilst by 1979 significantly lower prices were offered on machines in the consumer market segment.

Market Segmentation

Between 1977 and 1978, there were dramatic shifts in the structure of the overall personal computer market. During 1977, hobbyists brought most of the 23,000 to 25,000 units sold.[48] By the end of 1977, the growth rate in the hobbyist segment was slowing down and the new generation of personal computers were attracting new categories of end-users.

Equipment vendors therefore looked towards the three emerging market segments, namely, professional users, very small business users and mass consumers, as illustrated in Table 3.7. All three groups differed from computer hobbyists in one very important respect: they were primarily interested in applications, rather than equipment operations, experimentation or software program creation.

Professional users included engineers, business analysts, market researchers, scientists, educators and accountants. As such, they represented the innovative users in their respective professions, since the performance of the personal computers was still limited by RAM capacity and a lack of good applications software. Using BASIC, many of the professionals wrote their own applications programs. During 1977/78, most professionals bought equipment identical to hobbyists' equipment and consequently, market data for this period generally combined the two groups into one category, namely, technology-based users.

Professionals generally tended to purchase systems which included a VDU, keyboard and disk drive, with prices depending on the model and configuration. In many instances, the purchase was financed by the company within a single department's budget. By late 1978 and early 1979, a number of improved business applications were coming to the market, especially in word processing and accounting functions, which further boosted demand. However, it must be stressed that the power of the personal computer in 1978/79 was still fairly limited and therefore restricted the utility of software to a relatively narrow range of applications.

The very small business users were similar to the professionals in that they represented the innovative users in their particular group. Also,

Table 3.7. Personal computer market segments: 1978-1979.

MARKET SEGMENT	PRINCIPAL APPLICATIONS	TYPICAL 1978-1979 HARDWARE PRICE RANGES U.S. $
VERY SMALL BUSINESS USERS		
SMALL MANUFACTURERS RETAILERS SERVICE ORGANISATIONS	ACCOUNTING WORD PROCESSING INVENTORY CONTROL SALES ANALYSIS	$4,000 - $15,000
TECHNOLOGY-BASED USERS		
HOBBYISTS PROFESSIONAL USERS	CREATIVE EXPERIMENTATION SOLUTION OF PROFESSIONAL APPLICATIONS PROBLEMS	$1,000 - $4,000
MASS CONSUMERS		
ADULTS CHILDREN	EDUCATION ENTERTAINMENT PERSONAL MANAGEMENT	$300 - $500

NOTE: 1. Manufacturer's level.

Source: Arthur D. Little, Inc., *The Personal Computer Industry* — An update, 12 October 1979, p.3. Reproduced by permission of Decision Resources, Inc., © 1979.

as with many professionals, they tended to regard programming as a necessary evil. Furthermore, unlike the hobbyist, the small business user was investing in a personal computer to perform a task in a cost-effective manner. As a result, product reliability, clear documentation and sources of help or advice were important issues in the minds of the purchaser. Although many vendors promoted their products as providing productivity tools, in reality, the software lacked the sophistication to appeal to the mass small business market at this stage. Indeed, most "off-the-shelf" applications were restricted to accounting, inventory control, word processing, mailing lists and sales analysis. They were not therefore representative of solutions for general management functions and hence could only appeal to a limited number of small business users, many of whom could equally well be classified as professionals.

Thus in 1978, the technology-orientated user segment, including both professionals and hobbyists, constituted approximately 80 per cent of the total market in units, buying some 192,000 units; but within this category, hobbyists represented fewer than 35,000 units. In terms of sales revenues, technology-based users accounted for approximately 47 per cent of the total market. Very small business users accounted for 10 per cent in units and 47 per cent of dollar revenues, whilst the mass consumers accounted for 10 per cent in units and 6 per cent in dollars. These variations reflect the different average equipment prices of personal computer systems in the three major segments.

The emergence of both the professional and very small business user segments during 1978 can be directly attributed to the repositioning/reconfiguration of the personal computer into an integrated piece of hardware, priced at an attractive level. However, although product innovation opened the new segments, the innovative users represented only a small percentage of the potential market. In order to penetrate the new market segments effectively, suppliers needed to better understand the needs and wants of the potential users in these emerging markets.

In this respect, incumbents and new entrants had to enhance their innovations, not only in hardware but particularly in software applications and various areas of marketing. To shift the product from one segment to another therefore involved overcoming distinctive market segment barriers, which necessitated suppliers shifting or broadening their areas of functional competence to meet market requirements. Fig. 3.12 illustrates the areas of functional activity important to end-users of the three market segments. It emphasises the fact that a supplier would need distinctive competence in a different set of functions, depending upon the market sector being served. Although perhaps obvious, such distinctions were overlooked by a number of competitors at the time.

As can be seen in Fig. 3.12, the professional and very small business market segments based their needs upon applications. Hence, availability of suitable applications software was a primary need, which initially was not satisfied. Furthermore, such users (being technically less knowledgeable than the hobbyists), also needed advice on their choice of equipment,

MARKET SEGMENTS	AREAS OF FUNCTIONAL COMPETENCE						
	HARDWARE	OPERATING SYSTEMS	APPLICATION PROGRAMS	DOCUMENTS	PROMOTION	MARKETING DISTRIBUTION	SERVICE SUPPORT
VERY SMALL BUSINESS USERS			●	●	●	●	●
PROFESSIONAL USERS	●	●	●	●			●
HOBBYIST USERS	●	●					

AREAS OF FUNCTIONAL COMPETENCES

N.B. ● indicates area of activity important to users in the particular market segment and functional area.

Fig. 3.12. Market segment barriers and functional competences.

software programs and general "hand-holding" after purchase. In order to satisfy these needs, suppliers had to establish closer links with the customer. The combination of strong demand for the new generation of personal computers and the need for closer customer contact and ongoing service, created a change in the percentage mix of the structure of distribution channels. Furthermore, the importance of clearer (non-technical) documentation and supporting promotional material and advertising began to gather recognition amongst selected suppliers.

Marketing and Distribution

Neither industry leaders, Tandy Radio Shack and Commodore, had to establish a new marketing or distribution organisation for their personal computers. Tandy was provided with ready access to both the professional and hobbyist market, whilst Commodore had access to the small business office products market. The follower companies, including Apple, Cromemco, Vector Graphic, Southwest and others, relied upon establishing networks of franchise and independent stores. For these companies, the quality of their product, strength of demand amongst users, profit margins for dealers and support services were all critical factors in competing for shelf space and establishing a national scale of distribution. It was in this area that Apple and Vector Graphic proved highly successful. Apple's strategy was to adopt a general-purpose machine approach, with applications software aimed at the professional, education, games and small business market. Vector Graphic took a more focused position on the small business market, in close association with a regional dealer network. Cromemco also focused on the professional market. The majority of remaining followers, both new entrants and incumbents, were less focused, offering general purpose machines to all market segments capable of running the rapidly expanding range of applications software.

The four major channels of distribution are illustrated in Fig. 3.13. The channels through which a particular product moved to a particular user group were functions of the market segment and the technical characteristics of the product. Three major changes took place in the structure of distribution channels during the take-off stage:

(i)   retail computer stores (originally serving the hobbyist segment) moved into the small business user segment;

(ii) speciality electronics stores such as Tandy Radio Shack, together with Heath and Lafayette, actively began merchandising personal computers;

(iii) the franchise groups of the Byte Shop and Computerland (both started in 1976 and 1977 respectively) had grown at a rapid pace. In late 1977, there were some 24 Computerland stores in the U.S.A.: a year later this figure had risen to 59 stores.

Whilst Tandy kept distribution exclusively to its own chain of over 800 Radio Shack Stores, the remaining major vendors relied heavily upon independent computer dealers, or in the case of MITS, its own stores. With the shift away from the hobbyist segment, mail order gradually went into decline as a major distribution channel during 1977, although many vendors and dealers continued to use this as an additional outlet through 1978.

Two points were significant in the structural changes. The first lay in the competitive advantage gained by Tandy, which had control over its own exclusive and extensive distribution network. The second lay in the feedback from the small business market to the dealers and their suppliers. Many of the computer stores (dealers) were founded during 1976 and 1977 by technically orientated owners, who were motivated by the apparent success and demand for the early first generation of hobbyist personal computers. As such, they were able to provide product demonstrations, technical help in understanding and selecting equipment,

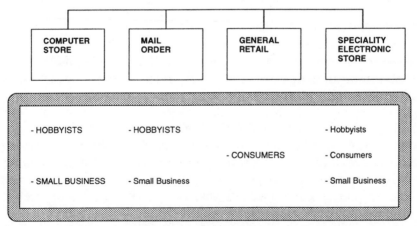

KEY: CAPITAL LETTERS OF CUSTOMER GROUPS = PRIMARY CHANNELS USED TO SERVE CUSTOMER GROUPS.

Lower Case Letters of Customer Groups = Secondary Channels Used to Serve Customer Groups.

Fig. 3.13. Personal computer distribution channels during the late 1970s.

together with repair and support of products, including the emerging range of applications software. In providing such services, they also catered for the needs of the small business user segment. However, although the technical product knowledge of such dealers was extensive, at this stage, relatively few of them possessed significant knowledge in business applications or about the most suitable choice of software. Pressures from this segment in the form of user needs and expectations therefore began to shift the emphasis of necessary functional competence from purely technical issues towards capabilities in advising of solutions and understanding business problems. These were a set of skills which not only involved business knowledge, but also required greater clarity of documentation, less technically orientated selling and advertising, together with improved levels of promotional activity. As such, they represented a higher set of market barriers for both dealers and suppliers.

SUMMARY

The previous two sections have argued that the newgame strategies of Tandy, Commodore and Apple changed the underlying asset structure of the industry's dominant pattern of value chains. In so doing, they created a new set of strategic groups and raised generic industry barriers together with specific mobility barriers. As a result of their strategies, the incumbent firms were forced to adopt new strategies, either similar to those of the new entrants or focused upon a niche market. The new products, marketing and distribution elements of the newgame strategies also led to expansion of the overall market and development of new market segments in the areas of professionals and small business users. It was also shown that the needs of users and buyers within those new segments were distinctly different from the hobbyist segment and therefore required an alternative set of functional areas of competence, which were reflected in the marketing mix of the competitors. This last section considers what costs and payoffs the new entrants had to face in this stage of the newgame environment's evolution.

The competitive advantages held by Tandy, Commodore and Apple over the incumbents led to their rapid penetration and expansion of the market. The leading incumbents lacked the management and resources necessary to respond and to defend their position and therefore rapidly lost market share. Given that the barriers to industry entry were low, the new entrants were sufficiently differentiated in their structure and strategies to create new strategic groups whose value chains shifted the areas of core competition from technology alone into marketing and distribution activities. Furthermore, given the relative maturity of the organisation structure of both Tandy and Commodore, as well as the product differentiation created by their integrated machines and lower prices, both companies were easily able to overcome the market barriers of incumbents' installed base of users and distribution networks. Apple achieved similar success, due largely to its integrated product, with high expansion board capacity, low price and highly effective promotion/marketing campaigns.

The impact of these new entrants, with differentiated product marketing strategies, was to significantly increase demand for personal computers and generate a shift in the pace and direction of market growth. Whereas in 1976 – 1977, most industry observers had forecast the major growth potential to be in the home segment for personal computers, the impact of the new generation of machines was greatest upon the professional and small business market segments.

These changes in the structure of the industry and market reflected in the costs facing the new entrants. However, analysis of the issue of costs highlighted that both Tandy and Commodore encountered "negative entry barriers", since part of their asset structures were already in place. Certainly the costs of setting up assembly plant facilities were higher for Tandy than when MITS entered the market, but for two reasons. Firstly, Tandy immediately made use of volume assembly operations (whereas MITS employed something more similar to a batch process) and secondly, Tandy set up a larger scale of production. Thus the risks to Tandy were greater, but the pay-offs were much larger, since Tandy rapidly built volume sales and market share. Hence, Tandy chose (like Commodore and Apple) to focus its investment on volume manufacturing of integrated systems for merchandising through its distribution channels on an aggregated, broad market front. In contrast, MITS had focused upon a narrower market segment (hobbyists) and subsequently failed to effectively adjust its product profile for the broader market.

Commodore's resources included its semiconductor company and therefore it was able to exploit a marginal cost advantage from its microprocessors, which was to place it in a strong position when it later focused on the low-price (commodity type) end of the market. However, Apple's success was achieved without ownership of microprocessor or semiconductor production and supports the argument that ownership of these factors was not a pre-requisite for competing in the industry, (at least not in the higher-value business market segments). Indeed, the entry of a number of the semiconductor manufacturers into the production of 8-bit microprocessors had made such components price-competitive and readily available. Furthermore, the standardisation by many personal computer companies upon the Z-80 microprocessor (except by Commodore and Apple) meant that this technology was easily available.

The real cost increases therefore came in scale and quality control improvements necessary at the assembly plant stage, together with the need for greater investment in marketing promotion activities. At the time of entry by Apple, Tandy and Commodore, even these costs were still relatively small. However, as a result of their successful product positioning and the significant acceleration and expansion of the market into volume sales, the scale of operations grew rapidly during the next two years up to 1979. Thus the cost of broad market entry rose considerably during

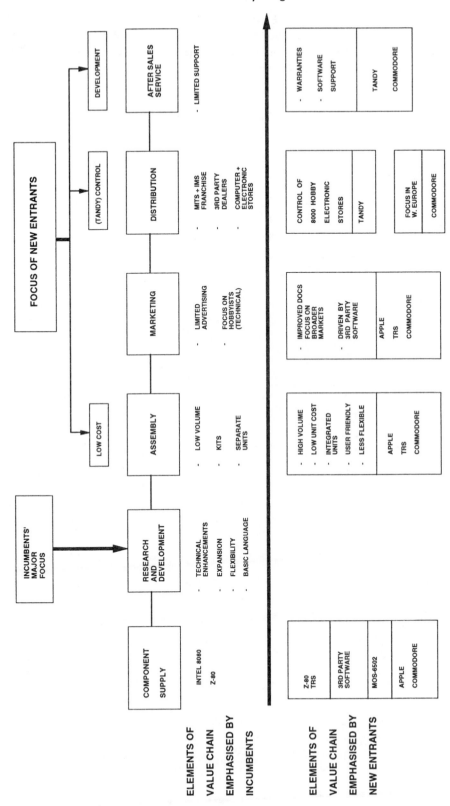

Fig. 3.14. The focus of newgame strategies between the embryonic and take-off stages.

the period of the take-off stage. This did not discourage entry, but forced entrants in the later period and subsequent growth stage to require larger resources or to "focus" their position of entry upon a market segment. These changes are illustrated in Fig. 3.14.

Chapter Four

FROM TAKE-OFF TO GROWTH

"Most people suspend their judgement till somebody else has expressed his own and then they repeat it".[1]

INTRODUCTION

Following on from the developments in the Take-Off stage of the microcomputer industry outlined in the previous chapter, the industry moved on to take a somewhat different structure, which is known as the Growth Stage. One important change during this period was the growing acceptance of the term 'personal computer' to refer to what previously had been largely known as the 'microcomputer'. Naturally, the change of usage took some time. However, given that the Growth Stage represents the period when the personal computer industry really was established, it seems therefore appropriate to refer throughout the remainder of this book to the 'personal computer' and to thus drop usage of the term 'microcomputer'.

The Growth Stage lasted from approximately early 1979 to mid-1981 and was characterised by a number of changes some of which are illustrated in Fig. 4.1, which shows the key issues and relationships which are explored within the following sections of this chapter and represents a continuation of the evolution of the newgame environment.

In the first section, analysis of the Growth Stage commences with identifying the major forces for change during the period under consideration. The key patterns that emerge suggest that technological change continued to be a major driving force, with developments in microprocessor performance and peripherals opening the opportunity for development of the small business and professional market segments. In addition, one witnesses the rapid rise in the importance of software in the industry and its ability to shape the focus of market activity by hardware manufacturers. Responding to the technological developments,

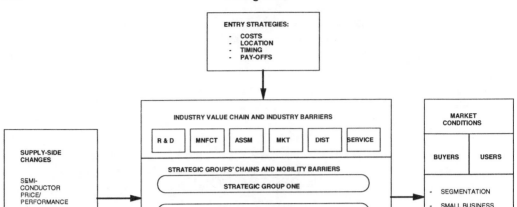

Fig. 4.1. Newgame issues and relationships from the take-off to growth stage.

one also sees that the strategic behaviour of the major competitors now changes towards an increasing emphasis upon marketing activities. These are largely directed at the emerging business markets, which in turn require new channels of distribution.

Having provided an overview of the forces for change, the next section moves on to analyse the major technological changes in more detail. The focus of this section is to illustrate how competition amongst semiconductor manufacturers had now led to two dominant families of microprocessor in the industry. This in turn allowed the evolution of an industry operating standard whose stability led to the explosion of new applications software. The combined developments in hardware and software thus improved the quality and value of personal computers in terms of their appeal to the growing markets.

Therefore, the next section considers the changes in the markets in more detail and highlights the impact that such developments had upon the structure of the overall market. Two key patterns emerged. Firstly, the overall size of the market expanded significantly, whilst secondly, the small-business and professional segments began to emerge as the key focus for the major players. Towards the end of the period, entry into the corporate market was also gaining importance for the leading competitors.

From changes in technology and descriptions of the overall market evolution, the following section focuses upon the key patterns of evolution that take place amongst the competitors in the industry. This commences with a look at the competitors overall strategic positioning and the associated changes that occurred in the composition of their respective value chains. Next, the strategic group patterns that resulted during the period are highlighted and four major groups are identified amongst the competitors. Finally, the strategic behaviour and performance of the key players is considered by reviewing the product–market strategies of the major incumbents and new entrants. In particular, the period witnessed the first wave of large established companies from the electronics and computing industries.

Taken together these developments are then summarised at the end of the chapter, where it is suggested that the overall industry became established in its own right during the Growth Stage. Furthermore, the continuing technological developments were leading to more powerful machines that were able to run software programs[2] suitable and of value to the business community. Thus the period witnessed an explosion in new software companies and a shift towards recognition of the growing importance that software was to play in the industry. Yet if such products were to be successful, it was also evident that marketing was to become a significantly more important activity amongst competitors. This therefore led to changes in the value chains of major competitors and the rapid growth of new independent channels of distribution, which in turn further stimulated growth within the industry. Furthermore, the entry of major companies such as Texas Instruments, Hewlett Packard and Zenith increased the scale of investment in marketing activities and forced incumbents to allocate increasing resources in promotion and distribution. Thus as illustrated in the lower part of Fig. 4.1, the developments in technology continued to create new strategies amongst established and new competitors that changed the nature of the industry and its markets, hence continuing to drive the process of newgame evolution.

Indeed, by the end of the period from 1979 to 1981 the industry is shown to have increased its overall size and scale of resources to a level that marked it as being established in its own right. However, its very success in the small business and professional markets together with its leading competitors' ambitions to gain a foothold in the larger corporate business market were to stimulate further major changes in the industry and lead to the next stage of evolution in the newgame environment.

FORCES FOR CHANGE

In the previous chapter it was shown that during the Take-Off Stage, Apple, Tandy and Commodore entered the personal computer market in 1977 and as the industry leaders, the strategic behaviour of these companies had a significant impact upon the evolution of the industry during the growth stage. Overall, the impact of these companies, together with other competitors resulted in continuing expansion of the market and thereafter the industry moved into a period of accelerating growth. As mentioned above, this growth stage lasted from early 1979 to mid-1981, during which

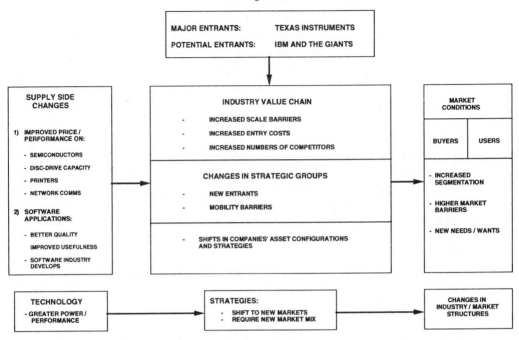

Fig. 4.2. Overview of developments during the growth stage.

time the industry continued to change as a result of a number of key factors. These factors centred upon technological changes, the emergence of new market segments and the strategic behaviour amongst competitors. Combined together they resulted in two significant changes in the nature of the newgame environment. Firstly, the emergence of fully fledged businesses focusing upon the personal computer industry and secondly, although the industry continued to be technology driven, the markets became much larger and marketing activities started to play an increasingly important role in competitive strategies. Fig. 4.2 provides an overview of some of these changes and highlights the major events that will be discussed in the remainder of this chapter.

On the supply side, two areas of technological development led to changes in the product/market strategies of both entrants and incumbents. The first involved technological changes and developments in hardware, especially in basic communications networking[3] and hard disk technology.[4] The resulting products provided the business user with the opportunity to develop local area networks (LAN's) and improved capacity storage of off-line data. Coupled with increased RAM (Random Access Memory), improved processor speeds and better quality printers, the personal computer was becoming a more legitimate business machine. The second feature involved the rapid establishment of a software industry. Based on the emerging industry operating system of CP/M-80, software developers began to produce more reliable and improved applications packages for the business market; these included accounting, payroll, inventory control, word processing and the important, innovative spreadsheet. This combination of improved hardware and more powerful software packages, with no significant increases in price, stimulated growth in demand. Software now increasingly moved towards becoming the defining feature of the computer and as such offered the opportunity for specialisation in particular market segments. This in turn drove the market structure towards greater segmentation.

However, whilst demand strengthened and grew, so too did the competitors, both in terms of numbers and also in their overall scale of resources. In particular, the period witnessed the entry of the major semiconductor company Texas Instruments and this fuelled the expectation that further major companies, such as IBM and other computer giants would soon be joining the competition. Shifts in strategies led to movements in asset configurations and resulted in changes to the membership of the various strategic groups. At the same time, standardisation on families of microprocessors and operating systems forced companies to seek product differentiation through higher performing software and integrated hardware packages. Research and development costs also began to rise, whilst economies of scale started to become apparent in both production and distribution. As a result of these events, a number of physical and psychological barriers began to develop around the emerging business segments. Some of the major market barriers included:

(i)   increased price sensitivity;
(ii) lack of product knowledge amongst buyers, on which to base their purchase decisions;
(iii) limited data transfer ability between different software applications and machines, and
(iv) varying standards of service and support by third-party distribution channels.

In order to overcome such barriers and to exploit the potential demand, competitors shifted an increasing scale of resources into marketing and support activities. In addition, the emerging software products became a key feature in the total package, with some companies starting to "bundle" both hardware and core applications software in the purchase price.

For the major competitors at this stage, such as Tandy, Apple and Commodore, the development of the professional segment was seen as a gateway to entry into the corporate marketplace. Yet to enter the corporate market required a totally different product mix from those applied to the hobbyist, home or small business segments. As they were to discover, significant market barriers existed which even the industry leaders, Apple and Tandy, were to find extremely costly and difficult to try to overcome. This was largely due to the fact that the personal computers were entering an established market domain, the world of the data processing giants, where the expected potential entry of companies such as IBM began to influence the behaviour of both suppliers and customers.

Thus, the key patterns to emerge during the growth stage reflected major improvements in peripheral product technology, which led to development and expansion of the small business and professional market segments, both of which required shifts in strategic behaviour of the competitors. In particular, there was the need to shift more resources into marketing activities, especially in seeking new channels of distribution and higher spending on advertising and promotion. Such moves created further changes in the structure of the personal computer industry and its markets. It is these key patterns that are now examined in more depth within the following sections to this chapter.

TECHNOLOGICAL CHANGE

As shown above, during the growth stage technological change continued to be a major driver in the evolution of the newgame environment. However, in addition to hardware developments there also occurred major advances in the performance of software technology.

Whilst hardware developments continued to reflect improved price/ performance in the core-semiconductor technology, they also involved improvements in the reliability and performance of peripheral equipment, especially in disk-storage and printer technologies. The synergistic effects of these technology/product developments meant that the input/output capabilities of the personal computer were significantly improved. As a result, the potential for personal computers to provide more effective services for end-users in business applications was greatly increased. However, whilst hardware developments were being made, their potential could only be realised if suitable software application programs were also developed and made available.

For the above reason, the period 1979 to 1981 was perhaps most significant in the evolution of personal computers, because it witnessed a major shift in the power and quality of applications software, the catalyst for which was a combination of the potential demand for more powerful software, together with improved low-priced hardware performance. These conditions led to the emergence and creation of a number of highly successful software companies, whose leverage in the personal computer industry has continued to increase through subsequent stages of evolution. Indeed, it is generally accepted that by 1983, software had become the key driving force in the personal computer industry, a position it has continued to enjoy, only more so in the 1990s. Yet only five years earlier, in 1978, the personal computer manufacturers' product lines:

> "... were largely bereft of meaningful applications software, and
> although there were scores of fledgling start-up software houses, only
> a few were viable enough to become serious suppliers... ".[5]

The development of the personal computer software industry presents an interesting and rich illustration of a newgame environment in its own right, which cannot be reported here.[6] However, the story about certain important relationships between software and hardware developments need to be highlighted at this stage, in order to understand the impact of software development upon the personal computer industry and its markets during the subsequent stages of evolution.

Firstly, it is important to reflect upon the previous 20 years of software evolution. The story can be retraced to the fact that mainframe and minicomputers were initially only able to run software developed for a specific machine family. Therefore this type of vertical or upward compatibility emerged as the key strategic approach for computer manufacturers and is illustrated in Fig. 4.3. The advantage to the computer manufacturers was that the high switching costs incurred by a user for changing to a competitor's system effectively locked their users into the supplier's future products. Furthermore this allowed premium pricing that was seen as necessary to support further research and development, due to an absence of opportunity for volume-based economies of scale. However, as the scale of software investment by users increased, this became an increasingly unacceptable situation for customers in the mainframe market. It was not really until the mid-1970s that an acceptable solution appeared for the mainframe industry. This involved the emergence of companies producing systems that could run operating and applications software developed for the IBM 370 family.[7] Such machines were known as "plug-compatible" since they could plug-into an existing IBM 370 system and included peripheral products as well as central processors. This development allowed a customer to buy elsewhere than from IBM, who still dominated the market and at the same time went a long way to protecting the user's large software investment, thus creating a strong source of competition for IBM from plug-compatible manufacturers, especially Amdahl.

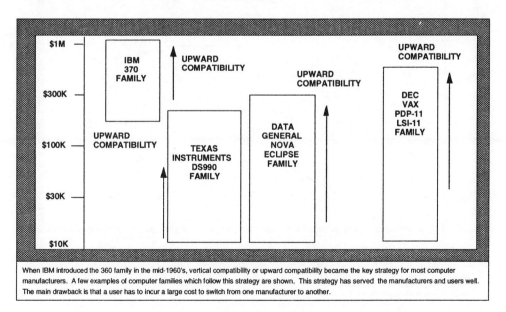

When IBM introduced the 360 family in the mid-1960's, vertical compatibility or upward compatibility became the key strategy for most computer manufacturers. A few examples of computer families which follow this strategy are shown. This strategy has served the manufacturers and users well. The main drawback is that a user has to incur a large cost to switch from one manufacturer to another.

Source: March, 1981, Future Computing Inc., 634 South Central Expressway, Richardson, Texas 75080. Permission sought.

Fig. 4.3. Vertical compatibility in mainframe and minicomputer software and systems development.

However, whereas mainframe and minicomputers had a fairly long period of incompatibility between systems at both the hardware and software levels, personal computers started from an entirely different position that was known as horizontal software compatibility[8] as illustrated in Fig. 4.4. The development of CP/M-80 as the initial industry operating system standard in 1976 soon allowed various personal computers to run the same operating systems software and hence the same applications programs. This development become a major driving force in the industry, since it provided users with some degree of software portability.[9] This also meant that hardware and software were decoupled from the beginning of the industry's development and hence gave customers a greater choice of hardware, since a number of machines would run the same applications software. However, this did not mean that the actual software disc was portable between different machines. Instead the same applications program was developed to run on different machines, but each machine had a special format and hence could only operate discs manufactured for use on that particular type of personal computer. Hence, the portability was in practice quite limited, although if a user knew what type of applications software was wanted, then there were a number of personal computers that could run that particular program. The most important result of uncoupling the hardware and software was that it allowed hardware manufacturers to build an "instant software base" and avoid the high costs of their own software development.

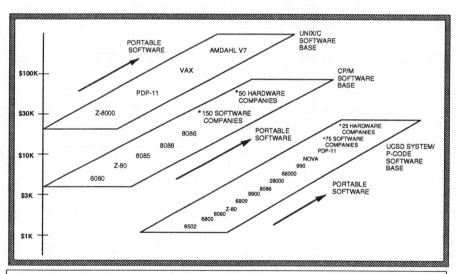

The personal computer and microcomputer industry have evolved along horizontal compatibility lines. This allows application software to be portable across systems made by different manufacturers. Three key portable software bases are shown. The CP/M software base which must use the 8080/Z80/8086 microprocessor family has over 50 hardware manufacturers and about 150 software companies. The UCSD system or P-code software base is portable across the largest number of microprocessors and minicomputers but has a 1-2 year lag on the CP/M base. The UNIX base is just starting to appear on microprocessors.

Source: March, 1981, Future Computing Inc., 634 South Central Expressway, Richardson, Texas 75080. Permission sought.

Fig. 4.4. Horizontal compatibility in mainframe, mini and micro software and systems development around 1980.

The impact of this situation is significant, yet paradoxical, since in one respect it reduces the industry barriers to entry for a manufacturer, by removing the costs of software development. On the other hand, it also removes a source of product differentiation. This is due to the fact, that if one manufacturer's product runs CP/M and a particular popular applications program, then that same program should also run on another CP/M-based machine, thus effectively reducing the switching costs to the customer. However, it must be stressed that at this stage of the industry's development, as mentioned above, portability was not so readily achieved in practice and hence one should not overplay the degree of flexibility available to customers. Nevertheless, it set a trend that was in time to lead to full portability, but this was only to come after the establishment of the IBM operating standard, which is covered in the next chapter.

Thus, the hardware manufacturers were faced from an early stage in the industry's development with three major technical choices, all of which are central to the product's technology market strategy. The first involves the choice of microprocessor; the second, the operating system; and the third, the decision whether to develop applications software "in-house" or buy-in from outside through third-party software developers. The choice of permutations is illustrated in Table 4.1. If a manufacturer chose a low cost, low-risk entry, then the product differentiation was minimal. However, if the manufacturer sought to achieve a product innovation, this could come from one level or a combination of the three levels. Although apparently obvious after the event, it must be remembered that the personal computer manufacturers' decision was ex ante, the launch of a new machine, hence the outcome of a particular strategy was not known in advance and carried a considerable amount of risk at the time of making the investment decision, as it still does today.

As shown in Table 4.1 whilst the take-off stage had been based upon 8-bit microprocessors, by 1979 16-bit microprocessors had become commercially available. These offered the opportunity for manufacturers to develop personal computers with significantly greater processing power and speed than their 8-bit predecessors. As a result, this new generation of microprocessors released both manufacturers and software developers from the constraints and limitations of the 8-bit environment. However, software development has tended to lag behind the pace of development of the hardware, since as described in the last two chapters, at both the embryonic and take-off stages of the personal computer industry's evolution, most applications software was still limited and generally of poor quality.

During 1978, applications packages emerged for accounting, inventory management, word processing and handling of mailing lists, which could appeal to the relatively undeveloped small business market. Yet the development of such programs signalled a "sea-change" in the forces driving the industry. Although hardware innovations would continue to be a major driving force, the launch, in 1979, of the first spreadsheet program, Visicalc from Visicorp., signalled that the range of applications programs available on a manufacturer's machine could significantly influence market

Table 4.1. The 3 key technology strategy choices in growth to legitimisation stages.

	EXAMPLE	COST	BENEFIT	DISADVANTAGES	RISKS
1) CHOICE OF MICROPROCESSOR:					
- 8 BIT	Z 80	LOW	- well tested - well supported by software development	- state of art technology - lower performance than 16-bits	- little differentiation - becoming obsolete
- 16 BIT	8086	HIGH	- higher performance - potential to support better software	- less software available - peripherals costly - no clear industry leader	- unknown which will be backed by software industry
2) CHOICE OF OPERATING SYSTEM:					
- PROPRIETARY	APPLEDOS	HIGH	- include special features - customise to own chip design	- requires special staff and restricts initial range of applications software	- may not be supported by software developers
- INDUSTRY STANDARD	CP/M-80	LOW	- wider range of applications software available at launch - appeal to users (known)	- less differentiation - lower performance than MS-DOS	- may become obsolete from MS-DOS or due 16-bit micros
- NEW STANDARDS	MS-DOS*	MEDIUM	- more powerful system for future development of applications software	- unknown level of support - limited applications immediately available	- may not become an industry standard
3) CHOICE OF APPLICATIONS:					
- IN-HOUSE	TANDY	HIGH	- good source of differentiation - greater control of focus in markets	- need own staff - spread costs over smaller volume - carry entire risk	- may not be a success - carry entire risk
- 3RD PARTY	VISICALC	LOW	- readily available if use CP/M-80 - wide software choice of programmes	- no differentiation - may not be able to attract software developers for special programmes	- may not be able to compete an anything but systems price

Note: *MS-DOS was launched in 1981 and therefore represents an example of a new operating system standard from that time onwards. However, by 1983, it was clear to industry participants that MS-DOS would supersede CP/M 80 and its 16-bit version of CP/M-86 as the new industry standard. Hence, this choice of technology must be viewed ex-ante these later developments.

performance, as measured by sales. Hence, the development of industry standards in the adoption of CP/M as an operating system led to relatively low entry barriers for software developers during 1978/79. The result was an explosion in the number and range of software application programs. However, with a few exceptions the quality of the software was limited, although by 1979 there were emerging recognised key players in the software industry.

At the applications level, the hardware manufacturers therefore tended to market software that was developed outside their own organisations by third-party companies. Yet in making this choice, a given manufacturer's leverage with software developers became a crucial factor to potential success. The situation represented a "vicious" or "virtuous circle", which is illustrated in Fig. 4.5. For example, Apple Computer had initially established a large installed base, due to its easy-to-program microprocessor, together with a large capacity for expansion boards that could run special peripherals or operating functions. This flexibility had attracted a large number of software developers. As a result, Apple gained over competitors as time passed, since its increasingly large range of software allowed it to maintain a better price/performance on hardware. This point is illustrated in Fig. 4.6.

The existence of proprietary operating systems on both the market leaders' machines, namely TRS-80 Model 1 and Apple II, together with the emerging Z-80 CP/M family of machines, provided three possible choices of installed bases for a software developer. Initially, Tandy had deliberately been less active in seeking third-party software developers than Apple. This accounted for the fact that in 1979, more applications software was being developed by third-party software houses for the Apple II than any other machine. Since the applications software determined the use of the personal computer, it also meant that the availability of popular applications packages could significantly improve sales performance for the hardware manufacturer. A clear illustration of just such a relationship and its effect is provided in the availability of Visicalc, which initially could only run on the Apple II machine. Sales of Apple II were boosted significantly during the early life-cycle of Visicalc, reflecting the joint elasticity of demand between both products.

Thus, from 1979 onwards, the relationship between microprocessor families, operating systems and applications software came to form a fundamental set of decision parameters for personal computer manufacturers. The choices made in those three areas of technology were to mould the product/market strategy of entrants and incumbents, and in turn, greatly influence their performance in their respective market segments. The next section will therefore look at how the market segments developed during the growth stage, before proceeding to look more closely at the strategies that the major competitors pursued and their relative performance and impact upon the industry.

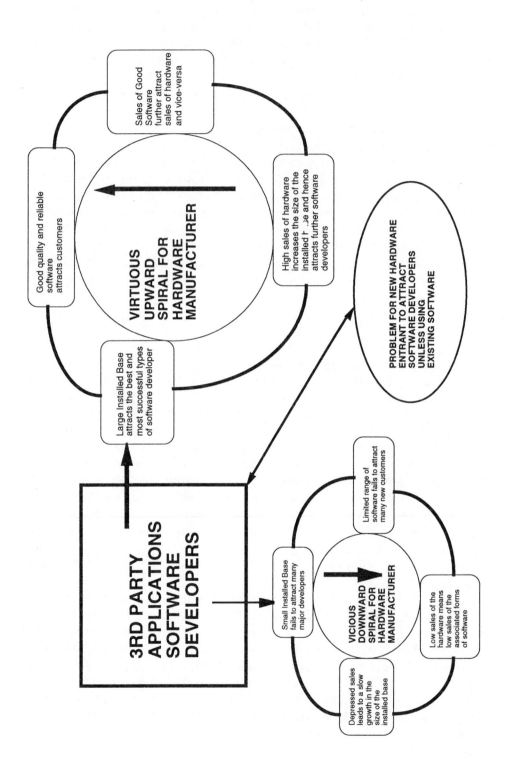

Fig. 4.5. Competitive positions in the software circle.

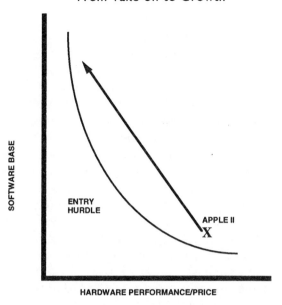

SOFTWARE BASE

ENTRY
HURDLE

APPLE II
X

HARDWARE PERFORMANCE/PRICE

PERSONAL COMPUTER ATTRACTIVENESS DEPENDS
ON BOTH HARDWARE PERFORMANCE AND THE EXTENT
OF THE AVAILABLE SOFTWARE BASE.

AS A MACHINE GAINS A LARGER SOFTWARE BASE, IT
CAN MAINTAIN MARKET POSITION WITH A WEAKER
HARDWARE PERFORMANCE/PRICE CHARACTERISTIC.

Fig. 4.6. Relationship between size of software base and hardware performance/price ratio.

CHANGING MARKET CONDITIONS

From 1978 to 1980 annual U.S. sales of personal computers increased from 190,000 to an estimated 345,000 units, whilst retail dollar volume increased from $235 million to $1.07 billion.[10] During this period market segmentation increased, with specific segments attracting both new entrants to the industry, as well as expansion across segments. The pattern of segmentation was brought about largely due to developments in the technology and the subsequent expansion of demand in new user groups responding to improved product performance.

As shown in the previous chapter, the take-off stage witnessed the entry in 1977 and consolidation in 1978 of low cost assembled systems from Apple, Commodore and Radio Shack. These strategies forced the S-100 bus-type systems to move from the hobby market into the small business and education markets. Thus during 1978 to 1980, the S-100 based systems became more involved in the traditional, small business computer market and greatly expanded the retail distribution channels for such systems. In addition, by this time the promotion by IBM of its 5110 system had started to awaken both users and suppliers to the potential of the under-$20,000 computer systems for small business users. In effect, systems used in large companies such as the IBM 5110 (which were to become known as the "office computer"), were configured with higher storage capacity and processing capabilities than the basic machines offered by Tandy and Apple. Office computers could be used in single stand-alone or multiple-user systems and as such formed a bridge from the personal computers such as the Apple II and TRS-80 Model I to the multi-station small business computers such as the IBM System 34. For reasons outlined in the previous section, during 1978 a number of new software suppliers introduced applications software for the business market. At the same time, the add-on peripherals market grew rapidly as the earlier "hobby" users upgraded their systems with floppy disks, printers and modems.[11] It was during this period that personal computing crossed over from a purely entertainment or hobby activity to serious applications in a commercial environment, as shown in Fig. 4.7. By the end of 1979, some of the personal computer suppliers had acknowledged this shift from recreation to work-related uses and therefore commenced heavier expenditure on advertising and activities supporting such systems. Figure 4.8 highlights the migration path during 1980 of some major competitors towards the very small business systems and office computer markets.

These emerging patterns of segmentation are illustrated in Table 4.2 in terms of the user groups, principal applications and dominant personal computer price bands. More broadly speaking the market consisted of three distinct categories: a low-end segment, in which computers priced at $300

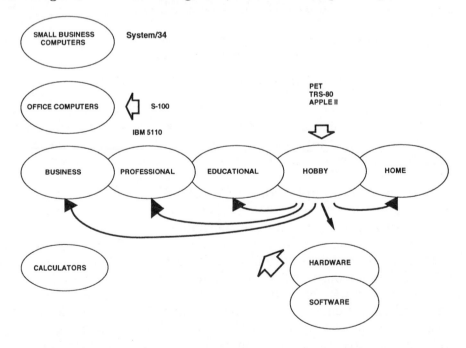

Source: 1980 Personal Computer Forum, *The Rosen Electronics Letter*, Rosen Research Inc., July 21, 1980. Reproduced by permission of Benjamin M. Rosen, © 1980.

Fig. 4.7. Strategic moves in the personal computer market during mid-1979.

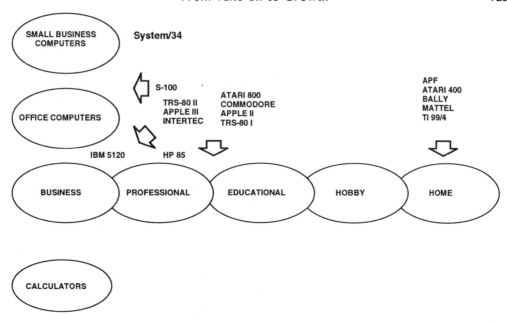

Source: 1980 Personal Computer Forum, *The Rosen Electronics Letter*, Rosen Research Inc., July 21, 1980.
Reproduced by permission of Benjamin M. Rosen, © 1980.

Fig. 4.8. Strategic moves in the personal computer market during 1980.

– $1500 were sold to the mass consumer and education markets; a medium-range segment, in which computers priced at $1000 – $4000 were sold to business professionals, scientists, engineers, industrial users and computer hobbyists; and a high-end segment, in which computers priced at $4000 – $15,000 were sold to very small businesses.[12] As illustrated in Table 4.3 growth in all three segments during 1978 to 1980 was strong,

Table 4.2. Personal computer user groups during the growth stage.

USER GROUP	PRINCIPAL APPLICATIONS	RETAIL HARDWARE PRICE RANGE, 1980-81 (US$)
CONSUMERS Adults and children	Education, entertainment, personal management	300 - 1,100
PROFESSIONALS Engineers, scientists, analysts, managers	Solution of individual applications problems related to profession	1,000 - 4,000
HOBBYISTS	Experimentation	1,000 - 4,000
VERY SMALL BUSINESSES Retailers, service organisations, and small manufacturers	Business management operations	4,000 - 15,000
EDUCATORS Elementary schools, high schools, universities, commercial education	Computer instruction and programming, computer-aided instruction and drills, administration	600 - 1,500
INDUSTRIAL USERS Process/plant engineers, electronic equipment suppliers	Process monitoring/control, quality control, resale activities	600 - 2,000

Source: *The Outlook for the U. S. Personal Computer Industry*, Arthur D. Little, Inc., December 1981, p.13.
Reproduced by permission of Decision Resources, Inc., © 1981.

particularly in the small business and technological/professional user categories. According to one report,[13] the worldwide installed base of personal computers at year end 1980 was 979,500 units of which 64.3 per cent was domestic, whilst 35.7 per cent was foreign. The same report indicated that almost eight out of ten personal computers were installed in 1978, 1979 or 1980. Furthermore, the more recently acquired fully-assembled machines tended to be of a higher value than the older kit-based machines and were supplied largely by the second wave of entrants, particularly Tandy, Apple and Commodore. In terms of market share in both the installed base and annual sales, all three companies held strong positions and had displaced the previous market leaders, MITS and IMSAI as illustrated in Tables 4.4 – 4.6. It can be seen from these tables that although Tandy held the largest installed base, by 1980, Apple's shipments were catching up with Tandy. It is also clear that Commodore's foreign market sales far exceeded its position in the United States. The concentration of 58.2 per cent of the installed base in the top three companies, together with their distinctive lead over the second tier of competitors, such as Cromemco, emphasises the extent of their market power at this time.

Table 4.3. Estimated United States retail sales to personal computer market segments: 1978 - 1981.

MARKET SEGMENTS	1978		1979		1980		1981	
	$M	%	$M	%	$M	%	$M	%
CONSUMER	15	6	30	5	85	8	130	9
TECHNOLOGICAL/ PROFESSIONAL	135	58	360	57	550	51	745	53
VERY SMALL BUSINESS	85	36	240	38	435	41	545	38
TOTAL	235	100	630	100	1,070	100	1,420	100

Source: Extracts from table in *The Outlook for the U. S. Personal Computer Industry*, Arthur D. Little, Inc., December 1981, p.11.
Reproduced by permission of Decision Resources, Inc., © 1981.

In order to develop market share, hardware manufacturers needed to implement distinctly different marketing mixes between segments. Furthermore, the changes in the nature of the personal computer to an integrated system, which were brought about by incorporating the personal computer with associated peripherals and software, also created the need for adjustments in manufacturers' value chains. Thus during the growth stage, competitors were forced into rapidly changing market conditions. The traditional hobbyist was no longer of major significance and competitors

Table 4.4. United States personal computer shipments (000's): 1980.

	DOMESTIC		FOREIGN		MANUFACTURER TOTAL	
	'000	%	'000	%	'000	%
RADIO SHACK	80.0	30.7	20.0	15.4	100.0	25.5
APPLE	63.8	24.4	21.2	16.2	85.0	21.7
COMMODORE	10.0	3.8	40.0	30.8	50.0	12.8
OTHERS	107.3	41.1	49.3	37.6	156.6	40.0
INDUSTRY SHIPMENTS	261.1	100.0	130.5	100.0	391.6	100.0

Source: Venture Development Corporation, PC Industry Report, 1981.
Reproduced by permission of Venture Development Corporation, © 1981.

Table 4.5. United States personal computer shipments (US$M): 1980.

	DOMESTIC		FOREIGN		MANUFACTURER TOTAL	
	$M	%	$M	%	$M	%
RADIO SHACK	154.4	20.3	38.6	9.1	192.9	16.3
APPLE	112.5	14.8	37.5	8.8	150.0	12.7
COMMODORE	17.0	2.3	66.0	15.6	83.0	7.0
OTHERS	476.2	62.6	282.0	66.5	758.3	64.0
INDUSTRY SHIPMENTS	760.1	100.0	424.1	100.0	1,184.2	100.0

Source: Venture Development Corporation, PC Industry Report, 1981.
Reproduced by permission of Venture Development Corporation, © 1981.

Table 4.6. United States personal computer installed base (000's): 1980.

	DOMESTIC		FOREIGN		MANUFACTURER TOTAL	
	'000	%	'000	%	'000	%
RADIO SHACK	200.0	31.8	50.0	14.3	250.0	25.4
APPLE	120.0	19.0	40.0	11.5	160.0	16.4
COMMODORE	43.0	6.8	117.0	33.5	160.0	16.4
CROMEMCO	11.7	1.9	11.6	3.3	23.3	2.4
OTHERS	255.5	40.5	130.7	37.4	386.2	39.4
TOTAL UNITS INSTALLED	630.2	100.0	349.3	100.0	979.5	100.0

Source: Venture Development Corporation, PC Industry Report, 1981.
Reproduced by permission of Venture Development Corporation, © 1981.

that had developed a position in the consumer and educational markets sought to consolidate their positions. However, the major growth opportunities developing in the professional and small business markets attracted a number of key players towards penetrating these new and expanding segments. Furthermore, by 1980, the new products being introduced were not only intended to compete against the established incumbents, but were also intended to gain the advantage of earlier entry over the anticipated entry of the major established mainframe and minicomputer companies. Hence, a number of competitors such as Tandy and Apple created strategies to develop the market for professionals, as a pathway to larger markets in the corporate sector. As such, these moves represent the first signs of a sequential entry strategy being pursued by the personal computer companies into the established corporate business market. Thus whilst the technology continued to drive the industry's overall development, the growth in the size of the markets and their associated segmentation meant that competitors needed to develop more sophisticated marketing strategies to succeed and survive. How these strategies developed and their impact upon the evolution of the industry are considered in the next section.

PATTERNS OF INDUSTRY EVOLUTION

During the growth stage, the industry developed in a number of directions. As has been shown developments in both hardware and software technology created new and expanded markets. At the same time, the industry itself witnessed a number of new entrants together with changes in the value chains of various competitors. Overall the period was characterised by changes amongst the leading companies from being relatively small entrepreneurial activities into substantial fully fledged businesses.

This section will therefore focus on the strategic behaviour of the major competitors. Firstly by looking at how the competitors' value chains developed during the period and then by proceeding to trace the pattern of changes in the strategic groups within the industry.

Competitors Strategies and Value Chains

During the growth stage, the value chains of competitors began to stabilise, as sources of components, assembly, marketing and distribution links became more firmly established between respective companies. However, the elements along the chain continued to shift, both in terms of content and relative importance. Such developments reflected both changes in technology and a desire by companies to develop a position in the expanding segments of the business market. Some of the key events are illustrated in Fig. 4.9, which highlights the following points.

Firstly, stabilisation of the two main families of microprocessor, namely the Z-80 and MOS-Technology's 6502, together with the emergence of CP/

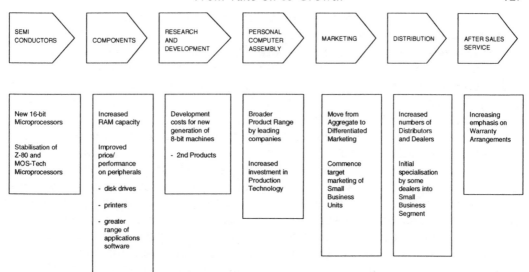

Fig. 4.9. Changes in the elements of the personal computer manufacturers' value chains during the growth stage.

M-80 as an industry standard meant that the opportunity existed for hardware suppliers (both microprocessors and peripherals) together with software developers to start developing systems based around these microprocessor families that could be sold onto an increasingly expanding user base. In this sense, the levels of risk in product development were somewhat reduced. However, the advent of 16-bit microprocessors also heralded the death-knell of the 8-bit microprocessors. What was uncertain was how quickly the 16-bit families would penetrate the market. At the time, the industry was highly confident that 8-bit technology had a reasonable life-span, especially since it had the perceived added advantage of a relatively large installed base. Hence, as was shown earlier in Table 4.1 competitors faced a choice between developing products on the established microprocessors or seeking to differentiate by moving to the 16-bit environment.

Most companies chose the former strategy, largely because the potential of the 8-bit microprocessor families had still to be realised through the new improved peripherals technology that was becoming available in the form of printers, storage disks[14] and increased RAM capacity. Competition from peripheral suppliers was still largely focused on 8-bit microprocessors, with opportunities to be realised in both the consumer, professionals and small business markets. Furthermore, as already shown, the fast expansion of software applications, providing higher performance and quality was mainly focused upon the 8-bit environment, again largely directed at these same market segments.

Hence a number of competitors, including Tandy, Apple and Commodore started to expand their product range by introducing machines aimed at the increasingly important professional and small business users. However, given the "off-the-shelf" nature of the majority of components making up personal computers, the investment in research and development still remained relatively low and was largely focused upon refining internal systems and some aspects of software enhancements. Where investment did increase was in production technology, which reflected both a need to improve the quality and reliability of products and also to manage a much larger scale of volume production.

In response to the emerging market expansion and segmentation, competitors found it necessary to move towards a more focused form of marketing mix, details of which are discussed shortly. In particular, the undifferentiated strategies pursued through the earlier embryonic and take-off stages were no longer suitable, especially for penetrating the professional and small business market segment, but also in the consumer market which was now demanding lower priced, but more well packaged and easier to use machines. As well as developing products and pricing them for the various market segments, increasing importance shifted towards the distribution channels. In most cases, this element of the value chain was not directly controlled by the personal computer company, with the notable exception of Tandy. However, the traditional technical hobbyist shop was clearly not appropriate for access to either the consumer market or professional and small business markets. Hence a number of new distribution channels began to emerge. For similar reasons to the need for new distribution channels, the manufacturers and distributors began to shift their attention to other aspects of merchandising. In particular, the need for warranties and guarantees on product reliability began to gain importance. However, it should be stressed that such developments were very *ad hoc* in nature and certainly were not industry wide during the growth stage. Instead, such developments, although well tried and tested in other industries and markets, were still experimental in nature within the growing personal computer industry. Because they were still a novelty, marketing and distribution therefore offered opportunities for differentiation at a most basic level. Thus as some competitors moved towards more emphasis upon marketing activities in their value chain, the industry began to witness changes in the pattern of its strategic groups.

Strategic Group Patterns

During the growth stage, the number of strategic groups increased in the industry, reflecting both new entrants and shifts in the position of various incumbents. Furthermore, whilst a number of small companies and start-ups entered during this period, the growth period also witnessed the first wave of larger established companies entering the industry. These included Texas Instruments (a major semiconductor and electronic calculator manufacturer), Hewlett Packard (a major scientific instruments and minicomputer manufacturer) and Zenith Radio Corporation (a major television and electronics components manufacturer).

The pattern of emerging strategic groups is illustrated in Fig. 4.10.

It must be emphasised that this diagram merely illustrates the relative strategic position and moves of the major companies in the industry at the time. Overall, there were well over one hundred companies competing in the industry by this time, however, in most cases their scale and impact upon the overall competition was insignificant. In Fig. 4.10, the matrix reflects the activities of the various companies only as they relate to the personal computer industry. It is divided along the vertical axis between companies offering or developing a narrow or broad product range. The horizontal axis suggests the focus of activity by companies along the value chain and was divided into three categories. Firstly, those companies where their main focus of strategic effort was upon product and/or production technology. Secondly, there were companies that although making efforts in product technology, placed an increasing effort into marketing activities, whilst lastly, there were some companies that focused their strategies upon the marketing of their products.

Four major strategic groups emerged that reflect each of the four quadrants occupied in Fig. 4.10. They are referred to as being the broad product-technology group, the narrow product-technology group, the broad integrated marketing group and the narrow integrated marketing group.

The main patterns show that the narrow product-technology group of companies focused mainly upon manufacture and assembly issues and included the previous industry leader, MITS (that had been acquired by the disk-drive manufacturer, Pertec). However, Pertec failed and exited the industry. A number of small entrants also occupied this group, together with the new entrant Hewlett Packard, Cromemco and Vector pursued a niche strategy aimed at selected market segments that demanded high standards of technological performance. During this stage, Apple migrated from this quadrant into a wider product range and at the same time, placed increasing emphasis upon marketing activities in its value chain.

As a new entrant, Texas Instruments formed the major player amongst companies of the broad product-technology group. It was subsequently joined by Zenith, which entered the industry by the acquisition of the incumbent Heath Computers. Heath had previously been a member of the narrow integrated marketing group of companies, occupying a niche position in the hobbyist (kit-based) market. Zenith broadened Heath's range of products, but at the same time initially placed more emphasis on technology than marketing issues. IMSAI, the other initial industry leader in the embryonic stage also exited the industry from this position. Whilst Commodore had occupied a position in the narrow integrated marketing group, during the growth stage it broadened its product range and moved up into the broad integrated marketing group, where it joined with Apple and Tandy. Tandy itself had originally been mainly using its traditional merchandising and marketing arm of Radio Shack shops to sell its personal computers. However, as Tandy developed into the industry leader, then it effectively integrated backwards, taking greater control of various assembly and product design issues, but at the same time remaining strong in its marketing activities.

The major characteristics of these groups could be defined as follows:

Broad Product-Technology Strategic Group

Texas Instruments (entry)
Zenith Radio Company
(acquired Heath at entry)

via

Forward vertical integration from semi-conductor or electronic components manufacture
- Mass production experience
- Mass consumer marketing experience

third-party outlets
- Large scale R&D resources
- Access to related technologies
- Access to large funds
- Multiple product range.

Narrow Product-Technology Strategic Group

Hewlett Packard (entry)
and
Small Entrants
and
Cromemco plus Vector

- Horizontal product development from minicomputers/calculators
- Technical Focus for differentiation
- Targeted at traditional scientific engineering market segments
- High focus upon R & D resources
- Some access to related technologies
- Single product offering

Narrow Integrated Marketing Strategic Group

Commodore (early)
Heath (pre-acquisition)
Small start-up companies
IMSAI (before exit)

- Single product offering
- Limited financial resources
- Limited R & D capabilities
- 'Me-Too' products
- State of art technology
- Marketing focus

Broad Integrated Marketing Strategic Group

Tandy (new position)
Apple (new position)
Commodore (new position)

- Multiple product range
- Strong Marketing focus
- Integrated Production and Assembly
- Reasonable Financial Resources
- Marketing Focus for Differentiation
- Strong Brand Name

Overall, the trend in the strategic groups reflected a growing concentration of companies offering broader product ranges. Some of these chose to retain a strong technology focus as their key source of differentiation, whilst others migrated into a stronger emphasis upon marketing activities. Clearly few companies were to remain for long in the narrow product range position.

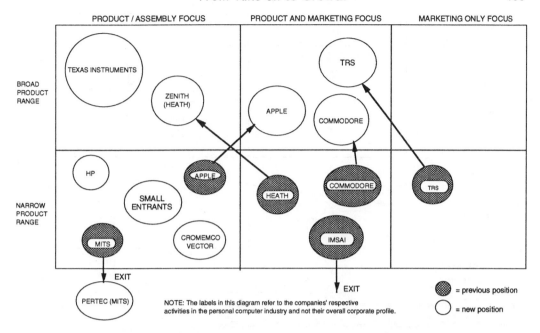

Fig. 4.10. Strategic groups in the personal computer industry during the growth stage.

Strategic Behaviour and Performance

As a result of the developments in technology and market expansion outlined previously, personal computer manufacturers recognised that their products were now becoming suitable for the basic computing needs of small businesses and professionals. However, the real power of the product could only be realised if suitable applications software were available to run on their machines. Furthermore, in order to successfully penetrate these markets, the personal computer manufacturers needed to develop new strategies and improve their capabilities along various dimensions of their respective value chains. Interestingly, the field research survey[15] preceding this book, showed that many of the competitors were attracted to these segments due to the potential for higher margins and less volatile growth patterns than were being experienced in the consumer market.

The strategies pursued by the major competitors shown on the strategic group matrix in Fig. 4.10 were of course dynamic in nature. In reality, there were many moves and counter moves between companies, however, some of the key strategic product-market moves during the growth stage can be understood by consideration of Fig. 4.11. This diagram plots the product position and price of various competitors for the time frame of 1979 and 1980 against the market segment targeted by the product. Two points concerning price in this diagram are noteworthy at the outset. Firstly, the majority of products for the consumer segment were priced around and below the $1000 level. Secondly, most of the products aimed at the small business and professional market segment were priced at over $3000.

Overall, the pattern that emerges in Fig. 4.11 reflects the observation from Fig. 4.10 that many competitors were developing a broader range

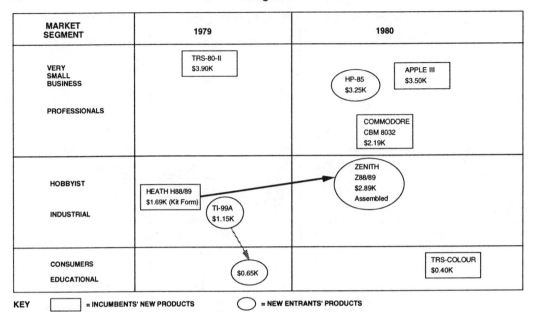

Fig. 4.11. Strategic product–market moves in personal computers during the growth stage: 1979 - 1980.

of products during the growth stage. However, an additional feature is also apparent, namely that the major competitors were now targeting their products towards specific market segments and thus moving their product-market strategies to a more focused approach. Amongst the incumbents, Tandy was the first to produce a desktop computer[16] specifically for the business market, the TRS-80 Model II, which it launched at $3,899 in May 1979. The machine used a fast Z-80A microprocessor, making it faster than some of the 16-bit processors available at the time. It represented part of its overall move to develop a broad product line in personal computers, as seen by the introduction in 1980 of the TRS-80-III, which effectively replaced the TRS-80-I. The original machine served the earlier hobbyist and home markets, but was gradually moved more into the small business and educational segments. In late 1980, the TRS-Colour computer was launched to the lower end mass consumer market. In March 1980, Commodore announced its CBM 8032 machine to penetrate the small business and professional markets. Priced at a very competitive level, the machine was not successful in the market, firstly because of performance limitations and secondly due to Commodore's continued focus upon the European marketplace. A few months later, Apple launched its Apple III machine. However, due to numerous production problems and no software (except for the Apple II emulation disk), the Apple III was relaunched in late 1981, with little enthusiasm from the dealership networks. In addition to the three key industry players, other early industry participants also moved their position more squarely into the commercial markets. Cromemco launched the System 3; Exidy, the System 80/1; North Star, the Horizon; and Vector Graphic, their Series 3. In terms of strategic moves, none of the incumbents pursued newgame strategies during the growth stage. As a result, the structure of the industry's dominant company value chains were not changed as significantly as in the previous take-off stage. However, it is clear that Tandy and Apple, together with some of the smaller incumbents, were attempting to broaden their product line and link specific products to the emerging segments through the development of new distribution channels.

As far as the new entrants were concerned, Texas Instrument's (T.I.) entry to the personal computer industry was less successful than might have been expected. The industry competitors had anticipated that as a leader in technological innovation, T.I.'s cost advantage as a mass manufacturer of semiconductor components might encourage the company to pursue the same kind of ruthless, cost-cutting leadership strategy as it had employed to decimate competition in the electronic hand-held calculator market during the early 1970s. However, this was not to be the case. In terms of corporate profile, T.I. represented the first "giant" to enter the industry. Internally, the company had planned to launch three products, each aimed at a specific market segment, namely, the mass market, professional and the business markets. Each machine was designed to use T.I.'s own family of 9900 microprocessors, which were 16-bit as opposed to 8-bit. However, technical problems forced the company to postpone plans for the professional and business machines. The company then chose a compromise product, the T.I.-99/4. This was announced in June 1979, at an initial price of $1,150 (including display) and was primarily aimed at the mass market, although software for business applications was also available. However, the price was too high for the mass market; yet the product was too restrictive in its performance for the professional/ business segment. Although shipments started in October 1979, they were in limited supply and T.I. missed the important Christmas sales period. During 1980, T.I. started selling the console separately to the monitor, thus reducing the entry price, yet slow sales and lack of dealer support forced the company to offer a three-month rebate programme. By this time, the positioning of the T.I.-99/4 was clearly outside the business segment and T.I.'s impact on the mass market was much less than it might have been, given its potential competitive advantage.

Hewlett Packard represented the first of the established computer companies to enter the personal computer industry with the HP-85, in January 1980. This machine was specifically targeted at scientists and engineers, many of whom already owned HP programmable calculators. Compact and lightweight, it was a totally self-contained unit and allowed Hewlett Packard to fill a gap in its scientifically oriented product line between the smallest of its scientific desktop computers. Although not aimed at the business segment of the personal computer market, nevertheless HP's entry represented the first edge of the wave of the traditional computer companies that were to follow into the personal computer industry within the next two or three years.

Zenith Radio Corporation, the major U.S. television and electronics components manufacturer, acquired the Heath Company in October 1979. At the time of the acquisition, Heath was marketing two personal computer products, the H-8 and H-11 systems, both of which had been aimed at the hobbyist market, in which Heath had been a leading supplier of electronics kits for a number of years. In early 1979, Heath had introduced its H-88/H-89 "all-in-one" personal computers in both kit and assembled form, since they perceived the competition as thinning out in this segment. Zenith soon established a separate division, Zenith Data Systems (ZDS), to market the H-88/H-89 as fully assembled products under the names Z-89 and Z-90. The consumer kit products continued to be marketed under the Heathkit name and sold via direct mail order catalogues and Heath electronics retail stores at a lower price. By using its merchandising and mass production experience, Zenith hoped to position the Z-89 and Z-90 machines into the small business segment.

When analysing the performance of the leading competitors, namely, Tandy and Apple during the growth stage, certain points clearly emerge. They both continued to invest in 8-bit technology, avoiding the higher costs which would have been associated with 16-bit leading edge technology. Apple's entry into the small business market and corporate professional sector with the Apple III was not successful and had to be withdrawn for nine months. By the time it was relaunched, it was too late, since it was now following after IBM's entry. Initially, the TRS-80 Model II aimed at the business market was not considered suitable because of inadequate memory capacity, so the less powerful version of the model was dropped. Thus, neither Tandy's nor Apple's new product offerings for the small business markets represented major technological innovations. However, both Tandy's TRS-80 Model I and the Apple II machine continued to enjoy strong sales in the educational and small business segments. Indeed, Apple's most significant achievements during the growth stage resulted from its strategic decision to add performance to the Apple II, rather than lowering the price of the unit. As a result, Apple created a $3000 price umbrella. It also became clear, that for Apple to move away from its hobbyist/home market position it needed to phase out its 16K machine and concentrate on moving the Apple II strongly into the professional and small business segments. The success of Visicalc significantly boosted Apple II sales in this segment, so much so, that by 1980 Apple II became market leader in terms of annual sales.

Although the above range of new machines offered better processing speeds and greater memory storage, the most significant impact in product development was made in applications software. By 1980, according to one report,[17] more than 3000 application programs were available to run on personal computers, most of which were designed to run on Apple II, PET and TRS-80 machines. Since the small business market was a major target for the hardware manufacturers with a growing installed base, this naturally led a number of software developers to also focus on the area, especially given that business applications offered far greater margins for the developers.

In addition to software developments, the other major changes in the industry value chain during the growth period occurred in the expansion of distribution channels. The proliferation of channels reflected the increasing segmentation of the industry, each of which developed to serve particular needs of users in various segments. Table 4.7 illustrates selected vendors' principal channels of distribution in the late 1970s and early 1980s. What is apparent from Table 4.7 is that most of the major competitors made use of a wide variety of channels. The independent computer stores tended to carry products for two or three manufacturers and represented the dominant share of the market. Apart from Tandy, manufacturers' retail outlets tended to be the preserve of the "giants" such as IBM, DEC, Texas Instruments and Xerox. Interestingly, this was their first point of entry into the personal computer market and was a move made partly to expand sales of electronic office products in general and partially a defensive move.

Texas Instruments, together with Atari and Commodore made use of department stores for sale of their low-end machines to the consumer market. Office equipment stores tended to focus mainly upon the small business sector and like independent computer stores tended to carry two or three manufacturers' products. Although recorded in the table, systems houses tended to play a very small role in distribution of personal computers at this stage of the market's evolution. As far as direct manufacturers' sales forces were concerned, these were used mainly by Xerox, DEC, Hewlett Packard and IBM in the next stage of evolution. However, Apple did start to make some tentative efforts in direct selling at this stage, but on a very small scale. Alongside independent computer stores, authorised dealers gradually moved into becoming the most important source of distribution channel. These gave manufacturers a greater degree of control of their access to the market and were to form the backbone of future strategies for companies such as Apple and Commodore. Lastly, mail order retailers had tended to slip from prominence as the market developed new channels. However, companies with lower priced products aimed at the mass consumer market, such as Apple, Commodore and Texas Instruments tended to continue to make use of mail order.

It should be noted that the relatively new channel of computer stores had grown in response to the special problems involved in selling to neophytes. Not only did they develop expertise to aid customers in learning how to use personal computers, but they also sought to offer advice on combinations of hardware and software. In this task, they became similar to systems houses, except that most of the software was packaged or "shrunk-wrapped"[18] as opposed to tailor-made. Overall, the major change in this channel involved an increased standard of professionalism amongst selected stores as they sought to establish more of a consultative role for small businesses. However, standards were extremely varied and since most stores were small businesses in their own right, few had the necessary

Table 4.7. Selected vendors' principal channels of distribution: late 1970s to early 1980s.

	INDEPENDENT COMPUTER STORES	MANUFACTURERS' RETAIL OUTLETS	DEPARTMENT STORES	OFFICE EQUIPMENT AND SUPPLY STORES	SYSTEMS HOUSES	MANUFACTURERS' DIRECT SALES FORCE	AUTHORIZED DEALERS OR DISTRIBUTORS	MAIL ORDER RETAILERS
APPLE	X			X	X	X	X	X
ATARI	X		X				X	
COMMODORE	X		X	X	X		X	X
DATA GENERAL	X			X			X	
DEC	X	X			X	X	X	
HEWLETT-PACKARD	X			X	X	X	X	X
IBM	X	X			X	X		
NORTH STAR					X		X	
OHIO SCIENTIFIC	X			X	X		X	X
TANDY		X			X		X	
TEXAS INSTRUMENTS	X	X	X		X		X	X
XEROX	X	X				X	X	

Source: The Outlook for the U. S. Personal Computer Industry, Arthur D. Little, Inc., December 1981, p.19. Reproduced by permission of Decision Resources, Inc., © 1981.

resources to develop ancillary services, such as training activities. In effect, this created a gap in the market, which was filled by the larger franchised chain stores, such as Computerland.

Overall therefore, during the growth period the industry showed a marked shift towards expansion of new types of distribution channels. In most instances, and with the notable exception of Tandy, channel expansion took place independently of the personal computer manufacturers. Instead it was driven by entrepreneurs and businesses seeking to capitalise on the opportunities presented by market expansion. In so doing, the channels helped also to expand the demand in these markets by providing more effective and efficient means of access and support to customers.

SUMMARY

In summary, the key changes of a strategic nature in the personal computer industry during the growth stage occurred in the following areas:

(i) the emergence of two families of microprocessor based computers: 6502 and Z-80;

(ii) two approaches to operating systems: CP/M-80 based and proprietary DOS[19] from the leaders, Apple, Tandy and Commodore;

(iii) rapid expansion of applications programs for CP/M and Apple machines;

(iv) low impact entry by two "giants", namely, Texas Instruments and Hewlett Packard;

(v) introduction of new, but non-innovative products by the industry leaders, expanding their product range to focus upon the small business market and consumer markets;

(vi) rapid development of the dealer networks and emergence of computer stores specialising in the small business market, including the entry of mass merchandisers such as Sears and computer or office products suppliers such as DEC and Xerox;

(vii) increasing expenditure upon promotional activities, especially magazine and business journal advertising.

In reflecting these developments, the value chains of various competitors moved towards increased emphasis upon the development of low-cost, high-volume manufacturing to produce improved hardware peripherals and capacity. In addition, expanded software applications drove the development of new markets which required better standards of distribution and support. These in turn necessitated higher costs of promotional activity. Each of these factors increased the industry's barriers to entry, as well as creating new sets of mobility barriers around the respective strategic groups. These various points are illustrated in Fig. 4.12, where it can be seen that essentially for those companies competing in the small business and professional markets, their value chains were clearly moving towards a systems orientation and away from the more basic sale of boxes.

However, towards the end of the growth stage whilst these developments were taking place, the entry of companies such as Texas Instruments and Hewlett Packard heralded a new threat to earlier incumbents such as Apple, Tandy and Commodore. With expansion of the personal computer market into the business and professional segments, the large established mainframe and other minicomputer companies began to recognise the significant opportunities that lay in entry to this related but increasingly significant industry. For by 1980, the personal computer business was quite clearly becoming an industry in its own right. Not only did this represent an opportunity, it also represented a threat. For companies such as IBM, the memory of late entry into the minicomputer industry was not forgotten. Furthermore, the trend towards an increasing number of individual managers and professionals purchasing machines from Apple, Commodore, Tandy, Texas Instruments and Hewlett Packard for their own use in large companies, created a position of serious threat to IBM, DEC and other major computer manufacturers in the mainframe and minicomputer industries. Thus as the major competitors shifted positions and as the size of the personal computer markets continued to expand, the industry was set to enter its next and in some ways most significant stage of development, namely, "The Entry of the Giants and Legitimisation".

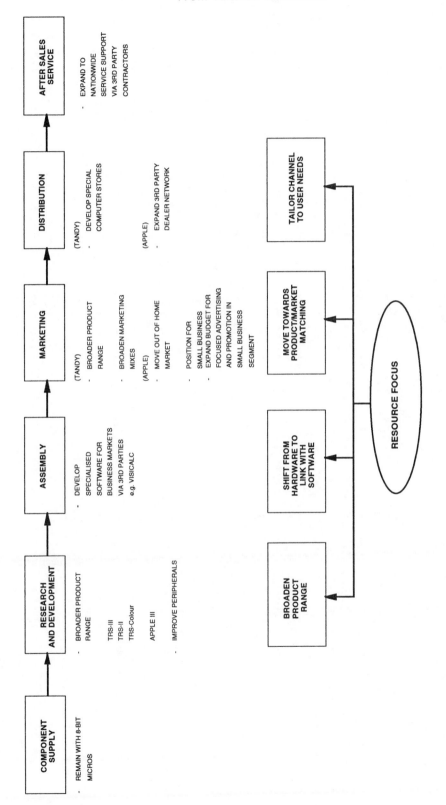

Fig. 4.12. The focus of strategic resources by industry leaders during the growth stage.

Chapter Five

ENTRY OF THE GIANTS AND LEGITIMISATION

"There is nothing that IBM has presented [in the Personal Computer] that would blow the industry away".[1]

INTRODUCTION

Following from the events of the "Growth Stage", the personal computer industry moved onto its next stage of evolution, which represents the "Legitimisation Stage" that forms the subject matter of this chapter.

The "Legitimisation Stage" is really divided into two phases. The first lasted from late 1981 to the end of 1982, whilst the second followed on from late 1982 to 1984. The first phase was marked by the "Entry of the Giants", that included companies from the computer, office products and consumer electronics industries. These included Xerox, IBM, DEC, Wang, NEC, Sanyo and others. What made them different to the earlier large entrants such as Texas Instruments, H.P. and Zenith was their experience and market focus upon the corporate sector. As will be shown later, some of the entrants were not as successful as they may have wished. However, the impact of IBM on the corporate sector was such that it dramatically altered the structure of the industry and changed the rules of competition. In so doing, through the market power of IBM, the personal computer was legitimised as a serious and important product within the broader computing requirements of corporate customers. In addition to IBM, a much smaller start up company, Osborne Computer also entered the market during the first phase and laid the foundations for development of the portable sector of the personal computer industry.

Following from this first phase, a number of companies responded to the impact of IBM, which within a year of its entry was already rapidly changing the industry standards for microprocessors, operating systems and applications programs. Amongst the incumbents, a variety of strategies were pursued. Apple chose to compete through technological differentiation, whilst Tandy, Commodore and others, although initially remaining outside the IBM standard were eventually forced to adopt it. Thus as IBM's success grew, it attracted a number of competitors to develop machines that were compatible with the IBM standards, this included a number of clones,[2] that were in time to become a source of major competition to IBM. Just as IBM created a central focus for the desktop personal computer industry, Osborne Computer created and stimulated interest in the portable sector. Therefore during the second phase, a number of new entrants chose to follow Osborne by developing portable machines aimed at the business market.

Overall, the "Legitimisation Stage" witnessed significant changes which are explored within this chapter. It commences by looking at the patterns of entry in more detail. It then proceeds to review the technological developments that took place in microprocessor technology, operating systems and applications programs which formed the basis for new product developments. This then leads onto an analysis of how new value chains were created by entrants such as IBM and Osborne Computer and how they and Apple Computer created new concepts about the nature and role of personal computers. In addition, it highlights the shift towards an increasing number of resources being allocated to marketing activities within the value chain. These shifts are also illustrated by consideration of the changes that took place in the nature and overall positioning of strategic groups.

In addition to developments in technology, new products and new competitors, the "Legitimisation Stage" was also marked by significant changes in market conditions. These are explored in terms of the trends in size, structure and growth within the overall business markets, together with an analysis of the changing pattern of needs for office users and small business customers. At the same time, the creation and nature of the portable computer market is also presented and illustrates some of its differences to the desktop market. Having presented the major changes that took place in the structure of the industry and its markets, the latter part of the chapter focuses upon the nature of the competition and market performance. This looks in more depth at the strategies pursued by a number of competitors, including some that failed and some that succeeded. In addition, the performance of these companies is considered in terms of their sales and market share in specific market segments. The chapter finishes with a summary, which draws out the major patterns that emerge from the content of the various sections and highlights the overall characteristics of the "Legitimisation Stage" of the evolution of the personal computer industry and its markets.

PATTERNS OF ENTRY

The first of the major companies or giants to enter the market in the legitimisation stage was the office copier giant, Xerox Corporation in June 1981, just a few months before IBM. However, although Xerox Corporation represented the vanguard to this new wave of major entrants, the most significant entry was undoubtedly made by IBM, which ranked as the largest entrant, with revenues of $26 billion in 1980 and an R&D budget for its total computer business of $1.5 billion. The relative size of IBM to the industry is well illustrated when one remembers that the combined personal computer revenues of all other personal computer manufacturers in 1981 was approximately $950 million. The second largest data processing[3] company at the time, Digital Equipment Corporation (DEC) followed in early 1982, whilst Wang Laboratories, which had pioneered and subsequently became the market leader in word processing followed a year after IBM's entry. The common feature amongst all the giant U.S. entrants was their overall size, whilst their distinguishing features lay in their strategic backgrounds and market positioning. At the same time, the period witnessed the first wave of European manufacturers to enter the U.S. market, including ICL, Philips and Olivetti, together with the Japanese companies NEC, Toshiba and Fujitsu. Other Japanese companies included Sanyo and Sony, however, their focus was on the small business sector and also included smaller handheld machines. In most cases, the U.S., West European and Japanese entrants were both vertically integrated and international in nature, although their percentage of sales from computer products was extremely varied.

Table 5.1 illustrates the pattern of strategic entry amongst the giants during the first phase of the legitimisation stage. The pattern which emerges highlights the fact that the nature of the entry move was usually due to segment expansion or related business expansion, but what is more striking is that virtually all the entrants were targeting their main efforts upon the business segments of the market. Field research[4] amongst these companies indicated that the motivation for entry was a mixture of offensive and defensive factors. Furthermore, the research data also showed that the opportunities identified through the success of companies such as Apple, Tandy, Vector Graphic and Victor Technologies, in the small business and professional segments, stimulated interest in the potential profits to be gained in these market segments. The apparently low mobility and market entry barriers further created optimism about the probabilities for success and hence the level of risk attached to such ventures. Many of the large entrants indicated a need to defend their installed base of computer users in the lower end of the small business systems market. This was because the rapid development in the product technology of personal computers indicated the possibility that by the mid-1980s, personal computers could form a significant part of the purchases for electronic office equipment in large corporations. At the time, it was felt that if this were to happen, then it would pose a real threat to the major computer companies which were unable to satisfy the need for such equipment.

For most of the European entrants, the nature of their entry move and strategic positioning appears to have been motivated by three factors.[5] Firstly, the desire to be present and close to the U.S. market and its technology. Secondly, to offer their own personal computer to their limited, installed base of mainframe or minicomputer business customers and lastly as an opportunistic move in a rapidly growing market. However, little evidence exists to suggest a well-planned strategy for their entry into the U.S. market, in either specific product design or major aspects of the marketing mix. In contrast, the Japanese entrants pursued a wider variety of approaches and yet were more focused in their strategic direction. For the Japanese, the small business and professional segments represented enormous potential markets, which they appeared willing to penetrate gradually over the long term, rather than by rapid means of price leadership to gain market share.

In addition to the giants, one other significant group of entrants during the first phase of the legitimisation stage were the small start-up companies that targeted the portable computer segment. The first entrant to establish the portable computer market segment was Osborne Computer, which was a start-up venture that launched its first product, the Osborne 1, just a month before IBM's entry. Yet similarly to IBM, Osborne was to create significant changes in the industry and led the way for development of portable computers by a wide range of companies. These initially included two small companies, namely, Otrana and Non-Linear Systems with their highly successful Kaypro machine, with others following later during the legitimisation stage and subsequent consolidation stage.

This second phase began between late 1982 and 1983. It is distinguished by the fact that following from the entry of IBM and Osborne

Table 5.1. Patterns of strategic entry amongst the giants: 1981 - 1982.

NAME OF COMPANY	DATE OF ENTRY	NATURE OF PARENT	NATURE OF ENTRY MOVE	ENTRY LAUNCH PRICE $*	TARGET MARKET SEGMENTS					
					H	E	I	C	S	B
NEC	JUN 1981	REL. BUSINESS	SEGMENT EXPANSION	3415					x	x
XEROX	JUN 1981	DOM. BUSINESS	RELATED EXPANSION	3195					x	x
IBM	AUG 1981	DOM. BUSINESS	SEGMENT EXPANSION	3580		x			x	x
DEC	OCT 1982	DOM. BUSINESS	SEGMENT EXPANSION	3245					x	x
SANYO	MAR 1982	UNREL. BUSN.	RELATED EXPANSION	4995					x	x
SONY	MAY 1982	DOM. BUSINESS	RELATED EXPANSION	3000		x			x	x
SHARP	FEB 1983	UNREL. BUSN.	RELATED EXPANSION	2500					x	x
EPSON	JAN 1983	REL. BUSINESS	RELATED EXPANSION	800					x	x
TOSHIBA	NOV 1981	REL. BUSINESS	GEOGRAPHICAL EXP.	5000					x	
OLIVETTI	MAY 1982	REL. BUSINESS	SEGMENT EXPANSION	3560					x	x
WANG	MAY 1982	SGL. BUSINESS	SEGMENT EXPANSION	5000					x	x

KEY TO MARKET SEGMENTS:

H = Hobby; E = Education; I = Industry; C = Home Consumers; S = Small Business and Professionals; B = Medium and Large Business.

* This figure reflects the average price of hardware for a fully configured system, suitable for basic business applications.

Source: J. W. Steffens, 'Entry Behaviour', unpublished doctoral thesis, The University of London, 1988.

Computer, the industry and its markets underwent rapid and significant changes, which are described later in this chapter. Most importantly, IBM established a new industry standard which was to be imitated by a number of competitors. This was a direct result of the rapid penetration of the business market segments by IBM, which created an enormous demand for its machines and which could not be satisfied for approximately eighteen months after its launch in late 1981. This shortfall created a market opportunity which was filled by two groups of entrants. The first were IBM clones or look-alikes and included companies such as Eagle Computers, whose machines not only emulated the IBM PC,[6] but were virtually identical in design. The second group consisted of companies producing machines that whilst different in physical design could emulate the IBM PC. In time, the majority of incumbents were also to adopt the IBM standard, the implications of which are discussed in a later section.

In addition to the clones, further Japanese competitors entered the U.S. market during this stage from a number of industry sectors. These included companies such as Sharp, Casio and Matsushita, which already marketed a multiple range of consumer electronics goods in the United States with well-established dealer networks and strong brand recognition for their products. Minolta, Canon, Ricoh and Oki also entered the market from their respective backgrounds in camera, copier and peripheral products. Each of these companies was undertaking a geographical expansion of their personal computer activities that they had developed previously in the Japanese and Far Eastern markets.

Osborne Computer's highly successful entry into the personal computer market by introducing the first portable personal computer, stimulated interest in this segment. In 1982 the market was flooded by a host of new entrants, which included the start-up company Compaq Computer, so that more than 20 new full-featured portable computer systems were introduced during the following year up to mid-1983. This represented a marked change in the pattern of entry during the period from 1982 to 1983, since in the latter period, sixty per cent of all personal computer start-up companies were in the portable computer segment. Furthermore, as the market developed, it also witnessed a substantial growth in the handheld personal computer market, which effectively created a further subsegment in the portable marketplace.

Overall therefore, the legitimisation stage witnessed two large waves of entrants. The first was made up of a number of large established international companies which entered the U.S. personal computer market and as will be shown later, with varying degrees of performance. However, within this group of entrants, the impact of IBM upon the industry was substantial and legitimised the personal computer in both the corporate and other business segments. Furthermore, by establishing a new industry standard, it led to a large number of clone and compatible entrants, some of which were highly opportunist in their strategies. At the same time, the lead by Osborne Computer created a major new market segment in portable personal computers that led to rapid entry by a large number of start-up as well as some established companies. Thus the legitimisation period created a number of major changes in both the structure of the industry and its markets. These changes reflected a continuation of the newgame's evolution and were generated by a combination of technological developments, shifts in market behaviour and the strategies pursued by the major competitors, both entrants and incumbents. To follow the pattern more closely, it is first of all necessary to look at the changes that were taking place in the core technologies at this time, since these formed the platform on which the competition chose to develop their strategic positions.

TECHNOLOGICAL DEVELOPMENTS

Over the legitimisation stage, the technology moved through a number of stages of development at different levels. The most significant change surrounded the introduction of the new generation of hybrid 8/16-bit microprocessors, which were duly followed by the full 16-bit families. The opportunity for creating a technological improvement or innovation led competitors to pursue a wide variety of product-technology strategies. As will be shown shortly, in some cases, the outcome of these strategies was to have a significant impact both upon the structure of the industry and its markets.

The New Generation of Microprocessors

During the period up to 1981, with the exception of Texas Instruments, incumbents and new entrants alike had chosen Intel, Zilog and MOS-Tech 8-bit microprocessors. However, this pattern changed when IBM chose to depart from the 8-bit standard by using the Intel 8088, which represented a compromise between some aspects of the 8-bit microprocessor and some of the more powerful 16-bit microprocessors. To begin with, it cost 70 per cent less than full 16-bit microprocessors, yet at the same time offered much better speed and power than the 8-bit microprocessors. Most importantly, the Intel 8088 was compatible with earlier Intel 8080/85 software and peripherals and therefore by choosing the Intel 8088 for its PC, IBM did not lose out on the wide range of 8-bit input/output devices and peripherals which were more readily available and cheaper than 16-bit based hardware. Furthermore, the hybrid could be expanded up to one megabyte[7] of Random Access Memory (RAM) and represented a significant increase over the standard 64Kb available on the 8-bit microprocessors. The only disadvantage was speed, since the hybrid was approximately 60 per cent slower than the 16-bit Intel 8086.

The choice of whether to invest in full 16-bit technology or remain with older 8-bit technology was beginning to become a major issue for competitors in the legitimisation stage and the three key technology-strategy choices available to competitors after IBM's entry are illustrated in Fig. 5.1. The three levels consisted of the choice of microprocessor, the choice of operating system and the choice of applications programs, all of which were interlinked. In the case of the microprocessor, whilst IBM initially chose the hybrid route, by 1982, a number of the semiconductor companies had moved into delivery of 16-bit microprocessors and included Zilog's Z8000 and Intel's 8086. By late 1982, Motorola was offering a 16/32 bit hybrid in the shape of the MC68000. This latter development, signalled that the potential power of personal computers was moving squarely into the realm of the minicomputer's territory. Thus in 1982, newer products introduced by DEC, NEC, Zenith and Wang all chose the Intel 8086, which made them compatible with the 8088-based IBM PC.

Technology Choices and Risk Assessment

As far as the choice of microprocessor was concerned, this was largely influenced by cost, performance and compatibility issues and these decisions had to be made in relation to the benefits, disadvantages and overall risks as illustrated in Fig. 5.1. The importance of these issues lies in their strategic implications for entrant and incumbent alike. As pointed out in a previous chapter, all such decisions were made in an uncertain environment. To begin with, during the year after IBM's entry it was by no means clear to everybody that a new industry standard was going to be created in the short term. By 1980, CP/M-80 had become the industry operating standard, so much so, that even Tandy and Apple, both of which sold their machines with proprietary operating systems, sold a significant number of CP/M-80 expansion boards which allowed non-proprietary software to run on their systems. During 1981 and 1982, CP/M-80 continued to represent the largest installed base of 8-bit microprocessor machines. At the time, the idea of abandoning this standard appeared to many as a ludicrous option, especially given the lack of 16-bit software and peripherals, which placed the newer machines under a severe cost disadvantage compared to the earlier 8-bit models. However, it was also evident that by 1980, the 8-bit microprocessor market was reaching maturity, as personal computer manufacturers recognised the next generation of machines would be defined by their applications software. They also appreciated the opportunities that 16-bit microprocessors would offer to users, especially in the business and professional market segments, where processing speed and user memory capacity[8] would enable software developers to produce more powerful and "user-friendly"[9] programs.

A further consideration involved the question of whether the MS-DOS standard would emerge as a clear winner over the successor to CP/M-80, namely CP/M-86, which was developed for the 16-bit microprocessor environment. Some believed that there would be loyalty amongst users of CP/M-80 to remain in the CP/M family, although in the end this did not prove to be the case. Thus manufacturers had a choice between developing proprietary operating systems, backing one of the competing industry standards or moving into a more sophisticated operating system such as UNIX, which although highly powerful and well recognised in larger computer systems, was still perceived by the market as a specialised system

	EXAMPLE	RELATIVE COST	BENEFIT	DISADVANTAGES	RISKS
1) CHOICE OF MICROPROCESSOR: - 8/16 BIT HYBRID	INTEL 8088 MOTOROLA 6809	MEDIUM	- standard on IBM - higher performance than 8-bit, but less cost than16-bit	- represents a temporary measure - lower performance than 16-bit	- may soon become obsolete in face of true 16-bits
- 16 BIT	INTEL 8086 ZILOG Z8000	HIGH	- support more powerful software - high performance - future standard	- initially less software available - more costly peripherals	- may not develop quickly over 8-bits
- 16/32 BIT	MOTOROLA 68000	VERY HIGH	- very high performance - minicomputer level - multi-tasking capabilities	- little software available - perhaps too advanced	- too advanced for needs of users
2) CHOICE OF OPERATING SYSTEM: - PROPRIETARY	APPLE LISA	HIGH	- include special features - customise to own chip design	- requires special staff and restricts initial range of applications software	- may not be supported by software developers
- INDUSTRY STANDARD ?	CP/M-80/86 MS-DOS	LOW LOW	- may attract software developers - most likely standard	- still limit base of applications programs	- may lose to MS-DOS - may lose to CP/M-86
- NEW STANDARDS	UNIX	MEDIUM	- high performance for multi-tasking and sophisticated software	- very limited base of applications programs - force own development	- possibly too advanced for current general business community
3) CHOICE OF APPLICATIONS: - IN-HOUSE	LISA	HIGH	- good source of differentiation - greater control of focus in markets	- need own staff - spread costs over smaller volume - carry entire risk	- may not be a success - carry entire risk
- 3RD PARTY	LOTUS 1,2,3.	LOW	- readily available if MS-DOS based - increasing wide range of programs	- delay, since IBM held monopoly for 9 months on best programs, e.g. 1,2,3.	- increased comp. amongst software companies increases risk of backing a loser

Source: J. W. Steffens, Entry Behaviour and Competition in the Evolution of the United States Personal Computer Industry (1975-1983), unpublished doctoral thesis, The University of London, 1988.

Fig. 5.1. Key technology-strategy choices post-IBM's entry.

which was not suitable for use in the general personal computer. Once again, the choice of systems software was to have a significant impact upon choice of applications software. The virtuous and vicious circle models outlined in the previous chapter in relation to programs developed for 8-bit microprocessors, is now applied to the software development associated with the new 16-bit machines. From the software suppliers' perspective, computers which *could* run CP/M using the closely related microprocessors offered reasonable software portability. In 1981 to 1982, such machines provided the largest customer base and for this reason Xerox, IBM, DEC, Hewlett-Packard, Zenith, Televideo and Wang all initially supported CP/M, since this provided them with the benefit of access to a large installed base of applications programs. However, by 1983, PC-DOS/MS-DOS was rapidly becoming the new industry standard and thereafter, applications software for the business market tended to be developed mainly for this environment.

These developments once again created the familiar pattern in the industry's evolution, whereby changes in the core microprocessor technology led to opportunities for hardware competitors to develop a new generation of personal computer. However, the pace and direction of development for each competitor depended very much upon their attitudes and resources in relation to the associated operating systems and applications programs as illustrated in Fig. 5.1. Thus the various technology strategies chosen by the different competitors directly determined a number of major changes that occurred in the industry. The pattern of changes that were brought about centred upon four major developments.

Major Product Developments

The Creation of New Industry Standards

The most significant development involved the speed with which two new industry standards emerged following from the entry of the IBM PC. The first involved the establishment of an IBM hardware protocol, whilst the second centred upon the associated operating system. The enormous latent demand for the IBM product only became apparent after its launch, but very quickly, a number of competitors began to imitate the IBM protocols adopted by IBM in its hardware and jointly between IBM and Microsoft in its operating system. As the IBM hardware standard became more strongly established, software developers began to introduce increasingly powerful applications making use of PC-DOS and MS-DOS. These tended to focus upon the products aimed at the newly emerging corporate marketplace, together with the still rapidly expanding small and medium sized business markets. Amongst the leading products to be launched during this period was Lotus 1,2,3 which represented the first integrated business program[10] developed by the new start-up company, Lotus Development Corporation. The Lotus programme allowed the user to mix word processing, graphical, spreadsheet and database[11] capabilities and in so doing gained considerable success in the corporate market.

However, on the early IBM PCs, the operating memory[12] or RAM was too small to make full use of the programs many features. As a result, RAM memory started to increase and further programs began to be developed that made use of the added capacity of the machines. In addition, as graphics became an increasingly important part of the tools used by customers in the corporate and professional environment, then improvements started to take place in the quality and size of high resolution screens[13] and monitors. Similarly, the diffusion of personal computers around large corporations led to a realisation that their power could be increased by setting up local communications networks that would allow the machines to share and exchange data. Furthermore, the needs of such users for high capacity long-term memory drove the demand for development of more powerful disk drive systems. In practice, the products developed in communications, high resolution monitors and high capacity storage devices were usually very expensive and aimed at a limited market. However, their development represented an important change of perception as to how the personal computer could be used in business. No longer was it viewed as a games machine or home entertainment device, instead the technology was driving rapidly towards the centre of computing activity in the business community, representing the legitimisation of the personal computer.

In response to IBM's entry, Commodore began using the same Intel 8088 microprocessor as IBM, whilst Tandy adopted the full, yet more expensive 16-bit Motorola 68000. Initially, Commodore made use of proprietary operating systems, but also continued to support the CP/M-80, whilst Tandy supported its software base for the previously highly successful Tandy TRS-80 Model II. However, relatively few CP/M-86 software applications were available in 1982 and Tandy's Model-16 had virtually no programs available for the 16-bit processor. Hence, both these incumbents were to some degree constrained in their new product offerings by the lack of available software or high price. Both of these factors created a major market barrier around the incumbents, since by 1983, IBM was supporting over 1000 programs for the PC, which included the new and more popular integrated programs such as Lotus 1,2,3. Faced with this situation Tandy and Commodore along with a number of smaller incumbents, were eventually forced to adopt the IBM standard and to begin producing IBM compatible[14] machines. However, there was one notable and major exception, namely, Apple Computer.

Technology Innovation: The Apple Lisa

Apple Computer's technology strategy represents the third significant development to occur during the legitimisation period. By the time of IBM's entry, Apple had become the industry leader, overtaking sales of Tandy in 1980. Like Tandy, Apple had attempted to pre-empt the IBM entry with its launch into the business market with the Apple III machine. However, this was not a success for reasons given in the previous chapter. Then, in January 1983, some sixteen months after IBM's entry, Apple responded with its launch of the Lisa, which was based on Motorola's 16-

bit 68000 microprocessor. Ironically, many of the features were similar to the Xerox Star workstation,[15] but priced at $10,000 it nevertheless represented a true technological innovation for the personal computer industry. At a technology level, what made the Lisa so different to its competitors was that its development was based on an integrated design of hardware and software, in order to produce a highly "user-friendly"[16] machine that made use of "icons"[17] to replace keyboard commands for commonly used functions, as well as a "mouse" for cursor controls.[18] At the time, this represented a step-change in product design and operation. The combined development of a proprietary operating system in conjunction with the design of the hardware meant that Apple was able to make significant advances in the overall system, compared to the IBM compatible based products. As a result the system was designed from the beginning with the user in mind in an industry that traditionally had been virtually entirely technology driven. Thus Apple pursued a high-risk newgame strategy with its technology, but one that was in time to change the concept of how personal computers interacted with their users. It was with this product that the concept of user-friendliness first began to have real meaning. Overall the Lisa was most significant since it formed the product that was to subsequently lead to development of the Macintosh family of personal computers.

The Osborne 1: The creation of the portable

The fourth development in technology centred around the creation of the portable computer. This segment started with the introduction of the Osborne machine and rapidly attracted a large number of entrants. In itself, the Osborne 1 relied purely on conventional technology. However, the product stimulated a number of other companies to enter the portable market niche as distinct from the desktop personal computer market. Over time, entry was made at three distinct product levels, which were categorised as follows:

(1) *Transportable Computers:* units which were generally light enough to be lifted by most individuals (15–40 lbs), but which were too bulky for use in restricted space. The distinctive features of such machines were that they operated off alternating current; battery packs were generally available as optional add-on products; and CRT displays, minifloppy drives[19] and detachable keyboards were usually in the overall package. Examples of such machines were the Osborne 1 and the Otrona Attache and later on included products from Compaq and IBM.

(2) *True Portable Computers:* units that could be carried like a tablet and could be operated on the user's lap. Such machines provided integrated battery power; flat-panel displays;[20] full keyboards; and mass storage in one single unit. The weight of these computers was such that they could be carried with comfort (5–15 lbs) and examples included the Epson HX-20 and the Grid Compass. These were the forerunners of the "laptop" computers

that became very popular by the late 1980s and were led by Toshiba.

(3) *Handheld Computers:* were units capable of being held in the hand; and usually weighed less than 5 lbs; and could easily be stored in a briefcase. Examples of handheld computers included the Hewlett-Packard HP-75 and the Tandy TRS-80 Pocket Computer and products from Japanese manufacturers such as Sanyo, Sharp and Casio. These were also to become increasingly popular during the 1980s.

Table 5.2 illustrates the distinguishing features between hand-held computers and the two categories of portable at the time. In effect, by developing three types or levels of portable personal computer, the industry redefined its boundaries and also created three new market segments. During the legitimisation stage, the largest technological challenges for portables surrounded overcoming the problems of limited battery life, small and poor quality screen displays, lack of compatibility with the IBM standard and weight. Although the heavier transportable machines were soon able to offer IBM compatibility and reasonable screen displays, this was only achievable at the cost of weight and often without independent battery power. With the exception of the Grid Compass, Epson's HX-20, Teleram's portable and the Toshiba T-100, most of the "portables" were too heavy and could only be truly described as "transportables". The key problem lay with the cathode ray terminal (CRT) displays, whose large tubes, heavy circuitry and substantial power supplies prevented radical loss of weight. As a result of this limitation, those companies offering more lightweight products made use of LCD[21] or in Grid's case electroluminescent displays.[22] However, although this technology was improving in quality all the time, its display size was still not able to support a full-sized screen in mid-1983 and the cost of panel displays was extremely high. In addition, these earlier true portables tended to have limited battery life and lacked compatibility with desk-top systems, whilst handhelds remained a fairly discrete product group in their own right and were often viewed as fancy calculators and hence not really connected to the world of personal computing.

Thus the development of a new generation of microprocessor led to four major changes in personal computer technology during the "Legitimisation Stage". This included the establishment of the IBM standard in hardware compatibility, the sweeping away of the previous industry operating system standard of CP/M-80 and its replacement by IBM's PC-DOS and Microsoft's MS-DOS. These events were accompanied by the associated new generation of applications software for the business market and the early challenge of Apple's innovative Lisa machine, which was the forerunner to its Macintosh family of personal computers with their proprietary operating systems but easier and more advanced user interface.[23] In addition, a range of portable personal computers were developed which created three further types of product category. What impact these events had upon the development of the industry are next explored in terms of

Table 5.2. Distinguishing features between handheld calculators and portable computers.

PRODUCT CHARACTERISTICS	HANDHELD CALCULATORS	PORTABLES
SIZE	paperback book	notebook to briefcase
PRICE	less than $500 (base price)	$795 - $8,150
KEYBOARD	calculator style	typewriter
RAM MEMORY	less than 16K	16K - 256K
FLOPPY DISK	not at present	3.5" & 5.25"
HARD DISK	no	3.8" - 5.25"
EXPANSION SLOTS	none, except for ROM and RAM cartridges	0 - 6
WEIGHT	less than 3 lbs.	up to 30 lbs.
DISPLAY	LCD	LCD, CRT or EL
BATTERY PACK	standard	optional or unavailable
OTHER	numerous peripherals	few peripherals

Source: Yankee Group Report 1983, p.111.
Reproduced by permission of Yankee Group., © 1983.

the various changes that took place in the value chains of the major competitors and the associated pattern of strategic groups that emerged during this period.

CHANGES IN VALUE CHAINS AND STRATEGIC GROUPS

New Types of Value Chains

In the last chapter it was demonstrated that during the Growth Stage none of the entrants pursued a newgame strategy and that the only major change to take place in the dominant companies' value chains occurred in the area of distribution. As shown in the previous section, with the development of the legitimisation stage, first Osborne Computer, then IBM and later Apple Computer all created newgame strategies. What made these strategies newgames as opposed to simply new product strategies, was the fact that in each case, they were to change the concept of personal computing, each in a unique manner, and in so doing, they also changed the underlying structure of their respective company's value chains.

Furthermore, the new value chains created strategic responses amongst competitors that led to changes in the strategic groups' configurations within the industry. The first part of this section will therefore focus upon the value chain patterns, before proceeding to consider the strategic groups. Further discussion of the overall product market strategies of these and other competitors will follow later in the chapter.

Although not the first newgame strategy of the legitimisation stage, IBM's entry strategy had such a significant impact on the market that it merits primary consideration. IBM's strategy reflected a major reconfiguration of both the focus and scale of asset structures as compared to the incumbents' value chains. Fig. 5.2 illustrates the areas of IBM's impact. As shown in the previous section, IBM chose to adopt the Intel 8088 microprocessor for its personal computer. In so doing and due to its success in the market, it upset the existing industry standards by forcing both hardware competitors and software developers to recognise that the future major installed base would no longer lie in the previous microprocessors and associated operating system of CP/M-80. Instead, IBM was able to eventually force major competitors to invest in developing a new generation of machines that were either IBM compatible, or as in the case of Apple, to develop a system based upon an alternative proprietary system with all the risks inherent in such a decision. As the production of IBM personal computers increased, the company also gained economies of scale in both its automated manufacturing and its leverage of supply in components and microprocessors. Unlike, most of the incumbents, IBM launched its personal computer to manufacture in high volume and invested heavily in automated equipment for testing quality control, as well as high speed assembly. It thus increased the scale of investment required by the major competitors in production facilities at the same time as achieving its own position as a low cost manufacturer.

In marketing, the company invested heavily in advertising and public relations activities, so much so, that its first twelve months' advertising budget exceeded the total advertising spend of the industry's six year history. In addition, since IBM targeted the corporate sector as one of its primary markets, it made major use of its direct corporate sales force. These changes in the promotion mix once again raised the costs involved for personal computer manufacturers who were aiming to promote their products to the small and medium sized business market. Meanwhile, IBM's direct sales force gave the company a distinctive advantage over incumbents such as Apple and Tandy Radio Shack in its entry to the corporate marketplace.

For its distribution strategy, IBM instituted a set of "standards" criteria for any dealer that wished to carry IBM products. These included minimum capital base, training facilities and general point of sale displays. Dealers were required to attend a three-day training program at IBM facilities and agree to a minimum sales quota. Whilst both Apple and Tandy had set similar requirements, the demand for IBM PC's was so strong that there was an excess supply of outlets wishing to become IBM-appointed

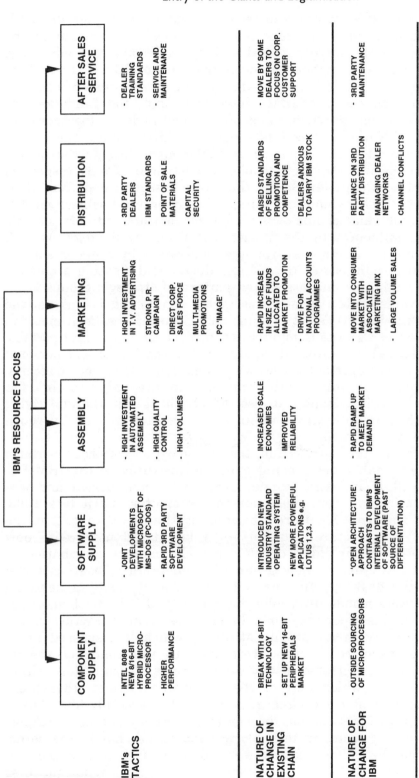

	COMPONENT SUPPLY	SOFTWARE SUPPLY	ASSEMBLY	MARKETING	DISTRIBUTION	AFTER SALES SERVICE
IBM's TACTICS	- INTEL 8088 NEW 8/16-BIT HYBRID MICRO-PROCESSOR - HIGHER PERFORMANCE	- JOINT DEVELOPMENTS WITH MICROSOFT OF MS-DOS (PC-DOS) - RAPID 3RD PARTY SOFTWARE DEVELOPMENT	- HIGH INVESTMENT IN AUTOMATED ASSEMBLY - HIGH QUALITY CONTROL - HIGH VOLUMES	- HIGH INVESTMENT IN T.V. ADVERTISING - STRONG P.R. CAMPAIGN - DIRECT CORP. SALES FORCE - MULTI-MEDIA PROMOTIONS - PC 'IMAGE'	- 3RD PARTY DEALERS - IBM STANDARDS - POINT OF SALE MATERIALS - CAPITAL SECURITY	- DEALER TRAINING STANDARDS - SERVICE AND MAINTENANCE
NATURE OF CHANGE IN EXISTING CHAIN	- BREAK WITH 8-BIT TECHNOLOGY - SET UP NEW 16-BIT PERIPHERALS MARKET	- INTRODUCED NEW INDUSTRY STANDARD OPERATING SYSTEM - NEW MORE POWERFUL APPLICATIONS e.g. LOTUS 1,2,3.	- INCREASED SCALE ECONOMIES - IMPROVED RELIABILITY	- RAPID INCREASE IN SIZE OF FUNDS ALLOCATED TO MARKET PROMOTION - DRIVE FOR NATIONAL ACCOUNTS PROGRAMMES	- RAISED STANDARDS OF SELLING, PROMOTION AND COMPETENCE - DEALERS ANXIOUS TO CARRY IBM STOCK	- MOVE BY SOME DEALERS TO FOCUS ON CORP. CUSTOMER SUPPORT
NATURE OF CHANGE FOR IBM	- OUTSIDE SOURCING OF MICROPROCESSORS	- 'OPEN ARCHITECTURE' APPROACH CONTRASTS TO IBM'S INTERNAL DEVELOPMENT OF SOFTWARE (PAST SOURCE OF DIFFERENTIATION)	- RAPID RAMP UP TO MEET MARKET DEMAND	- MOVE INTO CONSUMER MARKET WITH ASSOCIATED MARKETING MIX - LARGE VOLUME SALES	- RELIANCE ON 3RD PARTY DISTRIBUTION - MANAGING DEALER NETWORKS - CHANNEL CONFLICTS	- 3RD PARTY MAINTENANCE

IBM'S RESOURCE FOCUS

Source: J. W. Steffens, 'Entry Behaviour and Competition in the Evolution of the United States Personal Computer Industry (1975–1983)', unpublished doctoral thesis, The University of London, 1988.

Fig. 5.2. IBM's value chain and newgame entry strategy.

dealers. As a result, IBM was able to easily set and obtain higher standards of professionalism from its dealers than had previously existed in the industry. Overall, IBM therefore gained a distinctive competitive advantage by creating a perceived higher value on the part of IBM PC's and its support services in the minds of its existing and new customer base.

Thus, during the year after IBM's entry, both Apple and Tandy adopted higher profiles in their advertising and promotional budgets, together with the setting up of National Accounts programs. Furthermore, the nature of distribution channels was impacted by IBM's entry through the raising of standards in the industry as a whole. In particular, Tandy responded by opening further Computer Stores that were distinguished from their earlier Radio Shack shops and focused specifically on the business market segment. Hence the value chains of the major incumbents and new entrants were all heavily influenced by the impact of IBM's entry strategy. As such it represented a clear example of a newgame strategy by a major entrant changing the underlying structure of the industry and creating a new set of competitive conditions and associated pattern of strategic groups.

However, whilst IBM's impact was highly significant, it was not the only change in the industry's set of value chains during the Legitimisation Stage. In the case of Osborne Computer, its introduction of the first portable machine represented a significant change in the concept of the personal computer. This is an important aspect when identifying newgame strategies, since a newgame not only creates changes in the value chain of a competitor, but most importantly, it also reflects changes in the underlying perceptions that people have about the product or service–both manufacturers and customers.

As shown in the previous section, the technology in Osborne's portable was very conventional. Indeed, being launched just prior to the IBM PC, it adopted the CP/M industry standard that was then current and was non-IBM compatible as were most personal computers until late 1982. However, the Osborne 1, offered a product that was to excite the imagination of manufacturers and users alike. It did not create new production processes, nor did it develop new channels of distribution or support, but it did create a new group of competitors whose focus was no longer on the desktop, but instead was upon developing personal computers that were mobile. Ironically, the majority of Osborne 1 machines were not used in their portable role. In fact the great attraction of the Osborne portable lay in its pricing strategy, which is discussed later. However, the seeds of the concept were sown by this company and its product and in so doing created new strategic groups of competitors within the industry, some of which were start-up companies, whilst others were large established computer and electronics companies, especially from Japan.

In sharp contrast to Osborne, the newgame strategy pursued by Apple Computer was deeply rooted in technological innovation, but like Osborne, the impact upon the value chain was based upon a change of concept, rather than major changes in the elements of the chain. What the Lisa and subsequent Macintosh family provided was an easier way for users to actually operate their machines. Instead of dependency on various coded alphanumeric entries to get the computer to do something, as was necessary for all CP/M-80 and IBM machines, the Lisa and early Macintosh provided the opportunity for the user to point to commands that were displayed in English and could be activated by "clicking"[24] on a mouse. This ease of use was to revolutionise the development of applications software and in so doing laid the foundation for the evolution of market segments, such as desk-top publishing[25] and graphics design[26] which would generate a whole new range of peripheral products and systems over the next stage of the industry's evolution. Although the Lisa was not a great success, it was to provide the platform for the development of its successor, the Macintosh and the family of products belonging to the Macintosh range that emerged during the next ten years. At first, the Macintosh was not viewed as a serious competitor to the business market against IBM and its competitors' compatible machines. However, as will be shown in later chapters, in time, the Macintosh was to become an even more important product family in its own right which gained increasing acceptance in the business market place. Hence, the Macintosh created a strategic group in its own right, which ultimately was to challenge the approach adopted by IBM in its product and systems design.

About eighteen months after IBM's entry, as well as the launch of Apple's Lisa, further changes started to take place in the value chains of the major competitors, many of which were initiated by IBM, although not in all cases. Overall, this second wave of changes focused largely on shifts in the marketing elements of competitors' value chains and are illustrated in Fig. 5.3. At the product level, a number of more powerful 16-bit based machines were introduced, together with further more "user-friendly" software, especially the introduction of the Lisa and Macintosh from Apple. As more IBM PCs began to enter the corporate work place,

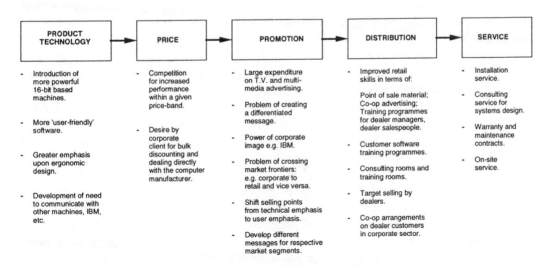

Fig. 5.3. Changes in the competitors' value chains: 1982 - 1983.

then issues surrounding communications between personal computers and other data processing systems began to take-on greater importance.

However, it was in pricing, promotion, distribution and service that some of the greatest changes took place. Price competition against the IBM standard began to intensify from clones and IBM compatibles as the shortfall initially created by IBM was overcome. Demand for IBM or IBM compatible machines by large corporations led to heavy discounting. As the market became more competitive, promotional expenditures continued to expand in an effort to gain market share. In particular, the industry witnessed during 1983 to 1985 huge expenditures on T.V. and magazine advertising. The problem however, was how to create a differentiated product message against the enormous brand power carried by IBM. At the same time, the smaller personal computer companies ran into problems of positioning when seeking to enter the corporate marketplace. Furthermore, a number of the large computer companies found it equally problematic trying to gain a foothold in the various markets served through third party distribution channels. All of which created a need for competitors to shift their marketing messages from a technical to a user perspective and develop different messages for their respective market segments.

In order to develop the business market, from corporate to medium and small sized companies, the industry was forced to significantly improve the quality and service of its distribution channels. This was a lead taken by IBM, whose market power allowed them to dictate terms to dealers wishing to carry their products. Thus by 1983, the structure of the U.S. market reflected seven clearly identifiable channels of distribution to the end-user, which are shown in Fig. 5.4. The two most dominant paths were computer retail and direct sales, which together represented an estimated 70–80 per cent of total market sales to all segments in 1982[27] and included an estimated 2000 computer retail outlets in addition to 1000 Tandy stores. Within the retail distribution two types of outlet were present, which reflected the transition taking place in this element of the industry's value chain structure. On the one hand were the older, more established technical retail outlets, whilst on the other there were the growing number of the more modern, sophisticated commercially-oriented outlets. As competition increased, manufacturers' margins on products were being squeezed in their battle for shelf-space, which forced retailers into price wars with one another and even fiercer competition in low-end machines[28] against mail-order houses. Thus although rising support and service standards were expected by the business segment buyers, these facilities cost extra money and unfortunately the price war generated amongst manufacturers and in between dealers squeezed retailers' margins against these rising costs. Those dealers wanting to carry leading manufacturers' products such as from IBM, also found the manufacturer expected investment in support and sales, thus raising the capital base and working capital requirements to obtain dealer contracts. In addition, the development of vertical market segments was creating a wide range of new specialised software, which in turn demanded the retailer to undertake an increasingly consultative role and

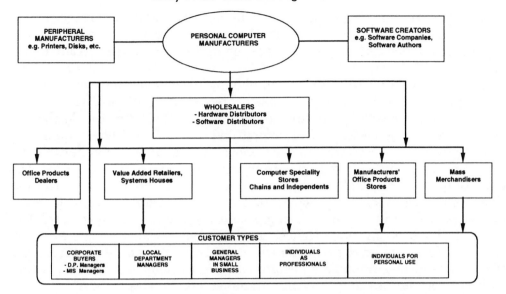

Fig. 5.4. Channels of distribution to personal computer business markets: 1983.

invest more time and money in sales and product training. In these circumstances, a process of consolidation began to take place in the distribution channels as the smaller and less efficient dealers were forced out of the market.

In this environment, Tandy continued to maintain a competitive edge in distribution to the low-end and small business market through its extensive network of stores. However, the corporate market was better reached via direct sales forces which were already in place and adopted by the giants such as IBM and DEC. Thus, IBM and the giants held the competitive advantage for distribution and selling to the corporate segment, whilst Tandy and Apple (through their established and loyal dealer networks) held the advantage in the small business/professional segments. In order to strengthen their positions, an attempt was made in 1982 by Tandy and Apple to penetrate the corporate segment by establishing special national accounts programmes for the larger companies, since it was believed that such companies wanted to deal directly with the manufacturer, rather than the local dealer. However, given their relatively limited resources in terms of the number of sales representatives and to reduce channel conflict, Tandy and Apple chose to employ their sales staff to gain orders and offer discounts, whilst allowing the local dealer to conduct installation and service support.

In addition to distribution and selling, the other elements of the marketing mix which changed significantly during this period were advertising and public relations. The effect of IBM's intensive campaigns surrounding its PC stimulated incumbents and subsequent entrants to make greater use of advertising and to increase their expenditure in this area. Within this context, promotional competence and the level of activity did much to drive the development of the industry and generate increased awareness, stimulating demand in the various market segments. Indeed, the personal desktop computer was changing its nature from being a machine whose capabilities could be measured in terms of technical performance to a system for use in solving problems. However, given the developments in technology already discussed, the hardware of such machines was increasingly taking second place to the software. Furthermore, as more machines became IBM compatible, the new software applications being developed were available on most makes of leading hardware, so that the problem of product differentiation came to the fore. Thus, advertising began to take on a new dimension of importance in the value chain, since the message now needed to sell a complex product, yet one that was outwardly similar to competitors' systems amongst a relatively neophyte business market. Hence, the emphasis began to move away from technical functions and performance towards user-friendly features, range of software, price, ergonomic design, communications capabilities, together with support for training and maintenance warranties.

Overall therefore, during the legitimisation stage, the value chains of the major competitors changed in both technological and marketing areas. In technology, the new generation of microprocessors created new products ranging from the IBM PC to Apple Lisa. The creation of the IBM standard and the PC-DOS and MS-DOS environment generated an enormous level of competition, which sought in particular to capture a share of the corporate and small to medium sized business markets. However, as will be shown in a later section of this chapter, these were markets that still required education amongst buyers and users as to the potential role of the personal computer and as such demanded higher standards of marketing. Hence, it was in the areas of pricing, promotion, distribution and support that the competitors' value chains underwent the greatest change. Essentially, for the reasons outlined above, they were required to move towards a much more professional approach to their marketing activities, although in practice, as will be shown later, their degrees of commitment and success in implementation were extremely varied. Before turning to look at their respective strategies and performance in more detail, it is useful to first of all gain an overview of the evolution of the industry during this period, by considering the pattern of strategic groups that formed during the legitimisation stage.

Patterns of Strategic Groups

Following from the entry of IBM, the industry's strategic groups changed considerably during the legitimisation period and set a pattern that was to remain intact for most of the 1980s. Two plots of strategic variables for the key competitors around 1983 are shown in Figs. 5.5 and 5.6. The first illustrates the relationship between the degree of business diversification of the parent company and the degree of vertical integration of the company in its personal computer activities. The measures for

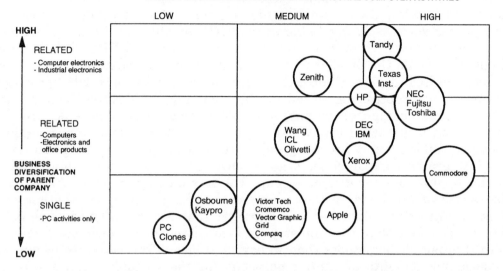

DEGREE OF VERTICAL INTEGRATION IN PERSONAL COMPUTER ACTIVITIES

Source: J. W. Steffens, 'Entry Behaviour and Competition in the Evolution of the United States Personal Computer Industry (1975-1983)', unpublished doctoral thesis, The University of London, 1988.

Fig. 5.5. Strategic group business configurations in the personal computer industry: 1983.

business diversification are in three sectors. The first and lowest level on the diagram represents the single company, where at least ninety per cent of its resources are dedicated to the personal computer industry. Above this category, parent companies are shown with at least fifty percent of their revenues generated through related activities in either the computer and electronic office products industry or the consumer and/or industrial electronics industry. In those situations where there is a degree of overlap between the two sectors, the dominant sector has been chosen for the illustration. On the horizontal axis, the degree of vertical integration may reflect backwards and/or forwards from personal computer manufacturing activities. Naturally, the diagram does not distinguish between the two, since it is merely intended to illustrate the range of activities along the value chain in which a company is directly participating.

Compared to earlier stages of the industry's evolution, Fig. 5.5 highlights the enormous increase in competitors with activities in the areas defined outside personal computers. In the majority of cases, such companies also exhibited a higher degree of vertical integration than most of the earlier incumbents. Overall, the number of strategic groups have increased, although in practice it must be remembered that there were a very large number of companies in the group defined as small limited scale players. These included a large number of the clones, although some of these were also to be found in the group of clones from the electronics industry sector. In one respect, IBM could be construed as a strategic group in its own right, however, given the variables under consideration, it shares a similar position to DEC. As a major electronics office products company Xerox stands somewhat alone, since it did not have the computer interests of companies such as Wang Laboratories, ICL or Olivetti. In the consumer and industrial electronics sector, new entrants such as NEC, Toshiba and Fujitsu, straddle the divide between computers and electronics, but all share a common high degree of vertical integration, especially since NEC produced its own microprocessors. Amongst the companies dedicated primarily to the personal computer business, Apple showed the highest degree of integration in its activities, whilst a group of smaller competitors including Compaq followed in a further group with less integration and finally, the low integrated companies such as Osborne and Kaypro from the portable sector occupy another discrete group. The key message to come from these measures of strategic variables centres not so much upon whether one type of strategic position provided a greater source of competitive advantage, but on the fact that the industry now consisted of a much more widely varied group of competitors than in earlier stages of the newgame evolution. Indeed, membership of similar positions for the variables shown was no guarantee of success. One has only to look at the similarity of IBM and DEC, or between Compaq and Vector Graphic to see the differences in subsequent performance could not be accounted for by these factors. In addition, the broadening and inclusion of competitors from the computer and office products industries, together with the consumer electronics industry represented a harbinger of the fact that in time the personal computer industry would increasingly find its industry and market boundaries being drawn into, and attacked from these sectors.

Another set of strategic group variables are illustrated in Fig. 5.6 where the degree of technological innovation is related to the marketing power

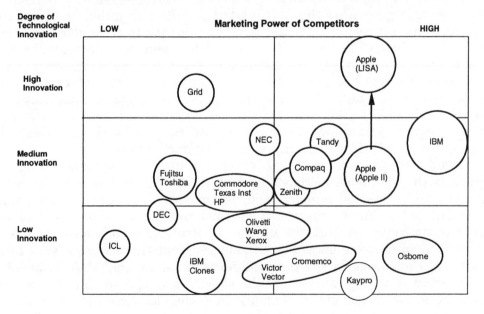

Fig. 5.6. Strategic groups by marketing power in personal computer business markets: 1983.

of the respective competitors around the period of 1983. The measure of technological innovation reflects the latest product that the company had developed in relation to the market in 1983. Thus Apple is seen as a high innovator, given the launch of its Lisa system, although it had moved from a more moderate level of innovation with its Apple II. Since, although at the time of its launch, the Apple II was relatively innovative, by 1983, this represented a mature technology. Along the horizontal axis is measured the degree of marketing power enjoyed by the competitor in the personal computer business marketplace. This is a fairly wide measure and although it reflects the scale of resources spent on advertising and promotional activities, it also incorporates the image of the company and its products as generally perceived by customers in this market. It is also a measure of the degree of differentiation the company created in terms of its product concepts. Thus Grid Computer was also a highly innovative company with its high performance portable computer system, based on proprietary technology. However, certain specifics about its operating concept were not readily adopted by the market and together with its relatively low promotional spend, the company was not so widely known outside its specialist niche market in the defence and government sectors.

What is interesting to note from Fig. 5.6 is that broadly speaking, those companies that developed relatively strong degrees of marketing power in this period, such as IBM, Apple, Tandy, Compaq and Zenith were the companies that went on to dominate the market by the late 1980s. The exception to this pattern being Osborne Computer, which failed due to reasons which are explained later. The clusters of companies such as the giants, Xerox, Wang and Olivetti, or Commodore, T.I. and H.P., together with smaller companies such as Victor Technologies, Vector Graphic and Cromemco, although successful up to this stage, increasingly thereafter found their fortunes declining. DEC is shown to have relatively low innovation in its personal computer products, but more importantly, its marketing power never really developed to the extent it had hoped at the time of its entry. According to field research, the problem for DEC, along with companies such as Wang and Xerox lay in internal politics, degrees of commitment and most importantly, the way in which the company and its personal computers were viewed by the business market, beyond their respective installed base of other electronic office and computer products.[29] Failure to make the transition from their established business sectors in computing and office products could possibly have therefore been due largely to a misunderstanding about the nature of the value chain involved in personal computers.

In particular, many of these larger companies were slow to appreciate the fact that although they were highly sophisticated in producing products, many of which were far more complex than personal computers, success in the business markets for personal computers ranging from the corporate to medium and small sized businesses was also dependent upon their competence in marketing activities. Many of them lacked the ability to project a powerful and differentiated image to these markets and to convince purchasers and users alike, that they would obtain better value from their products than from the competition. IBM achieved this without doubt on their initial PC, but failed with some later models. Apple had achieved this with their Apple II, but failed with the Lisa which was too expensive, yet succeeded in the long run with the Macintosh family. Osborne achieved this with its first machine as did Kaypro and Compaq. Tandy achieved this in the small and medium sized markets, but was unsuccessful with the same products in the corporate marketplace.

However, changes in the structure of value chains were not just a phenomenon driven by developments in technology or strategic thinking within the competing companies. As with all stages of a newgame industry's evolution they were also driven by significant changes that were taking place in the structure of the marketplace and amongst the behaviour of purchasers and users of personal computers. Indeed, the importance of these type of market conditions lay behind the need for competitors to increase their resources in marketing activities along their value chains. Therefore, the next section will move on to consider the nature of market conditions during the legitimisation stage, firstly looking at the overall structure and size of the market and then proceeding to consider the characteristics of the major emerging groups of business users.

MARKET CONDITIONS

Size, Structure and Growth

At the time of IBM's entry, an industry analyst forecast that unit shipments of desktop personal computers would grow at 60% annually from 1981 to 1983, with revenues growing at 40% for the same period.[30] The same report forecast numerous foreign vendors rushing into the market, such that their rate of growth in units would be 106% annually for 1981 to 1983. Given these types of forecast (which were typical for the period), it is not surprising that the forecasts became a self-fulfilling prophecy, at least in their effect of attracting a large number of entrants.

In terms of product segmentation, the market could be divided into five categories of machine or system type. These are illustrated in Table 5.3 which shows the number of models and unit shipments for the years 1982 and 1983, together with the growth in unit shipments between these two years. A number of important observations can be made from this data. Unlike in previous stages of the industry's evolution, the market had branched out from a basic single stand-alone desktop product into five categories. Firstly, there was the creation of two new product categories, namely, transportable computers and the smaller portable (notebook) computers.[31] However, overall the market was dominated by personal desktop computers with a substantial growth rate of 76% from an already large installed base. High-end machines[32] were enjoying a much faster growth rate, which reflected the improvements in technology and also the enormous demand for such products in the corporate business sector, which were the same reasons that accounted for the increase in the number of

Table 5.3. Worldwide personal computer market by system type: 1982 - 1983.

SYSTEM TYPE	NUMBER OF MODELS 1982	NUMBER OF MODELS 1983	UNIT SHIPMENTS 1982 (000's)	UNIT SHIPMENTS 1983 (000's)	GROWTH RATE 1982-1983
HIGH-END HOME COMPUTERS	2	8	215	680	215%
PORTABLE (NOTEBOOK) COMPUTERS	5	11	35	164	370%
TRANSPORTABLE (SAMPLE CASE) COMPUTERS	4	10	98	199	103%
PERSONAL (DESKTOP) COMPUTERS	38	48	1,550	2,735	76%
PROFESSIONAL (MULTI-TASK) COMPUTERS	2	5	2	90	N/M*
TOTAL: PERSONAL COMPUTERS	51	82	1,900	3,868	104%

* Not Meaningful

Source: InfoCorp Personal Computer Report, 1983, p.9.
Reproduced by permission of Computer Intelligence InfoCorp., © 1983.

multi-task professional computers. The data also highlights the rapid growth in demand and the increase in the number of notebook and transportable computers produced during this period.

Table 5.4. Estimated United States market for personal computers: 1977–1984.

		1977	1978	1979	1980	1981	1982	1983	1984
UNIT SHIPMENTS	(Thousands)	41.0	120.7	181.2	246.1	380.0	792.4	1,764	3,324
IF-SOLD-VALUE	($M)	74.5	223.8	302.5	495.0	926.9	2002.3	4,718	8,958
AVERAGE SELLING PRICE	(000's)	1.82	1.85	1.67	2.01	2.44	2.53	2.68	2.69
YEAR-END UNIT INSTALLED BASE	(Millions)	0.048	0.169	0.346	0.583	0.947	1.711	3.418	6.617
PORTION OF WORLDWIDE UNIT CONSUMPTION	(%)	85.4	66.0	64.5	56.7	52.2	52.1	51.2	50.8

Note: The 1983 and 1984 figures in italics are forecasts made in 1983, the remaining figures are estimated actuals.

Source: Extracts taken from Dataquest, 14 Oct 1983, SCIS. Vol II.
Reproduced by permission of Dataquest, Inc., © 1983.

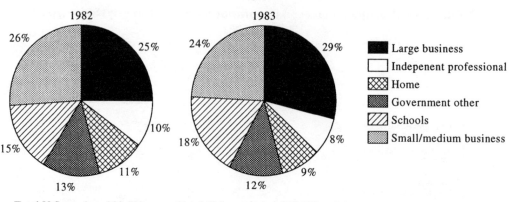

Total U.S. market: 880,000   Total U.S. market: 1,930,000 units

Source: InfoCorp Personal Computer Report, 1983, p.12.
Reproduced by permission of Computer Intelligence InfoCorp., © 1983.

Fig. 5.7. United States personal computer market purchases by customer type, $1,000-$5,999 price segment: 1982 - 1983.

To appreciate just how much the market had changed from 1977 to 1983, Table 5.4 illustrates the trends and forecasts for the size of the personal computer market for the period, from which it can be seen that instead of the 48,000 units estimated as installed in 1977, by the end of 1981 there were an estimated 947,000[33] desktop personal computers installed in the United States, which were expected to triple to over 3.4 million units by the end of 1983. During the same period of the legitimisation stage, the value of units sold was to quadruple. This explosion in the size of the market was largely accounted for by the enormous demand for IBM and IBM compatible personal computers in the corporate and small to medium sized business segments. This pattern is illustrated in Fig. 5.7, where in 1982 and 1983 it can be seen that purchases of personal computers in the $1000 to $5999 price range were dominated by large businesses, independent professionals and small to medium sized businesses.

The growth in unit sales of these categories of machine both in the United States market and worldwide is shown in Table 5.5, which segments the overall market into four price bands. At the low-end were units priced below $1000 for products which were aimed mainly at the home consumer marketplace, whilst at the high-end, products priced over $5999 included small business multi-user systems, with the majority of machines being sold in the $1000 to $5999 range, which were mainly for the large corporation, independent professional and small business user groups. Thus during the legitimisation stage, these three groups grew to represent some sixty one per cent of the market. Given their dominance of the market, it is important to understand some of the characteristics of the two business user groups.

Table 5.5. Personal computer market by price segment: 1982 - 1983.

PRICE CLASS	WORLDWIDE		U.S.	
	1982	1983	1982	1983
	(000's)	(000's)	(000's)	(000's)
$500 - $999	245	840	155	510
$1,000-$2,999	1,155	1,750	625	1,085
$3,000-$5,999	545	1,300	255	845
SUBTOTAL UNDER $6,000	1,945	3,890	1,035	2,440
$6,000-$24,999	288	340	180	227
TOTAL: ALL MICROSYSTEM UNITS	2,233	4,230	1,215	2,667

Source: InfoCorp Personal Computer Report, 1983, p.5.
Reproduced by permission of Computer Intelligence InfoCorp., © 1983.

Types of Customer

The Office User

During the growth stage, Apple, Tandy and other competitors had been successful in selling a limited number of their personal computers into the corporate or large business segments, consisting of the Fortune 1000 and their non-manufacturing equivalents. Fig. 5.8 compares the marketing, sales and distribution channels used by industry leaders Tandy and Apple, prior to the entry of the giants, for accessing and penetrating the corporate segment. Sales were made mainly via local dealers to individuals who were able to purchase a personal computer on their departmental budgets. Many managers and professionals had turned to personal computers during the growth period (particularly after the launch of spreadsheet programs and improved word processing packages), in order to provide data handling facilities at the local level. As a result, many DP[34]/MIS[35] managers in large organisations had no idea of the range of brands of personal computers being used by employees within their respective organisations. Whilst personal computers remained limited in their performance capabilities there was no problem, but from 1979 onwards their growth accelerated rapidly, so that both DP and senior financial executives became alarmed at the loss of control and costs involved in this area of resource allocation. The entry of IBM further exacerbated the situation, but also provided a catalyst for change, which would work against the incumbents in favour of the new larger entrants. Companies such as IBM, DEC and Wang started selling personal computers directly to their large corporate accounts and switched the focus of marketing to the DP or MIS department.

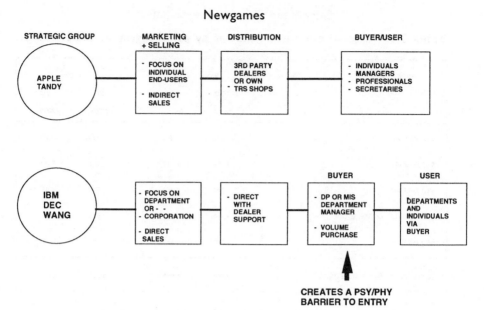

Source: J. W. Steffens, 'Entry Behaviour and Competition in the Evolution of the United States Personal Computer Industry (1975-1983)', unpublished doctoral thesis, The University of London, 1988.

Fig. 5.8. Creation of barriers in the corporate segment: 1981-1983.

The advantage to the large corporation was that it could now start to bring the purchase and diffusion of personal computers under some form of control and hence begin to plan more carefully how to incorporate personal computers into the corporate data/information system. The net effect was that a major barrier was raised against the smaller incumbent firms such as Tandy and Apple, whose machines were not always considered on their own merits, but in the context of their compatibility with the mainframe computer system used by the client corporation. In effect, both Apple and Tandy had to establish a team of direct salespersons (new costs), which needed training for representing the companies on a National Accounts programme. Furthermore, they then had to overcome the psychological barriers encountered amongst DP and MIS managers, who needed convincing as to why they should consider switching from their mainframe supplier. Given the scale of these barriers, many of the smaller incumbents chose to avoid the corporate market segment and concentrate instead on the small business sector, but this too proved to have its own new set of problems.

The Small Business User

Some estimates suggested that by 1986 small businesses and professionals such as dentists, lawyers, doctors and writers would buy over 2.4 million personal computers, worth approximately $4.4 billion.[36] Such projections intimated that small business/professional sales would pass corporate sales by 1984. Given the enormous potential forecast demand, many of the smaller entrants and incumbents in 1981 chose to focus their resources in this segment, in particular, Northstar, NEC, Victor and Fortune. What distinguished the existing and potential structure of the small business/professional segment from the corporate segment was the variety of sub-segments and vertical markets. This feature offered the ex-ante possibility for the smaller competitors to pursue a successful niche strategy, away from the direct competition of the giants.

This perception reflected a key difference between the corporate market segment and the small business/professional segment. The corporate sector machine was dependent upon improving productivity in generic functions such as word processing, spreadsheet analysis and specific accounting tasks. In theory, what was good for Exxon would also be good for Ford or General Electric. The key to success rested upon being able to offer effective and price-competitive software. For the reasons identified earlier, the "software circle" dictated that those personal computers capable of generating a large installed base were most likely to attract the best software developers, namely, IBM and the larger competitors.

In contrast, the small business/professional segment offered the opportunity for considerable vertical market segmentation. In addition to the more generic software packages for word processing or spreadsheet analysis, many smaller personal computer manufacturers saw an opportunity to market their personal computers as systems, made up of their hardware and specialised applications software. Thus, a number of the smaller competitors focused their systems on providing support for specific industry sectors, such as travel agents, hoteliers or estate agents, together with professionals such as dentists and doctors. This strategic development led to increased segmentation in the user market for small businesses and professionals.

Creation of Portables

The entry of Osborne Computer with the Osborne 1 "transportable" computer in March 1981 led to the creation of a new product-market segment. During the following two years, the portable computer market divided into three distinct segments, and sales grew to more than $250 million, with a number of new entrants following Osborne into the market. Osborne became the established market leader, only to become subject to Chapter 11 of the United States bankruptcy code by the summer of 1983, for reasons that are described later in this chapter.

The worldwide number of shipments for portable computers during the period of March 1981 to mid-1983 was estimated to grow from 8000 units to 400,000 units.[37] The fast growth resulted from two developments:

(1) the increased usage of computers by managers and professionals who spent much of their time away from the office;

(2) the growing number of applications that were being identified by both vendors and users as suitable areas for use of a portable computer as an intelligence-gathering and transmission device. Normally, such applications fell into

dedicated vertical markets such as salesmen or on-site stock control analysis.

However, IDC (International Data Corporation) noted in their mid-1983 report on Personal 'Computer Markets' that based on a survey of personal computer users, the majority of users of portables did not use the system as a portable computer. Instead the early success was resultant as much, if not more, from the pricing and packaging as from any greater need for portable computing.[38] In addition, despite such spectacular performances, the period up to the end of 1983 merely represented the early stage of this segment's development. Table 5.6 shows the actual and forecast growth in the market. Although even at this early stage, certain features of this segment were becoming clear factors necessary for success. These included capabilities in rapid technological innovation in display and component technologies; low cost, high volume manufacturing capabilities; IBM PC-DOS compatibility and powerful communications capabilities.

The Portable Segment

As already mentioned, the development of portable personal computers created a new market segment, which in the long-term was expected to experience significant growth and attract many vendors as illustrated in Table 5.6. The first year of the market's existence was dominated by Osborne Computer's machine, whilst in 1982 the market grew ten-fold as other entrants entered the competition. However, in the short term the actual rate of market growth was constrained by a number of factors.

First of all, it should be recognised that the products offered during the early first half of the 1980s were really somewhat limited in their

Table 5.6. United States portable computer shipments in US$ and units: 1981 - 1986.

YEAR	UNIT SHIPMENTS	GROWTH RATE	AVERAGE PRICE	REVENUES US$ M
1981	8,000		$1800	$14.4
1982	95,000	1090%	$1800	$171.9
1983	191,500	100%	$1650	$316.0
1984	344,700	80%	$1400	$482.6
1985	620,500	80%	$1150	$713.6
1986	1,116,800	80%	$900	$1005.1
CUM. AVERAGE GROWTH	168%	—	-15%	134%

Note: Actual figures in Normal Typeface. Forecast figures at the time of 1983 in italics.

Source: Yankee Group Report, p.128.
Reproduced by permission of Yankee Group., © 1983.

performance and characteristics since they suffered severe technological limitations, some of which were described earlier in this chapter. As illustrated in Table 5.6 portable computers were not low priced machines and therefore, their appeal was restricted mainly to specialised niches within the business segment. Secondly, most of the early vendors were new start-up companies, whose marketing power and in some instances, planning capabilities were somewhat limited. Furthermore, these small companies made use of the same distribution channels as the larger and more established desktop personal computer manufacturers and therefore had to fight hard to gain shelf-space. Moreover, the margins available were slim due to the high costs of producing smaller sized units and unless significant volumes could be generated, sustained profitability was difficult to achieve. In addition, the marketing window for the earliest entrants was relatively short and before long, some of the larger companies such as IBM and the Japanese, launched competitive products that further disrupted the conditions of competition.

The Handheld Segment

The handheld computer market evolved as an outgrowth of the calculator market. Specifically, handhelds emerged from a particular segment of the calculator market, namely, the programmable calculator market in which 600,000 units were shipped in 1981. The major applications of handhelds were in laboratory monitoring, engineering and data collection in business markets. At the time, it appeared that the handheld was gradually displacing the programmable calculator market, which had strategic implications for the incumbents in this sector.

Handheld portable computers had started to be marketed by Tandy and Sharp during the growth stage of the industry in 1980. However, the market started to develop rapidly from 1981 onwards as illustrated in Table

Table 5.7. United States handheld computer shipments in US$ and units (000's): 1981 - 1986.

YEAR	TOTAL UNITS (000's)	MACHINES (US$ M)	AVERAGE PRICE	PERIPHERALS (US$ M)
1981	52	$11.4	$219.75	$5.3
1982	162	$35.6	$219.75	$17.1
1983	335	$63.6	$189.85	$31.8
1984	608	$103.3	$169.95	$56.8
1985	1102	$176.1	$159.80	$105.7
1986	2000	$300.0	$150.00	$195.0
CUM. AVG. GROWTH	107%	92%	-8%	106%

Source: Yankee Group Report 1983, p.110.
Reproduced by permission of Yankee Group., © 1983.

5.7, growing from $11 million to $63 million in 1983. Furthermore, estimates suggested the market could grow to around $300 million by 1986. Priced at around $200 the handheld computer was distinct, in terms of prices and features, from other types of portable computer. Nevertheless the importance of the handheld computer was not so much in its immediate relationship to other systems, but more in its potential to represent a realistic platform for entry into the portable or even the desktop computer market. This was especially true, given the fact, that handheld computers were being used increasingly in business applications and were potentially of great interest to Japanese consumer electronics companies.

Overall, the conditions in the personal computer market changed dramatically during the legitimisation stage with rapid growth in the business sectors. It witnessed the development of new product groups, in the form of high-end machines and portables. Segmentation of the market by price and user group suggested that the corporate, professional and small to medium sized business sectors were growing rapidly in the aftermath of the entry of IBM and major players. In turn, the patterns of purchase and role of the personal computer was taking on a significant position in user companies. Thus the market was now moving from a relatively uncomplicated environment to one of increasing complexity and rapid change. Having now seen the nature of technological developments, patterns of strategic groups and market evolution, it is now appropriate to proceed to look at how the strategies and performance of the major competitors developed during the entry of the giants and legitimisation stage.

COMPETITION AND MARKET PERFORMANCE

As was shown earlier, the legitimisation stage was divided into two phases. The first witnessed the entry of a number of companies, including two competitors, namely, IBM and Osborne Computer whose entries represented newgame strategies that dramatically changed the conditions of competition in specific sectors of the industry. The second phase followed about eighteen months later, when the industry experienced substantial competition in response to the impact of IBM and Osborne Computer.

This section will therefore look at examples of strategies pursued by some of the competitors during both periods and try to identify the features that distinguish the failures from the success stories. Five different types of competitive strategy are illustrated in Table 5.8, which highlights the strategic elements applicable to each. These include the Innovator, Leader, Look-Alike, Speciality and the Installed Base. For clarity, the first part of this section will look at the strategies surrounding the giants and the response of the incumbents, before moving on to consider Osborne Computer's strategy and its role in stimulating the creation of the portable computer market.

During late 1979 and 1980, the increasing success of companies such as Apple, Tandy, Commodore and others, together with the entry of Texas

Table 5.8. Competitive strategies in the personal computer industry during the legitimisation stage.

TYPE OF STRATEGY	STRATEGY ELEMENTS				
	PRODUCT DEVELOPMENT	MARKETING	DISTRIBUTION	PRICING	RISKS
INNOVATOR e.g. Apple 'Lisa"	Define New Product Class	High Advertising, Front-End Investment	Selective or Broad Coverage	Target Level, Minimal Discounting	No Market, Miss Window, Requires Changing People's Behaviour - Expensive
LEADER e.g. IBM-'PC'	Conservative within the Product Class	Follow-Through Economies of Scale	Selective, Control and Co-operation	Competitive, No Open Discounting	Potential Product and Image Impact
LOOK-ALIKE e.g. Kaypro to Osborne Franklin Ace to Apple II	Identifiable Improvements, Quality	Follow-On Innovative Products	Intensive Distribution	Aggressive Pricing, with Perceived Value and Quality	Leader Moves, Inadequate Resources
SPECIALITY e.g. Cromemco or Convergent Technology	Leading-Edge within Class	Identifiable, Accessible Customer Prospects	Direct, Representatives, Limited Nos. Dealers	High Margin Pricing	Not Differentiated, Over-Designed Product
INSTALLED BASE e.g. Apple IIe	Improvement of Old Product	Reliability, Proven Features	Committed and Loyal Dealers	Aggressive Pricing Against New Technology	Quick Product Obsolescence

Instruments and Hewlett Packard began to be viewed as an important strategic issue for major competitors in the computer and office products industries and led to many of them making a subsequent entry during 1981 to 1984. Although some of their characteristics can be mapped on to strategic group maps that might suggest similarities and differences in their behaviour, in fact, the strategies of each company also had a high degree of uniqueness. What this section will try to illustrate therefore is how these unique features came into play and largely determined their relative performance in the personal computer industry.

Earlier it was shown that the overall market for personal computers continued to grow apace during the legitimisation stage. In Table 5.9, the relative market shares of the leading U.S. competitors in the U.S. market are therefore illustrated during the period 1980 to 1982. The data highlights a number of changes. Firstly, Apple took the market lead from Tandy in 1981, but was rapidly challenged for this position by IBM. Commodore lost significant market share during the period, whilst HP and Zenith/Heathkit both declined in their respective market positions. Franklin represented an Apple II clone that enjoyed reasonable success after its entry in 1982. Xerox Corporation went into rapid decline in this business after its entry in 1981, whilst Osborne Computer enjoyed significant growth during the first two years of its business.

Naturally, the data in Table 5.9 is highly generalised, although it does provide some insight into the key patterns and trends at the time. Table 5.10 highlights the fact that the competitive position of these and other competitors tended to vary considerably between two price bands that had emerged in the market at this time. The lower band consisted of machines in the $1000 to $2999 range, whilst the upper were in the $3000 to $5999 range. Data from this table will be referred to during the following discussion of the various competitors' strategies.

Table 5.9. Estimated United States market shares of leading personal computer competitors: 1980 - 1982.

	Percent of Units Shipped			Percent of If-Sold-Value		
	1980	1981	1982	1980	1981	1982
Apple	29.27	41.00	28.44	33.80	41.20	26.99
IBM	0.00	5.01	22.18	0.00	7.09	27.16
Tandy/Radio Shack	37.60	22.52	10.10	23.60	14.78	10.39
Osborne	0.00	1.42	8.17	0.00	1.04	5.97
Hewlett-Packard	5.28	6.06	4.65	11.49	11.20	5.42
Commodore	15.85	10.63	3.58	13.29	8.59	2.88
Franklin	0.00	0.00	2.50	0.00	0.00	2.23
XEROX	0.00	3.94	2.45	0.00	5.65	2.66
Zenith/Heathkit	1.87	1.71	1.03	3.00	2.35	1.53
Others	10.13	7.71	16.90	14.82	8.10	14.77
Total	100.00	100.00	100.00	100.00	100.00	100.00

Source: Dataquest Incorporated, *SCIS* Volume II, 29 July 1983.
Reproduced by permission of Dataquest, Inc., © 1983.

Table 5.10. United States personal computer market estimated unit shipments by leading vendors: 1982 - 1983.

COMPANY	MODELS		TOTAL 1982	MARKET SHARE	HALF 1983	TOTAL 1983	MARKET SHARE
$1000-$2999	PRICE RANGE:						
APPLE	IIe		350	30%	330	800	46%
TANDY	III/4		180	15%	110	250	14%
NEC	PC-8000		200	17%	90	160	9%
H-P	80 Series	}	43	4%	38	90	5%
	120 Series	}					
NON-LINEAR	KAYPRO-11/4		20	2%	40	80	5%
OSBORNE	O-1	}	73	6%	27	75	4%
	EXEC	}					
HITACHI	MBE/6000	}	66	6%	35	70	4%
	BM3	}					
COMMODORE	P-Series	}	103	9%	34	62	4%
	B-Series	}					
FRANKLIN	ACE		20	2%	20	40	2%
OTHERS			100	9%		123	7%
TOTALS			**1,155**	**100%**	**724**	**1,750**	**100%**
$3000-$5999	PRICE RANGE:						
IBM	PC	}	180	33%	200	550	42%
	XT	}					
DIGITAL	RAINBOW	}	0	0%	40	102	8%
	PROFESS	}					
VICTOR	9000		19	3%	30	80	6%
FUJITSU	MICRO-8		80	15%	30	60	5%
OLIVETTI	M-20		29	5%	23	55	4%
TANDY	11/2		32	6%	20	50	4%
APPLE	III		28	5%	18	40	3%
SHARP	MZ-80	}	52	9%	21	37	3%
	XY3200	}					
NON-LINEAR	KAYPRO-10		0	0%	5	35	3%
WANG	PROFESS		5	1%	11	30	2%
ZENITH	Z100		3	1%	11	30	2%
OKI	PC		25	5%	12	25	2%
TEXAS INST.	PROFESS		0	0%	6	25	2%
OTHERS			92	17%	73	181	14%
TOTALS			**545**	**100%**	**500**	**1,300**	**100%**

Source: Adapted from InfoCorp Personal Computer Report, pp.7-8.
Reproduced by permission of Computer Intelligence InfoCorp., © 1983.

The Xerox Strategy: A Case of Mistaken Identity

Xerox was the first of the major competitors to lead the entry of the giants at the beginning of the legitimisation stage and illustrates an example of a strategy that was less than successful.[39] However, what is most surprising about the Xerox entry, is that ex ante, Xerox actually looked as though it had the potential to be a winner, that was until implementation issues became a problem. In essence, Xerox intended to

expand its efforts to tackle the corporate U.S. market for office automation
by launching a personal computer ahead of IBM that made use of the
existing industry operating standard of CP/M-80 and to allow the machine,
known as the Xerox 820 to be linked to other desktop units by means of
Ethernet,[40] which was the Xerox developed local area network. What is
surprising in this decision, was the fact that Xerox had developed an
advanced workstation, known as the "Star" in the late 1970s which
incorporated a number of the "user-friendly" features that were to be
adopted by Apple Computer a few years later, when it launched its Lisa
machine, the forerunner to the Macintosh family. However, the "Star" was
priced at around $15,000 and Xerox needed a personal computer that could
be priced competitively against the Apple II machines, that were becoming
the most popular form of personal computer amongst professionals in
corporate locations, prior to the entry of IBM. Thus Xerox chose to launch
a product, that was essentially "me-too" in nature, with little technical
differentiation.

Yet although the Xerox 820 had little technical advantage, Xerox itself
believed it could gain competitive advantage in other areas, not available
at the time to the established competitors such as Apple, Tandy, Commodore
and others. In production, Xerox knew it could compete as a low cost
manufacturer, given its experience in its other products such as copiers
and typewriters. Where it believed its greatest strength resided however,
was in marketing activities. The Xerox brand name and image was well
known and respected in corporate America and the company had a
substantial direct sales force and field service support staff. Thus, so the
theory went, if Xerox (with its significantly larger resources than companies
such as Apple or Tandy) launched a personal computer targeted at the
corporate market, then with sufficient promotional and selling effort it
was expected to become a significant success. Further market development
was planned through the existing chain of Xerox Stores into the small
and medium sized business segments.

However, in practice a number of things did not fall into place. To
begin with, by the time Xerox launched in June 1981, it was barely two
months ahead of the planned launch by IBM, thus its window of opportunity
was limited. Xerox also faced a problem in identifying and choosing the
appropriate decision makers in large corporations. Traditionally, it had
sold its copiers and typewriters to office managers, purchasing managers
and those responsible for office supplies. Now it was trying to sell computers
to corporations, which needed to develop relations with a completely new
group, namely, the DP and MIS management. These people were used
to dealing with the established computer companies and to make matters
worse, in 1981, most of them did not want to know about personal
computers. Finally, for reasons that were as much political as anything
else, the planned advertising and promotion budget was dramatically
reduced a few months before launch, so that the company was unable to
make the kind of impact that IBM enjoyed a few months later. The net
effect, was that although Xerox entered the personal computer market,

it failed to make the impact necessary to become an established player. After the entry of IBM and its subsequent impact upon industry standards, Xerox rapidly found itself with a somewhat obsolete product. Lack of commitment to the market by failure to rapidly develop a competitive machine to IBM, together with its sale of the Xerox stores in 1983 meant that the company was unable to gain significant market share. This poor performance was illustrated previously in Table 5.9, where it can be seen that its market share declined after its first year of entry and significantly undersold the levels of production.

The IBM Strategy: A Leader in the Industry

A few months after the entry of Xerox, and in complete contrast, IBM's entry was a significant success. As shown in Table 5.9, its overall share increased from approximately 5 to 22 per cent during its second year in the market. As far as price position, the IBM PC dominated the $3000 to $5999 price range as illustrated in Table 5.10 which reflects the enormous market share the IBM PC had gained in this sector by 1982 and which was further increased to 42 per cent in 1983. Interestingly, IBM's strategy for its personal computer represented a complete departure from its traditional practices. The company chose to utilise a high degree of factoring, both in supply of hardware components, peripherals and software, as well as in selling and distribution. The company adopted a low cost leadership position by establishing a highly automated, high-volume assembly plant which provided significant economies of scale. This immediately reduced average unit costs for similar performance machines in the industry. By adopting an "open architecture",[41] IBM encouraged third-party software houses to carry the cost and risk of software development, but by using an 8/16 bit processor with 256K RAM it offered the opportunity for higher performance software to be developed and hence set a trend towards 16-bit applications software.

By collaboration with Microsoft, IBM introduced and effectively endorsed a new operating system, PC-DOS, to challenge the development of CP/M as the major operating system on the new generation of 16-bit based machines. Although IBM's price point was higher than the Apple II for a basic unit, in the case of a fully configured system the difference was marginal. IBM positioned its PC for both the large corporate sector and smaller business user and offered a different marketing mix for each. In so doing, it launched a direct attack against the major incumbents, Tandy and Apple, the key points of which are illustrated in Fig. 5.9.

In the case of the corporate segment, the company made use of bulk discounting in an effort to switch the purchasing channel from individual users to corporate buyers — most usually, managers of data processing or MIS departments. It was in this activity that IBM effectively legitimised the personal computer in the minds of data processing managers in large organisations. In so doing, IBM broke down a major psychological marketing barrier, namely the attitude that had existed within many DP departments

	SEMICONDUCTOR MICRO-PROCESSOR	OPERATING SYSTEM	APPLICATIONS SOFTWARE	MARKETING	DISTRIBUTION	POST-SALES SERVICE	BUYER	USER
APPLE II	8-bit MOS 6502	Appledos CP/M-80	3rd Party Largest Base Apple II (emulation)	Corporate - Individuals	3rd Party Dealers	3rd Party Contractors		Individual managers and professionals purchasing on departmental budgets for
APPLE III	8-bit MOS 6502A	Appledos CP/M-80						own use
TANDY								
TRS-80 II	8-bit Z-80A	TRS DOS	Internal Restricted Base	Small Cos. - Individuals	Tandy Computer Stores	In-House		
TRS-80 III	8-bit Z-80A	CP/M-80						
IBM PC	8-bit INTEL 8088	CP/M-80 PC-DOS	3rd Party Strong Support (Open Architecture)	Corporate - DP Mgrs - Direct Sales Small Cos. - Snr Mgrs - Heavy Adv - Heavy Prom	- Direct - 3rd Party Dealers	- 3rd Party Contractors	CORP: DP Managers for corporate scale purchase and volume discounts. SMALL COS: Financial and Senior Managers	
COMPETITIVE IMPACT OF IBM	FASTER AND BETTER PRICE PERFORMANCE	EASIER AND MORE POWERFUL O/S	RAPID MOVE FROM CP/M TO PC DOS AS INDUSTRY STANDARD	RAISED MAJOR COST BARRIERS FOR: - DIRECT SALES - ADVERTISING - PR	RAISED THE INDUSTRY STANDARDS - CREATED SHELF SPACE PRICE WAR		REMOVED CORP. DP RESISTANCE TO PC'S RAISED PSYCHOLOGICAL BARRIER AGAINST NON-IBM MACHINES	

Fig. 5.9. IBM's newgame strategy and attack on industry leaders, Tandy and Apple.

Source: J. W. Steffens, 'Entry Behaviour and Competition in the Evolution of the United States Personal Computer Industry (1975-1983)', unpublished doctoral thesis, The University of London, 1988.

that personal computers were an unfortunate nuisance and certainly not part of the corporate management information system. It should be pointed out that IBM's market power in the corporate DP world was reflected by the fact that in 1981, IBM still delivered sixty-one per cent[42] of the worldwide general purpose shipments for mainframes within large organisations. Thus development in communications for networking personal computers to one another and linking up to mainframes meant that IBM was in a position to offer a product that could be maintained and serviced under the same organisation as that which handled the large corporation's mainframe systems. As data processing managers saw that the potential improvements in technology could lead to personal computers becoming high performance intelligent workstations, then their acceptance of an IBM personal computer developed rapidly. As such, this represented an acknowledgement by DP personnel that it was only a matter of time before personal computers were to become integral units within the corporation's management information systems. Interestingly, although IBM broke down the psychological marketing barrier with DP managers, they also created a new marketing barrier that was initially to IBM's advantage. This involved the fact that the same DP managers who used IBM mainframes, although now willing to accept IBM PC's, were still somewhat wary of non-IBM equipment, unless it was one hundred per cent compatible.

Once IBM personal computers had been launched, their penetration of the corporate market was so fast that IBM were unable to supply sufficient quantities to satisfy total levels of customer demand for approximately eighteen months. This opened an opportunity for a number of small start-up companies to develop IBM clones (look-alikes) which were claimed to be able to run IBM software. Furthermore, many subsequent entrants and incumbents moved towards developing IBM compatible machines. Hence, the rapid development of a large customer base, together with the forecast penetration of IBM into the small business market, had the effect of creating an industry standard — namely the IBM PC-DOS family. In addition, IBM also raised the physical marketing barriers in the corporate segment through the use of their expensive, yet already established direct sales force.

Within the small to medium business segments, IBM affected the standards and structure of the indirect channels of distribution. Strategically, the personal computer was the first product (excluding turnkey systems)[43] to be sold directly to customers by non-IBM personnel. However, IBM were keen to ensure they maintained control over the standards and hence the image of their company projected by dealers in the retail sector. Given that there were no shortage of dealers willing to stock the IBM PC, IBM was able to sign up dealers under its own terms and conditions. Dealers were required to demonstrate sufficient capital base for security, minimal facilities (both for maintenance and selling floor space), to achieve certain target sales, etc. In addition, IBM insisted on attendance at IBM in-house training courses on small business management and sales techniques. In effect, IBM set the quality control standards similar to those introduced by major franchise dealers such as Computerland. However, as a result of their entry into this segment, standards within dealer distribution channels showed a marked improvement towards a more professional style and approach.

A further effect was that as IBM continued to gain market share in the small business segment, the battle for shelf space intensified amongst the second level suppliers. Whereas prior to IBM's entry, manufacturers had generally been able to control discount level, post-IBM conditions forced many companies to accept lower margins in order to gain shelf-space. Yet another feature of IBM's entry strategy was the fact that its advertising expenditure during the initial launch period was greater than the total budget for all other manufacturers during the previous year. Hence, the cost of maintaining a distinctive image was greatly increased as other entrants and incumbents imitated IBM. This in turn created a rising cost spiral for the industry, as companies fought through increasing advertising budgets to overcome the "noise" level in an effort to both inform and differentiate their respective products.

The pull-through effect of IBM's advertising, together with the power of its corporate image, significantly stimulated both demand and awareness of personal computers. The corporate image was managed in such a way that it maintained the air of confidence associated with the large multinational, yet at the same time cultivated an image to portray a "caring" giant. The clever use of the "Charlie Chaplin" lookalike in its advertising appealed to the general public, conveying a product that was user-friendly, easy to use, productive and yet backed by the world's acknowledged leading computer company.

Most of all, IBM's entry strategy moved the personal computer into the minds of both corporate buyers and the general public. By well-orchestrated technology, production and marketing strategies, IBM gained rapid market penetration and significantly expanded the business market segments. At the same time, IBM broadened the critical factors for success from being mainly product and distribution issues to include higher standards of distribution, larger scales of advertising and promotion and direct selling. In so doing, new market and mobility barriers were raised, whilst at the same time increasing the segmentation of the market.

Finally, IBM, especially in the corporate sector, began to redefine the nature of the personal computer. As the personal computer was linked to mainframe computers or clustered[44] in networks, it ceased to be a stand-alone machine or system. Rather, it was becoming an integrated component with flexible software-driven functions within corporate information systems. As such, it was no longer marketed merely as a computer, but as a productivity tool, designed to provide solutions and to be incorporated into much larger systems. In so doing, IBM extended the personal computer industry upwards into the much larger electronic office products (office automation)[45] industry, which effectively stimulated a response from many of the other large established communications and data processing companies active in the wider industry arena of information systems' suppliers.

Follower Strategies: Wang and DEC

Although the various effects of IBM's strategy took some time to work their way through the industry, nevertheless, the following eighteen months witnessed a number of strategic developments amongst competitors in response to IBM. These included further entry by giant companies such as DEC and Wang Laboratories together with new product launches amongst the leading incumbents. That IBM should decide to enter the personal computer industry took few incumbents by surprise. What did surprise many was the scale, style and pace of entry, together with the resultant rate of market penetration.

Wang Laboratories launched its personal computer in May 1982 and represented the most focused strategy of the giants. This involved the introduction of a 16-bit machine which included in-house design of hardware and software, together with product positioning which was primarily limited to Fortune 1000 accounts. The product was supported at the same level as other Wang office computers and peripherals and it could also form part of Wang's local area office network. The Wang PC was therefore an integral part of its office products range of equipment for use by its installed base of users. At the same time it provided an entry point for new customers. However, Wang never really appeared to significantly expand its personal computer sales beyond its established customer base. In particular it experienced some problems in its sales force organisation and pricing policy, together with a lack of strong commitment to a broad base of dealer channels. It was also subject to a limited range of general software in its earliest machines. Taken together, it appears that these conditions could account for why Wang's PC did not filter down to the lower price band segments. Therefore, after some unsuccessful attempts to broaden its market base, Wang ended up pursuing a speciality position linked to its installed base, with relatively limited commitment to developing or supporting markets outside this domain. In this respect, Wang's PC strategy could therefore be viewed as primarily defensive and in practice turned out to be somewhat less effective. In terms of performance, Wang never gained more than 2 per cent market share in the $3000 to $5999 price range as already illustrated in Table 5.10.

Although Wang's commitment to personal computers waned and ebbed, the second largest computer company in the world at the time, namely DEC, was determined to ensure that IBM would be given some serious competition in the corporate market for personal computers. However, whilst starting with high ambitions and although more successful than Xerox or Wang, DEC's strategy also suffered from a number of problems in the implementation process. These were created by some of the following factors. Firstly, in launching three personal computers simultaneously, there was a feeling amongst selected analysts that many potential buyers were possibly confused by the positioning of the company's respective products. The company then ran into serious delays in delivery of announced software, which caused frustration and disenchantment amongst dealers and customers. On all its models, DEC charged a price premium, which although acceptable to its corporate user base, failed to be justified in the small business and professional user segments. Lastly, and very significantly, DEC's ambitions included substantial inroads into the indirect sales and distribution channels for access to the small business and professional market. However, in these market segments its brand name was not so well known as IBM and consequently DEC had a very difficult time trying to overcome the psychological barrier that this represented. Unlike Xerox, however, DEC maintained a consistent and long-term perspective on its presence in this market. It gained considerable economies of scale in manufacturing production costs and obtained strong loyalty from a large installed corporate base willing to buy its machines. In addition, the company launched innovative products in terms of technical performance and ergonomic design. In terms of performance, the combined market share of the Rainbow and Professional reached 8 per cent in the $3000 to $5999 market. Although many of these sales were to DEC's large installed base of existing customers, nevertheless in mid-1983, most industry observers felt that once it expanded its software base, then DEC's performance would improve significantly, especially given its international scale of operations. However, as things turned out, DEC was not to be so fortunate.

Response of the Incumbents: Apple, Tandy and Commodore

Whilst Xerox, Wang Laboratories and DEC were making their efforts to capture a share of the personal computer market, the incumbents in the industry responded to IBM's entry with a number of new product launches, which brought mixed results.

At the time of IBM's entry, Apple was overall market leader, but based its income largely on one product family, namely the Apple II, which after seven years, was moving towards the end of its product life-cycle. Since its Apple III had faced serious problems in its introduction, the product had lost dealer support and credibility in the market and hence was no match for the IBM PC. However, although Apple was still a small company, it had raised $82.8 million in a stock offering during 1980, so that the company was able to undertake extensive R&D activity. Using these funds Apple's product response to the IBM PC rested on technological innovation in both hardware and software. Time taken to develop the technology meant that the product was somewhat later in its launch during early 1983 than the response of the other major incumbents. However, when it arrived, the Lisa represented a step change in product technology as outlined earlier. Initially, Apple positioned the Lisa squarely to challenge IBM in the corporate marketplace and to develop its penetration through its national accounts sales force. However, since there was little software available and the price was nearly three times as high as the IBM machine, its technological differences were initially too highly priced for the market.

Yet although not in itself particularly successful in terms of sales, the importance of the Lisa was that it formed the technological platform for Apple to subsequently develop and launch its highly successful Macintosh family of computers.

On the surface, Apple's performance was the best of all three major incumbents during this period. As was shown in Table 5.9, the company maintained high growth in earnings and took over leadership of the small business market segment in 1982 from Tandy. Most of Apple's sales were generated by its Apple II and Apple IIe machines, which dominated the $1000 to $2999 market as illustrated in Table 5.10. Sales for 1983 were expected to reach $1 billion, yet strategically the company was in a critical position. Given its own success with the Apple II and IIe, Apple was the natural target for IBM. During 1982, the relative failure of the Apple III in the small business/professional segment is illustrated in Table 5.10, where it can be seen that in the $3000 to $5999 range the sales actually declined from 5 to 3 per cent between 1982 and 1983. Given this performance, the need to penetrate the corporate market stimulated Apple's response. Although Apple's immediate strength lay in its installed base of users and wide range of software, together with a loyal and well-established dealer network, these were not advantages with sufficient value on which to base all its future growth and development. Apple believed it therefore needed an innovative and broader range of products, together with more extensive market presence.

For these reasons, the company appointed a new president to lead the battle against IBM, namely, John Sculley, who came with extensive marketing experience from the soft-drinks giant Pepsi Cola. Sculley's appointment was apparently intended to inject a more professional style of management and expertise into the company's marketing activities. For reasons explained earlier, it was generally recognised that Apple's potential weakness at the time lay in a limited and non-IBM compatible product range, weaknesses in management experience and systems, together with a lack of focus in market positioning. Given its strengths from the long period of success enjoyed by its Apple II family of computers, these factors had not previously been crucial, but in the post-IBM entry environment their continuation could be disastrous. The company was thus in a state of flux. Whilst the introduction of the Lisa represented an innovative lead in hardware and software technology, it clearly came at too high a price. Furthermore, the barriers to direct entry into the corporate segment were high for Apple, since it was not viewed as a major computer company by DP and MIS managers. Thus by late 1983, much of Apple's future performance was to rest upon whether it would be able to succeed with its then forthcoming Macintosh, which although much cheaper, nevertheless was to incorporate many of the software features of the Lisa and be squarely targeted at both the small business/professional and corporate segments with extensive communications facilities. The fact that Apple's stock value fell in August 1983 to a level of $33 from a 1983 high of $55 tended to reflect the financial community's somewhat pessimistic view of Apple's long term position at this point in the industry's evolution. What Apple had to prove was that it was not just another highly successful one product company. Although it had shown its ability to develop an extremely innovative product in the Lisa, what would be critical to its success in the future was whether it could market such technology effectively and at a price that the market felt gave value.

Tandy also responded to IBM by trying to consolidate a position in the corporate segment. Following the success of its earlier TRS-80 Model II, Tandy announced its Model 16 in February 1982. Although less sophisticated and less expensive than Apple's subsequent Lisa, it proved Tandy's ability to innovate and offer a differentiated product. However, the Model 16 was also positioned against stiff competition from new entrants such as Fortune System's 32:16 and The Corvus Concept, offering similar features in the same price range. Notwithstanding its high price, sales of TRS-16 computers were high, due both to its strength in distribution and promotion as well as its software. Thus within the market at the time, Tandy offered the broadest range of products of any competitor and controlled the largest direct distribution channel through its chain of stores. However, as illustrated in Table 5.9 during 1981–1982, Tandy lost its sales market leadership to Apple in the small business/professional segment. Yet overall Tandy continued as a profitable and rapidly growing company and reflected an increasing percentage of its revenues and profits from the sale of its microcomputers. This was because Tandy's competitive strengths lay in its expertise in merchandising, distribution and strong market presence in all but the corporate segment. Its extensive service network, in-house software development and proprietary operating systems meant that the company generated value in all these areas, as well as maintaining a low unit cost structure on a per unit basis.

Commodore was perhaps the least affected by all these changes, since it had chosen to compete in the lower price segments and was more active in Western Europe. In late 1981, Commodore made a renewed commitment to the U.S. market, based upon the strong financial position it had established in overseas markets. Commodore introduced five new computers in June 1982, two of which were aimed at the business market segments to replace the PET, SuperPET and CBM machines. However, as illustrated in Table 5.9 the company's overall market share declined significantly between 1980 and 1982. In the $1000 to $2999 market its P-Series and new B-Series machines declined in sales and market share to 4 per cent by 1983. However, amongst the three major incumbents, Commodore was the only vertically integrated incumbent and based its strategy upon low-cost manufacturing and aggressive pricing. Its broad product range positioned it well to compete in the consumer and education markets in addition to the small business/professional market segments. Competing across a range of products and low-end market segments gave Commodore an edge in learning curves, economies of scale, brand name and trade-up potential. However, in the small business/professional segment, Commodore held little competitive advantage over Apple's IIe, Tandy's 80-II, IBM's PC or the DEC Rainbow. Indeed, the company's success in the mass consumer market created certain market barriers, even in the small business segment, where its small software base and less-established dealer networks may have caused doubts amongst some analysts in the market about the company's serious capability to develop within this segment.

Response of Smaller Incumbents: Good Times, Bad Times

For other competitors faced with the impact of IBM's entry, 1981 to 1982 represented an optimistic and boom year for competitors in the business segment of the personal computer industry. Competitors found readily available venture capital and maturing distribution channels. Many of the companies positioned themselves in the upper price range of systems, with specialised strategies based upon penetrating both medium and large sized businesses, either in vertical markets or in established customer bases for related peripheral products. However, by 1983, things were looking quite different and just as in Apple's case above, a severe downturn in performance occurred for many of the companies, which were still relatively small, with a limited capital base. Three examples are Vector Graphic, Victor Technologies and Fortune Systems.

The first shock to the industry occurred outside the business market segments when, in the spring of 1983, a number of major home computer manufacturers (priced under $1000) ran into major problems. Atari, Texas Instruments and Mattel suffered multi-million dollar losses due to market miscalculations. During the summer of 1983, sales of Sinclair's machine, distributed through Timex, fell by as much as fifty per cent, even though its price had been cut from $99 to $49.45. These events sent shock waves through the industry and financial community as analysts recognised the bubble had burst and speculated as to the future of smaller suppliers in the business computer market. Rumours started to abound as companies such as Apollo Computers (1982 sales: $18 million), which was positioned with workstations in the scientific and engineering market, experienced a fall in sales of over 50 per cent during the first half of 1983.

Vector Graphic, one of the earlier and more successful entrants to the small business market, found itself in a declining position as IBM's effect began to penetrate the market. With 1983 sales at $33.6 million, the company had to lay-off a quarter of its workforce as 1982 sales fell $2.5 million and a $2.4 million profit turned to a $3 million loss. Victor Technologies (1982 sales: $6.5 million) decided to attack IBM head on in 1981 with enormous investments in establishing its own sales force and dealer network. The strategy did not pay off. The company recorded an $11 million loss in the second quarter of 1983 and had to lay-off 350 staff. A more specialised competitor was Fortune Systems, (1982 sales: $26 million) which had introduced an innovative low-cost multi-user office systems machine. Initially, the product was a success, but delays in development of new software led to a sharp fall in sales and a switch from a $3 million profit to a $3 million loss in the second quarter of 1983.

Stock values of these companies were severely affected, as shown below:[46]

	1983 High	Aug 26 Close
Fortune Systems	$22.50	$ 9.00
Victor Technologies	$22.13	$ 8.00
Vector Graphics	$14.00	$ 4.63
Apollo Computer	$50.50	$33.00

The downturn in performance of these companies highlighted above points to a number of features about the industry, the business market segment and the competitors' strategies at this time. In particular, the risks associated with a head-on confrontation strategy by a relatively small competitor with the industry leader. It also highlights the disadvantage of low scale production in trying to match the major competitor's cost structures. Even where a niche is developed, failure to deliver software on time or lack of leverage with dealers can also be detrimental to performance. Finally, it makes it apparent how important it is to keep one's strategy in tune with developments in the marketplace.

Another feature of the industry which hit the smaller competitors badly as a result of IBM's presence was the tight supply of personal computer components — microprocessors and data storage devices[47] in particular. Consequently, they were often forced to buy their parts on the spot market and pay a premium. On the spot market in 1983, parts normally costing 20 cents were costing $2, whilst $1.50 parts could cost as much as $10.[48]

For many of the smaller competitors, the situation had became a vicious circle, in which lack of strategic differentiation led to falling sales and associated losses. With virtually no leverage over cost of supply items, margins were squeezed further or deliveries delayed by months. These conditions disenchanted dealers who were keen to carry the more successful products and hence valuable shelf space for distribution was withdrawn, further damaging sales. These events further reduced stock market confidence in the companies, whose limited size and management resources were further stretched in a downward spiral of crisis management. In such a position, public confidence amongst dealers and potential customers was severely weakened, so that even new product introductions lacked a credible launch platform. As a result of these developments, the stronger companies such as IBM, Apple and Tandy were able to gain further market shares, especially when some of the weaker competitors were eventually forced out of business. Perhaps the most spectacular and in some ways most significant of the small personal computer entrants to rise to success and subsequently fall during this period, was by a company that created a whole new segment of the personal computer industry with a newgame strategy. That company was Osborne Computer.

Osborne Computer: The Creator of the Portable Computer

Osborne was a start-up company which introduced its portable computer, the Osborne 1, at the West Coast Computer Fair in March 1981, with commercial shipments commencing four months later in July 1981. The Osborne 1 gained rapid market acceptance with 8,000 units being shipped in the first six months. By the end of 1982, as shown in Table 5.10, Osborne had gained 6 per cent market share in the $1000–$2999 price segment of the market and held 94 per cent of the portable market segment. The rapid acceptance of the product and the resulting success of the company created significant media interest and attracted start-up companies and existing firms into this newly-established market segment.

In effect, Osborne pursued a newgame strategy which made use of existing state of the art technology, but marketed the products in a novel manner to a new market segment. Although described as setting the trend towards creation of the portable computer market, much of Osborne's sales directly penetrated the established desktop personal computer market and so took market share from entrenched companies such as Apple and Tandy Radio Shack. Although not quite so dramatic and long-lasting as the IBM personal computer, nevertheless, the entry of the Osborne 1 was one of the more significant marketing innovations within the personal computer industry since the launch of the early models from Apple, Commodore and Tandy. Clearly, the Osborne 1 differentiated itself from other competitors in a distinctive manner that was characterised by the following features:

(1) *Price Competition:* the Osborne 1 initially cost 25 per cent less than any competing unit, although its price was subsequently eroded by later entrants' products.

(2) *Hardware Bundling and Integration:* the completeness of the system allowed the prospective buyer/user to make a single purchase decision and a single installation action of just plugging it in. This was a significant step forward in the ease of use of computers, which was of particular benefit to neophytes in the area of personal computing.

(3) *Software Bundling:* this innovation enhanced the ease of the single purchase decision and effectively intensified price competition by offering the dealer the opportunity to promote the Osborne 1 with "nearly free hardware" or "nearly free software". A further effect of bundling software was to stimulate the demand for integrated, intercommunicating families of software products in the main productivity applications.

The success of these marketing techniques is reflected by the fact that so many companies copied Osborne's lead in a number of areas, especially in bundling of hardware and software. However, it must be pointed out that the credit for being the first to bundle hardware was due to Tandy Radio Shack. What Osborne did that was different was to put a convenient carrying handle on its all-in-one, suitcase-enclosed computer. Although third-party companies had produced carrying cases for Apple II machines, the ease of transportability of the Osborne 1 with its built-in visual display unit meant that users were presented with a truly self-contained transportable machine. The benefit of such a machine was that the user could actually take his computer relatively easily from one work location to another. However, as pointed out earlier, whilst the Osborne 1 was not a true portable in today's meaning of the term, given its weight and size, nevertheless it did stimulate other companies to try and produce a machine that would fit the key characteristics of a truly portable machine.

Osborne's initial success could be attributed to its pursuing a leadership position in a specialised product-market niche. However, it was not long before the company encountered a number of internal and external problems, which it failed to successfully manage. The result was a downturn in performance and subsequent withdrawal from trading in the United States market. Several factors accounted for Osborne's downturn in performance. Firstly, the package was at the blunt end of technology and hence easily imitated, e.g. Kaypro. Secondly, innovative technology soon provided more compact and lighter machines and lastly, it appears as if there may have been weaknesses in the internal management of the company. However, these factors represented longer-term threats. The real failure of Osborne occurred due to a premature announcement of its follow-on product. Many dealers immediately cancelled future orders of the Osborne 1, but unfortunately, unforeseen technical delays on the intended follow-up machine, named the Executive, forced the company into a cash flow crisis. In fairness, it is important to note that Osborne was forced to develop the Executive sooner than expected due to the rapid adoption in the market of the IBM standard. Osborne's plan was to respond with the Executive, which was intended to be IBM compatible and hence "piggy-back" the developing IBM installed base.

The First Wave of Portable Computer Competitors

Whilst Osborne was trying to remain solvent, the portable computer market witnessed a number of new entrants. The most successful of which was Compaq Computers. From an early stage the company looked set to capture and subsequently did obtain a large share of the portable market with their IBM (look-alike and compatible) machine. In the first nine months of 1983, Compaq generated sales of $59 million on more than 28,000 units and the story of the company's growth is followed in later chapters.

A year after Osborne's launch, there were at least a dozen competitors in the portable market and by 1983, over forty new portable products had been launched. Following closely behind Osborne were Otrona and Non-Linear Systems with their highly successful Kaypro II. Their relative success was illustrated earlier in Table 5.10, where the Kaypro gained a 3 per

Table 5.11. United States portable computer unit shipments by vendor: 1981 - 1983.

COMPANY	1981	1982	1983
DYNALOGIC	---	300	5,500
EPSON	---	750	1,500
GRID	---	550	9,500
NON-LINEAR	---	1,200	6,000
OTRONA	---	1,000	1,000
OSBORNE	8,000	90,000	155,000
TELERAM	---	600	4,000
TOSHIBA	---	700	3,500
OTHER	---	400	5,500
TOTAL	8,000	95,500	191,500

Source: Yankee Group Report 1983, p.127.
Reproduced by permission of Yankee Group, © 1983.

cent market share of the $3000 to $5999 market in its first year of sales from 1982 to 1983. But these companies were joined during 1982 by a further group of entrants with competitive product offerings, including the Dynalogic, Jonos Ltd. and Seequa Computer Corp. Sales performance of the major competitors is given in Table 5.11. What is important to note, is that approximately sixty per cent of all the personal computer start-up companies during 1982 to 1983 were in the portable computer segment, which tends to reflect the fact that venture capital was beginning to dry-up for start-up ventures in the desktop market, in light of the events described earlier. Instead, portable computers were seen as the next great event, where fortunes were to be made by those willing to take the risk.

Therefore, to some extent, the small start-up companies entering this market were similar in nature to Apple and Commodore at the time of their entry, or subsequent early entries such as Vector Graphics. However, although the portable computer market represented a new segment, as things turned out at the time, it was not sufficiently distinct from existing desktop personal computers to generate new channels of distribution or marketing techniques in the way that personal computers had done during the late 1970s relative to mini- or mainframe computers. In addition, since many portable computers in the transportables range were not purchased for their portability but for their price/performance advantage, they were subject to competition from the base products of Apple and Tandy, which involved heavy discounting. In reality, the new companies therefore found themselves competing directly with the incumbents of the desktop personal computer market.

To some extent, it could be argued that the portable computer segment was perhaps limited in its potential for growth at this time in the industry's evolution. This assumption is based upon the fact that although demand initially grew strongly, the conflict with desktop competitors meant that the product group was not really differentiated on portability, but more on price/performance. Only when the technology advanced further and allowed the development of more reliable and truly portable computers would the sector be able to support its own competitive group of companies.

The Handheld Competitors

It was due to their clear differentiation from both desktop and the larger types of portable computer that handheld computers managed to develop without competition from the companies in these other sectors, except for those which deliberately chose to enter the market. Sales in the handheld market were dominated by Radio Shack. However, all of Radio Shack's units were privately labelled with manufacture being carried out by Sharp. Tandy held 77 per cent of the market in 1982, as Table 5.12 shows. Other major competitors included Sharp, which sold two products under its own name, whilst Matsushita sold "top of the line" handhelds under the Panasonic and Quasar name. Both the Panasonic and Quasar models could fit into a briefcase with all the peripherals, including a printer, bus expansion,[49] extra memory packs,[50] modems, colour TV interface[51] and CP/M operating language. However, when compared to the Osborne these machines were not particularly price-competitive.

Tandy focused much of its marketing effort into developing the home and educational markets as well as the small business and hobbyist markets. The existing distribution channels exclusively available to Tandy accounted for much of its success in these market segments. In contrast, it appeared that failure to develop an effective marketing and distribution network was one of the prime reasons for Matsushita's relative failure to penetrate this market. Sharp was the leading manufacturer in the handheld market and as a Japanese company with sales operations in the United States, overcame the distribution problem by selling 86 per cent of its units through Radio Shack stores. In addition, the remaining 14 per cent of its sales were achieved through a variety of other distribution outlets. Furthermore, Sharp made extensive use of mail order houses and clearly defined its intention to move an increasing proportion of its handhelds though these alternative outlets and gradually reduce its dependency on the Tandy outlets. Sharp's entry strategy to this segment illustrates well the leverage that could be obtained in the United States market by making use of strong third-party distribution channels and a U.S. brand label. In so doing, Sharp was both able to build up significant market share and experience in the distribution of handheld computers to the major market segments in the United States and thus gave itself

Table 5.12. United States handheld computer unit shipments, (000's): 1981 - 1983.

YEAR	TANDY	SHARP*	MATSUSHITA**	OTHERS+	TOTAL
1981	45	5	-	2	52
1982	125	20	12	5	162
1983	250	45	25	15	335

*   This unit shipment figure is for Sharp-brand HHCs only.
        (Tandy also sells Sharp HHCs, but with the Radio Shack brand name.)

**   Matsushita sells its HHCs under the Panasonic and Quasar brand names; these
        unit shipment figures represent the sum total of both products.

+   Includes Casio's FX702P, Sanyo's PHC8000 and Olympia's HHC (which was
        OEMed from Matsushita), and others.

Source: The Yankee Group, 1983.
Reproduced by permission of Yankee Group, © 1983.

time to build up its own brand name. This type of strategy, not uncommon in consumer electronics, was viewed by a number of U.S. competitors as a possible method of entry that some of the Japanese personal computer companies might take during the 1980s. As such it provided a clear illustration of the Japanese willingness to take the long-term strategic view of market entry and development.

However, the other Japanese handheld companies, Casio and Sanyo Business Systems, were less successful in this market, largely due to their limiting initial distribution to mail-order houses and a few retailers. To some extent, mail-order was an inappropriate channel for distribution of these products (at least as a major channel), since the mail-order companies did not provide even the minimal support needed for these products, which contrasts to the needs of the basic programmable calculator such as the Texas Instruments or Hewlett Packard machines. However, by the end of 1982, the Japanese dominated the manufacture of handhelds marketed in the United States market. Even the announcement by Olympia, the German office products manufacturer, of their entry into the United States market in 1983 was to be based upon a Matsushita product.

By the end of 1983, the handheld market remained relatively immature in its level of development. However, its importance at the time lay in its position at the peripherary to a potentially major growth segment of the personal computer market, namely, the portable computer market. Japanese competence in the miniaturisation of electronic components was clearly demonstrated in this market. As mentioned above, the potential of the portable market would only be realised as the technology allowed it to happen. A key part to that technology centred upon components initially developed in the handheld market. A further reason why it is important to consider the handheld market at this stage of the personal computer industry's evolution, is that it emphasises the fact that through increased technological advancement in microelectronics technology, the computer had now reached a stage where it spanned in size from the handheld to the giant mainframe. But most relevant to this story is the fact that competitors in the handheld market could reasonably be expected over time to impact the programmable calculator market, the emerging portable computer market and even the desktop computer market in specific market segments.

The Foreign Competitors

Indeed, during the legitimisation stage, a further important change in competitive conditions occurred, which involved the entry of a number of foreign competitors to the United States market, many of whom were Japanese in origin. NEC, the Japanese computer and telecommunications giant was the most successful foreign entrant to the U.S. market during this stage. However, NEC also came from a strong established base in personal computers, since at the time, it held over sixty per cent of the Japanese market. The estimated number of personal computers shipped in the U.S. market during the period 1978 to 1982 is illustrated in Table 5.13 and includes the number sold by foreign competitors from Europe and the Far East. It can be seen from the data that most entrants were relatively new to the U.S. market and as described in the previous section, many Japanese competitors were focusing on the portable and handheld computer market segments. Amongst European entrants, only Olivetti appeared to be making a serious investment to gain a share of the U.S. market. Although little specific performance data was available on the Japanese entrants, certain features could be noted in their strategic behaviour. Japanese vendors as a group held little market share. However, during 1982 certain events occurred which suggested the direction of their longer-term strategy. Firstly, there was the announcement of a number of products in the portable computer segment, making use of non-cathode ray tube display technology. Secondly, there was evidence of refinement in older technologies to compete as stable products with newer 16-bit based products, yet cautious development of the 16-bit market. The latter moves were accompanied by aggressive pricing and distribution strategies in competition with U.S. competitors.

At the time, opinions were mixed as to how well the Japanese would eventually do in the United States personal computer market.[52] The optimists amongst U.S. observers believed that somehow personal computers would be different to consumer electronics, where the Japanese already dominated the world market. The key difference was felt to exist in three areas of the value chain. The first involved the hardware itself, where it was argued that the rapid pace of change in the technology was unsuitable

Table 5.13. Estimated personal computer unit shipments in the United States market, (000's): 1978 - 1982.

SUPPLIER	1978	1979	1980	1981	1982
Apple Computer	11	38	72	156.2	226.5
Commodore BMI	12	28	39	40.5	28.5
Digital Equipment Corp.	0	0	0	0	7.5
Eagle Computer	0	0	0	0.8	5
Franklin	0	0	0	0	20
Hewlett-Packard	0	0	13	23.1	37
IBM (PC 5150)	0	0	0	19.1	176.5
Intertec Data	0	0.8	4	6	4.5
Morrow Designs	0	0	0	0	16
Kaypro Corp.	0	0	0	0	12.3
Osborne Computer	0	0	0	5.4	65
Otrona Corp.	0	0	0	0	5.7
Tandy/Radio Shack	60	87	92.5	85.8	80.5
Xerox Corporation	0	0	0	15	19.5
Zenith/Heathkit	1.3	3.3	4.6	6.5	8.2
Other U.S.	36.7	22.9	16.1	11.9	47.9
Subtotal U.S.	121	180	241.2	370.3	760.6
Olivetti	0	0	0	0	2.9
Philips Data	0	0	0	0.2	0.4
Triumph/Adler	0	0	0	0	0
Other European	0	0	0.8	2.2	2.7
Subtotal European	0	0	0.8	2.4	6
Epson Inc	0	0	0	0	3
Fujitsu	0	0	0	0	2.1
Hitachi	0	0	0	0	0
NEC	0	0.9	3.5	7	11
OKI Electric	0	0	0	0.3	0.5
Panafacom Ltd	0	0	0	0	0
Sanyo Business Systems	0	0	0	0	4.2
Sharp Electronics	0	0	0	0.1	2.8
Sony Corporation	0	0	0	0	4.2
SORD Computer	0	0	0.3	0.5	0.9
Other Japanese	0	0.1	0.3	0.5	0.8
Subtotal Japanese	0	1	4.1	8.4	29.5
Grand Total	121	181	246.1	381.1	796.1

Source: Dataquest Incorporated, SCIS Volume II, 29 July 1983.
Reproduced by permission of Dataquest, Inc., © 1983.

for the Japanese to develop their advantage in stable well matured technologies in the same manner as they had done in T.V.'s or Hi Fi. The second stemmed from the increasing need to develop effective applications software in order to succeed in a market. In the view of some observers within the industry, this would be a problem for the Japanese, since it was felt that they did not understand the American way of doing business, and hence, so it was argued, Japanese software developers would not be able to create effective software for the American business market. Lastly, some felt that the Japanese would be unable to penetrate American business, due to weaknesses in their sales and distribution operations. In contrast, the pessimists believed the exact opposite of these arguments. They believed the Japanese had already demonstrated their ability to be innovators in electronics technology and quite capable of matching, if not leading U.S. competitors. Clearly, if large Japanese companies wanted to, then it seemed quite feasible for them to either acquire U.S. software houses or set up software companies in the U.S. with American software developers. Only on the sales and distribution issue was there a sense of weakness, but here again, the experience in distribution of Japanese consumer products in the American market tended to suggest that this would only be a question of time. However, the fact was that at the end of 1983, all except NEC and Epson were still at early stages of entry and the future was anybody's guess.

SUMMARY

The changes that occurred during the "Entry of the Giants and Legitimisation Stage" as described in this chapter once again illustrate the pattern of relationships that exist between technological change and competitive behaviour and their combined impact upon the structure of the industry and its markets.

On the supply side, the key patterns to emerge occurred in technological change, new product development, new types of competition and hence new value chains and strategic groups. Whilst on the demand side, the market conditions changed to reflect new types of customer groups and the legitimisation of the personal computer in the corporate segment.

At the base of the industry's evolution, lay the new range of developments in microprocessor technology by semiconductor manufacturers, which offered competitors the opportunity to make use of faster and more powerful systems in their personal computers. This opportunity was taken up by a number of new entrants to the industry. However, what was significant about the entrants was that for the first time they included a number of large established companies that came from the computer, office products or consumer electronics industries. Furthermore, they included large foreign competitors from Europe and Japan. Therefore companies such as IBM, Xerox, DEC, Wang Laboratories, NEC, Olivetti and Sanyo brought with them experience and market power, especially in the corporate segment. At first glance, it might appear that such companies would find it easy to gain market share and to compete with the smaller incumbents such as Apple, Tandy and others, yet as was illustrated in this chapter, entry from a related industry or even the same market segment of corporate customers was no guarantee for success.

Amongst the entrants, it was shown that IBM made use of its enormous market power and committed significant resources to launch its PC and in so doing created a new value chain from those of the previous incumbents. The success of the IBM PC rapidly eroded the industry's existing choice of microprocessors, operating systems and applications programs. As a result, competitors found that their earlier products could no longer compete and were forced to launch new products. Their choice of product development was between either adopting the new emerging IBM standards or creating their own proprietary systems. Although a few initially tried to differentiate their product systems, eventually, most moved towards developing IBM compatible systems. One exception to this pattern was Apple Computer which had overtaken Tandy as industry leader during the first year after IBM's entry. However, Apple now found itself as a prime target of IBM and chose to respond by launching an innovative and proprietary product to penetrate the corporate market.

Whilst IBM effectively legitimised and drove the growth of the corporate marketplace, it also had a significant impact on the small and medium sized segments of the personal computer market. In all these segments, IBM not only forced competitors to develop new products, but more importantly, it changed the content and scale of resources in other elements of the value chain. Thus competition in the industry found itself investing more heavily in marketing activities, especially in advertising, distribution and service support. The adoption of IBM compatible machines also meant that differentiation became increasingly difficult to establish at the product level alone. Furthermore, the needs of the corporate sector and the increasing expectations of customers in the small and medium sized business markets forced competitors to improve their standards of marketing. Once again, IBM and some of the other large entrants tended to lead in this area. In particular, competitors found themselves having to pay more attention to creating product and corporate images in the markets and ensuring that their channels of distribution reflected this image and provided the higher standards of service necessary for the business markets. Overall, the changes represented a process of increasing professionalism in the industry, which itself put considerable pressure on competitors and distributors alike, since the increased competition that came from clones and amongst different types of distribution channel consequently put greater pressure on operating margins. All these changes therefore led to new types of strategic groups being formed and shifts in the sources of competitive advantage.

In addition to developments in the desktop market, the entry of Osborne Computer created a new market segment in the shape of portables. Although Osborne's product technology was conventional, its marketing was innovative and rapidly led to a number of other companies entering the competition for this sector. Portable personal computers then evolved into various subsegments, with transportables, laptops and handhelds developing separate markets. However, whilst laptops and handhelds created discrete product markets, transportables found themselves in competition with desktops, since their portability was somewhat limited and their main appeal lay in lower prices compared to the desktops. For this reason, the true significance of portables was not to develop until much later, when the technology improved sufficiently to allow them to perform reliably as lightweight units on remote locations.

In terms of performance, the "Entry of the Giants and Legitimisation Stage" witnessed a number of failures and successes in the industry. Furthermore, the industry overall reflected some significant variations in performance between competitors in different strategic groups. Clearly, IBM enjoyed considerable success during its first few years in the industry, however, other giants such as Xerox, DEC and Wang Laboratories were less successful. Indeed, this provides an important strategic lesson, namely, that many entrants may have failed to understand that the personal computer market required far greater resources and commitment for success than merely treating the entry as a new product launch. What they failed to appreciate was that the value chain for their traditional products could not be used to project a satisfactory value to customers in the personal computer marketplace. Instead, this would require a different value chain that was specifically tailored to the business.

Overall, during the "Entry of the Giants and Legitimisation Stage" the industry and its markets continued to enjoy rapid growth, especially as a result of IBM's entry, which led to the stimulation of large scale demand in the corporate sector. Although companies such as Apple and Tandy lost market share to IBM, nevertheless, the overall market grew at a pace to support their growth. However, another group of competitors that experienced a dramatic change in their fortunes were the smaller companies that had previously succeeded in the personal computer industry by pursuing niche strategies that focused upon the small to medium sized businesses. Whilst also initially benefiting from IBM's stimulus to the industry's growth, they were unable and ill-prepared to subsequently compete directly with the giant, when IBM began to allocate more effort towards these segments. Thus the desktop personal computer industry witnessed a number of small and medium sized failures during and after 1983, which had the effect of seriously curtailing the interest and funds available from the venture capital community to support new start-ups. Instead, the interest of investors shifted to the portable computer segment of the industry, which attracted a number of new entrants.

In summarising the "Entry of the Giants and Legitimisation Stage" it can be seen that IBM and Osborne had a significant immediate impact on the industry and its markets with their newgame strategies. To a lesser degree, Apple Computer's newgame strategy laid the foundations of changes that would take effect later in the industry's evolution. What is important to appreciate is that the critical factor in each of these companies' newgame strategies was that they changed the concept of the personal computer amongst hardware manufacturers, software developers, distribution channels and customers. As an industry, the competition became much more intense and spread over a wider range of markets and products. Hence the complexity of strategic management increased for the competitors. This itself forced many of the smaller companies to adopt more professional styles of management and ways of running their businesses. Those that survived enjoyed considerable growth during this period. However, many failed, including the personal computer ventures of some of the larger companies.

In effect, the "Entry of the Giants and Legitimisation Stage" therefore signalled the first signs of maturing to take place within the industry. However, the maturing refers to the management of the companies and the ways in which they projected their images to the market. If maturity means slowing down, this certainly did not apply to the technology or the complexity of the industry. Following on from the "Entry of the Giants and Legitimisation Stage" technological change continued apace, whilst the management of the competitors were next faced with the challenge of surviving in an increasingly complex and competitive environment, which represented the "Consolidation Stage". The next chapter will therefore show how far technology developed during the 1980s and what types of products and new competitors entered the competition during this period, together with the impact that these had upon the shape of the industry and its markets.

Chapter Six

FROM CONSOLIDATION TO MATURATION AND SATURATION

"The big change in networking came in the mid-1970s when we decided that we'd have to network in a very standardised way. Everything we did used the same networking protocols and the same networking technologies. That really made networking a major part of our organisation. It's these standardised ways that we've been encouraging the world to accept so that we and they can all work together on the same network. We've been pressing for standards to make this possible for a long time."[1]

INTRODUCTION

The title of this chapter is based upon what is considered to be the most important pattern of change that took place in the nature of the personal computer industry and its markets during the period following on from the Entry of the Giants and Legitimisation Stage described in the last chapter. The scope of the chapter is wide, both in terms of its range of subject matter and in that it covers a whole decade from the period around the mid-1980s up to the beginning of 1993. In terms of stages of evolution in the newgame environment, the chapter covers two periods, namely, the consolidation stage, which was followed by the maturation and saturation stage. However, these stages also incorporate two other dimensions of change, which involved the development of internationalisation and the move towards globalisation of the industry. In order to avoid confusion, this chapter therefore focuses attention upon the dynamics of consolidation, maturation and saturation as it applies to the United States marketplace, whilst the next chapter, gives attention to the patterns of foreign competition and market developments. The purpose and content of this introductory section is therefore to provide a bridge between the last chapter and the subject matter of this chapter. In particular, it provides the reader with an insight into the significant degree to which the personal computer has grown as a separate industry sector within the overall computer industry. Following on from the introduction, there is then a review of the key changes that have taken place in the technology during the past decade, which highlights the fact that during the consolidation stage, hardware technology gave way to software technology as the most important driver of technological change. Next, the subsequent discussion moves on to consider how these and other technological developments have influenced the industry's market conditions and evolution. In particular, it highlights the enormous growth in the size of the personal computer market and its increasing interaction with other product markets in the computer industry, which has led to a new set of competitive conditions across a wide range of these respective industry sectors. The performance of some of the key players is reviewed in the light of these developments. This section also illustrates how the corporate segment has moved towards smaller sized systems, based upon networking personal computers and workstations, which in effect, produced a shift in perceptions by customers and manufacturers alike as to the concept and role of the personal computer. From market evolution, the chapter moves on to consider how the industry's overall structure and nature of competition has changed during the period. The main focus in this section is upon the key elements of the industry value chain and illustrates how they have changed during the period of the late 1980s and early 1990s. The chapter finishes with a summary of the major points emerging from the content of the previous sections.

Connections Between Decades

Before launching into discussion of the changes in technology that took place between the mid-1980s and the early part of the 1990s, it is important for the reader to appreciate some of the key developments that occurred in the personal computer industry and its markets during this time. Most importantly it must be realised that during this decade, as an example of an evolving newgame, the personal computer industry had changed in a number of fundamental ways. Firstly, the sheer size of the United States industry had grown enormously, reaching an estimated 10 million shipments in unit terms and $25 billion in value terms in 1992. The pace of this growth can be appreciated if one considers that in 1981, the personal computer represented an installed base in the United States of some 1.7 million machines, whereas by the end of 1992 the installed base had grown to just under 63 million machines. The real significance of its size lay in its growing importance as a major part of the overall information technology industry. This is illustrated in Table 6.1 where it can be seen that between 1987 and 1991 its market share by product segment grew from 10.6 per cent to 15.2 per cent. However, what is interesting to note is that in 1992, along with all other hardware categories, the market share of personal computers shrank, which was a first for this product category. Declines in hardware were offset partially by growth in software, but largely by growth in service activities reflecting major long term structural changes within the overall computer industry. In 1988, workstations began to count towards the total of desktop machines, so that if one combines personal computer and workstation sales, then in 1990 sales of desktop computers outranked those of mainframes and midrange computers put together. This increasing level of importance in sales reflects the "sea change" that took place within the overall computer industry between the decade which ran from the early 1980s to the early 1990s.

Such an enormous expansion in sales of personal computers was due to a variety of reasons, not least of which were the significant improvements in the power and performance of the core microprocessor technology, together with developments in the associated software. Based upon the improved systems that this technology provided, suppliers within the industry, including peripheral manufacturers, software developers and distributors, began to develop new product marketing strategies, which in the main reflected their increasing emphasis upon marketing activities. Thus whilst technological developments continued to drive the pace and direction of change, at the same time, the market itself began to have a greater influence on the pattern of evolution. In particular, the growing

Table 6.1. Computer industry market share by product segment: 1987-1992.

PRODUCT SEGMENT	1987 % SHARE	1988 % SHARE	1989 % SHARE	1990 % SHARE	1991 % SHARE	1992 % SHARE
LARGE-SCALE SYSTEMS	12.6	11.5	11	9.6	9.5	9
MIDRANGE	10.7	9.3	8.1	7.7	7.6	6.9
PERSONAL COMPUTERS	10.6	12.3	14.2	14.7	15.2	14.3
WORKSTATIONS	0	1.4	2.8	3.8	4.7	4.5
SOFTWARE	8.1	8.8	9.7	10.2	11.5	11.6
PERIPHERALS	25	24	22	22.3	20.9	20.3
DATA COMMUNICATIONS	7.1	7.3	7.7	6.3	5.3	5.5
SERVICES	7.6	8	9	10.1	11	15.6
MAINTENANCE	13	12	11.4	11.5	11.1	8.8
OTHER	5.3	5.4	4.1	3.8	3.2	3.5
TOTAL	100	100	100	100	100	100

Source: Based upon Charts displayed in DATAMATION – June 15, 1992, pp. 26–27 and DATAMATION – June 25, 1993, pp. 22–23.
Reproduced by permission of DATAMATION, June 15, © 1992 and DATAMATION, June 15, © 1993 by Cahners Publishing Company.

importance of personal computers in the large corporation meant that the role of the personal computer began to change as more machines ceased to be stand-alone products and increasingly became part of the organisation's overall information network. However, as these changes evolved, they also began to alter the nature of the personal computer, not just in terms of its technology, but also as a concept within the broader computer industry.

The Changing Nature and Concept of the Personal Computer

At one level the changes in the personal computer can be viewed in terms of its basic product technology, which continued to increase in power and mobility that was reflected in its ability to be used in new and different ways. At the same time from a marketing point of view significant changes took place in the pricing of personal computers that meant that although portables and high-end machines were still relatively expensive, the vast majority of personal computers shipped came down in price, so that they were priced from around $500 up to about $2000. These types of machine were no longer viewed as special products worthy of premium prices, instead, they were taking on the form of commodity items, which demanded much greater efforts by manufacturers to differentiate their products through marketing activities, rather than simply on technological benefits. Meanwhile at the top-end of personal computers, their increased performance brought them into direct competition with technical and commercial workstations, so much so, that most examples of industry analysis began to group personal computers and workstations together under the heading of personal desktop computers. Thus a number of the Figures and Tables in the remainder of this book adopt this convention.

However, it is at another level that the change in the concept of the role and function of the personal computer has probably had the greatest impact on the industry and its markets. This is especially true in large organisations, for it is here that the most significant changes in the personal computer have taken place. Whereas the early use of personal computers involved giving greater freedom to individuals to determine their own computing needs, developments in communications technology[2] and political considerations within organisations, increasingly witnessed personal computers being linked together to form local and company wide networks. At first such developments were viewed by many of the established computer manufacturers as being supportive of their mainframe or minicomputer activities. But as the power of the personal computer continued to increase, then customer organisations began to use the personal computer for sharing data and communications in a way that offered more flexibility, more cheaply than their larger computer systems. This process of choosing personal computer solutions over and above larger systems became known as "downsizing" and accelerated the demand for personal computers during the late 1980s. In so doing, not only did this pattern of purchase further stimulate the level of demand for personal computers, but it also depleted the demand for mainframe and minicomputers. Unfortunately, this downturn in demand for larger systems in the late 1980s and early 1990s, coincided with the development of what was to become a major recession. So much so, that by 1991, even the demand for desktop personal computers had slowed considerably and began to show signs of a saturated market. Hence it is important to appreciate what impact the downturn in the economic cycle has had on the personal computer industry and to identify the key characteristics in this stage of the industry's newgame evolution.

From Newgame to Samegame

As was shown in the first chapter, a newgame environment goes through a number of stages of development which are driven by various forces for change. However, as personal computers have grown in importance in the overall computer industry, they have also been affected by structural changes within this wider industry. During the 1960s and 1970s, mainframe computers enjoyed strong growth, as did minicomputers during the 1970s and most of the 1980s. Meanwhile, personal computers and then workstations enjoyed strong growth during the 1980s. Taken together the result of this cumulative diffusion of computing power in its various formats meant that by 1992 the top 100 U.S. companies in the information systems industry[3] generated $187.4 Bn in revenues, thus exceeding the size of the U.S. petroleum industry.[4] Another significant pattern to emerge by the early 1990s has been the increasing interface that personal computers have developed with the consumer electronics industry. So much so, that the United States Commerce Department estimates suggest that combined, the U.S. computer and electronics industry sectors now represent a $287 Bn business, thus exceeding the combined motor vehicle and parts industries at $205 Bn.[5] Not surprisingly it is estimated that in 1993, the combined U.S. computer and electronics industries will constitute the largest industry in the United States and exceed the previous leader, namely chemicals. All of which tends to suggest that the structure of the overall computer industry for hardware products is now reaching maturity, with the common characteristics of market saturation, an excess number of suppliers and heavy price competition. Most significantly, within the overall computer industry, the personal computer has itself gone a long way towards achieving the success predicted by Steven Jobs by proliferating into a large number of households and most businesses,[6] but in so doing it has also reached saturation point in the U.S. market in its current desktop form. It is therefore estimated that in 1993 nearly 90 per cent of the demand for computers in the business sector represents replacement business. Thus whilst niche segments may exist for certain products, overall the demand for computers is now more like that of the car market, where competitors are selling to customers who already own one. This is not to deny the fact that many households do not yet own a personal computer, however, the likely demand for units from this segment is not going to be significant enough to boost the industry's overall situation in the short term. Growth in computer demand is mostly dependent upon the corporate sector and unlike in the early 1980s, this sector is now saturated. This does not mean that the industry will not maintain healthy demand, however, the annual rate of growth in the overall United States personal computer market is predicted by most industry observers to remain below double digits.

In addition to the changes in the overall computer industry, the prolonged recession of the late 1980s and early 1990s has further dampened demand in the overall U.S. computer market. Set against this background, many corporate computer users have begun to look carefully at the type of solutions offered to them by the computer manufacturers, especially of larger systems. The rapidly changing and relatively hostile business environment has meant that companies have been seeking to reduce costs and improve efficiency and at the same time maintain a high degree of flexibility. Corporate decision makers are increasingly sensitive to the complexity with which they are faced and are influenced by ideas about re-engineering organisations,[7] critical time management of product life cycles[8] and time to market,[9] together with greater autonomy from the centre and team approaches to management.[10] In this environment, personal computers have been at an advantage, since in conjunction with networking technology they allow companies to seek an alternative concept or solution to their computing needs. In this respect, the personal computer and its kindred spirit the workstation are now reaching the top of their ascent to power. They increasingly provide a different solution for the computing needs of companies that threatens and indeed has already destroyed much of the old order of the established mainframe and minicomputer companies.

Thus, both this and the next chapter will show how through developments in technology, the structure of the industry and the markets of the personal computer newgame have moved through their consolidation stage and onto the latter stages of maturation and saturation. In so doing, the newgame for personal computers moves towards its potential close, before becoming a samegame. But it must be remembered that the newgame under discussion refers solely to personal computers themselves and does not directly include personal computer software. Furthermore, the impact of the personal computer upon the mainframe and minicomputer industries is developing along the pattern of the model illustrated in Chapter One. This suggested that ultimately if the newgame is successful (as it has been for personal computers), then over time, it will destroy or at least severely diminish the existing samegame, represented in this case by the mainframe and minicomputer industries. In so doing, the newgame will thus turn into the dominant samegame. The late 1980s and early 1990s are now witnessing this process and the following sections will provide an analysis of some of the key changes that have taken place in this process of industry evolution, starting by consideration of how technological change developed during this period.

FROM HARDWARE TO SOFTWARE TECHNOLOGY

As a basis for the discussion of technological change during this period of consolidation, maturation and saturation, Fig. 6.1 provides a focal point for discussion. The purpose of the diagram is to give the reader an overview of some of the areas of competition surrounding the personal computer in the early 1990s. Thus at the base, core technology components are built on top of the "Next Generation" of microprocessors to create the technical hardware platforms around which various input and output products are connected and which are controlled or driven by the appropriate processing and bus architectures.[11] Seated on the personal computer hardware are the various components of the operating environment, which includes the operating systems, networking and various types of user interface. This now represents a critical level of competition within the industry and forms the "Battle of the Systems". Applications software includes a variety of functions, but of course can only include a few of the more dominant varieties in the diagram. At this level, competition is very much concerned with trying to create a product that will "leap-frog" the existing methods and systems in a manner that creates an entirely new way of using the personal computer. Past examples include the introduction of the first spreadsheet by Visicorp, or the first integrated package by Lotus 1,2,3 and then the creation of desktop publishing by Aldus. Although thousands of new applications programs are developed each year, few of them can claim to achieve the success or impact of these type of "change agents". Hence software developers and customers await the introduction of an operating system or applications program that might achieve "The Next Breakthrough".

Nearer the top of the tower, the nature of the personal computer itself appears to be stretched forever further, ranging from convergence at the high-end with technical workstations, through to the various types of portables, including PDA's or Personal Digital Assistants.[12] Here the product segmentation identifies that although portables represent the high growth area, the main competition during this stage of the 1990s is being fought out between personal computer and workstation manufacturers in the "Battle of the Desktops", which is made even more competitive in the saturated market conditions. Finally, as mentioned in the introduction, personal computers and their technology can no longer be viewed as stand-alone products, instead they form part of a complex end-user environment requiring a mix of communications systems[13] and networks, varying degrees of mobility, stand-alone units and links to other larger computers, with a variety of general and specialised applications. For some customers and perhaps some competitors this could be best described as the level of "Information Chaos". In one respect the "Technology Tower" presented here reflects the complex range of suppliers and partners, through the variety of components and products which they sell to the personal computer companies. At another level this is also representative of the technological

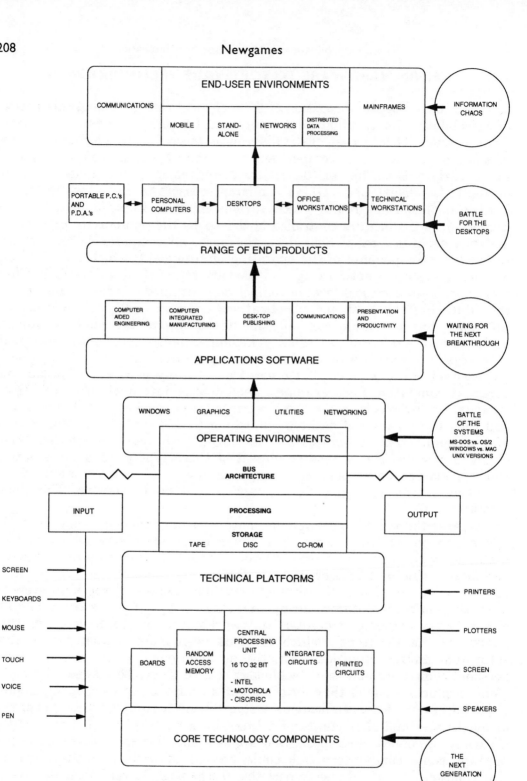

Fig. 6.1. Forces for change around the "Technology Tower" of the personal computer in the early 1990s.

elements of the value chain, at least from the supplier to the personal computer company. However, for our purposes it is meant to highlight the complexity of the range of technologies involved in the personal computer industry and to allow the reader to appreciate that competition is taking place at a number of levels within the "Technology Tower".

During this section, the principle discussion surrounds the strategic battles that are being fought out by competitors at three key levels. These are firstly amongst the suppliers of the core technology, namely the microprocessor and tracks the battles between semiconductor manufacturers and their influence upon the personal computer companies, some of whom are also manufacturing microprocessors. The discussion then moves on to the level of the operating environment and looks at the battle between suppliers of operating systems, some of which are software developers, whilst others are once again personal computer companies. Finally, whilst other areas of competition are acknowledged at the end of the section as having an important part to play in the industry's technological developments, the other key area of change is identified as being in the battle of the standards. Developments in the major software applications and various types of personal computers are discussed later in the chapter in the context of how they have changed the conditions of competition or market structure.

Competition in the Semiconductor Industry

The previous chapter described how IBM adopted the Intel 8088/86 microprocessor for its first personal computer known as the PC. Then as a result of the rapid adoption of the PC in the market, IBM created an industry standard that was based upon compatibility with IBM machines. Since IBM based its PC family upon Intel microprocessors, the 1980s witnessed an enormous growth in sales for Intel, as illustrated in Table 6.2. Whilst working closely with IBM, at the same time Intel was keen to maintain its competitive lead ahead of other semiconductor companies, especially Motorola. Thus in 1984, it began shipping its next generation of microprocessor, the 80286. At this time, as can be seen in Table 6.2, Intel shipments were still catching up with those of Motorola and others. However, by 1986, when it introduced its 80386 microprocessor, just two years after its predecessor, Intel had taken the lead in terms of annual shipments. Then in 1988 it introduced its low priced version of the 80386 in the form of the SX and further boosted sales of Intel microprocessors, when the following year it introduced its new generation of 80486 microprocessors. With each new generation of microprocessor, Intel provided IBM and its competitors the opportunity to develop more powerful machines, which in turn could run higher performance applications software.

As the figures show in Table 6.2, by 1992, Intel microprocessors accounted for approximately 83 per cent of microprocessor shipments in the U.S. personal computer marketplace, whilst Motorola microprocessors that were used mainly in the Apple family of Macintosh computers accounted for nearly 13 per cent of the market total. Most significantly,

Table 6.2. (Page 1 of 2) United States personal computer unit shipments and installed base by processor type (000's): 1981-1992.

VENDOR AND PROCESSOR	1981 Ships.	As a % of Annual Total	1981 Installed Annual Total Base	As a % of Annual Total	1982 Ships.	As a % of Annual Total	1982 Installed Annual Total Base	As a % of Annual Total	1983 Ships.	As a % of Annual Total	1983 Installed Annual Total Base	As a % of Annual Total
8088/86	35	4.49	35	2.01	192	6.32	227	4.75	698	12.81	925	9.07
80286	-	0.00	-	0.00	-	0.00	-	0.00	-	0.00	-	0.00
80386SX	-	0.00	-	0.00	-	0.00	-	0.00	-	0.00	-	0.00
80386	-	0.00	-	0.00	-	0.00	-	0.00	-	0.00	-	0.00
80486SX	-	0.00	-	0.00	-	0.00	-	0.00	-	0.00	-	0.00
80486	-	0.00	-	0.00	-	0.00	-	0.00	-	0.00	-	0.00
80586	-	0.00	-	0.00	-	0.00	-	0.00	-	0.00	-	0.00
Total Intel	35	4.49	35	2.01	192	6.32	227	4.75	698	12.81	925	9.07
680X0	3	0.38	7	0.40	13	0.43	20	0.42	44	0.81	64	0.63
RISC	-	0.00	-	0.00	-	0.00	-	0.00	-	-	-	0.00
Other	742	95.13	1,698	97.59	2,835	93.26	4,533	94.83	4,708	86.39	9,211	90.30
Total PCs	780	100.00	1,740	100.00	3,040	100.00	4,780	100.00	5,450	100.00	10,200	100.00

VENDOR AND PROCESSOR	1984 Ships.	As a % of Annual Total	1984 Installed Annual Total Base	As a % of Annual Total	1985 Ships.	As a % of Annual Total	1985 Installed Annual Total Base	As a % of Annual Total	1986 Ships.	As a % of Annual Total	1986 Installed Annual Total Base	As a % of Annual Total
8088/86	1,920	28.83	2,845	16.92	2,125	36.89	4,970	22.32	2,252	32.88	7,222	25.62
80286	22	0.33	22	0.13	393	6.82	415	1.86	1,021	14.91	1,436	5.09
80386SX	-	0.00	-	0.00	-	0.00	-	0.00	-	0.00	-	0.00
80386	-	0.00	-	0.00	-	0.00	-	0.00	61	0.89	61	0.22
80486SX	-	0.00	-	0.00	-	0.00	-	0.00	-	0.00	-	0.00
80486	-	0.00	-	0.00	-	0.00	-	0.00	-	0.00	-	0.00
80586	-	0.00	-	0.00	-	0.00	-	0.00	-	0.00	-	0.00
Total Intel	1,942	29.16	2,867	17.06	2,518	43.72	5,385	24.18	3,334	48.67	8,719	30.93
680X0	391	5.87	455	2.71	338	5.87	793	3.56	484	7.07	1,275	4.52
RISC	-	0.00	-	0.00	-	0.00	-	0.00	-	0.00	-	0.00
Other	4,327	64.97	13,488	80.24	2,904	50.42	16,092	72.26	3,032	44.26	18,196	64.55
Total PCs	6,660	100.00	16,810	100.00	5,760	100.00	22,270	100.00	6,850	100.00	28,190	100.00

Source: International Data Corp., 1992.
Computations on Market Percentage Share of Total by Author.
Reproduced by permission of International Data Corporation, © 1992.

Table 6.2. (Page 2 of 2) United States personal computer unit shipments and installed base by processor type (000's): 1981-1992.

VENDOR AND PROCESSOR	1987 Ships.	As a % of Annual Total	1987 Installed Base	As a % of Annual Total	1988 Ships.	As a % of Annual Total	1988 Installed Base	As a % of Annual Total	1989 Ships.	As a % of Annual Total	1989 Installed Base	As a % of Annual Total
8088/86	2,989	35.93	10,211	29.07	2,485	28.73	14,511	32.26	1,757	19.55	15,951	30.60
80286	2,827	33.98	4,263	12.14	3,421	39.55	7,836	17.42	3,759	41.84	11,595	22.24
80386SX	-	0.00	-	0.00	97	1.12	97	0.22	567	6.31	664	1.27
80386	265	3.19	326	0.93	766	8.86	1,094	2.43	1,285	14.30	2,379	4.56
80486SX	-	0.00	-	0.00	-	0.00	-	0.00	-	0.00	-	0.00
80486	-	0.00	-	0.00	-	0.00	-	0.00	3	0.03	3	0.01
80586	-	0.00	-	0.00	-	0.00	-	0.00	-	0.00	-	0.00
Total Intel	6,081	73.09	14,800	42.14	6,769	78.26	23,538	52.32	7,371	82.04	30,592	58.69
680X0	745	8.95	2,021	5.75	988	11.42	3,006	6.68	886	9.86	3,880	7.44
RISC	-	0.00	-	0.00	14	0.16	14	0.03	41	0.46	55	0.11
Other	1,494	17.96	18,299	52.10	878	10.15	18,430	40.97	687	7.65	17,601	33.76
Total PCs	8,320	100.00	35,120	100.00	8,649	100.00	44,988	100.00	8,985	100.00	52,128	100.00

VENDOR AND PROCESSOR	1990 Ships.	As a % of Annual Total	1990 Installed Base	As a % of Annual Total	1991 Ships.	As a % of Annual Total	1991 Installed Base	As a % of Annual Total	1992 Ships.	As a % of Annual Total	1992 Installed Base	As a % of Annual Total
8088/86	967	10.36	15,883	28.98	224	2.38	13,665	23.04	25	0.25	11,134	17.66
80286	3,000	32.13	14,595	26.63	1,610	17.13	16,144	27.22	289	2.86	15,934	25.27
80386SX	2,039	21.84	2,703	4.93	3,602	38.32	6,305	10.63	3,925	38.85	10,230	16.23
80386	1,730	18.53	4,108	7.50	1,814	19.30	5,922	9.99	1,299	12.86	7,222	11.46
80486SX	-	0.00	-	0.00	96	1.02	96	0.16	1,423	14.08	1,519	2.41
80486	99	1.06	102	0.19	558	5.94	660	1.11	1,406	13.92	2,066	3.28
80586	-	0.00	-	0.00	-	0.00	-	0.00	-	0.00	-	0.00
Total Intel	7,835	83.91	37,391	68.22	7,904	84.09	42,792	72.16	8,367	82.82	48,105	76.30
680X0	1,035	11.08	4,871	8.89	1,133	12.05	5,613	9.46	1,296	12.83	6,571	10.42
RISC	95	1.02	150	0.27	167	1.78	317	0.53	300	2.97	617	0.98
Other	372	3.98	12,395	22.62	195	2.07	10,581	17.84	140	1.39	7,752	12.30
Total PCs	9,337	100.00	54,807	100.00	9,399	100.00	59,303	100.00	10,103	100.00	63,045	100.00

Source: International Data Corp., 1992.
Computations on Market Percentage Share of Total by Author.
Reproduced by permission of International Data Corporation, © 1992.

shipment of other microprocessors had declined from their peak of 4.7 million in 1983 to 140,000 by 1992, when they represented just over one per cent of the market. As Intel's dominance of the personal computer microprocessor market grew during the 1980s, so too did their market power. Since IBM was the lead customer for Intel microprocessors, competitors to IBM were faced with two options in terms of microprocessors. Firstly, to either behave as IBM clones by using Intel microprocessors and hence lack any core product differentiation, or alternatively to use a competing microprocessor, such as the case in Apple's use of the Motorola family or to develop one's own, as in the case of the DEC Alpha chip.

However, with the rapid growth of desktop workstations[14] from the mid-1980s onwards and with their convergence to battle with high-end personal computers, a new type of microprocessor entered the competition in 1988. This took the form of RISC[15] technology (reduced instruction set computing) which differed from the Intel and Motorola technology which was based upon CISC,[16] standing for complex instruction set computing. Leading the attack on the Intel standard was the workstation manufacturer Sun Microsystems with its Sparc microprocessor. The key advantage of the RISC technology lies in its speed of processing, so that in principle, a RISC based PC or workstation would be faster than a similarly priced and configured CISC machine. Thus various PC and workstation manufacturers followed Sun in the development of RISC based machines in order to break away from the Intel family, including Hewlett Packard and the ACE (Advanced Computing Environment) consortium led by Compaq, Microsoft and MIP Computer Systems Inc. However, by referring to Table 6.2 it can be seen that in 1992, half a decade after introducing the technology, only about 617,000 desktop machines carried RISC microprocessors versus the 48.1 million installed by Intel.

This dominance and level of performance was further emphasised by the fact that by 1992, Intel's sales had grown four-fold since 1986 to $4.8 billion with earnings of $819 million. In the process, Intel displaced Motorola Inc. as the largest U.S. semiconductor supplier in terms of worldwide sales.[17] However, Intel's attitude towards the market went through some dramatic changes in the late 1980s under the leadership of CEO, Andrew S. Grove. For whilst dominating the microprocessor market, the 1990s promised severely increased competition for Intel. To begin with Intel's bread and butter technology came under attack from Cyrix Corp. plus Chips and Technologies Inc. with their improved re-creation of the 386, without apparently infringing copyrights or patents.[18] Similarly, Advanced Micro Devices Inc. (AMD), clones of Intel microprocessors, won 40 per cent of a market during 1991 to 1992, that had earned Intel $2 billion in profits since 1985. Whilst involving itself in court cases for copyright and patent infringement, Intel then decided that its best strategy would be to come out on the offensive against the high-end RISC technology and the lower and mid-range clones. The form of this offensive being based upon a faster pace of technological innovation. A decision that seemed all the more appropriate, when in October 1991, Intel's major customer IBM, announced to the world that it was joining forces with its previous arch rival, Apple

Computer, to jointly develop hardware and software technologies and included a new family of RISC chips based upon IBM's Power RISC architecture and developed jointly between IBM, Apple and Motorola.

These changes carry the seeds of significant implications for the personal computer industry and promise to lead to even greater changes during the rest of the decade. Firstly, it has meant that the dominant industry standard of Intel/IBM-compatible based machines is no longer likely to remain the norm. As will be shown later in this section, this situation has created a great deal of confusion in the market, as competing personal computer and workstation manufacturers battle to convince customers that their choice of microprocessor is going to become an industry standard. However, at present, this claim can sometimes ring somewhat hollow, since 20,000 applications programs run on Intel based microprocessors, which represents five times the amount available for the most successful RISC based microprocessor from Sun Microsystems Inc. Furthermore, this difference creates quite a significant switching cost for those customers who might consider abandoning their investments in Intel based machines. Yet whilst competitors lay claims for their microprocessor technology against the giant Intel, the company itself has reacted to the competition by "doubling-up" on its speed of time to market.

According to one report,[19] the decision to increase the speed and hence reduce the time between the introduction of new generations of microprocessors holds enormous potential impact on the personal computer industry and its markets during the 1990s. In mid-1990, Intel announced that work would begin on the 80686 family of microprocessor, due for public unveiling towards the end of 1993 or early 1994, two years before its unveiling of the 80586 family, which is now called Pentium by Intel. This was an unprecedented move, since Intel and its competitors have traditionally waited until completion of development and introduction of the previous microprocessor family, before commencing design on a successor. The result of the new order, leads to the product development cycle being reduced from the introduction of a new family of microprocessor every three or four years to one every two years. Furthermore, in 1992, Intel introduced more than 30 new variants of its leading edge 80486 microprocessor, as opposed to an average of one or two variants during the mid-1980s. Thus Intel is firmly set upon exploiting its key competitive advantage, namely speed to market. Its ability to achieve such acceleration in product development is apparently based upon its proprietary design automation software and indeed Intel is confident that its system will be able to carry over to subsequent microprocessor families for most of the decade, thereby reducing the usual four year development cycle. With two teams of development working concurrently, Intel proposes to introduce its 80686 and 80786 microprocessor families before the mid-1990s. The increased pace of product introductions by Intel is clearly illustrated in Fig. 6.2.

The immediate impact of this speed-up in performance severely dented the attack by the RISC and clone manufacturers. At the high-end, emulation displays[20] of the 80586 microprocessor persuaded Compaq Computer Corp. to drop its plans for a RISC based personal computer, as competitors

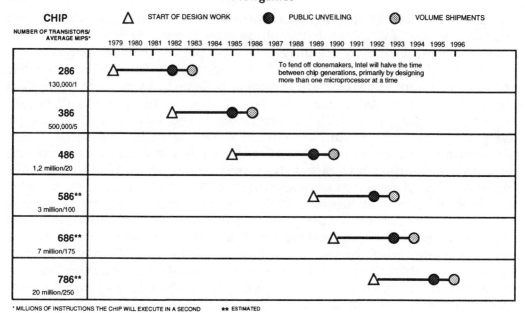

Source: "Intel Picks up the Pace of Product Innovations", *Business Week*, June I, 1992, p. 50.
Reprinted from June I, 1992, issue of *Business Week* by special permission, copyright © 1992 by
McGraw-Hill, Inc.

Fig. 6.2. Intel picks up the pace of product introductions.

realised that the speed advantages held by current RISC technology over
386 and 486 technology would be eroded by Intel's next generation of
microprocessor. At the same time, Intel's attitude to its customers was
dramatically altered when it became involved in concurrent engineering,
that involved working with customers and manufacturing early in the 586
development cycle. However, not all RISC products have been set back
by Intel's actions, as demonstrated by the latest RISC designs such as
DEC's Alpha and Texas Instruments SuperSparc, which still clearly keep
the lead in speed. The overall impact of Intel's strategy therefore appears
to have intensified the degree of competition amongst the microprocessor
manufacturers. Yet to keep up this pace of development requires enormous
R&D funds. Thus Intel spends more than any of its competitors in its
efforts to stay in the number one position and reinvests a phenomenal
30 per cent of its overall revenues into research and development. Yet it
should be remembered that this is in an industry sector, where 20 per
cent of sales is the necessary spend on R&D simply to keep in the race.
What allows Intel to make such large investments both on R&D and new
manufacturing facilities is its huge market share, which has generated
significant profits for inclusion in its reserves and a loyal customer base
willing to stay with Intel technology and hence not lose use of their existing
software systems.

This speed-up in the pace of new product introduction amongst
microprocessor manufacturers, naturally already has had major effects on
everyone further down the value chain in personal computers. Firstly, it

has put greater pressure on the personal computer manufacturers themselves, who have been faced with a shorter product life cycle for their own products. As can be seen from Fig. 6.2, shipments of the 386 and 386SX family began to impact sales of the 286 about three years after their introduction. Similarly for the 486 introduction and its impact on the 386 family. In each case, the new generation of microprocessor provides the personal computer manufacturers with an opportunity to offer the market a faster and more powerful type of machine, albeit at a higher price than existing models. However, since the prices of microprocessors fall quite rapidly, such differences are accepted as adding value in the market. One outcome of a faster pace of new microprocessor introduction is that personal computer manufacturers are not only forced into managing a broader product portfolio, but are also having to face a faster pace of product obsolescence. In the future this situation is likely to arise more frequently, since they themselves will be more closely involved with Intel from an earlier stage of product development, thus allowing them to introduce new products more quickly. But in so doing, they will naturally squeeze the product life cycle of earlier machines, which will in turn put greater pressure on margins.

Further down the value chain, the attack by Intel with its 80586 has included offering more help to software developers to permit them to write software applications for the microprocessor more quickly than in the past by the use of compilers.[21] Indeed, the lack of compilers is one reason that software has often lagged a generation behind the hardware chip, so that developers have frequently failed to take advantage of the full power of the earlier families of microprocessors such as the 286 and 386. By providing assistance to the software developers, Intel is effectively creating an even faster pace of product obsolescence in personal computers, since the 586 family and subsequent families will take less time to develop applications programs for the new generation of machines, which in turn, is likely to attract customers to buy the more powerful systems in order to take advantage of the better software. Such developments are based of course upon the phenomenal increases in both the density of transistors and their processing speed, which is illustrated for the various families of microprocessors in the left hand column of Fig. 6.2. But even more significant will be the increases expected in the next few years as the 486 gives way to microprocessors with the power of the 786, whose 20 million transistors will be able to process 250 million instructions per second (MIPS),[22] which is more than ten times faster than the first 486. Most significantly if Intel achieves these future goals, it will have almost doubled its speed of new product development and in so doing considerably increased the pace of competition in the overall personal computer industry.

Thus both the development of Intel's dominance of the microprocessor market for personal computers and its more recent impact on competition from other companies has greatly shaped the competitive process for personal computers over the past decade. By achieving dominance of the market, it effectively created an industry standard based on its major customer IBM. This industry hardware standard has had a great impact on competition between the personal computer manufacturers. However, the industry's evolution has also been driven by competition between software operating systems that represent the "Operating Environments" platform shown earlier in Fig. 6.1 and to which we next turn our attention.

Operating Systems and the New Platform for Competition

During the past decade operating systems have formed a key area for competition between a variety of personal computer manufacturers. Initially the competition was between clearly defined camps. However, as the industry continued to evolve, then the range and choice of operating systems has become much more complex, until eventually, by 1993, the situation is one of confusion. How and why such a pattern of confusion should arise is an important part of the story that illustrates the increasing impact that software technology has had upon the personal computer industry and its markets.

In the earlier description of the "Entry of the Giants and Legitimisation Stage" of the personal computer industry's evolution it was shown how the operating system, CP/M-80, which had become the initial industry standard was superseded by MS-DOS. Combined together, the various families of Intel microprocessors used by IBM and MS-DOS (PC-DOS on the IBM platform) became the dominant industry standard through much of the 1980s, since IBM clones and compatibles used both Intel and MS-DOS for their respective platforms. As was shown in the previous chapter, this copycat type of strategy was largely adopted by competitors in order to gain access to the enormous potential market of business customers that would normally buy IBM equipment. In addition, it provided competitors access to the vast range of applications programs developed for the MS-DOS environment. Thus by the mid-1980s, MS-DOS began to dominate operating systems as the industry standard, in much the same way as Intel was beginning to dominate the microprocessor sector of the industry's value chain.

However, MS-DOS did not enjoy a complete monopoly. In 1984, based upon systems technology from its Lisa personal computer, Apple Computer launched the Macintosh range of computers, which were based upon a proprietary operating system. Apple thus isolated itself from the industry trend, staking its fortunes upon the market's hoped for recognition of the distinctive advantages of its system. Initially, this looked like a strategy that was to backfire, since neither Apple nor the Mac[23] were taken seriously by large corporate accounts on whom the company depended for its longer term growth and success. In addition to the Mac operating system, one other operating system which was aimed at the personal computer industry was UNIX. However, although it was strongly favoured by scientists and engineers who had initially used it on small to mid-range systems, UNIX was seen by many as being too complex for broader acceptance in the commercial marketplace, especially on personal computers. In an effort to bury this arcane image, AT&T, Xerox and the workstation manufacturer Sun Microsystems launched a version of UNIX called "Open Look" in 1988, which attempted to present the user with a friendlier Macintosh like interface. By the mid-1980s, five years or so after IBM's entry, the industry was therefore dominated by MS-DOS, with Apple's Mac system and UNIX trailing in second and third positions.

Increasingly Intel and Microsoft were therefore enjoying rapid growth based upon sales of their products expanding beyond use by their major customer, namely IBM, into the growing number of various IBM clones and compatibles. Quite clearly however, what was good for these two companies was not working out to be quite so good for IBM. Having broken new ground by developing an "open-system"[24] with its PC, IBM's major challenge did not come at this stage by a riposte from industry incumbents defending the CP/M standard, nor from Apple's Macintosh. Instead, it came from the clones and compatibles that were adopting the IBM standard and riding on the coat-tails of IBM's success and market power. As a result, IBM began to lose market share at a rapid rate. Customers, including corporate clients, increasingly turned to the competitors' products, either because they were cheaper, as in the case of Far Eastern manufacturers, or because they were perceived as being better performance machines, such as those from Compaq Computer. Unlike with their experience in mainframes or minicomputers, IBM could not protect its customer base by means of proprietary hardware or software. In personal computers, the IBM system was perceived as being the de facto industry standard and as such was easily emulated by competitors. Faced with the prospect of losing still further market share on what was clearly becoming an increasingly important market segment of the overall computer industry, IBM chose to develop a completely new system. The new product was still based upon Intel microprocessors and an operating system developed jointly with Microsoft, however, it was also no longer a completely "open system". With the hardware named as PS/2 and an operating system known as OS/2, IBM hoped to recapture a large share of the market by encouraging its customers to upgrade to the new system, which could not be so easily emulated by the earlier clones and compatibles.

In order to further its differentiation, IBM also attempted to establish a new industry bus standard in the shape of its Micro Channel Architecture (MCA).[25] However, this was quickly challenged by a consortium of nine leading personal computer manufacturers[26] — headed by Compaq Computer, which announced plans to develop a rival PC bus architecture known as the Extended Industry Standard Architecture (EISA).[27] In each case, these new generation of bus architectures were intended to allow the personal computer to perform more like minicomputers in terms of the complexity of computing task that they could handle. What is significant in this pattern of events lies of course in the fact that IBM was not allowed to dominate in this aspect of personal computer technology, anymore than it had done in terms of its microprocessor base. Similarly, another key area where IBM was no longer able to dominate was in the area of its new operating system that was jointly developed with Microsoft.

Launched in April 1987, from IBM's viewpoint OS/2 claimed several operational advantages over DOS in terms of speed of processing and memory handling capacity, all of which were able to support more powerful applications and tasking capabilities. However, many customers initially remained sceptical as to how much added value the new systems would actually create for them. Many were just content to remain in the DOS environment and make use of their existing software investments, without bothering to face the switching costs involved in retraining and reinvesting in the new systems. Furthermore, IBM's new bus architecture (MCA) did not have the desired impact on the market due largely to the high entry cost of licensing agreements with IBM. Faced with slow sales a year after the launch of its new system, IBM therefore embarked on a major price cutting campaign across the range of its products from the PS/2 downwards, in order to stimulate demand and fight off the clones.

However, by this time, the industry had changed significantly from its earlier structure and conditions. Whereas in 1981, IBM's market power was sufficient to focus the industry around its systems, by 1988 things were very different, so that customers, both large and small had come to recognise that they did not have to buy everything from IBM, nor did they need to buy solely from anybody else for that matter. Instead, for much of their standard equipment requirements they were attracted to other Intel/MS-DOS products, whilst specialist tasks requiring graphical user interfaces[28] found them increasingly drawn towards Apple's Macintosh family and the more competitive priced workstations. This change of attitude was revolutionary and contributed to the creation of a completely new set of competitive conditions in the personal computer industry that were to emerge in the early years of the 1990s. In essence, what was happening was that the market dominance of IBM was giving way to a much more competitive market, where many customers no longer believed that IBM held all the solutions. But more competition and the erosion of the IBM de facto standard also meant that product choice became more complex.

From the point of view of product innovation, this development could be viewed as a good thing, especially for the customers, since it meant that they would be offered a wider choice of systems to choose from in the market. In particular, so long as Intel and Motorola had formed virtually 99 per cent of the microprocessor market, most personal computer platforms could be defined as IBM, IBM compatibles or Apple's Macintosh. This situation provided a high degree of stability for software developers, thus companies such as Microsoft, Lotus, Aldus and other leading developers were in a position to develop their programs for either the MS-DOS and/or Macintosh operating systems environment, knowing that their products would be marketed to a large installed base. However, when IBM tried to force the industry and its markets to a new standard of hardware and software, instead of succeeding, it set up a chain reaction of events that was to completely destabilise the industry's conditions of competition. Some might consider that in so doing IBM rather shot itself in the foot. However, this would be a rather cruel judgement, since other forces were at play that would most probably have had the same effect given some extra time. IBM merely accelerated the process. Part of the destabilisation was caused by the various RISC based microprocessors introduced into the market by Sun, DEC, Hewlett Packard and others as described in the previous section. But in addition, it was caused by the strategies of the major software developer, namely Microsoft, together with customers' increasing recognition of the benefits to be gained by the Macintosh type of graphical user interface. Taken together, these factors led to the situation whereby instead of remaining with a dominant industry standard, the personal computer industry was showing signs of changing to one of many standards.

How such a situation has arisen in the industry can best be seen by understanding how market power shifted from hardware to software during the late 1980s. The seeds to the change were laid in the early 1980s when the software company Microsoft, developed MS-DOS for the IBM PC and at the same time collaborated in the development of aspects of the graphical interface on the Apple Macintosh system. In so doing, Microsoft was seen as an ally of both manufacturers. However, with Microsoft's licensing of MS-DOS to a number of IBM's competitors, the writing was on the wall. However, IBM failed to see it, or take notice of it, since in developing its PS/2, Microsoft was once again contracted by IBM to help in the development of its operating system, OS/2. Yet around this time, according to a report in Business Week,[29] Microsoft is alleged to have pursued two strategies at the same time, which were to later cause changes in the market. The first involved publicly pushing OS/2, whilst the second involved a strategy for Windows, which was a competing method for giving PCs many of the graphical interface qualities associated with the Apple Macintosh. Thus in 1988, Apple Computer launched a lawsuit against Microsoft in an effort to restrain the launch of Windows,[30] claiming that it was an infringement of various copyrights. With the launch of Windows 3 in 1990, IBM began to recognise that friends and foes were beginning to change and later that same year, IBM and Microsoft effectively terminated their association, leaving IBM to market its own development versions of OS/2. In the twenty months following its launch, Windows sold over nine million copies, creating a one billion dollar business in Windows and related applications programs, of which Microsoft controls the major share. By providing Windows for MS-DOS users, Microsoft has effectively delayed the decision for many customers to upgrade to IBM's desired PS/2. At the same time, it has dramatically and effectively reduced the perceived differentiation and associated competitive advantage of the Macintosh over the MS-DOS environment.

Faced with this type of alienation by a former strategic partner, both IBM and Apple realised that they were both victims of the same competitor. Thus whilst it shocked the industry at the time, it is not really surprising that the two rival personal computer manufacturers, namely IBM and Apple Computer, should have decided to announce to the industry in late 1991, that they believed it was in their best interests to collaborate. This was to be in conjunction with Apples's long-time microprocessor supplier, Motorola. It was to be based upon upon the development of Power PC, a series of RISC based microprocessors using IBM's POWER (Performance Optimisation with Enhanced RISC) architecture. From then onwards, for both IBM and Apple, the major competitor became Microsoft and the technological battle moved firmly from being primarily a battle dominated by issues surrounding hardware, to one in which hardware, although still important would increasingly be a commodity item and where software would become the dominant force of competition. This took the form of the announcement of the Taligent joint venture project, which is intended to create an object-oriented[31] development environment. However, such developments made the battleground become increasingly complex and confused. Furthermore, as a result of other developments that had been taking place during the same period, the battle for personal computers now moved into a much larger arena involving other types of computers, ranging from mainframes and mid-range systems to workstations. Ironically, the problems of complexity now centred on an issue that had been created by the rise of the personal computer. The issue was one of standards.

From IBM Compatibility to Multiple Standards and Confusion

As an increasing number of different RISC based microprocessors were introduced from MIPS, Motorola, Hewlett Packard, Sun Microsystems and even IBM, they were complemented by a widening variety of operating systems to run on the various platforms. Furthermore, as shown in Table 6.3, on both the Intel and Motorola CISC based platforms, companies such as Apple, Santa Cruz, AT&T, NeXT and Sun Microsystems had developed operating systems to challenge the dominant MS-DOS and its heir apparent, OS/2. Then on top of the operating systems, an increasing range of graphical interface systems began to emerge alongside Microsoft's Windows and the long established Apple Mac system. However, such developments cannot be viewed in the context of the personal computer industry alone. Part of the problem was created outside in the related technologies of mainframe and midrange computers, together with technical workstations. In this respect, personal computers merely stimulated a major shift in thinking in these other areas of the computer industry. However, as a result of the shift, personal computers were drawn increasingly into these other areas of technology and in so doing became subject to their traditional problems.

The key to the problem of a plethora of different industry standards rests in the traditional way in which mainframe and midrange computer manufacturers competed with one another. As was shown in a previous chapter, companies such as IBM, DEC, HP and others traditionally tried to "lock-in" their customers by high switching costs based upon proprietary hardware and software systems. The experience of the 1980s with personal computers and the de facto standard of IBM compatibility gave companies

Table 6.3. Hardware and software standards in the United States personal computer industry around 1992.

HARDWARE PLATFORMS	OPERATING SYSTEM SOFTWARE	GRAPHICAL USER INTERFACES
CISC-BASED		
Intel 80X86		
IBM PCs and clones NCR large systems Sequent minicomputers	**MS-DOS** (Microsoft) **OS/2** (Microsoft/IBM) **XENIX*** (Santa Cruz Operation) **AIX*** (IBM) **DYNIX*** (Sequent)	**WINDOWS** (Microsoft) **PRESENTATION MANAGER** (IBM) **DESQVIEW** (Quarterdeck) **MOTIF** (Open Software Foundation)
Motorola 68000 Series		
Apple Macintosh Hewlett-Packard workstations NeXT workstations Sun	**MACINTOSH OS/SYSTEM 7** (Apple) **AUX*** (Apple) **UNIX V.4*** (AT&T) **MACH*** (NeXT) **SUN OS*** (Sun)	**MAC OS** (Apple) **MOTIF** (OSF) **NEXTSTEP** (NeXT) **OPENLOOK** (Sun)
RISC-BASED		
IBM RS/6000	**AIX*** (IBM)	**PRESENTATION MANAGER** (IBM) **MOTIF** (OSF)
MIPS R3000 Series		
DEC workstations Silicon Graphics workstations Compaq workstations (due out 1992) Pyramid Systems minicomputers	**ULTRIX*** (Digital) **OSx*** (Pyramid) **OSF/1*** (OSF)	**WINDOWS** (Microsoft) **MOTIF** (OSF)
Motorola 88000		
Data General workstations, minis Unisys workstations	**DG/UX*** (Data General) **UNIX V.4*** (AT&T)	**MOTIF** (OSF)
Precision Architecture		
Hewlett-Packard	**HP/UX*** (Hewlett-Packard)	**MOTIF** (OSF)
Sun Sparc		
Sun workstations Solbourne workstations Fujitsu workstations	**SUN OS*** (Sun) *Variants of UNIX	**OPENLOOK** (Sun)

Source: "Computer Confusion", *Business Week,* June 10, 1991, p.35.
Reprinted from June 10, 1991 issue of *Business Week* by special permission, copyright © 1991 by
McGraw-Hill, Inc.

their first exposure to an environment where transfer between suppliers of computer hardware and software was no longer a problem for customers. However, having tasted the benefits of such a situation, large corporations began to demand that such a condition should be extended to other elements of their computing systems, including their mainframe and midrange systems. At first, the manufacturers of such systems tried to ignore the demands of their customers, but by the late 1980s it was obvious to most observers that the trend was rapidly and clearly moving towards acceptance of this mode of thinking. The idea behind having standards for hardware, software and communications interfaces hinged on the premise that this would make them easier to purchase, to connect to other systems and simpler for the customer to learn to use. Furthermore, since they were thought to reduce the risks of entry, standards were believed to stimulate more competition. From this assumption it followed that since the resulting increased competition would reduce price, this would expand the size of the overall market and hence benefit suppliers and customers alike. Although great in theory, in practice it has so far turned out to be an unmitigated disaster.

The idea of moving towards a set of standards in the late 1980s quickly gave currency to a previously known but little used term, namely "Open-Systems". The concept found its origins in the late 1970s when non-IBM manufacturers created Open Systems Interconnect (OSI)[32] which represented a set of protocols to allow easy transfer of data between different systems. Unix was originally designed as such an early operating systems protocol, but the IBM compatibility available on PCs went much further, since this incorporated much of the computer's hardware, which permits a disk to go from one machine to another. However, many would argue that the IBM standard was still essentially a closed system, since it did not permit easy transfer or connection to non-IBM systems. This last point highlights a key problem surrounding the idea of open-systems, namely, that there are practically as many different definitions and solutions as there are companies willing to manufacture a system. Thus although customers clearly want open-systems that will allow easy connection and communication between different manufacturers' machines with all the associated advantages, not all manufacturers may share their enthusiasm, unless one happens to be the manufacturer who controls the industry standard. Therefore although manufacturers may say that they support the idea, in practice the issue is clouded by market power and politics.

What must be appreciated is the fact that standards apply across the entire computer and telecommunications industry. In other words, it cannot be entirely settled within the confines of the personal computer industry. Furthermore, as was shown earlier in Fig. 6.1 standards need to be applied to a number of different aspects of the personal computer itself, including microprocessors, electronic interfaces, peripherals, operating systems, graphical interfaces and applications software. To try and create a standard in any one of these areas alone, takes enormous resources and the development of significant market power as illustrated by the cases of Intel, IBM, Apple and Microsoft. Companies trying to challenge these industry leaders are in effect trying to break their technological domination of the market. Three options exist. Either adopt the dominant manufacturer's protocols (assuming that they are non-proprietary) or alternatively try and create a rival standard in much the same way that Apple did with IBM. Lastly, create a consortium of companies to establish an agreed standard. Unless the industry is regulated by quasi-government bodies as in the case of telecommunications, then there may be little incentive for major manufacturers to all agree as to which consortium or set of standards to adopt. An example that illustrates this last point is in the case of the arrangement between AT&T and Sun Microsystems to establish a UNIX based industry operating standard. However, in 1988 IBM, DEC and HP set up a rival programme since they did not want to lose control of such a critical technology to their rivals. Thus they established Open Software Foundation that would duplicate the efforts of AT&T and Sun, but at the same time would not be compatible.

Thus attempts so far in this direction suggest that standards may become the platform for the establishment of competing strategic groups during the 1990s. Given the vast investments required to establish a standard and the risks of failure, as illustrated by IBM's efforts with PS/2 and OS/2, then the only way forward looks increasingly to spread the risk and increase the market power by means of consortia and strategic alliances. Unfortunately the net result may be that the industry moves towards an era of multiple standards, which far from simplifying the market conditions will actually create further confusion. Ironically, it may be that the key area of battle over standards will be fought at the leading edge of communications itself, in other words in control of the network, for this reflects the area of greatest change in the way that personal computers and workstations are used in organisations. It is also in this area that software is going through its greatest changes. However, developments in networking software are still in their early stages and hence discussion of their implications on the industry and its markets are left to the last chapter, when some of their potential features are discussed in more detail.

Naturally, in an industry rooted so deeply in rapidly changing technology, it is difficult knowing where to draw the boundaries of discussion about the technology itself and where to begin to discuss its implications. Clearly, a number of other developments took place in personal computer technology during the past decade, some of the most significant of which are illustrated in Table 6.4. These included advances in screen technology and the use of low power microelectronics which have been instrumental in developing more reliable, lighter and more compact portable computers. Advances in printer technologies have seen the spread of laser and ink-jet printers to replace the earlier dot-matrix machines and the establishment of Canon and Hewlett Packard as world leaders in this field. The growth of Mac systems and the rapid diffusion of Windows have led to the much greater use of various input and output devices that facilitate graphical and visual presentations. Furthermore, the convergence of high-end personal computers with technical workstations has led to greater use of these machines with technical and scientific peripherals, which in turn has boosted demand for such products. Indeed, the entire trend towards development of multimedia[33] has also meant that personal computer technology is increasingly embraced by or involved with other forms of digital technology from the consumer electronics industry, especially in the areas of audio equipment and photographic and video systems. Personal computers can now be found with voice-recognition systems, voice synthesisers and built-in CD-ROM[34] drives. At the same time, memory storage devices continue to expand so that RAM capacities of over 20 Mb[35] as opposed to less than 1Mb in 1983 are not uncommon and hard-disk storage of over 2 gigabytes[36]

Table 6.4. Evolution of the personal computer — some significant issues in product technology: 1984 - 1990.

	1984	1987	1988	1989	1990
SOFTWARE	Establishment of MS-DOS as industry standard Operating Software, replacing CPM-80; Integrated Programs: Lotus 1,2, 3.; Communications Packages (Limited); Low awareness of MAC type Graphics Interface; Growth of Vertical Business Markets leading to specialised applications.	Success of Apple and software developers in the establishment of the Desktop Publishing market. Increased attention on high performance custom packages for vertical markets. Introduction of O/S-2; Menus/Icons Interface.	Desktop Publishing becomes major growth segment; Development of new graphics programs for the "Presentations" market; Increasing emphasis on Executive "Productivity" Tools; Spill-over from CAD;	Increased development of "Software suites" to allow easy learning and cross transfer of data, e.g. Microsoft packages. Growth of Utilities and Tools for Customised facilities; Networking Software for Multi-user environments.	Introduction of Windows 3; Apple System 7 both with multitasking capabilities; Increasing Networking and Multiuser programs; Unix vs. OS-2; Development of Multi-media programs.
PERIPHERALS	Increasing power of Off-Line Storage to 800K; Move towards 3.5 inch discs away from IBM and industry standard 5.25 inch discs; Improved speeds on daisy-wheel high-quality printers; Increasing range of peripherals for 16-bit based machines;	Laser-printers move to become the standard for high quality printing output; Ink-jet printers substitute dot-matrix printers; "Mouse" Input/Output; High-resolution monitors for large screen display; Improved ergonomic features and ease of use.	Growth of CD-ROM for audio input/output and visual learning methods; Increasing linkage between 3rd party software and appropriate peripherals into artistic and creative vertical markets, e.g. music synthesizers; Increasing use of Modems and Local Area Networks, plus database access.	Image Processing systems for Professionals; Introduction of Individual priced laser printers; Growth in "Scanners" and Digitisers for Input of data; Storage expansion up to levels of 650 MB; Tape storage up to 80MB.	Move towards the development of standards for multimedia systems; This will involve linking conventional input/output personal computer devices to more exotic units for purposes of computer control, data storage and manipulation in both the video, audio and tactile sense realms. e.g Hi-Fi; Photographic; T.V.; Fax; CAD; Phones;Voice; Touch and Simulators.
CENTRAL COMPUTER AND PROCESSING UNIT	Increasing RAM power to levels of 126K as a norm; Extension boards allowing upgrades to 258K; IBM PC gaining dominant industry position enormous growth in IBM compatible "Clones";	Demise of IBM vis "Clones"; Growing acceptance of the Apple MAC "Interface" and use of 32 bit processors; RAM power top range up to 2MB; Introduction of IBM PS-2 system.	Growth of high performance portable computers with high quality screen display; RAM power top range up to 4-6MB;	Increasing range of Lap-top machines with IBM compatibility; RAM power top range up to 16MB; Convergence of Top-end PC and low-end workstation;	The personal computer continues to grow in top end performance rapidly converging into a personal workstation. Whilst in mid to low range machines prices drop or customers receive an increasing level of power for constant price levels.

is now available, dwarfing the 10–20 Mb systems available in the mid-1980s. Thus the personal computer itself has really taken on the nature of a true hardware platform onto which manufacturers, third party suppliers of peripherals and many users are able to bolt on a whole variety of accessories and systems to make their machine perform whatever range of functions they choose to select.

With so many technologies, products and companies involved in the industry, it is not surprising that the market appears complex and confusing to many manufacturers and their users. However, whilst many new forms of hardware peripheral and software systems continually redefine the nature of the personal computer and its functions, the industry still revolves around the core product, namely the personal computer. Furthermore, for the purpose of this story, we are concerned to identify the key patterns of change that took place during the past decade between the major personal computer manufacturers and to see how their behaviour impacted the evolution of the industry and its markets. It is these issues that we now move on to consider in the next two sections.

MARKET CONDITIONS AND EVOLUTION

During the previous section it was shown how changes in technology had driven the industry to a much greater degree of complexity. What this section will show is how the market structure evolved during the late 1980s and early 1990s as a result of some of these changes in terms of market segmentation by user and product group. It will then proceed to see how competitive performance evolved over time, before finally considering some of the changes in strategic perceptions and orientations.

Market Development and Evolution

Patterns of Market Segmentation

Between 1985 and 1992 the United States personal computer market went through a number of changes in its structure and overall size, growing from $1.3 billion in 1985 to $22 billion in 1992. However, these figures exclude any single-user workstations, which when included increases the figure to $25 Bn. Indeed, as was discussed at the beginning of this chapter, the nature of the personal computer has changed quite significantly over time. Thus whereas in 1985, personal computers were mainly desktop stand-alone machines, by the early 1990s a number of different product types had emerged, so that when analysing the market in particular, as was shown in the last section, single-user workstations and high-end personal computers began to converge until they were really indistinguishable in terms of product/market characteristics.

Indeed, by 1988, the U.S. workstation market was rapidly converging with the top-end of personal computers to form a new category of desktop computer in the form of personal workstations. In general, this type of machine was based upon a 32-bit microprocessor and priced between $5000 and $15,000 as a stand-alone unit. The lead into workstations had been held by Sun Microsystems, Apollo Computers, DEC and Hewlett Packard during the mid-1980s and had been met by high-end machines from IBM, Apple and Compaq. The zone of confrontation between the personal computers and workstations is illustrated in Fig. 6.3,[37] where it can be seen that the workstation market was made up mainly of machines used in the technical marketplace. However, companies such as Sun, DEC and HP recognised the enormous potential that their products might have if software was developed for the commercial market and this motivated them to move in this direction. Furthermore, it was evident that the size of the technical workstation market was limited and therefore expansion into commercial applications seemed a logical move. The impact of these moves upon the competition in the personal computer industry are discussed later in this and the next chapter.

In terms of evolution, the United States personal computer market moved from its legitimisation stage into those of consolidation, maturity and saturation. This was most clearly marked by the slow down in the rate of growth in the overall market. However, during the mid-1980s up

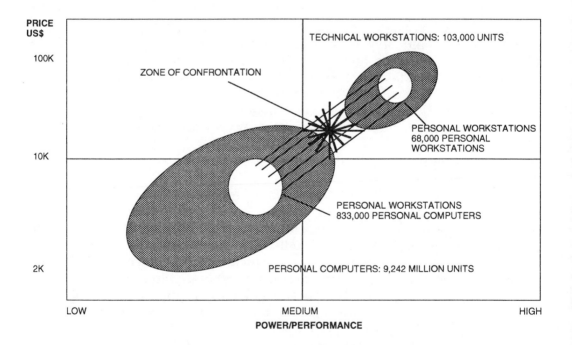

Source: Based upon data provided by and with the permission of International Data Corporation.
Note: This figure is not to scale, but is merely intended to illustrate the overall pattern and point of convergence between the two markets.

Fig. 6.3. Relative sizes and positions of the personal computer and workstation markets
(United States shipments of United States-based vendors): 1988.

to around 1988 the desktop market had enjoyed strong growth as an increasing number of companies moved towards personal computer systems for their information systems solutions, which was further stimulated by the introduction of the more powerful 386 based systems shown earlier in this chapter. The prospect of strong growth attracted a number of new entrants, some of which were in effect playing a newgame strategy. These were the low cost manufacturers and distributors such as Dell, Packard Bell and Gateway 2000. As a result, excess capacity began to develop. At the same time, the market itself began to mature as an increasing number of purchases shifted to replacement units. It should also be remembered that the market consisted of a large variety of different types of users ranging from large corporations to small businesses, whose patterns of demand were at different stages of maturity and based upon a different set of requirements. It is also important to appreciate that the slow down varied by user market segment as illustrated in Table 6.5, which shows the evolution of the market for the period between 1987 and 1992. No new major user segments emerged during this period. For each segment, Table 6.5 illustrates the level of unit shipments, active installed base, the value of shipments and the average selling price for each year, together with the annual change in these measures. In addition, each measure is shown as a percentage of the total market for the particular year. This presents a rich database and the reader will find a number of interesting points to observe. However, the key patterns to emerge centre upon the following.

Firstly, the trends in the overall market should be noticed, where it can be seen that after 1987, the annual growth rate in total shipments slowed rapidly from 20.8 per cent between 1986 to 1987 down to single digit numbers thereafter. Although lagging somewhat behind, the total installed base of units followed a similar pattern, so that it grew only 7.6 per cent during 1991 to 1992. However, it is in the growth of the value of shipments that the true scale of the slow down can be seen. In 1986 to 1987 this grew at 32.2 per cent, which was a faster rate than growth in unit shipments and was reflected in the increased average selling price (ASP) from $2340 to $2470. Indeed, although it slowed during the next two years to single digit figures, it still remained ahead of growth in unit shipments, continuing to reflect an increasing average selling price, which was largely due to the expanding number of single-user workstations and high-end personal computers being sold, especially in the scientific/ technical and business/professional market segments. However, in 1991, the value of unit shipments collapsed and actually declined, not just for one year, but again in 1992, which is forecast to continue in 1993. A number of factors accounted for this dramatic change and will be discussed in more detail shortly. However, the key culprit was a severe drop in unit prices, which is reflected in the decrease of average sales price. Indeed, the average selling price of personal computers is forecast to continue to decline and reflects very much the technology forces driving down the price of microprocessors and associated components described later in this chapter.

Table 6.5. (part 1 of 2) United States PC/SU workstation market by application segment, unit shipments (000's) and dollar value of shipments (US$M): 1987 - 1992.

	1987	% of Total Market	% Change 86/87	1988	% of Total Market	% Change 87/88	1989	% of Total Market	% Change 88/89
BUSINESS/PROFESSIONAL									
Shipments	4,806	58.60	40.5	5,595	64.08	16.42	6,029	67.10	7.76
Active Installed Base	16,822	47.90	39.1	22,169	51.47	31.79	27,095	55.28	22.22
$ Value of Shipments	13,285	69.30	41.8	14,759	68.49	11.10	15,483	67.10	4.91
ASP ($000s)	2.76		1	2.64		-4.35	2.568		-2.73
HOME/HOBBY									
Shipments	2,203	26.86	-4.3	1,685	19.30	-23.51	1,266	14.09	-24.87
Active Installed Base	14,171	40.35	9.8	15,381	35.71	8.54	14,910	30.42	-3.06
$ Value of Shipments	2,665	13.90	16.3	1,853	8.60	-30.47	1,223	5.30	-34.00
ASP ($000s)	1.21		21.5	1.1		-9.09	0.966		-12.18
SCIENTIFIC/TECHNICAL									
Shipments	430	5.24	47.3	595	6.81	38.37	720	8.01	21.01
Active Installed Base	1,317	3.75	40.6	1,895	4.40	43.89	2542	5.19	34.14
$ Value of Shipments	2,166	11.30	14.9	3,686	17.11	70.18	4938	21.40	33.97
ASP ($000s)	5.04		-22	6.2		23.02	6.86		10.65
EDUCATION									
Shipments	763	9.30	-1.5	856	9.80	12.19	970	10.80	13.32
Active Installed Base	2,810	8.00	24.6	3,627	8.42	29.07	4,470	9.12	23.24
$ Value of Shipments	1,054	5.50	10.2	1,250	5.80	18.60	1,431	6.20	14.48
ASP ($000s)	1.38		11.8	1.46		5.80	1.474		0.96
Shipments Total	8,202		20.80	8,731		6.45	8,985		2.91
Total Active Installed Base	35,120		24.60	43,072		22.64	49,017		13.80
Total $ Value of Shipments	19,170		32.20	21,548		12.40	23,075		7.09
ASP	2.34		9.40	2.47		5.59	2.57		4.06

Notes on Installed Base:

a.) Assumes a seven-year life cycle for PCs in the business/professional and education segments.

b.) Assumes a six-year life cycle for machines in the scientific/technical segment.

c.) Assumes six-year life cycle for machines in the home/hobby segment beginning for machines shipped in 1986. The retirement rate for home/hobby machines in 1990 - 1992 has been accelerated to account for substantial shipments that occurred in the mid-1980s. As a result, the installed base of home/hobby machines is declining as new shipments total less than retirements.

Source: International Data Corporation, 1992.
Reproduced by permission of International Data Corporation, © 1992.

Table 6.5. (part 2 of 2) United States PC/SU workstation market by application segment, unit shipments (000's) and dollar value of shipments (US$M): 1987 - 1992.

	1990	% of Total Market	% Change 89/90	1991	% of Total Market	% Change 90/91	1992	% of Total Market	% Change 91/92
BUSINESS/PROFESSIONAL									
Shipments	6,536	69.84	8.41	6,851	70.65	4.82	7,361	71.55	7.44
Active Installed Base	31,580	59.14	16.55	35,846	61.51	13.51	40,466	64.54	12.89
$ Value of Shipments	17,086	66.76	10.35	17,089	67.20	0.02	17,089	67.50	0.00
ASP ($000s)	2.616		1.87	2.5		-4.43	2.32		-7.20
HOME/HOBBY									
Shipments	936	10.00	-26.07	863	8.90	-7.80	859	8.35	-0.46
Active Installed Base	13,343	24.99	-10.51	12625	21.66	-5.38	11,182	17.83	-11.43
$ Value of Shipments	896	3.50	-26.74	763	3.00	-14.84	620	2.45	-18.74
ASP ($000s)	0.957		-0.93	0.88		-8.05	0.72		-18.18
SCIENTIFIC/TECHNICAL									
Shipments	866	9.25	20.28	955	9.85	10.28	1,039	10.10	8.80
Active Installed Base	3,271	6.13	28.68	4,003	6.87	22.38	4,750	7.58	18.66
$ Value of Shipments	6,079	23.75	23.11	6,103	24.00	0.39	6,152	24.30	0.80
ASP ($000s)	7.023		2.38	6.4		-8.87	5.92		-7.50
EDUCATION									
Shipments	1,020	10.90	5.15	1,028	10.60	0.78	1,029	10.00	0.10
Active Installed Base	5,201	9.74	16.35	5,802	9.96	11.56	6,305	10.06	8.67
$ Value of Shipments	1,534	5.99	7.20	1,475	5.80	-3.85	1,455	5.75	-1.36
ASP ($000s)	1.504		2.04	1.44		-4.26	1.41		-2.08
Shipments Total Total Active	9,358		4.15	9,697		3.62	10,288		6.09
Installed Base	53,395		8.93	58,276		9.14	62,703		7.60
Total $ Value of Shipments	25,595		10.92	25,430		-0.64	25,316		-0.45
ASP	2.74		6.50	2.62		-4.12	2.46		-6.17

Notes on Installed Base:

a.) Assumes a seven-year life cycle for PCs in the business/professional and education segments.

b.) Assumes a six-year life cycle for machines in the scientific/technical segment.

c.) Assumes six-year life cycle for machines in the home/hobby segment beginning for machines shipped in 1986. The retirement rate for home/hobby machines in 1990 - 1992 has been accelerated to account for substantial shipments that occurred in the mid-1980s. As a result, the installed base of home/hobby machines is declining as new shipments total less than retirements.

Source: International Data Corporation, 1992.
Reproduced by permission of International Data Corporation, © 1992.

If one looks at the pattern user segments, it can be seen that some significant differences in the various measures occur. In terms of relative size, the business/professional segment has remained the dominant sector, but its importance has grown significantly. Whereas in 1987 it represented 58.6 per cent of the overall market in terms of unit shipments, by 1992 it had increased to 71.6 per cent; not surprisingly therefore, many of the competitors during this period concentrated their main efforts in this area. This focus upon the business segment had already become apparent by the late 1980s, as illustrated in Table 6.6. What is evident is that companies such as Hewlett Packard, Sun Microsystems, DEC and Apollo were naturally focused upon the scientific/technical marketplace, whilst Amstrad focused upon the education segment and Commodore, Atari and Laser Computer focused their efforts on the home/hobby segment. For the remaining competitors, the business segment was their major area of activity. Indeed, referring back to Table 6.5 it can be seen that the original market size of the home/hobby segment declined rapidly during the late 1980s both

Table 6.6. Percentage of mix across segments in the United States personal computer market by major competitors in unit shipments (000's): 1988.

COMPANY	MARKET SEGMENTS									
	Business/ Professional		Home/Hobby		Scientific/ Technical		Education		U.S. Total	
	Units	% of Mix	Units	% of Mix	Units	% of Mix	Units	% of Mix	Units	% of Mix
IBM	1,170	75.00	78	5.00	156	10.00	156	10.00	1560	100.00
Apple	480	50.00	192	20.00	48	5.00	240	25.00	960	100.00
Zenith	461	85.06		0.00	49	9.04	32	5.90	542	100.00
Compaq	319	85.75		0.00	53	14.25		0.00	372	100.00
Tandy	273	60.13	136	29.96		0.00	45	9.91	454	100.00
Epson	184	85.19	15	6.94		0.00	17	7.87	216	100.00
Toshiba	173	100.00		0.00		0.00		0.00	173	100.00
Everex	145	100.00		0.00		0.00		0.00	145	100.00
Packard Bell	135	80.36	25	14.88		0.00	8	4.76	168	100.00
Hewlett Packard	130	70.27		0.00	55	29.73		0.00	185	100.00
Wyse	123	100.00		0.00		0.00		0.00	123	100.00
AST	116	95.08		0.00	6	4.92		0.00	122	100.00
NEC IS	111	100.00		0.00		0.00		0.00	111	100.00
Laser	97	100.00		0.00		0.00		0.00	97	100.00
Leading Edge	95	74.80	19	14.96		0.00	13	10.24	127	100.00
Dell	91	90.10		0.00	10	9.90		0.00	101	100.00
Acer	89	89.90		0.00		0.00	10	10.10	99	100.00
CompuAdd	79	79.80	20	20.20		0.00		0.00	99	100.00
Commodore	53	9.93	428	80.15		0.00	53	9.93	534	100.00
Atari		0.00	154	100.00		0.00		0.00	154	100.00
Laser Computer		0.00	60	100.00		0.00		0.00	60	100.00
Amstrad		0.00	30	60.00		0.00	20	40.00	50	100.00
Sun		0.00		0.00	41	100.00		0.00	41	100.00
DEC		0.00		0.00	28	100.00		0.00	28	100.00
Apollo		0.00		0.00	14	100.00		0.00	14	100.00
Others	1,667	59.34	645	22.96	175	6.23	322	11.46	2809	100.00
Total	5,991	64.12	1802	19.29	635	6.80	916	9.80	9344	100.00

Source: Adapted from data provided by International Data Corporation, 1990.
Reproduced by permission of International Data Corporation, © 1990.

in unit and value terms of shipments, so that its installed base shrank from 40.4 per cent of the market in 1987 to less than 18 per cent by 1992 and is predicted to decline still further. Clearly the most rapidly growing sector in terms of shipments has been the scientific/technical segment, which reflects the growing demand for high-end personal computers and workstations in this community of users, that have been rapidly shifting away from mainframe based systems. Remaining at around 10 per cent of the share of market shipments, the education segment has grown steadily, but slowly throughout the period. Broadly similar patterns can be seen in terms of the changes of the value of shipments, except that not surprisingly, given their higher average selling price, the relative size of the scientific/technical segment grew to 24 per cent of the market by 1992, whilst representing only 10 per cent in unit shipments. In contrast, yet complementing this pattern, the relative importance of the business/ professional, home/hobby and education segments were not so great as in unit terms.

However, the most significant factor related to the changes that took place in the average selling prices of units in the different segments during the period, since these fundamentally altered the financial model of the competitors and heavily influenced the behaviour of buyers in the respective markets. The first market to be affected was the home/hobby segment, which as can be seen from Table 6.5 experienced continuing decline in both the volume of demand as well as the average selling price, which fell from an ASP of $1210 in 1987 to around $760 by 1992, nearly halving in five years. At the same time, the importance of this segment has shrunk dramatically as mentioned above. In contrast, the ASP for the education segment has actually increased over the period, from $1380 in 1987 to $1410, although the trend is now downwards. Thus with comparatively slow but constant demand in unit shipments, the relative size of this segment has remained stable. In much the same way, the average selling price in the scientific/technical market also increased during the period from $5040 in 1987 to $5920 in 1992, although looking at the figures, just as with the education segment, the trend is now downwards from a 1990 peak.

However, given the importance of the business/professional segment, it is in this segment that the most significant changes for the industry as a whole have occurred, since this is where many of the competitors have focused their main resources and efforts. This is also their premium market. Whilst between 1987 and 1990 the average selling price dropped only 5 per cent from $2760 to $2616, in 1991 it dropped 4.7 per cent and a further 7.1 per cent the following year. Since this coincided with a slowing in the rate of unit growth to less than 5 per cent growth, then the value of unit shipments in the market as a whole experienced no growth at all during 1991 and 1992. Overnight, the conditions of the major market segment in the personal computer and single-user workstation market had changed dramatically and as a result, competition in the industry went through some significant changes.

In terms of product segmentation, it is worth noting how by 1990, the product range offered by competitors had expanded to include notebooks, battery-laptops, AC portables, desktops and towers,[38] which were divided between Intel based and non-Intel based machines as illustrated in Table 6.7. Most importantly, what this data reflects are the changes that have taken place during the 1980s in the life cycles of the different types of product. Whereas in the mid-1980s the market consisted primarily of desktop and AC portables, both of which were enjoying strong market growth, by 1990 the pattern had changed considerably. Although desktop machines clearly still dominated the overall market, growth in this product type had already reached maturity. In contrast, stand-alone workstations and high-end tower personal computers were enjoying strong growth at 40 per cent or above. Similarly, although the portable segment represented

Table 6.7. United States PC/SU workstation shipments by product type: 1989-1990.

Processor	1989 Shipments	1989 % Share	1990 Shipments	1990 % Share	% Change 1989/90
Intel:					
Notebook	42,550	0.5	255,790	2.7	501.2
Battery-laptop	555,239	6	583,584	6.2	5.1
AC-Portables	142,629	1.6	134,003	1.4	- 6
Total Intel Portables	740,418	8.1	973,376	10.3	31.5
Desktop	6,652,391	72.3	6,707,279	70.8	0.8
Tower	189,066	2.1	280,633	3	48.4
Desktop/Tower	6,841,456	74.4	6,987,912	73.8	2.1
Total Intel PCs	7,581,874	82.5	7,961,288	84.1	5
Non-Intel:					
Notebook	30,500	0.3	34,045	0.4	11.6
Battery-laptop	12,220	0.1	28,640	0.3	134.4
AC-Portable	200	0	850	0	325
Total Non-Intel Portables	42,920	0.4	63,535	0.7	48
Desktop	1,508,471	16.4	1,351,611	14.3	-10.4
Tower	62,409	0.7	87,521	0.9	40.2
Desktop/Tower	1,570,880	17.1	1,439,131	15.2	-8.4
Total Non-Intel PCs	1,613,800	17.5	1,502,666	15.9	-6.9
Total Portables PCs	783,338	8.5	1,036,911	11	32.4
Total Desktop/Tower PCs	8,412,336	91.5	8,427,043	89	0.2
Total PCs (excl SU Workstations)	9,070,856	98.6	9,288,913	98.2	2.4
Total SU Workstations	124,818	1.4	175,041	1.8	40.2
Total PCs/SU Workstations	9,195,674	100	9,463,954	100	2.9

Source: International Data Corporation, 1991.
Reproduced by permission of International Data Corporation, © 1991.

just over 10 per cent of the market and although older AC portables were no longer significant, they had given way to the newer battery powered laptop and notebook machines which were enjoying significant rates of growth that attracted a number of competitors, many of them from Japan, Korea and Taiwan. Thus it can be seen that by 1990, whilst the product life cycle for desktops was maturing rapidly towards saturation, high-end machines and the newer mobile personal computers were in a fairly early stage of their respective life-cycles. However, whilst representing rapidly growing sub-segments of the industry, they were also still quite small and could not provide sufficient sales to offset the decline in the maturing desktop segment.

Forces for Market Development

Having looked at the overall pattern of market segmentation and its relative rates of growth, both for user applications and product types, it is appropriate to move on to consider what were the factors that drove the industry and its markets from the legitimisation into the consolidation, maturation and saturation stages. In other words, what were the forces responsible for the patterns of change in market growth. Naturally, some of these factors are supply driven, whilst others are demand driven.

On the supply side, technological change together with increasing and new types of competition, plus subsequent over capacity in the industry underpinned many of the problems that were to occur in the early 1990s. As was shown in the previous section, technological change revolved around a number of events, including the battle between IBM and the clones, when IBM launched its PS/2 and OS/2; the conflict surrounding industry standards on operating systems and other protocols; plus the development of RISC based systems in the high-end personal computer and single-user workstation market. It also involved the development of the tower type systems, servers[39] and laptop and notebook products. In each of these product markets, different groups of competitors fought for market share, some were specialised into one segment, such as Sun Microsystems in workstations or Toshiba in portables, whilst others such as IBM and Compaq fought across the range. Furthermore, although competition was intense in all sectors, as was previously shown, it was only in the desktop segment that the life-cycle was moving through consolidation into maturity and saturation. However, given that this represented the major share of the overall market, a downturn in growth of demand in this segment was bound to have a major impact on the overall industry and it is upon this segment that our discussion of events is mainly focused.

The battle between the clones and IBM in the desktop market intensified in the late 1980s as low cost manufacturers from the Far East such as Goldstar and Hyundai, together with United States companies such as Dell, Packard Bell, AST and others began to change the rules of the game. Essentially their strategies were based upon development of low cost manufacturing and in particular, low cost distribution. Details of these changes in the industry's value chains are discussed a little more fully towards the end of this chapter. However, the impact of these strategies was to put increasing downward pressure on average selling prices as a result of the development of mass distribution channels and declining component costs, which reflected the advanced stage of the life-cycle in this segment. In addition, an increasing percentage of purchases of desktop machines were for replacement purposes. Given the over capacity that had developed in the industry, it was not long before competition on price rather than brand name became the dominant feature of sales activity.

This change was significant since it was to act in favour of many of the lower priced clones and was to have a serious impact on the performance of the brand leaders such as IBM and Compaq. It resulted from the fact that during the late 1980s, an increasing number of business customers found themselves questioning the value of paying the enormous price premiums that they were facing from leading companies such as IBM, Hewlett Packard and Compaq in standard desktop machines. Competing in a rather more select market, Apple Computer also found itself under increasing criticism for its high prices, although in Apple's case, the added value of the easier to use Mac system did carry some weight with many of its customers. However, even Apple needed to attract new customers if it was to continue to grow and increasingly many of these would need to be drawn from the classical MS-DOS environment, where Apple's prices were particularly high on a comparative basis. As a result of their shift in attitude, a number of customers began switching to the low cost clones. By 1990, the United States personal computer market was no longer driven by double digit growth with customers hungry for new equipment and systems. Instead it had matured into a saturated condition, where economic conditions became a far stronger driver of growth rates.

Unfortunately, the United States economy was by this stage entering into a significant downturn that was to turn into a full-blown recession during the early 1990s. However, the severity of the economic downturn and its duration was something that few had anticipated in the industry. Companies that a few years earlier had been willing to invest heavily in new personal computer systems, or to upgrade from older systems to the newer 386 based systems were now looking to cut costs in this area. As a result, customers became far more price sensitive and determined to gain value for their money. The newgame strategies of the low priced clones suited the requirements of those customers that were looking for cheaper boxes to do a particular job. Greater knowledge on the part of customers, both in the corporate and small end of the business market, also meant that they were far more confident to go out and choose products from other lesser known suppliers. Furthermore, as the recession began to take hold, a number of corporate customers started to shift their purchasing patterns towards trying to make their existing installed base of desktop personal computers work more effectively for them. This involved investment in connectivity technology in an effort to streamline and increase the value of information being used in their organisations. Overall a clear trend was developing in the desktop market, which consisted of low levels of demand for new equipment; except at the high-end, a large dominance of replacement purchases; a desire to upgrade the productivity of existing systems through new systems and applications software; together with improved communications capabilities. Furthermore, this trend underlied the drive towards improved networking technology by major hardware and software companies discussed in the previous section. At the same time, it was clear that traditional brand names could no longer command the scale of premium prices they had enjoyed a few years earlier. Furthermore, distribution of such products was moving rapidly towards an increasing reliance upon mass market channels such as mail order and superstores, whilst for systems requirements, the VARs[40] were becoming more important. Traditional dealer channels were seen to be going into decline.

As a result of these events and developments, competitors were forced to make a number of major changes in their operating and marketing strategies. In particular, the brand leaders such as IBM, Compaq, Apple and other brand competitors such as Zenith Data Systems, Hewlett Packard and DEC had to restructure their operations and product offerings towards a new financial business model. Gone were the high priced, high margin conditions which could support high overheads. Instead, the new financial model would have to be based upon meeting the new competitors such as Dell, Packard Bell, AST and others in low cost manufacturing and distribution with lower priced products sold in volume at lower margins. Furthermore, to meet such challenges, the companies would need to achieve major changes in their organisations within a short space of time and develop new relationships in the market, both with distribution channels and with customers. Similarity between strategic intent and strategic action are notoriously difficult to achieve and for many of the competitors cultural factors in their organisations presented a major obstacle to change. Such obstacles were not specific just to the larger established companies. A number of the younger companies, including Compaq were initially of the opinion that their downturn in performance could largely be attributed to the poor state of the economy. However, as 1991 moved into 1992, it became apparent to the vast majority of industry observers and competitors alike that the desktop personal computer business was going through a major restructuring, which was consistent with the predictions of the newgame model outlined at the beginning of this book. Indeed, as will be more fully described in the next chapter, the entire computer industry was now moving into a major period of Schumpeterian "creative destruction".[41] Furthermore, as will also be seen in the next chapter, such conditions were not only developing in the United States market, but were occurring overseas in foreign markets, so that competitors could not seek significant growth and expansion outside the domestic market. In addition, the changes in American foreign policy with the fading of the cold war also meant that the defence industry and associated government sectors were cutting back on investment in their traditional activities. As a result, demand from this segment for personal computers also went into decline and more importantly, offered little hope of assisting in economic recovery.

Competitive Performance of Major Players

Just how severe these changes in competitive conditions became can best be appreciated by taking a look at the performance of some of the leading players in the overall market during the period 1990 to 1992. During 1991, one study indicated that gross margins dropped from 33.8 per cent in the first quarter of 1991 to 29.2 per cent a year later.[42] This translated into a year over year drop in operating profit of 3.6 percentage points from 8.6 per cent to 5 per cent. Although some of these declines may not appear so high, it must be remembered that on a price basis, some of the product price reductions were in the order of between 30 to 50 per cent. Set against this background of declining margins, it is not surprising therefore that personal computer companies have been forced to cut their operating costs. This naturally put considerable pressure on manufacturers of such products as well as their channels of distribution. Thus even some of the low cost competitors are realising that the only way to survive in such an environment is to ensure that expenses as a percentage of revenues are continuously kept low. Furthermore, it is also important to appreciate that the pattern of growth in the different price segments was also quite varied and significant. This is illustrated in Fig. 6.4 which shows the rate of growth in the respective price bands for personal computers in terms of unit shipments between 1990 and 1991. The pattern for value shipments is quite similar. What stands out from this diagram is that products in the $1000 to $1999 range enjoyed strong growth during the period at 38.8 per cent, with the next band up of $2000 to $3999 enjoying moderate growth at 6 per cent. Together machines in these two segments represented 68 per cent of the total market in shipment terms, but only 47 per cent in value terms. In the low-end of below $1000 the segment shrank by nearly 30 per cent, whilst similar declines were

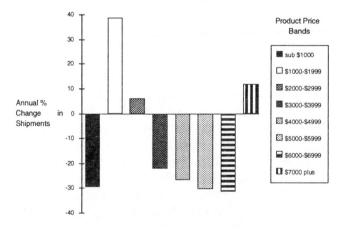

Source: Based upon data provided by International Data Corporation, 1992.
Reproduced by permission of International Data Corporation, © 1992.

Fig. 6.4. United States PC/SU workstation growth in unit shipments by price band: 1990 - 1991.

felt in all other sectors, except in high-end systems worth over $7000. Hence, the product mix, in terms of price ranges for a particular company could produce vastly different results. Thus competitors such as Sun Microsystems, whose workstations converged to compete with high-end personal computers enjoyed a market experiencing strong growth in unit and value terms, as did competitors with products above $1000 but under $4000. However, competitors' products outside these ranges faced the heavy price cutting and severe competition discussed earlier.

Within such a depressed overall market, it is therefore not surprising that a number of competitors have stepped up their efforts in the more rapidly growing segments of high-end and portable notebook machines. In effect, they have been forced to learn the importance of focus in their strategies. However, strong competition in both these segments has also meant significant price cuts. In notebooks, the resulting price war and oversupply has been advantageous to customers and Apple Computer's products in this segment have gained it rapid growth in market position, whilst new channels of distribution have expanded the market further into the consumer market. In high-end systems, Windows 3 has been a powerful driver for some customers to invest in the more powerful 32-bit based machines and increasingly Windows and the latest version of DOS are being preloaded onto systems. In addition, the networking of personal computers helps drive demand for mid-range and high-end machines, so that unit shipments of PC-based LAN[43] servers grew over 15 per cent from 1990 through 1992.

Set against this background, competitors have shown mixed levels of performance and Tables 6.8 and 6.9 illustrate the level of unit shipments and their value for the top twenty competitors in the overall United States PC/SU workstation marketplace for the period 1989 to 1991. Clearly a number of interesting patterns emerge from this data, but it must also be remembered that this data represents a broad overview of the market and for reasons explained earlier, there exist considerable variations in the performance of the respective competitors in particular market segments. However, the overview is nonetheless valid, since it provides an indication of some of the key patterns to develop during the period. To begin with these companies represented 65 per cent of the total market in unit shipments in 1991 and 71 per cent in value terms. Interestingly these amounts were rising, indicating a growing level of concentration in the industry for the period between 1989 and 1991.

Firstly, to provide an overview of the position of the key players during 1991, it can be seen that in terms of shipments the top five players in the market were IBM, Apple, Packard Bell, Compaq and Tandy/Grid which together represented 40.3 per cent of the total market. In value terms, Packard Bell and Tandy Grid were replaced by the workstation manufacturer Sun Microsystems and Hewlett Packard with its joint involvement in personal computers and workstations. Together these five represented 41.3 per cent of the market in value terms. However, if one excludes workstations, the top five competitors for both value and shipments

Table 6.8. United States PC/SU workstation market share of United States based vendors in unit shipments (000's): 1989 - 1991.

1989 Units Ranking	1990 Units Ranking	1991 Units Ranking	Name of Company Operating in the United States	1989 Unit Ships "(000)"	1989 Mkt Share (%)	1990 Unit Ships "(000)"	1990 Mkt Share (%)	% Change in Market Share 89/90	1991 Unit Ships "(000)"	1991 Mkt Share (%)	% Change in Market Share 90/91
1	1	1	IBM	1,544,000	16.79	1,525,800	16.31	-1.18	1,370,400	14.13	-10.18
2	2	2	Apple	980,100	10.66	1,019,120	10.89	3.98	1,340,045	13.82	31.49
7	5	3	Packard Bell	301,200	3.28	371,500	3.97	23.34	455,000	4.69	22.48
4	4	4	Compaq	400,000	4.35	425,300	4.54	6.33	390,000	4.02	-8.30
3	3	5	Tandy/Grid	460,850	5.01	468,600	5.01	1.68	349,250	3.60	-25.47
11	12	6	AST Research	157,350	1.71	172,200	1.84	9.44	261,490	2.70	51.85
36	18	7	Gateway 2000	22,170	0.24	94,950	1.01	328.28	246,774	2.54	159.90
-	9	8	VTech Computers (1)		0.00	206,850	2.21	.	220,000	2.27	6.36
5	6	9	Groupe Bull/ZDS	386,100	4.20	216,100	2.31	-44.03	202,761	2.09	-6.17
10	8	10	Toshiba America	171,100	1.86	209,600	2.24	22.50	181,500	1.87	-13.41
20	17	11	Dell Computer	77,865	0.85	96,850	1.03	24.38	158,880	1.64	64.05
21	13	12	NCR/AT&T(2)	76,095	0.83	155,109	1.66	103.84	147,267	1.52	-5.06
8	10	13	Commodore	295,000	3.21	196,000	2.09	-33.56	146,000	1.51	-25.51
18	14	14	CompuAdd	86,446	0.94	141,300	1.51	63.45	142,400	1.47	0.78
9	11	15	NEC Technologies	197,375	2.15	190,370	2.03	-3.55	139,520	1.44	-26.71
13	19	16	Everex Systems	152,500	1.66	92,550	0.99	-39.31	123,930	1.28	33.91
14	15	17	Hewlett-Packard/Apollo	132,115	1.44	129,100	1.38	-2.28	122,525	1.26	-5.09
-	37	18	Premier Innovations (3)		0.00	37,200	0.40	.	110,000	1.13	195.70
6	7	19	Epson America	302,300	3.29	211,000	2.25	-30.20	105,500	1.09	-50.00
22	20	20	Phillips Consumer Electronics	63,500	0.69	92,500	0.99	45.67	100,550	1.04	8.70
			Other	3,389,608	36.86	3,305,612	35.33	-2.48	3,383,611	34.89	2.36
			Total	9,195,674	100.00	9,357,611	100.00	1.76	9,697,403	100.00	3.63

Notes:
1) VTech Computers is the American subsidiary of Hong Kong based Video Technology. This comprises Laser Computer and Leading Technology. During 1989 Laser Computer shipped 154,600 units whilst Leading Technology shipped approximately 30,000 units.
2) NCR/AT&T reflect the figures for AT&T only in 1989, when NCR's shipments were 41,266 with 0.49 % market share which ranked in 32nd position. The 1990 and 1991 figures reflect the combined shipments after AT&T's takeover of NCR's computer operations.
3) Premier Innovations shipped approximately 20,000 units during 1989.

Source: International Data Corporation, 1991 and 1992, with percentage figures calculated by the author.
Reproduced by permission of International Data Corporation, © 1991 and 1992.

Table 6.9. United States PC/SU workstation market share of United States based vendors in value of shipments (US$M): 1989 - 1991.

1989 Value Ranking	1990 Value Ranking	1991 Value Ranking	Name of Company Operating in the United States	1989 Value Ships ($000)	1989 Mkt Share (%)	1990 Value Ships ($000)	1990 Mkt Market Share (%)	1990 % Change in Share 89/90	1991 Value Ships ($000)	1991 Mkt Market Share (%)	1991 % Change in Mkt Market Share 90/91
1	1	1	IBM	4,559,800	19.52	4,742,080	18.53	4.00	4,348,250	17.10	-8.31
2	2	2	Apple	2,131,384	9.13	2,647,066	10.34	24.19	2,659,677	10.46	0.48
3	3	3	Compaq	1,587,900	6.80	1,547,850	6.05	-2.52	1,231,700	4.84	-20.43
7	6	4	Sun Microsystems	858,215	3.67	1,046,298	4.09	21.92	1,175,530	4.62	12.35
6	4	5	Hewlett-Packard/Apollo	950,778	4.07	1,102,220	4.31	15.93	1,083,902	4.26	-1.66
11	9	6	Packard Bell	478,780	2.05	660,650	2.58	37.99	820,560	3.23	24.20
5	5	7	Tandy/Grid	974,402*	4.17	1,066,498	4.17	9.45	804,615	3.16	-24.56
13	12	8	AST Research	385,220	1.65	578,506	2.26	50.18	796,677	3.13	37.71
14	7	9	NCR/AT&T (1)	313,575	1.34	721,375	2.82	130.05	657,315	2.58	-8.88
36	19	10	Gateway 2000	59,443	0.25	239,248	0.93	302.48	618,034	2.43	158.32
8	10	11	Digital Equipment	773,640	3.31	658,009	2.57	-14.95	590,070	2.32	-10.32
4	8	12	Groupe Bull/ZDS	1,097,800	4.70	703,400	2.75	-35.93	576,962	2.27	-17.98
12	13	13	Toshiba America	445,745	1.91	532,380	2.08	19.44	494,800	1.95	-7.06
17	16	14	Dell Computer	255,156	1.09	309,172	1.21	21.17	458,231	1.80	48.21
20	31	15	Intergraph	200,685	0.86	109,860	0.43	-45.26	385,560	1.52	250.96
30	17	16	CompuAdd	109,046	0.47	300,243	1.17	175.34	336,101	1.32	11.94
-	20	17	VTech Computers (2)	0	0.00	232,128	0.91		312,801	1.23	34.75
18	18	18	Silicon Graphics	222,420	0.95	239,907	0.94	7.86	277,973	1.09	15.87
15	21	19	Everex Systems	307,739	1.32	230,916	0.90	-24.96	276,924	1.09	19.92
10	11	20	NEC Technologies	515,348	2.21	628,765	2.46	22.01	264,826	1.04	-57.88
			Other	7,129,169	30.52	7,299,119	28.52	2.38	7,260,565	28.55	-0.53
			Total	23,356,245	100.00	25,595,690	100.00	9.59	25,431,073	100.00	-0.64

Note:
1) NCR/AT&T reflect the figures for AT&T only in 1989, when NCR's value of shipments were US$188.6M which ranked in 22nd position.
The 1990 and 1991 figures reflect the combined shipments after AT&T's takeover of NCR's computer operations.
2) VTech Computers - value of shipments not known for 1989. However, see Table 6.8. (Note: 1) for volume of unit shipments.

Source: International Data Corporation, 1991 and 1992, with percentage figures calculated by the author.
Reproduced by permission of International Data Corporation, © 1991 and 1992.

of personal computers remain the same. Behind the top five competitors, in shipment terms come a number of the clones such as AST Research, Gateway 2000, Dell Computer, together with some of the more established companies including Groupe Bull/Zenith Data Systems, Toshiba America, NCR/AT&T, Commodore, NEC Technologies and Hewlett Packard/Apollo, each of which held approximately 1 to 2.7 per cent market share. Then further down and below the top twenty come another group of competitors, made up of competitors with less than 1 per cent market share each. However, not surprisingly, if one looks at the ranking in value terms, it can be seen that a number of the competitors with high-end machines or workstations such as Sun Microsystems, Hewlett Packard/Apollo, NCR/AT&T and DEC are much higher in the league.

What is most apparent if one looks at these figures over the period 1989 to 1991 is to see the changes in relative market share amongst certain key players. Clearly, there were winners and losers during the period, both in terms of rates of growth relative to the market average and in terms of actual profitability. Amongst the top five players, the greatest loser in terms of overall loss of unit shipments was IBM, whose dollar share in the PC/SU workstation market dropped dramatically due to a 10 per cent reduction in its personal computer shipments, which resulted largely from over-priced products, together with a lack of notebook products to compete in this rapidly growing segment. Compaq also lost heavily, especially in value terms of its market share. However, IBM managed to just maintain market leadership, whilst Tandy/Grid not only lost significant market share, it also slipped from third to fifth position. Much of this was due to intense competition in Tandy/Grid's core customer market of households and small businesses. The company also lost market share in its portable business. Although not so dramatic in its decline and able to maintain its market ranking, Compaq Computer lost sales in its portable business to heavy competition and in its desktop business to lower priced competitors such as AST and Dell.

In contrast, Apple Computer enjoyed a strengthening of its position due to the reductions in prices of its existing products, the introduction of competitive low-end products such as the Classic and LC, together with a highly successful launch of its Powerbook into the notebook market. Altogether this was reflected by a huge 56 per cent jump in its unit shipments of Macintosh products between 1990 and 1991. However, like other competitors, Apple's average systems value for all Macintosh models fell from $3115 in 1990 to $2514 in 1991. As a result, the company's total increase in value of shipments was less than one per cent, reflecting a major shift in Apple's financial business model. Another company to enjoy high growth in shipments was Packard Bell, which came from seventh position in 1989 to take third position in the league during 1991. Much of this gain was based upon its successive growth of over 20 per cent per annum in unit shipments during 1990 and 1991, which reflected the fact that the company's products fell into the high-growth $1000–$1999 price range, which was shown earlier in Fig. 6.4.

Outside the top five, AST made significant gains in sales, growing by 52 per cent in 1991 over 1990 shipments and as a result moved up from outside the top ten to number six in the league and number eight in value terms. Much of AST's success was based upon its growth in the high-end market and with its success in the notebook market. Following behind AST, Gateway 2000 achieved astounding growth through its mail-order channel operations, with a jump from thirty-sixth position and a growth of nearly 160 per cent over its 1990 sales, both in unit shipments and value terms. Gateway's strategy was based upon price leadership in mid- and high-performance desktop machines. For example, Gateway came a close second to IBM in the 486 processor segment. Once again, this highlights the variation that different competitors may achieve, when viewed across their various product market segments, or measured in terms of processor type or price range. Another company from a background in low-cost distribution was VTech Computers, which was the American subsidiary of the Hong Kong based Video Technology and comprises of two widely distributed consumer brands. The first is Laser Computer which actually underwent a slight downturn in shipments, whilst the other, Leading Technology was amongst the fast-rising brand names making use of alternative mass distribution channels.

In ninth and tenth places respectively were two of the established computer companies. Groupe Bull/Zenith Data Systems which was formed by the former's acquisition of Zenith Data Systems in 1989[44] and the Japanese computer giant and market leader in portable personal computer's, Toshiba. The French company's operations in the United States market centred mainly upon the activities of Zenith Data Systems, which had enjoyed fifth position in the market at the time of its acquisition, but had subsequently suffered major declines in annual shipments, both in unit and value terms and which had consequently halved its market share. Although its notebook line enjoyed some success, the company lost share heavily in its desktop/tower business. In 1991, Toshiba America experienced a downturn in its performance, due largely to increased competition from strong, low-priced products from AST Research, Texas Instruments and Dell Computer. Although not in the top ten in unit shipments, but included in value terms, at the time, the recently merged AT&T/NCR business saw a decrease in its business of nearly 9 per cent due to heavy price competition in its price segments of activity.

Outside these top ten competitors, a number of companies managed to grow ahead of the market average of 3.6 per cent in 1990 to 1991 including Dell Computer, Everex Systems, Premier Innovations and Philips Consumer Electronics. However, Commodore, NEC Technologies, Hewlett Packard/Apollo and Epson America actually lost market share in both years in terms of unit shipments. In value terms, DEC and NEC Technologies also experienced a significant downturn in sales, although DEC also gained in unit shipments. Outside the top twenty, well known competitors such as Acer, Hyundai and Wang sustained decreases in shipments in unit and value terms, with Atari losing heavily in unit shipments. Meanwhile,

Goldstar and Texas Instruments enjoyed strong growth. It is also worth noting the degree of foreign involvement in the market.

Below the top ten players a number of Far Eastern competitors had gained a position in the low end of the IBM compatible market during the late 1980s. These included companies such as Hyundai Electronics America, the South Korean electronics giant; Acer/Altos, in which the Taiwanese conglomerate Acer had acquired the small business systems manufacturer Altos; Samsung Information Systems and Goldstar Technology. Whilst these foreign players had grown in importance in the market, other European competitors that had been hoping for success in the United States market in the early to mid-1980s were far less successful. Olivetti had virtually dropped out of the market, after its marketing agreement with AT&T collapsed. L. M. Ericsson had withdrawn from the market, whilst Sinclair Computer had gone out of business in the United States. The once highly successful Amstrad had also failed to maintain a position in the United States market, which was somewhat of a harbinger of the downturn in performance it was later to experience in its home market in the United Kingdom. During the early 1990s the slow revenue growth in the United States market had damaged the business of a number of the more successful offshore competitors. So that in 1992, Philips Consumer Electronics exited the market. Indeed a number of the South East Asian manufacturers from Taiwan and South Korea have decided to switch their focus to monitors and subassemblies away from the personal computer market, since as will be shown in the next chapter, their own domestic markets have become so price competitive.

Overall therefore, it can be seen that the performance of competitors was extremely varied, with few enjoying any degree of success in the market under their own brand names, with the exceptions of Toshiba America, Epson America and NEC Technologies. Most other foreign competitors have failed in the market, except by acting as OEM contractors for domestic suppliers and distributors. Furthermore, when looking at the list of competitors in the top league, excluding the workstation competitors such as Sun Microsystems, Hewlett Packard/Apollo and Digital Equipment, it is apparent that a number of the low-cost manufacturing/distribution companies have gained significant market share from established players, especially after 1990. However, it is also interesting to note that in 1982, as was shown earlier in this book, the United States market was dominated by IBM, Apple, Tandy, Commodore and Osborne. Ten years later, although IBM, Apple and Tandy/Grid still held a position in the top five players, Commodore had in the meantime slipped significantly and of course Osborne had also fallen from the scene. The great rising star of the mid-1980s, namely Compaq Computer had gained a reputation as IBM's major adversary in the clone world and developed a strong market position. However, whilst IBM and Apple now competed for market dominance, it is apparent that the second tier of competitors with around two to four per cent market share consisted of two distinctly different types of competitor. On the one hand there were the established players such as

Compaq, Tandy/Grid, Groupe Bull/ZDS and Toshiba America, whilst on the other were the newgame low cost players, such as Packard Bell, AST Research, Gateway 2000, VTech Computers and Dell Computer. If one considers the trends in shipments and market share just described, then it is apparent that the former competitors were generally struggling to maintain market share, whilst the latter were making enormous and rapid gains. This is most clearly illustrated in Fig. 6.5 which plots the 1990 to 1991 growth for volume of unit shipments and value of shipments using data from Tables 6.8 and 6.9, and which includes those companies which appear in the top twenty competitors in either set of data. Four types of competitor emerge, which are divided between established companies and new companies, with the former consisting of computer companies that were operating in the personal computer industry prior to 1981, whilst the latter are companies that have subsequently entered after that date. Within each category, they are divided between poor and good performance, which is an indication of negative or positive growth in their shipments during 1990 to 1991. As such the former established competitors would appear to be clearly under attack from the newer entrants. Indeed, by these measures, although enjoying market dominance, IBM actually ranks as one of the losers. However, for the moment its most immediate threat to market dominance comes from Apple Computer and even with the most

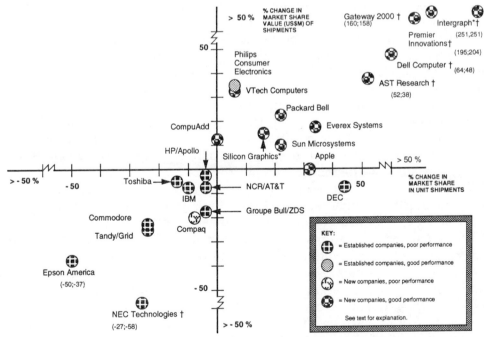

* These companies have been plotted on their actual unit value growth but, in the absence of data, the unit shipment terms have been assumed as equal.
† These outlying companies have their growth values shown in brackets with shipments growth as the first figure. Based on data shown in Tables 6.8. and 6.9.

Fig. 6.5. Strategic position of major competitors in the United States PC/SU workstation market in terms of the growth in volume and value of unit shipments: 1990 - 1991.

extreme projections, it will be a few years before IBM is overtaken by one of the second tier players. Naturally it should also be appreciated that such an event is not unthinkable in the volatile competitive conditions that characterise the United States personal computer industry during the 1990s.

Taken together, all these developments create an increasingly complex environment within the business/professional segment, which involves manufacturers of personal computers (both desktop and portable), technical workstations, minicomputers and mainframes, together with the various software companies. To some extent this environment is broadly similar to the conditions in the information systems business marketplace during the late 1970s, which was more commonly known as the office automation (O.A.) environment. The newgame analysis developed in the research behind this book suggests that the strategic direction, behaviour and performance of personal computer manufacturers within the business/professional segment can be better understood by considering at least two aspects of the evolutionary process. The first concerns the structure of the market and its pattern of development. In this respect, the data presented above attempts to provide a picture which reflects the segmentation that took place in the United States personal computer market during the late 1980s up to 1992, together with an indication of the relative position of the major competitors within the overall marketplace.

The second aspect of the evolutionary process considers the strategic behaviour of the major competitors over time and is dealt with by analysis of changes in the structure of competitors' value chains and the pattern of strategic groups. However, it would be naive and wrong to suggest that the pattern of strategic behaviour and subsequent performance of leading competitors in the business/professional segment of the United States (or indeed worldwide) personal computer market, can be understood entirely by consideration of the personal computer market alone. In addition, one must also understand the position which each of the competitors occupies within the much broader office automation environment. Given that the strategic vision of the major competitors is strongly influenced by their historical process of development not only within the various personal computer market segments, but also by their process of development within the broader office automation environment, then a better understanding of these patterns should strengthen our ability to assess the potential performance of these companies. Therefore, before moving on to present a summary of the strategic behaviour of the top competitors within the business/professional segment of the United States personal computer market during the eighties and early nineties, we shall briefly consider the position and pattern of development of these companies within the broader context of the United States office automation marketplace.

Strategic Perceptions and Orientations

Perhaps the potentially most powerful competitive weapon of any company is its strategic vision. Conversely, it may be its Achille's heel.

As explained in the introduction to this chapter, the development of the personal computer is not only a newgame in its own right, but is also a catalyst, forcing the potential of newgames into other sectors of the industry. Hence, the relative performance of major competitors in the personal computer marketplace is best understood by adopting a broad vision of both the generic product and its potential applications.

Personal computers have increasingly performed a two-way process of market exchange. In one direction, the successful applications of personal computers to what were initially stand-alone environments attracted the range of companies described in Chapters 3 to 5. As the 1980s unfolded, a reverse process was at work, in which personal computers were drawn into an increasingly wide range of alternative markets. However, whereas before the markets for personal computers were relatively new to computing, the alternative markets into which personal computers have expanded present new challenges, not least of which is the need to integrate with and/or substitute existing computer technologies and systems. The manner in which major competitors have made their strategic moves reflects much more than simple product-marketing implementation. Indeed, on intuitive grounds alone, there appears ample evidence to support the proposition that the performance of many major competitors has been determined as much by their strategic perceptions and orientation, as by the wizardry of their technology or marketing skills.

In order to illustrate these ideas more clearly, Fig. 6.6 depicts how during the past fifteen years the computer industry has defined and redefined its perceptions of key issues driving the industry's overall direction. The lower horizontal axis measures time, whilst the upper heading

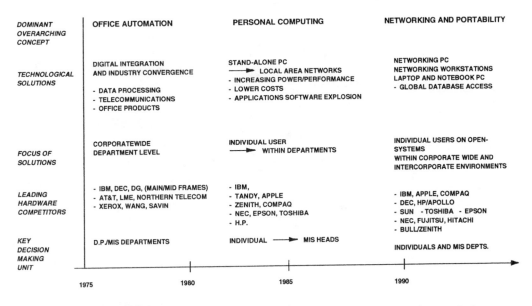

Fig. 6.6. Key perceptual issues driving the commercial markets of the computer industry: mid-1970s to early 1990s.

reflects the dominant overarching concept driving the computer industry at the time. On the vertical axis are indicated the technological solutions and their focus in respect of the overarching concept, whilst lower down are the major competitors and the key area of decision making in the respective types of customer organisation. Thus the latter half of the 1970s was characterised by technological convergence and the strategic drive towards office automation. This brought technologies, competitors, markets and concepts into contact that had previously been independent of one another. By the early 1980s, the dream of office automation was somewhat tarnished and superseded by the vision of giving computing power to the individual through personal computing. This created new competitors, new markets and most importantly a new concept of computing. However, by the late 1980s personal computing was being somewhat eclipsed by increasing concern for other issues, such as networking, software integration, personal workstations and the like. It was also characterised by a fair degree of confusion and uncertainty as to what the 1990s would hold in store. The point to be made here is that although personal computers have undoubtedly been a major agent of change, it does not follow that they are necessarily a permanent feature of the electronic office environment, at least not in their present form. Indeed some would argue that other forces and products are already rising up to take their place.

A further factor is illustrated in a simple format in Fig. 6.7. This involves the conceptual difference between the mainframe, minicomputer

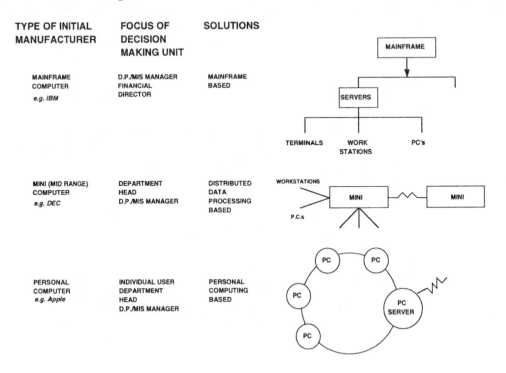

Fig. 6.7. Conceptual solutions to computing by different types of manufacturers.

and personal computer. Other products such as small business systems or technical workstations could equally be incorporated into the analysis. The point being made in this illustration focuses upon the impact that the historical technological trajectory of a given competitor will have upon its strategic vision and hence actual strategy in the broad environments depicted previously in Fig. 6.6. The strategic vision matrix reflects the strategic approach of the major computer manufacturers towards the office automation marketplace. The diagram is merely intended to clarify the strategic background of the companies. However, behind this pattern of development, it is suggested that there exists a more powerful conceptual view or vision of the office automation marketplace, which is reflected in the strategic behaviour of the major competing companies.

Hence, the office automation environment of the late 1970s represented a competitive environment, wherein each of the major players held a specific perception of the future of the market evolution and its own competitive potential. Each company held a vision that "their way" or "their solutions" would serve the customer best. As things turned out, office automation slipped from the collective industry mindset, as more and more evidence accumulated to suggest that the technological issues, including standards, interoperability and portability might delay the dream for a decade or so. None of the major players were forced out of business during this time frame, since demand for their core products remained healthy and strong. However, their success in developing their core business created a conceptual block in their perceptions of how the market was changing and in particular, how rapidly the market was to change during the late 1980s. This change was brought about both by the demands of users for networked personal computing and increased standardisation of systems interfaces, together with the continued drive towards smaller systems solutions by the personal computer and workstation manufacturers. By the early 1990s, failure to recognise the pace of the downsizing process in corporate business clients, together with the developing saturation of the industry and the growing depth of the economic recession was to take its toll amongst some competitors from the mainframe and mid-range computer manufacturers, details of which are discussed in the next chapter.

The legacy of office automation presented above has been provided to draw attention to the converging technologies and competitor/market sets. However, office automation solutions of the 1970s and early 1980s amongst the major competitors were still based upon proprietary systems. At the time, such "closed systems" were a mere continuation of the industry's classical mode of competition. With the evolution and increased importance of personal computers in the corporate marketplace, the focus moved first towards the individual and then later towards collections of individuals communicating with each other through some form of network. On the surface, the net result may not look very different from the classical office automation solution of local area networks, hooked up to mini and mainframe computers as illustrated in Fig. 6.7. However, an important and subtle shift in user requirements and perceptions has taken place in this evolutionary change. The era of "power to the user" initiated through personal computing has created a major conceptual shift in the customer market. Most significantly, it has broken the belief in the need for "closed systems" and in its place has developed an increasing pressure for "open systems". Secondly, it has broadened the size of the market in terms of the numbers and types of people using computers, which has in itself created new patterns of demand. The process is continuing to change, as one witnesses the drive towards greater portability and miniaturisation of personal computers. Although recognised by some competitors, the scale and implications of these changes have still not been fully internalised amongst all the major players. How the industry structure changed in response to and as a cause of these changes in the United States market is therefore the topic of the next section, whilst the pattern of industry development in the international marketplace is reviewed in the following chapter.

STRUCTURAL CHANGES WITHIN THE INDUSTRY

The period of the mid-1980s to the early 1990s witnessed significant changes in the structure of the personal computer industry. Some of these changes have been gradual, whilst others have been much more sudden. Yet whatever the pace of change they have all contributed to a significant restructuring of the personal computer industry. But as mentioned in the introduction to this chapter, what happens in the personal computer industry can no longer be separated from its impact and relationship to other parts of the overall computer industry. For reasons of clarity in the storyline, some of the latest developments are left until the last chapter, leaving this section to focus upon the changes that have taken place in the value chain of competitors in the personal computer industry up to 1992. The key structural changes that have occurred within this market in terms of the evolution of the elements of the industry's overall value chain, are dealt with under the following headings:
— Research and Development;
— Manufacturing;
— Marketing;
— Distribution;
— Service and Support.

Research and Development

Although it is possible to extract figures on the level of investment in research and development amongst competing companies within the computer industry from annual reports, this data is extremely limited for industry wide comparisons within the personal computer sector. Data for companies such as Apple Computer Inc. or Compaq Computer Corporation are satisfactory, insofar as these companies are single business operations, with virtually all their activities directed towards the personal computer sector. However, companies such as IBM, DEC and HP have a vast spread of other computer or non-computer related research that makes analysis somewhat meaningless in the specific context of their spend on R&D towards personal computers.

What is clear from the data is that companies such as Apple have a larger spend on R&D than Compaq, largely because Apple has chosen to compete on a proprietary set of technologies, whereas Compaq has in the main worked within an IBM industry standard. Similarly, IBM, Apple, Compaq and HP are examples of companies that spend large amounts on R&D activities, since they have to try and maintain a leadership position in the industry. However, it is important to recognise that for many competitors investment in R&D is a non-event in comparison to the companies mentioned above. Instead, as clones of the IBM standard they will assemble a personal computer from the basic components based upon an Intel microprocessor and ancillary components. Such machines are finding an increasing market share at the low-end of the market and have forced makers such as IBM and Compaq to respond with their own low priced products.

However, when looked at in aggregate, since the mid-1980s, overall investment in R&D has increased amongst all the major competitors as a result of the increasing need for personal computers, not only to deliver more power and higher performance, but also to interface with the more sophisticated environment of larger networked systems. This was not a requirement when personal computers operated in a stand-alone configuration. Furthermore, whilst competition at the low-end of the market is highly price sensitive and less concerned about brand names, the costs of developing leading edge hardware and software technology continue to spiral upwards. As a result, the industry has witnessed a growing number of strategic alliances between companies on a global scale. Details of these alliances are discussed more fully in the following chapter. However, for the moment it should be noted that companies such as IBM, Apple, DEC, AT&T, Sun Microsystems, HP and many others have all set up some form of partnership with either other hardware or software companies within the past few years and the number of such arrangements are growing at a rapid pace. Some of these alliances are built around consortia based upon establishing common standards for "open-systems" as discussed earlier in this chapter. Others are based upon sharing technology as in the case of the deal between IBM and Apple, which will involve initiatives to help both companies expand their current technologies and also involves the establishment of two new companies to develop technologies for products likely to come on-stream during the mid- to late-90s. Whether the alliances are on this grand scale or more specific to a particular product development, as between Apple and Sony, what they point to is the fact that the scale of resources necessary to develop leading edge products in the personal computer industry are no longer small enough to be carried by a single company, even if that company is the size of IBM. The risks and the range of technologies involved have simply become too large.

Hence, technological development continues to be an increasingly expensive part of the value chain for leading competitors. Yet, this pattern is not without its critics and it should be noted that there are some industry analysts who reflect the sentiments of many major customers, when expressing their concern that perhaps the major competitors are over extending their investments in new technology, when the markets are still trying to catch up with effectively utilising the existing technology. So far, this is a viewpoint that has had little impact upon the R&D efforts of the major competitors, but nevertheless represents an important consideration.

Manufacturing

Since neither the original study nor the subsequent examination of the industry was focused upon details of manufacturing technology or processes, it is necessary to keep this section relatively brief. A great deal has been written about changes taking place in manufacturing systems and management within high technology industries, some of which has included references to the personal computer industry.

In terms of structural change, the major competitors in the U.S. personal computer market appear to have followed a conventional pattern of investing heavily in modern production technology, incorporating high degrees of automation and minimising unit costs. Although labour costs vary across the global market, the major competitors are generally able to take advantage of such opportunities in terms of location and proximity to markets. In particular, due as much in part to political pressures as economic, the industry has witnessed an influx of Japanese and some South East Asian competitors into the United States as a location for assembly operations of personal computers. Furthermore, as shown in the next chapter, U.S. manufacturers have increased their share of output for foreign markets, especially in Europe, by locating manufacturing or assembly operations outside the United States. These changes in development have once again created the need for management amongst the major competitors to be able to handle both more advanced production processes and a more complex portfolio of supply and manufacturing logistics.

Outside the technical and managerial issues of production technology, the major personal computer manufacturers are increasingly faced with a more difficult task and one which creates a greater potential source of differentiation. This involves the interface between production, research and development together with marketing. Here the issue is increasingly concerned with understanding management of the phenomenon of "time to development" and its impact upon frequency of product introductions and life-cycle management. As was discussed in an earlier section, the increasing pace of new product introduction by Intel and its competitors as suppliers of the core semiconductor technology have forced an increased pace of technological obsolescence onto the leading personal computer manufacturers, who in turn have had to respond by speeding-up their own rate of new product introduction. These forces and pressures have their most direct impact upon the efficiencies of technical research and development. However, research and development also needs to respond to rapidly changing patterns of demand, such as the latent demand for efficient laptop or notebook personal computers. Competitors' desire to "leapfrog" the competition in product-technology has meant that production technology itself has to be increasingly flexible, in order to remain cost efficient and form an effective link between R&D and the marketplace.

Hence, although manufacturing is perhaps not the key element in gaining a sustainable competitive advantage, due to similar technologies being available to major competitors, nevertheless, it demands both increasingly high levels of capital investment and more sophisticated methods of management in the personal computer industry of the 1990s. Thus any major competitor wishing to succeed in the industry and its markets must ensure competence in this element of its value chain, both in terms of cost of operations, logistics and locations management, as well as an increasing degree of integration between the company's research and development and marketing activities resulting from faster product development and changing customer patterns of demand. However, it should be noted that these high capital costs mainly represent a barrier to any entrant aiming to establish itself as a major player in the industry. Ironically, the barriers to entry into the industry overall are relatively low, as witnessed by the large number of small clone type companies that compete on a smaller scale and assemble industry standard components off-the-shelf.

Marketing

As far as the overall industry is concerned, the fact that whilst it is evident that technology continues to be a central driving force, the success of any competitor is now highly dependent upon its marketing capabilities. This shift of emphasis in the value chain of competitors probably represents the most significant change to take place in the structure of the industry and its competitive behaviour during the past five or six years. The marketing capabilities refer to the entire range of activities within the marketing mix, from an aptitude to develop products that match market needs, through to pricing strategy, image creation, distribution and services. The latter two issues are dealt with under separate headings below.

In the context of the major competitors, personal computer manufacturers are in a way serving a number of market requirements, not all of which are concerned with the end customers. This tends to contrast sharply with the situation in the mid-1980s, when the market structure was much simpler and consequently the marketing activities could be less sophisticated. By the early 1990s, marketing activities had to be concerned with issues surrounding the development of global scale, which necessitates the development and implementation of integrated and coordinated product marketing campaigns, as well as corporate image building programmes. Now the competition is not just based upon the technological performance of the product, but also upon overall image of the company, both to its various distribution channels as well as to its various types of end customer. This naturally includes the brand name of the company, such as IBM or Apple and the bundle of attributes that different domains of the market feel towards this image. For example, the image based upon experience held amongst dealers is extremely important. Similarly, the high prices associated with Apple products were for a long time advantageous to its dealers, however, when sales declined this was not such a good situation and has caused some confusion in this channel. Issues concerning the image of the company's distribution, support and service are all linked to the ability of the personal computer company to effectively manage a complex set of relationships with various third party organisations. Product image also can quickly make or break the success of a particular launch. IBM, Apple, HP and many others have all had their share of "flops" within the marketplace during the past five years. Acceptance or non-acceptance of a new product tends to be fairly rapid in a market that has decreased its product life-cycle to such short periods.

However, in the early 1990s the market has become increasingly complex, for although a great deal of emphasis has been placed upon developing the business segment by the major competitors, other market segments are increasing in their importance. In particular, the convergence based upon digital technology between computers, telecommunications and consumer electronics is creating a huge potential mass market for all sorts of products and services that will cut across the conventional barriers of business, home and education. Such developments are discussed in more detail in the last chapter. However, for the moment it should be noted that already in the period between 1990 and 1992, companies such as IBM, Apple and Compaq were discovering that at the low-end of the personal computer market, brand name was not so important to many customers as in higher end equipment and the nature of the personal computer in this segment was very much like that of any commodity type consumer electronics item. In a recent study of the market, price and warranty were seen as the key factors for influencing buying behaviour.[45] Given such differences in market condition, major personal computer manufacturers are therefore having to learn that the comfortable conditions of the mid-to late 1980s have now left the industry. Maturation and saturation have brought lower margins and more competition. As the personal computer becomes more like a commodity item, market power and marketing competence therefore becomes an increasingly important part of the value chain activities.

Amongst the various elements of the marketing mix, the issue of pricing strategy, both as a final customer retail price and amongst the different distribution channels has therefore become increasingly important, particularly in these lower and mid-range positions of the market described above. As a result of its continuing loss of market share up to 1987, IBM launched an aggressive posture in this element of the marketing mix after its introduction of the PS/2 system and so forced its compatible-product competitors into a price war with decreasing margins. This war has continued into the 1990s and has been made possible, not only by economies of scale in personal computer assembly, but also by the continuing decline in component costs. These component costs include the microprocessors and logic sets[46] that make up the motherboard, the memory chips, the videoboard subsystem,[47] the storage devices and supplemental components.[48] However, the changes in such components on a year to year basis vary considerably depending upon their age of maturity in the market. On average, the cost decrease is dependent upon the type of system configuration and Table 6.10 provides a broad comparison of the total cost elements estimated for four levels of Intel based system over the period 1991 and forecast up to 1993. What is evident from this data is that the trend is towards continuing decline in component costs for each of the type of systems illustrated, but that these average rates of decline in component cost between 1991 and 1992 have been far exceeded by declines in price. Hence, all personal computer manufacturers have found themselves having to cut their margins drastically during this period. Even Apple Computer, which managed to maintain a high price premium on its products during the 1980s was forced to drastically cut its prices as it came under increasing competition from low-end machines using Microsoft Windows and so emulating many of the features that had previously been unique to the Apple Macintosh family. Since then, Apple has continued to push its prices down at the low-end of its product range and on its more recently introduced highly successful range of Powerbook portables, but in so doing it is having to operate with an entirely different financial model of its business, which now turns on high volume and falling margins.

Of course Apple is not alone in this situation. Compaq Computer was a victim of price wars that found it slipping in 1989 from a strong market leader to a languishing competitor under heavy price competition from cheaper IBM clones such as Dell Computers and AST Research. However, under new leadership the company bounced back in early 1993 with major changes in its strategy from emphasis upon leading product technology towards building high quality personal computers at low prices. In 1992, the company made price cuts of up to 32 per cent across its range and announced forty one new products supported by a major expansion in its number of channels of distribution. Using its economies of scale the company launched a new family of low priced products, the ProLinea and Contura, with a $799 machine at the bottom of its range. It also abandoned its programme on RISC development. However, the type of price war waged by companies such as Compaq can create its own problems, for whilst it has led to a significant upturn in volume shipments, its net operating margins have sunk from a level of 18 per cent in 1988 to an estimated 5 per cent in 1992.[49] This means that its earnings may be more than halved from its 1990 position. The problem that this creates for Compaq and similarly for IBM, Apple, HP and other previously premium priced

Table 6.10. Average cost of worldwide desktop computer system components: ASP 1991 - 1993.

Processor Type: 80286	1991 ASP ($)	1992 ASP ($)	1993 ASP ($)
Total motherboard	66.20	55.28	48.05
Total memory	59.37	53.56	45.03
Total video	18.05	16.98	16.43
Total storage	288.65	297.30	309.45
Total supplemental	105.65	95.96	87.93
Total 80286	**537.92**	**519.08**	**506.89**

Processor Type: 80386SX	1991 ASP ($)	1992 ASP ($)	1993 ASP ($)
Total motherboard	123.48	112.44	102.80
Total memory	83.71	89.51	89.60
Total video	19.35	18.13	16.91
Total storage	346.50	361.15	364.60
Total supplemental	111.05	98.37	89.09
Total 80386SX	**684.09**	**679.60**	**663.00**

Processor Type: 80386DX	1991 ASP ($)	1992 ASP ($)	1993 ASP ($)
Total motherboard	241.12	214.39	184.90
Total memory	156.82	161.07	164.69
Total video	18.65	15.88	14.53
Total storage	405.00	404.15	398.50
Total supplemental	136.25	124.24	85.73
Total 80386DX	**957.84**	**919.73**	**848.35**

Processor Type: 80486	1991 ASP ($)	1992 ASP ($)	1993 ASP ($)
Total motherboard	513.07	404.09	321.75
Total memory	268.21	260.93	278.67
Total video	30.00	27.50	25.00
Total storage	529.39	546.60	545.35
Total supplemental	153.05	145.63	81.86
Total 80486	**1493.72**	**1384.75**	**1252.63**

Note: * 1993 data shown in italics are forecast figures.
     ** Total figures are calculated by author.

Source: International Data Corporation, 1992.
Reproduced by permission of International Data Corporation, © 1992.

manufacturers is that they have much smaller funds with which to finance research and development projects on technology that traditionally has given them the competitive edge. Indeed, as mentioned earlier this is a viable reason for why we are seeing an increased level of strategic alliances in the industry. But at the same time the trend towards lower margin products reflects the major structural changes taking place in the industry, witnessed by competitors seeking to develop new strategies and desperately attempting to reduce organisational overheads in order to remain profitable as the newgame takes on the characteristics of a samegame environment.

Faced against the low cost manufacturers, in late 1992 companies such as Compaq were still carrying much larger fixed costs in the order of 6 per cent, compared to say 1.5 per cent for a company like Dell. This means that even on their lowest priced computers, Compaq were still 30 per cent more expensive than some of the lowest priced equivalent powered products such as the Gateway brand.[50] Admittedly, Compaq's research and development budget was still 5 per cent of sales and about six times larger than Dell's, however, the price wars have and indeed continue to force many companies into a very uncomfortable and potentially disastrous position. On the one hand, there are the low cost clones that exert their power through low prices, whilst on the other, there are the established personal computer giants of the 1980s, led by companies such as IBM, Apple, Compaq and Hewlett Packard, all of which have large commitments to the corporate marketplace, but are also increasingly drawn into competition by low cost manufacturers. Part of the battle is fought in the business marketplace, where brand name and heavy advertising, together with leading edge technology still count towards market success. However, an increasing part of the battle is taking place in lower end machines, some of which are used in business, but some of which are used in the home and in this segment things are different. Price is the dominant factor. Yet if a company like IBM or Compaq commit themselves to this mass market, they are then in danger of being drawn more deeply into the 'Catch 22 position', where leading edge technology is not the most important selling point and margins cannot support the high level of research and development usually invested in their upper end machines. At one level, this might seem a simple problem, since a competitor could continue to invest heavily in technological research in its high-end machines and simply adopt off-the-shelf technology for the low-end of the market. However, such separation of markets, although fine in theory is far from simple in practice. Unfortunately, the general momentum of the market today, due partly to the saturated state of the desktop segment and the added burden of the recession is instead driving prices down across the entire range of products. Margins are therefore squeezed in all product categories. Indeed, some industry participants foresee the possibility of the personal computer industry suffering the same fate as the electronic handheld calculator market in the early 1970s. In such a scenario, the price war will continue to spiral downwards, reducing margins still further, until eventually for companies competing across the broad range of markets, only the most efficient low cost competitors will survive and companies with high overhead costs will fail, unless they are able to provide the market with proprietary products that are perceived as highly differentiated and of value to their customer base.

In these types of market conditions, the traditionally premium priced competitors also have to avoid cannibalisation of their higher end products. This is probably one of their most difficult challenges, as IBM learned with their PS/1 which was targeted at the home market and limited in its upgrade capabilities to avoid PS/2 users buying the machine and upgrading it into a cheaper version of the PS/2. This part of the strategy worked, but the limitations on the PS/1 also discouraged home consumers from purchasing it, since they chose the more powerful clones from Packard Bell, Dell and others. In its latest attempt to enter the low-priced market,

IBM has held back on entry and launched its family of four ValuePoint machines towards the end of 1992 directly to attack Compaq's ProLineas. Whilst likely to be popular in the IBM corporate environment, at the time of writing this section, it still remained to be seen how they would fare in the wider mass market.

Faced with such an increasing pressure of competition and price warfare in the mid- to low-end of the market, it is therefore in the high end of the market that Apple, IBM, DEC, HP and others have put their hopes for maintaining reasonable margins. Such hopes already appear to be fading fast, at least in terms of the actual hardware, whether it be personal computers or their peripherals. Indeed, a key characteristic of the saturation stage of the desktop market is that margins on most generic hardware products are becoming increasingly thin. Thus the nature of the competition has increasingly moved towards seeking volume sales for replacement products making use of new, higher performing technology or in some cases, as in the case of portable notebooks, sustaining a temporary price premium. True, products such as Apple's Newton "Personal Assistant" can potentially hold a price premium so long as there is limited competition and a novelty value, but this is the exception and will soon be eroded by competition from Japanese consumer electronics companies. Higher margins in the personal computer industry are no longer to be found in the hardware, instead the value added is to be made in software and ancillary activities such as systems integration[51] and systems development or service and support. Here is the arena in which the major personal computer and workstation manufacturers such as IBM, Apple, Compaq, DEC, HP and Sun Microsystems may be able to increasingly make their main profits in the future. For it is in the corporate market that business buyers are not only concerned about price, for they are buying systems and systems need support. However, whilst personal computer manufacturers may provide the hardware, as was shown in the technology section of this chapter, it is in software systems, especially networking and operating systems that user companies will place their greatest investments. How this change will effect the personal computer companies in the future is given further consideration in the final chapter.

Reflecting the complexity of the pricing situation and market segmentation outlined above, advertising for personal computers has gone through a number of changes during the past decade. Following IBM's enormous promotional campaign for the launch of its original PC, the industry has invested a significant share of its resources in advertising and promotional activities. However, since the mid-1980s when it seemed that almost every other television advert was about another competitor's personal computer product, large scale spending has tended to become the preserve of the major competitors. Detailed data for advertising specific to personal computers is not always available, however, the figures presented in Table 6.11 illustrate the advertising spend of selected companies in the industry for 1990 ranked by their size of spend in 1990. These are also plotted against the value of unit shipments for the respective companies during 1991, as well as their ranking in the overall league of competitors. Finally, the 1990 advertising spend is expressed as a percentage of sales in 1991.

A number of points emerge from this data. Firstly, AT&T, IBM and to a lesser extent Hewlett Packard and NEC, enjoyed considerable advantages of image development through their corporate and total advertising over their smaller rivals such as Compaq and Apple Computer. However, in the personal computer market specifically, which starts with the IBM Personal Computer spend, established competitors such as IBM, Apple, Compaq, Toshiba and Epson have a much higher spend than companies such as Tandy, Zenith or NCR and clearly treated advertising as a major part of their promotional budget and activities. However, what is particularly interesting is the high percentage of their sales that the new low cost competitors such as Dell, Zeos International, Gateway 2000 and CompuAdd spend on advertising to support their sales efforts, thus reflecting their policies of high profile promotion to encourage "pull-through" of enquiries into their distribution channels, through which they sell the majority of their products. The second observation concerns the heavy commitment to advertising and brand development by the major Japanese companies: Toshiba (portable focus); NEC Technologies and Epson America. Although not statistically verified, one intuitively senses the importance of heavy advertising and promotional activity within the industry to either create or support a high profile of corporate and/or brand awareness. Furthermore, the occupation of the top positions by U.S. and Japanese competitors in the industry once again emphasises the absence of a significant European presence in the marketplace.

Thus, although one might expect such a pattern, it is evident that both for the leading established competitors and the newer entrants, whether making use of direct or indirect distribution, the scale of investment in promotional and advertising activity is substantial. For whilst it is accepted that "brand name" in some market sectors that are heavily price dependent will count for little, it still remains true to say that in historical terms, as the market for personal computers continues to segment across an increasingly complex range of customer groups, it is important for competitors and entrants to recognise that having a "brand name" in general purpose computers or indeed even in general personal computers, will not be sufficient to guarantee an effective brand presence in another market segment, such as notebooks or other forms of mobile machine. Indeed, this lesson was illustrated in the case of IBM's earlier attempts to compete in the portable segment and DEC's initial efforts to move successfully into personal computers. There exist other examples which may well come into play during the 1990s, for example the transition by leading workstation and personal computer companies between their respective core segments. Also, one can envisage the moves that could be made by consumer electronics companies from their traditional markets into multimedia or mobile computers which represents an area where careful brand development will be a key factor for success. Careful management and

Table 6.11. Selection of leading computer advertisers in United States personal computer market: 1990 and 1st Half of 1991.

Rank 1990 by Advertising Spend	Name of Company	1990 Advertising Spend US$000	** 1991 Value of Shipments US$	¥ Rank in 1991 PC League	1990 Advertising as a % of 1991 sales
1	AT & T Total*	73,895	657,315	9	11.24
2	IBM Total*	45,714	4,348,250	1	1.05
5	HP Total*	30,817	1,083,902	5	2.84
7	NEC Total*	26,715	264,826	20	10.09
9	IBM Corp.*	26,180	4,348,250	1	0.60
10	Northgate Computer Systems*	25,445	141,744	30	17.95
11	DEC Total*	22,889	590,070	11	3.88
12	NEC Technologies	22,669	264,826	20	8.56
13	IBM Personal Computers	19,534	4,348,250	1	0.45
14	Apple Computer Inc.	19,076	2,659,677	2	0.72
15	Dell Computer Corp.	18,474	458,231	14	4.03
16	HP Printers/Scanners*	17,226	1,083,902	5	1.59
17	Compaq Computer Corp.	16,052	1,231,700	3	1.30
18	Zeos Intl. Ltd.	15,415	203,200	24	7.59
19	Toshiba America, Inc.	15,189	494,800	13	3.07
26	Epson America, Inc.	10,779	256,463	21	4.20
35	Gateway 2000	8,570	618,034	10	1.39
38	CompuAdd Corp.	7,607	336,101	16	2.26
41	HP Corporate*	7,314	1,083,902	5	0.67
48	Sun Microsystems	6,638	1,175,530	4	0.56
51	Texas Instruments*	6,529	116,625	36	5.60
52	Everex Systems, Inc.	6,288	276,924	19	2.27
54	AST Research Inc.	5,875	796,677	8	0.74
59	Tandy Corp.*	5,432	804,615	7	0.68
63	Zenith Data Systems	4,838	576,962	12	0.84
64	Bull HN Info. Systems*	4,769	576,962	12	0.83
71	WYSE Technology	4,370	115,234	37	3.79
76	Advanced Logic Research	4,045	236,990	22	1.71
81	NCR Personal Computer Div. †	3,881	657,315	9	0.59
122	HP Workstations*	2,240	1,083,902	5	0.21

Note:

*   This indicates that the advertising budget is for the entire company or group and not just personal computers.

**   The value of shipments is for personal computers alone and does not include other areas of the respective company's business.

¥   This ranking does not include all companies, since advertising data was not available on certain competitors such as Packard Bell.

†   The AT&T and NCR value of shipments are for their combined AT&T/NCR value of personal computer shipments.

Source: From Adscope Inc., 1991 and with 1991 Value of Shipments and PC League from International Data Corporation, 1992.
Reproduced with permission of Adscope, Inc., © 1991 and International Data Corporation, © 1992.

understanding of brand issues is already showing signs of becoming a major challenge during the 1990s and illustrates the growing changes in the market structure as reflected by the increased levels of segmentation. At the same time, strategic emphasis by existing and potential major competitors and entrants into the personal computer market upon effective "corporate and market segment" brand development will further shape the changing structure of the overall business.

Distribution

Not surprisingly, the growing segmentation of the personal computer market suggested previously has meant that the element of distribution has become an increasingly important part of the value chain within the personal computer industry. By the late 1980s, the personal computer industry and its markets in the United States had developed a multiple range of channels between the manufacturer and the customer. These included:

— Manufacturer (Direct Outbound)
— Manufacturer (Direct Response)
— Systems Integrators[52]
— Retail/dealer
— Superstore
— Value Added Reseller (VAR)[53]
— Mass Merchant
— Consumer Electronics
— Mail Order

Overall, the breakdown of different types of channel is not particularly unique, in that most of them occur in other industries or sectors of the computer marketplace. As the markets have developed one would expect to see an evolution of the basic categories of wholesaler and retailer, which were already fairly well developed by the mid-1980s. Yet since that time a number of additional factors have come into the distribution arena, some of which are common to distribution channel evolution, whilst others are a little more specific to the nature of personal computers. Table 6.12 illustrates the pattern of distribution for personal computers and stand-alone workstations in terms of their total value and number of shipments for the period 1987 to 1993 in the United States market, whilst Table 6.13 provides a breakdown of the U.S. personal computer shipments by major manufacturing competitors through the seven main categories of distribution channel in 1990, and Table 6.14 provides similar data in value terms. In Table 6.12 each column reflects the percentage of annual total shipments in value or unit terms for the appropriate type of channel. The pattern that emerges shows a significant decline in direct outbound distribution, which represents direct sales force activity. However, direct response increased substantially and reflects the increased activities of companies in this channel. Similarly, dealers have declined in importance relative to Value Added Resellers (VARs). Not surprisingly, the value of

Table 6.12. Total United States PC/SU workstation market by distribution channel: value of shipments (Total in US$M) and units (Total in 000's): 1987 - 1993.

	Direct Outbound	Direct Response	Systems Integrators	Dealer	Super-store	VAR	Mass Merchant	Consumer Electronics	Mail Order	Other	Total
Percentage of Total Value of Shipments											
1987	18.2	7.3	1.6	52.9	-	13.2	1.4	1.8	2.3	1.3	19,230
1988	17.1	8.1	2	51.1	-	14.2	1.7	1.9	3.2	0.7	21,830
1989	16.3	9.9	2.5	46.7	-	15.9	1.9	2.1	3.7	1.1	23,356
1990	16.8	10.5	3.5	42.9	0.7	15.1	3	2.5	3.5	1.5	25,771
1991	15.3	12.3	3.7	38.5	1.9	16.5	4	3.3	3.5	1	25,431
1992	11.6	14.2	4.9	37.8	2.5	15	4.9	4	4	1.1	24,661
*1993**	*11.3*	*12.3*	*5.7*	*37.7*	*3.1*	*15.9*	*4.7*	*4.2*	*3.9*	*1.1*	*25,214*
Percentage of Total Unit Shipments											
1987	10.4	8.9	1	55.9	-	11.3	3.4	4.1	4.3	0.7	8,320
1988	9.5	9.9	1	53.9	-	12.4	3.9	4.3	4.4	0.7	8,935
1989	8.6	11.9	1.6	50.3	-	13.8	4.1	4.7	4.3	0.7	9,196
1990	8.3	13.2	2.1	44.1	2	14.8	5.1	5.2	4.4	0.9	9,359
1991	7.3	15.2	2.4	40.4	2.4	15.8	6.2	5	4.4	0.9	9,697
1992	5.1	15.6	3.2	39.1	2.9	15.3	7.5	5.9	4.5	0.8	10,288
*1993**	*4.5*	*14.3*	*3.7*	*38.6*	*3.4*	*15.4*	*8.1*	*6.3*	*4.7*	*0.8*	*10,738*

Note: **1993 data shown in italics are forecast figures.

Source: International Data Corporation, 1992.
Reproduced by permission of International Data Corporation, © 1992.

shipments through VARs was somewhat greater than the number of shipments, since VARs tend to focus on installation of high value systems, whereas dealers would include a fair amount of box shifting. From 1990 onwards, the value and number of shipments through the newly developed superstores and the other mass merchandisers, including consumer electronics stores and mail order operations starts to rise significantly. This trend is forecast to continue during 1993 and reflects the price war issues discussed above in the previous paragraphs.

Essentially, the change in pattern in 1990 illustrates the large number of companies that started to market low priced products and that adopted low price distribution strategies to support their marketing campaigns. Some of the companies producing such low priced products are illustrated in Tables 6.13 and 6.14, where it can be seen that Acer, CompuAdd, Dell, Epson, Hyundai, Leading Tech, Packard Bell and Toshiba were key users of the superstores, whilst most of these and others, including IBM were major users of the mass merchant outlets. This shift in emphasis created fundamental changes in the relative importance and role of the retail/dealer and the consumer/mass merchant channels, the former of which has a significant impact upon the marketing strategies of personal computer manufacturers operating in the business segment. The consumer/mass merchant channels, although not traditionally relevant to the business segment to any large extent, began to emerge as a more significant channel during the 1990s. Although not offering the same levels of service as the established computer dealers, the development of superstores and the increasing importance of the consumer/mass merchandisers signalled a new departure in the patterns of customer buying behaviour by certain segments of the business marketplace. Whereas, the latter type of store had long sold low priced consumer type personal computers for the home market, the new trend reflected the growing demand from professional and business users to be able to shop around for the lowest priced supplier of standard "bolt-on"[54] products to the basic personal computer. Such items could include peripherals such as printers, or ancillary components such as video boards or special electronic components to improve the performance of the computer that could easily be fitted to the machine or items of software, such as Windows or applications programmes. By reading the respective computer magazines that were by now full of product advertisements and product profiles, the relative enthusiast could easily determine the "best buys" and go out to look for them. Thus a small business may decide that it needs a couple of 486 Intel based computers and would go to a mass distribution channel to buy a unit significantly cheaper than the price of a comparative IBM product. As the reputation of the leading low priced products such as Dell, Packard Bell, AST and Goldstar began to be developed as good value products, so their popularity grew and mail order delivery became an increasingly important channel for this market segment.

This competition from "box-shifters" has been an increasing problem for the established traditional dealers who supported Apple, IBM, Compaq and other leading brand name products during the 1980s and early 1990s,

Table 6.13. United States personal computer unit shipments (000's) by major competitors and distribution channels: 1990.

	Direct Units	%	Dealer Units	%	Super Store Units	%	VAR Units	%	Mass Merchant Units	%	Consumer Electronics Units	%	Mail Order Units	%	Other Units	%	Total Units	%
Acer	0	0	37,873	55	3,443	5	13,772	20	10,329	15	3,443	5	0	0	0	0	68,860	1
Apple	122,294	12	815,296	80	0	0	81,530	8	0	0	0	0	0	0	0	0	1,019,120	11
AST Research	0	0	110,663	65	0	0	59,587	35	0	0	0	0	0	0	0	0	170,250	2
Atari	0	0	32,480	58	0	0	2,800	5	11,760	21	8,960	16	0	0	0	0	56,000	1
AT&T	51,450	49	16,800	16	0	0	15,750	15	0	0	0	0	0	0	21,000	20	105,000	1
Commodore	0	0	89,190	45	0	0	9,910	5	9,910	5	89,190	45	0	0	0	0	198,200	2
Compaq	0	0	361,505	85	0	0	63,795	15	0	0	0	0	0	0	0	0	425,300	5
Dell	38,740	40	0	0	3,874	4	13,559	14	0	0	0	0	40,677	42	0	0	96,850	1
Digital	9,499	75	0	0	0	0	2,406	19	0	0	0	0	0	0	760	6	12,665	0
Epson	0	0	116,050	55	4,220	2	21,100	10	37,980	18	31,650	15	0	0	0	0	211,000	2
Everex	0	0	93,300	50	1,866	1	52,248	28	0	0	0	0	16,794	9	22,392	12	186,600	2
Gateway	0	0	0	0	0	0	0	0	0	0	0	0	94,950	100	0	0	94,950	1
Goldstar	0	0	23,130	45	0	0	7,710	15	10,280	20	10,280	20	0	0	0	0	51,400	1
Hewlett-Packard	15,538	17	57,582	63	0	0	18,280	20	0	0	0	0	0	0	0	0	91,400	1
Hyundai	0	0	63,900	60	4,260	4	5,325	5	21,300	20	6,390	6	5,325	5	0	0	106,500	1
IBM	125,864	8	1,242,907	79	0	0	141,597	9	62,932	4	0	0	0	0	0	0	1,573,300	17
NEC Technologies	0	0	150,363	82	0	0	33,007	18	0	0	0	0	0	0	0	0	183,370	2
Packard Bell	0	0	112,950	30	7,530	2	3,765	1	112,950	30	139,305	37	0	0	0	0	376,500	4
Samsung	0	0	53,933	85	1,269	2	8,249	13	0	0	0	0	0	0	0	0	63,451	1
Tandy	98,571	21	326,517	69	0	0	48,812	10	0	0	0	0	0	0	0	0	473,900	5
Toshiba	0	0	167,680	80	6,288	3	25,152	12	0	0	0	0	10,480	5	0	0	209,600	2
Wyse	0	0	5,789	12	0	0	42,456	88	0	0	0	0	0	0	0	0	48,245	1
Other	193,555	6	1,638,948	47	68,056	2	658,006	19	218,223	6	205,705	6	411,931	12	75,115	2	3,469,539	37
PC subtotals	**655,511**	**7**	**5,516,856**	**59**	**100,806**	**1**	**1,328,816**	**14**	**495,664**	**5**	**494,923**	**5**	**580,157**	**6**	**119,267**	**1**	**9,292,000**	
Single-User Workstations																		
Digital	25,478	79	0	0	0	0	4,838	15	0	0	0	0	0	0	1,935	6	32,251	0
Hewlett-Packard	19,578	52	0	0	0	0	18,072	48	0	0	0	0	0	0	0	0	37,650	0
IBM	5,976	72	0	0	0	0	2,324	28	0	0	0	0	0	0	0	0	8,300	0
Intergraph	3,010	100	0	0	0	0	0	0	0	0	0	0	0	0	0	0	3,010	0
Silicon Graphics	3,760	65	0	0	0	0	1,678	29	0	0	0	0	0	0	347	6	5,785	0
Sun Microsystems	28,718	42	1,368	2	0	0	35,555	52	0	0	0	0	0	0	2,735	4	68,376	1
Other	11,735	71	1,002	6	0	0	2,316	14	0	0	0	0	0	0	1,576	9	16,629	0
WS subtotals	**98,255**	**57**	**2,370**	**1**	**0**	**0**	**64,783**	**38**	**0**	**0**	**0**	**0**	**0**	**0**	**6,593**	**4**	**172,001**	**2**
Totals	**753,766**	**8**	**5,519,226**	**58**	**100,806**	**1**	**1,393,599**	**15**	**495,664**	**5**	**494,923**	**5**	**580,157**	**6**	**125,860**	**1**	**9,464,001**	**1**

Source: International Data Corporation, 1991.
Reproduced by permission of International Data Corporation, © 1991.

Table 6.14. United States personal computer value of shipments (US$M) by major competitors and distribution channels: 1990.

	Direct Units	%	Dealer Units	%	Super Store Units	%	VAR Units	%	Mass Merchant Units	%	Consumer Electronics Units	%	Mail Order Units	%	Other Units	%	Total Units
Acer	0	0	90,355	55	4,928	3	41,070	25	22,999	14	4,928	3	0	0	0	0	164,280
Apple	397,060	15	2,064,711	78	0	0	185,295	7	0	0	0	0	0	0	0	0	2,647,066
AST Research	0	0	282,158	63	0	0	165,712	37	0	0	0	0	0	0	0	0	447,870
Atari	0	0	45,952	64	0	0	4,308	6	12,206	17	9,334	13	0	0	0	0	71,800
AT&T	260,415	54	67,515	14	0	0	62,693	13	0	0	0	0	0	0	91,628	19	482,251
Commodore	0	0	68,056	47	0	0	10,136	7	5,792	4	60,816	42	0	0	0	0	144,800
Compaq	0	0	1,269,237	82	0	0	278,613	18	0	0	0	0	0	0	0	0	1,547,850
Dell	129,852	42	0	0	12,367	4	43,284	14	0	0	0	0	123,669	40	0	0	309,172
Digital	58,807	75	0	0	0	0	14,898	19	0	0	0	0	0	0	4,705	6	78,410
Epson	0	0	224,744	55	8,173	2	53,121	13	65,380	16	57,208	14	0	0	0	0	408,626
Everex	0	0	187,631	47	3,992	1	123,756	31	0	0	0	0	35,929	9	47,906	12	399,214
Gateway	0	0	0	0	0	0	0	0	0	0	0	0	239,248	100	0	0	239,248
Goldstar	0	0	50,596	45	0	0	16,865	15	22,487	20	22,487	20	0	0	0	0	112,435
Hewlett-Packard	77,123	21	205,660	56	0	0	84,468	23	0	0	0	0	0	0	0	0	367,251
Hyundai	0	0	103,440	60	6,896	4	8,620	5	34,480	20	10,344	6	8,620	5	0	0	172,400
IBM	381,140	8	3,668,473	77	0	0	571,710	12	142,928	3	0	0	0	0	0	0	4,764,251
NEC Technologies	0	0	464,224	75	0	0	154,741	25	0	0	0	0	0	0	0	0	618,965
Packard Bell	0	0	213,272	32	13,330	2	6,665	1	193,278	29	239,931	36	0	0	0	0	666,476
Samsung	0	0	81,877	82	1,997	2	15,976	16	0	0	0	0	0	0	0	0	99,850
Tandy	271,796	25	714,152	65	0	0	114,440	10	0	0	0	0	0	0	0	0	1,100,388
Toshiba	0	0	420,580	79	15,971	3	69,209	13	0	0	0	0	26,619	5	0	0	532,379
Wyse	0	0	12,674	11	0	0	102,546	89	0	0	0	0	0	0	0	0	115,220
Other	605,167	9	3,232,248	47	113,733	2	1,411,812	20	255,310	4	242,311	4	876,484	13	159,892	2	6,896,757
PC subtotals	2,181,360	10	13,467,555	60	181,387	1	3,539,938	16	754,860	3	647,359	3	1,310,569	6	303,931	1	22,386,959
Single-User Workstations																	
Digital	497,253	83	0	0	0	0	71,892	12	0	0	0	0	0	0	29,955	5	599,100
Hewlett-Packard	404,234	55	0	0	0	0	330,737	45	0	0	0	0	0	0	0	0	734,971
IBM	117,296	78	0	0	0	0	33,084	22	0	0	0	0	0	0	0	0	150,380
Intergraph	86,820	100	0	0	0	0	0	0	0	0	0	0	0	0	0	0	86,820
Silicon Graphics	168,519	70	0	0	0	0	60,186	25	0	0	0	0	0	0	12,037	5	240,742
Sun Microsystems	466,249	47	24,801	3	0	0	471,210	48	0	0	0	0	0	0	29,761	3	992,021
Other	271,017	66	5,553	1	0	0	103,487	25	0	0	0	0	0	0	27,910	7	407,967
WS subtotals	2,011,388	63	30,354	1	0	0	1,070,596	33	0	0	0	0	0	0	99,663	3	3,212,001
Totals	4,192,748	16	13,497,909	53	181,387	1	4,610,534	18	754,860	3	647,359	3	1,310,569	5	403,594	2	25,598,960

Source: International Data Corporation, 1991.
Reproduced by permission of International Data Corporation, © 1991.

since with their higher cost structures they have been unable or have found it extremely difficult to meet the lower prices of the more efficient distribution channels. The situation has been made increasingly difficult as product margins on these established manufacturers' products have been continuously trimmed, thus putting greater pressure on the dealers' margins. Yet the problems for traditional dealers are more complex than simply fighting a price war with mass merchandisers, where they may win customers on the basis of their value added provided through service support and training. For most dealers their major market is in the business segment, ranging from the small to large sized business. In the former case they are often involved in supplying a relatively simple system along with after sales support. However, in medium to large accounts, their role is much less straightforward. To begin with they may find that the manufacturer is directly involved with the customer and that their role is to supply and support various products. However, if the customer has a complex information system based on existing mainframe and/or minicomputer systems linked to local area or even company wide networks, the dealer is rarely able to cope with the complex tasks of systems integration that may be required by the customer. It is in this area that the traditional dealer finds itself in competition with a Value Added Reseller or Systems Integrator. These have been in existence for a number of years in the broader computer industry, especially in serving the major minicomputer manufacturers, such as DEC, Hewlett-Packard, Data General, Prime and Wang. However, as personal computers have increased in power and performance, then they have found themselves at work in networked environments, where they have to interface with a wide range of other manufacturers types of products, ranging from printers, modems and plotters to mainframe computers. Most of the traditional dealers for personal computers, simply do not have the technical knowledge or skills to effectively handle such locations. Gradually therefore, the manufacturers have been forming links with traditional VARS and systems integrators, who have themselves been forced to come to terms with the new personal computers and to incorporate them into their clients' MIS environments. Indeed, it can be seen from Tables 6.13 and 6.14 that the workstation manufacturers such as DEC, HP and Sun Microsystems still distribute these products to the market mainly via their direct operations or through VARs.

However, not all the personal computer dealers are losing, since the more ambitious, financially strong and forward looking dealers have been investing in personnel and support resources, such as service engineering facilities to take advantage of the opportunities offered by this more lucrative end of the market. Naturally, this is a long term learning process and not all the dealers are up to the task. Furthermore, if networking continues to increase in importance by involving the installation of complex and customer dedicated network systems or platforms, then even fewer dealers are likely to be able to compete in this market segment. Hence, the traditional channels of distribution are already very much under threat, at the low-end by mass merchandisers and from VARs at the high-end.

Personal computer manufacturers themselves are caught in the position of trying to determine what types of channel to use for their ever widening range of products. In some cases, this involves their direct distribution of complex systems, which has been a traditional source of high margins for the established mainframe and minicomputer companies such as IBM and DEC. This is unlikely to be an area that they would be willing to give up. Indeed, after many years of standing on the sidelines, during the early 1990s Apple Computer began making major investments in the type of technical teams and support staff needed to service major accounts directly. Alongside the hardware manufacturers, it must also be remembered that systems integrators, information consultants and software houses are also involved in trying to capture the lucrative business of systems integration and support. In the middle, there are a range of products that can still reach small and medium sized businesses, some parts of the educational market and the home consumer market via traditional dealers. However, these dealers are increasingly undercut by mass merchandisers, who will carry products from IBM, Apple and Compaq alongside products from low priced producers such as Dell, Goldstar and Packard Bell.

The net result of these developments is that achieving effective relations and management of distribution channels has become a major preoccupation of the leading personal computer manufacturers. Part of their task is to develop an optimal mix of channels to handle the various market segments targeted by the manufacturer. However, since this necessitates the creation of different types of channel, offering variation in their range and levels of service, quality of staff, degrees of technical knowledge, overall image and standards and competence of management, the task is not easy. Furthermore, many channel owners have a different set of goals or perspectives to the manufacturer and creation of consistency and harmony of objectives is an important starting point. Yet assuming such qualitative issues can be resolved, there still remains the problems of pricing policy. With so many different levels of service and types of channel, it is very difficult to maintain a consistent pricing strategy across all channel categories. Although manufacturers may like to project an image of egalitarian treatment of their range of channels, in reality, most people in the industry are only too well aware of the need to strike special deals, in order that they can compete effectively. What is often forgotten by manufacturers is that most dealers, whilst declining in relative importance, still represent the major channel for sales. Furthermore, they do not simply regard the competition as consisting of another computer manufacturer's product. For the dealer, the competition is the other dealer down the road, who might well be selling similar products from IBM, Compaq, Apple or a second-tier lower priced player. These differences in perspective partially account for the inability of dealers and manufacturers to see totally eye-to-eye over certain factors such as margins, range of products to be carried, etc. Furthermore, as Tables 6.13 and 6.14 illustrate, although dealers are declining in their relative importance as new channels expand in the marketplace, nevertheless, for many competitors, including Apple, Compaq,

IBM, NEC, Samsung and Toshiba, in 1992, they still represented more than 75 per cent of channel throughput for these particular manufacturers in the United States. Thus they are still the most important channel for these companies and may need to be nurtured and developed, rather than ignored.

In addition to the forces acting between manufacturers and the range of distribution channels, it must be remembered that a major force also comes from the changes taking place in the patterns of user and buyer demand. These range from the sophisticated requirements of large and medium sized companies, whose decision makers involved in management information systems are often highly skilled technical buyers, to the individual business professional interested in buying an easy to use mobile personal computer. Requirements for levels of pre-sales information, price sensitivity, product awareness, implementation of usage and post-sales technical and service support will all be extremely varied from segment to segment. Furthermore, the majority of customers are now generally much better educated about and aware of product differences, as well as the various deals and bargains on offer in the market. Hence, understanding the needs of buyers and the resulting patterns of segmentation requires careful consideration, not only by the manufacturers, but also by the distribution channels, for they are now faced with a much more discriminating group of purchasers. In this context, the increasing power of major distribution channels (either on a broad or focused market basis) also needs to be recognised by manufacturers, since this might block some of them out from the market and reduce their levels of information about their intended customers.

For these and the other reasons given above, distribution has become a major element of the value chain and critical to competitive position and success in the personal computer industry of the early 1990s. Furthermore, as the range of products continues to expand, major manufacturers are already and will increasingly find themselves in a wider range of personal computer markets. These will stretch from the low-end products priced below $500 and sold through mass distribution channels to consumer type markets and to the sophisticated top-end personal workstations that form part of the complex networks of the large corporation's information system. As a result of this trend, the personal computer industry has discovered that success in a more developed newgame environment also requires a sound understanding and management of the distribution channel. Furthermore, at a structural level, the market power of certain types of distribution channel is likely to increase during the 1990s. Only those manufacturers who fully understand the magnitude and significance of this change are likely to develop strategies that ensure their survival. Whereas in the early 1980s distribution was seen as primarily a delivery system for hardware boxes and software packages, the 1990s provides the distribution channel with the opportunity to offer a wide variety of non-hardware products that carry higher margins such as systems consulting, training and maintenance services. In so doing, the emerging pattern of the 1990s potentially places the manufacturer further from the end-user customer. As seen in other industries, only those manufacturers who work effectively to develop efficient long term relationships with their distribution channels, that are based upon a sound understanding of the end-user markets, are likely to succeed.

Service and Support

As just mentioned, another element of the value chain that has increased significantly in importance within the personal computer industry's broad value chain has been technical services and support activities. Again, the degree of importance has largely been determined by the level of sophistication of the product and/or the installation site. This in turn has reflected whether the service has been carried out by the manufacturer or a third party agent.

Since the mid-1980s the personal computer industry has developed a much more sophisticated set of service arrangements for the benefit of its major markets, especially within the business sector. These developments are reflected in both the nature and range of services that are available to the various market segments and also in the structure and growing importance of companies that provide the services. As far as the nature of the services are concerned they include:

— pre-sales consulting advice and planning;
— procurement and implementation of systems;
— monitoring upgrades and technical support of systems;
— training for technical and user groups;
— helpline facilities.

Many of these activities have been the historical preserve of both manufacturers, VARs and systems integrators within the traditional mainframe and midrange computer businesses. Furthermore, they have been a significant source of profits and represented an important incentive for "locking-in" a customer to a particular manufacturer, hence the role of proprietary operating systems.

However, the emergence of new segments reflecting different types of users and buyers has opened up a whole range of opportunities for providing these services through alternative channels. An increasing share of service activities are therefore being conducted by specialised technical service companies or departments within the various types of distribution channel indicated in the previous section.

From the point of view of strategic management of services by personal computer manufacturers, it once again raises the question of how best to support the needs of various customer segments in a profitable manner. The fundamental issues involve both design and provision of services, but also the pricing of services. Here again there are lessons to be learnt from other industries. These revolve around responding to the questions which :

— highlight the nature of service and what it now involves;
— problems of pricing for service;
— consulting/training service and whether to bundle or separate;
— customer attitudes towards service (concern over viability of small suppliers);
— growth of dedicated service companies and their power, especially when linked to distribution activities;
— scope for innovation: lessons from other industries;
— high value added: who should gain? the vendor or dealer?
— operations issues: what works best in terms of vendor control or third party association.

Answers to these questions will vary from company to company. What is clear in analysis of the changes taking place in the personal computer industry and its markets, is that service activities will become an increasingly important part of the revenue sources within the industry during the 1990s. What share of these activities are obtained by manufacturers has yet to be determined. However, once again, it illustrates that to succeed in the personal computer market of the 1990s (especially in the business segment, where the mix and variety of subsegment needs are becoming increasingly complex), management of personal computer companies will have to be highly sophisticated in their appreciation of this area of the business. In addition, even more than with distribution issues, it raises the spectre of competition for service revenues, not only coming from other computer companies, but also from third party distribution and specialised service companies. Such new competitors for this particular niche of personal computer activities may well have superior qualities in both their level of technical knowledge and also in customer knowledge relating to patterns of buyer/user behaviour. As a result, they could present a significant source of threat to income streams that might otherwise go to the computer companies themselves.

SUMMARY

In summary, this chapter has highlighted the major changes that took place within the United States personal computer industry during the period 1984 through to the beginning of 1993, with particular focus upon the business/professional market segment.

In terms of the newgame environment, it was shown that significant changes had occurred in a number of areas, which included:

(i)   a shift in balance of importance from hardware to software as being the major technology platform;
(ii) a move from consolidation into a maturing and saturation of the desktop market structure and patterns of segmentation;
(iii) changes in the concept and role of the personal computer in various market segments;

(iv) major shifts in the competitive strategies and performance of key players;

(v) a significant shift in the value chains of many industry competitors from a strong technology bias towards an increasing emphasis upon marketing activities;

(vi) the development of an increasingly complex pattern of products, prices, distribution channels and third party competitors involved in the value added activities further down the industry's value chain;

(vii) a recognition that the personal computer newgame for hardware products was entering its final stages for its conventional form of desktop products and was transforming towards a commodity type of activity.

The introduction to the chapter provided an initial connection between the industry conditions in the mid-1980s at the end of the "Entry of the Giants and Legitimisation Stage" and the broad pattern of developments since that time during the 1980s up to the early 1990s. Overall, the key patterns to emerge reflected a thirty-fold increase in the size of the personal computer industry. But more significant was the fact that personal computers had become an increasingly integral part of the overall computer industry. Part of these changes were due to technology developments which significantly increased the power and performance of the personal computer. As a result, it was shown that the concept of the personal computer had changed in a number of respects. At the high-end, personal computers had converged with technical workstations, which when linked together on a network, provided large corporations with an alternative solution to their computing needs. This change in the role of personal computers had not only brought them into technical relationship with mainframe and minicomputers, it also threatened to challenge the future of the revenue and profit streams of the larger type of computer suppliers as an increasing number of corporate customers began to "downsize" their computer systems. However, the personal computer industry itself had reached a stage of maturity and saturation in its own right, which meant that a large share of its market was now a replacement market, at least for desktop machines, although it was also noted that strong growth could still be measured in the portable marketplace. Furthermore, for companies in all sectors of the overall computer industry, from mainframes to personal computers, the effects of a long deep recession on a worldwide scale further dampened demand. Hence, by 1992 and early 1993, the desktop personal computer industry was seen to be in its final stages of a newgame environment, namely that of saturation and as such showed signs of transforming into a samegame environment.

However, although evolving into a samegame environment, the personal computer industry was still subject to rapid technological change. Indeed, the next section focused upon the pattern of changes that had taken place in technology surrounding the personal computer during the period under consideration. In particular, it gave attention to the competition in the semiconductor industry, changing operating systems and the confusion in industry standards. A key pattern to develop during the second half of the 1980s was the rise of Intel Corporation, which established itself as the clear market leader supplying microprocessors to over 80 per cent of personal computer manufacturers. However, from 1990 onwards, although still clearly the market leader, competitors were at work to break its dominance, including its major customer, IBM. Many of the competitors were switching from CISC technology to the newer and supposedly faster RISC technology, whilst other significant competition came from clones of the Intel microprocessors. In response to these challenges, Intel was shown to have dramatically stepped up its pace of new product introductions and in so doing forced further pressure upon the personal computer manufacturers. Thus microprocessor technology has continued to be a major driving force within the industry, however, whilst its importance is undeniably real at the core of hardware developments, its relative importance in the overall personal computer industry was somewhat eclipsed during the period by the increasing influence of software technology. Although software technology clearly was shown to be influential at a number of levels, its most dramatic impact was in operating systems, for it was here that the major software developer, Microsoft, gained its strategic advantages that have taken it to become what is generally now accepted as the personal computer industry's most powerful single player, even more so in many respects than the major personal computer manufacturers themselves. This situation came about since development of MS-DOS as the industry standard on IBM machines led to further proliferation of the system to virtually all Intel based machines. Then with IBM's attempt to block out the clones, Microsoft was once again involved as the developer of the new operating system, OS/2. However, Microsoft also had other plans, which came in the early 1990s with Windows, which effectively emulated the Apple Macintosh environment. Thus by 1992, Microsoft MS-DOS dominated the operating systems environment, with strong growth in Microsoft's Windows, whilst Apple's OS for Mac, IBM's OS/2 and Unix followed behind in terms of unit shipments and installed base.

Thus the 1980s witnessed the personal computer industry develop into one which was dominated by the IBM standard based upon Intel microprocessors and Microsoft's MS-DOS, but one in which IBM itself was continuing to lose market share to the clones. As a result of this deteriorating situation, IBM chose to develop and introduce its new personal computer system in the shape of the PS/2 hardware platform, running the OS/2 operating system. However, since its entry in 1981, in the intervening years, IBM's market power had been severely eroded as customers discovered both in large corporations and in smaller businesses that competitors' products, such as those from Compaq and subsequently the low cost clones such as Dell and Packard Bell often offered better value than an equivalent IBM machine. Thus IBM's attempt to shift the industry standard led to other competitors and consortia to try and create their own standards to replace MS-DOS. At one level, the goal of such moves was to create an environment of "open-systems" that would ideally allow users to link computers and systems, regardless of manufacturer, thus creating a "seamless environment"[55] for the user. However, it was shown that in fact quite the opposite has happened. Instead, the proliferation of different standards at the level of hardware, operating systems and user interfaces has led to an increasingly complex and at times highly confusing marketplace. The net result has been that in 1992, whilst Intel and Microsoft still dominate the industry, customers, especially in the corporate segment are facing an uncertain future in the area of choosing a particular standard. What does seem certain is that "open-systems" are unlikely to develop in the near future, unless one particular player or consortia can convince the market that they should be the dominant power. At present, this is a position closely guarded and defended by Intel and Microsoft. The implications of which are significant for the personal computer manufacturers wishing to break with this pattern.

Given the developments in technological change, the next section then moved on to consider the nature of market evolution during the period and how market conditions had changed as a result of competitive strategies and customer patterns of demand. Data for the industry showed that the major user groups were still made up of the business professional, home/hobby, scientific/technical and educational segments and that the business professional sector was by far the largest of all four. In terms of product segmentation, high-end personal computers had increasingly converged with technical workstations to create personal workstations, whilst portable computers were clearly the fastest growing category. Overall, the market for personal computers had moved into much slower levels of growth at the beginning of the 1990s, which partly reflected the stage of saturation of the industry for desktop machines in addition to the impact of the recession. Within these markets, a number of new entrants had come into the competition during the 1980s including Sun Microsystems and Apollo Computers in workstations, with Compaq moving into the strongest clone position. But Compaq was subsequently joined by a number of manufacturers of low priced machines, who made use of low cost distribution channels and gained significant market share, such companies included Dell Computers, Packard Bell and AST Research, along with Far Eastern manufacturers such as Hyundai, Acer, Goldstar and Samsung. Less successful competitors were the earlier incumbents, DEC, Texas Instruments, Wang Laboratories and Commodore. Aggregate figures need careful interpretation, since the market was dividing into a number of segments, particularly in terms of product category and microprocessor/price category. Thus the overall market leaders in the shape of IBM, Apple and Compaq faced very different competitor groups in each of the various segments. For example, whilst Toshiba was not amongst the top five overall competitors in 1990, it nevertheless dominated the portable market for most of the late 1980s and early 1990s. These patterns also reflected the product maturity and life cycle of different microprocessors, so that the older units such as the 826 family were gradually going into decline, whilst newer based systems such as the 386 and 486 families were the focus of most new product introductions by the personal computer manufacturers. Similarly, competitors that were dominant in one user market segment such as business, were not necessarily dominant in other segments such as education. In terms of the nationalities of competitors, whilst details of the international market are discussed in the next chapter, what was common in the market segments illustrated was the absence of strong European competitors and the growing presence of Japanese and other Far Eastern competitors, especially from South Korea and Taiwan. Overall, the expanding segmentation of the markets, the varied performance of an increasing number of competitors, together with the changing patterns of technological development described earlier meant that the personal computer market had evolved into a much larger, yet more slowly growing environment, but one which was made up of a significantly more complex market structure.

However, within this complex market it was also shown that the personal computer had become the principle agent of change outside the immediate boundaries it had occupied in the early 1980s. During the following decade, personal computers had not only developed in power and performance, whilst at the same time declining in price, but they had also changed in the role which they performed in many organisations, especially large corporations. Initially used as stand-alone units, they had evolved into multipurpose systems, linked to other personal computers, workstations, mainframe and minicomputers, together with an ever increasing range of peripheral products ranging from printers to multimedia systems. As a result, the upper end machines could perform tasks similar to technical workstations and minicomputer systems, but most importantly, when linked together in networks, it was shown that they became a viable alternative to minicomputer based systems and even some mainframe systems. For networked personal workstations and computers offered to customers in large and medium sized corporations much greater flexibility for structuring their organisation's computing requirements was perceived as giving a higher value than many of the larger sized computer systems. Naturally, personal computers could not do all the things possible on larger machines. However, with the continuing trend of improvements in digital technology being used in computers, telecommunications and consumer electronics, a greater number of companies were recognising that their future organisation structures would need to be based upon networked organisations that would be better served by personal computers and networked systems, rather than highly centralised systems. This is a process that is being driven even further by developments in miniaturisation and increased portability. In effect, this change of perception about the concept of the personal computer also signalled the beginning of the final stage of the personal computer newgame. This is because as was shown in Chapter One, when the newgame reaches its more mature stage of development, competitors from the newgame, which in this case is the personal computer business, will increasingly compete with competitors in the samegame environment, which in this industry is made up of the mainframe and minicomputer suppliers. Such competition does not refer to IBM competing with Apple in personal computers, since that was a much earlier stage of evolution. Instead it refers to competition at the concept level and hence, at the solution level. In this respect, personal computers and workstations linked on networked server-based systems are competing directly for business that was traditionally the preserve of mainframe and minicomputer suppliers. This manifests itself in the industry today in the form of "downsizing" and represents the major restructuring of the entire computer industry referred to earlier in this chapter and developed further in the next chapter.

Restructuring of the personal computer industry was therefore the next topic of the chapter and focused upon the major changes that had taken place in the overall industry's pattern of competitors' value chains during the period of the mid-1980s up to the early 1990s. The key findings of this review were based upon the various changes that had taken place in research and development, manufacturing, marketing, distribution and service support in the industry. At a general level, it was shown that whilst investment in technology, both for research and development as well as production had grown significantly, nevertheless there had been a clear shift towards an increasing proportion of resources and effort being directed towards marketing activities. However, notwithstanding this general shift in the value chain, research and development budgets for the market leaders such as IBM and Apple had grown significantly and the risks associated with new product development had become larger as industry standards had become more confused. For this reason, the industry witnessed an increasing number of strategic technology alliances, both between semiconductor companies, personal computer manufacturers and some software developers. At the same time, it was also pointed out, that industry clones did not invest heavily in R&D, instead, they chose to achieve their competitive advantage through low cost manufacturing and distribution. As a result, the industry was divided between technology leaders such as IBM and Apple that invested heavily in R&D, ranging through moderately high investors such as Sun Microsystems, Hewlett Packard and Compaq to the low cost followers such as Dell, Packard Bell and Goldstar.

A further feature of the industry's evolution was that during the late 1980s and early 1990s, the rising levels of competition, together with the greater degree of customer awareness and education, as well as the effects of a saturated market coinciding with a recession, all combined to make the personal computer market an increasingly complex environment. In such a situation, it is not surprising that companies such as IBM, Compaq, HP and Apple that had previously relied heavily on their technical leadership and brand names were forced, together with many other competitors to adopt a more sophisticated approach to their markets. Competition came mainly in the form of a price war that dramatically and rapidly reduced margins for many of the key players. Whereas in 1987 to 1988 a number of competitors could hope to achieve premium price margins of 35 to 40 per cent on their products, by 1992, many found their margins had been cut to less than 10 per cent. As the market developed, an increasing proportion of sales came from the low priced end of the market that were able to cut deeply into the market share of companies such as IBM and Compaq. The resulting price wars, then spread over to effect the Apple Macintosh market, so that by 1991 the industry was faced with a very different type of financial model for competition. Instead of enjoying the high growth, high margin, premium priced conditions of the mid-1980s, competitors were faced with having to adjust their strategies and organisations to trying to maintain high volume business, with much lower margins in a more slowly growing marketplace. The effect of these changes has been to reduce profit levels and force many competitors to reduce their overhead costs, especially in terms of their number of employees. Under the new competitive conditions, personal computer manufacturers have therefore found themselves increasingly involved in a business, wherein the lower end has virtually already turned into a commodity type of market, with clear signs that much of the middle part of the business is rapidly following in the same direction. Even high-end machines are under increasing price pressures, as they battle out their positions with workstation competitors. However, in the corporate sector where such systems are mainly sold, the personal computer manufacturers are concerned to ensure that they do not lose out on the value added to be gained from other elements of the computer system, such as systems integration, training and service support.

Trying to supply and service the increasingly complex range of customer groups and market segments has therefore become a major issue for the industry during the past decade. This has focused increased attention upon the distribution channels, which have not only grown in numbers, but have also expanded in terms of type of channel. In particular, it was shown, that once again, in response to the development of the low priced end of the market for business personal computers, competitors such as Dell and Packard Bell have placed a large share of their sales through alternate consumer and mass market channels and even IBM has followed with a significant volume of its sales through these types of channel. As a result, traditional dealers were placed under increasing pressure from the lower priced volume channels and from the decreasing margins of their major suppliers. In addition, it was also shown that in the case of larger accounts, dealers found themselves sometimes ill equipped to compete with VARs, or alternatively found themselves potentially blocked out by a major manufacturer such as IBM or HP, which was already established with the customer through their mainframe or minicomputer activities.

Thus distribution, witnessed a significant shift in its structure and conditions of competition, that are still far from resolved at the time of writing. However, the fact is that dealers still represent the major channel for many of the established previously premium priced manufacturers and this is not going to change overnight. Equally well, a number of the larger dealers have responded to the opportunities in the business market, by developing their range of technical services and training facilities to support larger types of account. Thus in this type of environment, the challenge for personal computer manufacturers is to manage the development of their dealer channels in an honest and sympathetic manner, trying to reduce channel conflict and trying to develop a portfolio of channels suitable for serving their respective target markets. In practice, although extremely important, this is not going to be an easy task. Failure to do so however, may leave certain competitors more distanced than ever from the customer bases that they believe should be the focus of all their attention.

In conclusion, faced with such significant changes in the industry and its markets, it is not surprising that virtually all the major competitors have not only had to make major changes in strategy, but have also been forced to rethink some fundamentals in the nature of their business organisations and their underlying structures. Some of the major issues that competitors are therefore now facing include:

Organisational Factors

— Use of information technology as a competitive weapon;
— search for more flexible and flatter organisations;
— rationalisation of component sourcing and production locations;
— understanding the cycle of time to development and product cycle frequency;
— internal sales operations between personal computer/ workstation business versus other computer business sales;
— distribution channel evolution with alliances and co-operation of third parties.

Strategic Factors

— Evolution towards an integrated strategy for developing an appropriate scope of computer product mix;
— evolution from technology driven, product sales perspectives towards a genuine customer driven approach to the business;
— more sophisticated understanding of market segmentation;
— linkages between technology R&D with the other elements of the marketing mix;
— more careful consideration and understanding of positioning and cross market migration;
— development of longer term strategic direction against ever shortening product life-cycles and how to develop effective life-cycle management in such an environment.

Overall, such issues and the challenges involved in their solutions emphasise the broad scope of changes that have been generated both within and around the United States personal computer industry during the consolidation, maturation and saturation stages of its evolution. Although technology has still continued to be a major driver of change (if not the most significant driver), what has also become apparent, is that technological leadership has clearly not been a sufficient condition for success in these final stages of the newgame environment as it has evolved into the early 1990s. In addition, competitors need to recognise that whilst the newgame environment for desktop personal computers is transforming into a samegame environment, there still exist new opportunities to develop other parts of the industry such as the portable segment or those interfacing with the consumer electronics industry that can create fundamental shifts in the dominant underlying business value chain. Recognition of the direction and ability to respond to such changes is strongly reliant upon understanding the nature of market evolution and the speedy implementation of effective marketing strategies. Hence, the key change that one can observe in the evolution of the personal computer newgame as it moved from the conditions of consolidation around an IBM standard in the mid-1980s to a much more complex and multivariate environment of the early 1990s, was one of transition from technological to marketing competition. Naturally, many aspects of this pattern are not just specific to the U.S. industry and marketplace, but are intrinsically linked to the international scope of the major companies' strategies. Therefore, we now turn in the next chapter to consideration of the West European and Japanese personal computer industries and their markets.

Chapter Seven

THE EVOLUTION OF INTERNATIONAL COMPETITION

"A major problem in a world of increasing global commonality is how to organize and manage in the face of persistent differences in the context of a generalized drift toward and preference for standardization".[1]

"U.S. and Japan will start thousands of joint ventures. Europe '92 will be the toughest trade challenge to U.S. U.S. trade with Canada and Mexico will nearly triple. A U.S.–Pacific Rim trade deal will be worked out in '90's. Third world debt will be stretched out and written down. The Soviet economy won't get on its feet by 2000. China will emerge as the new manufacturing hub of Asia. Small Asian nations will grow the fastest in the next decade."[2]

INTRODUCTION

Chapter Six ended by indicating that a major change taking place in the United States marketplace for personal computers during the past few years has been the increasing shift of resources by U.S. competitors towards their international business activities. In particular, this trend has been mainly towards their European markets. At the same time, the last chapter also showed that the low end of the United States market has come under increasing competition from lower priced machines manufactured in the Asia/Pacific Rim and marketed by both United States and South East Asian competitors. This chapter therefore examines some key issues concerning the evolution of the personal computer industry and its markets in the West European and Asia/Pacific regions, with particular attention placed upon how United States companies have developed their positions overseas, in comparison to local competitors. In addition, the chapter also addresses the issue of trying to establish how far the personal computer industry and its markets has become global in nature and what forces are driving this process of change.

The treatment of these issues is divided into three sections, the first of which commences with a commentary on the overall pattern of evolution of the worldwide personal computer marketplace during the late 1980s and early 1990s. Data is presented whose findings suggest the existence of a triad of market areas comprising the United States, Western Europe and the Asia/Pacific Rim, which is itself dominated by Japan. Given its importance as one of the major three regions of the worldwide market, the next section proceeds to look at the pattern of evolution during the 1980s and early 1990s of the West European marketplace. The analysis focuses upon the patterns of competition and customer behaviour in different countries throughout the region. What emerges in the findings is the fact that the West European market is still highly heterogeneous in nature, with significant differences existing between different country markets. Furthermore, specific strategic groups are identified, some of which are Pan European in nature, whilst others are much more local. The third major region of the worldwide marketplace is that of the Asia/Pacific group of countries. Thus the third section analyses the pattern of evolution of competition and market development in these various countries. Japan is seen to clearly dominate the region. The rest of the region is made up of a very mixed group of economies and hence markets for personal computers, which harbour a number of strategic groups of competitors, many of which dominate their local markets, but which are less pronounced in other parts of the region.

Having reviewed these two major regions, the final section considers the pattern of competition that has developed across all three major regions of the worldwide personal computer market. The analysis sets down various databases to help provide an overview of the pattern of performance amongst the major competitors in the evolution of the international marketplace. This includes reference to changes in the overall computer industry, whose development has become increasingly linked to the growth of the personal computer as was shown in the previous chapter. Some observations are also made relating both to the patterns of mergers and acquisitions, together with an increasing number of strategic alliances that have taken place in the industry in the past few years. The chapter closes with a summary section which draws some conclusions about the process of internationalisation within the personal computer industry and its markets and reflects upon the trend towards globalisation.

PATTERNS OF WORLDWIDE MARKET EVOLUTION

A detailed overview of the development of the worldwide personal computer marketplace for the period 1989 to 1992 based upon a country segmentation is provided in Table 7.1. The data matches the level of annual

Table 7.1. Worldwide PC/SU workstation unit shipments (000's), value of shipments (US$M) and installed base (000's): 1989 - 1992.

Region/Country	1989			1990			1991			1992*		
	Shipments	Value	Installed	Shipments	Value	Installed	Shipments	Value	Installed	Shipments	Value	Installed
US	8,985	23,074	49,017	9,356	25,595	53,395	9,698	25,430	58,277	10,287	25,310	62,703
W.Europe	7,216	18,031	26,225	7,961	23,807	29,672	8,827	23,296	32,387	9,365	21,545	35,217
Japan	1,861	7,746	6,665	2,293	9,592	8,476	2,304	10,458	10,384	2,447	11,137	12,352
Rest of World (ROW)												
Canada	708	1,376	4,137	771	1,399	4,909	799	1,737	5,707	836	1,711	6,543
Latin America:												
Argentina	42	59	117	84	147	197	91	167	287	120	234	405
Brazil	120	341	344	177	397	447	202	395	648	245	488	890
Chile	33	61	94	36	55	124	48	63	169	60	80	224
Mexico	153	299	428	217	459	659	311	642	970	415	828	1,383
Venezuela	16	38	138	49	101	183	66	136	249	82	160	329
Other	36	96	112	56	139	168	72	70	240	92	90	332
Total Latin America	400	894	1,233	619	1,298	1,778	790	1,473	2,563	1,014	1,880	3,563
Asia/Pacific Rim:												
Australia	535	1,313	2,273	579	1,532	2,707	591	1,070	3,127	646	1,100	3,573
Korea	325	590	705	501	646	1,192	591	829	1,757	650	837	2,352
Taiwan	266	264	722	277	272	996	292	344	1,280	331	379	1,602
China (PRC)	75	230	410	86	254	496	98	550	594	112	664	706
Thailand	49	105	130	64	132	193	94	188	288	151	293	423
Hong Kong	46	123	160	51	134	195	62	164	243	67	192	297
Malaysia	30	58	97	57	115	150	80	146	222	100	164	311
Singapore	30	88	121	35	105	150	43	119	186	48	134	225
Total Asia/Pacific	1,356	2,771	4,618	1,650	3,190	6,079	1,851	3,410	7,697	2,105	3,763	9,489
India	75	210	193	110	250	303	154	268	457	185	343	642
Eastern Europe:												
Hungary	21	43	54	48	110	99	43	173	137	50	140	182
Czechoslovakia	32	97	50	42	117	89	42	64	126	44	73	164
Poland	42	76	104	54	91	154	180	122	251	102	134	345
Yugoslavia	18	61	60	24	73	•82	28	76	106	29	87	130
Soviet Union	100	500	350	130	600	470	150	660	603	164	759	747
Other E.Europe	15	75	30	20	90	45	21	95	59	23	104	74
Total E.Europe	228	852	648	318	1,081	939	464	1,190	1,282	412	1,297	1,642
Other ROW (Mid.East and Africa)	345	750	1,245	376	745	1,581	432	650	1,969	484	704	2,403
Total ROW	3,112	6,853	12,074	3,844	7,963	15,589	4,490	8,728	19,675	5,036	9,698	24,282
Total World	21,174	55,704	93,981	23,454	66,957	107,132	25,319	67,912	120,723	27,135	67,690	134,554

Note: 1) US$ values based upon 1992 base year.
        * 1992 data are forecast estimates.

Source: International Data Corporation, © 1992.
Reproduced by permission of International Data Corporation, © 1992.

shipments of personal computers in unit and value terms, plus the size of the installed base in unit terms for every major country that is involved in the sale of personal computers. Certain key patterns can be observed from this data. Firstly, it can be seen that for all three measures, the United States, Western Europe and Japan all rank significantly larger than any other single country or region and together represented 82 per cent of the installed base and 81 per cent plus 86 per cent of shipments in unit and value terms respectively during 1992. For this reason, to complete the analysis of the worldwide markets outside the United States, the major part of this chapter will focus upon the West European and Japanese marketplace. However, it will also include an analysis of a number of countries in the Asia/Pacific Rim region, since this represents approximately 40 per cent of the fourth region referred to as the Rest of the World. Furthermore, and most significantly it includes countries which are the home to a number of increasingly important competitors in the worldwide market.

Nevertheless, before moving on to look at these major regions, it is worth making a few observations about the remaining countries in the Rest of the World region. In North America, Canada forms a relatively important market in its own right, however, it is dwarfed by its larger neighbour to the south and tends to be treated as an overflow market for the United States, since it does not support its own indigenous personal computer industry. Latin America is a rapidly growing market especially in Argentina and Venezuela, however, the installed base of the region is still relatively small and once again lacks any significant indigenous industry, although Mexico has become an important source for the manufacturing of electronic components, due to its low labour costs. With the formation of the North American Trade Area, both Canada and Mexico may attract further investment in these activities during the future. Despite their enormous populations, both India and mainland China support a small installed base for personal computers. In the aftermath of 'perestroika' Eastern Europe has experienced great difficulties in its respective economies that is reflected in its personal computer markets. Much of East Germany's manufacturing capacity has now been absorbed into the new unified Germany and has in some instances provided lower cost facilities. Czechoslovakia has shown little growth, Poland has actually declined, whilst the break-up of Yugoslavia has virtually meant no growth in the region. Only Hungary appears to have maintained some growth. These conditions, as with the former Soviet Union reflect the much greater economic difficulties facing the region as a whole for the foreseeable future and suggest that growth in these markets will remain slow or even non-existent, until such time as their economies are able to show strong positive growth and are supported by sufficient levels of foreign investment.

It therefore follows that by focusing upon the United States, Western Europe, Japan and selected countries within the Asia/Pacific Rim, one is able to gain a fairly complete picture of the overall worldwide personal computer marketplace and its industry, since not only do they account for the majority of the market demand, but they also account for the majority of the worldwide industry's manufacturing capacity. Furthermore, Ohmae's model[3] of a Triad is well supported by the data which suggests that in 1992, between them, North America, Europe and the Asia/Pacific Rim accounted for approximately 94 per cent of the installed base and shipments in volume and value terms within the overall world or global market for personal computers.

In order to summarise the worldwide data Table 7.2 illustrates the personal computer shipments in unit and value terms for the four main regions during the period 1989 to 1992. However, in addition Table 7.2 also shows the annual percentage growth in each region for the respective measures. Clearly, from this it can be seen that the United States has remained the dominant market in terms of size of shipments throughout the period, both in value and unit terms, followed in second place by Western Europe and third place by the Rest of the World. However, as was shown in Table 7.1, Japan effectively ranks as the third largest single market, given that it is much larger than any of the independent countries which go to contribute to the Rest of the World segment. Furthermore, whilst the annual percentage share for each region has remained relatively stable over the four year period, certain trends can be detected in terms of changes in relative worldwide market share. For example in the United States and Western Europe, whilst shipments have continued to grow throughout the period, in 1991 and 1992, the value of shipments has actually declined. Furthermore, although Western Europe enjoyed much higher growth in value terms than the United States during 1990, it declined even more rapidly in 1991. Meanwhile, Japan's growth remained strong in both unit and value terms throughout most of the period, although it slowed dramatically in terms of unit shipments during 1991, whilst the Rest of the World also showed signs of a slow down, due largely to the economic recession. As we shall see in the next section, even though these figures only reflect a very broad pattern of the size and relative rates of growth in the worldwide market, many United States personal computer manufacturers increased their scale of operations within the West European market during the period 1989 and 1990, due to the opportunities created by the stronger growth in the region and also due to the increased levels of competition and lower margins available in the United States. However, in 1991 and 1992, the recession has hit both the United States and Western European markets, so that the differential in rates of growth between the two regions have been largely eroded.

Some of the reasons why Western Europe looked attractive to United States companies during the 1989 to 1991 time frame were partly due to the weak U.S. dollar at the time, giving U.S. manufacturers a competitive advantage on cost and hence price levels, but more particularly, the West European market began to demand a higher level of performance in personal computers, which was best provided by the major U.S. manufacturers. A similar situation began to emerge in the Japanese market during 1993. In addition, the United States market was more developed and closer to

Table 7.2. Worldwide personal computer shipments by four major regions in unit (000's) and value (US$M) terms: 1989 - 1992.

	1989				1990			
	Shipments	Growth (%)	Value	Growth (%)	Shipments	Growth (%)	Value	Growth (%)
US	8,985		23,074		9,356	4.13	25,595	10.93
WESTERN EUROPE	7,216		18,031		7,961	10.32	23,807	32.03
JAPAN	1,861		7,746		2,293	23.21	9,592	23.83
REST OF WORLD	3,112		6,853		3,844	23.52	7,963	16.20
WORLDWIDE TOTAL	21,174		55,704		23,454	10.77	66,957	20.20

	1991				1992*			
	Shipments	Growth (%)	Value	Growth (%)	Shipments	Growth (%)	Value	Growth (%)
US	9,698	3.66	25,430	0.8	10,287	6.07	25,310	-0.47
WESTERN EUROPE	8,827	10.88	23,296	8.6	9,365	6.09	21,545	-7.52
JAPAN	2,304	0.48	10,458	24.6	2,447	6.21	11,137	6.49
REST OF WORLD	4,490	16.81	8,728	17.5	5,036	12.16	9,698	11.11
WORLDWIDE TOTAL	25,319	7.95	67,912	1.43	27,135	7.17	67,690	-0.33

Note: 1) US$ values based upon 1992 base year.
   * 1992 data are forecast estimates.

Source: Based upon data shown in Table 7.1. and provided by permission of International Data Corporation, © 1992.

saturation, whereas both the West European and Asia/Pacific Rim markets still had significant growth potential. A further boost to the West European market was the growing awareness amongst members of the business community in the late 1980s of the coming Single European Market in 1992. Rightly or wrongly, many U.S. manufacturers were convinced that it would be important to establish a strong base in the West European market prior to 1992, in order to take advantage of greater freedom of movement and trading between member states and also to avoid any risk of being "closed out" of the market. This was an idea held by those who believed in the possibility of a "Fortress Europe" trading block developing after 1992.[4] Then in 1991 to 1992, both the United States and West European economies went into recessionary conditions that depressed sales of personal computers, which was a trend that also became apparent in the Japanese market and some of the other Asian/Pacific countries.

In terms of the broad Triad regions, the impact of these changes can be most clearly seen by reference to Fig. 7.1 which illustrates the growth in the installed base for the period 1989 through to 1992, for the major four regions. What stands out most clearly, is that the historical dominance of the United States market no longer applies, as its relative share has been shrinking quite rapidly. Already, the size of the Asia/Pacific Rim and Europe combined exceeds that of the United States in value terms and is very nearly equal in volume terms. This was one of the reasons why, starting in the mid- to late 1980s, many United States manufacturers decided to increase their focus on foreign markets. Indeed, one might argue that on a purely arithmetical basis, any global personal computer company should be one which attains a similar market share in all three regions and is able to distribute its products in proportion to the relative size of the three major markets as expressed as a percentage of the overall size of the worldwide or global marketplace. In other words, a U.S. manufacturer should be aiming at achieving approximately 50 per cent of its global revenues from outside the United States, similarly a West European,

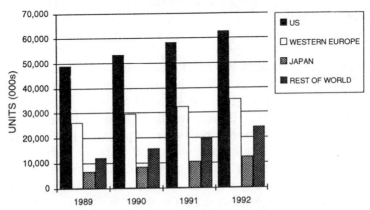

Source: Based upon data provided by and with permission of International Data Corporation, © 1992.

Fig. 7.1. Worldwide personal computer installed units base by major regions, (000's): 1989 - 1992.

Japanese or other Far Eastern competitor should look to develop at least 50 per cent of its global revenues outside its own home region. How far this pattern has yet evolved will be a topic of investigation later in this chapter.

Of course, these types of broad statistics can only show a very general pattern for the personal computer market in each country or region, regardless of user market segment. As will be shown later, the business segment dominated all of the countries discussed in the following sections. However, data provided in this chapter will look at the overall personal computer market within each country, with an indication of what percentage of the market consisted of business users. Indeed, on a worldwide basis, it is the business/professional segment that has undergone the most significant growth in overall size during the five year period. In value terms, it has grown to be over seven times larger than the home/hobby segment, twice as large as the scientific/technical segment and twenty one times larger than education. It is hardly surprising therefore, that many United States manufacturers have seen such major opportunities for foreign market growth being mainly in the business/professional segment. Thus the overall general picture for international sales of personal computers by United States manufacturers over the past five years suggests a strong strategic emphasis upon the business/professional segment. As far as the patterns of buying behaviour amongst customers in the business sector from different countries around Europe and the Pacific Rim markets are concerned, in the main, these tend to be fairly similar in their product requirements. For this reason, major competitors are able to produce virtually identical products for global distribution. Where differences do exist at the product level, they involve customising the keyboard, documentation and modifying software to the local language. However, whilst the basic product is relatively standard in nature across borders, it must be recognised that major differences do exist between country market conditions and centre upon issues surrounding government policies, payment systems, levels and methods of training, the process and responsibility for maintenance support, together with variations in the mix and type of distribution channels. Further discussion of these issues is provided later in the chapter.

Another important feature of the worldwide market is that although there exist similarities in the general hardware product requirements of markets in the major regions, it should be appreciated that the state of product market maturity is extremely varied in terms of the level of user sophistication based upon processor types. This is best illustrated by reference to Table 7.3 which shows the rate of diffusion of the various processor types and families on a worldwide basis into the four major regions on a percentage basis. All sorts of interesting patterns emerge from this data and indeed, more specific data will be provided on a country basis later in the chapter. For the moment, Table 7.3 serves to illustrate that not surprisingly, the United States is the fastest adopter of new families of Intel processors. However, the data also reveals that the older

Table 7.3. Worldwide personal computer unit shipments (000's) by processor type and regions: 1989 - 1992.

Processor	Region	1989	1990	1991	1992*
8088/86	US	1,819	967	224	42
	W.Europe	1,445	922	357	159
	Japan	132	79	28	10
	ROW	887	665	565	315
	Worldwide	4,283	2,633	1,174	526
80286	US	3,931	3,000	1,610	279
	W.Europe	2,437	2,484	1,799	996
	Japan	1,014	1,023	473	278
	ROW	1,074	1,461	1,436	1,294
	Worldwide	8,456	7,968	5,318	2,847
80386SX	US	500	2,039	3,602	3,918
	W.Europe	254	1,360	2,937	3,970
	Japan	93	478	886	1,057
	ROW	104	538	1,185	1,662
	Worldwide	951	4,415	8,610	10,607
80386	US	1,328	1,729	1,814	1,299
	W.Europe	652	856	1,015	965
	Japan	220	365	509	465
	ROW	216	327	494	529
	Worldwide	2,416	3,277	3,832	3,258
80486SX	US	0	0	96	1,423
	W.Europe	0	0	61	591
	Japan	0	0	18	130
	ROW	0	0	18	101
	Worldwide	0	0	193	2,245
80486	US	3	99	558	1,406
	W.Europe	0	53	239	583
	Japan	0	1	60	122
	ROW	2	10	112	166
	Worldwide	5	163	969	2,277
Total Intel	US	7,581	7,834	7,904	8,367
	W.Europe	4,788	5,675	6,408	7,264
	Japan	1,459	1,946	1,974	2,062
	ROW	2,283	3,001	3,810	4,067
	Worldwide	16,111	18,456	20,096	21,760
680X0	US	886	1,055	1,491	1,662
	W.Europe	1,061	1,302	1,393	1,424
	Japan	123	103	165	225
	ROW	374	423	314	554
	Worldwide	2,444	2,883	3,363	3,865
RISC	US	41	95	152	186
	W.Europe	25	55	106	159
	Japan	7	18	30	43
	ROW	18	27	36	60
	Worldwide	91	195	324	448
Other	US	688	373	151	72
	W.Europe	1,342	929	920	518
	Japan	272	226	136	117
	ROW	438	394	328	355
	Worldwide	2,740	1,922	1,535	1,062
Total PCs	US	9,199	9,357	9,698	10,287
	W.Europe	7,216	7,961	8,827	9,365
	Japan	1,861	2,293	2,305	2,447
	ROW	3,115	3,845	4,488	5,036
	Worldwide	21,391	23,456	25,318	27,135

Note: * 1992 data are forecast estimates.

Source: International Data Corporation, © 1992.
Reproduced by permission of International Data Corporation, © 1992.

8088/86 technology has remained in Western Europe and the Rest of the World far longer than in the United States or Japan, whilst 286 technology has remained longer in Japan than in Western Europe, which like the United States has been quicker to adopt the SX version[5] of 386 technology. Such patterns reflect differences in competition within the four regions. For example, during the past few years, the rate of adoption in the United States and Western Europe of more powerful processors has been based upon the increased demand by users to obtain hardware to drive Microsoft Windows based programs. Similarly, Japan's relatively slow adoption of Intel 486 based technology can be explained by the generally low level of networking and the use of indigenous based microprocessors. However, one type of product that appears to enjoy a similar importance in all four regions is that of RISC based machines, which up to now have mainly consisted of workstations. This trend seems to suggest that as in the United States market, competition in the technical/scientific and increasingly at the high-end of the business market will continue to increase from workstations on a worldwide basis. At the same time, high-end personal computers are likely to converge with these "personal workstations",[6] and lead to the situation described in the last chapter, where more "power-users"[7] choose personal computer and workstation networks[8] as an alternative solution to their computing needs, instead of mini or mainframe based computer solutions. Indeed, as will be shown shortly, this pattern of behaviour in "downsizing" has been happening in both Western Europe and parts of the Asia/Pacific Rim region during the past few years.

In conclusion of this overview, naturally all of the above data merely reflects the patterns of competitive conditions in the respective market regions. Much of the remainder of this chapter will set out to explain the causes of these patterns. Furthermore, although the data has so far treated the regions of Western Europe and the Asia/Pacific Rim as homogenous markets, as already mentioned, in practice they contain a number of significant differences in terms of competitive and market conditions. In order to better appreciate the differences and also to recognise the similarities, the next two sections will therefore turn to look at the patterns of evolution and competitive conditions in these two important regions of the worldwide market for personal computers outside of the United States.

THE WEST EUROPEAN MARKET AND PATTERNS OF COMPETITION

The Structure of the Overall Market

The first thing to appreciate about the structure of the West European personal computer marketplace is the fact that it has evolved on the basis of a number of quite distinct country markets. Thus although it is possible to analyse data for the aggregate of the various country segments, such an approach, if taken alone, can be misleading, especially in light of events during the early 1990s. The issue of Pan European versus local European is of course central to the events surrounding the economic development of the region during the period. On the one hand, Western Europe's economies have been moving towards a unified market as a result of the 1987 Single Market Act, whilst on the other hand, many cultural and institutional differences still exist that give advantage to competitors concerned with and catering for local market conditions.

However, suggestions that differences should exist in the West European personal computer market may appear strange to people who observe that hardware standardisation appears to be the order of the day and the product itself seems to be moving rapidly towards taking on the characteristics of a commodity item, at least at the lower end of the market. Indeed, whilst it is true that a product manufactured for the German market may be almost identical to a product manufactured for the Spanish or Swedish market, such an assessment overlooks the important fact that the market consists of customers as well as competitors and their products. The facts are that virtually no customer purchases their personal computer simply on the basis of technology alone. Instead, they purchase on the basis of their particular needs and their perceptions of how these needs are best met by a specific personal computer supplier. Given these variations in market conditions, the analysis which follows will therefore incorporate both aggregate and country specific data into the discussion and starts by tracing how the overall market has evolved during the late 1980s up to 1990. It then follows on to look at the startling developments which have taken place during 1991 and 1992.

For an overview of the level of sales of personal computers within the different major country markets in Western Europe for the period during 1988 to 1992, Table 7.4 provides data on unit shipments, whilst Table 7.5 provides the equivalent value shipments. As can be seen, both tables include the top thirteen countries in terms of personal computer sales and excludes smaller countries, such as Portugal, Greece and Turkey. Looking firstly at the overall dimensions of the market, it can be seen that following the trend of the late 1980s, the value of annual shipments grew rapidly at nearly 30 per cent in 1990, whilst unit shipments grew around 10 per cent. Then in 1991, although unit shipments maintained around 10 per cent, the value of shipments collapsed dramatically, with 1992 showing even worse performance. The reasons for this pattern are explained more fully later in this section. For the moment, what should be noted are the differences in the rates of growth for the various countries within Europe, together with the fact that both in volume and value of shipment terms, the largest four country markets are made up of West Germany, the United Kingdom, France and Italy, with a second group of countries consisting of Spain, the Netherlands, Sweden and Switzerland, followed by a group of smaller countries, namely, Belgium, Finland, Denmark, Norway and Austria. Behind the figures rest some significant variations in market conditions, which determine the relative sizes of the markets. The most obvious differences are the relative populations of the countries, but it is also true that some of the countries have a higher per capita utilisation

Table 7.4. West European personal computer market shipments — all sectors — in specific country markets, (units 000's): 1990 - 1992.

	1990	1991	Growth (%)	1992*	Growth (%)
West Germany	2,008	2,396	19.32	2,576	7.51
France	1,213	1,318	8.66	1,392	5.61
U.K.	1,416	1,544	9.04	1,615	4.60
Italy	800	867	8.38	909	4.84
Netherlands	495	520	5.05	544	4.62
Belgium	232	240	3.45	258	7.50
Sweden	283	302	6.71	322	6.62
Denmark	177	194	9.60	219	12.89
Norway	157	192	22.29	207	7.81
Finland	166	146	-12.05	142	-2.74
Switzerland	312	344	10.26	362	5.23
Austria	138	156	13.04	170	8.97
Spain	564	608	7.80	648	6.58
Western Europe	7,961	8,827	10.88	9,364	6.08

Note * 1992 data are forecast estimates.

Source: International Data Corporation, © 1992.
Reproduced by permission of International Data Corporation, © 1992.

of personal computers than others. Such results reflect the variation in levels of general education, the levels of computer literacy in the working population and the marketing efforts and strategies of different competitors. In addition, attitudes of customers towards personal computing, range and mix of distribution channels, pricing and promotional campaigns, have all helped to influence the relative sizes of these markets. Quite clearly therefore, the West European market cannot simply be viewed as a single market (at least not in terms of its relative internal infrastructure). Thus when various U.S based companies decided to increase their involvement in the West European marketplace, they were faced with a number of decisions concerning what elements of their marketing mix to make global, Pan European or country specific. Naturally, these questions have had major implications for their strategies and are considered further later in this chapter.

Within each country, the business/professional segment represented the major share of the market, whilst overall this segment grew appreciably faster than other user segments. Figure 7.2 illustrates to just what extent the installed base of this segment dominates the remaining segments and underlines clearly why competitors have focused and will continue to focus so much of their attention on gaining a share of the business market.

Table 7.5. West European personal computer market shipments —all sectors — in specific country markets, (value US$M): 1990 - 1992.

	1990	1991	Growth (%)	1992*	Growth (%)
West Germany	5,057	5,130	1.44	5,137	0.14
France	4,207	3,953	-6.04	3,699	-6.43
U.K.	4,081	3,921	-3.92	3,273	-16.53
Italy	2,259	2,077	-8.06	2,041	-1.73
Netherlands	1,381	1,340	-2.97	1,300	-2.99
Belgium	698	684	-2.01	663	-3.07
Sweden	1,097	1,040	-5.20	895	-13.94
Denmark	563	544	-3.37	504	-7.35
Norway	532	624	17.29	474	-24.04
Finland	610	505	-17.21	452	-10.50
Switzerland	1,333	1,330	-0.23	1,073	-19.32
Austria	403	357	-11.41	363	1.68
Spain	1,586	1,791	12.93	1,671	-6.70
Western Europe	23,807	23,296	-2.15	21,545	-7.52

Note   1) US$ values based upon 1992 base year.
        * 1992 data are forecast estimates.

Source: International Data Corporation, © 1992.
Reproduced by permission of International Data Corporation, © 1992.

Not surprisingly, the relative size of the different country markets for the business/professional segment followed the same pattern as before, with West Germany, the United Kingdom, France and Italy estimated to account for some 66 per cent of the total for Western Europe's annual growth in units shipped and 63 per cent in value terms, whilst the same group accounted for 66 per cent of the installed base of the business/professional segment in 1992. At the same time, the relative size and importance of shipments in the business/professional segment for each country market was high in all cases, ranging between 42 per cent in Germany to as high as 74 per cent in Finland, whilst the overall average for the region was 57 per cent.

At a technology level, the evolution of the market in terms of its use of different processor families is illustrated in Fig. 7.3, where it can be seen that in 1988, the overall market was still dominated in terms of unit shipments by the older 8086/88 technology and other 8-bit processors, although clearly the newer 286 and Motorola 680X0 families were rapidly gaining market share and already dominated in value terms, being more expensive units. Then during the next five years, the Intel 386 technology, in the cheaper version of the SX and the more powerful version of the

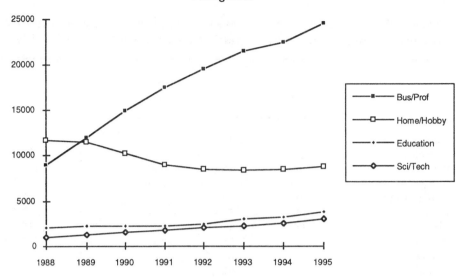

Source: Based upon data provided by and with permission of International Data Corporation, © 1992.

Fig. 7.2. West European personal computer installed base of shipments by user sector, (000's): 1988 - 1995.

DX[9] began to rapidly gain market share. Thus by 1992, the market was dominated by 386 based processors, whilst the non-Intel environment was mainly made up of Motorola 680X0 processors, with an increasing number of RISC based processors gaining market share as workstations developed more acceptance in the business market segment. The overall pattern therefore is not dissimilar to that of the United States, although lagging somewhat behind in the speed of adaptation to the new technology. However, it must also be remembered that the pace of introduction of new processor technology varied greatly between different countries within Europe, so that Sweden for example was generally well ahead of most countries, whilst Italy or Spain would be less developed in terms of their overall use of processor technologies. Further details of these specific country patterns are shown later in the review of the market after 1990.

Evolution of the West European Marketplace up to 1990

From the early stages of the personal computer industry's evolution and during most of the 1980s, the West European marketplace has generally lagged somewhat behind the United States market in terms of overall size and growth rates. This was largely due to the fact that the technology and hence the worldwide market was led from the United States and that the majority of personal computer companies active in Western Europe were mainly American in origin and therefore tended to regard the European market as part of their international operations, which were often treated as simply an overflow for their home market production. Thus product R&D was focused on the United States market, with production overseas usually consisting of no more than "screwdriver assembly plants".

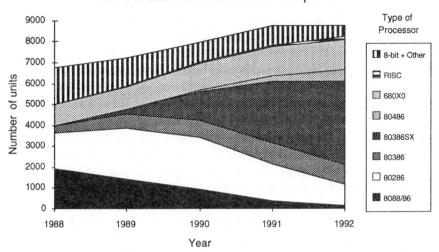

Source: Based upon data provided by and with permission of International Data Corporation, © 1992.

Fig. 7.3. West European personal computer unit shipments by processor type (000's): 1988 - 1992.

Such a pattern was not surprising, nor uncommon in the pattern of international market development. The task was made somewhat easier by the fact, that in the main, the U.S. companies faced relatively limited competition from indigenous European companies, except on a country by country or market niche basis. However, during the late 1980s as U.S. companies found their home market moving into increasing maturity and saturation, as described in the last chapter, then they started to focus more attention on development of their overseas markets, especially in the highly developed economies of Western Europe. In order to understand these patterns more clearly, it is useful to reflect briefly upon how the West European market and its competition developed up to 1990.

In the early stages of the market's evolution, first amongst the U.S. competitors were companies such as Commodore, Apple and Tandy, together with some of the lesser known companies of the "take-off" and "growth stages" of the industry's evolution, such as Vector Graphic. Commodore in particular, with a wide network of office equipment distribution outlets already established in Western Europe concentrated its efforts on this market and for a while enjoyed clear market leadership ahead of its other American rivals. However, with the entry of IBM into the European market in 1982, a year after its U.S. entry, things began to change. By making use of its global brand name and market power, together with its reputation in the U.S. personal computer market, IBM very quickly moved to the number one position in most West European countries and has remained there ever since, at least in value terms. Then on the back of its success with the Apple II machine, Apple Computer began to develop a more consistent European strategy in the mid-1980s, as it recognised the potential for its Macintosh family outside the home market. From the mid-1980s onwards, other U.S. competitors began to step up their efforts in the various

European markets. Compaq Computer in particular developed an extensive dealership network and a strong reputation that saw it challenging IBM in certain countries. Similarly, Hewlett Packard, using its reputation and strength in the minicomputer and workstation markets began a concerted effort to gain market share, which was complemented by its highly successful marketing of its laser and ink-jet printers. In the late 1980s, with the slow down in their home market, U.S. companies stepped up their efforts in Europe, so that by 1990, U.S. dominance of the West European market was virtually assured as competitors such as IBM, Apple, Compaq and Commodore enjoyed continued growth and looked set to develop Pan-European approaches to the marketplace. Indeed, strong performance of the U.S. competitors and the somewhat weaker performance of the indigenous West European competitors meant that only the Italian and French computer giants Olivetti and Bull respectively, held a position in the overall top ten competitors in value terms, whilst Amstrad also held a position in volume terms. Except for the Japanese company, Toshiba, which was the market leader in laptops, the remaining positions were held by U.S. companies.

At this stage of the market's development, although a number of West European companies enjoyed a strong market share in their home market and one or two other countries, it could be asked how was it that the West European personal computer industry, with its heritage of computer companies such as ICL, Siemens, Nixdorf, Olivetti, Bull, Norsk Data and others failed during the 1980s to achieve the kind of Pan-European leadership in their home markets of Western Europe enjoyed by IBM, Apple and Compaq, especially after they had previously seen the American's dominate the overall West European mainframe and minicomputer markets? One possible explanation lies in the fact that many of Europe's larger computer makers, like many of their American counterparts, were slow to recognise the potential market for personal computers and more significantly, were slow to recognise its potential threat to their core businesses. In the main, with the notable exception of Olivetti, their initial approach to personal computers was mainly defensive, so that many of their product offerings were on an OEM basis and geared mainly to serve their installed base of corporate accounts. Secondly, the focus of the European competitors, large and small, tended to be heavily biased towards their own national home markets, with slow development of Pan-European market presence or marketing capabilities.

However, it must also be remembered that the West European personal computer industry did not consist purely of the established computer companies, quite the contrary. In point of fact, a number of start-up companies took seed in Western Europe during the take-off and growth stages of the industry's evolution. Amongst the more successful were companies such as Acorn, ACT and Sinclair, all of which enjoyed a period of high success in their home markets of the U.K., but also in some other parts of Europe and in the case of Sinclair even in the United States, when Sinclair set up distribution arrangements with Timex. However, none of these companies survived as independent concerns in the manufacture of personal computers for the long-term. Other entrants to the market that have survived, include the U.K. computer and consumer electronics company Amstrad and the Dutch company, Tulip. Yet although both these companies enjoyed strong home market positions during the 1980s, neither of them have managed to capture the type of market spread of their American counterparts. Instead they have remained mainly regional, occupying strong positions in two or three countries in Europe. As such, with the exception of Amstrad, such smaller start-up or diversification entrants to the market have never really managed to gain the broad European customer awareness necessary to establish a strong brand name and market position. Thus by 1990, the West European market was dominated by the U.S. manufacturers, with European competitors being more local in their presence, where many enjoyed quite a strong market position. Japanese and Far Eastern competitors, with the exception of Toshiba as the market leader in portable machines and Fujitsu through its ownership of ICL, held much smaller market shares.

Clearly, given the demographic differences together with the economic and social variations between countries in Western Europe, it is only natural to expect the type of differences in the size and scale of the country markets that were shown earlier in this chapter. However, the relative position of competitors in local country markets and their presence across Europe has significant implications for the patterns of competition and market development. One such implication concerns the answer to the question of whether Pan-European or more local country strategies work best in the personal computer marketplace. Evidence from the 1980s seemed to suggest that U.S. companies present in a large number of countries enjoyed the stronger overall performance, than many of the West European competitors competing on a more local or regional basis. At least up to 1990, this appeared to be true, however, during 1991 things changed dramatically and this was largely caused by the new competition which entered the market in the form of local competitors. Although not the first to pursue this type of strategy, one of the most successful companies is illustrated by the German competitor Vobis. In addition, it was also due to the variation in the buying behaviour between countries, both in terms of the type of processor and machine required together with differences in attitudes towards suppliers and institutional characteristics which are discussed more fully below.

By 1990 therefore, the structure of the West European personal computer market presented somewhat of a conundrum. On the one hand the dominance of U.S. manufacturers with a presence across a wide range of markets and strong overall market position in Europe, tended to suggest that the market was rapidly moving towards a single homogeneous structure, wherein standardised products and marketing strategies could be developed on a Pan-European basis. No doubt many of these beliefs were assisted by the "hype" and confusion surrounding the concept of a single market after 1992 and a tendency amongst many multinationals in the computer business to believe that this pattern of development had a certain degree of historical determinism about it, which would therefore make it inevitable. On the other hand, others believed that the market was much more heterogeneous in nature and would not move quite so rapidly in this direction towards a Pan-European structure. In fairness, most competitors accepted that even in a single market environment, there would still need to be a fair amount of localisation of products, especially in areas such as software and local support. However, few of the leading U.S. competitors at the time questioned their "right to dominate" and as a result, to some extent they miscalculated the importance of local competitors in specific major country markets. Furthermore, some were too simplistic in their understanding of the differences in buying behaviour amongst different nationalities.

Turbulence in the West European Marketplace after 1990

Part of the reason why established market leaders such as IBM, Compaq and others were slow to react was the fact that the process of competition in Western Europe changed rapidly and very dramatically. This "sea change" after 1990 into a more volatile and turbulent set of market conditions was caused by a number of factors. Firstly, the previous few years of rapid growth in the market meant that many markets were approaching saturation and hence buyer demand for personal computers became more dependent upon replacement purchases. This stage of market maturity was also set against the onset of a major economic downturn in most of Western Europe, led by the U.K. market. In such a climate, it is not surprising that buyers became more careful in their purchasing behaviour. However, similar to the case of the United States, buyers were now much better educated about the market and more aware of the various deals on offer from different competitors. As the market slowed down, a number of competitors in Western Europe therefore began to turn from competition based upon technological differentiation towards marketing based competition, with the emphasis very much on price. For the reasons given in the last chapter, with Intel's increased rate of new product introduction and the promotion of Windows 3.0, demand for higher performance machines based upon 386SX and DX, together with 486 technology exploded as can be seen from Fig. 7.3, which was shown earlier. But the competition providing these machines was no longer a stable set of established competitors, instead it now included a highly fragmented group of small competitors, some of which have enjoyed enormous rates of growth in a short period of time. These competitors included companies such as Vobis in Germany, Elonex and Viglen in the U.K., with Kenitech in France, which now forms the brand name for the PC Warehouse company. What these companies had in common was a low cost structure, both for assembly operations and most importantly in distribution, since here they could go direct and avoid all the overheads of dealer channels. What is interesting to note, is the fact that it was the different way in which these factors combined in the various countries in Western Europe that accounts for the high degree of heterogeneity from market to market. Indeed, practically the only thing that was Pan European in nature during late 1992 was the significant growth in notebook computers across all markets.

Just how significant the slow down in growth has been for the West European personal computer market can best be appreciated by reference to Fig. 7.4, where it can be seen that although annual unit growth was relatively stable during the late 1980s up to 1992, the growth in market value definitely was not. The spike shown in 1988 reflected a significant shift in the user base towards the more powerful 286 based machines from 8086/88 and 8-bit machines, which was shown earlier in Fig. 7.3. However, between 1988 to 1991, value growth crashed from 46 per cent to -3 per cent. Worse still, in 1991, both unit shipments and value growth declined, which manifested itself in a dramatic free-fall in prices. Naturally, this pattern represents a European aggregate and within individual countries the relative growths and declines during 1991 and 1992 ranged dramatically between negative growth in some instances, to quite healthy growth in other cases. Such patterns, once again point to the significant variations and heterogeneity in competitive conditions across the different country markets.

Clearly, the sharp fall in prices cannot be explained purely in terms of an increased number of competitors or fragmentation in the overall market reducing advantages of scale to larger companies such as IBM, Compaq or Apple. Part of the reason was due to changing patterns in buyer preferences. Research[10] on European personal computer buying behaviour shows that between 1990 and 1992, "price" rose from being the third most important item to the most important item. However, other data from the survey also confirmed that past experience with the

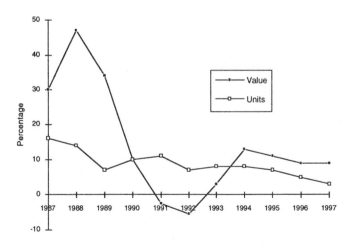

Source: Based upon data provided by and with permission of International Data Corporation, © 1992.

Fig. 7.4. The slow down in West European personal computer market growth — units and value: 1987 - 1997.

Table 7.6. (1 of 2 pages) Vendor Shipments in major West European markets, ranked by unit shipments, (000's): 1991.

COUNTRIES	WESTERN EUROPE			UNITED KINGDOM			GERMANY			FRANCE			ITALY			NETHERLANDS			BELGIUM		
COMPANY	Rank	Units	% Share	Rank	Units	% Share	Rank	Units	% Share	Rank	Units	% Share	Rank	Units	% Share	Rank	Units	% Share	Rank	Units	% Share
Commodore	1	1,229.736	13.97	4	99.645	6.43	1	666.300	27.88	4	93.400	7.10	3	125.000	14.45	1	75.200	14.68	1	37.141	15.48
IBM	2	1,099.450	12.49	2	152.858	9.87	3	166.890	6.98	2	175.800	13.37	2	141.050	16.30	2	63.111	12.32	2	35.142	14.65
Apple	3	592.527	6.73	5	88.627	5.72	8	74.400	3.11	1	180.000	13.69	6	48.100	5.56	6	23.900	4.66	3	22.500	9.38
Amstrad	4	538.532	6.12	1	287.002	18.53				5	92.700	7.05	4	72.500	8.38						
Compaq	5	425.350	4.83	3	119.171	7.69	6	79.060	3.31	3	97.000	7.38	10	21.300	2.46	5	25.101	4.90	5	11.300	4.71
Olivetti	6	372.315	4.23	8	44.799	2.89				7	52.150	3.97	1	145.910	16.86	8	20.700	4.04	4	14.392	6.00
Vobis	7	240.000	2.73				2	240.000	10.04	9	38.000	2.89				11	11.300	2.21			
Toshiba	8	223.037	2.53	9	44.500	2.87	10	51.390	2.15				9	23.700	2.74				7	8.470	3.53
Atari	9	165.797	1.88				4	97.000	4.06				5	56.000	6.47						
ZDS/Groupe Bull	10	157.344	1.79	10	42.406	2.74				6	73.740	5.61	7	29.900	3.46				8	7.002	2.92
Tandon	11	142.577	1.62	13	34.112	2.20	9	52.920	2.21							12	11.000	2.15			
Hewlett-Packard	12	126.211	1.43	15	15.649	1.01	12	24.750	1.04	8	40.780	3.10	12	2.900	0.34	9	13.013	2.54	9	6.023	2.51
ICL/Nokia	13	101.389	1.15	6	50.565	3.27															
S.N.I.	14	81.530	0.93				5	81.530	3.41												
Aquarius	15	74.690	0.85				7	74.690	3.13												
Tulip	16	69.700	0.79													3	59.700	11.65			
Tandy/Grid/Victor	17	55.751	0.63	16	12.975	0.84	13	18.130	0.76	10	31.000	2.36	13	2.300	0.27						
Digital Equip.	18	50.236	0.57													13	4.330	0.85			
Actebis	19	48.600	0.55				11	48.600	2.03												
Elonex	20	47.004	0.53	7	47.004	3.04															
Investronica	21	46.210	0.52																		
Philips	22	40.390	0.46													7	23.801	4.65	6	10.000	4.17
Opus	23	40.315	0.46	11	40.315	2.60															
Dell	24	39.123	0.44	12	39.123	2.53															
Sun Micro.	25	37.981	0.43	17	11.292	0.73	14	9.604	0.40	11	9.568	0.73				14	2.606	0.51			
Goldstar	26	33.949	0.39	14	33.949	2.19															
Laser Comp.	27	29.800	0.34													4	29.800	5.82			
Olidata	28	28.000	0.32										8	28.000	3.24						
Acer	29	27.799	0.32																		
Asem	30	17.500	0.20										11	17.500	2.02						
Copam	31	16.753	0.19																		
AST Research	32	16.042	0.18																		
Mitac	33	15.542	0.18																10	6.000	2.50
Sirex	34	12.960	0.15													10	12.960	2.53			
Mandax	35	10.400	0.12																		
CPU Datasuperm.	36	10.000	0.11																		
NCR Corp.	37	9.108	0.10																		
Mega	38	8.000	0.09																		
Osborne	39	7.375	0.08																		
Unisys	40	1.828	0.02																		
OTHERS NOT NAMED		2,514,750	28.56		384.702	24.84		704.436	29.48		430.859	32.77		151.100	17.46		135.878	26.52		81.900	34.14
TOTAL		8,805,601	100.00		1,548,694	100.00		2,389,700	100.00		1,314,997	100.00		865,260	100.00		512,400	100.00		239,870	100.00

Table 7.6. (2 of 2 pages)Vendor Shipments in major West European markets, ranked by unit shipments, (000's): 1991.

COUNTRIES	SWEDEN			DENMARK			NORWAY			FINLAND			SWITZERLAND			AUSTRIA			SPAIN		
COMPANY	Rank	Units	% Share	Rank	Units	% Share	Rank	Units	% Share	Rank	Units	% Share	Rank	Units	% Share	Rank	Units	% Share	Rank	Units	% Share
Commodore	3	31,600	10.47	2	43,945	22.92	2	24,320	12.63	1	21,840	15.10	1	53,060	15.47	1	33,185	21.26	1	110,100	18.20
IBM	1	66,450	22.02	1	56,190	29.31	1	31,178	16.19							2	25,781	16.52	6	31,280	5.17
Apple	2	37,499	12.43	3	14,336	7.48	4	11,600	6.03	3	10,650	7.36	2	41,500	12.10	5	8,135	5.21	2	81,484	13.47
Amstrad																8	4,846	3.11	8	13,865	2.29
Compaq	6	15,000	4.97	7	6,500	3.39	8	7,173	3.73	10	3,000	2.07	3	22,000	6.41	7	4,880	3.13	4	42,003	6.94
Olivetti				4	13,361	6.97	7	9,221	4.79	6	6,788	4.69	4	18,357	5.35	10	4,634	2.97			
Vobis																					
Toshiba	7	8,095	2.68	8	5,250	2.74	9	6,496	3.37	5	7,055	4.88				9	4,760	3.05	7	14,021	2.32
Atari																4	12,797	8.20			
ZDS/Groupe Bull																					
Tandon																12	4,296	2.75			
Hewlett-Packard	9	3,820	1.27	10	3,315	1.73	11	4,000	2.08	9	3,375	2.33	8	8,400	2.45	11	4,342	2.78	5	31,803	5.26
ICL/Nokia	5	22,983	7.62	9	4,382	2.29	12	3,605	1.87	2	19,854	13.73	9	6,541	1.91	14	2,045	1.31			
S.N.I.																					
Aquarius																					
Tulip	4	24,751	8.20																		
Tandy/Grid/Victo.	10	1,375	0.46				13	2,100	1.09	8	3,800	2.63	10	2,850	0.83	13	2,376	1.52	9	10,000	1.65
Digital Equip.																					
Actebis																					
Eionex																					
Investronica																			3	46,210	7.64
Philips																6	6,589	4.22			
Opus																					
Dell																					
Sun Micro.	8	3,850	1.28				14	1,061	0.55												
Goldstar																					
Laser Comp.																					
Olidata																					
Acer							3	12,645	6.57							3	15,154	9.71			
Asem																					
Copam							5	10,803	5.61	7	5,950	4.11									
AST Research							10	4,075	2.12	11	2,950	2.04	7	9,017	2.63						
Mitac							6	9,542	4.96												
Sirex																					
Mandax				5	10,000	5.22							5	10,400	3.03						
CPU Datasuperm.																					
NCR Corp.				6	8,000	4.17							6	9,108	2.66						
Mega										4	7,375	5.10									
Osborne																					
Unisys																	1,828	1.17			
OTHERS NOT NAMED		86,373	28.62		26,435	13.79		54,711	28.42		52,000	35.95		161,751	47.16		20,421	13.08		224,184	37.06
TOTAL		301,796	100.00		191,714	100.00		192,530	100.00		144,637	100.00		342,984	100.00		156,069	100.00		604,950	100.00

Source: International Data Corporation, © 1992.
Reproduced by permission of International Data Corporation, © 1992.

manufacturer, together with service and support programmes were also highly important. What this tended to suggest therefore is that brand name still had a value for many buyers, but that the price premium was now worth only 10 to 15 per cent as opposed to the much higher figures which many of the leading companies enjoyed during the late 1980s. For this reason, a number of local low cost manufacturers were able to gain substantial market share from the established competitors, so long as they were able to undercut them by significant levels. As a result, during 1991 to 1992, industry leaders such as IBM, Compaq and Olivetti effectively lost control of the market, as users began to migrate en masse towards the low priced clones. The pattern was not dissimilar to the competitive pressures placed upon industry leaders in the United States market from low-end manufacturers such as Packard Bell, Dell and Far Eastern competitors. However, the extent to which price competition damaged the traditionally premium priced companies varied greatly between different country markets, again reflecting the significant economic, social and cultural differences between the European member states.

The significance of these differences should not be underestimated for they are highly influential upon the patterns of buying behaviour and consequent performance of different competitors in the respective markets. For example, the Italian economy is significant for its high percentage of small businesses, relative to somewhere like France. Meanwhile, in the French market, buyers are generally much more conscious about brand value than say the German market. Equally, in Germany, companies generally seem much less willing to make use of indirect channels than U.K. companies, the latter being culturally more similar to the United States patterns of buying behaviour. On some occasions, a company may enjoy a high market share in a particular country due to its position as the indigenous manufacturer, which can generate strong market loyalty from its nationals. Examples including Bull in France and Olivetti in Italy. These patterns can be seen most clearly by reference to Tables 7.6 and 7.7 which illustrate the ranking and performance of the major competitors in each of the main West European country markets,[11] as well as for the overall West European marketplace in terms of unit shipments by volume and value. The data illustrates three important points. Firstly, on a Pan European basis, ranking the top ten competitors suggests that U.S. companies dominate the market in value terms, although this is not so pronounced for volume figures, given the performances of Amstrad, Olivetti, Vobis and Bull. However, if one looks on a country by country basis, two other points emerge. To begin with, there appear to be three categories or groups of competitors in terms of geographical spread. These consist of companies such as IBM, Compaq, Apple, Commodore, Olivetti, Hewlett Packard and Toshiba, which have significant sales in all or nearly all of the countries; then there are regional companies, which cover approximately twenty-five to seventy-five per cent of the countries, such as DEC, ICL/Nokia, Zenith Data Systems/Bull or Atari. Lastly, there are the local companies that tend to cover one or two countries only, examples being

Siemens Nixdorf, the Dutch company Tulip, Dell, Goldstar from South Korea and Tandy/Grid/Victor, together with the European clones such as Vobis or Elonex. For arithmetic reasons, quite naturally companies in the third category do not show up as significant players on a Pan-European league table. However, if one looks more closely on a country by country basis, it can be seen that quite often, these local competitors, and indeed some of the regional competitors have gained significant market share in specific countries. Furthermore, another point to observe is the fact that due to this phenomenon of successful local or regional competitors in selected countries, the market share and hence performance of many of the larger competitors is extremely varied across different countries.

These patterns all emphasise the fact that there exist significant differences between the various country markets around Western Europe, both in terms of strategic groups and market conditions. Thus during 1991, in Germany, the home/hobby segment was still quite strong, and Commodore enjoyed strong volume sales in the small business market, along with local companies such as Vobis, Aquarius, Actebis and Schmitt. Whilst not so adversely affected by the recession during 1991, Germany has also faced harder economic conditions due to its absorption of its Eastern half that has put increasing strains upon investment. France has traditionally been a strong market for Apple and Compaq who are both major players in this country. However, the French market also witnessed the penetration of new players, such as Kenitech and IPC. One of the markets to be hardest hit by the recession has been the U.K., which suffered a fall in demand during early 1991. As demand fell, so did prices, which led to heavy discounting, that then created a stimulus to demand later in the year. However, much of the gain went to companies such as ICL/Nokia, Elonex, Dell and Opus who are active in direct channels, whilst other players, including Amstrad have suffered significant losses. The Italian market, has been traditionally dominated by Olivetti and IBM, however, "no-name" brands have been gaining market share. In the Netherlands, although a much slower rate of growth took place in the market, unlike in the big four countries, the major brand names continued to do well, whilst only the two domestic companies, Philips and Tulip, together with Laser lost ground. Belgium was similar to the Netherlands in its performance, growing slowly but giving sales to the major brand companies, with virtually no other competition. However, the market is much less developed than its larger neighbours. Scandinavia reflected the best and the worst in terms of market growth rates. The largest market in the Nordic region is Sweden and the most developed, although the collapse of the Soviet Union has severely depressed its economy. IBM and Apple both continued to dominate this market, whilst amongst the local companies, ICL/Nokia has enjoyed strong growth, whilst, Tandy/Grid/Victor has continued to decline. Denmark's market growth has been strong, but unlike in Sweden, the main growth has come from local competitors, new to the market, such as Mega and CPU Data Supermarket and from Olivetti, Commodore and ICL/Nokia. Norway's market was strong due to the increased oil prices surrounding

Table 7.7. (1 of 2 pages) Vendor Shipments in major West European markets, ranked by unit shipments, (Value US$M): 1991.

COUNTRIES / COMPANY	WESTERN EUROPE Rank	Value	% Share	UNITED KINGDOM Rank	Value	% Share	GERMANY Rank	Value	% Share	FRANCE Rank	Value	% Share	ITALY Rank	Value	% Share	NETHERLANDS Rank	Value	% Share	BELGIUM Rank	Value	% Share
IBM	1	4149.8	18.03	1	581.6	15.00	1	747.9	14.77	1	613.9	15.54	1	528.2	25.27	1	233.7	18.09	1	141.4	20.83
Compaq	2	1772.6	7.70	2	392.1	10.11	3	329.1	6.50	2	510.4	12.92	6	82.9	3.97	3	103.4	8.01	4	42.3	6.23
Apple	3	1708.3	7.42	4	239	6.16	4	292.8	5.78	3	475.4	12.03	3	127.3	6.09	4	75.3	5.83	2	64.8	9.54
Olivetti	4	1064	4.62	12	99.5	2.57				7	144	3.65	2	423.7	20.27	7	61.1	4.73	3	55.4	8.16
Commodore	5	864.7	3.76	6	148.3	3.82	5	287.7	5.68	10	80.5	2.04	4	114.7	5.49	5	72.7	5.63	5	38.8	5.72
Hewlett-Packard	6	858.9	3.73	14	92.5	2.38	6	239.1	4.72	5	218.5	5.53	10	48.1	2.30	6	72.1	5.58	6	29.9	4.40
Toshiba	7	765.9	3.33	5	176.5	4.55	10	146.5	2.89	6	155.6	3.94	8	57.2	2.74	10	35.6	2.76	7	26.6	3.92
Amstrad	8	559.3	2.43	3	326.2	8.41				11	80	2.03									
Sun Micro.	9	477.2	2.07	7	141.1	3.64	13	120	2.37	8	119.5	3.03	9	55.4	2.65	12	32.6	2.52			
Digital Equip.	10	475	2.06	9	125.3	3.23	8	156	3.08				11	45.3	2.17	13	30.6	2.37	9	18.2	2.68
ZDS/Groupe Bull	11	472.2	2.05	13	97.2	2.51				4	241.4	6.11									
Tandon	12	374.9	1.63	15	83.7	2.16	9	154.9	3.06				5	105.9	5.07						
S.N.I.	13	358.6	1.56				2	358.6	7.08												
ICL/Nokia	14	335.8	1.46	8	139.2	3.59										14	30.3	2.35			
Vobis	15	225.8	0.98				7	225.8	4.46												
Atari	16	221.7	0.96				11	129.4	2.56				7	78.5	3.76						
Tandy/Grid/Victo	17	182.4	0.79							9	103.2	2.61				2	129.5	10.03			
Tulip	18	167.6	0.73																		
Aquarius	19	126.8	0.55				12	126.8	2.50												
Dell	20	123.7	0.54	10	123.7	3.19															
Opus	21	118.5	0.51	11	118.5	3.06															
Actebis	22	111.1	0.48				14	111.1	2.19												
Investronica	23	105.9	0.46																		
Philips	24	86.6	0.38													9	48.6	3.76	8	26.3	3.87
Elonex	25	83.6	0.36	16	83.6	2.16															
Goldstar	26	83	0.36	17	83	2.14															
Acer	27	68.5	0.30																		
AST Research	28	55.3	0.24													8	53.4	4.13			
Laser Comp.	29	53.4	0.23																		
Mitac	30	46.6	0.20										12	45	2.15				10	13.9	2.05
Asem	31	45	0.20																		
Mandax	32	44.1	0.19																		
Olidata	33	43.5	0.19										13	43.5	2.08						
Copam	34	43.2	0.19																		
Sirex	35	33.8	0.15													11	33.8	2.62			
NCR Corp.	36	28.6	0.12																		
Osborne	37	20	0.09																		
CPU Datasuperm.	38	18.3	0.08																		
Mega	39	17.3	0.08																		
Unisys	40	10.7	0.05																		
OTHERS NOT NAMED		6,611.00	28.72		827.50	21.34		1,636.40	32.33		1,207.80	30.58		334.60	16.01		278.90	21.59		221.30	32.60
TOTAL		23,015.20	100.00		3,878.50	100.00		5,062.10	100.00		3,950.20	100.00		2,090.30	100.00		1,291.60	100.00		678.90	100.00

Source: International Data Corporation, © 1992.
Reproduced by permission of International Data Corporation, © 1992.

Table 7.7. (2 of 2 pages) Vendor Shipments in major West European markets, ranked by unit shipments, (Value US$M): 1991.

COUNTRIES	SWEDEN			DENMARK			NORWAY			FINLAND			SWITZERLAND			AUSTRIA			SPAIN		
COMPANY	Rank	Value	% Share	Rank	Value	% Share	Rank	Value	% Share	Rank	Value	% Share	Rank	Value	% Share	Rank	Value	% Share	Rank	Value	% Share
IBM	1	240.5	23.85	1	196.1	37.52	4	125	20.35	2	74.3	15.29	1	227	17.17	1	70.2	19.38	1	370	20.99
Compaq	5	71.8	7.12	5	26.9	5.15	6	31.5	5.13	10	13.4	2.76	3	94.5	7.15	11	11	3.04	8	63.3	3.59
Apple	2	126.8	12.57	4	39.3	7.52	5	30.6	4.98	3	31.2	6.42	2	123.5	9.34	4	16	4.42	6	66.5	3.77
Olivetti				3	39.8	7.62	9	30.4	4.95	5	22.7	4.67	5	54.1	4.09	10	12.8	3.53	2	120.3	6.83
Commodore	9	21	2.08	2	46.3	8.86	7	26.9	4.38							2	32.7	9.03			
Hewlett-Packard	7	25.1	2.49	9	16.5	3.16	10	21.8	3.55	7	19.2	3.95	4	55.1	4.17	5	15.9	4.39	7	64.3	3.65
Toshiba	8	25	2.48	7	17.8	3.41				4	24.3	5.00				7	14.7	4.06	4	88.2	5.00
Amstrad																14	9.5	2.62			
Sun Micro.	6	50.9	5.05				13	13.1	2.13												
Digital Equip.	10	20.5	2.03				11	16.5	2.69	8	18.3	3.77	6	47	3.55	6	15.5	4.28			
ZDS/Groupe Bull																15	9.5	2.62			
Tandon													10	27	2.04	13	9.5	2.62			
S.N.I.																					
ICL/Nokia	3	88.4	8.77	10	16	3.06	14	12.4	2.02	1	79.8	16.42							5	69.5	3.94
Vobis																					
Atari																8	13.8	3.81			
Tandy/Grid/Victor	4	79.2	7.85																		
Tulip																			9	38.1	2.16
Aquarius																					
Dell																					
Opus																					
Actebis																					
Investronica																					
Philips													9	28.6	2.16	9	13.7	3.78	3	105.9	6.01
Elonex																					
Goldstar																					
Acer							2	36.5	5.94	11	10.9	2.24	8	30.7	2.32	3	32	8.83			
AST Research							12	13.7	2.23												
Laser Comp.																					
Mitac							3	32.7	5.32				7	44.1	3.33						
Asem																					
Mandax																					
Olidata																					
Copam							8	26.7	4.35	9	16.5	3.40									
Sirex																					
NCR Corp.				6	18.3	3.50				6	20	4.12									
Osborne				8	17.3	3.31															
CPU Datasuperm.																12	10.7	2.95			
Mega																					
Unisys																					
OTHERS NOT NAMED		259.30	25.71		88.30	16.90		174.30	28.38		155.30	31.96		590.80	44.68		74.80	20.65		776.40	44.05
TOTAL		1,008.50	100.00		522.60	100.00		614.10	100.00		485.90	100.00		1,322.40	100.00		362.30	100.00		1,762.50	100.00

Source: International Data Corporation, © 1992.
Reproduced by permission of International Data Corporation, © 1992.

the Gulf War. IBM, Mitac, Olivetti and AST were the main gainers in this market, with Acer also being a significant player. The disastrous state of the Finnish economy, due to its significant loss of trade with the Soviet Union meant a decline in the market during 1991. Both Apple and Olivetti managed to hold their positions, however, Toshiba and ICL/Nokia, for whom Finland is Nokia's major home market, both lost heavily. Both the Swiss and the Austrian economies are closely tied to developments in their neighbours in central Europe. These have generally been much more traditional markets. However, the performance of competitors was varied between them. For example, Compaq ranked third in Switzerland but eleventh in Austria. Similarly, Toshiba, Amstrad and Zenith Data Systems/Bull held a significant market share in Austria but not in Switzerland. Lastly, Spain has been a relatively large market with IBM and Investronica providing growth at the head of the market, with Tandon, Tulip and Toshiba also providing growth as major second tier players.

Naturally, the above pattern of market conditions is specific to the one particular year of 1991 and if one looks at the data provided earlier in Tables 7.4 and 7.5 it can be seen that the estimated growth in the various country markets during 1991 shifts quite dramatically, which is of course bound to reflect upon the relative performance of different competitors. However, the snapshot of the 1991 market is intended to provide the reader with a deeper appreciation of just how varied the ranking and performance of the different competitors are across these different country markets in Western Europe. Naturally, performance of competitors and the rate of market growth are closely linked to local economic conditions, but at the same time, the strategies of competitors in specific markets can also strongly influence the pace of growth of the local personal computer marketplace. When combined with some of the cultural and customer differences, plus variations in government and commercial procurement policies, together with distinctions in the mix and maturity of distribution channels described earlier, it can be appreciated just how different the country segments are within the West European personal computer marketplace.

In order to appreciate the scale of some of the changes in competitive performance during the period of the late 1980s up to 1992, Table 7.8 illustrates the variation in rates of growth amongst the major competitors. From this data it can be clearly seen that virtually all these major competitors, (with the notable exceptions of Apple Computer and ICL/Nokia) have been losing market share to companies such as Vobis and Aquarius in Germany, Elonex in the U.K. and other low cost manufacturers within the different country markets, which were described in the previous paragraphs. What became increasingly important to many customers during the early 1990s was value for money. For many customers, it appeared that IBM was unable to provide this with its high price and over centralised approach to the market and so the company lost market share quite dramatically. In contrast, Compaq continued to gain market share until early 1992, when it dropped quite rapidly. The decline in market share

Table 7.8 Leading vendors shares in West European personal computer market, percentage unit shipments: 1988-1992.

	1988 Per Cent %	1989 Per Cent %	1990 Per Cent %	1991 Per Cent %	Q1 and Q2 1992 Per Cent %
Intel Architecture					
IBM	21.3	19.4	18.5	17.1	15.1
Compaq	6.8	5.9	6.4	6.7	6
Olivetti	8.6	7	7.4	6.3	4.9
Amstrad	4.3	6.8	4.6	5.1	4.2
Vobis		1.1	2.1	3.9	4.1
Toshiba	3.2	3.4	3.8	3.6	3
ZDS	5.6	4.1	3.4	3.2	2.8
ICL/Nokia		2	2	2.1	2.7
Tandon	3.9	4	3.4	2.8	2.5
SNI	3.6	2.6	2.1	1.9	2.3
H-P	2.9	2.5	2.3	1.7	1.8
Sub-total	60.2	58.8	56	54.4	49.4
Share of Total Market					
Apple	5.4	4.1	5.7	6.7	6.7

Source: International Data Corporation, © 1992.
Reproduced by permission of International Data Corporation, © 1992.

for these competitors and others like them, including Zenith Data Systems and Hewlett Packard has been due largely to the rise of companies such as Vobis, which has enjoyed rapid growth on the basis of its low price of assembly and distribution to the local market. One key reason for this change in performance has been due to the increasing fragmentation of the marketplace in Europe, which has taken the advantage away from the Pan European players and given it to the local players who cater for local customers' needs more effectively than their larger competitors. As already mentioned, even Amstrad, which has traditionally competed heavily on price has found its market share reduced as a result of heavy price competition. In contrast, ICL/Nokia has competed more on selling its personal computers into a highly focused group of accounts in the U.K. market, where its position as the leading mainframe and minicomputer supplier has allowed its sales force to leverage sales into major accounts and gain market share. Finally, Apple Computer's price cuts in late 1990 and its launch of low-end Macs, such as the Classic and LC range have helped increase the company's market share, since although more expensive than the low priced Intel based machines, the Mac system was perceived by many customers throughout Europe as offering a product differential that was of sufficient value to merit the extra cost, namely, a simple and user-friendly system.

Thus for these leading Intel based suppliers, the decline in market share during the past five years has been significant and has dropped from 60.2 per cent to 49.4 per cent. Clearly, the decline cannot be attributed to the success of just a few low cost manufacturers such as Vobis, Elonex and Kenitech. Instead, one has to appreciate that these companies represent the tip of an iceberg. Research[12] on the number of active brands in the West European marketplace suggests that the failure by many of the major players to lower prices sufficiently during 1990 and 1991 encouraged a vast explosion in the number of small brands marketed. Most of these small brands were assembled by dealers and distributors (which were the origins of Elonex and Vobis) and were motivated by two main reasons. The first was based upon a survival strategy. Due to the increasing price competition in the market and the shift in some markets towards low cost distribution outlets, many dealers felt that the only way to survive was to join the competition and assemble their own branded machines. In this manner they were no longer constrained by the pricing policies of the majors and the associated shrinking margins. The second reason was less concerned with price and more with marketing power. For those dealers that did not wish to merely be box shifters, their strategies were directed to creating greater value added by involvement in systems integration and implementation, training, consulting and after-sales support. Since they felt that they wanted to be perceived as providing the total solution, it naturally follows that branding the boxes in their own name enhanced their position with customers and helped to block out other competitors, whether they were manufacturers, other dealers or VARs. As a result of these activities, it has been estimated that the number of own brands grew to approximately one thousand five hundred by mid-1992.[13] However, the loss of market share resulting from these activities for the established vendors meant that although slow to react at the beginning, IBM and Compaq then responded by launching their new low cost machines, in an attempt to regain control of the market and reverse their losses.

As a result of the competitive turbulence and downward pressure on prices in the early part of the 1990s, one interesting feature to emerge in the market has been the way in which users have been expecting to pay less for the same type of equipment each year. This pattern of downward expectations is illustrated in Fig. 7.5. But at the same time, this data also reveals two other patterns. Firstly, it shows the pattern of significant differences that users were prepared to pay for the same type of system in the four different countries shown in the diagram during 1991. However, the second pattern to emerge, suggests a trend towards a growing convergence between the prices expected in these different major geographical markets. Thus it would appear that whilst prices have spiralled downwards during 1991 and 1992, by 1993 they are likely to start levelling out and indeed may even begin to rise, particularly, when one takes account of the exchange rate problems being encountered in a number of West European economies. Such shifts in both the internal European exchange rate system and in relation to overseas currencies in the United States

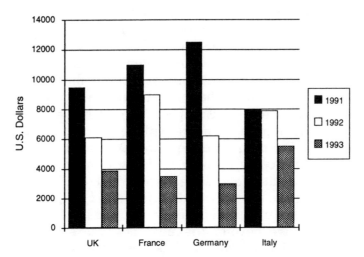

Source: Based upon data provided by and with permission of International Data Corporation, © 1992.

Fig. 7.5. What Users expect to pay for 80486 personal computers: 1991 - 1993.

and Far East, can significantly move the price advantage in either direction.

Given such a high degree of volatility in the West European marketplace and such differences between the various geographical market conditions, as described above, the established competitors such as IBM, Compaq, Apple and others have of course been faced with major organisational challenges during the period. The downward price spiral naturally put enormous pressure on margins, which led to significant losses for many of the larger companies which were caught with somewhat inflexible and costly overhead operations. Hence, 1991 and 1992 have witnessed significant staff lay-offs in Western Europe from companies such as IBM, DEC and even Apple. It has also been accompanied by the introduction of lower priced machines from these companies, since the conditions of the West European market have much in common with the United States, in terms of low-end price competition. However, unlike in the United States, some of the large competitors are beginning to realise, that although 1993 is meant to herald a Single European market, in reality, it still has some way to go — at least in the personal computer industry. Clearly, the evidence does seem to suggest that prices may be converging towards a Pan-European norm and indeed European wide or even global brand image for companies such as IBM, Compaq, Hewlett Packard and Apple still counts for a great deal, at least with certain types of customer. However, it is also evident that for the moment, the West European personal computer markets are still sufficiently different to merit a local approach to each country or region. This of course may change in time and future patterns are discussed in a little more detail in the last chapter. What does appear certain is that during the late 1980s and early 1990s the major competitors learnt that brand name and product technology alone were not enough to win the PC battles in Europe. Instead, careful attention to local market conditions has been a winning strategy. But at the same time, it must also be recognised that the market has not only become more fragmented between countries, but it has also become more fragmented between different product groups and customer groups. For these reasons, in such an environment, competitors are being forced to rethink their marketing strategies and also their organisational structures.

Overall therefore the West European market has evolved into a highly competitive, yet fragmented marketplace in which the major U.S. competitors IBM, Compaq and Apple have been faced with strong competition on a country by country basis by local indigenous companies. Yet, if one takes the total size of sales across Western Europe, IBM, Compaq and Apple are still the leaders and it is not at all clear that many of the low cost manufacturers, especially the mass of branded low scale assemblers will survive beyond the next few years. Clearly, the loss of market share by IBM and Compaq has been a cause for concern within these companies, however, based upon the data shown in this chapter,[14] it would be fair to say that Western Europe's indigenous personal computer industry including the large established companies and newer low-end manufacturers have failed to develop on anywhere near the scale of their North American competitors. This weakness applies even within their home market of Western Europe. Whilst it is true that on a country basis certain companies have done very well and even outperformed the U.S. leaders, nevertheless, it is important to remember that when looked at on a Pan-European basis, the evidence clearly points to some fundamental weaknesses.

Although many reasons can account for why European companies have been unable to develop stronger Pan-European market positions, what does stand-out for scrutiny is the fact that there appears a strong correlation between those companies that have achieved a broad geographical spread throughout Europe and those that occupy a strong overall market position. The strategy of focusing heavily upon a limited number of markets may have rewarded a few companies well in their home markets, but it does not place them well for the longer term, either in what should be their home market of the 1990s, namely Western Europe, nor in the wider global marketplace, which is discussed more fully later in this chapter. Naturally, part of this pattern can be explained by the limited resources available to the companies concerned and their time of market entry. However, other factors must account for the poor performance of the majority of the Europeans in this context, not least of which could be the weaknesses in their marketing strategies and a limited sense of vision, which are issues discussed more fully towards the end of this chapter. However, before discussing such matters, it is necessary to look carefully at the competitive and market conditions in the third major region of the international personal computer marketplace, which goes to make up the Triad, namely, the Asia/Pacific Rim.

THE ASIA/PACIFIC MARKET AND PATTERNS OF COMPETITION

The third largest region of the world's personal computer market is found around the Asia/Pacific Rim. The group of countries which go to make up the geographical subsegments within this region vary depending on one's source of reference. However, for the purposes of this analysis the countries considered consist of Australia, China (PRC),[15] Hong Kong, Japan,[16] Korea, Malaysia, Singapore, Taiwan and Thailand. From Fig. 7.6, it can be seen that the overall size of annual unit and value .shipments for the region as a whole has increased significantly between 1988 and 1992. Thus in 1992 the region represented approximately 17 per cent of the worldwide market for unit shipments and 22 per cent in value terms. Furthermore, a number of analysts predict that by 1995, shipments may well have reached a level of $25 billion on eight and a half million units, creating an installed base value of $126 billion made up of nearly 38 million units. Such rapid historical and projected patterns of growth are based upon the fact that in general terms, with the exception of Australia, the economies of this Asia/Pacific region exceed and in many cases far outstrip the average for those of the OECD group of countries. Even allowing for the recession of the early 1990s, they are therefore expected to well exceed the growth of both the United States and West European personal computer marketplaces, especially since the general market for computers amongst these countries is growing significantly faster than GDP. If this happens, the region will represent over a quarter of the worldwide market by 1995.

Certain features of the region can clearly influence the general levels of economic activity and hence the sales of personal computers. For example, during the past decade, much of the growth in the overall region has been due to strong Japanese direct investment in high technology offshore operations, which has boosted demand for computer systems. However, for

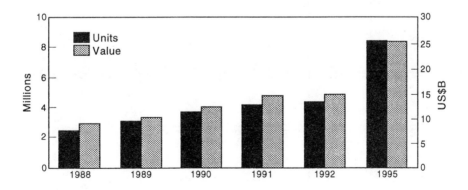

Source: International Data Corporation, © 1992.
Reproduced by permission of International Data Corporation, © 1992.

**Fig. 7.6. Asia/Pacific region personal computer unit shipments (000's)
and value (US$M): 1988 - 1995.**

Table 7.9. Asia/Pacific region personal computer market unit shipments (000's): 1989 - 1992.

COUNTRY	Unit Ships. 1989	% Change	Unit Ships. 1990	% Change	Unit Ships. 1991	% Change	Unit Ships. 1992*	% Change
Japan	1,861	24.90	2,293	23.21	2,304	0.48	2,447	6.21
Australia	535	28.30	579	8.22	591	2.07	646	9.31
Korea	325	70.16	501	54.15	591	17.96	650	9.98
Taiwan	266	24.30	277	4.14	292	5.42	331	13.36
China (PRC)	75 No 1988 data		86	14.67	98	13.95	112	14.29
Thailand	49	44.12	64	30.61	94	46.88	151	60.64
Hong Kong	46	27.78	51	10.87	62	21.57	67	8.06
Malaysia	30	50.00	57	90.00	80	40.35	100	25.00
Singapore	30	20.00	35	16.67	43	22.86	48	11.63
TOTAL	3,217	32.50	3,943	22.57	4,155	5.38	4,552	9.55

Note: * 1992 data are forecast estimates.

Source: International Data Corporation, © 1992.
Reproduced by permission of International Data Corporation, © 1992.

Table 7.10. Asia/Pacific region personal computer market, unit shipments (000's), shipment value (US$M) and installed base (000's): 1992.

Country	Rank	Unit Shipments	% Share of Total	Rank	Shipment Value	% Share of Total	Rank	Installed Base	% Share of Total
Japan	1	2,447	53.76	1	11,137	74.74	1	12,352	56.55
Korea	2	650	14.28	3	837	5.62	3	2,352	10.77
Australia	3	646	14.19	2	1,100	7.38	2	3,573	16.36
Taiwan	4	331	7.27	5	379	2.54	4	1,602	7.33
Thailand	5	151	3.32	6	293	1.97	6	423	1.94
China (PRC)	6	112	2.46	4	664	4.46	5	706	3.23
Malaysia	7	100	2.20	8	164	1.10	7	311	1.42
Hong Kong	8	67	1.47	7	192	1.29	8	297	1.36
Singapore	9	48	1.05	9	134	0.90	9	225	1.03
TOTAL		4,552	100		14,900	100		21,841	100

Note: US$ values based upon 1992 base year.

each country within the region, there exist very distinctive political–economic conditions. Given these types of distinctive political–economic patterns amongst the member countries, it is not surprising that they help to create significant differences in the value of shipments due to variation in levels of competition and in trade and tariff practices. Hence, as illustrated in Table 7.9, if one looks at the specific levels of growth on a country by country basis within the region, it can be seen that there are substantial differences, not only between the respective countries, but also, within a number of the countries over the period. The reasons for these changes are explored later in this chapter, for the moment, it is important for the reader to appreciate that the region reflects very different country markets and conditions. However, whilst rates of growth are varied, Table 7.10 highlights the relative importance of each of the countries in the region in terms of their market shares of unit and value shipments, together with the size of the installed base in unit terms of 1992. Clearly, it can be seen that Japan dominates the region, especially in the value of shipments. Australia and South Korea the second and third tier places, followed by Taiwan. However, Taiwan along with the remaining countries in the region are all relatively small markets, even though in most cases they are growing rapidly.

In terms of development, overall the Asia/Pacific personal computer market is far less saturated than either the United States or even the West European markets and exhibits greater variation in its patterns of competition and customer demand for personal computers between the different countries in the region. On closer investigation, it appears that six key factors are driving the differences between these various country markets. These include pricing, government influence, competition by and in-between foreign and local personal computer vendors, lack of copyright laws and the importance of local area networks. The variation that these factors cause within the region can best be understood by taking a look at how they affect the personal computer industry and its markets throughout the respective countries in the region. The analysis will therefore make use of region wide data, that breaks down the patterns of competition, market structure and distribution on a country segment basis. This regional data will be presented by a series of Figures and Tables which illustrate the overall patterns of market segmentation by product microprocessor category (Fig. 7.7), market shares of competitors (Tables 7.11 and 7.12), the pattern of distribution (Table 7.13) and by applications segments (Table 7.14) in each of the various countries. Readers are therefore asked to refer back to this information, as they study the following analysis of this Asia/Pacific region. However, given the importance of the Japanese market, both in the region, and in the worldwide marketplace, the analysis will commence with a specific more in-depth look at Japan's personal computer industry and its market, before moving on to a more general survey of the rest of the region.

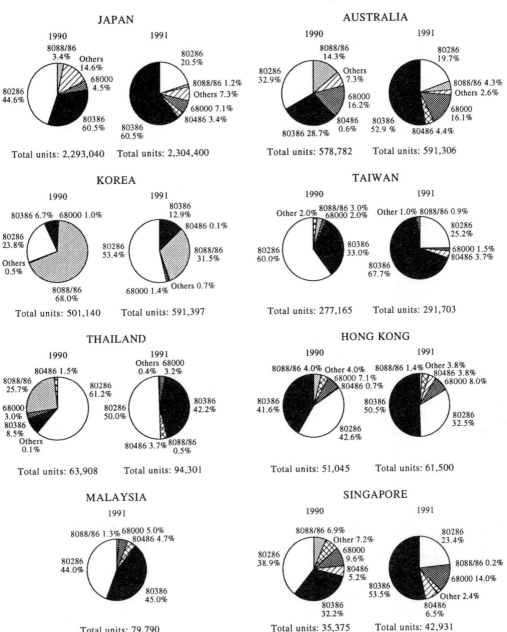

**Fig. 7.7. Asia/Pacific region personal computer market unit shipments
by processor: 1990 - 1991.**

Table 7.11. (pages 1 of 4) Asia/Pacific region personal computer market shares of leading vendors, unit shipments (000's): 1991.

COUNTRIES	ASIA/PACIFIC RIM REGION			JAPAN			AUSTRALIA			KOREA			TAIWAN		
COMPANY	Rank	Units	% Share	Rank	Units	% Share	Rank	Units	% Share	Rank	Units	% Share	Rank	Units	% Share
NEC	1	1,162,196	28.64	1	1,132,700	49.15	11	17,201	2.91						
Fujitsu	2	239,200	5.90	2	239,200	10.38									
Apple	3	239,389	5.88	3	133,000	5.77	1	77,070	13.03	10	8,043	1.36	9	4,223	1.45
IBM	4	225,960	5.57	4	147,500	6.40	2	32,255	5.45	6	15,000	2.54	7	10,935	3.75
Toshiba	5	216,849	5.34	5	193,000	8.38	9	20,529	3.47						
Seiko	6	172,000	4.24	6	172,000	7.46									
Samsung Electronics	7	117,520	2.90				15	7,537	1.27	1	108,358	18.32			
Trigem	8	105,350	2.60							2	105,350	17.81			
Daewoo Telecom	9	101,014	2.49							3	101,014	17.08			
Goldstar	10	88,275	2.18							4	88,275	14.93			
Acer	11	56,000	1.38				25	4,005	0.68				1	34,800	11.93
Hyundai	12	49,272	1.21							5	47,622	8.05			
Hitachi	13	40,100	0.99	7	40,100	1.74									
Matsushita	14	36,000	0.89	8	36,000	1.56									
Sun	15	29,006	0.71	12	23,100	1.00	26	2,720	0.46	13	1,200	0.20	10	1,150	0.39
Commodore	16	28,655	0.71				3	28,655	4.85						
Sony	17	28,500	0.70	9	28,500	1.24									
Ricoh	18	28,000	0.69	10	28,000	1.22									
Hewlett-Packard	19	27,999	0.69	15	14,500	0.63	22	5,041	0.85	11	1,350	0.23	11	880	0.30
Total Peripherals	20	27,331	0.67				4	27,331	4.62						
Compaq	21	27,244	0.67				10	18,834	3.19				12	454	0.16
Copam	22	25,818	0.64										2	23,218	7.96
Osbourne	23	25,321	0.62				5	25,321	4.28						
Mitsubishi	24	25,000	0.62	11	25,000	1.08									
Sharp	25	23,615	0.58	14	19,000	0.82	24	4,227	0.71						
Ipex	26	23,520	0.58				6	23,520	3.98						
Arrow	27	23,132	0.57				7	23,132	3.91						
Amstrad	28	23,111	0.57				8	21,511	3.64						
DTK	29	22,506	0.55										3	22,506	7.72
Sanyo	30	21,000	0.52	13	21,000	0.91									
Mitac	31	19,803	0.49				14	9,586	1.62				4	18,211	6.24
Olivetti	32	16,271	0.40				21	6,000	1.01						
AST	33	15,638	0.39										13	435	0.15
Twinhead	34	15,565	0.38										5	12,065	4.14
ALR	35	15,209	0.37												
DEC	36	14,683	0.36	16	6,600	0.29	17	6,923	1.17	14	400	0.07	14	310	0.11

Source: International Data Corporation, © 1992.
Reproduced by permission of International Data Corporation, © 1992.

Table 7.11. (pages 2 of 4) Asia/Pacific region personal computer market shares of leading vendors, unit shipments (000's): 1991.

COUNTRIES / COMPANY	ASIA/PACIFIC RIM REGION Rank	Value	% Share	JAPAN Units	% Share	Rank	AUSTRALIA Units	% Share	Rank	KOREA Units	% Share	Rank	TAIWAN Units	% Share	Rank
Qnix	37	13,600	0.34							13,600	2.30	7			
MCS (Optima)	38	13,470	0.33												
Epson	39	12,558	0.31				13,470	2.28	12						
Tatung	40	12,300	0.30				7,448	1.26	16				11,528	3.95	6
FIC	41	10,307	0.25										10,307	3.53	8
Bull/Zenith	42	10,166	0.25				10,166	1.72	13						
Dongyang (Hyosung)	43	8,800	0.22							8,800	1.49	8			
Koryo Systems	44	8,500	0.21							8,500	1.44	9			
Laser	45	8,360	0.21				4,840	0.82	23						
Atari	46	6,100	0.15				6,100	1.03	18						
Unisys	47	6,043	0.15				6,043	1.02	19						
Wang	48	6,029	0.15				6,029	1.02	20						
KT Technology	49	5,100	0.13												
GES (Datamini)	50	5,052	0.12												
Gabil Electronics	51	4,900	0.12												
IPC	52	4,740	0.12							4,900	0.83	11			
South East Asia (Intec)	53	4,200	0.10												
Advanced Computer (Aztech)	54	4,143	0.10												
Wearnes	55	4,100	0.10												
MCS (Optima)	56	3,810	0.09												
Hamson	57	3,400	0.08												
APC	58	2,830	0.07												
Easy Data	59	2,470	0.06												
Sherry	60	2,174	0.05												
Porro	61	2,000	0.05												
Philips	62	1,830	0.05												
Deltron	63	1,800	0.04												
Neatron	64	1,200	0.03												
Wyse	65	1,035	0.03												
Amiga	66	763	0.02												
Arche	67	735	0.02												
Tandon	68	635	0.02												
ICL	69	600	0.01												
Intergraph	70	285	0.01												
MIPS	71	260	0.01							285	0.05	15			
Dell	72	250	0.01							260	0.04	16			
Silicon Graphics	73	102	0.00												
OTHERS NOT NAMED		527,629	13.00	45,200	1.96		175,812	29.73		78,440	13.26		140,681	48.23	
TOTAL		4,057,328	100.00	2,304,400	100.00		591,306	100.00		591,397	100.00		291,703	100.00	

Source: International Data Corporation, © 1992.
Reproduced by permission of International Data Corporation, © 1992.

Table 7.11. (pages 3 of 4) Asia/Pacific region personal computer market shares of leading vendors, unit shipments (000's): 1991.

COUNTRIES / COMPANY	ASIA/PACIFIC RIM REGION			THAILAND			HONG KONG			MALAYSIA			SINGAPORE		
	Rank	Units	% Share	Units	% Share	Rank	Units	% Share	Rank	Units	% Share	Rank	Units	% Share	Rank
NEC	1	1,162,196	28.64	2,085	2.21	9	4,650	7.56	4	3,500	4.39	9	2,060	4.80	9
Fujitsu	2	239,200	5.90	2,300	2.44	7=	4,900	7.97	3	4,000	5.01	5	4,853	11.30	1
Apple	3	238,389	5.88	6,295	6.68	1	6,450	10.49	1	3,800	4.76	7	3,725	8.68	5
IBM	4	225,960	5.57	320	0.34	24	3,000	4.88	6						
Toshiba	5	216,849	5.34												
Seiko	6	172,000	4.24	1,625	1.72	12									
Samsung Electronics	7	117,520	2.90												
Trigem	8	105,350	2.60												
Daewoo Telecom	9	101,014	2.49												
Goldstar	10	88,275	2.18												
Acer	11	56,000	1.38	5,882	6.24	2	2,080	3.38	9	5,200	6.52	1	4,033	9.39	3
Hyundai	12	49,272	1.21	1,650	1.75	11									
Hitachi	13	40,100	0.99												
Matsushita	14	36,000	0.89												
Sun	15	29,006	0.71	174	0.18	25	380	0.62	16				282	0.66	13
Commodore	16	28,655	0.71												
Sony	17	28,500	0.70												
Ricoh	18	28,000	0.69												
Hewlett-Packard	19	27,999	0.69	955	1.01	14	770	1.25	15	1,800	2.26	17	2,703	6.30	7
Total Peripherals	20	27,331	0.67												
Compaq	21	27,244	0.67	1,281	1.36	13	2,640	4.29	7	2,000	2.51	15	2,035	4.74	10
Copam	22	25,818	0.64							2,600	3.26	11			
Osbourne	23	25,321	0.62												
Mitsubishi	24	25,000	0.62												
Sharp	25	23,615	0.58	388	0.41	23									
Ipex	26	23,520	0.58												
Arrow	27	23,132	0.57							1,600	2.01	20			
Amstrad	28	23,111	0.57												
DTK	29	22,506	0.55												
Sanyo	30	21,000	0.52												
Mitac	31	19,803	0.49	792	0.84	16	800	1.30	14	3,700	4.64	8			
Olivetti	32	16,271	0.40	685	0.73	20	850	1.38	13	1,200	1.50	22	1,450	3.38	12
AST	33	15,638	0.39	1,703	1.81	10	6,300	10.24	2						
Twinhead	34	15,565	0.38	3,500	3.71	4									
ALR	35	15,209	0.37	2,975	3.15	5	3,200	5.20	5	4,300	5.39	3	4,734	11.03	2
DEC	36	14,683	0.36				252	0.41	17				198	0.46	14

Source: International Data Corporation, © 1992.
Reproduced by permission of International Data Corporation, © 1992.

Table 7.11. (pages 4 of 4) Asia/Pacific region personal computer market shares of leading vendors, unit shipments (000's): 1991.

COUNTRIES	ASIA/PACIFIC RIM REGION			THAILAND			HONG KONG			MALAYSIA			SINGAPORE		
COMPANY	Rank	Units	% Share	Rank	Units	% Share	Rank	Units	% Share	Rank	Units	% Share	Rank	Units	% Share
Onix	37	13,600	0.34												
MCS (Optima)	38	13,470	0.33												
Epson	39	12,558	0.31	22	600	0.64	8	2,310	3.76	13	2,200	2.76			
Tatung	40	12,300	0.30	17	772	0.82									
FIC	41	10,307	0.25												
Bull/Zenith	42	10,166	0.25												
Dongyang (Hyosung)	43	8,800	0.22												
Koryo Systems	44	8,500	0.21												
Laser	45	8,360	0.21	3	3,520	3.73									
Atari	46	6,100	0.15												
Unisys	47	6,043	0.15												
Wang	48	6,029	0.15												
KT Technology	49	5,100	0.13							2	5,100	6.39	4	3,752	8.74
GES (Datamini)	50	5,052	0.12							21	1,300	1.63			
Gabil Electronics	51	4,900	0.12												
IPC	52	4,740	0.12							16	1,900	2.38	6	2,840	6.62
South East Asia (Intec)	53	4,200	0.10							4	4,200	5.26			
Advanced Computer (Aztech)	54	4,143	0.10	7=	2,300	2.44				14	2,200	2.76	11	1,943	4.53
Wearnes	55	4,100	0.10							18=	1,800	2.26			
MCS (Optima)	56	3,810	0.09							6	3,810	4.78			
Hannson	57	3,400	0.08							10	3,400	4.26			
ARC	58	2,830	0.07	6	2,830	3.00									
Easy Data	59	2,470	0.06							12	2,470	3.10	8	2,174	5.06
Sherry	60	2,174	0.05												
Porro	61	2,000	0.05				10	2,000	3.25						
Philips	62	1,830	0.05	15	860	0.91	12	970	1.58						
Deltron	63	1,800	0.04							18=	1,800	2.26			
Neatron	64	1,200	0.03							23	1,200	1.50			
Wyse	65	1,035	0.03				11	1,035	1.68						
Amiga	66	763	0.02	18	763	0.81									
Arche	67	735	0.02	19	735	0.78									
Tandon	68	635	0.02	21	635	0.67									
ICL	69	600	0.01							24	600	0.75			
Intergraph	70	285	0.01												
MIPS	71	260	0.01				18	250	0.41						
Dell	72	250	0.01				19	102	0.17						
Silicon Graphics	73	102	0.00												
OTHERS NOT NAMED		527,629	13.00		48,676	51.62		18,561	30.18		14,110	17.68		6,149	14.32
TOTAL		4,057,328	100.00		94,301	100.00		61,500	100.00		79,790	100.00		42,931	100.00

Source: International Data Corporation, © 1992.
Reproduced by permission of International Data Corporation, © 1992.

Table 7.12. (pages 1 of 4) Asia/Pacific region personal computer market shares of leading vendors, value of shipments (US$M): 1991.

COMPANY	ASIA/PACIFIC RIM REGION			THAILAND			HONG KONG			MALAYSIA			SINGAPORE		
COUNTRIES	Rank	Value	% Share	Value	% Share	Rank	Value	% Share	Rank	Value	% Share	Rank	Value	% Share	Rank
NEC	1	3973.3	29.21	6.7	3.56	7	9	6.21	4	6.8	4.66	7	5	4.20	8
IBM	2	1606.1	11.81	27.7	14.73	1	18.7	12.90	1	12.9	8.84	1	10.1	8.49	4
Fujitsu	3	1408.7	10.36												
Apple	4	911.7	6.70	9	4.79	4	16.4	11.31	2	10.9	7.47	2	12.9	10.84	2
Toshiba	5	601.8	4.42	1.2	0.64	24	7.6	5.24	6						
Epson	6	532.3	3.91	1.3	0.69	23	4.2	2.90	10	3.6	2.47	14			
Hitachi	7	398	2.93												
Sun	8	349.3	2.57	2.7	1.44	15	3.8	2.62	11				5.3	4.45	7
Hewlett-Packard	9	310.8	2.28	4.6	2.45	12	7.2	4.97	7	5.9	4.04	8	25	21.01	1
Mitsubishi	10	189.9	1.40												
Matsushita	11	188.9	1.39												
Sony	12	167.9	1.23												
Ricoh	13	141	1.04												
Samsung Electronics	14	128.9	0.95	4	2.13	13									
DEC	15	124.1	0.91				2.9	2.00	14				4	3.36	11
Trigem	16	120.3	0.88												
Sanyo	17	118.1	0.87												
Sharp	18	107.7	0.79	0.9	0.48	25									
Goldstar	19	106.1	0.78												
Compaq	20	101.2	0.74	5.5	2.93	10	8.4	5.79	5	7.5	5.14	6	4.5	3.78	9
Acer	21	83.6	0.61	13.9	7.39	2	3.7	2.55	12	9.2	6.30	3	6.4	5.38	5
Daewoo Telecom	22	73.4	0.54												
Ipex	23	51.6	0.38												
Osborne	24	49.1	0.36												
Total Peripherals	25	46.4	0.34												
Arrow	26	41.6	0.31												
Hyundai Electronics	27	40.1	0.29	3.1	1.65	14									
AST	28	39.7	0.29	4.7	2.50	11	15.3	10.55	3						
Olivetti	29	37.7	0.28	1.8	0.96	20	2.2	1.52	17	2.9	1.99	17=	2.9	2.44	13
ALR	30	33.3	0.24	7.3	3.88	6	5.9	4.07	8	7.8	5.34	5	11.4	9.58	3
Copam	31	32.9	0.24							8.7	5.96	4			
Commodore	32	29.1	0.21							4.8	3.29	12			
Amstrad	33	28.9	0.21							2.4	1.64	20			

Source: International Data Corporation, © 1992.
Reproduced by permission of International Data Corporation, © 1992.

Table 7.12. (pages 2 of 4) Asia/Pacific region personal computer market shares of leading vendors, value of shipments (US$M): 1991.

COUNTRIES COMPANY	ASIA/PACIFIC RIM REGION Rank	Value	% Share	JAPAN Value	% Share	Rank	AUSTRALIA Value	% Share	Rank	KOREA Value	% Share	Rank	TAIWAN Rank	Value	% Share
DTK	34	24.8	0.18										4	24.8	7.21
Mitac	35	24.7	0.18										5	20.5	5.96
Bull/Zenith	36	24.6	0.18				24.6	1.66	15						
MCS (Optima)	37	24	0.18				19.1	1.29	17						
Twinhead	38	22.7	0.17										8	13.5	3.92
Qnix	39	17.5	0.13							17.5	2.31	10			
Wang	40	16.7	0.12				16.7	1.13	18						
Tatung	41	16.4	0.12										6=	15	4.36
Laser	42	15.1	0.11				7.6	0.51	26						
Konyo Systems	43	13.7	0.10							13.7	1.81	11			
Unisys	44	13.6	0.10				13.6	0.92	22						
Dongyang (Hyosung)	45	12.9	0.09							12.9	1.70	12			
Sharp	46	11.6	0.09				11.6	0.78	23						
FIC	47	11.5	0.08										9	11.5	3.34
Intergraph	48	10.5	0.08							10.5	1.38	13			
Atari	49	9.5	0.07				9.5	0.64	24						
Wearnes	50	9	0.07												
MIPS	51	8.3	0.06							8.3	1.09	15			
GES (Datamini)	52	8.1	0.06												
IPC	53	7.2	0.05												
Gabil Electronics	54	6.3	0.05							6.3	0.83	16			
ARC	55	6.1	0.04												
Advanced Computer (Aztech)	56	5.4	0.04												
KT Technology	57	5	0.04												
Philips	58	4.9	0.04												
South East Asia (Intec)	59	4.9	0.04												
Hannson	60	4.7	0.03												
Porro	61	4.6	0.03												
Sherry	62	3.7	0.03												
Deltron	63	3.1	0.02												
Wyse	64	2.4	0.02												
Silicon Graphics	65	2.4	0.02												
Tandon	66	2	0.01												
Amiga	67	1.9	0.01												
Neatron	68	1.7	0.01												
ICL	69	1.7	0.01												
Easy Data	70	1.7	0.01												
Arche	71	1.4	0.01												
Dell	72	0.6	0.00												
OTHERS NOT NAMED		1063.1	7.81	280.20	2.69		443.00	29.97		106.20	13.99			116.00	33.72
TOTAL		13603.50	100.00	10424.50	100.00		1478.00	100.00		759.00	100.00			344.00	100.00

Source: International Data Corporation, © 1992.
Reproduced by permission of International Data Corporation, © 1992.

Table 7.12. (pages 3 of 4) Asia/Pacific region personal computer market shares of leading vendors, value of shipments (US$M): 1991.

COUNTRIES	ASIA/PACIFIC RIM REGION			THAILAND			HONG KONG			MALAYSIA			SINGAPORE		
COMPANY	Rank	Value	% Share	Rank	Value	% Share	Rank	Value	% Share	Rank	Value	% Share	Rank	Value	% Share
NEC	1	3973.3	29.21	7	6.7	3.56	4	9	6.21	7	6.8	4.66	8	5	4.20
IBM	2	1606.1	11.81	1	27.7	14.73	1	18.7	12.90	1	12.9	8.84	4	10.1	8.49
Fujitsu	3	1408.7	10.36										2	12.9	10.84
Apple	4	911.7	6.70	4	9	4.79	2	16.4	11.31	2	10.9	7.47			
Toshiba	5	601.8	4.42	24	1.2	0.64	6	7.6	5.24						
Epson	6	532.3	3.91	23	1.3	0.69	10	4.2	2.90	14	3.6	2.47			
Hitachi	7	398	2.93												
Sun	8	349.3	2.57	15	2.7	1.44	11	3.8	2.62	8	5.9	4.04	7	5.3	4.45
Hewlett-Packard	9	310.8	2.28	12	4.6	2.45	7	7.2	4.97				1	25	21.01
Mitsubishi	10	189.9	1.40												
Matsushita	11	188.9	1.39												
Sony	12	167.9	1.23												
Ricoh	13	141	1.04												
Samsung Electronics	14	128.9	0.95	13	4	2.13	14	2.9	2.00						
DEC	15	124.1	0.91										11	4	3.36
Trigem	16	120.3	0.88												
Sanyo	17	118.1	0.87												
Sharp	18	107.7	0.79												
Goldstar	19	106.1	0.78	25	0.9	0.48									
Compaq	20	101.2	0.74	10	5.5	2.93	5	8.4	5.79	6	7.5	5.14	9	4.5	3.78
Acer	21	83.6	0.61	2	13.9	7.39	12	3.7	2.55	3	9.2	6.30	5	6.4	5.38
Daewoo Telecom	22	73.4	0.54												
Ipex	23	51.6	0.38												
Osborne	24	49.1	0.36												
Total Peripherals	25	46.4	0.34												
Arrow	26	41.6	0.31												
Hyundai Electronics	27	40.1	0.29	14	3.1	1.65	3	15.3	10.55	17=	2.9	1.99			
AST	28	39.7	0.29	11	4.7	2.50									
Olivetti	29	37.7	0.28				17	2.2	1.52	5	7.8	5.34	13	2.9	2.44
ALR	30	33.3	0.24	20	1.8	0.96	8	5.9	4.07	4	8.7	5.96	3	11.4	9.58
Copam	31	32.9	0.24	6	7.3	3.88				12	4.8	3.29			
Commodore	32	29.1	0.21												
Amstrad	33	28.9	0.21							20	2.4	1.64			

Source: International Data Corporation, © 1992.
Reproduced by permission of International Data Corporation, © 1992.

Table 7.12. (pages 4 of 4) Asia/Pacific region personal computer market shares of leading vendors, value of shipments (US$M): 1991.

COUNTRIES / COMPANY	ASIA/PACIFIC RIM REGION			THAILAND			HONG KONG			MALAYSIA			SINGAPORE		
	Rank	Value	% Share	Rank	Value	% Share	Rank	Value	% Share	Rank	Value	% Share	Rank	Value	% Share
DTK	34	24.8	0.18												
Mitac	35	24.7	0.18	16	2.4	1.28	18	1.8	1.24						
Bull/Zenith	36	24.6	0.18												
MCS (Optima)	37	24	0.18							10=	4.9	3.36			
Twinhead	38	22.7	0.17	3	9.2	4.89									
Qnix	39	17.5	0.13												
Wang	40	16.7	0.12												
Tatung	41	16.4	0.12	21=	1.4	0.74									
Laser	42	15.1	0.11	5	7.5	3.99									
Koryo Systems	43	13.7	0.10												
Unisys	44	13.6	0.10												
Dongyang (Hyosung)	45	12.9	0.09												
Sharp	46	11.6	0.09												
FIC	47	11.5	0.08												
Intergraph	48	10.5	0.08												
Atari	49	9.5	0.07												
Wearnes	50	9	0.07	8=	6.1	3.24				17=	2.9	1.99			
MIPS	51	8.3	0.06												
GES (Datamini)	52	8.1	0.06							21	2	1.37	6	6.1	5.13
IPC	53	7.2	0.05							17=	2.9	1.99	10	4.3	3.61
Gabil Electronics	54	6.3	0.05												
ARC	55	6.1	0.04	8=	6.1	3.24									
Advanced Computer (Aztech)	56	5.4	0.04							17=	2.9	1.99			
KT Technology	57	5	0.04							9	5	3.42	14	2.5	2.10
Philips	58	4.9	0.04	18=	1.9	1.01	13	3	2.07						
South East Asia (Imtec)	59	4.9	0.04							10=	4.9	3.36			
Hannson	60	4.7	0.03							13	4.7	3.22			
Porro	61	4.6	0.03				9	4.6	3.17						
Sherry	62	3.7	0.03												
Deltron	63	3.1	0.02							15	3.1	2.12	12	3.7	3.11
Wyse	64	2.4	0.02	17	2	1.06	15=	2.4	1.66						
Silicon Graphics	65	2.4	0.02	18=	1.9	1.01	15=	2.4	1.66						
Tandon	66	2	0.01												
Amiga	67	1.9	0.01												
Neatron	68	1.7	0.01							22=	1.7	1.16			
ICL	69	1.7	0.01							22=	1.7	1.16			
Easy Data	70	1.7	0.01							22=	1.7	1.16			
Arche	71	1.4	0.01	21=	1.4	0.74									
Dell	72	0.6	0.00				19	0.6	0.41						
OTHERS NOT NAMED		1063.1	7.81		53.70	28.56		24.90	17.17		24.20	16.58		14.90	12.52
TOTAL		13603.5	100		188.00	100.00		145.00	100.00		146.00	100.00		119.00	100.00

Source: International Data Corporation, © 1992.
Reproduced by permission of International Data Corporation, © 1992.

Table 7.13. Asia/Pacific Region personal computer market shipment value by distribution channels: 1990 and 1991.

	1990 Direct Channel Per Cent %	1991 Direct Channel Per Cent %	Percentage Change Between 1990-1991	1991 Breakdown between Various Indirect Distribution Channels DISTRIBUTOR Per Cent %	DEALER Per Cent %	VARS Per Cent %
JAPAN	15	15	0			
AUSTRALIA	15	24	9	1	87	12
KOREA	24	24	0	1	97	2
TAIWAN	29	35	6	36	60	4
THAILAND	13	2	-11	78	21	1
HONG KONG	14	10	-4	10	83	7
SINGAPORE	17	14	-3	38	52	10
MALAYSIA	5	5	0			
Average	18	16	N/A	27	67	6

Source: International Data Corporation, © 1992.
Reproduced by permission of International Data Corporation, © 1992.

Japan's Personal Computer Industry and Marketplace

Dominating the region of the Asia/Pacific Rim personal computer marketplace is Japan, as shown previously in Table 7.10. However, when considering the Japanese personal computer marketplace, certain general economic, social and political factors should first of all be remembered concerning its place in the Pacific Rim region, especially when comparing its position to that of the United States and European markets. Japan's economic wealth makes it one of the highest per capita income nations in the world, at around the same level as Germany, the U.K. and France. Unlike these European countries where trade within the European Community holds over 55% of total imports and exports amongst member states, Japan is not yet surrounded by countries with similar levels of economic wealth in the immediate region. Hence, it has historically needed to export heavily to both the U.S. and Europe, which in itself has been a source of economic friction during the 1980s and early 1990s. For example, the U.S. imposed 100 per cent import taxes on selected Japanese products, including personal computers during 1987. However, despite the favourable movement of the Yen/Dollar exchange rate during the late 1980s, Japanese companies in the IT[17] industry began to change their methods of international market expansion by investing offshore in both U.S. and European based production/assembly facilities. Hence major Japanese personal computer and workstation manufacturers including NEC, Toshiba, Seiko-Epson and Sony established such overseas sites during this period. Furthermore, a number of Japanese computer companies maintain OEM manufacturing contracts for U.S. and European companies that are marketing worldwide. Historically, Japan has also played host to mainframe and minicomputer companies from the U.S. and Europe, whose production of computers and peripherals are marketed through exports, as well as in the Japanese market. Nowadays, Japan provides a major source of components to computer companies in the U.S. and Europe as well as being a significant centre of research and development in leading edge component technologies and more recently, Japan has attracted further investment from foreign companies, especially in the software sector, which has involved a number of joint ventures and Japanese funded software projects. However, Japan's IT industries have (like the United States and Western Europe) found themselves increasingly affected by recessionary conditions. Therefore as was illustrated in the earlier worldwide overview in Table 7.2, the Japanese personal computer market has experienced considerable variation in its growth rates between 1988 and 1991.

Generally, it has been far more buoyant than either the United States or West European markets achieving a 30 per cent growth in 1990. However, in common with the United States and Western Europe, this pace of growth was severely reduced in 1991, when as shown in Table 7.2, for the first time since the late 1970s the nation's personal computer markets hit a plateau, showing virtually no growth rate in unit shipments and only 1.2 per cent value terms.[18] A number of economic factors in Japan's business community accounted for this slowdown, however, the sudden decline in growth also reflected changes in customers' attitudes and behaviour in the marketplace. In terms of installed base, Japan is by far the largest in the region, however, in relative terms its size of active installed base makes it small compared to the U.S., which is nearly five times larger and Western Europe, which is two and a half times as large. Yet at the same time, it should also be remembered that Japan's market is significantly larger than any of the markets for an independent European country.

In Japan's personal computer market, as shown in Table 7.14 the business/professional has grown to become the dominant sector, representing 62 per cent of unit shipments and 52 per cent of value in 1991. Meanwhile, the second largest sector consisted of the technical/scientific market, followed by the home/hobby segment. Overall, the Japanese personal computer market is far less saturated than in either the United States or the West European markets. Indeed, whilst Japan has the world's second largest economy, the number of personal computers per capita is less than half that of the United States or many countries in Western Europe. This is a pattern that can be explained by several factors which may account for why personal computers remained a relatively small market in Japan, until the late 1980s, especially in the business segment. On the supply side, these factors include high hardware prices, together with a lack of compatibility between many Japanese competitors' machines and limited availability of software modified to Japanese requirements, especially by the U.S. computer companies. It has also been suggested that additional factors that may account for the small size of Japan's personal computer market development include a shortage of software engineers at the end-user level for customer support and systems development, limited office

Table 7.14. Asia/Pacific Region personal computer market, unit shipments by application segments: 1990 and 1991.

COUNTRY	1990 Business Per Cent %	1990 Technical/ Scientific Per Cent %	1990 Education Per Cent %	1990 Home Per Cent %	1990 Number of Shipments	1991 Business Per Cent %	1991 Technical/ Scientific Per Cent %	1991 Education Per Cent %	1991 Home Per Cent %	1991 Number of Shipments
JAPAN	61.00	18.00	4.00	17.00	2,293,040	62.00	19.00	9.00	10.00	2,304,400
AUSTRALIA	68.30	6.20	16.10	9.40	578,782	67.60	5.80	16.80	9.80	591,306
KOREA	32.00	5.00	28.00	35.00	501,140	47.00	7.00	30.00	16.00	591,397
TAIWAN	42.00	8.80	11.20	38.00	277,165	44.60	8.90	12.40	34.10	291,703
THAILAND	77.40	3.30	13.10	6.20	63,908	67.10	2.90	20.80	9.20	94,301
MALAYSIA						85.50	2.70	4.00	7.80	79,790
HONGKONG	72.20	5.10	14.70	8.00	51,045	72.30	4.10	9.10	14.50	61,500
SINGAPORE	63.00	11.00	17.00	9.00	35,375	67.00	6.00	11.00	16.00	42,931
Average	59.41	8.20	14.87	17.51	542,922	64.14	7.05	14.14	14.68	507,166

Note: Data not collected for Malaysia during 1990.

Source: International Data Corporation, © 1992.
Reproduced by permission of International Data Corporation, © 1992.

space and high communications tariffs. On the demand side, factors such as keyboard aversion and a general preference for centralised systems[19] amongst many of Japan's older managers have often been cited as reasons for the slow growth of the personal computer market. In addition, the unique nature of the Japanese language with its complex form of kanji,[20] has made the acceptance of typing much more difficult than in many other countries.

Another important feature to account for the relative small size of Japan's personal computer market relates to the structure of Japan's overall information technology or IT market, especially as it affects the corporate business market. The total size of the IT market in 1991 for Japan was estimated at U.S.$60 billion, representing about 19 per cent of the worldwide market. For hardware alone, large mainframe computers held a much more significant share at 30 per cent than in the U.S. or European markets, where they occupied only 20 per cent. Conversely, personal computers and workstations as a percentage of the overall market in Japan are small at 20 per cent compared to 40 per cent in the U.S. and Europe. In addition, historically, word-processors known as wahpuros have maintained a much stronger position in the Japanese office than in the west and this has therefore slowed the adoption of personal computers in this major applications area, which until recently have been much more expensive machines. Hence the corporate business market for computer systems has been dominated by large-scale mainframe systems which are attractive to the needs of Japanese organisations and management style of decision making. A further feature has been the fact that in 1990 only some 3 per cent of PC/workstations were connected on LANs in Japan, compared to a figure of 12 per cent in the U.S. This was due largely to the slow implementation of new technologies such as ISDN (integrated services digital network) by the Japanese telecommunications common carrier,[21] Nippon Telegraph and Telephone Corporation (NTT). However, major investment in the infrastructure started to take place in the early 1990s and industry estimates[22] suggest that by 1996 some 20 per cent of the installed base of personal computers will be connected to a LAN.

Historically Japan's personal computer market has also tended to consist of a much higher percentage of older equipment than in the United States or West European markets. For example, in 1989, Japan's personal computer market was dominated by the much older 80286 based machines which accounted for 55 per cent of unit shipments. However, the market for 80386 based machines grew rapidly from a small base during 1989 when it represented 17 per cent of unit shipments to 45 per cent by 1992, thus making it much closer in the mix of its product families to the United States and Western Europe. During 1991 and 1992, several 80486-based personal computers have been launched in Japan with prices on the low-end SX version competing heavily with the 386 machines, thus as illustrated in Fig. 7.7, the market is experiencing a major transition from lower powered machines to faster, higher capacity systems for networking environments.

Other changes taking place in the Japanese personal computer market include a number of developments in operating standards, which has witnessed a complicated adoption of MS-DOS, with many vendors adopting proprietary versions of the software to fit their systems. As the market leader, NEC's version of MS-DOS has come under attack from IBM Japan's new "open" system designated DOS/V,[23] which has attracted followers and has led to over 130 DOS/V machines being launched on the market. However, sales have been slow and problems exist as to the portability of the new system between different vendors' products. In an effort to overcome these problems, IBM Japan and the Open Architecture Developers Group (OADG) are attempting to develop a standardised version of OADG DOS/V. At the time of writing, how long this will take is a matter of conjecture, however, it is likely that in the future, the new operating systems should help to stimulate demand for applications software, since Japanese users of personal computers have for a long time had to put up with a limited choice of Japanese-language software for the primary business applications. The new operating systems are decreasing the time required for Japanisation of software packages, which is further supported by the entry of a number of foreign software companies into the bilingual PC/AT market. Furthermore, the significant increase in sales of Apple Macintosh equipment has also stimulated developments in this area. Probably the most significant software development in Japan's personal computer market has been the unveiling of Windows 3.1J in May 1993. According to one report,[24] it is claimed to be bilingual and able to run on most types of IBM-compatible hardware, as well as NEC's proprietary 9800 line. Potentially, Windows 3.1J could change the conditions of competition in the Japanese market significantly by opening up opportunities for U.S. competitors to take on the Japanese in their own market, especially NEC.

Historically, Japan's personal computer industry has been dominated by domestic companies. Tables 7.11 and 7.12 illustrate that in the top five positions, the U.S. penetration of the market is restricted to Japan IBM and Apple, both in unit shipments and in the value of shipments. Most of the remaining competitors are also Japanese with the exception of Sun, Yokugowa Hewlett Packard (YHP) and DEC which have managed to gain small shares with their workstation/PCs. Noticeable by their absence from the ranking are Compaq and Zenith that figure strongly in both the United States and West European markets, along with clones such as Dell or Packard Bell. Similarly, South East Asian and West European competitors do not figure in this market. Amongst the Japanese competitors, it can be seen that NEC dominates the market, followed by Fujitsu, Toshiba and Seiko Epson. The top six vendors accounted for 80 per cent of revenue on 88 per cent of unit sales during 1991, representing an extremely high level of concentration in these top brand name companies. However, only NEC, IBM Japan, Apple Japan, Sun Microsystems and YHP managed to achieve an increase in revenues during fiscal 1991, which reflected how hard the economic recession and downturn in demand for personal computers hit the competition during this period. This can be seen in the fact that during fiscal 1991 the combined revenue of the remaining competitors declined by an average of 3 per cent. Most successful was Apple Computer which enjoyed a huge increase in revenues of 122 per cent which moved it into the top five competitors in the Japanese market.

However, 1993 has not only witnessed Microsoft's moves to gain a stronger position in the Japanese market, it has also seen a much more aggressive stance by U.S. competitors. With the advantage of an effective Windows environment, Compaq, IBM and Dell are offering much lower priced machines in an effort to draw customers away from their word processors and higher priced Japanese personal computers. Meanwhile Apple continues to build up its market share, which currently places it well ahead of its other U.S. rivals in the Japanese market.

Table 7.13 illustrates the breakdown between direct and indirect sales for the market as a whole and emphasises the fact that the vast majority of personal computer sales are dependent upon indirect channels in terms of both unit and value shipments. These indirect channels consist of VARs and dealer/retail outlets, with retail outlets being used exclusively for the sale of personal computers rather than workstations, which tend to sell through VARs if not on a direct basis. In addition, many dealers are financed or owned by Japanese computer manufacturers. However, channel strategies in Japan are going through a number of changes in light of the stagnation in demand in the marketplace. For IBM Japan and Apple Computer, sales through indirect channels have increased significantly. In the case of IBM this has been generated by a switch of channel emphasis, whilst for Apple it has resulted from a new channel strategy and organisation that has supported increased sales of the Macintosh. In contrast, for most domestic competitors, the proportion of personal computers sold through indirect channels has been in decline. The main reason for this pattern is that such companies already have established extensive dealer networks throughout the country, whereas IBM and Apple have been involved in catch-up operations. In addition, companies such as NEC and Fujitsu have been making more use of their own direct sales force for sales of their high-end products to the corporate marketplace. Generally speaking the VARs channel in Japan is less developed than in the United States or Western Europe, however, as competitors move towards the marketing of more powerful high-end personal computers and LANs, distribution channels are likely to go through further and yet more drastic shifts in the next few years, as dealers and retail outlets struggle to cope with the newly emerging range of services required to sell and support such systems. Most recently, since late 1992, Dell Computer, which has made its success through low cost mail-order distribution in the U.S. market has set up a similar operation in Japan. Some analysts are sceptical as to whether this kind of marketing will catch-on in Japan, others see it as a trend for the future.

Overall therefore, the Japanese computer industry and its markets are still dominated by Japanese manufacturers with the exception of IBM

Japan and the growing importance of Apple Computer. The market itself is generally less mature and hence less saturated than the United States or West European markets, although somewhat stagnant. However, the accelerating investment in telecommunications infrastructure[25] for the office environment and the increasing demand for more productive use of personal computers, based upon newer hardware and software systems together with LANs has meant that the market is rapidly moving towards a process of "downsizing" which is likely to put considerable pressure upon competitors, both within the personal computer industry and the overall Japanese computer industry. How fast this process develops depends of course on a number of factors, not least of which will be the behaviour of companies in the continuing recessionary conditions and the impact of greater competition for Japanese based software applications. However, analysts are generally optimistic that the Japanese personal computer market still has the potential for significant growth as "downsizing" increases demand for LAN based systems and as the portable market continues to develop.

Key to Apple's success in Japan have been the use of local managers and their development of an effective distribution strategy. Whether new competition based upon Windows 3.1J and Apple's graphical user-interface will overthrow NEC's dominance of the market remains to be seen. One thing that does seem certain is that Japan's personal computer industry and marketplace will become an increasingly competitive environment during the 1990s.

Other Pacific Rim Markets and their Competitive Conditions

Given that Japan dominates the Asia/Pacific region, this section will provide an overview of the personal computer industries and markets for the remaining countries in the region. What is important to recognise about these other countries is that although currently collectively representing less than 50 per cent of sales in the region, as was shown earlier, their rates of growth in most cases are far higher than those found in the United States or Western Europe and even those of Japan. Hence, given that many of these countries are also forecast to maintain high rates of growth during the 1990s, then by the mid-1990s some of these markets are expected to become much more significant than today, especially in the case of South Korea. Secondly, in the case of Taiwan and South Korea, these countries are also home to an increasing number of successful competitors in the low-priced end of the market, not only in their home market or the Asia/Pacific arena, but also in the United States and West European marketplace.

With the exception of Australia and mainland China, the remainder of the countries in the region including South Korea, Taiwan, Thailand, Hong Kong, Malaysia and Singapore are frequently lumped together as the "Paper Tigers" of the region. As such they are expected to be the major engines of growth in the 1990s for the region. However, whilst this may be the case, it is also important to recognise and understand some of the differences between these countries, since these will account for how the overall personal computer industry and its markets develop during the 1990s. Mainland China will however, not form a significant part of the commentary, given its rather special economic market conditions. Furthermore, in relation to its population size, as yet it remains a very small part of the overall market in the region, on which there is limited data.

Standing somewhat apart from the rest of the region, in terms of culture, economic maturity, social demography and political systems is Australia. As such, the Australian personal computer market, whilst historically being the second largest in the region after Japan, is relatively small, as shown earlier in Table 7.10. During the late 1980s the market enjoyed strong growth. However, in the early 1990s, things changed and as shown earlier in Table 7.9, with the deepening and extension of the recession, growth in the personal computer market first slowed and then declined. As in most personal computer markets, Fig. 7.14 illustrates that in 1991 the business segment accounted for just under 70 percent of sales and is relatively sophisticated, although not so developed or close to saturation as the U.S. or Europe. However, during 1991 this segment went through significant changes which were caused firstly by reductions in the cost of components that resulted in the erosion of personal computer prices of up to 40 per cent on 1990 prices, thus dramatically improving price/performance ratios, which led to a shift in buying patterns towards the increasingly more affordable powerful systems. However, the demand for such systems was not only driven by lower prices, but also as in other mature markets, by the rapid acceptance of the value in adopting the Windows graphical interface,[26] that required these more powerful systems. In terms of processor segmentation, Intel dominates, although Motorola holds some 15 per cent, mostly due to sales from Apple Macintoshes and Commodore's Amiga family. However the changes in buying behaviour have meant that 8-bit processors have significantly declined as they are replaced by 386SX based systems at the low-end, as shown in Fig. 7.7. As for distribution, the direct sales became important during the late 1980s, since these were the preferred choice of a number of mainframe and minicomputer companies that entered the personal computer market. This trend has been further fuelled during the early 1990s as the poor economic conditions and price declines of personal computers have forced many vendors to remove their intermediaries and pass on their cost savings in the form of lower prices. Alternatively some vendors are making greater use of mass merchant retail channels. As a result, pressure is building upon the viability of dealer channels. Indeed, the degree to which direct channels are being used as an increasing proportion of total channel sales can be seen in Table 7.13 which illustrates the significant shift between 1990 and 1991. Thus the issues discussed earlier concerning channel conflict management in the United States and Western Europe are therefore gaining importance in the Australian personal computer marketplace.

Many of these market changes have both been encouraged and partially brought about by a significant expansion in the number of second and third tier personal computer vendors, who have taken market share away from some of the more established brand name competitors. As far as performance of competitors in the market is concerned, the record is extremely varied with over 200 brands available, many of which are sourced from Taiwan, Singapore or Korea. In some instances the completed product is imported and then relabelled under various brand names, whilst others, which go to make up the majority of local "home-grown" products arrive as semi-finished component units for final assembly. Thus shipments of Amstrad, Apricot, Compaq, IBM, NEC, Olivetti, Toshiba, Unisys and Wang have all either decreased or did not keep pace with the market. Demand for the lower priced products has been driven by changes in the buying policies of large organisations in the private and state sectors, which have now adopted much more liberal guidelines, thus boosting sales of products from Acer, Apple, Arrow, AST, DEC, Ipex, Osborne, Total Peripherals and Samsung. Hence, although Australia lacks any indigenous personal computer companies, by 1992 there were estimated to be upwards of twenty assembly plants claiming to be personal computer manufacturers, which tended to sell directly to the government and business sectors. Altogether they represented approximately 10 per cent of the market. Apart from such "home-grown" products, Australia's absence of any significant indigenous computer manufacturing industry has meant that the mix of competitors is internationally highly diverse as shown in Tables 7.11 and 7.12. Hence, U.S., Japanese and European companies compete for the major parts of the market share.

Amongst the "Paper Tigers", at a broad level, whilst the 1980s witnessed phenomenal double digit growth from these economies, the worldwide economic slump of the 1990s has now made itself felt even in these countries. Furthermore, each of these countries are sensitive to political change and face rather different conditions that can influence the nature of economic activity, especially in terms of overseas investment. Thus Hong Kong's growth has dropped and has been quite volatile with uncertainties about its future after 1997, whilst Taiwan and to a slightly lesser extent, South Korea, have also suffered from a sharp decline in their growth. In contrast, Singapore has been slowing off only gradually, with Thailand and Malaysia maintaining high rates of growth. Naturally, performance of the economies in these countries is closely linked with developments in their respective personal computer industries and markets, which will be the focus of the rest of this section.

During the late 1980s growth in unit shipments of personal computers was fastest in South Korea and slowest in Taiwan as shown in Table 7.9. As a result, the installed base of the different countries created the pattern shown in Table 7.10, where it can be seen that Korea and Taiwan are considerably larger in this respect than Hong Kong, Singapore, Thailand or Malaysia, which is one of the reasons why these last two have enjoyed such high growth, because of their relatively small starting positions. In all cases, the level of penetration of the personal computer markets is still relatively low, with the potential for considerable growth in the 1990s. Indeed, for this reason, the expected growth of shipments between 1990 and 1995 is expected to remain in double digits for both unit and value shipments, taking the total number of installed units from a level of some 22 million in 1992 to nearly 38 million in 1995.

Although part of the reason for differences in the size and rates of growth of the personal computer markets between these countries can be linked to the economic and political issues mentioned above, further differences in competitive and market conditions can be explained in terms of the structure of the local industry, the degree of competition between local and foreign companies, the development of local-language software and support, the lack of copyright laws and the patterns of market segmentation and buyer behaviour. On the supply side, government policies towards IT in general have had a major influence upon the personal computer markets, although their impact is varied between countries. For example, the Singapore, Taiwanese and South Korean governments have all pursued extensive programmes of investment to promote the use of information technology. In contrast, Thailand still has to formulate an IT policy, whilst Hong Kong maintains a laissez-faire approach to the issue. In all regions however, the government sector is a major buyer of personal computers, so that their influence is felt in the market both directly and indirectly.

As far as product market segmentation is concerned, there existed quite a lot of variation between different countries as to the relative mix of processors and their rates of growth. Fig. 7.7 illustrates the pattern of diffusion for each of the countries. Quite clearly, Intel dominates all of the markets, however, what is most interesting is to note how far newer 386 and 486 processors have penetrated in different countries, with the converse lower levels of use in older technologies. The pattern of diffusion of the processors also reflects the fact that virtually every market has experienced significantly increased price competition. Industry estimates suggest that the regional average system value for personal computers was U.S.$3,575 in 1988 and U.S.$2,975 in 1991. Much of this price competition reflected the desire by vendors to move older slower machines based on 8-bit processors or 286 technology in favour of 386 and 486 based systems. The extent to which this pattern has evolved can be seen to be most advanced in Hong Kong, Taiwan and Singapore, whilst South Korea, Thailand and Malaysia reflect less developed buying patterns. At the same time, some of the price competition has been undertaken by major competitors such as IBM, Compaq and Hewlett Packard trying to protect their market position against the cheaper clones. This is particularly true in Taiwan and Malaysia, which has resulted in faster increases in unit shipments than in value shipments. Thus like in the United States and Western Europe, the major companies have been facing a new financial model in these markets, as buyers switch their preference to lower priced clones. One exception to this pattern is in Korea, where prices have been held artificially high to subsidise exports of Korean manufactured personal computers. However, since 1989, this pattern has been changing due to the increased number of foreign competitors who have been allowed into the market offering better quality machines. Similar changes have been taking place in Thailand, where the indigenous clones have been losing market share to more expensive foreign competitors, who are better placed to serve the needs of corporate customers in terms of product quality, performance and reliability. Price has traditionally been the major driver of sales in Singapore and Hong Kong as has been the case in Taiwan, whose local manufacturers were forced in 1990 to dump much of their unsold surplus products for exports onto the local market as their foreign markets went into slower growth, which resulted in the lowest average selling price in the region of U.S.$980.

As far as competition is concerned, Tables 7.11 and 7.12 illustrate the diversity of conditions between the various countries. As in Japan, Korea's personal computer manufacturers enjoyed the protection of various government policies in their home market during much of the 1980s and thus the market is dominated by domestic and Taiwanese manufacturers such as Trigem, Samsung, Goldstar and Daewoo Telecom, with IBM being the only foreign company in the top five rankings. Apple and Hewlett Packard rank further down in the top ten, but many of the other competitors are local. Thus, although during the past few years liberalisation of the market has allowed a number of foreign entrants into the competition, the domestic manufacturers have managed to establish formidable barriers to entry centred upon their large installed base, marketing presence and distribution channels. In contrast, during the 1980s, Taiwan, Singapore and Hong Kong pursued much more open policies, which allowed foreign competitors to establish stronger positions in these markets. However, during the early 1990s the surplus supply of cheap machines in Taiwan has enabled the local manufacturers to gain significant market share. Similarly, in Singapore, local brands have been gaining market share during the past few years, whilst the Thai market shows signs of going in the same direction.

From the users point of view, in most countries the choice is between low cost, but poor quality domestically produced machines, versus the higher priced, but higher performance foreign imported products. For corporate buyers, the tendency is towards purchasing foreign products, whilst small businesses and home segment users are willing to accept the lower performance machines, but enjoy the benefits of lower prices. However, whilst foreign competitors may enjoy a technological lead at present, the increasing technological sophistication of local firms, together with their understanding of local markets may result in a shift of balance in the future. Nowhere is the importance of local market conditions made more explicit than in the area of local language software. Just as in Japan, personal computers cannot sell in the South Korean or Taiwanese markets without local language software. Similarly, in Thailand and Malaysia, growth of the personal computer market has been severely restricted due to a scarcity of this facility. Singapore's market is unaffected by this requirement, whilst in Hong Kong, the introduction of Taiwanese and Chinese-based software has significantly aided growth in these markets, especially in the small Chinese family run businesses.

One of the key reasons why local-language software has not been developed extensively by foreign software companies has been the fact that during the 1980s a cultural trait in the region was the large scale of piracy[27] on personal computer software. As a result of the limited protection from this problem, foreign software companies have been reluctant to invest in local-language packages[28] for fear that they would lose heavily from piracy of their products. In order to try and tackle the problem, governments across the region have commenced the introduction of copyright and patent protection laws. However, their impact has been varied, with enforcement remaining weak in South Korea and Taiwan and virtually non-existent in Thailand. Even in Singapore and Hong Kong, where greater resources have been committed to trying to overcome the crime, success has been very limited.

Whilst software piracy has somewhat dampened development in the region, the increased networking potential of personal computers has stimulated demand for such machines across the region, with the exception of Thailand, where the market has not yet reached this stage of sophistication. This pattern of networking has taken place mainly in the corporate business segment, where just as in the United States and Western Europe, large companies are assessing their current information systems and recognising that networked server/personal computer and workstation systems can offer effective alternative solutions to some of their mainframe or minicomputer based solutions. Downsizing has therefore begun to develop in the region and hence stimulated demand. Another factor stimulating demand has been the increasing availability of more powerful laptop and notebook computers, although at present, these have not begun to displace desktop machines in the workplace.

As far as the user segmentation of each country market is concerned, as can be seen from Table 7.14, the business segment dominates the personal computer market within every country throughout the region. Not surprisingly, those countries with a higher percentage of business users in the overall market, tend to also have the highest percentage of high-end machines in their product processor segmentation as shown earlier in Fig. 7.7. However, it can also be seen from Table 7.14, that the extent to which the business segment dominates each country varies quite considerably. Thus in Thailand, Malaysia, Hong Kong and Singapore the segment represents between 67 and 86 per cent of the total market, whilst in Korea, although the business segment is the largest and is expanding quite rapidly, here the education segment plays a significant role. Similarly, in Taiwan, the home market is much more significant than in other countries within the region. It can also be seen that the size and relative importance of the remaining sectors is therefore quite varied. Finally, distribution throughout these countries in the region has been dominated by indirect channels as can be seen from Table 7.13. However, once again it is evident from the data that there are significant differences in the degree to which different types of indirect channel are used in various countries. In all cases, indirect channels are the most important channel and increasingly so, in Thailand, Hong Kong and Singapore, although in Taiwan and Australia the trend is towards greater use of direct channels. Distributors, dealers and VARs go to make-up the indirect channel in each of the countries in different proportions. From the data it is also apparent that dealers dominate the Australian, South Korean, Taiwanese and Hong Kong markets, whilst in Thailand, distributors are the dominant channel. Singapore and Taiwan have a somewhat more even balance between distributors and dealers, with Singapore also showing a much higher than average number of VARs. All such differences are reflections of the variation to be found amongst country markets in the region and reflect distinctions, both in the local industry infrastructure, competitors' strategies and patterns of buyer behaviour.

In conclusion, when looking at the overall Asia/Pacific Region, it can be seen that the market area really consists of three market segments. The first and most dominant consists of Japan, which represents a sophisticated yet relatively under penetrated and somewhat stagnant market of late, which has been traditionally protected from excessive foreign competition. This has resulted in a competitive condition that is largely indigenous in nature and strongly dominated by NEC. It was also seen that whilst the Japanese market enjoyed strong growth during the 1980s, it slowed during the early 1990s and is now experiencing a process of downsizing in the corporate marketplace, together with increasing competition from U.S. companies. The second market segment consists of Australia, which really has no indigenous personal computer industry to speak of and has attracted a wide range of competitors from all over the world. In some ways, the Anglo-American nature of its business environment has meant that the business market is relatively sophisticated. However, given the depressed state of its economy it is not a rapidly growing market. Lastly, the remaining South East Asian countries go to make up the third segment. Here there are considerable variations in the competitive conditions, rates of market growth, patterns of buyer behaviour, levels of market maturity and the degree of competition between local and foreign manufacturers. However, generally speaking, notwithstanding political shocks to the system, growth of personal computers is much stronger in this segment than in either Japan or Australia, although it must also be remembered that such growth is based upon much smaller installed bases, which reflect much lower levels of market development. Whilst Japan is expected to continue to dominate the region, it is apparent that Australia is going to shortly be surpassed by South Korea in terms of installed market size and level of shipments. Overall the region is expected to more than double its size of shipments in unit and value terms between 1990 and 1995.

Hence, whilst still representing a fragmented and varied marketplace for personal computers, the Asia/Pacific region offers a significant source of market growth during the 1990s, that will ensure its growing importance in the overall worldwide marketplace. Furthermore, although already apparent, the strength of the major indigenous competitors in Japan, South Korea and Taiwan suggests that their competitive strategies are likely to bring them into further competition with United States and West European companies, not only in the Asia/Pacific region, but also in their own markets. Such developments have significant implications for the industry overall on a worldwide scale and for this reason, the next section of this chapter will look at how the overall pattern of competition and market structure is evolving on a worldwide basis.

COMPETITION IN THE WORLDWIDE PERSONAL COMPUTER MARKET

Having now analysed the general patterns of evolution in the market structures of the United States, West European and Asia/Pacific Rim, together with the market performance of the major competitors, this section will proceed to highlight some of the broader strategic observations that can be made about the major competitors from the U.S., West European and Asia/Pacific region in their position within the worldwide marketplace. In particular, it will look at one of the questions raised at the beginning of this chapter, namely, to what extent are the personal computer industry and its markets global in nature?

In effect, this question consists of two distinct but closely related parts. The first part concerns the degree of globalisation amongst the competitors in the industry, whilst the second involves the degree of globalisation in the markets themselves. Naturally, two of the key drivers towards a global market are firstly, globalisation of competitors' strategies and secondly, standardisation of customers' requirements on a global basis. Thus it is intended in this section to see whether any pattern of global competition is emerging in the industry and to explore the extent to which customers' requirements are becoming global in nature.

Broad Strategic Patterns

From the evidence presented in the last chapter and the two preceding sections of this chapter, it can be seen that there exist considerable differences between the extent to which United States, West European and Far Eastern competitors have developed their market presence outside their home territories. It also highlighted that whilst their exist similarities in product type between the regions, there are some very significant differences in the structure and stage of development of the respective markets. Based upon these observations, it is therefore suggested that the personal computer industry is made up of three distinctive groups of competitors. Firstly, those which have developed global value chains and operate in each of the three major regions of the marketplace. Secondly, those which are international in nature, but as yet have only established themselves in one or two of the regions and have little or no presence in the third. Lastly, are the regional or local competitors, which have most of their operations and marketing activity located in just one region. Thus there emerges a framework for looking at the extent to which the different competitors fulfil these various characteristics, which can be usefully employed to compare the international strategies of the major competitors. The framework presents their strategic position as measured along various dimensions, which includes, scale and scope of IT activities, together with their geographical scope.

Scale and Scope of IT Activities

In order to gain an overview of the scope of business activities undertaken by some of the major competitors, Table 7.15 illustrates the 1990 and 1991 ranking of the top 50 personal computer companies and year on change on a worldwide basis. It also indicates the size of the total information systems related revenues for each company and expresses the relative size of personal computer revenues, as a percentage of total IS revenues. Finally, ranking of the company in the overall top 100 data processing companies is also provided. The percentage of PC revenues as part of overall IS related revenues is perhaps a little less important, since clearly, although PC revenues are only 13.53 per cent of IBM's overall IS revenues, the sheer leading size of IBM and its PC revenues clearly makes it a formidable and powerful competitor. The strategic importance lies in the extent to which personal computers form an important part of the critical mass of activity by each company and hence both its strategic commitment to the personal computer business and the scale of resources available to carry personal computer activities into other areas of its overall IT business. One other interesting observation concerns the annual change in personal computer revenues between 1990 and 1991. It can be seen that some clear groupings exist. Given the average for the sample of 7.5 per cent, there are those that are high growth (more than 15%), which tend to consist largely of the Japanese hardware companies, together with the workstation manufacturer, Sun Microsystems. The upper mid-range group (from 7.5 per cent to 15 per cent) consists of Digital, Hewlett Packard, Apple Computer and Seiko Epson. What is most significant are the number of companies that posted declines in their overall IS revenues between 1990 and 1991, which reflects the problems in the overall computer industry discussed earlier. The companies included IBM, Unisys, Olivetti, Siemens Nixdorf, Groupe Bull, Wang Laboratories and even Compaq and Toshiba. This pattern reflects the slow down in growth for the whole industry, which has hit the mainframe and minicomputer companies in the United States and Western Europe particularly badly. However, as mentioned elsewhere, it also is a signal of the endgame for these sectors of the industry. In contrast, the Japanese during this period appeared to be maintaining growth, with strong home market development and financial reserves, although by 1992 even this position was changing as was seen in the previous sections. Thus, although this data merely represents a snapshot of two years trading, an extension of the pattern over the period 1985 to

Table 7.15. Personal computer and total IS revenues of major competitors in the worldwide personal computer industry and marketplace: 1990 and 1991.

1991 World Rank	1990 World Rank	COMPANY	1991 PC REVENUE	1990 PC REVENUE	PC REV % CHANGE	1991 TOTAL IS REVENUE	PC REV AS % OF TOTAL IS REV	1991* Ranking in Datamation Top 100 Cos
1	1	IBM	8505.00	9644.00	-12	62840.00	13.53	1
2	3	NEC Corp.	5280.00	3620.00	46	16171.00	32.65	3
3	2	Apple Computer Inc.	4900.00	3845.80	27	5740.00	85.37	10
4	4	Compaq Computer Corp.	3271.00	3598.00	-9	3271.40	99.99	19
5	7	Fujitsu Ltd.	2342.00	1419.60	65	19516.70	12.00	2
6	5	Toshiba Corp.	2044.60	2488.30	-18	4996.30	40.92	13
7	6	Ing C. Olivetti & Co. SpA.	1578.20	1791.70	-12	6050.80	26.08	11
8	10	Commodore International Ltd.	1038.50	995.70	4	1038.50	100.00	51
9	16	AT & T	950.00	700.00	36	8169.00	11.63	7
10	8	Unisys Corp.	900.00	1181.00	-24	8000.00	11.25	8
11	9	Groupe Bull	889.50	1142.90	-22	5929.80	15.00	12
12	14	Hitachi Ltd.	825.30	718.40	15	10310.20	8.00	6
13	21	AST Research Inc.	800.70	516.20	55	827.30	96.78	61
14	12	Tandy Corp.	750.00	850.30	-12	1070.60	70.05	50
15	18	Hewlett-Packard Co.	715.00	625.00	14	10726.00	6.67	5
16	13	Acer Inc.	708.90	739.60	-4	814.90	86.99	63
17	17	Seiko Epson Corp.	707.60	636.30	11	1572.50	45.00	39
18	20	Dell Computer Corp.	667.40	546.20	22	889.90	75.00	N/A
19	23	Packard Bell Electronics Inc.	641.00	518.00	24	675.90	94.84	70
20	26	Canon Inc.	612.50	426.80	44	4373.70	14.00	15
21	15	Siemens Nixdorf Informationssysteme AG.	596.75	709.90	-16	7308.60	8.17	9
22	N/A	Sanyo Electric Co. Ltd.	550.00	N/A	N/A	N/A	N/A	N/A
23	22	CompuAdd Corp.	513.60	515.60	0	513.60	100.00	90
24	27	Tandon Corp.	461.40	418.50	10	461.40	100.00	96
25	33	Gateway 2000 Inc.	444.50	275.00	62	635.00	70.00	75
26	34	Digital Equipment Corp.	425.00	250.00	70	14237.80	2.99	4
27	29	Ricoh Co. Ltd.	408.90	373.00	10	2548.40	16.05	28
28	30	Wang Laboratories Inc.	340.00	360.00	-6	1940.00	17.53	31
29	N/A	Victor Co. of Japan	311.30	N/A	N/A	N/A	N/A	N/A
30	N/A	NV Phillips' GL (now part of DEC)	307.60	N/A	N/A	N/A	N/A	N/A
31	35	Everex Systems Inc.	307.20	248.00	24	492.50	62.38	92
32	11	Intel Corp.	304.50	980.00	-69	1100.00	27.68	47
33	N/A	ICL PLC (part of Fujitsu Corp.)	297.40	159.00	87	3308.10	8.99	18
34	39	DTK Computer Inc.	290.00	230.00	26	290.00	100.00	N/A
35	24	Amstrad PLC	271.60	499.10	-46	313.40	86.66	N/A
36	N/A	Hyundai	268.81	N/A	N/A	N/A	N/A	N/A
37	42	Advanced Logic Research Inc.	250.00	172.00	45	N/A	N/A	N/A
38	38	Mitsubishi Electric Corp.	242.40	201.30	20	2203.70	11.00	26
39	28	Mitac International Corp.	235.00	416.00	-44	373.60	62.90	N/A
40	49	Zeos International Ltd.	230.90	127.10	82	230.90	100.00	N/A
41	N/A	TriGem Computer Inc.	217.10	147.00	48	318.50	68.16	N/A
42	N/A	Tulip Computers International B.V.	215.50	214.70	0	215.50	100.00	N/A
43	36	Memorex Telex NV	207.60	213.30	-3	1533.10	13.54	40
44	31	Atari Corp.	206.90	325.70	-36	258.00	80.19	N/A
45	N/A	First International Computer Inc.	204.30	116.70	75	214.67	95.17	N/A
46	44	Matsushita Electric Industrial Co. Ltd.	202.80	164.10	24	5068.80	4.00	14
47	46	Tatung Co.	199.80	150.20	33	667.30	29.94	71
48	N/A	Samsung Electronics Co.	198.90	N/A	N/A	835.70	23.80	N/A
49	N/A	Sharp Electronics Corp.	181.70	N/A	N/A	N/A	N/A	N/A
50	37	Northgate Computer Systems Inc.	167.14	203.40	-18	167.14	100.00	N/A

Note: * "Datamation Top 100 Cos. refers to the Datamation league table of all Information Systems companies.

Source: "The Datamation Worldwide PC Big 50", December 1, 1992, p.37.
All financial data based on calendar year end results.
PC revenues as a percentage of overall IS revenues calculated by the Author.
Reprinted with permission of DATAMATION, December 1, 1992, © 1992 by Cahners Publishing Company.

1990 reflects the development of the trend towards the computer industry's major change of fortunes between the mainframe, minicomputer and personal computer companies.

Whilst Table 7.15 provided an insight into the relative size of the overall IS business of the major personal computer manufacturers, Fig. 7.8 illustrates the relationship between the overall size of selected major companies, their IS revenues and personal computer revenues. The Y axis indicates the size of IS revenues in U.S.$ billions, whilst the X axis plots total size of revenues for the overall company, which includes any of its other businesses outside of IS. The position of each company is marked by a circle, the diameter of which reflects its level of personal computer revenues. This is meant to illustrate the relative size of IT related activities and to highlight the strategic importance (and/or commitment) of personal computers to the particular company. From Fig. 7.8 the sheer size and scale of IBM stands out, both in terms of its personal computer business, but also in terms of its overall revenues and IS revenues. Following behind IBM, it can be seen how large some of the Japanese companies are. In particular, Hitachi, Toshiba, NEC, Fujitsu and Mitsubishi tower above the remaining competitors, with the exception of the U.S. telecommunications giant, AT&T, which now also owns NCR. NEC and Fujitsu in particular

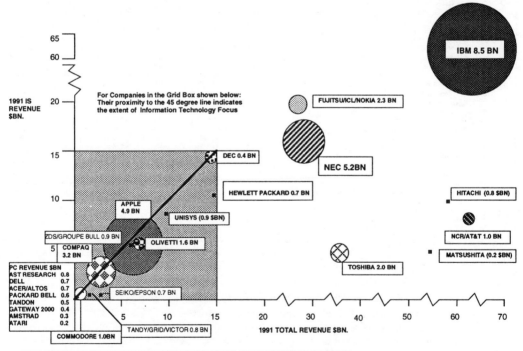

NOTE: THE SIZE OF EACH CIRCLE'S DIAMETER IS PROPORTIONAL TO THE COMPANY'S PC REVENUE

Source: Based on data from Table 7.15.
International Data Corporation and annual reports.

Fig. 7.8. Relative revenues of major competitors in the global personal computer market: 1991.

are not only large in overall size, but are also larger than all other competitors apart from IBM in information systems. Following the Japanese and AT&T/NCR come the group of companies within the grid-box in Fig. 7.8. These include companies with revenues of over U.S.$1billion up to around the U.S.$15billion mark of DEC and Hewlett Packard. Those companies sitting on the forty five degree axis have virtually all their revenues coming from information systems, whilst those to the right have other activities, such as Hewlett Packard's revenues from its scientific and measuring equipment business. The importance of this diagram lies not so much in whether any of the larger companies are inherently capable of producing better personal computers, since clearly a number of smaller companies, such as Compaq, Dell or Packard Bell are amongst the most successful companies in the industry. However, it does require one to recognise that for long-term strategies, some of the companies outside the grid have access to much larger resources with which to undertake core R&D development in areas such as semiconductor and electronic component technology, together with telecommunications technology or to buy market power, should they so decide, without the more critical cash flow problems that might face smaller competitors.

Having gained some insight into the scale of the major competitors, Table 7.16 illustrates the product/market scope of 20 major information technology computer companies in terms of their total information systems revenues and their component areas of activity. On a broad level, the data presents a clear picture of the strategic groups that form around various hardware products. For example, IBM still dominates in mainframes, with over 40% of this sector. However, we see here clearly the changes that have taken place (which are discussed later in this chapter, under mergers and acquisitions) in terms of the departure of many of the traditional U.S. manufacturers. Therefore, the key positions after IBM are held by the Japanese competitors, Fujitsu, Hitachi and NEC. Excluding Amdahl, whose overall revenues are not sufficient for this table, only Unisys (formed by the merger of Sperry-Univac and Burroughs) and AT&T reflecting its take-over of NCR remain as the other U.S. competitors,[29] whilst Groupe-Bull and Siemens Nixdorf, represent the European presence in this sector. Individually, they all tend to pale against IBM and the Japanese companies, which explains why some industry observers and government commentators are of the opinion that with the possible exception of Siemens, Western Europe lacks any serious global player in this sector and the United States industry is clearly in a relative and fairly rapid process of decline and increasing concentration. In the mid-range sector, we see a much broader and more balanced base of competitors from the U.S., Western Europe and Japan. However, both in terms of scale and performance both within and outside their home market regions, most of the United States and European competitors in this sector are relatively weak and making losses. As a result, a number of them, such as Prime, Data General and Wang Laboratories appear to lack the resources to expand their global operations. Even the traditional leader DEC, is now facing increasing problems in

Table 7.16. Business mix of major computer companies in the IT industry, revenues (US$M): 1991.

1991 Rank NAME COMPANY	Total IS Revenue	Large Systems Revenue	% of Total IS Revenue	Midrange Systems Revenue	% of Total IS Revenue	Personal Computers Revenue	% of Total IS Revenue	Work stations Revenue	% of Total IS Revenue	Software Revenue	% of Total IS Revenue	Other % of Total IS Revenue
1 IBM	62840.00	9100.00	14.48	5870.00	9.34	8505.00	13.53	1400.00	2.23	10524.00	16.75	9.12
2 Fujitsu	19516.70	4488.80	23.00	2634.80	4.19	2342.00	3.73	1366.20	2.17	2535.30	4.03	0.00
3 NEC	16171.10	3234.20	20.00	2096.70	3.34	4187.80	6.66	161.70	0.26	1933.10	3.08	0.95
4 DEC	14237.80	185.00	1.30	2730.00	4.34	110.00	0.18	1250.00	1.99	796.00	1.27	0.00
5 Hitachi	11167.30	3977.70	35.62	408.90	0.65	877.30	1.40	223.00	0.35	966.50	1.54	0.34
6 Hewlett-Packard	10726.00		0.00	832.00	1.32	715.00	1.14	1055.00	1.68	345.00	0.55	0.00
7 AT&T	8169.00	200.00	2.45	550.00	0.88	950.00	1.51		0.00	250.00	0.40	0.00
8 Unisys	8000.00	850.00	10.63	945.00	1.50	1061.00	1.69	100.00	0.16	600.00	0.95	0.99
9 Siemens Nixdorf	7308.60	964.40	13.20	934.30	1.49	602.80	0.96	211.00	0.34	964.40	1.53	0.00
10 Apple	6496.00		0.00		0.00	4900.00	7.80		0.00	250.00	0.40	0.00
11 Toshiba	4996.30		0.00	1301.10	2.07	2044.60	3.25	312.30	0.50		0.00	0.00
11 Olivetti	6050.80	115.60	1.91	478.60	0.76	1586.10	2.52		1.67	630.80	1.00	1.53
12 Matsushita	4769.20		0.00		0.00	202.80	0.32	1048.30	0.00		0.00	0.66
12 Groupe Bull	5929.80	830.20	14.00	355.60	0.57	889.50	1.42		0.00	593.00	0.94	0.00
13 Sun	3454.70		0.00		0.00		0.00	2455.30	3.91	175.00	0.28	0.00
13 Compaq	3271.40		0.00		0.00	3271.40	5.21		0.00		0.00	0.00
14 Mitsubishi	2178.40	198.30	9.10	459.60	0.73	242.40	0.39		0.00		0.00	0.00
14 Wang	1940.00		0.00	352.00	0.56	340.00	0.54		0.00	80.00	0.13	0.00
15 Seiko Epson	1572.50		0.00		0.00	707.60	1.13		0.00		0.00	0.00

1991 Rank NAME COMPANY	Peripherals Revenue	% of Total IS Revenue	Data-Coms Revenue	% of Total IS Revenue	Services Revenue	% of Total IS Revenue	Maintenance Revenue	% of Total IS Revenue	Others Revenue	% of Total IS Revenue
1 IBM	10278.00	16.36	2000.00	3.18	2018.00	3.21	7414.00	11.80	5731.00	9.12
2 Fujitsu	3025.10	4.81	585.50	0.93	1368.00	2.18	1171.00	1.86	594.80	0.00
3 NEC	2104.10	3.35	319.70	0.51	646.80	1.03	892.20	1.42		0.95
4 DEC	2900.00	4.61	275.00	0.44	1570.30	2.50	4421.50	7.04	215.80	0.00
5 Hitachi	3345.70	5.32	446.10	0.71	408.90	0.65	297.40	0.47		0.34
6 Hewlett-Packard	4370.00	6.95	450.00	0.72		0.00	2959.00	2.75		0.00
7 AT&T	2100.00	3.34	1790.00	2.85	600.00	0.95	1729.00	2.93	620.00	0.00
8 Unisys	1000.00	1.59	380.00	0.60	600.00	0.95	1844.00	2.30		0.99
9 Siemens Nixdorf	1733.00	2.76	150.70	0.24	301.40	0.48	1446.60			0.00
10 Apple	1346.00	2.14		0.00		0.00		0.00		0.00
11 Toshiba	713.80	1.14	624.50	0.99		0.00		0.00		0.00
11 Olivetti	1018.60	1.62	164.10	0.26		0.00	1094.50	1.74	962.50	1.53
12 Matsushita	2044.60	3.25	1189.60	1.89		0.00	283.90	0.45		0.66
12 Groupe Bull	1067.40	1.70		0.00	415.10	0.66	1363.90	2.17	415.10	0.00
13 Sun	524.40	0.83		0.00		0.00	300.00	0.48		0.00
13 Compaq		0.00		0.00		0.00		0.00		0.00
14 Mitsubishi	727.20	1.16	550.90	0.88	50.00	0.08	818.00	0.00		0.00
14 Wang	300.00	0.48		0.00		0.00		1.30		0.00
15 Seiko Epson	864.90	1.38		0.00		0.00		0.00		0.00

Sources: Datamation, June 15, 1992; Datamation, July 1, 1992 and September 1, 1992.
Reprinted with permission of DATAMATION, July 1, 1992 and September 1, 1992, © 1992 by
Cahners Publishing Company.

this its core business, leaving only Hewlett Packard as a profitable and strong business. In contrast, some of the Japanese have yet to expand globally, since they have the resource base as shown in the previous section, to support a long term process of strategic market development. But this may not be their way forward, since as has been discussed elsewhere, mid-range product technology is under increasing attack and pressure on margins from personal computers and workstations, which all reflects the continued trend towards "downsizing". For this reason, virtually all of the top fifteen hardware competitors in the global IT industry have some presence in either the personal computer and/or workstation product markets as illustrated in the relevant columns of Table 7.16.

Other broad observations arising from Table 7.16 include the high percentage of companies in the top fifteen global IT competitors who are involved in software development, peripherals, data-communications and maintenance, with a slightly smaller, but still significant share involved in services. Two comments can be made from this observation. Firstly, setting aside whether the specific competitor is involved in hardware manufacture of mainframe, mid-range, personal computer or workstation products, the vast majority have also invested many of their resources further downstream in hardware (peripherals and data communications)[30] and software or service activities (including maintenance). The reason behind this pattern can be explained both by the decreasing margins generated on "box manufacture"[31] versus the higher margins in these other activities, and also by the need of the companies to develop their capabilities to match the needs of their major customers in providing systems integration and support services. When priced on a bundled basis, it is these latter activities that traditionally generate the greater source of value added to the supplier company. This is especially true of companies like IBM, DEC, Unisys, Hewlett Packard and AT&T. It also identifies the area where many of the Japanese companies are still relatively weak and explains why they are currently so keen to invest in developing these areas of activity, often through the acquisition of specialist companies in such areas as peripherals, systems integration and service support/maintenance.

Geographical Scope

Having looked at the scale and scope of activities of some of the larger companies in the overall computer industry, the next point to consider relates to the question of degree of geographical coverage or scope of the major personal computer players. The geographical scope of the major personal computer manufacturers has been set down in some detail within Chapter 6 (relating to their U.S. market share) and earlier in this chapter for both the West European and the Asia/Pacific regions. However, in order to present a more concise picture for comparative purposes, the following two tables, Tables 7.17 and 7.18, have been compiled to reflect an overview of the unit shipments of personal computers by the top forty companies in 1991. It should be noted that the data set used in these tables is drawn from a survey conducted by International Data Corporation and breaks the regions into the United States, Western Europe, Japan and the Rest

Table 7.17. Geographical scope of major competitors in the personal computer industry: ranked by worldwide unit shipments, all regions: 1991.

Rank 1990	Rank 1991	Country of Origin	Name of Company	1991 United States	1991 % Share of United States Total	1991 Western Europe	1991 % Share of Western Europe Total	1991 Japan	1991 % Share of Japan Total	1991 Rest of World	1991 % Share of Rest of World Total	1991 Worldwide	1991 % Share of Total Worldwide
1	1	U.S	IBM	1,370,400	14.13	1,099,450	12.46	147,500	6.40	260,000	5.79	2,877,350	11.37
2	2	U.S.	Apple	1,340,045	13.82	592,527	6.71	133,000	5.77	410,000	9.14	2,475,572	9.78
3	3	U.S.	Commodore	146,000	1.51	1,246,339	14.12	0	0.00	343,000	7.64	1,735,339	6.85
4	4	Japan	NEC	139,520	1.44	7,743	0.09	1,132,700	49.15	40,000	0.89	1,319,963	5.21
5	5	U.S.	Compaq Computer	390,000	4.02	425,350	4.82	0	0.00	65,000	1.45	880,350	3.48
6	6	Japan	Toshiba	181,500	1.87	228,438	2.59	193,000	8.38	67,000	1.49	669,938	2.65
8	7	W.Europe	Amstrad	0	0.00	604,857	6.85	0	0.00	30,000	0.67	634,857	2.51
13	8	U.S.	Packard Bell	455,000	4.69	0	0.00	0	0.00	55,000	1.23	510,000	2.01
7	9	U.S.	Tandy/Grid/Victor	349,250	3.60	72,151	0.82	0	0.00	64,000	1.43	485,401	1.92
10	10	W.Europe	Olivetti	8,796	0.09	402,689	4.56	0	0.00	57,000	1.27	468,485	1.85
16	11	U.S.	AST Research	261,490	2.70	80,831	0.92	0	0.00	98,000	2.18	440,321	1.74
11	12	U.S.	Atari	46,000	0.47	357,313	4.05	0	0.00	28,000	0.62	431,313	1.70
12	13	W.Europe	ZDS/Groupe Bull	202,761	2.09	202,140	2.29	0	0.00	20,000	0.45	424,901	1.68
9	14	Japan	Seiko/Epson	105,500	1.09	72,714	0.82	172,000	7.46	45,000	1.00	395,214	1.56
15	15	Japan	Fujitsu/ICL/Nokia	1,086	0.01	149,585	1.69	239,200	10.38	2,000	0.04	391,871	1.55
14	16	U.S.	HP/Apollo	122,525	1.26	133,210	1.51	14,500	0.63	57,000	1.27	327,235	1.29
18	17	U.S.	Tandon	85,430	0.88	177,867	2.02	0	0.00	20,000	0.45	283,297	1.12
17	18	R.O.W.	Acer/Altos	67,728	0.70	76,822	0.87	0	0.00	138,000	3.08	282,550	1.12
21	19	R.O.W.	VTech/Laser	220,000	2.27	36,022	0.41	0	0.00	14,000	0.31	270,022	1.07
37	20	U.S.	Gateway 2000	246,774	2.54	0	0.00	0	0.00	22,000	0.49	268,774	1.06
25	21	U.S.	Dell Computer	158,880	1.64	72,159	0.82	0	0.00	17,000	0.38	248,039	0.98
31	22	W.Europe	Vobis	0	0.00	246,100	2.79	0	0.00	0	0.00	246,100	0.97
35	23	R.O.W.	Goldstar Technology	88,300	0.91	35,599	0.40	0	0.00	95,000	2.12	218,799	0.86
28	24	U.S.	NCR/AT&T	147,267	1.52	45,863	0.52	0	0.00	25,000	0.56	218,130	0.86
25	25	R.O.W.	Samsung	59,000	0.61	17,365	0.20	0	0.00	134,000	2.99	210,365	0.83
30	26	R.O.W.	Deewoo/Leading Edge/Cordata	87,190	0.90	1,000	0.01	0	0.00	111,000	2.47	199,190	0.79
26	27	R.O.W.	Sun Microsystems	86,900	0.90	44,471	0.50	23,100	1.00	39,000	0.87	193,471	0.76
19	28	W.Europe	Philips	100,550	1.04	85,836	0.97	0	0.00	7,000	0.16	193,386	0.76
23	29	R.O.W.	Hyundai	95,457	0.98	21,983	0.25	0	0.00	65,000	1.45	182,440	0.72
24	30	U.S.	CompuAdd	142,400	1.47	150	0.00	0	0.00	15,000	0.33	157,550	0.62
40	31	U.S.	Digital Equipment	72,400	0.75	59,756	0.68	6,600	0.29	10,000	0.22	148,756	0.59
32	32	U.S.	Everex Systems	123,930	1.28	1,126	0.01	0	0.00	17,000	0.38	142,056	0.56
29	33	W.Europe	Siemens/Nixdorf	500	0.01	119,126	1.35	0	0.00	4,000	0.09	123,626	0.49
36	34	W.Europe	Tulip	0	0.00	116,618	1.32	0	0.00	2,000	0.04	118,618	0.47
·	35	U.S.	Premier Innovations	110,000	1.13	0	0.00	0	0.00	0	0.00	110,000	0.43
·	36	U.S.	Wang Laboratories	62,115	0.64	22,958	0.26	0	0.00	22,000	0.49	107,073	0.42
·	37	U.S.	Advanced Logic Research	72,250	0.75	4,896	0.06	0	0.00	29,000	0.65	106,146	0.42
·	38	R.O.W.	Trigem	0	0.00	0	0.00	0	0.00	106,000	2.36	106,000	0.42
·	39	U.S.	Zeos International	87,000	0.90	0	0.00	0	0.00	7,000	0.16	94,000	0.37
·	40	U.S.	Wyse Technology	56,993	0.59	17,958	0.20	0	0.00	19,000	0.42	93,951	0.37
			Other	2,406,854	24.82	1,947,988	22.07	242,900	10.54	1,928,774	42.98	6,526,416	25.78
			TOTAL	9,697,691	100	8,827,000	100	2,304,400	100.00	4,487,774	100	25,316,865	100

Note: Computation of percentages by the Author.
Source: International Data Corporation, 1992.
Reproduced by permission of International Data Corporation, © 1992.

Table 7.18. Relative shares of major competitors for global regions in the personal computer industry: ranked by worldwide unit shipments, all regions: 1991.

Rank 1990	Rank 1991	Country of Origin	Name of Company	1991 United States	1991 % Share Company's Worldwide Total	1991 Western Europe	1991 % Share Company's Worldwide Total	1991 Japan	1991 % Share Company's Worldwide Total	1991 Rest of World	1991 % Share Company's Worldwide Total	1991 Worldwide	1991 % Share Company's Worldwide Total
1	1	US	IBM	1,370,400	47.63	1,099,450	38.21	147,500	5.13	260,000	9.04	2,877,350	100.00
2	2	US	Apple	1,340,045	54.13	592,527	23.93	133,000	5.37	410,000	16.56	2,475,572	100.00
3	3	US.	Commodore	146,000	8.41	1,246,339	71.82	0	0.00	343,000	19.77	1,735,339	100.00
4	4	Japan	NEC	139,520	10.57	7,743	0.59	1,132,700	85.81	40,000	3.03	1,319,963	100.00
5	5	US.	Compaq Computer	390,000	44.30	425,350	48.32	0	0.00	65,000	7.38	880,350	100.00
6	6	Japan	Toshiba	181,500	27.09	228,438	34.10	193,000	28.81	67,000	10.00	669,938	100.00
8	7	W.Europe	Amstrad	0	0.00	604,857	95.27	0	0.00	30,000	4.73	634,857	100.00
13	8	US.	Packard Bell	455,000	89.22	0	0.00	0	0.00	55,000	10.78	510,000	100.00
7	9	US.	Tandy/Grid/Victor	349,250	71.95	72,151	14.86	0	0.00	64,000	13.18	485,401	100.00
10	10	W.Europe	Olivetti	8,796	1.88	402,689	85.96	0	0.00	57,000	12.17	468,485	100.00
16	11	US.	AST Research	261,490	59.39	80,831	18.36	0	0.00	98,000	22.26	440,321	100.00
11	12	US.	Atari	46,000	10.67	357,313	82.84	0	0.00	28,000	6.49	431,313	100.00
12	12	W.Europe	ZDS/Groupe Bull	202,761	47.72	202,140	47.57	172,000	43.52	20,000	4.71	424,901	100.00
9	14	Japan	Seiko/Epson	105,500	26.69	72,714	18.40	239,200	61.04	45,000	11.39	395,214	100.00
15	15	Japan	Fujitsu/ICL/Nokia	1,086	0.28	149,585	38.17	14,500	4.43	2,000	0.51	391,871	100.00
14	16	US.	HP/Apollo	122,525	37.44	133,210	40.71	0	0.00	57,000	17.42	327,235	100.00
17	17	US.	Tandon	85,430	30.16	177,867	62.78	0	0.00	20,000	7.06	283,297	100.00
18	18	R.O.W.	Acer/Altos	67,728	23.97	76,822	27.19	0	0.00	138,000	48.84	282,550	100.00
21	19	R.O.W.	VTech/Laser	220,000	81.47	36,022	13.34	0	0.00	14,000	5.18	270,022	100.00
37	20	US.	Gateway 2000	246,774	91.81	0	0.00	0	0.00	22,000	8.19	268,774	100.00
25	21	US.	Dell Computer	158,880	64.05	72,159	29.09	0	0.00	17,000	6.85	248,039	100.00
31	22	W.Europe	Vobis	0	0.00	246,100	100.00	0	0.00	0	0.00	246,100	100.00
35	23	R.O.W.	Goldstar Technology	88,200	40.31	35,599	16.27	0	0.00	95,000	43.42	218,799	100.00
28	24	US.	NCR/AT&T	147,267	67.51	45,863	21.03	0	0.00	25,000	11.46	218,130	100.00
22	25	R.O.W.	Samsung	59,000	28.05	17,365	8.25	0	0.00	134,000	63.70	210,365	100.00
30	26	R.O.W.	Daewoo/Leading Edge/Cordata	87,190	43.77	1,000	0.50	0	0.00	111,000	55.73	199,190	100.00
26	27	US.	Sun Microsystems	86,900	44.92	44,471	22.99	23,100	11.94	39,000	20.16	193,471	100.00
19	28	W.Europe	Philips	100,550	51.99	85,836	44.39	0	0.00	7,000	3.62	193,386	100.00
23	29	R.O.W.	Hyundai	95,457	52.32	21,983	12.05	0	0.00	65,000	35.63	182,440	100.00
40	30	US.	CompuAdd	142,400	90.38	150	0.10	0	0.00	15,000	9.52	157,550	100.00
24	31	US.	Digital Equipment	72,400	48.67	59,756	40.17	6,600	4.44	10,000	6.72	148,756	100.00
20	32	US.	Everex Systems	123,930	87.24	1,126	0.79	0	0.00	17,000	11.97	142,056	100.00
29	33	W.Europe	Siemens/Nixdorf	500	0.40	119,126	96.36	0	0.00	4,000	3.24	123,626	100.00
36	34	W.Europe	Tulip	0	0.00	116,618	98.31	0	0.00	2,000	1.69	118,618	100.00
.	35	US.	Premier Innovations	110,000	100.00	0	0.00	0	0.00	0	0.00	110,000	100.00
.	36	US.	Wang Laboratories	62,115	58.01	22,958	21.44	0	0.00	22,000	20.55	107,073	100.00
.	37	US.	Advanced Logic Research	72,250	68.07	4,896	4.61	0	0.00	29,000	27.32	106,146	100.00
.	38	R.O.W.	Trigem	0	0.00	0	0.00	0	0.00	106,000	100.00	106,000	100.00
.	39	US.	Zeos International	87,000	92.55	0	0.00	0	0.00	7,000	7.45	94,000	100.00
.	40	US.	Wyse Technology	56,993	60.66	17,958	19.11	0	0.00	19,000	20.22	93,951	100.00
			Other	2,406,854	36.88	1,947,988	29.85	242,800	3.72	1,928,774	29.55	6,526,416	100.00
			TOTAL	9,697,691		8,827,000		2,304,400		4,487,774		25,316,865	

Note: Computation of percentages by the Author.
Source: International Data Corporation, 1992.
Reproduced by permission of International Data Corporation, © 1992.

of the World and links to the more detailed breakdowns which were shown
earlier for these respective markets. Furthermore, the data indicates
shipments of all personal computers into all market segments for the
companies, hence, certain companies appear that have figured significantly
in our discussion, since they are not really active or significant in the
business/professional segment, e.g. Commodore and Atari. Lastly, the
composition and ranking of companies is slightly different to Table 7.15,
due to the former being in terms of the value of shipments, whilst the
latter set are in unit shipments and both are based upon different sources.[32]
However, notwithstanding these qualifications, the overall picture that
emerges tends to confirm the main patterns outlined elsewhere in this
chapter and provides a useful cross-check of the respective databases.

   Table 7.17 highlights the variation in geographical scope amongst the
major competitors by indicating their country of origin, their relative share
of revenues (expressed in absolute figures and their percentage market
share) generated in each of the three major regions of the global market
and based upon their degree of geographical spread within each of the
fragmented markets of Western Europe and the Asia/Pacific Rim. Table
7.18 takes the same data-set as in Table 7.17, but expresses the information
in terms of the relative share of shipments by each company in percentage
terms across each of the major regions. Figure 7.9 then maps this pattern
by tracing the position of the top twenty companies along two dimensions.
The X axis plots the presence of a competing company in each of the three
regions of the United States, Western Europe and a combined region[33]
of Japan and the Rest of the World and indicates the share of each
particular company's shipments within each region as a percentage of the
region's total shipments. The Y axis plots the share that each company
enjoys within the particular region, expressed as a percentage of each
respective company's overall revenues across all three regions.

   The construction of Fig. 7.9 serves to directly look at the question
of how global are the competitors in the personal computer industry. It
is based upon classifying the various competing companies into three
strategic groups, which are global, international or regional in nature, along
the lines suggested earlier in this section. On consideration of what would
be a reasonable measure for each of these three categories, it was decided
that a company would need to be present in each of the three regions
with at least 10 per cent of its worldwide sales coming from each of these
three regions. If a company had only two regions with this level of sales
then it was signified as international, whilst a presence in only one region
counted as a regional competitor. In effect, this measure reflected the
strategy of each company in terms of its actual geographic scope. However,
the measure needed to be complemented by the relative share that the
company held in each of the three regions, to avoid including a company
that might have more than 10 per cent of its sales in a particular region,
but with virtually no market presence. Hence, a company also had to have
at least 1 per cent of the regional market in order to qualify as a potential
global player.

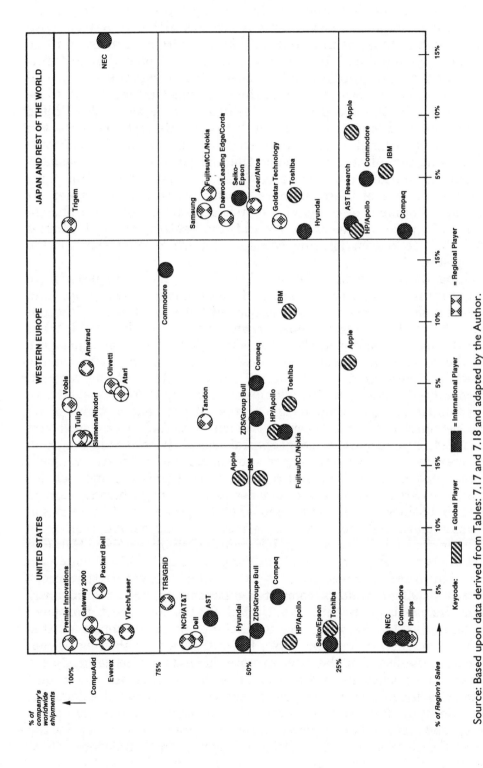

Fig. 7.9. Geographical scope and market share of major competitors in the worldwide personal computer regions: 1991.

Source: Based upon data derived from Tables: 7.17 and 7.18 and adapted by the Author.

It can be seen that a key point to emerge from the pattern in Fig. 7.9 is the fact that it tends to confirm that amongst the major competitors in the worldwide computer market, only a few are global in nature, with a reasonably high number of international players, although many of these have a strong regional focus. In particular, it can be noted that in terms of the scope of their geographical sales, most of the competitors still tend to have 50 per cent or more of their business focused in one of the three regions, which, with the exceptions of Toshiba and Seiko in the United States and Commodore plus Atari in Western Europe, reflects the companies' various original start-up locations. Conversely, no United States or West European manufacturer has more than 50 per cent of their business in the Japanese market, nor does any West European competitor have more than 50 per cent of their business in the United States market. At the same time, a number of companies do not appear in Fig. 7.9, although they are in the top forty players on a worldwide basis as shown in Tables 7.17 and 7.18. The reason for this being that their market share is too small to register.

By taking the data from Tables 7.17 and 7.18 it is also possible to plot various strategic groups in terms of their geographical scope and regional market share across the three regions of the United States, Western Europe and the combined region of Japan and the Rest of the World. What emerges is the pattern shown in Fig. 7.10 which plots the regional presence of each of the competitors along the vertical axis by showing in how many regions each company holds more than 1 per cent share of the regional personal computer market, whilst along the horizontal axis is shown in how many countries each company generates 10 per cent or more of its worldwide personal computer revenues, which is taken to be a measure of each competitor's respective geographical scope. Within this diagram, the companies in the top right corner are considered to be truly global in their geographic scope and scale of regional market presence and includes IBM, Apple, Hewlett Packard/Apollo and Toshiba. Although having a broad spread of their business in all three regions, AST Research and Seiko Epson lack sufficient market share in all three regions to be global, even more so in the case for the Taiwanese and Korean companies, Acer, Hyundai and Goldstar, together with Tandy/Grid/Victor and NCR/AT&T who each only have significant market share in one region. However, the recent acquisition in 1993 of Tandy's computer business by AST, significantly strengthens its position in both the United States and West European personal computer markets. In the weakest position in terms of this measure are Sun, DEC, Wang and Wyse. However, the poor showing by Sun is largely due to the fact that the measures are for units, which downplay the market share of workstations, which tend to be high value and lower unit volumes than many of the lower priced high volume personal computers.

Companies that have a significant share of their personal computer business spread across two regions, form the greatest number in the industry. At the closest to being a global competitor is Commodore, which has a strong market presence in all three regions, but fails to have more

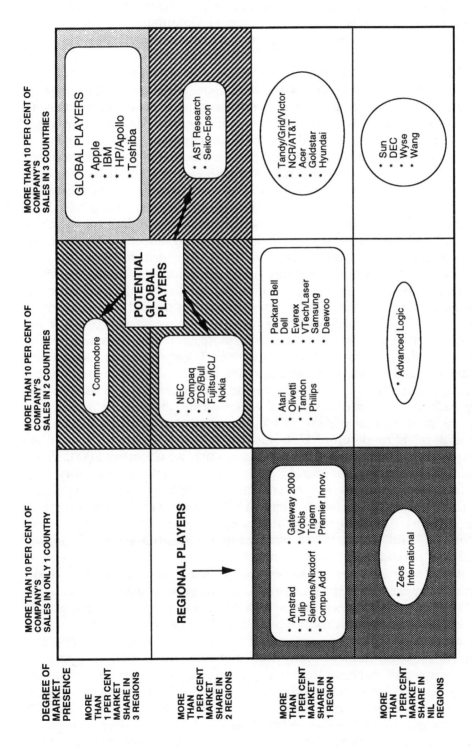

Fig. 7.10. Geographical strategic groups showing market scope and market presence in the worldwide personal computer marketplace: 1991.

Source: Based upon data derived from Tables 7.17 and 7.18 and adapted by the Author.

than 10 per cent of its business in the United States. Next comes the group of companies made up of Compaq, NEC, ZDS/Groupe Bull and Fujitsu/ICL/Nokia, which with the exception of Compaq are strong in the two regions where they have a significant market share, but very weak in their respective third regions with little market presence and levels of sales. What is interesting to note here, is the way in which two out of the four of these companies are now based upon international acquisitions that have strengthened the presence of each company in a second region. Occupying the position of the largest strategic groups are those companies that have a geographical spread across two regions, but only have a significant market share in one region. These include companies from every region and as such this is a very mixed group, since it includes some of the fastest growing companies such as Packard Bell, Dell, VTech-Laser and Everex, plus some of the more traditional competitors such as Atari, Tandon, Olivetti and Philips, together with Samsung and Daewoo. Finally at this level, Advanced Logic although having a spread of its business in two regions, registers less than 1 per cent market share in each region.

The final level of groups consist of companies that have a strong regional focus since they generate at least 81 per cent of their sales in only one region. This pattern can be particularly appreciated by referring back to Fig. 7.9, where many of these companies occupy the top box for their respective regions, but can also be seen to lack any presence in the other regions. Indeed, it is partly because their geographical focus upon their one particular region is so strong that they fail to gain more than 3 per cent market share in any other region. Although Zeos International is growing rapidly, it is still too small to generate more than 3 per cent market share in its home region. It can be seen that the main strategic group at this level is made-up of U.S. and West European based companies. Some of these include the fast growing clones such as Gateway 2000, Vobis and Premier Innovations, CompuAdd and Trigem which in time may well increase their geographical scope and market share in other regions. However, the group also includes some of the more established computer companies such as Amstrad, which is losing its geographical scope, and Siemens/Nixdorf, and Tulip, all of which have a limited scope of market presence in the personal computer marketplace.

Naturally, these measures are somewhat arbitrary and further data on a segment by segment basis would demonstrate some differences. However, the key point to recognise is that relatively few of the competitors in the worldwide personal computer industry can really claim to be global in their strategic geographical scope of operations, although clearly, the trend suggests that the numbers may well increase in the future, especially from those companies surrounding the top right corner. For the moment, the vast majority are still essentially international in nature and divided between those that need to increase their own internal spread of business across the regions and those that although present in a number of regions, need to increase their market share in order to move towards a global position. Furthermore, it is clear that some of these companies are profitable enough to maintain this strategy, whilst others are losing geographical scope and/or market presence. In addition, to these groups of international competitors, the data also underlies the fact that a number of competitors are still essentially regional in their nature and still have a considerable way to develop in terms of their own geographical scope of business mix or relative share of the three regional markets.

It should be emphasised that these observations concerning the geographical scope and relative scale of regional market shares amongst the major competitors is not intended as a test of correlation between the two sets of variables. Rather, it is to illustrate the particular pattern and level of evolution towards a global scale of operations achieved at the time by the major competitors within the overall personal computer market. However, the data does provide a general pattern of the degree of geographical scope and strategy amongst the major players in the global personal computer market and clarifies the fact that the industry is still very much in the process of evolving towards a global competitive situation, with a significant degree of development required in this direction by many of the players.

Indeed, when presenting material in this particular section of the book, the reader is cautioned to remember that we are forming subjective observations linked to other qualitative data collected from other sources (such as annual reports and news journals). It does however, provide a clearer picture of the relative strategic position of the major competitors. Furthermore, the analysis places emphasis upon trying to understand the position of the major personal computer competitors, not only in terms of their more obvious market share in the personal computer market, but also in relation to the broader Information Systems (IS) environment, within which much of the future development of personal computers as applied to the business market segment will continue to take place during the 1990s.

The Global Challenge and Strategic Responses

The analysis of the United States, West European, Japanese and other Asia/Pacific region markets for personal computers has shown that the worldwide market is at one level already global in nature, at least in terms of the ability to ship similar hardware to all three regions, with relatively little localisation, except at the software level. However, it was also shown that there exist considerable differences in the conditions of competition between the respective regions and especially within the West European and Asia/Pacific regions. These differences were seen to reflect in the relative performance of competitors and in the variations in market buying behaviour. The last section further proceeded to illustrate that few global competitors exist at this stage, although clearly a number of international competitors show signs of moving towards global coverage and market presence. Thus a somewhat paradoxical situation exists, wherein the basic hardware of the personal computer would appear to be relatively global in its nature. This fact is especially evident if one remembers that most elements on the supply side of the industry are already global in nature, with microprocessors and many of the electronic components being traded on a global basis, virtually as commodity items, with many of them controlled by Japanese companies. However, the markets appear to be highly fragmented. This raises the question of whether global economies of scale can be captured in this industry and if so, at what levels of the value chain do these become apparent.

One of the reasons that so much detail about the various markets and patterns of competitive performance have been provided in this chapter is to make the reader aware of how varied the markets actually are on a worldwide scale. Too often, observers focus purely on the product technology and seeing global components as a relatively heterogeneous product, then proceed to assume it is a global industry and marketplace. However, for personal computers, this is simply not the case, at least not yet, although it may well be that the trend is in this direction. Instead, based upon the evidence in this study, it is suggested that the personal computer industry is in the process of transforming towards a global industry and marketplace. Driving this transformation are three key factors. The first is technology that already provides a global source of supply for competitors within the industry and indeed, as was shown in the previous sections, small, local competitors in Western Europe and the Asia/Pacific region have been able to compete effectively with the major brand names, due to their ability to gain access to relatively cheap technology that is in the public domain. The second factor concerns the strategies of the competitors themselves, which choose various methods to try and develop competitive advantages either through "break-through" technology developed by their research and development activities, or through economies of scale in global production or through marketing and distribution. Finally, the growing convergence of users' needs and patterns of buying behaviour will also move the market towards a more global structure, as the levels of technology diffusion and market development become more similar.

Given that only a few competitors are anywhere near global in their personal computer operations together with the strong degree of heterogeneity between different market conditions, it may be that globalisation will not only develop through the further expansion of particular players into all three regions, but also through an increased level of alliances between major players from the different regions. In this way, competitors will be able to develop global scale research and development, together with manufacturing economies with local market knowledge and service facilities. There is much evidence to support this idea, since a clear trend has been developing in the industry, both for more strategic alliances on an international or global basis and through the high number of mergers and acquisitions. However, this trend does not result from a process of clear sighted planning or visions on the part of the majority of players in the industry, instead, it reflects a set of industry and market conditions that have forced the competitors to make such moves or risk going out of business.

Quite clearly, a number of factors have been driving these events for some time. Firstly, increased competition in personal computers has made weaker competitors ripe for acquisition. Secondly, the dramatic improvements in price/performance of personal computers, client server networks, workstations and various peripherals together with related software has fuelled the process of "downsizing" in large organisations. This has created the crisis in the mainframe and minicomputer industry sectors, which together with the global economic slowdown or recession has forced a major restructuring to take place in the industry, which still has some way to go. Then there is the process of convergence amongst the various digital based technology industries, ranging from computers to telecommunications, from broadcasting to publishing, from entertainment to consumer electronics, the implications of which are discussed more fully in the final chapter. However, for the moment, it should be noted that all of these factors effectively add up to the creation of other newgames, which are in large part symptoms of the development of the personal computer. In order to compete effectively in such an environment, requires more than just a competence in one area of technology or one market region. Instead, competitors have been forced to realise that their world is rapidly changing and that the only way to survive, or at least reduce their risks, at the same time as focusing their own resources is through cooperation with other companies, not only in their own industry, but in other relevant industries and not only in their own country or region, but on a global scale. Hence, another pattern that can be seen emerging that crossed the entire computer industry, from mainframes to personal computers, from software developers to peripheral suppliers and from systems houses to distributors is a rapidly increasing number of mergers and acquisitions. Initially developing slowly in the late 1980s, they have gathered pace during the early 1990s. Such developments are part of the process by which the personal computer industry is transforming the rest of the computer industry and at the same time going through its own major metamorphosis. We now therefore turn to analyse the pattern of major mergers and acquisitions that have taken place within the worldwide computer industry during the past five years.

Acquisitions and Mergers

Although it would be too simplistic to claim that many of the changes witnessed within the computer industry at this time are due entirely to the newgame created by personal computers, it does not appear an exaggeration to suggest that nevertheless they provide an important driving force. Essentially, the late 1980s provided a period when the increased power and performance of personal computers meant that they began to be used in large organisations in a different way to how they had been utilised during the early to mid-1980s, when they had been primarily stand-alone self-contained units for the benefit of individual users. As shown in Chapter 6, after the mid-1980s personal computers increasingly began to be used on a shared basis within local area networks, linked to file servers[34] and printing resources and able to perform multi-tasking capabilities. In such configurations, decision makers in the MIS function recognised the trend towards a more economical and flexible solution to their departmental and in some instances corporate information systems requirements. This could be achieved by substituting the technology of personal computer and workstation based networks to replace mainframe or minicomputer based systems linked to terminals, either in total, or more commonly, to complement existing systems. Hence, rather than expanding, the mainframe and minicomputer markets both experienced a slow-down in demand, in particular within the minicomputer business. This process of change in choice of MIS solutions has as mentioned in the previous chapter become generally known in the computer industry as "downsizing". However, it has been the speed and scale of the downsizing in large organisations throughout the world, initially in the United States and Western Europe, but increasingly also including Japan and other Asia/ Pacific based companies, that has sent shock waves through the worldwide industry.

Many of the established incumbents have simply been too slow in recognising the changes taking place in the patterns of market demand and have consequently been stuck with their conventional product/market strategies, which were based upon technological solutions that have been increasingly out of line with the developing trends. Hence, a number of minicomputer companies that enjoyed enormous growth during the early 1980s, due to strong demand at the earlier stage of the product life-cycle, suddenly found that their competitive edge, gained through proprietary operating systems (and in Europe and Japan due to a degree of government protectionism, either overt or indirect) was disappearing rapidly. The market trend was towards smaller and more "open systems", which demanded a new financial model of high volumes and lower margins. Pressure of the market required a greater investment further down the value chain in software development, systems integration, maintenance and support services. Many of these factors were well known in the industry, yet organisational inertia in the form of the "not-invented here" syndrome and resistance to change by both top and middle management, meant that many of the competitors failed to act sufficiently quickly. Hence companies which had invested enormous amounts on development of proprietary systems found themselves unable to develop the scale or size of market share initially anticipated in order to offset the costs through large volume sales, which could have reduced unit costs through the effect of economies of scale. This problem appears particularly acute for most of the U.S. and West European mainframe and minicomputer companies, since, unlike their Japanese counterparts, they traditionally have produced their systems purely for in-house consumption. In contrast, major Japanese corporations, based upon their Keiretsu[35] style of organisation have marketed their electronic components, not only in-house, but also on the open market, including to competitors. As a result, they have gained enormous economies of scale and gradually have forced other competitors from the United States and Western Europe out of the market. Hence in 1991, Japan's share of the worldwide semiconductor market exceeded 50 per cent and was still growing. Similar patterns exist in many of the electronic components used in computer systems. Indeed, companies such as Canon, Hitachi, Matsushita, NEC, Sharp, Sony and Toshiba are already world class players in the fields ranging from consumer electronics to computers and office products. As a result of these trends, some observers wonder whether the United States and Western Europe will be able to sustain a viable major worldscale computer hardware industry and indeed, there are those who argue in favour of the creation of U.S. and West European style of keiretsu organisations to compete in this marketplace.[36]

A further factor to complicate the issue was that whilst the global economy of the mid-1980s could be characterised as a high-growth period, the late 1980s witnessed a gradual slowing down of activity, which moved into recessionary conditions in the early 1990s. The pace of technological change in information systems and the increasing degree of global competition in all aspects of the technology from computers, through communications and office systems, meant that potential customer organisations began to be more cautious about their choice of investment path. For example, in larger computer operating systems, the issues surrounding the future of UNIX versus alternatives has delayed many investment decisions. Set against this background, the large scale of investment in research and development necessary to underwrite alternative technology solutions have forced even the largest companies in the industry to seek joint ventures or strategic alliances through technological or marketing agreements in order to share the risk and spread the costs necessary to develop key projects. However, as the industry moved into the 1990s, it became clear that the scale of changes would involve much more than cooperative ventures. Instead, the industry was witnessing a major realignment and reconfiguration of its resources that would go way beyond alliances and has taken the form of an increasing number of mergers and acquisitions. Clearly, not all such activity has been involving personal computer companies, however, given the increasing importance of both personal computers and workstations to the type of product mix offered by competitors within the overall IT industry, such patterns of behaviour have already had an effect on the relative position of companies in the global personal computer marketplace. Earlier analysis in this chapter has shown how personal computers already make up an important part of the product mix within many major computer companies. Fig. 7.11 illustrates selected patterns of major acquisitions and mergers that have taken place within the global computer industry for hardware manufacturers during the period 1987 to mid-1993. However, this is not an exhaustive illustration, since it does not include any of the smaller company developments. Nor does it map the hundreds of technical and marketing agreements and swaps that have occurred between companies within the industry, nor the various linkages being forged with other industry sectors such as software, nor the relationships with companies in related industries such as consumer electronics, all of which issues are considered in the next two chapters.

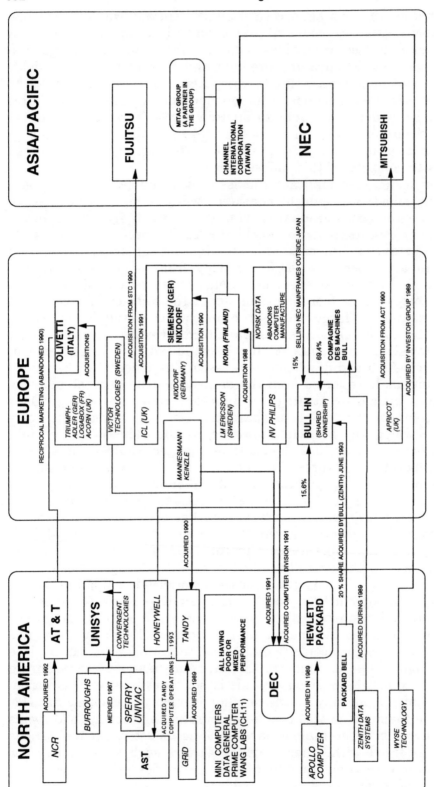

Fig. 7.11. Selected major acquisitions and mergers within the global computer industry for hardware manufacturers during 1987-1993.

Source: Company Annual Research and Market Research Reports.

However, it is intended to let the reader appreciate the significant scale of change of ownership and consolidation that has already taken place amongst the major mainframe, minicomputer, personal computer and workstation hardware manufacturers in this period on a worldwide basis.

Naturally a number of the mergers or acquisitions reflect the failure of companies to remain profitable in their computer business. Just how bad things have become is illustrated by the fact that even amongst the surviving companies, what initially appeared as temporary problems in 1990 have subsequently led to major losses and significant levels of unemployment within the industry as a whole, as companies that had never before experienced laying-off staff were forced to announce major redundancies in 1991, 1992 and early 1993. Indeed, rather than disappear, this pattern of restructuring and lay-offs is likely to continue for some time to come. The pattern that emerges from Fig. 7.11 is as follows:

Within the United States:

(i)   Mergers and consolidation amongst the major U.S. mainframe manufacturers. The traditional group of IBM and the BUNCH[37] has shrunk as Burroughs and Sperry Univac merged to form UNISYS in 1987, which proceeded to acquire Convergent Technologies. Honeywell, which was a major shareholder in Honeywell Bull, reduced its stake to a minority position and instructed the market to forget the name of Honeywell and switch allegiance to Bull. NCR was acquired by the telecommunications giant, AT&T.

(ii)   In the technical workstation market, Apollo Computer (the original leader of the workstation market) was acquired by Hewlett-Packard in 1989.

(iii) Tandy acquired GRiD Computers the portable and laptop personal computer manufacturer during 1989, giving it increased access to certain sectors of the corporate business market and the government sector.

(iv)   In mid-1993, AST acquired the personal computer business of Tandy Corporation, which of course included GRiD Computers. Thus one of the personal computer industry's earlier leaders bowed out of the competition. Hence, of the earlier traditional U.S. mainframe manufacturers they have shrunk to IBM, UNISYS and AT&T in general systems, joined by later entrants such as Amdahl. Meanwhile, many of the minicomputer companies are in financial and strategic difficulties, with questions over their future survival as independent concerns. Amongst the minicomputer manufacturers, the past few years have brought nothing but substantial losses. In 1989 losses were recorded at Prime Computers ($276.8 million), Wang Laboratories ($511.0 million) and Data General ($120.7 million). In 1991, whilst Prime had managed to make a profit, Wang Laboratories had sought protection from bankruptcy under Chapter 11, whilst Data

General had yet another year of heavy losses, which were repeated in 1992. Meanwhile, in 1991, the two giants of the U.S. industry, IBM and DEC suffered their first ever losses, with IBM declaring a total loss of $2.83 billion (including accounting changes) and DEC reporting a loss of $864 million, which included restructuring charges. By 1993 two of the high-flying personal computer companies, namely Everex and CompuAdd had sought Chapter 11 protection. In 1992, things got much worse. IBM suffered an even greater loss of U.S.$6.87 Bn, whilst DEC lost U.S.$2.50 Bn.

Within Europe:

(i)   L.M.Ericsson, the telecommunications giant that had set high goals based upon its strategy of combining telecom, data processing and office equipment manufacturers into a global scale office automation company, sold off its loss-making data processing division during 1988 to the Finnish electronics company Nokia. In turn, Nokia then proceeded to experience difficulties in the absorption process, which led to its selling its data processing operations to ICL during 1991.

(ii)   The previously highly successful German computer company, Nixdorf, ran into financial difficulties and was acquired during 1990 by the larger German computer and electronics giant, Siemens (that acquired the British electronics company, Plessey, from GEC a short while before).

(iii)   During the mid-1980s Olivetti's growth was partly developed through its acquisition of various European companies in the information technology field. However, by 1992, even this company was running into strategic problems with losses of $363 million and the prospect of a sale being rumoured within the industry.

(iv)   Norsk Data declared a major loss of $60.4 million in 1989, in the early 1990s it went through a major restructuring, that effectively took it out of its minicomputer hardware manufacturing activities to allow it to restructure purely as a distribution and service company.

Overall, the European computer industry therefore came under increasing pressure as a result of a downturn in the midrange market that hit the fortunes of a number of companies which had previously enjoyed high growth, especially Nixdorf and Norsk Data. The data processing division of NV Philips and Mannesmann Kienzle were sold off to the U.S. company, DEC, whilst Olivetti and Groupe Bull are under pressure to reduce costs and restructure, which is involving substantial reductions in their workforces. Groupe Bull has declared consecutive losses in 1989, 1990 and 1991 of approximately $42 million, $1246 million and $585 million. Much of the pressure has been due to the "downsizing" phenomenon, the increased pressure on prices and hence margins from Far Eastern competitors and European based brand clones, which has even forced

Amstrad into heavy losses.

Within Japan and the rest of the Asia/Pacific region:

(i)   Mergers or acquisitions between the major companies within the region have not occurred, largely, because the companies are financially strong.

In addition, the process of "downsizing" during the late 1980s was less of a problem in this region, since many large corporations were tending to adjust their MIS requirements more slowly, which gave manufacturers a little longer to make changes in their product mixes. Furthermore, companies such as NEC, Fujitsu and Toshiba were also active in a high level of technological innovations, especially in the areas of laptop personal computers and workstations. However, by 1992 the situation was beginning to change with Toshiba and Mitac, experiencing downturns in their revenue growth, and Acer and Oki suffering losses of approximately $4million and $23million respectively.

Although still highly profitable, many of the larger companies did experience the first chill winds of change during 1991, which continued during 1992 as Fujitsu's earnings in fiscal 1991 dropped 83 per cent, NEC's fell by 72 per cent and Hitachi's net income fell by 45 per cent. At the same time, the Japan Electronics Industry Association estimated that Japanese vendors' personal computer worldwide sales dropped nearly 8 per cent during 1991 on 1990 figures. However, despite these results, in the high-end of the computer industry, after IBM, the Japanese companies, Fujitsu, Hitachi and NEC now dominate the global mainframe industry and are profitable. Although much slower than in the late 1980s, NEC, Fujitsu and Hitachi still all experienced reasonable annual growth in revenues and represent some of the best positioned companies for expansion of their activities, especially given their experience and strengths in both the electronics components and telecommunications businesses.

If one indulges in some speculation, one could postulate that should they so decide, a number of the major Japanese companies are well positioned in terms of their financial strength to develop their global operations through acquisition of some of the weaker U.S. or European manufacturers during the rest of the 1990s. Such a move would give them faster access to these markets, both in terms of customer bases and distribution/sales channels. Indeed, one has seen instances of such moves in the maintenance and service fields, together with Japanese minority shareholdings developing in U.S. and West European companies. For example, NEC's 5% stake in Control Data Systems. Furthermore, the acquisition of U.S. and European computer companies would give the Japanese an opportunity to accelerate their competence in systems integration and software activities, for which they recognise a serious need in order to compete effectively outside of Japan, especially for corporate based systems.

Indeed, during the late 1980s and increasingly during the 1990s, these patterns are already occurring in terms of cross-regional acquisitions as witnessed by:

(i)   In 1989, the acquisition of Zenith Data Systems by Compagnie
             des Machines Bull of France, when it was sold by its parent
             company, the Zenith Group.
(ii)   Honeywell's sale of its majority stake in Honeywell Bull to
             Compagnie des Machines Bull, in which NEC (Japan) initially
             held a 15% stake. However, this was subsequently reduced
             to just over 4%.
(iii)   Channel International Corporation of Taiwan, a major investor
             group, which includes the personal computer manufacturer,
             Mitac, acquired the ailing Wyse Technology which lost $21.2
             million during 1989.
(iv)   Mitsubishi, the Japanese conglomerate, acquired the U.K.
             personal computer manufacturer Apricot Computer from its
             parent company ACT Ltd during 1990.
(v)   The sale of Britain's leading computer company, ICL, to
             Fujitsu of Japan by its parent telecommunications company
             STC Ltd.
(vi)   Tandy's acquisition of Victor Technologies of Sweden in 1990
             gave it access to a large established European distribution
             channel, with sales subsidiaries in eleven countries serving
             approximately 2,700 dealers and distributors.
(vii)   After a few years of speculation, in 1991 both NV Philips
             and the German computer company, Mannesmann Kienzle,
             which had been showing poor market performance, sold off
             their respective data processing operations to DEC.
(viii)   Bull sold just over a 5 per cent stake of its operations in
             1991 to IBM, in order to avoid undertaking large development
             costs in RISC technology.
(ix)   In June 1993, France's Groupe Bull took approximately a 20%
             share in the U.S. mass market personal computer company,
             Packard Bell, which needed cash after abandoning its stock
             market floatation. As such, Bull's struggling aquisition of
             Zenith Data Systems means that it gains access to 7,000
             retailers. At the same time it provides Packard Bell with funds
             to protect and develop is market position.

Clearly, these events are not all specific to personal computers, nor
do they include the significant number of mergers and acquisitions between
companies in other sectors of the overall industry, such as software or
systems integration. However, most of the companies illustrated are or
were ranked in the top 30 competitors in the global personal computer
marketplace and hence, the strategic realignment of assets between these
companies has the potential to significantly alter their competitive positions.
It also underlines the extent to which personal computers and workstations
have become a major focus for product/market development amongst any
of the companies wishing to compete within the global corporate and
business information technology marketplace during the rest of the 1990s.

Most importantly, these changes illustrate the significant scale of structural adjustment now taking place within the global computer industry, reflecting the pattern of change predicted within the newgame framework. Thus, the personal computer can be seen to have reached a further stage of development in its process of evolutionary impact upon the structure and nature of competition, not only amongst companies involved in the manufacture of personal computers, but also including computer companies that have to some extent ignored its presence and development. The changes in demand characteristics amongst corporate customers in the business segment have led to a realignment of preferences. In turn, those companies that have moved in harmony with such changes, whether in personal computers and/or workstations, generally include those that are enjoying growth in this sector of the industry, whilst the remainder are suffering significant downturns in performance, which in the more extreme instances has led or is likely to lead to their acquisition or extinction.

It does not seem fanciful therefore to suggest that, even if one assumes an easing of recessionary conditions, the mid-part of the 1990s are likely to reflect a continued pattern of acquisitions and mergers between some major competitors. This will be driven by the need to gain access to technology and markets, together with the opportunities available to the stronger global competitors to obtain assets at a reasonable price in the form of the weaker competitors. The rationale and makeup of the moves will not take place in terms of strictly defined product businesses, but will involve companies with activities from across the range of hardware products. Furthermore, the competitive and financial pressures upon the major computer hardware companies in the United States and Western Europe has forced those remaining, to run to the banner of strategic alliances as their salvation. In particular, shorter product-life cycles, together with increasing research and development costs are both forcing this as the only option available upon the majority of competitors. However, many such arrangements (as with the ICL–Fujitsu situation) may turn out to be harbingers of mergers or acquisitions. Such developments will effectively be a key driver to the globalisation of the industry, at least in terms of the supply of core technology and the assembly of the various forms of desktop and mobile personal computers and it is to this phenomenon that we next turn our attention.

Strategic Alliances

A very important strategic question that many of the computer industry's competitors are now having to address in relation to their strategies for the remainder of the 1990s, concerns the method they employ to expand within the global marketplace. Their choice of options will of course be partly determined by their existing and potential scale of resources and their potential trading positions. However, a deeper philosophical question also needs careful consideration, namely, do joint ventures and strategic alliances create the opportunity for a Trojan Horse? Clearly, a number of other U.S. and European companies have witnessed such patterns of behaviour within various industries when competing with the Japanese.

Perhaps the difference, in this instance, is that the horse may originate from Taiwan and/or South Korea as much as from Japan. For this reason, a number of observers have noted that in general government policy within the European Community, both individually and collectively, (especially in France, Germany and Italy), has tended to encourage cooperation with U.S. companies in preference to the Japanese. However, it should be remembered that in terms of patterns of international expansion and development, many of the Japanese companies are still at a relatively early stage of their international development investment cycle. Ironically, the broader tensions surrounding sensitivities to trade imbalance issues encountered by the Japanese during the late 1970s and early 1980s, have largely been responsible for encouraging their rapid acceleration in the establishment of international manufacturing factories in both the U.S. and West European regions. Towards the end of the 1980s and now in the 1990s one is witnessing a further extension and development of this process with their establishment of research and development facilities in both the United States and Europe, both for semiconductor and other electronic components manufacture, together with computer and telecommunications technologies.

A further feature of the pattern of strategic alliances for the computer industry, which is relevant to the personal computer industry is the increasing tendency for traditional hardware manufacturers in both the United States, Europe and Japan to seek to develop their line of activities beyond "box manufacturing". This is not a recent phenomenon. Indeed it has been apparent in the strategic behaviour of a number of mainframe and minicomputer companies since the late 1970s. What is now changing is the increased levels of investment being directed into these activities and the pressure within such companies to broaden the basic range of technologies to which they have access. Hence, a key strategic issue revolves around how best to organise access to different technologies in the field of information technology that have the potential to be relevant to possible future product and market development. Nowhere is this more dominant than in the area of personal computers.

In this instance, the major competitors in the personal computer field are being faced with choices concerning technology platforms which go beyond the basic traditional components of computer hardware. Areas such as audio technology, high-density storage mediums,[38] high-density transmission systems[39] as well as associated software are just a few examples which reflect the diversity of technologies that may be incorporated into personal computers. Nor are such technologies purely for the high-end performance machines, the growing potential for graphical animation[40] in simulation programs,[41] together with more advanced forms of integration with home-leisure systems suggest that a wide range of technology platforms will be incorporated into the home personal computer of the 1990s. Indeed, as the process of miniaturisation continues to proceed in conjunction with improvement in the price/performance characteristics of the various technologies, then it seems likely that the resulting achievement of higher levels of mobility associated from the resulting products will confuse the current distinctions between the various physical locations of personal computers as they are more easily transferred between the office and home environments.

Thus, although international marketing and distribution activities have become and will continue to play an increasingly important element of the structure of the value chain for major competitors in the global personal computer marketplace, it is also true to say, that the scale and range of technological innovation to which competitors will need access is likely to remain very significant. There are no signs yet that there is any form of slowdown in the pace of innovation, either in hardware or software and systems development. Hence, an important part of the strategic challenge facing major competitors during the 1990s will be to establish and develop effective strategic alliances in the form of technology agreements. However, such arrangements should be approached with caution by both parties, since in time, the leverage of one partner may shift to a level which could permit an acquisition of the other partner's resources and is a topic discussed somewhat further in the next two chapters.

SUMMARY

What this chapter has attempted to achieve is to provide the reader with a reasonably detailed overview of how the personal computer industry and its markets outside the United States have evolved during the latter part of the 1980s and during the early part of the 1990s. It has then proceeded to combine these findings with the previous chapter to illustrate the more recent pattern of evolution of competition in the worldwide marketplace. During the period, considerable changes were seen to have taken place, both in the industry and market structure, together with the modes of competition and customer behaviour. Table 7.19 provides a summary of the broad pattern of development of the international personal computer newgame environment. What it attempts to illustrate are the changes in the dominant business strategy characteristics that one might expect to find in market leaders at each respective stage of international evolution.

In terms of the structure of the worldwide industry and its marketplace, the following observations represent the major points that emerge from this chapter. Firstly, the worldwide marketplace for personal computers is dominated by three major regions consisting of the United States, Western Europe and the Asia/Pacific region, the latter which is dominated by Japan. The trend is towards a decreasing importance of the United States market in terms of relative size to the overall worldwide marketplace. Together, these three regions account for nearly 95 per cent of the worldwide shipments of personal computers and are home to the major personal computer companies. Furthermore, in each of these markets, the business segment dominated. Secondly, the stage of market maturity both in terms of processor usage and diffusion, plus aspects of market infrastructure in these three regions is quite different, accounting for the

Table 7.19. Illustration of development of international newgame business environment.

DOMINANT CHARACTERISTIC OF BUSINESS STRATEGY	STAGES OF NEWGAME INTERNATIONAL EVOLUTION				
	EMBRYONIC	GROWTH & EXPORT OPERATIONS	ENTRY OF GIANTS & LEGITIMISATION & OVERSEAS EXPANSION	CONSOLIDATION & INTERNATIONALISATION	SATURATION & GLOBALISATION
PRODUCT-MARKET SCOPE	SINGLE PRODUCT UNDIFFERENTIATED	SINGLE TO MULTI PRODUCT/MULTI SEGMENTS	MULTI PRODUCT MULTI MARKET	DIFFERENTIATED	MULTIPLE PRODUCTS MULTIPLE COUNTRIES
HORIZONTAL INTEGRATION	NON-EXISTENT	LIMITED	DEVELOPING	INCREASING	INTERNATIONAL
VERTICAL INTEGRATION	NON-EXISTENT	LIMITED	DEVELOPED	VARIABLE	INTERNATIONAL
GEOGRAPHIC SCOPE	DOMESTIC	EXPORTER WITH LIMITED FOREIGN SALES	INTERNATIONAL AND MULTINATIONAL	INTERNATIONAL AND MULTINATIONAL	INTERNATIONAL, MULTINATIONAL AND GLOBAL
INTERNATIONAL STRUCTURE					
R & D	DOMESTIC	DOMESTIC	DOMESTIC & FOREIGN	DOMESTIC & LIMITED FOREIGN	INTERNATIONAL GOING GLOBAL
PRODUCTION	DOMESTIC	DOMESTIC	DOMESTIC & FOREIGN	DOMESTIC & RISING FOREIGN	INTERNATIONAL GOING GLOBAL
MARKETING					
- PRODUCT	DOMESTIC	DOMESTIC & FOREIGN AGENT OR SALES	DOMESTIC & FOREIGN	DOMESTIC & FOREIGN	INTERNATIONAL GOING GLOBAL
- PRICE	DOMESTIC	DOMESTIC & FOREIGN AGENT OR SALES	DOMESTIC & FOREIGN	DOMESTIC & FOREIGN	REGIONAL VARIATIONS
- PROMOTION	DOMESTIC	DOMESTIC & FOREIGN	DOMESTIC & FOREIGN	INTERNATIONAL	LOCAL, REGIONAL AND GLOBAL
DISTRIBUTION	DOMESTIC	DOMESTIC & FOREIGN AGENT OR DEALERS	DOMESTIC & FOREIGN SALES AND DEALERS	DOMESTIC & FOREIGN CHANNELS	LOCAL, REGIONAL AND GLOBAL
SERVICE	DOMESTIC	DOMESTIC & FOREIGN AGENT OR DEALERS	DOMESTIC & FOREIGN AGENTS OR DEALERS	DOMESTIC & FOREIGN AGENTS OR DEALERS	MAINLY LOCAL WITH SOME REGIONAL CHAINS
PEOPLE TRANSFER	DOMESTIC	DOMESTIC	INTRA-COUNTRY	LIMITED INTERNATIONAL	INTERNATIONAL LIMITED GLOBAL
STRATEGIC ISSUES	SALES	PRODUCTION & SALES	PRODUCTION & SALES & DISTRIBUTION	R&D, PRODUCTION MARKETING SERVICE	GLOBAL COORDINATION & COMPLEXITY

Note: The above details are only meant as a guideline to some of the dominant patterns that might be expected amongst major competitors in the newgame environment.

variations in growth rate. The most mature is the United States market, which began to slow during the late 1980s, forcing home based competitors to expand their operations in the equally sophisticated, yet less saturated West European marketplace. However, during the early 1990s, the West European marketplace experienced a dramatic change as prices fell, margins were squeezed and competitor positions shifted significantly. The changes were due to increased competition, the impact of the economic recession and a maturing of the marketplace. During the same period, the Japanese market also experienced a dramatic slowdown in its rate of growth. Thus by 1992, competition in the three regions of the United States, Western Europe and Japan was faced with slow rates of market growth, whilst countries elsewhere in the Asia/Pacific region showing a mixture of growth rates, ranging from high to moderate.

It was also evident, that whilst the markets in each region showed different levels of development, there also existed significant differences in the market infrastructure, which largely accounted for substantial variations in performance amongst the major competitors. In particular, these differences appeared to be driven by a number of factors, some of which were supply related, whilst others were based upon patterns of demand. How much each of these factors came into play, depended not so much upon the region, but more on the specific country. On the supply side, government policy could play an important role, either through protectionism of indigenous manufacturers, such as in the cases of Japan, Korea or Taiwan. The degree of foreign versus local competition could also impact pricing structures in the market, as witnessed in parts of South East Asia or in Western Europe. Similarly, the degree of competition on price versus quality and performance could also strongly influence levels of profitability for both manufacturers and distribution channels, whose margins were effected by increasing volumes, but decreasing prices. Levels of training and customer support also affected the nature of competition and the levels of demand.

More specifically on the demand side, general demographics and the average levels of education naturally shaped the size and sophistication of the respective markets. This also reflected in the degree of personal computer market penetration, the numbers of computers per capita and associated levels of computer literacy. All of which influenced the pace of adoption and investment in newer technology, higher end processors, workstations, windows type environments, graphical user interfaces and local area networks. Attitudes and buying behaviour surrounding these issues were in turn closely linked to the degree and pace of "downsizing" found in the business segment of these markets, which was extremely varied and hence set the agenda for competition in each market. Culturally specific factors also played an important part, especially, where English was not the native language and thus necessitated localisation of software products. Attitudes towards software piracy in various Asia/Pacific countries was also an issue, whilst the degree of competition between foreign and local competitors also impacted the market, as did the procurement policies of large corporations. Finally, differences in the attitudes and preferences of buyers to various types of product, reflecting the degree of price sensitivity or brand loyalty all played a significant role. Hence, whilst the worldwide personal computer marketplace could be divided into three major regions, at the same time, it was also clear that there exists a high degree of homogeneity between selected features of the different country markets within each region.

Set against all these changes and variations in the worldwide marketplace for personal computers, it was also evident that relatively few competitors were as yet organised on a global basis. The majority were much more regional in their focus and indeed, during the early 1990s the smaller, local clones appear to have been more profitable than most of the larger established competitors. However, the fortunes of the more established computer companies, that are still largely regional in their strategies, were not so good. Here, it was seen that the impact of the personal computer newgame was similar throughout the major regions of the world, with a general trend, especially in large user organisations towards "downsizing" of their computer systems. As a result, the personal computer industry has been forcing the remainder of the computer industry into a major process of restructuring, which in the case of the mainframe and minicomputer sectors appears to represent an endgame situation. Thus commencing in the late 1980s and gathering pace into the 1990s, the overall computer hardware industry has witnessed a significant level of mergers and acquisitions amongst many of the historically key players, ranging through mainframe, mini, workstation and personal computer companies. Furthermore, a number of these unions have been international in nature crossing the three major regions, although it should be noted that Japanese and other South East Asian participants have all played the part of acquirers. Meanwhile, whilst "downsizing" has hit the performance of competitors in Japan as well as the United States and Western Europe, it is in the latter two regions that the process of restructuring has been most felt. For many of the established computer companies that have not merged, heavy losses and repeated internal reorganisations have become the order of the day. Even for the healthier competitors, survival appears dependent upon being able to strike the appropriate bargain in terms of strategic alliances, both for technology sharing and market access.

Thus, the worldwide personal computer industry shows signs of moving towards a global structure. One which is driven largely by the pattern of increasingly complex alliances, partnerships and mergers, rather than by the global expansion of all but a few of its most successful players. As for the markets, these show signs of converging towards more common patterns of demand in terms of basic product technology, although differences are bound to exist between the relative stages of market maturity for some time. However, the underlying differences in infrastructure and cultural dimensions are not likely to disappear, and as such will continue to force competitors to remain sensitive to maintaining a fine balance between the use of their global resources and their delivery at the local level. Overall therefore, the key pattern that emerges is one in which the dimensions of the international personal computer industry and its markets look set to become increasingly competitive and complex during the foreseeable future.

Chapter Eight

REFLECTIONS, PATTERNS AND CONCLUSIONS

"Let no one say that I have said nothing new;
the arrangement of the subject is new."[1]

INTRODUCTION

This penultimate chapter presents us with the opportunity to reflect upon the study of the evolution of the personal computer industry and its markets as it has been told in this book. It therefore draws together the main patterns that have emerged and suggests some conclusions that can be made about the nature of newgames. The chapter is divided into two halves. The first provides a review of the main developments in the evolution of the newgame environment for personal computers by identifying specific drivers, which have been responsible for creating changes in the underlying industry and market structure. These changes in structure have manifested themselves through specific developments in technological change, strategic competition and customer behaviour. From these patterns are drawn a set of conclusions about the nature of newgames, which provide a series of insights and lessons to be applied to competitive strategies in the future of the evolution of the personal computer industry. The second part of the chapter then applies the newgame framework to speculate on the next five years, by making suggestions as to what will be some of the major changes that are likely to take place in the personal computer industry and its markets as the final stages of a newgame give way to the establishment of a samegame. Once again it illustrates the trends amongst drivers such as technological change, strategies of semiconductor companies, software developers, personal computer competitors and distributors, together with customer behaviour. Furthermore, it suggests how they might all interact to shape changes in the structure of the industry and its markets. Within its predictions are included an endgame for mainframe and minicomputers resulting from the success of the personal computer newgame, together with continuing convergence of major industries, that not only include computers, telecommunications and consumer electronics, but also broadcasting, photography and others. Taken together these events are predicted to create yet more newgames, that will force competitors from the personal computer and other sectors of the computer industry to reorganise still further their value chains and corporate structures. Overall, the traditional industry barriers will be broken by the common element of digital based information technology,[2] but at the same time the resulting industry and market structures will require even more emphasis upon understanding the customer and the dynamics of the newgame environment.

LESSONS OF THE PAST FOR THE FUTURE

The Newgame Framework Revisited

The story of the development of the personal computer industry and its business markets as told in the previous chapters has provided a rich insight to the underlying factors which both caused the emergence and subsequent development of this particular newgame environment. Furthermore, the evidence gathered has supported the broad basis of ideas central to the concepts of newgame environments as expressed in the opening chapter. Clearly, a strong set of relationships exist between technological change, competitive strategies and outcomes, together with their impact upon the process of change within the shape, structure and dynamics of both the industry and its market evolution. However, with such a large mass of information over a fifteen to twenty year period, it can be difficult remembering just how each of these drivers for change affected the process of development. This section will therefore provide a framework for summarising the key drivers for change. The framework itself is based upon looking at two fundamental criteria for change, namely, structures and processes, which are identified as consisting of the following:

(1) Evolution in Hardware and Software Technology;
(2) Competitive Strategies between Suppliers, especially:
— Semiconductor Manufacturers;
— Software Developers;
— Third Party Peripheral Companies;
(3) Competitive Strategies between Personal Computer Companies;
(4) Competitive Strategies of Mainframe, Mini and Workstation Competitors;
(5) Competitive Strategies of Various Types of Distribution Channel;
(6) Behaviour of Customers both as Purchasers and Buyers.

Naturally each of these drivers for change have an actual and potential dimension, such as the threat of potential entrants or the potential behaviour of customers that might influence the strategy of a particular competitor. Furthermore, this list is not exclusive, since clearly other elements come into play, however, it is felt that it captures the most significant forces for change. Clearly structures included in the industry are made up of the suppliers, including semiconductor and component manufacturers, software companies, the personal computer competitors in terms of strategic groups and their associated value chains, together with the channels and the market in terms of its segmentation. The processes involve the strategies of the suppliers, personal computer companies, channels and the behaviour of different customer groups.

Since the purpose of this section is to clarify and summarise, rather than repeat a shortened version of the previous chapters in chronological order, it was felt that a more interesting and hopefully more informative structure could be obtained by presenting a summary of each of these drivers and reflecting upon what role they played in creating and driving change in the newgame environment. It also highlights how at each stage of development of the newgame evolution, a newgame strategy preceded the change in industry and market structure and involved one or more of these drivers. The section finishes with a set of conclusions about the observations made and with some suggested lessons and insights that they provide to our understanding of the evolution of newgame environments and the way in which they are driven by newgame strategies.

As a starting point to the summary of the various drivers for change, it seems appropriate to focus on the personal computer itself and to recap how it has evolved since its earliest days up to the present. However, this is not a review of the technology per se, which comes subsequently, but rather it is intended to provide an insight into the way in which the personal computer has been perceived by both competitors and customers alike during the process of its evolution. The reasoning behind this approach is to allow the reader to appreciate that the development of the personal computer industry and its markets is essentially dependent on how people perceive the product and its role in their activities. It is not simply a question of looking at a personal computer as a box or part of a system, instead it is a bundle of attributes that may or may not be perceived by customers as giving value. Over time, perceptions of the role, usefulness and value of a personal computer have changed, sometimes increasing, sometimes decreasing, which is important, for therein lies the key to what value personal computers in their various shapes, sizes and forms have created for the marketplace and for the companies that have competed for market share, whether they be suppliers, competitors or distributors. By looking at this pattern of perceptual change first of all, it should be easier to then appreciate why the following drivers for change developed the way they did during the evolution of the personal computer industry and its markets.

Perceptions of the Personal Computer over Time

How perceptions of the personal computer changed over time are illustrated in Fig. 8.1 which also suggests that there existed extreme variations in perceptions between different competitors and different market segments. In its earliest format as a hobbyist's kit, the microcomputer as it was then known was seen as a basic electronics machine, that could provide a source of entertainment and interest to those willing to take the time necessary to construct the computer. As the product evolved from a kit form into a preassembled unit, so the perception of its potential uses began to broaden from a simple hobbyist's machine into something that might be sold to other types of customer. Initially, limits on the technical performance of the product meant that it was really only suitable for running games, but this at least increased sales and gave personal computers greater public exposure and began to develop a home market. Indeed, such was the success of companies such as Atari and Commodore in this market, that many industry analysts forecast this as being the major growth market for the 1980s. In addition, some of the early competitors also focused their attention upon selling these microcomputers into the school level educational market. Indeed, some companies such as Apple Computer developed a strong presence in this segment from the beginning of their activities.

CUSTOMER PERCEPTIONS

HOBBY MARKET	GAMES AND EDUCATIONAL MARKETS	EARLY SMALL BUSINESS AND PROFESSIONAL MARKETS	EARLY CORPORATE MARKET	DEVELOPED BUSINESS MARKET	REFINING EDUCATIONAL AND EXPANDING CONSUMER MARKETS
* Hobby Activity	* Leisure Activity	* Business Activity	* Business Activity	* Business Activity	* Educational Activity
* Kit	* Games Machine	* Powerful Calculator	* Low-end Computer	* Standard Computer	* Leisure Activity
* Fun	* Fun	* Limited Word Processing	* Personal Usage	* Part of MIS	* Addictive
* Stimulating	* Entertaining	* Novel	* Department Budget	* Powerful	* Fun
	* Educational Activity	* Interesting	* Status Builder	* Fascinating	* Experience
	* Novel			* Essential	* Stimulating

VENDOR PERCEPTIONS

HOBBY MARKET	GAMES AND EDUCATIONAL MARKETS	EARLY SMALL BUSINESS AND PROFESSIONAL MARKETS	EARLY CORPORATE MARKET	DEVELOPED BUSINESS MARKET	REFINING EDUCATIONAL AND EXPANDING CONSUMER MARKETS
* Basic Electronics Machine	* Basic Consumer Product	* Basic Office Product	* Stand-alone Computers	* Server Based Network System of Computers	* Interactive Games Machine
* Limited Market of Hobbyists	* Large Software Market	* Needed greater support	* Expanding Software	* Integrated Solutions	* Interactive Educational and Learning Device
* Potential for Home Use	* Expand into other Home Areas and Education	* Large Potential	* Large Rapid Growth Market	* Saturated Market	* Home Office Market
		* Possible entry to Corporate market	* Substitute for Word Processors	* Substitute for Mainframe and Minicomputer Solutions	* Home Environment
				* Client/Server Enterprise Environments	* Entertainment System Controller
					* Communications Device

Fig. 8.1. Changing perceptions of the personal computer during its evolution.

Small business and office applications for the microcomputer were not considered major growth markets at the time, although a number were sold with relatively basic word processing or accounting packages. Then in 1979, the first spreadsheet application program, Visicalc was launched for use on the Apple II. Sales of both products were enormous and as a result, microcomputers began to be viewed as more than simply games or basic educational machines. Instead the public perception began to shift towards recognition that personal computers could be used for serious purposes in the office environment. Given the expectation that the technology curve for microcomputers would continue to improve in terms of cost and performance ratios, it became increasingly evident that these machines would diffuse into a growing number of businesses and perhaps eventually into large corporations. At the time however, it must be remembered that this path of progression was by no means a foregone conclusion, for although companies such as Apple, Tandy, Commodore, Texas Instruments and others had already started efforts to gain acceptance in the large corporations, it was not until the early 1980s with the entry of IBM into the marketplace, that microcomputers began to be sold in significant numbers into large corporate accounts.

This event created a fundamental shift in the way that people viewed the personal computer as it was now called and represented its legitimisation. From now on, personal computers began to increasingly be considered as low-end office machines. They were still not quite as good as dedicated word processors, but they were more versatile and whilst they could not handle the scale of analysis possible through terminals linked to mini or mainframe computers, they could at least allow the individual to manipulate and analyse data at a local and personal level. They were stand-alone units, but much cheaper than larger computers, including small-systems computers[3] and so they began to sell in large numbers to small and medium sized businesses, as well as to individuals in large corporations. However, in Fig. 8.1 it can be seen that as far as the large computer manufacturers of mainframes and minicomputers were concerned, including those who had now entered the competition for personal computers, these machines were essentially stand-alone products and as such not terribly different to word processors or electronic typewriters. They were definitely not an integral part of the large corporation's management information systems. This was also a view shared by the majority of data processing and MIS managers. However, it was not a view that could be maintained for long.

Following from their earlier efforts, during the mid-1980s companies such as Apple with their Macintosh machines, together with third party hardware and software companies began to push the idea of connecting personal computers together, so that they could share data and communicate with larger machines. Naturally, the idea of establishing communications between computers was not new, after all, this is precisely what terminals did with larger mainframes and minicomputers, all of which could be linked to talk to each other. DEC's concept of distributed data processing[4] did the same thing centred around their minicomputers. However, the increased power of personal computers that emerged in the latter part of the 1980s meant that they could be used as file servers and handle fairly large amounts of data in an autonomous local area network, which could be connected to other networks or larger computer systems.

It was at this stage that the personal computer once again went through a further stage of metamorphosis. As more and more machines were linked together on networks, it was no longer viewed as simply a stand-alone machine, instead it became an increasingly important part of the management information system of large corporations. As such it presented a real threat to small-business systems and even minicomputer based systems. Furthermore, at the high-end of the range, personal computers were increasingly converging with technical workstations that could run commercial applications, so that by the early 1990s that threat became a reality, as personal computer and workstation based networked systems became a viable alternative solution to minicomputer and even some mainframe systems in large companies. In large corporations, this has taken the form of enterprise systems, based upon the concept of client/server[5] systems.

Thus in less than twenty years, personal computers have changed in terms of their concept from being a hobbyist's kit, to a home games machine, to a stand-alone low performance word processor and accounting machine to a machine capable of handling the information needs of a small business single handed, or capable of handling the information needs of a sizeable organisation by means of linking together a large number of personal computers, based upon a client/server network. How this process has taken place has of course been described in great detail throughout this book and will be summarised below. What is important to appreciate however, is that not only has the microcomputer changed in terms of a concept to today's modern personal computer, it has also dramatically effected the business world's perception of the role and function of larger computers. In so doing, it has created a fundamental change in the structure, not only of its own industry, but also that of the entire computer industry and has therefore been a major contributing factor to the creation of yet more newgames. These changes are of course based upon digital technology and the changing needs and expectations of a business community that treats the personal computer as a ubiquitous object. At the same time they are also driven by the fierce competition, not only between the personal computer hardware companies, but also by the interests of software and peripheral competitors in the industry.

The preceding chapters have told how these events came about in terms of the chronological pattern of developments in technology, competition, industry and market structure. The next section will proceed to look at the drivers for change outlined above by applying the newgame framework to track their contribution to the pattern of evolution of the personal computer industry and its markets.

DRIVERS OF NEWGAME EVOLUTION

The starting point of this summary of newgame evolution will begin by consideration of the structure of the industry on the supply side, by firstly reviewing the role that technology and its suppliers have played in the evolution of the personal computer industry. This will then be followed by a reminder of how the personal computer itself has evolved from a technological perspective as a result of the preceding patterns of supplier behaviour, which is then followed by a summary of the pattern of competition between the personal computer companies in terms of their strategic groups and value chains, both of which reflect their strategic positioning. An important part of the industry's evolution has also been played by the distribution channels and this will also be reviewed in terms of the structure and type of channels that have been created to serve the various markets. Finally, the pattern of market segmentation is reviewed, with attention upon how it reflects changes in customer demands and behaviour. Our starting point is with the core technologies that have helped shape the evolution of the industry and its markets.

The Nature and Impact of Technological Change

Technology has undoubtedly been one of the key drivers to the evolution of the personal computer newgame since its very beginning. Clearly, a number of technologies have been involved in the development of personal computers, which are most easily divided between hardware and software categories. The former includes, microprocessors, electronic and other components and the ever expanding range of peripherals, whilst the latter consists mainly of operating systems, utilities and applications programs.

Competition amongst Semiconductor Manufacturers and the Rise of Intel

An important relationship was shown to exist between the technologies just mentioned, however, throughout the evolution of the personal computer the core technology has remained the microprocessor. Whilst it is true that other technologies such as software, or issues such as marketing have become more significant forces of competition, the microprocessor still remains a prime mover of change in the personal computer industry. The evidence in this book shows that with each step change to a new generation of microprocessor, such as 8-bit to 8/16-bit to 16-bit to 32-bit, there was a knock-on effect throughout the industry in terms of the other technologies involved with personal computers. Thus each new generation of microprocessor has led to the creation of a new generation of personal computer, from which was created a new generation of peripheral products, together with new operating systems and applications programs. In addition to creating new models of personal computers, this pattern of step-change also provided the opportunity for new entrants to the industry, as in the case of IBM, or for established competitors to shift their position as with Apple and its development of the Mac.

If one looks at the competition in the microprocessor industry itself, an interesting pattern emerges. Initially Intel enjoyed a short monopoly as the supplier of the world's first microcomputer which was produced by MITS, however, within a few years this sector of the industry was inhabited by a number of competing companies including Motorola, Texas Instruments, Zilog and NEC. Indeed, for a while Zilog, with its Z-80 processor was the dominant player. Personal computer companies used this multiple supply in an effort to gain product differentiation, but by the late 1970s, with the exception of Apple and Commodore, the majority of companies had opted to use the Zilog, which became a de facto industry standard. Incremental changes to the microprocessor families were not frequent. Then in the early 1980s a major change occurred in this sector of the industry, which was brought about by IBM's decision to use a new family of Intel microprocessors.

Due to the subsequent success of the IBM personal computer, Intel sales increased dramatically. Furthermore, by the mid-1980s as the IBM machine became the new de facto industry standard, then other personal computer manufacturers joined Intel's customer base, since they would find it impossible otherwise to produce an IBM compatible system at an economical price. As a result of IBM's rapid gain in market share, the earlier 8-bit microprocessors rapidly became phased out of the market and Intel's only rival remained Motorola, whose major customer was Apple Computer, but who represented less than 10 per cent of the personal computer market. However, Motorola's size as a major semiconductor manufacturer outside the personal computer marketplace, together with the continued presence of the giants Texas Instruments and NEC, stimulated Intel to continue to innovate with new processor families. Quite apart from the possible risk of being "leap-frogged" by one of these competitors introducing a faster and more powerful processor, Intel was also keen to maintain a high rate of growth in sales of new processors for its customers in high-end personal computers, which opened up new markets and provided higher margin sales. Thus by the second half of the 1980s microprocessor life-cycles were getting significantly shorter. In the strong growth of the consolidation stage amongst corporate customers of personal computers, Intel found no shortage of manufacturers such as Compaq, who were willing to push ahead with newer and faster machines. This put pressure on IBM to respond and carried the IBM compatible competitors along with it.

Then in the late 1980s, with Intel dominating this sector of the industry, new forms of competition began to emerge. For whilst Intel had benefited from the IBM standard in the way described above, competitors from the workstation industry sector such as Sun, DEC and Hewlett Packard were developing faster processors for their machines using a different type of technology based on RISC, as opposed to Intel's and Motorola's more conventional CISC technology. Since high-end personal computers were increasingly in competition with workstations, Intel saw a threat. Furthermore, other low cost processors were now coming onto the market that were seen by some customers as offering better value than Intel's products. As a result, Intel dramatically increased its pace of new product development and in so doing forced down the price of older processors. It has also meant that personal computer manufacturers are under more pressure to introduce a wider and newer family of machines. Thus by 1993, the microprocessor still continues to drive new product development, but at a pace that is far faster and accelerating. Intel still dominates, but is under attack from RISC based technology and low cost manufacturers. Intel is fighting back, but with the loss of its major customer IBM for the next generation of computer, this may be a tough battle. But then again, as will be shown later, IBM's market power is no longer what it used to be and Intel's installed user-base is very large indeed and could not be seriously challenged in the short-term.

The Changing Importance of Software and the Rise to Power of Microsoft

Whilst microprocessor hardware could be regarded as the brain of the personal computer body, software should be perceived as equivalent to its mind. For without software, a personal computer has always and will always be useless. As with all computers, personal computers are dependent upon two types of software, namely operating systems and applications programs. Each new generation of microprocessor has created the opportunity for the development of improved types of software. Better operating systems software has made it easier for software developers to create more powerful and in more recent times, more "user-friendly" types of applications. This pattern of relationship between each new succeeding generation of microprocessors and software has then led to increased demand for the particular type of software application, which in many cases has been accompanied by a boost to sales of personal computers as in the case of the first spreadsheet program which ran initially only on Apple II machines. In some instances, new types of applications program have also led to the creation of new market segments as in the case of Desktop Publishing Programs.

In the early stages of the personal computer industry's evolution, software was very much a do-it-yourself product. Many hobbyists were experienced in computer programming and enjoyed the challenge of creating simple commands for their kit based machines. Although important for making the computer work, software per se was seen as a secondary issue. As personal computers began to develop their power further and changed from kit based to pre-assembled machines, various operating systems began to emerge as did some basic applications programs. Initially with a large number of small personal computer manufacturers in the market, their was no standardisation on systems. Whilst the personal computer hardware industry was highly fragmented and very underdeveloped, the software industry could be described as almost anarchic in its nature. Most software was written by individuals or small partnerships, which then made copies of the programs for sale through direct mail. Quality and performance was very varied. However, as personal computers began to be used for games in the home and on a limited scale in educational establishments and small businesses, then greater effort began to be placed upon software development. It was therefore at about this time that the early personal computer industry moved in a direction that was to dramatically depart from the traditional patterns which had taken place in the mainframe and minicomputer industries.

Instead of maintaining proprietary operating systems for their personal computers, manufacturers began to adopt the increasingly popular system of CP/M-80 from Digital Research, which eventually became established as the industry standard during the late 1970s and early 1980s. As a result of developing an industry standard operating system, both manufacturers and applications software developers were able to benefit. Developers benefited because they were able to market their products to a far larger market than would have been possible in a world full of different operating systems, which in turn brought down the price of applications software and hence further expanded the market for personal computers, since buyers were now faced with the emergence of a mass produced software industry. The lower prices also served the interests of the personal computer manufacturers, since it stimulated demand for their machines and at the same time reduced their costs of having to develop applications software in-house on a proprietary basis. This development probably represents one of the most significant structural and process changes in the industry and laid the basis for its evolution into a high volume marketplace.

These structural and process changes in the early stages of the personal computer industry's development, meant that a specific type of relationship was established between hardware and software technology and the companies that produced such products were to shape the future pattern of evolution. For the hardware manufacturers, it meant that those with a large installed base or the potential for developing such a base by the use of strong market power would be able to attract the most successful software developers, who naturally wanted to market their products to the largest possible audience. This was a virtuous circle. However, for those companies that chose to ignore the industry standard, without significant market power, there was little chance of establishing a strong market position, either for a hardware or software company.

Interestingly, IBM was one such company which had the market power to be able to choose to ignore the prevailing industry standard operating system in the personal computer market at the time of its entry. Using the strength of its brand name, IBM successfully shifted the dominant industry operating system standard from CP/M-80 towards MS-DOS, which was jointly developed for IBM with Microsoft. By the mid-1980s, compatibility with IBM systems had become the new industry standard. As a result, just as Intel which had supplied the microprocessor for IBM's machines had enjoyed rapid growth, so too did Microsoft. By the late 1980s both companies had capitalised on the fact that they had successfully marketed their products to the vast majority of personal computer manufacturers. Only Apple Computer had chosen to avoid the IBM standard and survived as a result of developing a proprietary and more advanced "user-friendly" type of operating system, again in association with Microsoft, in the form of its Macintosh family of personal computers. As the 1980s unfolded, Apple began to slowly gain market share, whilst IBM began to lose market share. This was due largely to the fact that the industry standard core technology of Intel microprocessors, associated components and Microsoft operating systems could all be easily obtained by any competitors. Thus providing one could combine the various elements at a lower cost than IBM, then there was a ready market for IBM clones or look-alikes. The IBM clones were in the market almost the day after IBM's entry, but most of these were merely making up the shortage of supply on early IBM machines. However, by the latter half of the 1980s the clones were marketed by companies whose products were frequently assembled at low cost in the Far East.

As at the time of its entry, once again technology was seen as the core to IBM's retaliation against the clones, in the form of its PS/2 hardware platform and the associated OS/2 operating system. In order to maintain an upgrade path for its users, IBM chose its established partners, Intel and Microsoft to help develop these products. However, neither technology nor market power proved sufficient in this instance to gain the type of success IBM had hoped for in its strategy. Instead, IBM found itself increasingly in conflict with Microsoft, who had proceeded to develop a Macintosh "look-alike" system called Windows, that would effectively emulate the Mac's more "user-friendly" system. Thus during the 1980s, Microsoft had moved from the position of a small four year old software development company, that through winning the IBM contract to develop MS/DOS, then moved on to dominate the industry in terms of its control or influence over operating systems in the shape of MS/DOS, PS/2 and Windows. During this time, Microsoft's king maker, IBM, far from creating a new industry standard, had helped lay the seeds for a new stage of industry evolution as far as technology standards were concerned.

Whilst Microsoft grew to become the leading supplier of operating systems in the industry, it also developed a strong position in the related but more competitive field of applications software. Initially, under CP/M-80, applications software had been fairly restricted in its scope, due largely to the limited power of the microprocessors available at the time. However, during the 1980s MS-DOS based upon higher performance processor platforms offered software developers the opportunity to create a new generation of applications. Thus the 1980s witnessed the introduction of integrated programs, such as Lotus 1,2,3, desktop publishing programs, more powerful word processing packages and a whole range of graphical, presentation and accounting applications, that in turn opened new markets and uses for personal computers. Costs of applications software development rose dramatically and the packaging of "shrink-wrapped" programs became a mass market business. Gradually, customers became more interested in the type of software application that they needed and less interested in the hardware platform, providing it was IBM compatible, unless of course they happened to be Macintosh users. Apple's Macintosh machines frequently led the field however, in terms of attracting the most significant advances in applications software such as desk-top publishing, due to their "user-friendly" graphical user based system.[6]

Thus by the late 1980s applications software began to dominate the personal computer industry and was supplied by a large number of developers, ranging from individuals to large companies such as Aldus, Lotus or Microsoft and even Apple Computer, when it decided to join this sector of the competition by establishment of its software company Claris. For Apple now found itself like IBM taking note of the fact that its earlier relationship with Microsoft would be worth less as the company sought to develop Windows and hence reduce Apple's unique technical differentiation. It was also aware that in the not too distant future, the higher margins along the value chain would increasingly come from software and not hardware activities. Thus between the mid-1980s and early 1990s, the software sector of the personal computer industry expanded both in terms of its size and power.

Changes in both the competitive conditions and power of two of the major supplier sectors of microprocessors and software can be seen to have been responsible for many aspects of the evolution of the personal computer industry and its markets. However, it should also be recognised that whilst not so directly relevant as a significant driver of change within the industry, third party suppliers of components for end-users, such as fax boards[7] and other expansion boards, together with the peripheral suppliers have played an increasingly important role in the industry's development. Indeed, much of the potential of personal computers can only be realised in specialised markets by their linkage to other types of equipment such as plotters, optical character recognition units, bar-code readers, scanners, CD players and many other types of peripheral. Sales of such units now outstrip sales of personal computers and provide a lucrative sector to companies such as Hewlett Packard with its dominance of the laser printer market or to third party manufacturers such as Seagate for its disk drives and literally hundreds of other small to medium sized companies that go to make up this important sector.

Overall therefore, the 1980s allowed a pattern of evolution to take place in an environment wherein the de facto IBM standard (based upon the Intel and Microsoft standards) provided a stable and consistent base for product development, whether by other personal computer companies, third party suppliers or software developers. By the early 1990s this position shows signs of falling apart. The industry is in a "sea-change" as various companies and consortia of companies compete for establishing new industry standards. The watchword has moved from IBM compatibility to "open systems", wherein all systems are intended to be compatible with one another, at least to the user. However, the reality is somewhat different and filled with political and competitive pressures, that ensure that no single system is likely to be adopted as a new industry standard, since this will mean a return to the type of dominance enjoyed by IBM during the 1980s. Competitors would much prefer that their unique solutions are adopted, but are not so keen to adopt other competitors' solutions. This confusion has now spread through microprocessors, operating systems, graphical interfaces, communications protocols[8] and shows no signs of improving. Where it might lead to is touched upon in the following chapter. For the moment, having seen how microprocessor and software technologies have impacted the pattern of evolution of the personal computer industry, it is time to move on to look more carefully at how the personal computer itself has evolved as a product during the period, before proceeding to review the strategic development of the competitors.

The Personal Computer — from Hobbyist Kit to Mainframe Substitute

At a basic level of hardware, personal computers have been shown to be largely a product of their microprocessor, associated electronic components and related packaging, whilst in order to function, they must also include operating systems and applications software. Clearly, improvements in microprocessor performance and associated peripherals together with software have been instrumental in developing the power, shape and size of the personal computer. However, it is also important to remember that it is the design of the personal computer itself in terms of its various configurations that has directly determined the shape of the industry and its markets.

Initially, personal computers existed only as kits that could be assembled into relatively unattractive desktop boxes and were hardly ergonomically attractive. Some units contained all the parts of the machine in a single box, including keyboard, monitor and central processing unit, whilst others manufactured these as separate units. Gradually, as the market evolved further and the personal computer began to be sold as consumer electronics goods, or for use in the office, more attention began to be paid to issues of design. However, its basic desktop design did not fundamentally alter nor show any major difference between various market segments. Then in 1981, Osborne's portable computer marked the beginning of a new type of configuration that was effectively representative of a type of product that would over time develop into an increasingly important market, namely that of portable machines. Gradually the heavy transportable type of unit, gave way to battery driven units that could operate on remote locations, but it was only by the late 1980s that portable machines began to appear that had the power, size and weight ratios that could make them attractive for serious remote location working.

As the 1980s progressed desktop personal computers began to expand increasingly beyond being viewed as single stand alone-units into integrated systems. In some cases this was through their linkage to other personal computers where one of the machines would be used as a file-server, whilst others would be linked to the server on a local area network. This increased power of the personal computer enhanced its role in corporate locations. However, the other change in personal computers involved their linkage to a wider range of peripheral products that went beyond the standard printer or external disc drive to include scanners, cameras, CD-ROMS and Tape Back-up units.[9] As a result, the personal computer itself increasingly became perceived less as a single unit product and more as the core unit of a complex system.

By the early 1990s as a result of advances in high-end machines, with Tower based units and their convergence with workstations, personal computers have therefore become significant parts of the large company's information systems, in what is commonly referred to as enterprise systems. At the portable end, personal computers have been subjected to increasing improvements in the miniaturisation of various component technologies that have meant smaller and lighter machines. Add to this, the developments in communications technology in the form of fax, modems and cellular communications,[10] together with pen based technology.[11] Furthermore, the personal computer has most recently begun to be packaged as a handheld variety of personal digital assistant, which offers enormous power to its end-users and the potential to be used in a multitude of applications, some of the implications of which are considered in the following chapter. As a result of these developments the personal computer is therefore now set to become a competitive product in a broadening set of markets ranging from the technical and scientific to the consumer electronics arenas.

Thus the personal computer has evolved from a basic electronic kit to be configured in a wide variety of formats, including, desktop stand-alones, desktop networks, servers, tower units, portables, laptops and handhelds, which are summarised in their basic formats in Fig. 8.2. Each format has reflected developments in the core technologies within the computer, but at the same time, the type of configuration has created or responded to market demands. However, product segmentation is just one of the ways in which the personal computer companies have developed their strategies, other strategies have been based upon functional, user, geographic and price segmentation, the patterns of which are reviewed in the following section.

Patterns of Strategic Behaviour, Strategic Groups and Value Chains

In reviewing the patterns of strategic behaviour amongst competitors in the personal computer industry, it is intended to pick out the different types of strategy that occurred and show how they changed the process of competition and hence the structure of the industry and its markets. Essentially, it can be shown that newgame strategies had the greatest impact on the industry and its markets, since they deliberately sought to change the rules of the game, whilst samegame strategies mainly focused upon positioning with the existing competition. In effect, the industry's evolution can be viewed as a series of newgame strategies that created

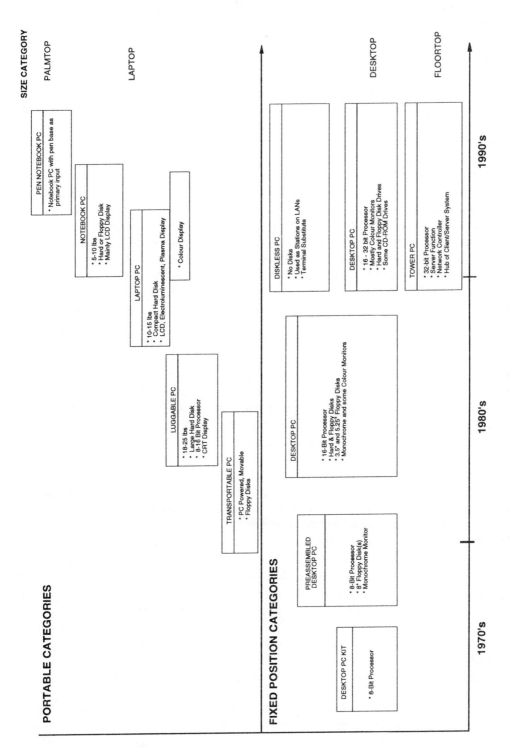

Fig. 8.2. The evolution of personal computer products.

new ways of competing, that where successful, led to expansion of existing or the creation of new market segments. Where a newgame was successful, it appeared that other competitors tried to imitate the newgame strategy and hence developed value chains that were similar, although not identical to that of the initial newgame player. As a result, strategic groups, reflecting the different value chain structures evolved over time. What is important to note, is that each successful newgame strategy led to the creation of a new strategic group. This can be shown by looking at the pattern of newgame strategies that emerged, considering the basis of their value chains and seeing how other companies copied their newgame strategy.

Overall, a number of newgame strategies emerged during the various stages of evolution of the personal computer newgame environment. Some of these were pursued by new entrants, whilst others were pursued by incumbents to the industry as illustrated in Fig. 8.3. The first newgame strategy was pursued by MITS, which had a very basic strategy and value chain. As was shown in an earlier chapter, it was quickly copied by a number of other entrepreneurial hobbyists who wanted to cash-in on the embryonic market that MITS had uncovered. What is important to note, is that the MITS strategy was totally unrelated in terms of technology, marketing or organisation to any of the established large companies in the core mainframe and minicomputer industry, who were in turn totally uninterested in this market segment. This initial move by MITS and other small competitors shown in Fig. 8.3 highlights the impact of the various newgame strategies on the structural evolution of the personal computer industry and its markets during 1975 to 1993. Together these early entrants effectively created a single strategic group. R&D was almost non-existent, production was very basic and distribution was initially via direct mail. Gradually as the market grew, a simple distribution channel in the form of technically oriented dealers started to become established. Although still relatively small, the MITS newgame strategy had the effect of creating the "Catalyst Stage" of the industry and led it into the "Embryonic Stage" which opened up the development of the hobbyist market.

However, MITS and most of its rivals were insufficiently well organised to face the competition of the next group of entrants. In particular, the competitive value chain created by Tandy Radio Shack and Commodore. Tandy led the field with a newgame strategy based upon its experience and resources in distribution and merchandising of electronic hobbyists kits and equipment, whilst Commodore led in Western Europe with its office products outlets. But in addition to their distribution skills, both companies, together subsequently with Apple Computer started to sell pre-assembled machines, which were attractive to both software developers and some small businesses and professionals. In effect, Tandy, Commodore and Apple changed the rules of the game once more. Tandy and Commodore quickly took the market lead in their respective major markets, whilst many of the members of the original strategic group surrounding MITS, tried to compete along the same lines as these new entrants or went out of business if they stayed in the hobbyist kit market. The industry now

	EMBRYONIC	TAKE-OFF	GROWTH	ENTRY OF THE GIANTS AND LEGITIMISATION	CONSOLIDATION	MATURATION AND SATURATION
SIGNIFICANT PLAYERS	- MITS - IMSAI - Other small start-up ventures	- Tandy Radio Shack - Commodore - Apple Computer - Other small start-up ventures	- Apple Computer - Tandy Radio Shack - Texas Instruments - Commodore - Other small companies - Xerox, H-P	- IBM - Apple Computer - Tandy Radio Shack - Osborne - Compaq - Commodore	- IBM - Apple Computer - Compaq - Zenith - Tandy Radio Shack - GRID - Amstrad - Epson - Packard Bell - Dell	- IBM - Apple Computer - Compaq - Dell - Toshiba - Packard Bell - NEC - Everex - Tandy/GRID - Gateway 2000 - Epson - Vobis - Olivetti - Fujitsu/ICL/Nokia - Bull/Zenith - AST/Tandy/GRID
INDUSTRY AND MARKET CHANGES	△ MITS launches the Altair microcomputer kit, thus creating the basis of the market. △ Other companies are created to enhance and develop the micro-kit. △ IMSAI a start-up company gains market share from MITS based upon its better quality and service support. △ The industry is fragmented with a large number of small scale start-ups competing on a range of incremental improvements. △ The market is simple and unsegmented, consisting largely of hobbyists who are interested in building and improving the hardware kits or developing simple software programmes. △ Marketing Promotion is small scale in the hobbyist press. △ Distribution is largely through Direct Mail with a limited number of technically orientated dealers.	△ Tandy, Commodore and Apple start to offer their machines as assembled units. △ All three companies start to gain market share as the quality and performance of their machines surpasses those of the incumbents. △ The Apple II machine gains popularity amongst software developers who now start to create games software programmes. △ The hobby and games programmes lead to development of a home market segment. △ Tandy's US chain of electronic kit and equipment stores expand the scale of distribution and further broaden access to the market, thus encouraging start-up dealers to support equipment from the other manufacturers. △ Tandy's merchandising skills lead to a higher standard of promotional and selling activity, geared mainly to the home market.	△ Apple takes over as the industry leader, whilst T.I. enters the market. Xerox makes a failed entry. △ Due to support from software developers and its short-term monopoly on the 1st spreadsheet programme (Visicalc). Apple takes over as market leader. △ Apple's success with Visicalc opens up the small business market as a new segment, attracting TRS, Commodore and others to follow. △ CP/M-80 becomes the standard industry operating system. △ The education market begins to take-off, as interactive programmes are created for this segment. △ The home market expands as TRS, Apple, T.I. and others improve the quality and levels of investment in mass merchandising. △ The hobby segment declines in importance in relative terms.	△ IBM creates a new industry standard around its PC platform and PC-DOS operating environment, thus displacing the previous CP/M-80. △ Demand for IBM PCs is so far ahead of supply, that a number of IBM clones are established by small start-up companies. △ IBM's major marketing promotion activities raises the scale of investment in these activities for major competitors such as Apple, TRS and others. △ IBM legitimises the PC in the corporate business environment and encourages further competition in this segment. △ Osborne creates a low cost bundled transportable machine, thus further stimulating demand for PCs in the small business and professional market segments.	△ Compaq creates a strong price/performance competitor for IBM and gain from the IBM standard. △ IBM fails to respond effectively to Compaq's transportable and fails with its low priced PC Junior. △ Apple launch the Lisa as a precursor to its Macintosh family. Whilst Lisa fails to attract support in the corporate market, the lower priced Macs gain rapid acceptance in vertical markets requiring high quality graphics and an easy user interface. △ The investment bubble for new PC hardware companies bursts as 1983 records small start-up failures. △ Low priced IBM compatibles, such as Amstrad and Far Eastern companies start to take market share from IBM. △ IBM market share declines and leads to its launch of a new family of machines for the corporate market with the PS/2 and OS2 family in order to create a new protected standard. △ GRID's portable becomes a major product in the high end market. △ Zenith Data Systems become a major player in the government sector. △ Corporate customers begin to adopt PC networks as a major part of their information systems.	△ Globalisation becomes the newgame for the industry. △ Global competitive pressures force an increase in the number of strategic alliances in technology and marketing agreements. △ The industry celebrates 10 years since the IBM PC launch and views the 1990's as a period of sea change. △ Mergers and acquisitions start to develop across the three global regions and between hardware and software companies. △ A "Downsizing" and the global recession restructure the overall computer industry. △ Industry standards become more fragmented as product/market boundaries become less clear between various user segments. △ A Discussion about "open-systems" creates ideas of further strategic alliances and consortia like EISA. △ A Top-end Corporate PCs begin to converge with technical workstations creating "client/server" systems. △ Price Wars force new business models upon PC competitors. Losses or lower profits become the norm for most competitors in the PC hardware business.
STAGE OF NEWGAME	EMBRYONIC	TAKE-OFF	GROWTH	ENTRY OF THE GIANTS AND LEGITIMISATION	CONSOLIDATION	MATURATION AND SATURATION
	1975 1976		1979	1981	1983	1988 1993

Fig. 8.3. The impact of newgame strategies on the structural evolution of the personal computer industry and its business markets: 1975 - 1993.

formed three strategic groups, those of the old group around MITS, those like Tandy and Commodore with their own distribution outlets or those that relied on dealers, like Apple, but nevertheless actively sold their products as pre-assembled units to a wider market than just hobbyists. One such company was Atari, which successfully capitalised on what was becoming the rapidly growing home/games market. Although a number of other companies entered the industry after Tandy, Commodore and Apple, most of them tended to pursue a samegame type of strategy. In other words, they copied the value chain of the established competitors and tried to compete on cost or differentiation along the value chain, but nothing significant enough to change the industry or market structure. Both Texas Instruments and Hewlett Packard were among such entrants, but for reasons already explained in earlier chapters, neither managed to offer a newgame strategy. Thus the industry was led out of the "Embryonic Stage" into the "Take-Off" and "Growth Stages" by the newgame strategies of Tandy, Commodore and Apple. During this latter period, Tandy's market leadership, began to give way to Apple, which offered a technically more flexible type of machine to both developers and users. Furthermore, Apple gained significantly from the fact that the launch of the first spreadsheet program Visicalc, was only available on their machine, which gave them half a year's clear monopoly on the most popular program, that was aimed squarely at development of the business market.

Nevertheless, Apple's lead was to be short-lived, for six years after the promotion of the first microcomputer from MITS, IBM led the "Entry of the Giants" and moved the industry onto the "Legitimisation Stage" of development. It is important to remember however, that IBM was not the first of the large established computer or office automation companies to enter the industry. Hewlett Packard's entry had been low key in 1979 but was not a newgame strategy, any more than were the strategies of Texas Instruments or Zenith. More interesting was the newgame strategy pursued by Xerox Corporation, which for reasons explained in this book, failed to gain success in the marketplace, largely due to problems of implementation.

Like all newgame strategies, IBM's entry strategy was not only new for the industry, but involved an entirely novel approach for the company itself in terms of being a complete departure from its traditional practices. In comparison to the existing incumbents, IBM's strategy reflected a major reconfiguration of both the focus and scale of asset structures employed in the process of competition. On the technological and product levels, IBM achieved improvements in price/performance through the adoption of a more powerful microprocessor, but avoided significantly higher costs by adopting a hybrid 8–16 bit unit. Costs of production were kept low by means of highly automated, large volume production and high standards of quality control. It thus shifted the cost of capital barrier upwards and achieved a position as a low-cost manufacturer. In addition, the company invested heavily in advertising and public relations activities, gaining a distinct competitive edge over incumbents, by spending more in these areas during the first twelve months after entry than the total industry competition had done since 1975. For its distribution strategy, IBM instituted a set of "IBM Standards" upon its dealers and made use of its direct sales force to develop the corporate market segment. It was also the first company which had the resources, infrastructure and effective implementation to enter the market across the entire range of business segments. In contrast to Xerox, the execution of its entry strategy was virtually flawless.

As a result, IBM was able to dramatically alter the process of competition and so change the structure of the industry and its markets. In terms of strategic groups, a number of other large established office automation companies in the United States and Western Europe such as DEC, Wang and Olivetti entered the market by trying to copy the IBM newgame strategy. Unlike the earlier established personal computer players, such as Apple, Tandy, Commodore and others, these new entrants made use of their direct sales force to focus upon corporate clients. They also invested heavily in advertising and promotional activities. This set of moves acted as a kind of pre-emptive strike against the potential encroachment by the smaller personal computer companies into the larger computer companies' domain. Although, at the time, relatively few would have been willing to argue that personal computers would one day become a serious threat to their traditional core businesses. In an effort to gain a significant foothold in the corporate market, companies like Apple and Tandy soon responded by trying to establish national accounts programmes, however, with limited success. Thus IBM's entry legitimised the personal computer in the corporate marketplace and stimulated demand in both medium and small sized businesses. As a result, many competitors began to either focus upon a specific market segment outside of the business environment such as technical, education or home use, or else they chose to go after one or both of the business markets, made up of corporates or the medium and small business sector. In so doing competitors developed value chains to try and best fit their business focus.

One such company, was Osborne Computer. Unlike many of the smaller company entrants who pursued samegame strategies based upon the value chains of companies such as Apple Computer, Osborne started its own newgame strategy. Using state of the art technology, but packaged in a novel manner as a portable machine, the company differentiated itself from other competitors in a distinctive manner in terms of price (costing 25% less than any competing units), and in the bundling together of hardware and software. Although described as setting the trend towards the creation of a portable computer market, many of its sales were to desktop users and unlike many other low cost machines for the games and educational markets, Osborne attacked the core of the business market. In addition, although many did not buy the machine for its portability, it nevertheless led to the creation of this significant and major new market segment, by stimulating a large number of subsequent entrants such as Compaq, Tandy, Hewlett Packard and Grid, who focused on this "niche" market. Sadly for Osborne, although it was quickly established as a market leader of this segment, its success was to be short lived due to internal management and marketing problems.

In their different ways, the newgame strategies of IBM and Osborne therefore created new ways of competing, new value chains, new market segments and a new set of competitors and strategic groups. Initially, the success of IBM meant that as shown in the previous section, a new industry standard emerged around hardware and software based upon the notion of IBM compatibility. IBM appeared to dominate every market of the industry, including education, technical and scientific as well as business. Observers began to fear that IBM's historical dominance of the mainframe industry would be repeated in the personal computer industry, since companies such as Apple were mere dwarfs in terms of resources when compared with IBM. Equally well, other larger companies such as DEC, HP and Xerox seemed unable to make a serious challenge to Big Blue. However, IBM had an Achilles' heel in this industry, which ironically had been a fact that had initially contributed to its success. By developing an "open architecture" approach as opposed to its traditional proprietary approach, IBM had made itself vulnerable to the clones.

Hence following the "Entry of the Giants and Legitimisation Stage" of the personal computer industry the "Consolidation Stage" reflected a number of significant changes in the process of competition. Foremost of which was the newgame strategy pursued by the clones, who based their competitive advantage on IBM's system, but produced and marketed it at a much lower price, such as Packard Bell or Dell or at a higher standard of performance, such as Compaq. The net result of these aggressive strategies was the business market exploded in the period of the mid- to late 1980s as customers increasingly recognised the value of buying from suppliers other than IBM, and gaining either a better or a cheaper machine and sometimes both. The traditional brand value of IBM was therefore in decline, at least in many companies, especially those that had no IBM mainframe. Now the industry was beginning to move into a much more complex structure, as IBM and strong competitors such as Compaq and Olivetti continued to market products with high margins, whilst other clones developed the low-end of the market. At the same time, the portable market was beginning to gain in size as technology improved sufficiently to make the product better value for money and unlike in desktops, this segment was ruled by Toshiba and not IBM. Alongside the IBM environment, Apple Computer was gaining market share as businesses began to take its Macintosh products more seriously. Although not creating a different value chain, Apple's Macintosh strategy could be viewed as a newgame, since it fundamentally departed from the industry and market norms for how a computer should work in relation to the end-user. Whilst slow at first to recognise the benefits, businesses began to recognise the unique value of working with such a system and hence the company began to dominate "niche" segments of the business market, such as desk-top publishing and other graphically based activities. At the same time, the increasing power in high-end personal computers meant that they were in competition with technical workstations, whose manufacturers showed increasing interest in the commercial markets. Hence, a strategic group consisting of workstation manufacturers joined the overall framework of competitors in the domain of the personal computer. The increasing number of strategic groups reflected the growing complexity of the industry and the variety of strategies being pursued.

In order to try and stop the decline in its market position, IBM launched its PS/2 system. In a way this was a newgame strategy, since IBM once again wished to change the rules of the game and create a demand for its new machines that would regain it market share. However, the market did not respond for reasons explained in the last section and in effect, IBM merely contributed to a further shift in industry conditions. But unlike in the "Legitimisation Stage", this time, with the development of the "Consolidation Stage", IBM was no longer in control and indeed, IBM simply had become one of a number of players who were to determine the new shape of the industry and its markets. At the same time, the late 1980s witnessed an increasing number of U.S. based companies focusing their attention upon development of their overseas markets, especially in Western Europe, since this offered higher growth rates than the home market, at least for a while. As a result, a number of competitors began to move towards development of multinational types of organisation structure. As the European market grew in size and importance, so the personal computer companies began to establish a greater variety of strategies. Some continued to view overseas markets as mere extensions of their home market activities, whilst others found themselves at various stages of development between international, multinational and in a few cases global organisation structures. What was happening in the United States market in terms of competitive performance was not always the same as in Western Europe, Japan or other parts of the world. Hence competitors began to develop a much richer range of strategies to try and cope with the various geographical and product market differences. One pattern concerning strategies and value chains that stands out during the late 1980s and early 1990s for virtually all the major competitors is the increasing scale of resources being invested further down the value chain. This not only included aspects of advertising and promotion designed to strengthen and develop product and corporate images or support of distribution channels, it also involved direct investment in after sales service and support. In a few cases, it has also either involved establishment of a software company, such as Apple with Claris, or it was taken in the form of investment in a third party company.

Thus in terms of strategic groups and value chains, the industry now took the form of an increasingly complex and at times volatile type of structure, set against the "Maturation and Saturation Stage", which itself was coloured by an increasing worldwide recession. International dimensions now played a larger role, competition was split between a greater number of product sectors, ranging from workstations, to desktops to portables. Indeed whilst the desktop personal computer sector was saturated, portables were seen as a growth business and hence attracted a large number of competitors. Technical standards no longer revolved simply around IBM and at the low-end of the business, personal computer hardware was becoming much more commodity-like in nature. As a result, the industry became subject to increasing price wars and declining profit margins. Thus by 1993, many competitors were facing substantial losses in their personal computer businesses. However, the significance of these events for the industry can only really be understood if one first of all remembers how these various changes affected the patterns of development in the market. Firstly, by considering how they were connected to the market, via its distribution channels and then secondly, by looking at how the market structure in terms of segmentation and customer behaviour evolved.

Channel Development — Strategies, Structure and Conflict

When considering the pattern of evolution in distribution, it is clear that the structure of the channels serving the personal computer market have become increasingly varied, more complex and in some respects more important as the industry has evolved. Initially, in the "Catalyst Stage" personal computer companies tended to use direct mail as their main form of distribution, not because this was more economical, but simply for the reason that no other channels existed at the time. As the industry moved into its "Embryonic Stage", it still had a kind of amateur club culture about it, in that many of the new start-up companies had been founded by individuals who were drawn from the hobbyist market itself. Similarly, the first dealers to emerge were mainly set-up by people who either had experience in selling other types of electronics kit and equipment, or who had a technical interest in microcomputers. Thus a large number of small dealers sprang up to begin selling the products of the various early entrants to the industry. MITS even went so far as to establish a franchise operation, but this was never very successful. In essence, the early dealers were therefore mainly interested in selling technical products to technically oriented buyers and users.

This pattern changed when Tandy and Commodore entered the market. Both companies were experienced retailers and wanted to expand their businesses beyond the classical hobbyist market. With its extensive chain of stores throughout the United States, Tandy was able to quickly gain a competitive advantage over the established competitors by selling its personal computers to a broader market on a more commercial and professional basis. Tandy's impact on the industry was largely to stimulate other dealers to improve their standard of service and move from offering a mainly technical to a more commercial approach to their businesses. Towards the end of the "Growth Stage" Tandy's advantage had been significantly eroded as other independent dealers began to match their standards of merchandising. Indeed, as the small business market expanded, Tandy found its traditional Tandy Stores inadequate for this new market and had to develop a new set of outlets geared to this segment and as such, the company was no better established than other independent dealers that had already started to develop outlets more suitable for the small business market. These new outlets employed better trained sales representatives who were more familiar with the business needs of small companies and offered a more professional standard of technical service, support and training facilities. Furthermore, as a greater number of competitors were now competing for shelf space, dealers began to become more selective in whose products they would be willing to sell and promote. Hence, manufacturers began to take more notice of issues relating to margins and cooperative advertising. For some dealers, the opportunity began to arise to expand their operations by acquisition of weaker dealers, thus some of the first dealer chains began to take shape and as a result, a shift started to take place in terms of negotiating power between manufacturers and the larger chains.

Then in 1981, with the entry of IBM, dealerships went through a revolutionary change. Prior to IBM, no personal computer manufacturer had been able to have such power over the channel. In the case of Tandy, its impact on dealers had been indirect. True, it owned its own stores, but over time, as the number of independent dealers grew, its share of the total channel became much smaller. Tandy merely set an example for others to follow. Similarly, Apple Computer was reliant entirely on its dealers for access to the market, but although it became market leader in 1980, its market power was still somewhat limited, since dealers were also willing to carry competitors products that could sell just as well. With IBM all this changed. Its enormous brand power in the corporate business marketplace meant that the early IBM personal computers sold themselves. Dealers were therefore desperate to carry IBM products. In this situation, IBM found it easy to set the standards it required from anyone wishing to become an IBM channel. As a result, IBM determined that personal computer dealers were to reflect the professional IBM corporate image, whether a dealer was selling into a large, medium or small sized business. As explained earlier, the IBM image consisted of more elaborate merchandising, better trained sales representatives, larger capital base, improved training facilities and properly trained technical staff. In their scramble to satisfy these requirements, a vast number of dealers significantly improved their operations and those that did not, tended to find themselves left with products from second tier manufacturers. Another attraction of the IBM product was that it was able to command high margins in the market, which were also enjoyed by its dealers, so that those who sold high volumes, soon found themselves growing stronger than the smaller or non-IBM dealers, which then became take-over targets for the larger dealers. This process of cannibalisation led to an expansion of the major dealer chains, such as Computerland and Computer World.

As the "Consolidation Stage" began to develop, dealer channels found themselves faced with the problem of choosing whether to support IBM alone, or whether to sell other products from clones or alternatively from Apple Computer. Those that chose Apple, found themselves frequently moving towards exclusive Apple sales, whilst IBM dealers, tried to balance their sales between IBM and clone products. However, whatever range of manufacturers they supported, by the late 1980s dealers found the nature of their business beginning to change. This occurred for two separate reasons, both of which involved the changing nature of the personal computer. Traditionally, dealers had been involved in selling personal computers as boxes, with associated peripherals and software. Increasingly from the mid-1980s onwards they had become active in aspects of training and customer after sales service, such as technical repairs or upgrades. But by the late 1980s for reasons that were explained earlier, the more powerful types of personal computers increasingly needed to be linked to other computers on some type of local or company wide network within medium to large organisations. Installation of such systems required a much greater knowledge of computer and network technology than was held by the majority of personal computer dealers and such work was the traditional territory of systems integrators who had developed their skills largely around minicomputer systems. Thus many dealers felt that in order to remain in the business market, they would need to change into systems integrators, which would be a costly and time consuming business. Others merely ignored or failed to recognise the threat, being content to enjoy their more immediate profits and assuming that they would be able to survive by serving small business customers who had less sophisticated requirements. However, the second reason why dealers found their business changing was caused by the increasing pressure upon their margins, which was itself caused by major changes in the strategic groups of competitors described in the previous section.

By 1990, the business market was sending clear signals that it was no longer prepared to pay the high prices associated with products from brand leaders such as IBM, Compaq, Hewlett Packard and even Apple Computer. Instead, they were quite willing to shop from companies offering lower priced clones such as Dell, Packard Bell, Amstrad and Vobis. Thus began the price wars that have pushed prices of personal computers in a downward spiral as explained in the last two chapters. Unlike the established manufacturers, the low priced clones were sold through low cost channels, such as superstores and direct mail. Traditional dealers were faced with falling margins from their established suppliers and at the same time were being undercut by the low cost clone distribution. In such circumstances, they have been forced to either start branding their own products or to move into higher value added services such as systems integration or maintenance services. Those unwilling or unable to make the move have found life becoming increasingly difficult, particularly in the recessionary conditions of the 1990s.

In such an environment, distribution channels have therefore become a vexed issue for many of the established manufacturers and as such, an ever more important force in determining the shape and size of the overall personal computer industry. This is because efficient distribution can ensure optimal growth in the size of the market and hence the industry, whereas inefficient distribution merely curtails the pace of growth. Gone are the comfortable days, when the only concern was to choose a dealer in the right location to carry and sell one's products. In their place, are a complex range of channels, whose level of service and economics reflect their appropriateness for different types of market segment. However, channels are mainly independent from the manufacturers and their prime source of competition and hence concern is from other types of channel — a fact often forgotten by a number of the personal computer companies. Given the complex range of products and systems now being marketed by the manufacturers, it is hardly surprising that there is considerable confusion and in some cases apprehension as to how distribution channels are likely to develop in the future. A great deal is at stake in the answer to this question, both for the manufacturers who need to decide on an efficient yet compatible set of channels for their various types of products and for the different channels, whose future is not only a question of what products to sell and support, but also, what type of channel should they become in order to survive. The answer to this question is not simple. Indeed it merely becomes more complex as one considers not only the pressures created from the manufacturers and other channels, but also the increasing complexity of the marketplace itself. Thus this is the topic to which we next turn.

Markets — Patterns of Customer Segmentation and Behaviour

In addition to developments in technology and competitor's strategies, customer behaviour probably ranks as one of the most important drivers to change in the evolution of any newgame environment and this is certainly true of personal computers. However, the relative power of customers has changed quite significantly over time and not just in one direction. Like competitors' strategies, customer behaviour is a process, whose results can be seen in terms of the market structure, the most obvious of which can be measured by the pattern of segmentation. Over time, the personal computer marketplace has evolved from a single unsegmented market to one which nowadays can be segmented into a multitude of categories, including geographical areas, product types, industry sectors, purchasing patterns, applications and user groups to name but a few. Broadly speaking, the preceding chapters have shown that the market for personal computers moved through some distinctive changes at each stage of the industry's evolution. In other words, since nearly every successive stage of the newgame environment was largely stimulated by a newgame strategy, it follows that the newgame strategy also created a change in market structure, which itself reflected a shift in existing conditions or the creation of new patterns of customer behaviour.

At the earliest stages of the market, it was shown that the market was unsegmented and consisted largely of hobbyists, whose knowledge of the technicalities of the basic microcomputer was generally high, as was their influence over manufacturers through their user groups. Customers were almost like members of a club. Furthermore, buyers were also the users and hence there was no separation between the two roles and if users were not happy with a product, they would either buy a competitor's product or were most likely go out and set up a company to manufacture the missing or faulty element of the machine. However, this easy going culture soon gave way to a more commercial environment and was further changed by the newgame strategies of Tandy, Commodore, Apple and others as they shifted towards pre-assembled units and away from kits. As a result of these strategies, customers began to favour the newer companies over the initial entrants such as MITS and IMSAI, who were soon out of business, hence changing the strategic group make-up of the industry. The extensive distribution channels of Tandy further attracted customers and as the microcomputer increased in performance it was soon being sold to enthusiasts outside the hobbyist marketplace. These were people who were less interested in knowing how the computer worked and more interested in discovering what the computer could actually do for them. As market segments they represented the home, education and small business. As customers, at one end they included children and adults wanting to use the computer to run games in the home and so complement the then current craze in video games arcades. Others saw the computer as more of a tool, that could help in basic business tasks such as word processing or accounting. This latter type of customer needed a machine that was simple to use and could provide value for money. Initially, neither were particularly forthcoming. However, competitors recognised that if they were to tap what could be an enormous demand for personal computers in the home and small business market, they would have to improve their products, whilst dealers would have to improve their service.

IBM's newgame entry strategy once again changed the pattern of customer behaviour and market structure. By legitimising the personal computer within the corporate business environment, IBM increased the segmentation of the market to include large corporations and endorsed the expansion of the small to medium sized business market segments. However, corporate customers also represented a different type of behaviour, both in terms of purchasing patterns and user requirements. Initially, buyers and users were the same people, but gradually, as personal computers became a more integral and important part of the corporations' information systems, then the purchasing function became more centralised. This shift in customer profiles created changes in the industry's structure of sales and distribution. Another feature during the "Legitimisation and Consolidation Stages" that affected the structure of the market was the fact that an increasing number of products began to be developed for the market by each of the major competitors. No longer did each company market only one or two products; instead, they began to develop a whole range of products reflecting differences in performance and price. Initially these were aimed at the major market segments of the home, education, technical and scientific or business. However, by the late 1980s they were increasingly targeted at specific types of user, which could be defined more in terms of how much power was required from a machine and what price they were willing to pay. For example, high-end machines would be required by large corporations such as financial institutions for their trading officers, whilst less powerful machines could be used for secretarial staff, with mainly word processing requirements. Similarly, portable computers, whether briefcase size or laptop could be aimed at specific types of customer with a need for various degrees of portability, performance and price levels. At the same time, the increasing international and multinational nature of the marketplace meant that major companies were faced with markets in the Far East that generally had a much lower percentage of newer types of machine say compared to the United States or Western Europe.

During this period in the second half of the 1980s competition from the clones created a situation where a number of customers decided to abandon IBM as their preferred source of supply in the corporate segment or to never use it, as in the case of a number of small to medium sized companies. IBM's retaliatory move with its PS/2 system, gambled on attracting back customers from the clones. However, in this instance, customers chose to maintain their freedom. In so doing, they reflected a profound change in the attitudes and behaviour of a large share of the market, which IBM and subsequently other high margin competitors such as Compaq, Olivetti and Hewlett Packard were somewhat slow to recognise. The change was that for medium to low-end products, established brand products could no longer expect to command the premium price margins of the past, nor the same levels of previous customer loyalty. Instead, for customers purchasing these type of machines, the issue was mainly one of price and value for money. Companies such as IBM could still command a premium, but this would have to be much smaller and based increasingly on concrete added value, such as after sales service and support. Such has been the power of the customers in these segments of the market, that IBM, Compaq, Apple Computer, Hewlett Packard, DEC, Olivetti and others have been forced to radically revise their product pricing strategies during the early 1990s. Now their financial models have to be increasingly based upon low margin, high volume business. However, for many, their high overhead costs and bureaucratic organisational structures and cultures has meant a period of savage cost cutting and staff reduction exercises, which in mid-1993 are still far from over. Thus the market structure and patterns of behaviour amongst different buyer and user groups served by the personal computer industry now presents a highly complex web of customer profiles.

Hence, although hardware and increasingly software technology can be seen to drive the industry forward in terms of its product development, it is also important to recognise the power and driving force of customer demand. Indeed, increased competition from the clones during the 1980s offered customers both greater freedom and choice of products which had the effect of shifting power away from the established market leader, namely IBM. As competition then became even more intense, in an effort to maintain or gain market share in an increasingly saturated and recessionary market, customers found themselves with even more power, since they were able to encourage greater discounting and price reductions. For this reason, it was argued in chapter six that competitors' strategies were forced away from simply reliance upon technological differentiation and competition, towards greater emphasis upon marketing activities. In many respects this interplay between technological developments and customer demand is a circular or symbiotic form of relationship, with neither party really holding the upper hand on a permanent basis. On some occasions a new technology or new way of packaging the technology has come into the market that then clearly released latent demand, such as in the case of IBM's original personal computer, Osborne's portable, Toshiba's laptop or Apple's more recent Powerbook. Equally, on other occasions a number of new products have done little to stimulate demand, including Apple's Lisa or IBM's famous PC Junior. The important lesson for personal computer companies to realise is that they cannot assume that just because it works, looks good and feels right, that a new product will create demand. Equally, it would be wrong to assume that a new product cannot create demand. It just depends on whether the product is 'right' for the market at the time. 'Right' meaning able to satisfy customers' demands, better than any competitors' products and/or services, which of course included the criteria of affordability.

Converging Industries and Markets

Before considering some conclusions to these various patterns of development amongst the major drivers of change in the evolution of the personal computer newgame environment, it is also important to add one last set of observations concerning its process of technological evolution, competition and buyer behaviour and their joint impacts on the structure of the industry and its markets. This concerns the impact that the personal computer has had upon the mainframe and minicomputer industry. As was shown in the last chapter, the increasing technological performance of high-end personal computers and their convergence with workstations to create personal workstations linked on a client/server network has meant that the role and value of larger computers is frequently under question in large corporations. In effect therefore, the changing concept of the personal computer and personal computing has meant that manufacturers of these products often find themselves, not just in competition with other personal computer or workstation companies, but also with companies selling mainframe or minicomputer solutions. Whereas ten years ago, such a situation would have appeared impossible, nowadays, a growing number of customers are deciding to choose the personal computer/workstation solution. In terms of the analytical framework, what this represents therefore is the first signs of confirmation that the personal computer newgame is beginning to diminish the power and performance of the companies or business units of companies active in the mainframe and minicomputer industries, which are now moving into an endgame situation.

Evidence provided in this book shows quite clearly, that already the process of "downsizing" computer systems in large organisations is gathering pace, on a worldwide basis. At the same time, as these events have been occurring in the overall computer industry, personal computers at the low-end of the desktop sector and special technology based personal computers such as portables and pen based systems[12] have found themselves drawn into yet another industry sector and market, namely that of consumer electronics. Both these sets of developments carry significant implications for the future of the personal computer industry and its markets. For this reason, any discussion which seeks to understand the potential pattern of change in the near future must be based upon a scenario that looks at a combined structure of the mainframe, minicomputer, workstation, personal computer and consumer electronics industry sectors, since it is within this much larger environment that the personal computer newgame now plays out its further stages of development. This will form the basis of the next chapter, which looks forward to the next five years. However, before proceeding to consider possible future scenarios, the remainder of this chapter firstly offers some reflections about the above patterns of the various drivers and their impact upon the evolution of the personal computer newgame environment.

REFLECTIONS ABOUT THE PATTERNS OF EVOLUTION

In summary, as one looks back at the story of the evolution of the newgame environment for the personal computer industry, so far it appears to have gone through seven distinctive stages of evolution, namely:
(1) catalyst stage;
(2) embryonic stage;
(3) take-off stage;
(4) growth stage;
(5) entry of the giants and legitimisation stage;
(6) consolidation stage;
(7) maturation and saturation stage.
Throughout each stage of this process of evolution developments have taken place in the conditions of competition that have manifested themselves through the following major drivers for change, namely:
(1) Evolution in Hardware and Software Technology;
(2) Competitive Strategies between Suppliers, especially:
 — Semiconductor Manufacturers
 — Software Developers
 — Third Party Peripheral Companies.
(3) Competitive Strategies between Personal Computer Companies;
(4) Competitive Strategies of Mainframe, Mini and Workstation Competitors;
(5) Competitive Strategies of Various Types of Distribution Channel;
(6) Behaviour of Customers both as Purchasers and Buyers.

As a result of the interaction and relationships between these drivers, fundamental changes have taken place in the structure of the personal computer industry and its markets. Over the different stages of the evolutionary process of the newgame, these factors have played varying degrees of importance. However, what seems to present a consistent pattern is the fact that the industry and its market structure has been moved at practically each stage of its evolution by some form of newgame strategy, that has changed the rules of the game and the concept of the personal computer or personal computing. Not every newgame strategy has worked, but then this may not have been a fault of the strategy, but more a problem of its implementation and that is a central issue of management in any environment. At one level the process by which these strategies feed through to the markets for personal computers was seen to be highly complex. However, within the various competitive processes the above review of the key drivers for change has highlighted the way in which technological progress has been a major driving force to development of the industry and its markets. Table 8.1 provides some of the key examples of how developments in product technology were used as a basis for newgame strategies, which in turn created changes in the pattern of evolution in the newgame environment.

The impact of technological change appears to have come in a variety of forms both from hardware and software. At the most significant level it is evident that a clear pattern of development exists in relation to the introduction of a new family of microprocessor, as this leads to new products, new types of operating system and applications programs. The new applications in turn have been seen to open up new market segments. These types of step-change have often been accompanied by new product developments that have been the basis of a newgame strategy, such as with MITS, IBM and Apple. However, it must also be appreciated that technological change in other electronic components, such as the miniaturisation or improvement of screen technology, has allowed companies such as Toshiba to pursue newgame strategies by creating compact laptop computers. Similarly, changing the existing technology to one's advantage, as with Osborne or the clones has created major changes in competitors' value chains. Thus, newgame strategies have not simply been based upon major technological innovations, but have also included clever reconfiguration of resources to fit a particular market need or to alter the concept of the personal computer.

Altering the concept of the personal computer has of course been a major feature of the evolutionary process. It was shown how this occurred as the machine changed from a kit, to an assembled unit, to a product that has eventually rivalled the much larger mini and mainframe computers, as can be seen in Fig. 8.4. As well as illustrating the product segmentation amongst the different types of computer that had developed by the early 1990s, Fig. 8.4 also highlights the stage of development of the different types of product in terms of whether they are newgame, samegame or endgame environments. Naturally, this is a subjective assessment and how

Table 8.1. Newgame strategies and their characteristics at various stages of the United States personal computer industry and market evolution: 1975 - 1992.

Stage of Evolution	Name of Company and Product	Type of Company (1)	Conceptual Change (2)	Focus of Change in Value Chain
Catalyst/Embryonic	MITS Altair	Small, single related business	Basic creation of the idea of a micro-computer for the individual	Creation of a basic chain Technical Design
Embryonic/Take-Off	Tandy TRS 1 Commodore PET	Medium, electrical goods and office products merchandising chains niche consumer mass market	Professional expansion of the market by development of mass merchandising	Distribution/Selling
Embryonic/Take-Off	Apple Apple II	Small, start-up	Easy to use (preassembled) personal computer; good for developers	Technical Design Promotion Image
Entry of Giants	IBM IBM PC	Large Corporation, Computer Industry leader	Professional expansion and legitimisation of the PC into the corporate market	Technical Design, through entire chain
Legitimisation	Osborne Osborne I	Small, start-up	Bundled marketing of hardware and software for niche business segment and a transportable unit	Marketing and Pricing
Consolidation	Toshiba Portable	Large corporation, vertically integrated electronics, industrial and consumer	True portability of the personal computer with global niche focused marketing	Technical Design Promotion Image
Consolidation	Compaq Portable	Small, start-up	An IBM compatible high quality/ portable machine	Perceived technical superiority and value over industry leader
Consolidation	IBM Clones	Large, Medium-sized and start-ups	Adopted the Intel microprocessor and MS-DOS enabling a lower cost copy of IBM machines, substitute	Production Pricing
Consolidation	IBM PS/2	Large Corporation PC industry leader	Attempt to re-align the business market behind a new industry standard, offering better performance	Technical R & D Marketing
Consolidation	Apple MAC	Established PC Company	Windows based integrated user friendly system. Easy to learn and good graphics capabilities	Technical R & D Marketing Service Support
Maturation/ Saturation	Dell Packard Bell Vobis	Start-ups, Distributors	Very low cost IBM clones. PC as a commodity type product, with easy access and low cost distribution	Production Assembly Marketing Pricing Distribution
Saturation	Atari Portfolio	Established PC Company Electronic Games Company	Light-weight, compact pen input palmtop machines for easy input and mobility	Technical R & D Marketing

KEY:
(1) Type of Company: refers to the nature of the company at the time of its commencement of the newgame strategy.
(2) Conceptual Change: refers to the basis of the new concept and hence basis of differentiation created by the newgame strategy.

this pattern was arrived at is discussed shortly. What Fig. 8.4 most strongly illustrates is how personal computers and workstations have now evolved into desktop supercomputers,[13] whose power to price ratio clearly offers a competitive alternative to minicomputers, just as mini-supercomputers[14] make a feasible alternative to some mainframe systems. Again the basis of these changes come from technology, but they also reflect knowledge and imagination on the part of designers who have reconfigured the technology in different ways to create products ranging from high-end servers,[15] to conventional desktops for the office or the home, down to laptop and now palmtop computers.[16] With each new configuration, the personal computer has moved into new market areas. Similar results have of course come from the ingenuity of software developers who have come to play an increasingly major part in the evolution of the industry and its markets. Applications programs now represent a major driver for change, since they essentially can define and create the range of possible uses for a personal computer with a given stage of technological development. As new types of software are developed, they naturally open up the opportunity for the peripheral suppliers, that in turn enhance the facilities of the personal computer with new and constantly improving products.

However, new products are not enough to develop the market. There is another important element in the development of technology driving the personal computer industry, whether it be in microprocessors, electronic components, the personal computer itself or its software and peripherals. This is the fact that not only has the performance of the technology constantly improved, but it has also continually been dropping in price. As a result, the personal computer has managed to penetrate an ever widening number of markets, especially in the business segment. To support this market development, new types of distribution channels have emerged, some of which have either offered better value than older types of channel,

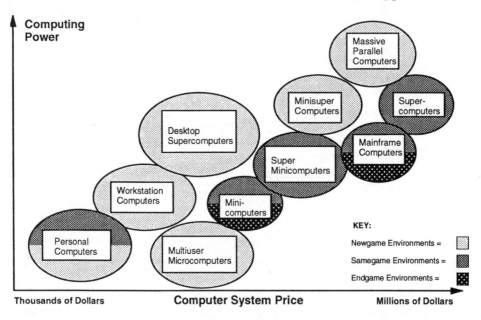

Based upon The Computer Industry Almanac 1992, published by Computer Industry Almanac Inc, p.9, 1992 and adapted to include the types of Competitive Environment by the author. Reproduced by permission of Computer Industry Almanac Inc., © 1992.

Fig. 8.4. Product segmentation in the computer industry during the early 1990s.

either through higher standards of service in areas such as training, systems integration and maintenance support, or as in the case of the mass market channels, through faster, cheaper and more reliable forms of distribution.

The resulting impact of these developments upon the structure of the industry is that it is now highly complex with a variety of competitors ranging from the older established computer companies such as IBM, DEC, NEC, Bull and Olivetti, through to the most successful personal computer start-ups which entered the industry during the earlier stages of its evolution and includes Apple, Compaq and Commodore, to the highly successful latter day clones such as Dell, Packard Bell, Vobis and their Far Eastern competitors such as Samsung, Goldstar and Hyundai, or global market niche players such as Toshiba. Sourcing of products takes place on a global basis, with many of the components available as commodity items. At the low-end of personal computers, the product itself is increasingly treated as a commodity, where local branding appears more powerful than global branding. In higher end markets, brand name is still of value, but no longer able to command high price differentials. Hence competition is intense as established competitors seek to maintain market share against the attacks of workstations at the high-end of the market, or from low price clones at the bottom end of the market. To make matters worse, the major market regions of the United States, Western Europe, Japan and selected areas in the Rest of the World are in recessionary or sluggish economies. Furthermore, the United States and West European business markets are now increasingly saturated. Thus competitors must seek to maintain or gain market share in a very slowly growing overall market, where much of the business is made up of replacement sales. This has forced competitors to seek new markets by entering the portable segment in its various forms of laptop and palmtop products.

Falling prices, decreasing margins, increased competition and slowly growing markets add up to falling profits or even losses. Yet the industry needs strong profits in order to invest in new technology. Thus competitors have found themselves cutting costs, reducing staff and reconfiguring their operations in an effort to establish more efficient types of structure. However, even with such improvements in operational efficiency, the industry still appears to be experiencing other major competitive pressures such as shorter product life-cycles, which in turn create a need to ensure shorter product development cycles and hence leave a shorter time to market. All of these factors are symptoms of the saturation stage of the newgame evolution and an underlying innovative and highly competitive industry and marketplace, which are summarised in diagrammatic form within Fig. 8.5. Where it might lead to is the topic of the next chapter.

However, it is also important to note that the saturation of the desktop personal computer industry and its markets does not mean that the industry is in decline or decay. Quite simply, for the desktop sector of personal computers, the present stage of evolution is merely reflecting a change from a newgame environment towards a samegame environment. Newgame strategies can be created in samegame or even endgame environments and

PRODUCT- TECHNOLOGY	ORGANISATIONAL	MARKET RELATED
- INCREASED PACE OF INNOVATION	- RIGHTSIZING	- INCREASING COMPETITION
- INCREASED SCALE OF R & D	- FLATTER STRUCTURE	- LIMITED HIGH END SEGMENT
- SHORTER PRODUCT LIFE CYCLE	- NETWORKING	- SATURATED DESKTOP SEGMENT
- SHORTER TIME TO MARKET	- BUREAUCRATISATION	- STRONG GROWTH NOTEBOOK SEGMENT
- INDUSTRY STANDARDS	- ALLIANCE AND JOINT VENTURES	
- PROPRIETARY SYSTEMS	- FEDERATED VERSUS INTEGRATED	- EMERGING PALMTOP AND PEN INPUT SEGMENTS
- OPEN SYSTEMS	- VERTICAL INTEGRATION	- DECLINING MARGINS
- PRODUCT MINIATURISATION	- HORIZONTAL INTEGRATION	- "DOWNSIZING" PHENOMENON
- PRODUCT RANGE	- UNDERSTANDING MARKETING	- NETWORKING DEMANDS
- PRODUCT INTEGRATION	- REDUCING OVERHEADS	- GREATER INTEGRATION
- PRODUCT COMPATIBILITY	- REDUCING COSTS	- UPGRADE PATHS
- SOFTWARE DOMINATION	- REDUCING HEADCOUNTS	- LOW-END COMMODITY BUYING
	- GREATER MARKET FOCUS	- CHANGING CHANNEL MIX
	- CHOOSING CHANNELS	- GEOGRAPHICAL VARIATIONS
	- IMPROVING SERVICE	- CULTURAL VARIATIONS

Fig. 8.5. Challenges and issues in the personal computer industry of the 1990s.

hence give rise to other newgame environments. In reaching this stage of evolution, the personal computer industry has also set in train the dawn of the endgame for the mainframe and minicomputer sectors of the overall computer industry. Thus as illustrated in Fig 8.6 the newgame of desktop personal computers began a sequential entry path into the domain of low-end minicomputers during the mid-1980s, whilst a newgame in luggable and early portable personal computers was beginning to become established as a separate sector or strategic group of competitors in the personal computer industry. Referring to Fig. 8.7, by the early 1990s, driven by the technology and patterns of market evolution, the growing pressure towards "downsizing" in large corporations meant that the mainframe sector, which had originally been attacked by high-end super minicomputers[17] (as shown earlier in Fig. 8.4) was now moving into a highly concentrated endgame environment with few competitors. At the same time, a newgame environment was developing at the high-end of mainframes, with the emerging development of massive parallel computers.[18] For the mainstream minicomputer environment things had moved from strong growth to one of rapid decline due to the sequential entry of powerful desktop supercomputers and workstations, which was forcing the core of the minicomputer industry rapidly towards an endgame environment. Meanwhile, the core desktop personal computer environment was moving from its final saturation stage of the newgame environment into the beginning of a samegame environment. However, whilst this was true of mid- to low-end desktop personal computers, it was not true of notebook computers, which were enjoying the rapid growth-stage of their newgame evolution. Whereas the early portables of the mid-1980s could only create a limited market due to their performance limitations, the new generation of notebook machines with high performance features and increasing communications capabilities could eventually represent a threat to even the desktop sector of the industry. Finally, competitors in the emerging palmtop sector of the industry, found themselves facing the embryonic stages of a newgame environment, which was likely to bring them into competition with new competitors from the consumer electronics industries.

Overall therefore, the personal computer industry and its markets now finds itself at the centre of major structural changes representing transitions not only in its own environment, but also in the computer industry as a whole. The situation is incredibly complex and reflects the penultimate stage of the current newgame for personal computers. However, further newgames may well emerge and already, in addition to laptop or notebook computers, new technology is taking competitors firmly into new industries and market areas. In high-end and portable machines this involves a vast range of technology for the development of more user-friendly systems, making use of multimedia techniques[19] and advanced communications. The future therefore holds the prospect of yet more newgames, that far from making the computer industry a mature and low growth environment, will add new sectors to the industry that will push the frontiers of the computer, in whatever form it takes, into new technologies and new markets. Where the industry may be heading over the more immediate future of the next five years thus forms the basis of the next chapter.

Clearly, all of these changes have created a complex pattern of competition. However, it is also important to remember that the picture is made somewhat more complex by the fact that it takes place against

MARKET SEGMENTS	SAMEGAME ENVIRONMENTS	SAMEGAME ENVIRONMENTS	NEWGAME ENVIRONMENTS	NEWGAME ENVIRONMENTS
CORPORATE	* SUPERCOMPUTERS * MAINFRAME COMPUTERS	* SUPER MINICOMPUTERS * MINICOMPUTERS	Sequential Entry Path * WORKSTATION COMPUTERS * DESKTOP PERSONAL COMPUTERS	
* TECHNICAL * PROFESSIONAL * SMALL BUSINESS				* LUGGABLE COMPUTERS * PORTABLE COMPUTERS

Fig. 8.6. Evolutionary patterns in the computer industry during the mid-1980s.

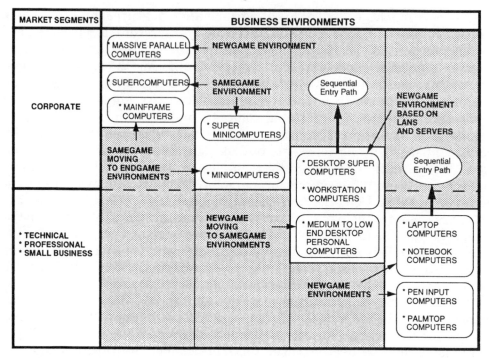

Fig. 8.7. Restructuring of the computer industry during the early 1990s.

an international environment. What the last chapter showed was that a major driver for change in the personal computer industry and its markets has been international competition and that this has followed a distinct pattern of development. Initially, in the early stages of the industry's evolution, the United States was both the dominant location of competitors and the major market. International markets in Western Europe and the Asia/Pacific Rim were treated as export markets. Gradually, both regions developed their own indigenous industries and a varied set of government policies emerged towards their domestic companies. For example in Western Europe, a liberal policy led to the situation where U.S. based companies such as IBM, Apple and Compaq gained market dominance, whilst in Japan, protectionist measures meant that even in 1992, the vast majority of suppliers are Japanese, although in 1993, U.S. competitors show signs of starting to gain market share. Other Asia/Pacific markets reflected a mix of liberal and protectionist policies, thus influencing the competitive situation that has emerged in the overall region.

During the 1980s the major competitors that emerged in the United States, Western Europe and Japan began to give more attention to the development of markets in the other regions. What emerged was a pattern of overseas market development that reflected three major types of organisational response. The first involved companies that were already established global scale computer, peripheral or electronics companies, that had diversified into personal computer operations, examples included IBM, Seiko-Epson or Toshiba. Secondly, there were dedicated personal computer companies that were evolving through a fairly conventional pattern of internationalisation, whilst lastly, there existed a few companies that had moved from international operations towards some form of global concern, such as Apple and Compaq. As a result of competition between these various types of company, the United States ceased to so clearly dominate the worldwide market towards the end of the decade, as the faster pace of growth in Western Europe, Japan and the remaining countries in the Asia/ Pacific region meant that its relative importance went into decline.

In effect, the personal computer industry has therefore evolved from being geographically fragmented into one in which there is multinational competition. However, it would not be fair to describe it as being global competition in the classical sense of the word. Certainly, certain elements of the industry are global in nature, for example the supply of microprocessors and electronic components. Indeed, the generic nature of the personal computer hardware has meant that excluding certain minor technical features, a machine sold in Taiwan can just as easily be sold in Paris or San Francisco, so here too there exists a global product. Yet to be a global industry it was pointed out earlier that there must be open competition in all regions of the world. This has not yet happened, although it is certainly moving rapidly in this direction and already a number of the major personal computer companies have now established or are in the process of establishing global supply chains.

When one looks at the market for personal computers, then what may appear global from a distance turns out to be very local in nature on closer inspection. To begin with the stage of product market development is quite varied, so that the United States market is virtually saturated with a low use of older technology, whilst somewhere like Thailand is still growing rapidly and making use of older technology. These patterns are due largely to the fact that outside the United States and Canada, there exist a vast range of different cultures that are set in very different types of economy. Hence, even in Western Europe, it was shown that there exist significant differences in aspects of customer behaviour, distribution channels and general social and political attitudes. Such differences are even more apparent when looking around the countries in the Asia/Pacific region. Although it is easy to regionalise the market into three major blocks, in reality, the worldwide personal computer market is much more complex. Furthermore, although the market for personal computer hardware may be treated as moving towards a global commodity type of environment, however, software is definitely not yet in this category. Indeed localisation of software applications is a major competitive issue in many markets.

In conclusion, the personal computer industry and its markets have clearly gone through a great many changes during the 1980s in terms of their international nature. The pattern that emerges is one of an industry whose major competitors' are increasingly multinational in the organisation of their resources, although at the same time, in Western Europe and the Asia/Pacific Rim many of the competitors remain distinctly regional in the scope of their geographical activities. Few competitors have a significant worldwide market spread across all three regions. As for the markets, they still maintain a high degree of regional or even local character in terms of structure and customer behaviour. This is not to deny similarities, but at the same time, any company wishing to advance its global ambitions will need to pay careful attention to the local market conditions if it is to succeed. In addition, the convergence of the various digital industries mentioned elsewhere, means that not only are competitors now faced with developing strategies for a complex international marketplace for personal computers alone, but they are also faced with the need to develop strategies to compete effectively in a number of other related industries and markets, some of which are multinational in nature, whilst some are already global.

CONCLUSIONS ABOUT NEWGAMES

In talking about the development of the newgame evolution of personal computers, this book has tried to present a framework that captures not only the changes in structure or content of technology, industries and markets, but has also recognised the fact that all these changes are created by specific drivers for change. Each of these drivers has made some contribution to the pattern of evolution and although technology may appear as the most important force for change, it must also be remembered that just as the markets could not evolve without customers willing to buy the products, so too products would never arrive at the market without the ideas and strategies of people within the competing companies.

Thus in drawing a set of conclusions to this chapter, which in itself has summarised the main events described in this book, it seems appropriate to focus attention upon what insights can be gained from the patterns that have been observed that would be of benefit to managers within the industry, who are responsible for making decisions about their respective company's strategies. This seems particularly appropriate, since in conducting the original research for this book, it was precisely these sorts of people who were kind enough to assist in the research process by sharing their views and strategic outlooks. Quite clearly, there are many strategic lessons that could be drawn from the story of the personal computer industry, but the most important seem to revolve around two key areas, namely, understanding the competitive environment and secondly the implementation of strategies.

On the first issue, it is apparent that for all the success stories, a number of companies, including some of those that have a high success record, have failed to fully appreciate the directions of change in the industry or its markets sufficiently quickly. Such understanding is needed at two levels. At a macro level, senior managers need to be more informed about the dynamics of a newgame environment. There is still a strong tendency to retreat into the comfort of looking at strong sales figures as a barometer for their company's health. But in a newgame environment this can be disastrous as competitive conditions can change very rapidly.

The increasingly complex interplay of technology, supplier, competitor and distributor strategies, together with the unpredictable behaviour of buyers and users mean that competition needs to be based upon a sophisticated understanding of the overall business environment, in order to identify potential trends. Clearly, with such complexity and volatility in the marketplace, it can sometimes appear foolhardy to try and develop models or predictions of the future. However, effective understanding of the competitive environment does not just mean simply accumulating vast amounts of statistical data. Ironically, as leaders in promoting the use of information technology, many computer companies are the most ineffective users of their own creation. In the kind of environment surrounding the industry today, not only do companies require to develop new types of organisation structure, but they also need to create new types of organisational systems. One of the most important of these systems is their information systems. But instead of basing these upon somewhat mechanical models of the environment, they need to rethink the basic principles of how they manage the whole process of information flows in the organisation. Solving these problems would also put them in a better position to sell their systems to corporate customers. At a micro level, research needs to be more sophisticated at the level of the product market. As competitors find themselves in an increasingly large number of different product market segments, geographical regions and with different types of customer groups, it is becoming imperative that they develop more sophisticated methods of market research. However, in addition to better market research in the field, they also need to think carefully about how that information is used within the organisation in terms of new product development. Here again, new ways of organising their business processes become of prime importance, especially in the management of complex product portfolios under the pressures of shorter product life-cycles and faster time to market. This emphasis does not mean to suggest that technology is not important. On the contrary, the lesson is that technology is important, but more important is the way that it is used. Products, production and information handling all represent aspects of technology in the company's value chain. However, people whether as employees, distributors or customers also play a large part in the process. Marrying the two effectively is the key to success.

Even assuming a company has a good understanding of today's competitive environment, the lessons of the evolution of the newgame environment, confirm ideas from many other industry and market studies, one of the most important of which is that a strategy is only as good as its implementation. During the development of the personal computer newgame it was apparent that a number of companies failed, not because they had the wrong strategy, but because they failed to implement it effectively. Two of the key reasons for this were firstly, lack of resources and secondly, lack of commitment by top management, the latter sometimes being the cause of the former (although not always). Senior executives as decision makers are of course dependent upon information that they are provided with by management lower down the organisation. This goes back to the previous issue about market research. If local managers in a particular country or responsible for a particular product market, fail to fully understand the competitive environment, then they will give poor advice to their bosses or whoever is responsible for making the resource allocation and funding decisions in the company. The net result of which will be insufficient resources.

Part of the implementation of strategy is of course linked to the issue of time. Here managers have to also remember that commitment of resources always takes place within a particular time frame. At a macro level, strategic decisions about business development necessitate the long-term view, but at the same time, at the micro level management is faced with shortening time horizons. Once again companies need to make increasing use of their information resources to manage these issues. Long term changes can be identified for companies willing to make the effort. Clearly, the demise of the traditional mainframe and minicomputer companies was not something that should have taken people by surprise, since it was forewarned in a number of circles.[20] However, the stumbling block for many managers has been their difficulty with changing their attitudes or their view of the world. This again points to the need for companies in the industry to appreciate the importance of ensuring that their management and staff are aware of new ideas and their implications to their business. However, it also points to the importance of developing new ways of helping management and staff to learn how to change, and having learnt, to then remember the experience for future occasions.

These then would appear to be the most important lessons for management resulting from this study of the evolution of the personal computer newgame environment.

(1) To recognise the importance of understanding the dynamics of the competitive environment;

(2) To make use of information technology in new ways to ensure that management at all levels is aware of market conditions and constantly alert to customer needs;

(3) To ensure that sufficient resources are available for effective implementation of strategy and within a useful time horizon;

(4) To look for new ways of helping management and staff and hence the organisation to learn to cope with change.

Naturally, it could be argued that these recommendations are appropriate for many businesses in today's world. Indeed, this is entirely true and underlines an important fact which is as follows. In 1975, when the first microcomputers were being assembled, the world was still in a relatively early stage of its transition into the information technology revolution. Now, in the 1990s that revolution is well under way and digital technology as the common element of the information age has diffused into a vast range of different businesses. With this diffusion has come change and with change, new ways of running various businesses. The result is that a large number of industries, both in product and service businesses have begun to experience similar changes in their industry and market structures as described in this book. In effect, the information revolution based upon digital technology has released a vast process of economic and social change, within which newgame environments are being created at an increasing rate. Personal computers happen to have been one of the most powerful manifestations of this change, but they are not unique in this respect. Furthermore, management within the personal computer industry must also recognise that behind every newgame, there is the possibility of another newgame. Successfully identifying and managing the transition to the next newgame from their core businesses in personal computers will most probably be the most important and challenging task facing any manager in the computer industry during the 1990s. What some of those newgames may involve is not the task of this book to reveal. However, the way in which some of today's drivers for change may effect the next five years of the personal computer industry and its markets does provide the basis of the final chapter which is appropriately entitled "Towards the Future".

Chapter Nine

TOWARDS THE FUTURE

"Time present and time past Are both perhaps present in time future
And time future contained in time past."[1]

INTRODUCTION

As one reflects on the patterns of change that have taken place in
the personal computer industry and its markets as described throughout
this book, it is with some caution that this last chapter looks forward
over the next five years. What appears to be happening is a process of
metamorphosis, that involves a variety of industries and not just personal
computers. Any discussion therefore about the future, must embrace
consideration of these other industries.

As far as desktop personal computers are concerned it would appear
that this industry is now nearing completion of its newgame evolution
and commencing a transition into a samegame environment. Mainframe
and minicomputers arrived at this situation many years ago as their
markets became saturated and revenues became increasingly dependent
upon replacement sales. However, unlike these industries before it, as was
shown in the last chapter, the personal computer industry has developed
a very different set of competitive conditions to these predecessors. As a
result, future developments are far less certain.

What does seem certain is the fact that the personal computer industry
is now very much party to an even bigger newgame than the one which
it has played out in the overall computer industry during the past fifteen
odd years. However, this other newgame is less product/industry specific,
since it involves, not only the entire computer industry, but also the
telecommunications and consumer electronics industries, plus a few more.
In effect, we are therefore entering a period of Schumpeter's "creative
destruction", but on a grand scale. In terms of technology, personal

computers will just be one of the parts in this performance, however, in terms of competition, a number of personal computer companies, both hardware and software will be central to the emerging battles. To understand therefore, what might happen during the next five years in the personal computer industry and its markets, it is first of all necessary to take a look at a much larger picture, namely that of the convergence and clash of the major information based industries.

THE CONVERGENCE OF THE INFORMATION BASED INDUSTRIES

Nobody today has any idea what the future of these industries will definitely look like tomorrow. Tomorrow being at the beginning of the 21st Century, which is less than ten years away. However, the framework of the newgame environment employed to look at the personal computer industry can be gainfully used to at least speculate on some of the major structural and process changes that could happen some time in the next five years or a little beyond.

To begin with it is clear that certain drivers will be at work in the process of evolution. One of the most important of which will be digital based technology. Already, a large number of industries in addition to computing are actively involved in developing or using products of this nature. Two of the largest and most relevant to this situation include telecommunications and consumer electronics. However, as illustrated in Fig. 9.1, a number of other important and large industries are also involved, these include the communications services of which broadcasting plays a major part, together with the publishing, printing, photographic and film industries, as well as the entertainments industry. The reason that all these industries are relevant to this newgame is the fact that none of them owns all the technology necessary to command or shape the development of the future information technology industry. In a way, this process has been evolving for some time. It was first apparent in the late 1970s, when it was predicted that an enormous office automation industry would emerge from the convergence of the computer, telecommunications and office products industries. This did not actually happen in quite the way forecast and certainly, not with the same predicted winners and losers. However, something similar has now evolved, albeit through a somewhat different process, one incidentally that was left out of the original scenario, namely the rise of the personal computer. Now, as has been shown, competitors in the computer and telecommunications industries find themselves in areas of mutual interest, namely, how to transmit large amounts of information rapidly along communications lines. Yet increasingly, the solutions to such problems are not only one of hardware but also one of software. Unlike in the 1970s when proprietary computer systems meant that software was owned by the hardware manufacturers, the evolution of personal computers has ensured that information software[2] has become a separate industry in its own right. However, what hardware and software

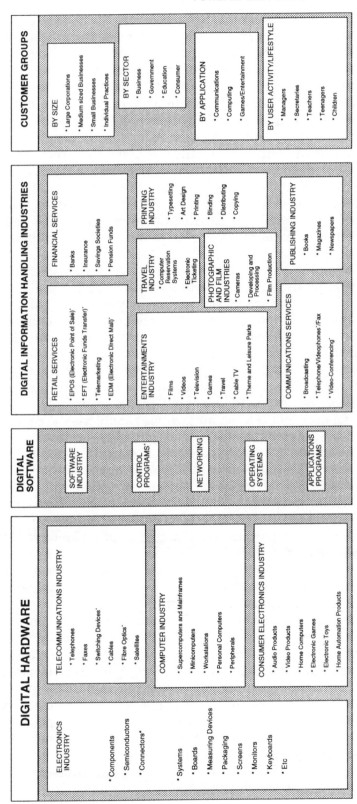

Fig. 9.1. The convergence of interests between digital based technology industries during the 1990s.

Notes: * See glossary where asterisk symbol appears after names for respective technical terms.

still share in common is their ability in different ways to handle digital based information. This has enormous implications for all the information based industries. During the latter part of the 1970s and 1980s computers and telecommunications led the field in the application of digital based technology to their information and communication products. However, during the latter 1980s other industries began to explore or shift to digital technology. For example, in the photographic industry, Kodak has launched a CD-based system for storage and transmission of still photos to a television screen. This will of course be further enhanced by the arrival of HDTV.[3] Digital technology has also been central to many products in the consumer electronics industry, but in the main, different types of video and audio equipment have been highly specific in their functions, such as radio, Hi-Fi, stereos, television, VCR, CD-ROM or computer games, with relatively little cross communication or transfer of data between different types of products.

What interests competitors in all these industries is the prospect that in the fairly near future, many of the different forms of audio and video technologies will be able to interact and hence cease to be seen by consumers and companies alike as being independent and unconnected products. For many would be competitors, capturing the high ground in this digital information technology environment is their major goal for the 1990s. However, the convergence does not just involve the manufacturers of the hardware. Already, software dominates the computer and telecommunications industries, but software itself can be incredibly varied in its format. In the computer and telecommunications industries it consists of computer code, but from another perspective it provides the intelligence and ability for a piece of hardware to perform a specific task. In the photographic industry, digital based software already drives the hardware of many cameras. Soon digital code[4] will form the software that will replace traditional film. Meanwhile, in the film, music or broadcasting industries, input into the design of the look and feel of visual and audio software plays an increasingly important part in the production of a final product. Hence this could explain one of the motives for Sony's long term interests in investing in Hollywood. Thus for competitors in all these present day industries, their future scenarios involve the convergence of a number of major industries, namely, computers, telecommunications, consumer electronics, broadcasting, publishing, music, film and the entertainments industry, as illustrated in Fig. 9.1.

What role each company might play is never certain, however, lessons of the past from the computer industry, would suggest that no single company can possibly command these heights alone and that software will play a greater part than hardware, although of course both will be essential. Furthermore, since this will represent the world's largest newgame, the risks and the rewards are both enormous. For this reason, the next five years are likely to see an increasing number of competitors from all of these industries creating various forms of alliance with competitors in other industries. Some of these alliances will involve joint development of new technologies, others will allow sharing of existing technologies and in some cases there will be licensing of production.

Apart from the activities of the competitors providing the technology, other forces will help shape this future. In particular, the suppliers of the core technology, namely microprocessors and other electronic components, together with software producers. In addition, such an expansion of activity between these different industries is going to revolutionise the patterns of distribution, both in terms of the type of channels and the processes involved, many of which will make increasing use of information technology. Last, but by no means least, customers, both buyers and users of these future products will of course have a major impact upon how the various industries and their markets develop. Given all these types of activity, industry boundaries will increasingly overlap and in some cases maybe even disappear, as newgames create new businesses that are still in their infancy or even not thought of at the present. However, what is clear about any newgame environment, particularly one on this scale is the fact that as these events develop, a number of the existing industries will go through enormous upheaval and that a significant number of today's leading competitors in their respective industries may not lead tomorrow, indeed they may not even exist. For success tomorrow is likely to be more dependent upon where a company is going, than where it has already been.

ENDGAMES, SAMEGAMES AND NEWGAMES IN THE COMPUTER INDUSTRY

Set against the above background, it is now possible to better understand the reasoning behind the description of some of the events that could take place in the personal computer industry during the next five years, as described below.

As previously discussed, during the past few years the computer industry itself has been going through enormous structural change. Clearly this process involves the direct effect of the personal computer and subsequent workstation newgames. Even in 1993, it is unlikely that the process will come to a halt in the next few years. The transition is a long-term and ongoing event, which will partly be driven by the impact of the convergence between different industries described above and partly by forces within the computer industry itself. It is this latter category that we will focus on first of all.

Within the computer industry overall, it appears likely that the traditional hardware manufacturers from mainframe to portable will have to continue to come to terms with a number of issues that will force ongoing changes in their organisations. These include technology drivers, strategies of suppliers, competitors and distributors together with the behaviour of customers. At a broad level, mainframe and minicomputers are expected to continue to experience declining sales and lower margins as corporate customers switch over to solutions based upon networks of personal computers, workstations and client servers. Looking specifically at personal computers, as was shown earlier, the core technology of the microprocessor is expected to continue increasing in power and reducing in cost, so that by the late 1990s desktop personal computers will surpass the performance of today's supercomputers.[5] At the same time, developments in disk storage technology are likely to provide significant increases in capacity and storage speed, offering standard systems with gigabytes of memory, together with the greater use of new peripheral products such as CD-ROMs for multimedia storage,[6] all of which will be at decreasing prices. All of these kinds of development will reflect major battles in different areas of the industry, the most important of which are illustrated in Fig. 9.2 and which are discussed below.

The Battle for Microprocessors

Domination of microprocessors will provide one of the key battlegrounds of the personal computer industry. Intel's strategy will be to have launched its 586, 686 and 786 processors by 1997. Motorola in conjunction with IBM and as part of their joint alliance with Apple will have launched its RISC processor for the Power PC in 1994 or 1995, whilst other RISC based chips from Sun, DEC and others will all be doing battle. Essentially the key issue will be whether RISC technology can take-over from CISC, and whether Intel being attacked from all sides can be toppled from its leadership position, not only by RISC based products[7] but also by low cost

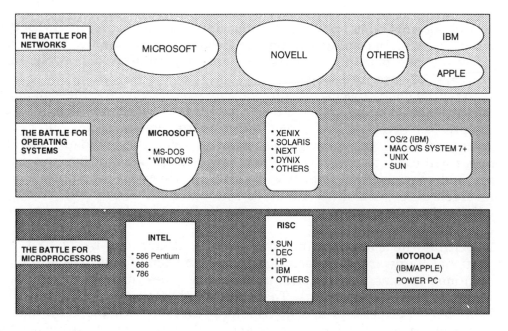

Fig. 9.2. The battle for dominance in personal computer technology during the 1990s.

clones. Clearly it is now faced with some heavy competition, but it also sits on top of an installed base of users worth over $340 billion and equally well, it has an ambitious strategy to maintain these customers and fight off the competitors. However, the impact of the increased competition is likely to be mixed. On the one hand, it may help to drive down prices of personal computers still further, but at the same time, it may fuel the development of two or three new processor standards, one based upon Intel, the other on the Motorola/IBM/Apple standard, with a third from a consortium of companies possibly led by DEC and Compaq. What effect such developments will have upon customer patterns of demand will depend upon whether "open-systems" get any closer to reality and that may depend largely on the battle amongst suppliers of operating systems.

The Battle for Operating Systems

Today's leader of operating systems software is well aware of the competitive threats it faces for the future. Having established itself, along with Intel as one of the two dominant forces in the industry and in so doing effectively stripping IBM of the role and at the same time alienating Apple as the industry's number two competitor, Microsoft has effectively set itself up as the primary target for these two companies. Already in the late 1980s it was clearly evident that software was becoming the most important element in the value chain for personal computer companies. However, relatively few had access to its supply or control. Apple was one of the few and now, in alliance with IBM is set upon developing the next generation of operating system to run the Power PC. Microsoft's strategy appears to be intended to provide an evolutionary path, with its products being engineered into its Windows environment. The launch of its Windows NT,[8] for New Technology is expected over the next few years to migrate users of MS-DOS to a more user-friendly environment, but one that will allow them to transport much of their existing software. Apple and IBM on the other hand are looking to develop a more revolutionary approach based on Object-Oriented Programming.[9] This represents a significant departure from current software programs and should make it easier to develop programs, especially using multimedia technology,[10] which would also be easier for customers to use. However, although promised to be a transparent system[11] to end-users, it will remain to be seen how portable older applications programs will be to the new system. With an estimated 70 million copies of MS-DOS and an unknown number of pirate copies, plus over 200 million applications programs running on it, Microsoft's installed base will not be easy to topple. IBM has already experienced how poorly its OS/2 was received by a market more willing to stay with a familiar system, apparently selling less than a million copies in three years after its launch, compared to over four million copies of Microsoft Windows. All this underlines the fact that customers are caught in an inertia of sunk investments and will only switch to alternative systems if it is not too costly and offers real value, assuming that they are willing to invest when the major economies have come out of the present recession. One of the issues that appears to be key in terms of customers' perceptions of value seems to be ease of use and simplicity of a system. This is an area in which Apple has excelled and is likely to be the forefront of its new joint operating systems with IBM.

Controlling the Network: The Ace Card?

During the next five years, it is network software technology that is likely to turn out to be the greatest battle ground, following the dictum that the company that controls the network, controls the system and therefore the customer. In this area, a number of companies are likely to come to blows. These include Novell, the leading company in this area of the industry which bases its main business on networks, whilst Apple and IBM intend to make Macs more integrated into IBM networks via a series of cross-licensing deals and product developments, whilst Microsoft is building networking into its Windows environment. The reason why networking is likely to be so crucial in the future hinges upon the way in which many large companies decide to operate their MIS departments. Only a short while ago, these consisted of highly centralised systems with remote terminals located around the organisation that were linked to the mainframe computer. Once personal computers had been accepted into the MIS environment, it meant that large organisations might have two or three thousand machines in a single building and anywhere between 20,000 and 80,000 machines in the entire organisation. Supporting such systems can be very time consuming and costly, especially in a company that is keen to use the latest versions of applications programs. One solution to this problem is to ensure that individual machines do not have to carry all the main programs. Instead, it will be increasingly easier to set up a number of local server based networks,[12] which would be connected to other networks and larger mainframes and minicomputers. In such client/server environments, the large organisation or enterprise with an appropriate networking system, will then be able to download all major software from a limited number of servers, which in time could be automatically downloading their software from other computers. Individual users could still load their own applications for specific tasks if they wished, but the principle programs would be server based and the personal computer would store less local software. Similarly, much of the corporate database that would need to be accessed by users in other areas of the company would be held in relatively central systems. Fast and intelligent networking might therefore return the corporate world to a pattern more similar to the days of minicomputers and mainframes, the difference being that the mainframes would be personal computers or workstations acting as servers to the overall system.

Naturally, this is only one possible scenario and some observers point to the problems of data security in such systems. However, it reflects the fact that personal computing no longer has quite the same meaning as when it was first developed in the 1970s. At that time, technology dictated that everything resided in the desktop machine in terms of basic processing power and software. With the development of local area and then company wide networking, data could be shared between users. Now it was becoming less personal and more communal. It should not come as a surprise therefore, if during the 1990s, personal computing, at least in large organisations gives way to this different terminology. Indeed, "groupware"[13] indicates the trend in this direction. This does not mean, as in the old days of the mainframe and early minis, that the individual has little or no control of the computer's processing or programming operations, instead it gives the user the best of both worlds. For the average user, if operating systems and networking move increasingly towards graphical and Windows based formats, it will merely mean that when requesting an application or a file,[14] this may well reside in a server or even a mainframe. Increasingly, communications have allowed users to access remote databases on a global scale. The advanced network, will ensure that certain corporate-wide or community-wide aspects of the machines will be located around the network. The ace therefore is that whoever controls the network, will have the ability to deliver the preferred choice of operating system and applications programs. Making it all work smoothly is of course another and more difficult challenge.

Personal Computers as Chameleons

With so many battles for control or dominance surrounding the various key elements of the personal computer, it is small wonder that analysts are open-minded as to the outcome. Indeed, the desktop personal computer itself is evolving into a number of rather different types of product, some of which could represent newgames in their own right. At the high-end, their convergence with workstations, future use of RISC and more powerful CISC processors means that the two classes of machine are becoming indistinguishable. Personal workstation is already a common term. Such machines are also used as servers for controlling networks and will do more of this task in the future as their power increases. As desktop machines their power will be phenomenal. However, much of this power will be needed to run the newly emerging programs that will be developed by the mid-1990s for multimedia type applications and functions. This will include greater use of visual materials, using photos, film and sound simulation. Handling the networking requirements of users will be a major area of computing power as will navigation of local and remote data bases. Limited voice communication will also require large amounts of processing power, whilst scanning[15] and compression[16] will need vast amounts of storage capacity. Therefore, during the next five years, a desktop workstation, will still be seen as needing further processing power to speed up handling these various activities.

For many customers, such sophisticated applications will still be a little way ahead in five years time—for them the key requirements will be for low price. In such markets, personal computers will have become like today's handheld calculators. The battle in this sector of the industry is likely to be extremely bloody, as IBM, Compaq, Apple, HP, Olivetti and a host of clones continue to bleed each other for market share. For those who argue that margins are already too low and competitors will see sense, they should remember the fate of the handheld calculator companies in their battle against Texas Instruments during the early 1970s or look at today's airline industry in Western Europe or the United States. These examples allow one to see how far competitors are prepared to accumulate losses, especially if they are protected by their government or by legislation and the equivalent of Chapter 11 in the United States. In such scenarios, eventually, a few are left, but those are usually the companies with the deepest pockets and the lowest costs of manufacturing, together with low cost distribution channels, except for those subsidised by their home governments.

Overall, these developments in the high-end and medium to low-end of the marketplace are likely to cause severe problems for the immediate competitors. However, they are also likely to cause even greater problems for the mainframe and minicomputer companies as a result of the continuing process of "downsizing" in large corporations. Therefore, during the next five years, the increasing power of desktop machines will mean more and more companies will make use of these machines linked to servers and that developments in networking software will make such options more attractive than ever to customers in the market place.

The Dawn of the Mainframe and Minicomputer Industry Endgames

In effect, what all mainframe and minicomputer companies will have to do in order to survive is to recognise that their organisational structures and processes will need major change. The process that began in the early 1990s of falling margins and decline in their core businesses is unlikely to desist. This represents the exact pattern that one would expect when a newgame moves into its final stages of completion. Personal computers are now replacing the traditional mainframe and minicomputer solutions at an increasing rate. Although mainframes and supercomputers have a future, many of their manufacturers do not look so likely to survive in the business. Up until now, a number of the companies manufacturing such products have been relatively slow to realise that their downturn in fortunes has less to do with the recession of the early 1990s and more to do with the fact that they are now under attack from a maturing newgame as illustrated in Fig. 9.3. However, the attack is nowhere near over. The pattern in the past five years of increasing mergers and acquisitions, corporate failures and hence industry concentration for mainframe and minicomputer companies is likely to continue, with still more U.S. and West European companies becoming casualties. Nor should one assume that all Japanese companies will be unscathed. Although their vast reserves and scope of other business activities make it unlikely that any Japanese giants will not survive and although these areas of their

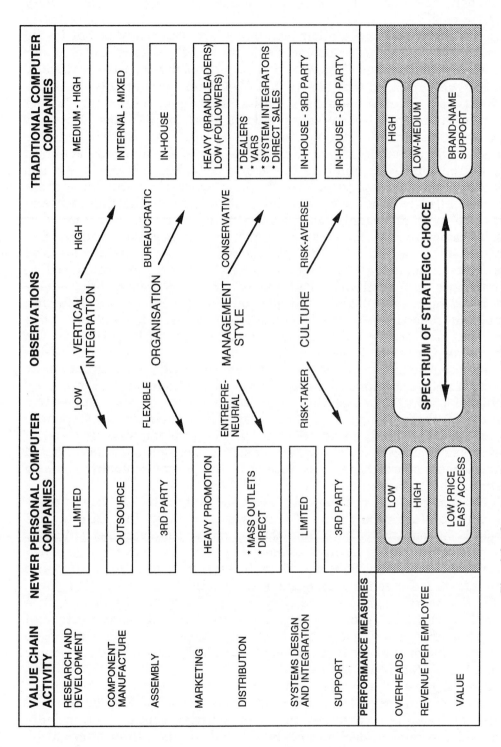

Fig. 9.3. Contrast between value chain organisations in the personal computer industry during the 1990s.

businesses have been somewhat slower to experience the "downsizing" phenomenon, however, now that it has started, it is likely to move very rapidly.

One of the reasons why other companies are still likely to fail in the mainframe and minicomputer businesses is that as the market comes under increased attack from more powerful desktop machines, then gradually total sales will shrink, at first slowly, but then later more rapidly. In effect, these industries are now entering a long-term endgame situation. Cutting margins to stay competitive can only provide a short term solution. However, cutting costs has to be the main strategy to stay competitive and this requires a different approach to their value chain. It cannot be achieved simply by reducing staff numbers or closing factories, although these are unfortunately also necessary. Indeed, the new approach to the value chain is a lesson already practised by a few competitors in the industry and reflects the type of organisation developed by a number of the more successful competitors in the personal computer and workstation industries. The contrasts between the value chains of traditional mainframe and minicomputer companies and the new value chains are illustrated in Fig. 9.3. Companies such as IBM, Unisys, Olivetti, DEC, Wang and others have always relied upon being highly vertically integrated organisations. However, the endgame conditions in their traditional businesses demand that with low margins and slow growth, these companies can no longer afford the cost of being vertically integrated. In effect they must federate, which involves subcontracting many of the activities which they have traditionally done, especially including manufacturing of components and probably assembly of products, unless they have some source of real competitive advantage in these elements of their respective value chains. Japanese companies are less likely to be affected by this problem, since in most of their Keiretsu type organisations, they consist of a complex web of affiliated companies, most of which not only supply to the parent company, but also compete on the open market.

Such changes are not easy to achieve. Not only do they involve enormously painful restructuring of the organisation, but they also involve major shifts in company culture from the top down. However, cost efficiency is only part of the battle, for at the same time, quality must be maintained or better still, improved. This again requires a very special relationship with suppliers and a sound management of logistics and information flows. Thus for the overall computer industry, except for a few companies, it is unlikely that sufficient profits will be generated from the manufacture of computers in five years time, since the vast majority of machines will be made from components that can be better made by specialised electronic component manufacturers and assembly companies. Similarly, distribution will become a game for the most cost efficient type of organisations. Direct selling may remain an option, but even here specialist distributors and even freight handling companies could be a better choice. Conventional dealers will continue to decline and be dependent upon their survival by either upgrading their services or moving into high volume operations.

As Fig. 9.3 illustrates the bulk of future profits will be generated on the value chain in software and systems design together with integration activities and services. This of course represents that area of the computer industry that is being focused upon by just about every type of competitor.

The Era of Software Systems Integration and Consultancy

Who wins and who loses in these areas is impossible to predict. In addition to operating and networking systems that were previously discussed, applications software is expected to enjoy strong growth during the next five years. In this area competition is much more varied with specific companies dominating particular types of software. What does seem likely however, is that the mass market of "shrink-wrapped software" will be subject to more competition in the future as some of the computer hardware companies step-up their interest in this sector, as Apple did with Claris. Additionally, mergers and acquisitions seem likely to increase as some competitors try to copy the strategies of Microsoft, Adobe and Claris by building up suites of applications[17] that share a common type of user-interface. In the corporate and medium sized business sector, with the various networking and issues of systems integration between different types of products still likely to be in full swing, systems design and integration is of course a major projected source of revenue and one that still offers high margins. As a source of consulting, it naturally falls into the category of being based upon high levels of expertise, but one that almost all competitors claim to possess. Expectations of their performance by many companies in this area are probably highly exaggerated and based on a failure to understand the nature of the business.

A number of opposing viewpoints exist as to who is likely to succeed if customers are looking for experience in these areas. One of which suggests that even with the rapid decline of mainframe and minicomputer installations, many of these traditional manufacturers still have the background of years of experience in handling the information requirements of client companies. These large client companies traditionally rely upon this knowledge of their particular business and systems requirements by the computer companies, as in the case of Unisys in the airline industry. Countering this argument is the idea that since the newgame involves a different type of concept about how to organise computing based upon very different types of hardware and software systems, then the experts should be seen as the newer companies who have originally developed this type of technology. Yet another viewpoint would dismiss both these options as being too biased and more than likely to push their own pet solutions, whatever they may claim about impartiality in their sales pitch. This school of thought would suggest that the only safe solution is to rely upon a professional systems integrator, who not only understands the technology options, but would also claim to be an expert in understanding the nature of a particular client's business.

Naturally, what actually happens in all these areas of the industry will not only be determined by the battles between different technologies, suppliers, competitors and distributors, but will also be largely influenced by the behaviour of customers. Since the recession of the early part of the 1990s may not actually end until the mid-1990s, it seems likely that the desktop computer companies, their hardware suppliers and distributors will be largely dependent during this period upon generating replacement sales in the developed markets of the United States and Western Europe, with some growth opportunities in Japan and the Rest of the World. Software appears as the great battleground, but one with continued growth potential, although the rate is dependent upon the developments in operating systems and networking. Growth potential in both areas will be enhanced by increased moves towards "downsizing", but of course this is not a costless investment. Even when and if the recession comes to an end, general demand for desktop computers in their present form is unlikely to rise significantly and nowhere near the rates experienced in the mid-1980s. Once again, this is entirely consistent with an industry whose major products are at a mature stage of the life cycle.

What the overall industry needs in order to really stimulate demand is the evolution of another newgame sector or the development of a newgame in the existing industry. Either option is a possibility, although the latter is more likely to come later rather than sooner. If it comes at all, it will be based upon some of the technology currently under development or shortly to be developed in areas such as object-oriented programming, advanced networking systems and high powered microprocessors that will dwarf the power of today's supercomputers. Such machines would need to form the platform for applications software that was sufficiently powerful, interesting and easy to use that it could even be considered valuable and possible for senior executives to use. Today's machines fall far short of this yardstick, since they are mainly used by people who are required to handle information in a structured manner. Tomorrow's dream will be to create machines that can handle unstructured information and convert it into structured formats. With such machines, that will incidentally probably no longer be called personal computers but personal assistants,[18] the user will be at liberty to communicate with the personal assistant by voice or handwriting or pointing to icons. The personal assistant will be able to send and receive messages on a worldwide basis, it will be able to access information from local, corporate and remote databases and will present information by voice and multimedia formats making use of video, photos, graphics, simulation models and a variety of hard copy materials, including micro disks,[19] transparencies or just plain paper. It may even be able to offer simultaneous translation and almost anything that can be reduced to a set of 1's and 0's for the microprocessor to handle. Such developments may sound far fetched or the stuff of science fiction, however, some of the technology to make such dreams come true is already in place or will shortly be available in the form of yet more sophisticated multimedia systems. One area where many of the components of multimedia technology is already in place and will become increasingly integrated into personal computers, is in the consumer electronics industry.

Multimedia, Personal Assistants and Personal Companions

Although personal computers have been sold alongside consumer electronics products for some time, they have always remained discrete products, sitting alongside Hi-Fi, stereo or computer games machines in department stores or consumer electronic equipment outlets. However, as mentioned earlier, the past few years have witnessed a major change in the type of component technology included in personal computers or their peripherals. Although still representing a relatively small percentage of shipments, more and more machines are carrying audio and video devices, that will permit them to "play" visual and sound signals from other types of machine. All of which represents the beginning of a development that is considered by some analysts and competitors to become the major growth area of the 1990s, namely, multimedia. Fig. 9.4 illustrates the converging paths of multimedia technologies during the mid-1990s. At present, nobody is really sure how to define multimedia beyond the somewhat tautological level of describing it as being the interactive linkage between television, audio and graphical personal computing.

However, the developments in the related digital based technologies, suggest that a strong inertia is being established to realise both a conversion of some of today's media to an electronic based format, as well as a convergence of various media to an interactive format.[20] The result will provide a linking together of the spectrum of information as it currently

TECHNOLOGIES	RECORDING	PROCESSING	STORAGE MEDIA
AUDIO			
RECORDS	Professional Sound Studio	Record Player (individual)	Rigid Read Only Memory
TAPES	Professional Sound Studio / Tape Recorder (individual)	Tape Player (individual)	Tape Reel, Tape Cartridge / Erasable, recordable (individual)
COMPACT DISC	Professional Sound Studio	CD Player (individual)	CD ROM; / Erasable, recordable (individual)
MULTI-MEDIA	*Static and Animated Cameras to record original or prerecorded images and file electronically into Personal Computers to permit manipulation of audio and video data.*	*Personal Computers using HDTV monitor displays to manipulate and edit various forms of audio and video data by means of cutting, pasting, modifying and altering software.*	*Erasable and Recordable compact discs and tapes. (Individual)*
VISUAL	**RECORDING**	**PROCESSING**	**STORAGE**
STILLS	Cameras (individual)	Film Projector (individual)	Film Slides or Prints / Rigid and Fixed
ANIMATED	Television Cameras (Professional) / Cine-cameras (individual) / Video Cassette Recorder (individual)	Television; HDTV (individual) / Cine-Projector (individual) / Video Cassette Recorder (individual)	Film Tape Reel / Limited Editing of Sequence / (Individual)
ADJUSTABLE	Personal Computers using graphics software and mouse or pen input devices (individual)	Personal Computers using graphical and animation software (individual)	PC Floppy/Hard Disc Storage (individual) or CD ROMs (rigid)

Note: The reference to "Individual" indicates that the recording and/or processing machine can be controlled by an individual or that the storage media can be partially or wholly manipulated and altered by an individual as opposed to a professional video or audio studio.

Fig. 9.4. Converging paths of multimedia technologies during the 1990s.

exists in its separate visual and audio formats and the resulting multimedia is expected to remove the boundaries, so that as illustrated in Fig. 9.4 each of the recording, processing and storage technologies will be able to transfer information across the different media and products based upon the common characteristic that their core information handling technology is digital in nature. Such developments would be similar to those experienced during the latter part of the 1980s in desktop-publishing, when previously cost-intensive systems were substituted by much lower cost personal computer based technologies. Hence, current high cost systems employed in sound and television studios look set to become accessible to the individual or at least for small groups of users at much lower prices based upon the next generation of personal computer systems. As mentioned at the beginning of this section, interest in the potential of multimedia is what has attracted so many companies from related industries to begin serious discussions about joint-ventures with computer hardware and software companies. Already, companies such as Philips Consumer Electronics and Commodore Computers are involved in developing the market with the initial systems in this field which represented a $5 billion market in 1991. Some estimates suggest that by 1995, multimedia will have grown into a $25 billion market. Such forecasts are what has attracted interest and product development strategies from other consumer electronic giants such as Sony, as well as IBM, Apple and Microsoft and a number of other companies. Thus, it is likely that many alliances will continue to cross the traditional industry boundaries between computing and consumer electronics during the next few years.

Another product segment of personal computers that continues to and is projected to enjoy growth over the next five years is portable machines. In particular, notebook machines are likely to maintain strong growth, especially since they will continue to improve in performance and power, both of which will broaden their market base. Some observers have even predicted that as these machines improve and gain more facilities such as modems, fax, inbuilt printer and cellular communications, then they will start to cannibalise desktop machines. Indeed, one could even argue that portables represent a newgame in their own right. This is especially true if one considers the next generation of portable that is only now coming to the market, but will include some of the technologies needed for the desktop personal assistant. These powerful handheld computers are known by various names, such as the "personal assistant" by Apple Computer, but referred to as "personal information processors" by competitors such as Tandy (prior to the take-over of its computer business by AST), Casio and Geoworks who have formed an alliance for its development, whilst AT&T and Go Corp. are working on a "personal communicator" that lets one send written notes. In all these machines they represent a form of palmtop computer that is not only expected to be marketed aggressively to blue collar workers and sales staff in remote locations, but also to the consumer market. This represents just one of a number of products that the computer industry plans to launch into the consumer market during the next five years. For it is here that many of them see a major market opportunity that they hope will compare to the success of the handheld calculator boom of the 1970s.

The importance of success in the consumer market is however not only based upon a desire to sell lots of palmtop computers. More importantly, it is necessary in order to establish a beachhead for launching subsequent products that will once again try to resurrect the effort to sell personal computers to the home market. Only this time, instead of being used for basic and fairly conventional home education or home office applications, the computer companies are banking on the belief that developments in digital technology in the telecommunications, broadcasting, cable TV and various other types of delivery systems will open up further developments in the infrastructure of financial services, retailing and entertainment that will provide the consumer with a range of products and services that will make use of powerful home based personal computers, which if not called personal assistants due to their business connotations, will probably be called "personal companions" or pc, thus giving a new meaning to the acronym of PC, only this time it will be in lower case.

However, as mentioned above computer hardware companies are not the only competitors interested in development of the "personal companion" marketplace. Not surprisingly the major consumer electronics companies such as Matsushita, Philips, Sony, Toshiba and Hitachi are all busily investing in activities that will strengthen their hands in this area. After all, they have the most to lose and are probably the best placed to succeed. Not only do they provide many of the critical components for consumer electronics products, as they do for portable computers, Japan is also the world leader in aspects of electronics hardware miniaturisation. For this reason many U.S. computer companies, both from the software and hardware sectors have teamed up with the Japanese to obtain access to these technologies. However, it is not all one sided, for the Japanese are nowhere near as strong in software systems and this is critical to any multimedia based system. Naturally, this does not overlook the fact however, that computer games companies such as Sega and Nintendo have considerable skills in this type of multimedia technology. Furthermore, they both enjoy an enormous brand awareness on a global scale. Who will win or lose, it is impossible to say, but as was illustrated earlier in this chapter in Fig. 9.1 the emerging pattern of converging industries and markets promises to force many industry leaders from the various sectors into major strategic choices about with whom they will choose to compete in the future.

What must be remembered however, is that taking on the major consumer electronics companies in their own territory may not be so easy for the personal computer companies as was the task of battling with the mainframe and minicomputer companies. In that case, although some of the incumbents responded by entering the personal computer industry themselves, they did not fully appreciate the scale of the threat or its potential speed of delivery. Furthermore, their traditional businesses were highly inefficient and protected by proprietary systems that restricted the choice of their customers. Hence whilst it lasted, they enjoyed large margins that could support high overheads. The consumer electronics industry is very different and consists of a group of global competitors who are used to low cost operations, with mass distribution channels and strong corporate and product images in the marketplace. Margins are very small compared to all but the lowest priced personal computers and even then heavy price discounting is common. Perhaps the most important lesson for personal computer companies to learn from the past when entering this market is that very few of the mainframe or minicomputer companies succeeded when they moved out of their core businesses. Many were very confident that they would succeed, but they failed to understand these new markets, which resulted in them developing inappropriate marketing strategies and under-resourcing their implementation efforts, both in terms of commitment and funds. On that occasion, they were taking on a group of relatively small incumbents who had little or no experience of large company growth or operations, yet in the case of Apple they were often outclassed, or failed to respond quickly enough to new competitors, ranging from Compaq through to later small entrants such as Packard Bell, Dell or Vobis. Learning not to make the same mistake would be an important lesson for any company planning to attack the consumer electronics industry at its centre.

THE UBIQUITOUS MICROCOMPUTER

In effect, the only thing that appears certain over the next five years for the personal computer industry and its markets is the fact that there will continue to be a considerable amount of change. As the above discussion has shown, major technology battles can be expected in a number of key areas, that will create and test alliances and competitors alike. In microprocessors, Intel will battle against Motorola and its IBM/Apple alliance, together with other RISC based competitors such as DEC, Sun and others maybe moving towards a common third standard. The result, may well therefore be a three sided ring. In operating systems and network systems, the software giant, Microsoft looks ready to do battle once again with the IBM/Apple consortium, but both will probably be joined by Novell and others who will form alliances with other software companies to strengthen their positions. The net result is likely to be a continual search for a somewhat elusive base of "open systems", which will be drawn ever further away as successive competitors launch new products in a bid to gain market share.

Set upon these various technological platforms, personal computer companies will be faced with the difficult questions of choosing which standards to support or to develop. There will be many more consortia formed, which in turn is likely to cause yet more confusion. However, for some time, at least until the next generation of microprocessors are established in the market, many competitors will be faced with the harsh realities of competing in markets with falling prices, decreasing margins and strong competitive pressures making it difficult to protect market share. At the high-end of the market competition between personal computers and workstations will intensify and increasingly engage-in battle with the mini and mainframe accounts. As a result, the mainframe and minicomputer industries will move into endgame environments. Competitors competing as hardware manufacturers in any sectors of the computer industry will be forced to reconfigure their value chains and organisation structures from vertically integrated to a federated model. This in itself will necessitate major cultural changes and some will fail. For those that succeed, strategic alliances, joint ventures, licensing and sub-contracting arrangements will be the order of the day.

As digital technology draws competitors together from a wide variety of industries, including the central core of telecommunications, computers, consumer electronics together with those connected with multimedia such as photographic, broadcasting, publishing and the entertainments industries, then their traditional business boundaries will be overlapped or destroyed. On a global scale, an extraordinarily complex web of partnerships is likely to evolve, which will be based upon strong brand name companies in respective market sectors being used by a consortia of companies to sell their products. However, the wide interplay between so many different companies is also likely to stimulate innovation and lead to an increasing range of new products in both the office and home environment. Distribution channels will continue to change in both type and service as they try to grapple with new markets and new products. At the high-end of the channel, increase in systems integrators and VARs for large and medium sized companies can be expected, whilst mass market stores are likely to increase to serve the consumer markets.

One final point that is worth emphasising is to appreciate that the nature of the industries that are converging is very varied in terms of their competitive conditions and markets. Therefore in such a complex and rapidly changing environment there are bound to be a few surprises both in competitor performance, technology and product developments together with market behaviour. Trying to forecast who will win and who will lose is a worthless venture. However, a few predictions about broadly based processes may seem valid. Firstly, technological innovation will clearly continue to be a key driving force in whatever form the personal computer industry and its markets may take. Secondly, as the industry converges with an increasing number of other industries, competitors will frequently be forced to create global strategic alliances and partnerships in order to survive. Thirdly, although the industry will be driven by technological change, the growing complexities of the range and types of markets served by competitors will require them to dramatically improve their marketing skills beyond their current capabilities. Fourthly, some large companies in the overall computer industry will be acquired or go out of business as the competition becomes more complex and intense. Fifthly, some currently unknown companies will rise up to become significant players

tomorrow. Whilst lastly, the personal computer will continue to evolve in a variety of different shapes, sizes and forms, although what it will be called remains anybody's guess. One other thing that is certain, few newgames, whatever their origins could possibly claim to have had such an effect upon society in such a short period of time as that of the personal computer. Hence, the idea expressed in the title to this book, namely:
— The PC Revolution.

EPILOGUE

"... such stuff,
As dreams are made on..."[1]

"Immediately the law of Copernicus was discovered and demonstrated the
mere recognition of the fact that it was not the sun but the earth that
moves destroyed the whole cosmology of the ancients. It might have been
possible by refuting the law to retain the old conception of the movements
of the heavenly bodies; but without refuting it it would seem impossible to
continue studying the Ptolemaic worlds. Yet long after the discovery of the
law of Copernicus the Ptolemaic worlds continued to be a subject of
study."[2]

During the late 1960s and early 1970s various sociologists and other writers began to observe that the industrialised world was entering a new revolution, similar in process to, yet potentially more significant than the previous agrarian or industrial revolutions. Initially, the term "post-industrial society" became the watchword for this phenomenon. However, by the late 1970s the now familiar phrases "information society"[3] and "information revolution" began to take over as the impact of microelectronics was increasingly seen upon the industrial landscape. In 1978, a former British government Chief Scientist, Sir Ieuan Maddock referred to the phenomenon as "The most remarkable technology ever to confront mankind."[4]

At the time, social observers were strongly influenced by two key developments that appeared to be moulding the patterns of change around them. The first was the remarkable speed of technological progress being made in the tiny yet powerful microprocessor accompanied by its reciprocal fall in costs. The second involved applications of the microchip to various products and machines that were dramatically altering the economics and performance of existing products and production processes and at the same time, stimulating the development of new products and processes. As observers contemplated the future, hardly an area of economic activity appeared likely to escape the impact of microelectronics.

During the 1980s, many of the predictions concerning the microelectronics revolution began to unfold as the technology diffused into our factory, office, education and home environments. Increasingly, patterns of employment have shifted towards information related industries and services, changing the complexion of our industrial landscape. The common element of the microprocessor has provided a pathway for the convergence of the major industries involved in the development and manufacture of information systems, namely, computers, telecommunications and consumer electronics.

By 1990 the world was increasingly seen as taking on the form of a global environment, as satellites circled the planet and linked organisations and people through their computers and their electronic communications devices. Change in the field of information technology has indeed been rapid during this brief period of time and its impact upon our economies and societies is becoming increasingly apparent.

Now as the mid-1990s are approaching, it is interesting to note that at the time of the observations made in the late 1970s, personal computers were only just emerging from their embryonic stage of development and beginning their growth stage. Most of their application was still in the home for computer games, with limited usage in the education and small business environments. The dominant perception in society was that computers were still essentially large central units around which clusters of users could link their terminals. IBM clearly ruled the world of computing and although futurologists acknowledged that computing power would be distributed more and more to individuals in the workplace and home, the method of dissemination was expected by many to be based upon centralised processing systems.

As things have turned out, perhaps more than any other product emerging from the core technology of the microprocessor, personal computers have, as illustrated in this book, fundamentally changed our concept of computing. In their essence computers have always been machines for processing data which in its more sophisticated format represents information. Information itself can be used as a source of considerable power. By changing the concept of computing, personal computers have more than anything else shifted the balance of power in our society. So far, most of this power has been economic in nature, as individuals have been able to use personal computers for developing, enhancing and providing their skills in a wide variety of applications ranging from software developers to school teachers, from accountants to commercial artists, from authors to publishers and many more.

Based upon the success of the personal computer to enhance the power of individuals and create new markets and applications, manufacturing and software companies have come into existence that are now multibillion dollar concerns. As a result of their success and their ideas, the structure of the computer industry and its markets have been dramatically altered during the past decade. Although some industry observers in 1978 foresaw the direction of change that was then only just beginning, few had the vision or understanding to recognise just how far it would go in so short a time.

Nobody should ever be blamed for missing out unexpected events in our futures. However, this does not exonerate one from the need to remember that the unexpected is always present in our lives and there are lessons to be learnt from our past experiences.

Thus as we look forward towards the millennium, it is perhaps worth taking time to remember how far personal computers have changed our lives during the past decade, since clearly they hold the potential to continue to further change our lives in the future. However, given the relationship between information and power, society should perhaps be looking carefully at the path down which we may be led by such machines. Whilst some may believe that technology in itself is essentially neutral, this is a debatable point. However, clearly it is the way in which it is applied that determines whether it be a benign or malevolent force. As the power of the personal computer increases, its potential impact upon our society becomes greater. In many respects the fact that personal computers have evolved from low powered individually used machines has meant that they have until now been seen as liberators within our society. To a large extent, this statement would appear to be perfectly valid. However, in the decade ahead, personal computers will increasingly be networked and will access large databases on a global scale. In such a scenario, it does not require too much imagination to identify some of the threats to individual freedom that might emanate from the abuse of power available from the misuse of personal computers. Even more significant are issues surrounding the potential effects of personal computer based virtual reality[5] systems. Naturally, such developments can be used to great benefit in our society, but we should also be aware of their potential for abuse by individuals, both to themselves and others around them.

Up to the present, in addition to technological forces, the personal computer industry has been largely driven by economic and commercial criteria of the marketplace. Whilst necessary to provide the parameters of competition and development, it is apparent that in the decade ahead, senior executives and government policy makers will need to be increasingly concerned with the social implications arising from this industry. As an area of industrial activity, it has in a very short space of time moved from being of little significance to one of considerable importance, both in terms of its size and influence. Hence, types and levels of employment, the nature of the infrastructure and patterns of international trade relating to the industry will all become more dominant issues of concern to those involved in the future.

However, it is perhaps in its more subtle areas that the personal computer industry will need responsible management, both from within and also from outside sources. As the industry develops products for the consumer mass leisure market to create alternative realities,[6] or as personal communicating video wrist units[7] become commonplace for all of us, society should ensure that it has carefully considered the implications of such systems before they infringe on our basic freedoms.

Up until now, the technology of microprocessors has run true to form in terms of providing the catalyst to change represented in our society by the information revolution. During the 1970s and 1980s its technological impact created major shifts in our economic systems. As the 1980s moved forward, personal computers rose up to become one of the most significant by-products of this technology and as their economic power has been released, so they have greatly influenced the patterns of social change taking place around us. To complete the cycle, political systems also now need to change in order to accommodate the new social order that is developing in this high technology society.

In this respect, we are approaching a turning point. Not so long ago, the development of the conceptual base of modern physics created a paradigm shift that moved the scientific community away from Newtonian based physics to operate in new dimensions of the science.[8] The practical and applied engineering achievements of such changes have manifested themselves in all sorts of fields. In particular, electronics and the derived products of the computing and telecommunications industries have in turn created a vast paradigm shift away from a mechanical solid based engineering world into an electronic and increasingly software based environment, perhaps the most significant developments of which have been associated with the personal computer.

As a result of the creation of the personal computer, the world is now shifting increasingly towards the channelling of ideas and innovations that were once the sole preserve of large institutions and organisations, but are for now shared by the individual. In so doing, personal computers have already created a shift in the conceptual base of what we understand to be the nature of computing. It is a trend that hopefully cannot be reversed. Naturally, personal computers represent only one of the many major forces for change in our society today. However, as such they are becoming increasingly ubiquitous and represent a powerful symbol of the information era. Therefore from this technological paradigm shift has been created the basis of a product that has itself created a paradigm shift in our society, the implications for which are only beginning to manifest themselves more openly. Clearly personal computers have now become much more than the mere "toys" that they were taken to be in the 1970s. They are agents of change that continue to not only transform the way that we do business, but also the way that we learn, how we communicate and increasingly, how we spend our leisure time.

Trying to predict how the personal computer will develop into the more distant future is pure guess work. However, whatever happens, it is to be hoped that the derivative of the personal computer, whatever form it takes, whatever functions it performs, should remain as an individual and personal item for the expansion and realisation of our existing and potential human capabilities. In this respect, the personal computer of the future has the potential to fulfil our most ambitious dreams.

NOTES

AUTHOR'S PREFACE

1. Washington Irving, "Notoriety", *Tales of a Traveller*, 1824.
2. Gerard Manley Hopkins, *Ecce Homo*.
3. See glossary for **Information Technology (IT)**.
4. George Gilder, *Microcosm, The Quantum Revolution in Economics and Technology*, Simon and Schuster, 1989. The reader is referred to this publication for an interesting look at the direction in which some people believe that information technology is moving society and business.
5. Robert N. Noyce, "Microelectronics", in Tom Forester (ed), *The Microelectronics Revolution*, B. Blackwell, 1980. This article and others in the edition draw out evidence both for and against the claim that we are involved in a revolution of social and economic as well as technological dimensions. It is also a good source of further references to the subject.
6. See glossary for **Personal Computer**.
7. See glossary for **Microelectronics**.
8. See glossary for **Computer Industry**.
9. See glossary for **Hardware**.
10. See glosary for **Microcomputer**.
11. See glossary for **Downsizing**. The process is discussed more fully later in the book, during Chapter Six. However, the reader is referred to R.H. Baker, *Downsizing: How to Get Big Gains from Smaller Computer Systems*, McGraw-Hill, Inc., 1992, for an explanation of the concept and its processes and one which also provides a good source of reference on the subject. A similar term, but one which claims to overcome the limitations of a technical approach to the topic by downsizing evangelists is that of "rightsizing". The reader is referred to C.H. Hendricks, *The Rightsizing remedy: How Managers can respond to the Downsizing Dilemma*, Business One Irwin, Illinois, 1992, for a presentatiuon of these ideas and a good source of reference on the subject.
12. See glossary for **Digital Technology**.
13. See glossary for **Telecommunications Industry**.
14. See glossary for **Consumer Electronics Industry**.

CHAPTER ONE: CONCEPTUAL FRAMEWORKS

1. Vauvenargues, *Reflections and Maxims*, p.3, 1746, from translation by F.G. Stevens.
2. See glossary for **Core Technology**.
3. See glossary for **Computer**.
4. See glossary for **Telecommunications**.
5. The background to this decision emanates from the topic chosen for the author's unpublished doctoral thesis of the title, J.W. Steffens, Entry Behaviour and Competition in the Evolution of the Personal Computer Industry, (1975–1983), The University of London, 1988.

6.   Michael E. Porter, *Competitive Advantage, Creating and Sustaining Superior Performance,* The Free Press, 1985, p.36. The concept of the value chain is described in great detail within this publication.

7.   J. McGee, Strategic groups: A useful linkage between industry structure and strategic management: In *Strategic Marketing and Management,* (H. Thomas and D. M. Gardner, Eds), Wiley, 1985.

8.   See glossary for **Software Developers**.

9.   For fuller details of this process and the background literature on the subject at the time, the reader is referred to the author's unpublished doctoral thesis on the subject, J.W. Steffens, Entry Behaviour, 1988.

10.   J. S. Bain, *Barriers to New Competition,* Harvard University Press, 1956.

11.   F. M. Scherer, *Industrial Market Structure and Economic Performance,* Rand-McNally, 1980.

12.   E. T. Penrose, *The Theory of the Growth of the Firm,* Basil Blackwell, 1959, is a good starter in this field, from which to draw further references.

13.   This objective was stimulated through discussions with my doctoral colleague, A. Ghazanfar whilst working on his unpublished doctoral thesis on the topic of Analysis of Competition in the Office Reprographics Industry in the U.K., The University of London, 1984.

14.   J. McGee and H. Thomas (Eds), *Strategic Management Research: A European Perspective,* John Wiley and Sons, 1986, p.14. This book presents an excellent overview of the literature in the field and the reader is directed towards the introductory chapter by the editors, pp.1–18.

15.   M. E. Porter, The contribution of industrial organisation to strategic management, *Academy of Management Review,* Vol. 6, No. 4, pp.609–620, 1981.

16.   Whilst there is a vast literature in this field, the reader is referred to the following for discussion of technological change and its relationship to the topics of strategic management and industrial evolution. The reader is referred to studies by: K. Pavitt, Some characteristics of innovative activities in British industry, *Omega,* Vol. 11, pp.113–120, 1983; K. Pavitt, Sectoral patterns of technical change: Towards a taxonomy and a theory, *Research Policy,* Vol. 13, pp.342–373, 1984; R. Nelson and S. Winter, *An Evolutionary Theory of Economic Change,* Harvard University Press, Cambridge, MA, 1982; G. Dosi, Technological paradigms and technological trajectories, *Research Policy,* Vol. 11, pp.147–162, 1982.

17.   D. B. Jemison, The importance of an integrative approach to strategic management research, *Academy of Management Review,* Vol. 6, No. 4, pp.601–608, 1981.

18.   M. E. Porter, How competitive forces shape strategy, *Harvard Business Review,* p.217, March–April 1979.

19.   In this model, the term "End-User" refers to the individual who actually uses the product or service that is provided by a competitor. The end-user may on certain occasions be the same person as the purchaser, as is the case for many consumer items. However, the end-user may not necessarily be the same person as the purchaser. This is especially true in large organisations, where a purchasing decision may be made by one individual or team of people, who do not comprise of the actual people who will be using the equipment concerned.

20.   M. Porter, The structure within industries and company performance, *Review of Economics and Statistics,* Vol. 61, pp.214–227, 1979.

21.   J. A. Schumpeter, *Capitalism, Socialism and Democracy,* Harper, New York, 1942.

22.   Porter, *Competitive Advantage,* 1985.

23.   McGee and Thomas, *Strategic Management Research,* 1986.

24.   *Ibid.,* 1986.

25. M. S. Hunt, Competition in the Major Home Appliance Industry 1960–1970, unpublished doctoral dissertation, Harvard University, 1972.

26. M. E. Porter, *Competitive Strategy: Techniques for Analyzing Industries and Competitors,* The Free Press, New York, 1980.

27. *Ibid.,* p.129.

28. J. McGee and H. Thomas, Strategic groups: Theory, research and taxonomy, *Strategic Management Journal,* Vol. 7, No. 2, pp.141–160, 1986.

29. J. R. Galbraith, *Designing Complex Organisations,* Addison-Wesley, 1973.

30. McGee and Thomas, *Strategic Management Research,* 1986; and again, J. McGee and H. Thomas, Making sense of complex industries. In: *Strategies in Global Competition,* (N. Hood and J.E. Vahlne, Eds). Routledge, Kegan Paul, 1988.

31. J. McGee and H. Thomas, Strategic Groups and Intra-industry Competition, *International Review of Strategic Management,* 1992.

32. K. O. Cool and D. E. Schendel, Performance differences among strategic group members, *Strategic Management Journal,* 1988.

33. A. Fiegenbaum, Dynamic aspects of strategic groups and competitive strategy: Concepts and empirical examination in the insurance industry. Doctoral dissertation, University of Illinois at Urbana-Champaign, 1987.

34. A. Fiegenbaum and H. Thomas, Strategic groups and performance: The US insurance industry 1980–1984, *Strategic Management Journal,* Vol. 11, pp.197–215, 1990.

35. B. Mascarenhas, Strategic group dynamics, *Academy of Management Journal,* Vol. 32, pp.332–352, 1989.

36. J. McGee and S. Segal-Horn, Strategic Space and Industry Dynamics: The implications for international marketing strategy, *Journal of Marketing Management,* Vol. 6, No. 3, pp.175–193, 1990.

37. J. McGee and H. Thomas, Analysis of sequential entry paths: Entry theory, technological change and industry dynamics, unpublished, 1990 (under review).

38. Bain, *Barriers,* 1956.

39. R. E. Caves and M. Porter, From entry barriers to mobility barriers, *Quarterly Journal of Economics,* Vol. 91, pp.241–261, May 1977.

40. McGee and Thomas, *Strategic Groups,* p.80, 1992.

41. McGee and Thomas, *Strategic Management Research,* p.150, 1986.

42. *Ibid.,* 1986.

43. C. K. Prahalad and G. Hamel, The core competence of the corporation, *Harvard Business Review,* pp.74–94, May–June 1990.

44. Penrose, *Theory of the Firm,* 1959.

45. S. Oster, Intra-industry structure and the ease of industry change, *Review of Economics and Statistics,* Vol. 64, August 1982.

46. A. D. Chandler, The enduring logic of industrial success, *Harvard Business Review,* pp.130–140, March–April 1990.

47. Intrapreneurism is a term developed to describe entrepreneurial behaviour within large corporations. It was apparently developed by Gifford Pinchot III in his book *Intrapreneuring: why you don't have to leave the corporation to become an entrepreneur,* Harper and Row, New York, 1985. In this book he wrote in the introduction that an intrapreneur is "Any of the "dreamers who do". Those who take hands-on responsibility for creating innovation of any

kind within an organisation. The intrapreneur may be the creator or inventor but is always the dreamer who figures out how to turn an idea into a profitable reality."

48. "Vertical thinking" contrasts with "Lateral thinking" which is a fundamental aspect of the approach employed for generating Newgame Strategies. Use of the lateral process is perhaps best described in the seminal work of the psychologist Edward de Bono. The reader is referred to: Edward de Bono, *The Use of Lateral Thinking*, p.5, Pelican Books, 1967.

49. Porter, *Competitive Strategy*, 1980.

50. It is interesting to note that in some cases of newgames, large established companies choose to develop their newgame operations outside their core business activities, which in a way is a similar separation as encountered by the creation of a new strategic group within an industry at an inter-company level, whereas in the company it is at an intra-company level.

51. Porter, *Competitive Advantage*, p.36, 1985.

52. See glossary for **Mainframe Computer.**

53. See glossary for **Minicomputer.**

54. K. R. Harrigan, "Strategies for Declining Industries." Unpublished doctoral dissertation, Harvard Graduate School of Business Administration, 1979. Harrigan's thesis did much to develop our understanding of the diverse nature of endgame environments and the heterogeneous nature of competing firms' strategies, within this specific set of industry life cycle conditions. Her ideas had a significant influence in directing my research to seek for similar homogeneity of patterns in the strategies of firms within the Newgame Environment.

55. Chandler, *Enduring Logic*, 1990.

56. *Ibid.*

57. B. Kogut, Designing global strategies: Comparative and competitive value-added chains, *Sloan Management Review*, Summer, 1985.

58. K. Ohmae, *Triad Power: The Coming Shape of Global Competition*, p.21, Free Press, New York, 1975.

59. E. M. Rogers, *Diffusion of Innovations*, Free Press, New York, 1962.

60. *Ibid.*, p.161.

61. Thomas V. Bonoma, *The Marketing Edge*, p.4, Free Press, 1985.

62. There are a number of good books which tell the story of product innovations, human organisation and leadership, and the reader is referred to some recommended examples in the footnotes of later chapters in this book. However, the importance of long-term vision and imagination are important qualities which have been reported on in the literature and which make a distinction between the classical approach to market research and trying to understand customer needs in established markets, versus the quite different approach which may often be necessary for creating a newgame market.

63. Christopher Lorenz, *The Design Dimension: Product Strategy and the Challenge of Global Marketing*, pp.33–39, Basil Blackwell, 1986.

64. *Ibid.*, p.33.

65. In practice, this may not necessarily involve studying more than a few market segments, since most companies will be constrained from total market coverage due to their pattern of historical development and limited scale of resources.

66. Note: This form of differentiation involves more than product differentiation as defined within the marketing literature. Instead, it entails trying to create a difference (relative to the competition) in chosen stages of the value chain. However, the conventional oldgame approach would not involve an attempt to restructure all or most parts of the chain with a

view to changing the dominant industry value chain patterns.

67. Strategic mix is defined as the combination of integrated strategic functions that focus a company's resources upon its chosen set of business activities, e.g. design, technology research and product development, production, marketing, etc.

68. Thomas V. Bonoma, *Marketing Edge*, p.4, 1995.

69. *Ibid.*, p.4.

70. K. Simmonds, Peaks and pitfalls of competitive marketing, Stockton Lecture at London Business School, *LBS Journal*, Vol. 10, No. 1, January 1985.

71. Michael Hammer, *Reengineering Work: Don't Automate, Obliterate*, Harvard Business Review, Jul-Aug 1990. This provides a good outline of the principle ideas on the subject by the author who coined the phrase and has popularised the concept.

72. Peter M Senge, *The Fifth Discipline: The Art and Practice of the Learning Organisation*, Doubleday/ Currency, 1990. This not only provides a clear description of learning organisations, but it also has a good bibliography on the subject.

73. John Steffens, *The Intelligent Organisation*, paper presented at the ITIMA 1993 conference in Malmo, Sweden. This sets out the principle characteristics of the type of organisation which are necessary to cope effectively in a newgame environment.

74. Chapter 11 applies under United States law. This allows companies that are in financial hardship to reorganise their capital structure without pressure from their creditors. Critics of Chapter 11 argue that it allows companies that are technically insolvent to continue to trade for unacceptable periods of time, whilst they often bolster their cash flow by severely cutting prices. This of course is seen to have a bad effect on the operating income of the more solvent companies, which are usually drawn into a price war in an effort to maintain market share, as can be witnessed in the continuing case of the United States domestic airline industry. Some blame the courts for such a situation, since a number of judges seem willing to grant debtor corporations repeated extensions of the 120-day deadline for filing restructuring and financing plans. Supporters of Chapter 11 argue that it is necessary to try to protect jobs that would otherwise be lost and lead to increased unemployment. However, reform of Chapter 11 although discussed, seems no nearer coming to fruition at the time of writing.

75. See glossary for **Computer Literacy.**

CHAPTER TWO: PERSONAL COMPUTER TECHNOLOGY

1. J. A. McCrindle, "The Origins of Today's Microcomputers". In *Microcomputer Handbook*, (J.A. McCrindle ed.), Blackwell Scientific, p.1, 1985.

2. See glossary for **Microprocessor.**

3. McCrindle, "The Origins of Today's Microcomputers", 1985.

4. See glossary for **Difference Engine.**

5. See glossary for **Analytical Engine.**

6. See glossary for **Switching Theory.**

7. See glossary for **Tabulator.**

8. Note: The reader is referred to the following texts for further information on the history of such developments. Herman H. Goldstine, *The Computer, from Pascal to Von Neumann*, Princeton University Press, 1972: M. Mosely, *Irascible Genius, A Life of Charles Babbage, Inventor*, London, 1964: (Lord Bowden, ed.)., *Faster than Thought*, Chap. 1, London, 1953: J. H. Blodgett,

"Herman Hollerith, Data Processing Pioneer", Master's Thesis, Drexel Institute of Technology, 1968.

9.   See glossary for **Comptometer.**

10.   J. A. McCrindle, *Ibid.,* p.9.

11.   See glossary for **Program.**

12.   Paul Kimberley, *Microprocessors: An Introduction,* p.212, McGraw Hill, 1982.

13.   See glossary for **Local Area Network (LAN).**

14.   See glossary for **Peripheral.**

15.   See glossary for **Portable.**

16.   See glossary for **Laptop.**

17.   See glossary for **Handheld.**

18.   See glossary for **Systems.**

19.   See glossary for **Central Processing Unit (CPU).**

20.   See glossary for **Memory.**

21.   See glossary for **Input Facilities.**

22.   See glossary for **Output Facilities.**

23.   See glossary for **Software.**

24.   See glossary for **Computer System.**

25.   See glossary for **Printer.**

26.   See glossary for **Disk.**

27.   See glossary for **Components.**

28.   See glossary for **Arithmetic Unit.**

29.   See glossary for **Logic Unit.**

30.   See glossary for **Control Unit.**

31.   See glossary for **Address.**

32.   See glossary for **Register.**

33.   See glossary for **Silicon Chip.**

34.   See glossary for **Integrated Circuit (IC).**

35.   See glossary for **Random Access Memory (RAM).**

36.   See glossary for **Read Only Memory (ROM).**

37.   The former hold their data as long as the power is applied, whilst the latter actually needs to be refreshed every few milliseconds. Dynamic RAM demands extra circuitry for the refresh action, but their lower cost has rendered them popular in the microcomputer field.

38.   See glossary for **Operating System (OS).**

39.   See glossary for **Mouse.**

40.   See glossary for **Storage Device.**

41.   See glossary for **Disk Drive.**

42.   See glossary for **Visual Display Unit (VDU).**

43.   See glossary for **Monitor.**

44.   See glossary for **Laser Printer.**

45.   See glossary for **Interface.**

46.   See glossary for **Stand-alone.**

47.   See glossary for **Multi-tasking** or **Multi-user.**

48.   See glossary for **Storage Capacity.**

49.   See glossary for **Bus.**

50.   See glossary for **Bit.**

51.   See glossary for **Byte.**

52.   See glossary for **Baud Rate.**

53.   See glossary for **Parallel Transmission.**

54.   See glossary for **Serial Transmission.**

55.   The major standards are the S100 bus, IEEE Standard 488 bus and the RS232 interface.

56.   See glossary for **Printed Circuit Board (PCB).**

57.   See glossary for **Computer Chassis.**

58.   See glossary for **Input/Output (I/O).**

59.   See glossary for **Interface Circuit.**

60.   See glossary for **Application Program.**

61.   This was in fact the case with the early versions of single-board processors available before the MITS Altair 8800.

62.   See glossary for **Off-line.**

63.   See glossary for **Floppy Disk.**

64.   See glossary for **Hard Disk Storage.**

65.   See glossary for **Paper-tape Read-out Printers.**

66.   See glossary for **Dot Matrix.**

67.   See glossary for **Ink-Jet Printer.**

68.   These terms are the standard classification used for the relative sizes of microprocessors. In this case the numbers 4, 8, 16 and 32, refer to the size of the data word used in their arithmetic and logic functions (as defined by their manufacturer).

69.   See glossary for **Network.**

70.   See glossary for **Language.**

71.   See glossary for **Software House.**

72.   See glossary for **User Base.**

73.   See glossary for **CP/M.**

74.   See glossary for **MS-DOS.**

75.   See glossary for **PC-DOS.**

76.   See glossary for **UNIX.**

77.   See glossary for **UCSD-p.**

78.   See glossary for **OS/2.**

79.   See glossary for **Application Package.**

80.   See glossary for **Spreadsheet.**

81.   See glossary for **Utilities.**

82.   See glossary for **Application Software.**

83.   See glossary for **Vacuum Tube Valve.**

84. See glossary for **Semiconductor.**

85. See glossary for **Transistor.**

86. Ernest Braun and Stuart MacDonald, *Revolution in Miniature: History and Impact of Semiconductor Electronics,* Cambridge University Press, 1978.

87. See glossary for **Planar Process.**

88. J. Tilton, *International Diffusion of Technology: The Case of Semiconductors,* The Brookings Institution, Washington, DC, 1971.

89. See **Planar Technique** for explanation of these other production processes in the glossary.

90. Robert Noyce, Microelectronics, *Scientific American,* Vol. 237, No. 3, pp.62–69.

91. See glossary for **Bipolar Logic.**

92. See glossary for **Large Scale Integration (LSI).**

93. See glossary for **Customised Circuits.**

94. See glossary for **Metal-Oxide Semiconductor (MOS).**

95. *Business Week,* 25 April 1970.

96. *Electronics,* 10 January 1974.

97. Robert W. Wilson, Peter K. Ashton and Thomas P. Egan, *Innovation, Competition and Government Policy in the Semiconductor Industry,* p.89, Charles River Associates, 1980.

98. See glossary for **Magnetic Core.**

99. See glossary for **K.**

100. See glossary for **Polysilicon.**

101. Lawrence Altman, Special report, MEMORIES, it's a user's paradise: Cheaper RAMs, reprogrammable ROMs, CCDs and bubbles coming along, *Electronics,* pp.81–96, 20 January 1977.

102. George Sideris, AMS brushes off blows, *Electronics,* pp.74–76, 30 August 1973.

103. Howard Wolff, 4096-bit RAMS are on the doorstep, *Electronics,* pp.75–77, 12 April 1973.

104. Mostek employed a 16 pin design, whilst TI and Intel had adopted a 22 pin design.

105 *Electronics,* 13 June 1974.

106. See glossary for **Silicon Gate Technology.**

107. Author's parenthesis.

108. G. L. Simons, *Introducing Microcomputers,* p.30, The NCC Publications, 1979.

109. *Fortune,* p.137, November 1975.

110. *Fortune,* p.137, November 1975.

111. *Electronics,* 1 March 1973.

112. This Motorola unit needed only one +5V power supply, compared to three for the Intel 8080.

113. See glossary for **Cathode Ray Tube (CRT).**

114. See glossary for **Controller Chip.**

115. See glossary for **Direct Memory Access (DMA).**

116. *Electronics News,* p.56, 8 March 1976.

117. *Financial World,* 15 March, 1977.

118. E. A. Torrero, *Focus on Microprocessors: Electronic Design,* Vol. 22, No. 18, p.57, 1974.

119. R. R. Noyce and M. E. Hoff Jr, A history of microprocessor development at Intel, *IEEE Micro,* February 8–21, 1981.

120. See glossary for **Processing Speed.**

121. See glossary for **Address-size.**

122. K. Pavitt, Technology, innovation and strategic management. In *Strategic Management Research: A European Perspective,* (J. McGee and H. Thomas, Eds.) John Wiley, 1986.

123. See glossary for **PROM.**

124. See glossary for **OEM.**

125. See glossary for **Light Emitting Diode (LED).**

126. Venture Development Corporation, 1976, p.24.

127. See glossary for **Toggle Switch.**

128. See glossary for **Motherboard (Backplane).**

129. See glossary for **Formatter.**

130. See glossary for **Interface Card.**

CHAPTER THREE: THE EARLY STAGES

1. Dostoevsky, *The Idiot,* translated David Magarshack, 1868.

2. During this chapter, the personal computer will initially be referred to as a microcomputer. This being the term originally applied to the early machines. Later, during the take-off stage of the industry's evolution, the term personal computer was introduced and is subsequently used from that period onwards within the text. However, when referring to the overall industry, the term personal computer will normally be used in the text.

3. Philip Kotler, *Marketing Management: Analysis, Planning and Control,* 5th edn, p.377, Prentice/Hall, 1984.

4. See glossary for **Terminal.**

5. See glossary for **Programming.**

6. See glossary for **Programming Language.**

7. See glossary for **Memory Board.**

8. See glossary for **BASIC.**

9. See glossary for **High Level Languages.**

10. See Glossary for **Machine Code.**

11. See glossary for **Interface Board.**

12. See glossary for **Single Board Systems.**

13. See glossary for **Kb.**

14. See glossary for **Printed Circuit Board Substrata.**

15. In Table 3.1 the Nature of Parent and Nature of Entry Move represent specific categories which are defined as follows:

    (1) **Nature of Parent Company:**

    (a) Single Business:

    A company that manufactures and distributes a single product, a line of products with variations in size and style, or a set of closely related products linked by technology or market structure.

(b) Dominant Business:

A company that derives 70–95% of sales from a single business (as defined above) or a vertically integrated chain of businesses.

(c) Related Business:

A company that has diversified into related areas, where no single business accounts for more than 70% of sales.

(d) Unrelated Business or Conglomerate:

A company that has diversified without necessarily relating new businesses to old, and where no single business accounts for as much as 70% of sales.

(e) No Parent Company:

Where there is a newly started company with no parent company.

(2) **Nature of Entry Move:**

(a) Geographic Expansion:

The new entry is the expansion of a personal computer market previously developed outside the United States.

(b) Segment Expansion:

The company was already competing in another market for computers, (e.g. mainframes, minis or small business computers) and entry into personal computers represents a new segment.

(c) Related Expansion:

The company was not already producing computers, but the entry was closely related horizontally to its pre-existing businesses (e.g. electronic calculators or computer peripherals).

(d) Forward Vertical Integration:

The new entry is related to pre-existing businesses and is at a stage closer to the end user (e.g. semiconductor manufacturer moving into personal computer manufacturing).

(e) Backward Vertical Integration:

The new entry is related to pre-existing businesses and is at a stage closer to the sources of supply (e.g. electronic specialist store moving into personal computer manufacturing).

(f) Unrelated Diversification:

The new entry is not closely related to its pre-existing businesses.

(g) No Pre-Existing Businesses:

The new entry is a start-up company with no parent company.

16.   See above footnote for explanation.

17.   See glossary for **Mass Storage.**

18.   See glossary for **Cassette Drive.**

19.   See glossary for **Paper Tape Reader.**

20.   See glossary for **Paper Tape Punch.**

21.   See glossary for **Plotter.**

22.   See glossary for **Voice Encoder/Decoder.**

23.   See glossary for **Optical Character Encoders/Decoders.**

24.   See glossary for **Magnetic Media.**

25.   See glossary for **Word Processor.**

26.   *The Personal Computer Industry,* Venture Development Corporation, 1976.

27.   See glossary for **Installed Base.**

28.   *The Personal Computer Industry,* Venture Development Corporation, p.61, 1976.

29.   *Ibid.,* p.64.

30.   Author's insert in parenthesis.

31.   See Freiberger and Swaine, *Fire in the Valley: The Making of the Personal Computer,* Osborne/McGraw-Hill, 1984, p.39.

32.   J.E.S. Parker, *The Economics of Innovation,* 1978, Longman, p.126. Various diffusion studies have classified adopters by the time of their first use of a new product. One such classification divides users into innovators, early adopters, early majority, late majority and laggards. See; E. M. Rogers, *Diffusion of Innovations,* Free Press, New York, 1962.

33.   See Chapter One, for further details of this proposition.

34.   See glossary for **Expansion Board.**

35.   See glossary for **Bundling.**

36.   *The Personal Computer Industry II : A Strategic Analysis: 1981–1985,* Venture Development Corporation, 1981, p.122.

37.   *Ibid.,* p.122.

38.   See glossary for **Controller Board.**

39.   See glossary for **Integrated System.**

40.   See glossary for **Disk Storage Device.**

41.   See glossary for **Integrated Computer Package.**

42.   J. McGee, "Barriers to Growth for Small Innovating Companies in the U.K. and the Role of Competitive Strategy", a paper prepared for the ACARD Study, *Barriers to Growth for Small Innovating Companies,* February 1987, pp.14–16.

43.   *Ibid.,* pp.14–16.

44.   Author's parenthesis and enclosure.

45.   McGee, *Barriers to Growth,* February 1987, p.16.

46.   See glossary for **Second Generation Computer.**

47.   Research Letter, *The Personal Computer Industry,* Arthur D. Little, L780901, 7 September, 1978.

48.   "Impact Services", *The Personal Computer Industry — An Update,* Arthur D. Little, L791002, 12 October 1979, p.2.

CHAPTER FOUR: FROM TAKE-OFF TO GROWTH

1.   Ernest Dimnet, *The Art of Thinking,* 1928.

2.   See glossary for **Software Program.**

3.   See glossary for **Communications Network.**

4.   See glossary for **Hard Disk Technology.**

5.   D. H. Fylstra, Software, the lever in personal computer sales, *The Rosen Electronics Letter,* p.40, July 21, 1980.

6.   For an authoritative account of developments in the software field, the reader is referred to Robert T. Fertig, *The Software Revolution: Trends, Players, Market Dynamics in Personal Computer Software*, North Holland, 1986.

7.   See glossary for **Computer Families.**

8.   See glossary for **Horizontal Software Compatibility.**

9.   See glossary for **Portability.**

10.   Decision Resources, *The Outlook for the U.S. Personal Computer Industry*, p.10, December 1981, Arthur D. Little, T811201.

11.   See glossary for **Modem.**

12.   In most market research reports reviewed by the author, very small businesses were defined as those with annual sales of less than $5million and/or under 10 employees.

13.   *The Personal Computer Industry II: A Strategic Analysis, 1981–1985*, p.56, Venture Development Corporation, May 1981.

14.   See glossary for **Storage Disk.**

15.   J. W. Steffens, Entry Behaviour and Competition in the Evolution of the Personal Computer Industry, (1975–1983), unpublished doctoral thesis, The University of London, 1988.

16.   See glossary for **Desktop Computer.**

17.   "Decision Resources", Arthur D. Little, December 1981, p.24.

18.   See glossary for **Shrink-Wrapped Software.**

19.   See glossary for **DOS (Disc Operating System).**

CHAPTER FIVE: ENTRY OF THE GIANTS AND LEGITIMISATION

1.   Quotation from a Tandy Corp. executive at the time of IBM's launch of the Personal Computer in August 1981. Source: *Business Week Cover Story*, 3 October 1983.

2.   See glossary for **Clone.**

3.   See glossary for **Data Processing (DP).**

4.   J. W. Steffens, Entry Behaviour and Competition in the Evolution of the Personal Computer Industry (1975–1983), unpublished doctoral thesis, The University of London, 1988.

5.   These were identified through the field research interviews in Steffens, Entry Behaviour, 1988.

6.   The IBM PC was the brand name adopted by the first IBM personal computer.

7.   See glossary for **Megabyte (Mb).**

8.   See glossary for **User Memory Capacity.**

9.   See glossary for **User-friendly.**

10.   See glossary for **Integrated Program.**

11.   See glossary for **Database.**

12.   See glossary for **Operating Memory.**

13.   See glossary for **High Resolution Screen.**

14.   See glossary for **IBM Compatible.**

15.   See glossary for **Workstation.**

16.   Apple Computer's definition of user-friendliness incorporated the idea that users should be able to operate the machine effectively within one hour.

17.   See glossary for **Icon.**

18.   See glossary for **Cursor Control.**

19.   See glossary for **Minifloppy Drive.**

20.   See glossary for **Flat-panel Display.**

21.   See glossary for **LCD.**

22.   See glossary for **Electroluminescent Display.**

23.   See glossary for **User Interface.**

24.   See glossary for **Clicking.**

25.   See glossary for **Desk-top Publishing (DTP).**

26.   See glossary for **Graphics Design.**

27.   M. M. Obenzinger, *The Personal Computer Market: A Profile for Growth Industry Review,* Lehman Brothers Kuhn Loeb, p.17, January 1983.

28.   See glossary for **Low-end Machine.**

29.   Steffens, Entry Behaviour, 1988.

30.   *Yankee Group Report,* Field Interview, 1983.

31.   See glossary for **Notebook Computer.**

32.   See glossary for **High-end Machine.**

33.   Source: Dataquest Incorporated.

34.   See glossary for **DP.**

35.   See glossary for **MIS.**

36.   *Yankee Group Report,* p.226, 1982.

37.   Source: *Dataquest Personal Computer Industry Report,* 1983.

38.   *IBM Data and Strategy Book,* p.45, International Data Corporation (IDC), 1983.

39.   The story of Xerox's entry into the personal computer industry is well documented in the book, *Fumbling the Future,* by D.K. Smith and R.D. Alexander, William Morrow and Co., 1988.

40.   See glossary for **Ethernet.**

41.   See glossary for **Open Architecture.**

42.   *IBM Data and Strategy Book,* p.31, International Data Corporation(IDC), 1983.

43.   See glossary for **Turnkey System.**

44.   See glossary for **Clustered.**

45.   See glossary for **Office Automation (OA).**

46.   Source: An Easy-Come: Easy-Go World, *Time Magazine,* p.44, September 5, 1983.

47.   See glossary for **Data Storage Device.**

48.   Based on a quote from George Morrow of Morrow Designs Inc. Source: *Businessweek,* p. 83, October 3, 1983.

49.   See glossary for **Bus Expansion.**

50.   See glossary for **Memory Pack.**

51.   See glossary for **Colour TV Interface.**

52.   Steffens, Entry Behaviour, 1988. The opinions of U.S. industry observers reported in this paragraph were based upon field research interviews by the author.

CHAPTER SIX: FROM CONSOLIDATION TO MATURATION AND SATURATION

1. Ken Olsen, founder of Digital Equipment Corporation, extract from *Digital at Work: Snapshots from the First Thirty-Five Years,* p.176, edited by Jamie Parker Pearson, Digital Press, 1992.

2. See glossary for **Communications Technology.**

3. Information Systems Industry here refers to companies competing in hardware and software activities.

4. *Datamation,* p.14, June 15, 1992.

5. *Ibid.,* p.33.

6. Whilst in the early days of Apple's development, Steven Jobs, one of its-cofounders is reputed to have expressed the desire to make the personal computer do for computing what Henry Ford did for the motor car, in other words to make it available for nearly everyone.

7. M. Hammer, "Reengineering Work: Don't Automate, Obliterate", *Harvard Business Review,* Jul-Aug 1990. This provides a good outline of the principle ideas on the subject by the author who coined the phrase "Reengineering".

8. George Stalk, "Time-The Next Source of Competitive Advantage", *Harvard Business Review,* July-August 1988; and G.Stalk and T. Hout, *Competing Against Time: How Time-Based Competition is Reshaping Global Markets,* Free Press, 1990. The book is a good source of further references on the subject. Also see J.D. Blackburn, *Time-Based Competition: The Next Battle Ground for American Manufacturing,* Business One Irwin, Illinois, 1991. This provides a clear insight into some practical strategies to achieve time-compression, especially in the manufacturing arena.

9. P.G. Smith and D.G. Reinertsen, *Developing Products in Half the Time,* Van Nostrand Reinhold, New York, 1991. This provides an explanation of how development cycles can be speeded up in different areas of management. It is a good source of further references on the subject.

10. Many books have been written on this subject, although it is once again receiving keen interest in the field of leadership management. J.H. Shonk, *Team-Based Organisations: Developing a Successful Team Environment,* Business One Irwin, Illinois, 1992, provides a contemporary and practical look at the subject.

11. See glossary for **Bus Architecture.**

12. See glossary for **Personal Digital Assistant (PDA).**

13. See glossary for **Communications System.**

14. See glossary for **Desktop Workstation.**

15. See glossary for **RISC.**

16. See glossary for **CISC.**

17. According to the Dataquest Inc. ranking, as reported in *Datamation,* p.84, 15 June 1992.

18. "Inside Intel", *Business Week,* p.49, June 1, 1992.

19. "Inside Intel", *Business Week,* June 1, 1992.

20. See glossary for **Emulation Display.**

21. See glossary for **Compiler.**

22. See glossary for **Millions of Instructions per Second (MIPS).**

23. See glossary for **Mac.**

24. See glossary for **Open System.**

25. See glossary for **Micro Channel Architecture (MCA).**

26. As well as Compaq – AST, Epson America, Hewlett Packard, NEC, Olivetti, Tandy, Wyse and Zenith participated in the EISA joint venture announcement.

27. See glossary for **Extended Industry Standard Architecture (EISA).**

28. See glossary for **Graphical User Interface (GUI).**

29. "Microsoft", *Business Week,* p.38, February 24, 1992.

30. See glossary for **Windows.**

31. See glossary for **Object-Oriented.**

32. See glossary for **Open Systems Interconnect (OSI).**

33. See glossary for **Multimedia.**

34. See glossary for **CD-ROM.**

35. See glossary for **Mb.**

36. See glossary for **Gigabyte.**

37. Note: This figure is not to scale, but is merely intended to illustrate the overall pattern and point of convergence between the two markets.

38. See glossary for **Tower Personal Computer.**

39. See glossary for **Server.**

40. See glossary for **VAR.**

41. J. A. Schumpeter, *Capitalism, Socialism and Democracy,* Harper, New York, 1942.

42. Study conducted by International Data Corporation, 1992.

43. See glossary for **LAN.**

44. Further details concerning this and other acquisitions that took place in the worldwide computer industry are presented in the next chapter.

45. Report on some 650 business and home computer buyers in the United States conducted by Frost and Sullivan Inc., appearing in "Savvy Consumers Keep PC Makers Hopping", *Business Week,* p.71, November 2, 1992.

46. See glossary for **Logic Set.**

47. See glossary for **Videoboard.**

48. See glossary for **Supplemental Components.**

49. Company Reports.

50. "Savvy Consumers", *Business Week,* p.71, November 2, 1992.

51. See glossary for **Systems Integration.**

52. See glossary for **Systems Integrator.**

53. See glossary for **Value Added Reseller (VAR).**

54. See glossary for **Bolt-on.**

55. See glossary for **Seamless Environment.**

CHAPTER SEVEN: THE EVOLUTION OF INTERNATIONAL COMPETITION

1. Theodore Levitt, *The Marketing Imagination,* The Free Press, p.41, 1983.

2. Austin H. Kiplinger and Knight A. Kiplinger, *America in the Global '90's,* The Kiplinger

Washington Editors, Inc., p.81, 1989.

3.   K. Ohmae, *Triad Power: The Coming Shape of Global Competition*, New York, Free Press, p.21, 1975.

4.   A large amount of literature has been generated within the past few years on the topic of 1992. The reader is referred to P.Cecchini, M.Catinat and A. Jacquemin, *The European Challenge 1992: The Benefits of a Single Market*, Wildwood House, 1988; for a favourable review of the changes involved. James Dudley, *1992: Strategies for The Single Market*, Kogan Page, 1989; presents a reasonable overview of the strategic options available to companies, whilst J. Kay (Ed.), *1992: Myths and Realities*, Centre for Business Strategy Report Series, London Business School, 1989; provides a set of five realistic essays on various aspects of the subject. Meanwhile, *Europe and the Multinationals: Issues and Responses for the 1990's*, edited by Stephen Young and James Hamill, Edward Elgar, 1992; is worth reading to gain an insight into the issues facing multinationals in Western Europe for the 1990's.

5.   See glossary for **SX.**

6.   See glossary for **Personal Workstation.**

7.   See glossary for **Power Users.**

8.   See glossary for **Workstation Network.**

9.   See glossary for **DX.**

10.   Research conducted by International Data Corporation in Western Europe during 1992 and reported with their permission.

11.   It should be noted that the data in Tables 7.6 and 7.7 are based upon country by country reporting. Thus certain companies may not show up in these tables, which nevertheless have a small market share in a number of countries, for example Dell Computer. Such companies could rank in other tables showing total sales for Western Europe. However, the purpose of these tables is to illustrate the variation in performance amongst the major players, both across Western Europe and within specific country markets.

12.   Research conducted by International Data Corporation in Western Europe during 1992 and reported with their permission.

13.   Based upon research conducted by International Data Corporation in Western Europe during 1992 and reported with their permission.

14.   A word of caution is necessary surrounding both the nature of this data and its interpretation. Firstly, it must be remembered that this data is representative of one research company's findings, however, these are generally born out by cross referral to other similar industry data sources. Furthermore, the fact that a company is not shown to have a level of sales in any particular country, does not necessarily mean that it is not active in marketing or selling its products in that particular country, but merely that its level of sales is not significant in terms of its share within the country market.

15.   Data for the Peoples' Republic of China was limited and therefore only general data is provided for this country, with little information on the details.

16.   Within all figures and tables shown in this Section of the chapter, it should be noted that all shipments and installed base figures for Japan (units and values) are for fiscal years, i.e. from April of the previous year through to March of the named year. Figures for the other countries are for the calendar year specified.

17.   See glossary for **IT.**

18.   The 1.2% figure for growth in shipments in value terms is based upon local currency figures, whereas US$ conversions showed a higher figure, which reflects a weaker yen, which moved

from US$1=Yen145 in 1990 to US$1=Yen135 in 1991.

19.   See glossary for **Centralised Systems.**

20.   Kanji represent the complex pictograms that form the basis of the Japanese language.

21.   See glossary for **Telecommunications Common Carrier.**

22.   IDC Report, August 1992, Japan Personal Computer Market Review and Forecast, 1991–1996.

23.   See glossary for **DOS/V.**

24.   *PC Wars in Japan*, Fortune, July 12, 1993, p.16.

25.   See glossary for **Telecommunications Infrastructure.**

26.   See glossary for **Windows Graphical Interface.**

27.   See glossary for **Piracy.**

28.   See glossary for **Local Language Packages.**

29.   Other U.S. mainframe computer companies such as Amdahl (US$2.5Bn turnover 1992) and Cray Research (US$0.8Bn turnover 1992) in supercomputers do not appear in the data, since they are not involved in the personal computer industry.

30.   See glossary for **Data Communications.**

31.   See glossary for **Box Manufacture.**

32.   Tables 7.15. and 7.16. are based upon data provided from Datamation, whose database tends to be constructed from the annual reports of companies and from data obtained from Dataquest, the market research company, thus reflecting financial year end figures. In contrast, Tables 7.17 and 7.18 are based upon data provided by International Data Corporation and was collected at the year end period, rather than on the financial year end. This largely accounts for the variations, although naturally, one would also expect differences in any figures collected by a number of independent research organisations in a market of this nature.

33.   This combined region of Japan and the rest of the World is largely made up of Japan and the Asia/Pacific region as was seen earlier in the introductory section to this chapter.

34.   See glossary for **File Server.**

35.   Keiretsu refers to highly diversified, vertically integrated corporate complexes, many of which are embedded in financial-industrial groups.

36.   C. H. Ferguson, "Computers and the Coming of the U.S. Keiretsu", *Harvard Business Review,* July-August, 1990, pp.55-70.

37.   The BUNCH is the acronym which was regularly used to refer to the five major U.S. mainframe computer companies that shared the market with IBM during the 1960s. It stood for Burroughs, Univac, NCR, Control Data and Honeywell.

38.   See glossary for **High Density Storage Medium.**

39.   See glossary for **High Density Transmission Systems.**

40.   See glossary for **Graphical Animation.**

41.   See glossary for **Simulation.**

CHAPTER EIGHT: REFLECTIONS, PATTERNS AND CONCLUSIONS

1.   Pascal, *Pensees,* p.22, 1670, translation by W. F. Trotter.

2.   See glossary for **Digital Based Information Technology.**

3.   See glossary for **Small-systems Computer.**

4.   See glossary for **Distributed Data Processing (DDP).**

5.   See glossary for **Client/Server.**

6.   See glossary for **Graphical User Based System.**

7.   See glossary for **Fax Board.**

8.   See glossary for **Communications Protocols.**

9.   See glossary for **Tape Back-up Unit.**

10.   See glossary for **Cellular Communications.**

11.   See glossary for **Pen Based Technology.**

12.   See glossary for **Pen Based Systems.**

13.   See glossary for **Desktop Supercomputers.**

14.   See glossary for **Mini Supercomputer.**

15.   See glossary for **High-end Server.**

16.   See glossary for **Palmtop Computer.**

17.   See glossary for **Super Minicomputer.**

18.   See glossary for **Massive Parallel Computer.**

19.   See glossary for **Multimedia Techniques.**

20.   These included articles in the computer trade press about the threat to the mainframe from minicomputers and likewise the threat to minis from low-end mainframes and high-end micros. They also included the doctoral research of this author, whose dissertation in 1988 clearly predicted the possible pattern of decline for the industry sectors described in this book.

CHAPTER NINE: TOWARDS THE FUTURE

1.   T. S. Eliot, *Four Quartets.*

2.   See glossary for **Information Software.**

3.   See glossary for **HDTV.**

4.   See glossary for **Digital Code.**

5.   See glossary for **Supercomputer.**

6.   See glossary for **Multimedia Storage.**

7.   RISC based products are computers or other electronic machines based on RISC type microprocessors.

8.   See glossary for **Windows NT.**

9.   See glossary for **Object-Oriented Programming.**

10.   See glossary for **Multimedia Technology.**

11.   See glossary for **Transparent System.**

12.   See glossary for **Server Based Networks.**

13.   See glossary for **Groupware.**

14.   See glossary for **File.**

15.   See glossary for **Scanning.**

16.   See glossary for **Compression.**

17. During the 1980s, software companies such as Microsoft, Claris and Lotus began developing their various applications programs with a high degree of compatibility in data transfer and user commands. This was to provide customers with easier to use systems and at the same time to encourage them to buy their range of applications from a common supplier. Accountancy packages, with their various modules have long been referred to as a suite of programs, that go to make up the complete set.

18. Today's use of the term personal assistant tends to refer to people who are usually responsible for assisting executives or managers in their tasks. These may include filing, taking dictation or audio-typing, producing letters, arranging meetings, acting as a gatekeeper, controlling information flows between their boss and the outside world. Tomorrow's use of this term is likely to grow from the current early versions of PDAs or Personal Digital Assistants, which are currently mobile compact machines, but which may eventually become a network of systems to support the individual on a worldwide basis. See glossary for more information on **PDAs.**

19. See glossary for **Micro Disks.**

20. An Interactive Format refers to a system that will permit the user of a computer to interact (as in a simulation). This ability of the system to be active on a real-time basis has been put to great effect in simulation and games programs. It has enormous potential in the educational marketplace.

EPILOGUE

1. William Shakespeare, *The Tempest,* Act IV, Scene I.

2. Leo Tolstoy, *War and Peace,* p.1442, Penguin Books edition, 1978.

3. Daniel Bell, *The Coming of Post Industrial Society,* Basic Books, New York, 1973; and Harper and Row, New York, 1976; Heinemann, London, 1974.

4. Reported in editor's introduction, Tom Forester, *The Microelectronics Revolution,* p.xiii, Blackwell, 1980.

5. See glossary for **Virtual Reality.**

6. Alternative realities in this context refers to the development of ideas and machines for the creation of Virtual Reality.

7. The idea of a personal communicating video wrist unit is based upon the proposition that electronics technology will: (1) continue to achieve significant advances in miniaturisation; (2) continue to reduce in price; (3) continue to increase in power. If these assumptions are met and if the global telecommunications infrastructure continues to develop at a competitive rate, then it seems highly probable that a form of video wrist unit will be developed that will perform the tasks of the currently evolving personal digital assistants. However, it will be more compact and more sophisticated in its performance.

8. Fritjof Capra, *The Tao of Physics,* Bantam, New York, 1980. This book provides a rich and fascinating look at the connections between modern physics with eastern philosophy, mysticism and religion in the context of paradigm shifts.

GLOSSARY OF TECHNICAL TERMS

Please Note: Items in *italics* indicate the term is presented elsewhere in this glossary.

Abacus: This is an ancient counting device, which consists of a frame within which rods are fixed and upon which same rods are located a specific number of beads, which can be freely moved by a user of the device. Depending upon its location, each bead represents a digit or a specific number of digits, whilst each rod represents a given denomination within the decimal system, such as tens, hundreds or thousands.

Address: An identification (a label, number or name) that designates the position of an item of data stored in *memory*.

Address-size: This refers to the width of the *address bus*, which determines the maximum size of the *computer's* main *memory*, because the number of wires in the *address bus* determines the maximum number of possible *memory* locations.

Analytical Engine: The intellectual design of this machine was undertaken by Charles Babbage between 1843 and 1846. The design anticipated many of the features of electronic computing devices which were developed much later in the late 1940s and early 1950s. The design envisioned a *memory* of a thousand 50-digit numbers and could do addition, subtraction, multiplication and division. Borrowing the Jacquard pattern-weaving loom, the overall calculations were to be controlled by a sequence of punched cards; the machine was thus to be directed through a variety of computations, and conditional branching was possible, including complex computations based upon nested loops. Although Babbage returned later in his life to try to make a test piece using die-cast *components* it was not completed at the time of his death in 1871.

Application: This refers to the use to which the *computer* is put by the user, such as *word processing, desk-top publishing* or education.

Application Package: See *Application Software.*

Application Program: See *Application Software.*

Application Software: *Programs* or packages designed to perform specific tasks or *applications*. To be distinguished from the *operating system* which controls the operation of the total *computer system*.

Arithmetic Logic Unit: That part of the central processor which performs arithmetic and logical operations required by an *input* command. In some *computer systems*, both the arithmetic and logic units exist as separate parts of the central processor.

Arithmetic Unit: See *Arithmetic Logic Unit*.

Auxiliary Storage: Often referred to as auxiliary *memory* or secondary storage, this consists of a non-volatile *memory* storage medium, which stores both programs and data, even when the power is switched off. The nature of the auxiliary storage medium is such that it is usually possible to rewrite without deterioration, although certain types of optical auxiliary storage are read-only formats. The range of such devices continues to grow. Earlier versions for *personal computers* relied on cassette tapes. However, in time these have expanded to include *floppy disks*, fixed-head and moving-head hard *disks*, video-cartridge *disks*, magnetic tapes (especially for back-ups), as well as solid-state memories and optical and laser *disks*.

BASIC: An acronym for Beginner's All-purpose Symbolic Instruction Code. Originally designed as an easy to learn, easy to use algebraic *programming language* at Dartmouth College, USA. BASIC has a limited range of commands and simple statement formats.

Baud Rate: The number of *bits* of data transmitted in one second. One baud is one *bit* per second.

Bipolar Logic: An *input* signal is defined as bipolar if different logical states are represented by signals of different electrical voltage polarity.

Bit: A binary digit. The basic unit of *computer* information that can be represented in binary notation (i.e. zero or one).

Boards: This is synonymous for *Printed Circuit Boards (PCBs)*.

Bolt-on: This refers to the addition of extra *components* or *peripherals* that enhance the *computer's* performance with little or no alteration to the basic system design.

Box Manufacture: This refers to the process by which some *computer* companies that produce low-end clones that are priced as commodity type items and involve the assembly of industry standard *components* into the machine. Their only differentiation is on price.

Bundling: This represents the marketing practice whereby the cost of a *computer* system may include both the CPU together with an operating system, selected *peripheral* devices and, on occasions, sales or service agreements, thus forming a complete *systems* purchase.

Bus: A passive interconnecting system path over which information is transferred, from any one of many sources to any one of many destinations. The devices involved are connected in parallel, sharing each wire with all other devices on the bus.

Bus Architecture: This refers to the way in which the *bus* is designed. Three major architectures dominate the industry during the early 1990s, namely, Industry Standard Architecture (ISA) *bus*, which was initially developed for IBM's AT (Advanced Technology) *computers*; *Micro Channel Architecture (MCA) bus*, which is a proprietary 32-*bit bus* used in high-end IBM PS/2 *computers*; and Enhanced Industry Standard Architecture (EISA), which is a competitive *bus* to MCA.

Bus Expansion: This represents an extension of the *computer's* data *bus* and *address bus* that includes a number of receptacles (slots) for fitting adapter *boards*.

Byte: A grouping of adjacent binary digits (*bits*) operated on by the *computer* as a unit. Normally shorter than a word, unless otherwise indicated, a byte is assumed to be 8 *bits* long.

CAD: An acronym for *Computer Aided Design*.

Cassette Drive: A tape transport for handling magnetic tape contained in cassettes.

Cathode Ray Tube (CRT): An electronic display device, similar to a television picture tube, upon which information is presented. Its surface provides the screen used in *visual display units* and *word processors*.

CD-ROM: This is an acronym for Compact Disk-Read Only Memory and represents the predominant form of *read only (ROM)* optical *disk*. Both *disk* and drive are based on the compact audio consumer product. The data on the *disk* is encoded in the form of a spiral of minute bumps impressed into the surface of the *disk* at the time of manufacture, and cannot subsequently be altered. Many commercial *databases* are now available on CD-ROM, often as an alternative to an on-line service.

Cellular Communications: This refers to the form of *communications systems* which have evolved from the theory developed at Bell Labs. Essentially, a large geographical area is divided up into small areas called cells. Each cell has a base station that transmits to and receives from all mobile phones within the area of the cell.

Central Processing Unit (CPU): This represents the "brain" of the computer. It contains the *arithmetic* and *logic unit*, the core *memory* and the *control unit* which directs and coordinates the operation of the *computer* and its *peripheral* units.

Centralised Systems: This refers to a *computer* based *network*, where the processing power is focused upon a single *computer*, such as a *mainframe* or super *mainframe*.

Chip: This is a common term for a miniaturised integrated circuit made of a *semiconductor* material, which is usually silicon. Through advances in *semiconductor* technology the density (or number of electronic components) has grown enormously over the past twenty years. Chips are square or rectangular in shape and measure about 1/16th to 5/8th of an inch on a side, whilst being only 1/30th of an inch thick. However, only the top 1/1000th of an inch actually holds the circuits and their millions of components. *Memory* chips and *microprocessors* are the two kinds of chips most commonly used in the *computer industry*, however, special-purpose customised chips are also built for other tasks, such as control of *disk* drives and chips for generating video and audio output.

CISC: An acronym for Complex Instruction Set *Computer*. It refers to the design of the *microprocessor* in which the instruction set has evolved to satisfy the needs of system *software* to enable generation of reliable efficient object code, often in a time-sharing environment governed by a specific *operating system*.

Clicking: This involves the action of pressing and quickly releasing a *mouse* button.

Client/Server: This represents a *computer systems* architecture in which a personal *computer* or *workstation* acts as a client which requests information from a *server*, which is the supplying machine and may range from being a powerful *personal computer* or *workstation* through to a *mini* or *mainframe computer*. The communication between client and *server* is usually achieved via a *local area network*. Most usually the client unit provides the *user interface* and performs most of the *applications* processing tasks. Meanwhile, the *server* maintains the *databases* and processes requests from the client to download data and update the *databases*. The *server* is also responsible for systems security and integrity. In practice, a *server* supports a number of clients, which may vary in size from two or three units up to many hundreds, depending upon the power of the *server*.

Clone: This represents a *hardware* device or other system that is claimed by its manufacturer or supplier to be a functional copy of a product from another company and will be capable of providing identical results when running a *software program*. The IBM *PC* attracted a number of clones.

Clustered: This refers to a group of *hardware* devices that are under the control of a single master *computer*.

Colour TV Interface: An *interface* for connection to a colour TV.

Communications Network: This involves a system whereby information can be transmitted between pieces of *hardware*.

Communications Protocols: A set of *hardware* and *software* standards that govern the transmission of data between *terminals* and *computers* using *telecommunications*.

Communications System: See *Communications Network.*

Communications Technology: This refers to the vast array of technologies used in the transmission and communication of data in its various forms. During the past decade the convergence between *computer* and communications technologies has blurred the previous distinctions. Nowadays, *digital technology* is at the core of both *computer* and *communication systems* providing for computerised control of *communications systems* and for the integral use of *communications systems* within *computer systems*. Modern communications technology is involved with a vast array of products, some of which are discrete, such as telephones or satellites, whilst others may be built into *computers*, such as *modems* or fax units. In addition, communications technology is now involved in handling the transfer of data in both narrow and wide band-width formats ranging from millions of *bits* of *computer* data per second, ranging through voice to moving visual images.

Compiler: A *computer program* which translates a *program* written in a high level *language* such as FORTRAN or COBOL into the binary code that *computers* can understand which is referred to as *machine code.*

Components: The basic elements that make up various electronic devices including *computers*. These may be either passive, such as resistors, capacitors etc. or active, such as valves, *transistors* or *chips* etc.

Compression: Any method in information *systems* whereby data can be coded or recoded in order to make use of redundancy in that data, as a result of which the data is packed into a smaller storage space.

Comptometer: An early specific design of mechanical computing device.

Computer: This is a general purpose machine, device or system that is capable of following instructions to carry out a sequence of operations in a distinctly and explicitly defined manner, some of which are without human intervention. *Hardware* refers to the computer itself and all the peripherals attached to it such as *printers* or *disk drives*. *Software* consists of the instructions which tell the machine what to do, which consists of an *operating system* and *applications programs.*

Computer Aided Design (CAD): This involves the use of a *computer* and design *software program*, which allows the user to create designs which range from architectural to specialised engineering, such as naval and aerospace technologies. Initially only available on *mainframe* and *minicomputer systems*, the development of more powerful *microprocessors* and associated graphics *software* has brought CAD *software* to technical *workstations* and the high-end of *personal computer* platforms.

Computer Aided Engineering (CAE): See *Computer Integrated Manufacturing.*

Computer Chassis: This refers to the frame within which *computers* are mounted. Originally, on *mainframe computers* it referred to the framework within which the various parts of the *computer* were assembled.

Computer Families: A group of *computers* that represent successive generations of a particular *computer system* and are likely to have similar but not identical architectures. e.g. the Macintosh family.

Computer Industry: In this context the computer industry refers to those companies involved in the manufacture and/or marketing of *computers* and *workstations*, *peripherals*, associated *computer software*, *data communications*, services and maintenance activities.

Computer Integrated Manufacturing (CIM): This normally refers to the process whereby *computers* assist in the design and manufacturing of products. This incorporates *Computer Aided Design (CAD)* and Computer Aided Manufacturing (CAM), which involves robotics and *computer* controlled manufacturing processes and control *systems*.

Computer Literacy: This is a term to describe the level of competence a person has in handling *computer* operations.

Computer System: A complete *computer* installation, which not only includes the basic *central processing unit*, but also the *peripherals*, such as a keyboard, *monitor, disk drives* and a *printer* in which all the *components* are able to work with each other.

Connectors: Within a *computer system* this refers to any cable or wire which links a *computer* to other *computers* or *peripheral* devices.

Consumer Electronics Industry: In this context the consumer electronics industry refers to those companies involved in the manufacture and/or marketing of a wide range of electronics products and systems which are traditionally sold to the general public. Historically, this has included Hi-Fi equipment, such as stereo amplifiers, speakers, record players, cassette players, CD-players, radios and televisions. With the diffusion of digital technology, the breadth of the industry widened to include digital watches and cameras. More recently, the development of home electronic games machines, together with the expansion of *personal computer* based games has led to a convergence of the *computer* and consumer electronics industries. New product development aimed at both the business and consumer market, such as *laptop* and *palmtop computers*, the latter being referred to as *personal digital assistants* has made the boundaries still more unclear between *computers* and consumer electronics products.

Control Unit: Part of the processor responsible for controlling sequences of operations.

Control Program: In contrast to an *application program*, a control program represents *software* that controls the operation of a *computer* and has the highest priority within its hierarchical structure of commands. Examples of control programs include *operating systems* and *network* control *systems*.

Controller Board: The *control unit* for a particular *peripheral* device which may contain considerable processing power and *memory*.

Controller Chip: This is a microcircuit that controls one or more devices of a particular kind. Its role is to regulate the flow of data between the *computer memory* and the device or devices.

Core Technology: This refers to the technology that is at the foundation of the *computer* or system. In particular it includes the *microprocessor* in terms of *hardware* and an *operating system* at the *software* level.

CP/M: An *operating system* which was used widely during the early stages of the evolution of *microcomputers* which specifies a standard for *memory* layout and file storage. Several versions of CP/M evolved including CP/M-80 for 8-*bit* machines, CP/M-86 for 16-*bit* micros, MPM (a *multi-user* version) and CPNET, a *network* version.

CRT: An acronym for *Cathode Ray Tube*.

Cursor Control: Typically a visible and flashing pointer on a display screen or *monitor* marking a position on the screen at which the next character will be placed.

Customised Circuits: This refers to electronic circuits produced for *computers*, as well as other industrial and consumer electronics products which are designed for a specific task. Special performance features on such circuits may often provide a source of differentiation in the market.

Daisy Wheel Printer: This is an impact type of *printer* that simulated the typeface produced upon office typewriters. The term daisy wheel refers to the plastic or metal hub, which has spokes on, at the end of which are located an image of the appropriate typing character. The daisy wheel itself spins around when a particular key is hit on the keyboard, so that a hammer will come down on the matching character of the daisy wheel, which presses against a typing ribbon. Before *laser* and *ink-*

jet printers, daisy wheel printers were used in preference to *dot-matrix printers* in order to produce letter quality typeface and were often used in conjunction with *word processors* and some *personal computers*.

Data Communications: The process by which data is sent between two or more *computers* via means of a *telecommunications system*.

Data Processing (DP): Involving the operations carried out on data, usually by a *computer* to derive information or to achieve order among *files*. It was also a generic term for the computing function in large organisations, hence the term Data Processing Department. However, many DP Departments are now known as MIS Departments.

Data Storage Device: A device or unit in which data is stored, e.g. a *floppy disk* or *hard disk*.

Database: A store of data on *files* to be made accessible to a *computer*. It is designed for operation in connection with an information retrieval system and is therefore not designed to satisfy a specific, limited *application*.

Desk-top Publishing (DTP): The use of a *personal computer* or *workstation* together with a page *printer* to produce typeset-quality text and graphics.

Desktop Computer: A *personal computer* or professional *workstation* designed to fit on a standard-sized office desk and equipped with sufficient *memory* and secondary storage to perform business computing tasks.

Desktop Supercomputer: This is a newly emerging category of *computer* that uses multiple high-performance *microprocessors*, which in some cases may be hundreds of *microprocessors*. In cases of maximum performance they are claimed to achieve levels similar to low-end *supercomputers*, hence their name.

Desktop Workstation: See *Desktop Computer*.

Difference Engine: This is a machine that automates the calculation of mathematical tables. In the context of the history of computing, the term normally refers to the Difference Engine designed by Charles Babbage. Contrary to popular belief, Babbage's Difference Engine was never built, save for the demonstration model. In 1833, Babbage ceased work on Difference Engine 1 and in 1847 he produced a design for a second Difference Engine which took advantage of simpler ideas, which he conceived in relation to his *Analytical Engine*. Technically, there was no obstacle to building the Difference Engine and indeed a replica based upon Babbage's drawings was constructed in 1991 at the Science Museum in London.

Digital Based Information Technology: This refers to devices and *systems* that handle information that is in digital format as opposed to analog format.

Digital Code: This is code used in *computers* and *communications systems* that is binary in its format.

Digital Technology: This refers to products and *systems* whose technology is based upon the use of *digital code*. It contrasts with analog technology.

Diode: This is an electronic *component* that is able to behave like a two-way valve. They are found as discrete *components* in electrical circuits or may be built into *semiconductor* materials. Frequently, they are used as sensors or *light emitting diodes (LEDs)*.

Direct Memory Access (DMA): A *data storage device* in which the access time to retrieve items of data is constant, relatively short and independent of the location previously addressed. Examples include *disk storage devices*. In contrast, the speed of access to data on tape storage is a function of the position of the data in relation to the last piece of data which was read by the *computer*.

Disk: This is a storage medium which is constructed as a circular plate. The data is stored via magnetic encoding. Disks can be constructed in *floppy disk* or *hard disk* form.

Disk Drive: This is a mechanical device which reads from, or writes to, magnetic *disks*. Also called a *disk* unit, or magnetic *disk* unit. It can also refer to the mechanism within a *disk* unit which performs the necessary movements of the magnetic *disk*.

Disk Operating System: This is a *program* that controls the operation of all activities related to the use of magnetic disks in a *computer system*.

Disk Storage Device: This is any *disk* based system for storing electronic data.

Distributed Data Processing (DDP): The concept whereby *data processing* resources are organised in a distributed manner, so that selected capabilities of the host *computer* are brought closer to the place where the data originates and/or processing is required. The idea was made famous by the *computer* company, Digital Equipment Corporation.

DOS: This is an acronym for *Disk Operating System*.

DOS/V: A specific version of *DOS*.

Dot Matrix: Method of printing characters in which each character is formed by a rectangular array of dots in a required shape. It has now been superseded by higher quality *ink-jet* and *laser* technologies.

Downsizing: Fundamentally this is the process within large corporations and other organisations of converting *mainframe* or *minicomputer* based *systems* to *personal computers, workstations* and *servers* linked together on a *local area network (LAN)*.

DP: An acronym for *Data Processing*.

DX: This refers to a specific version of the Intel 386 *microprocessor*, which communicates with *RAM* over a path which is 32-*bit* wide.

EDM (Electronic Direct Mail): This is a specific *application* of electronic mail (E-Mail) which usually transmits data, messages and documents across point to point systems or *computer* based *systems*. In EDM, the technology is used to transmit information that is concerned with selling a product or service and may take the form of an electronic advertisement or a consumer accessible booking or purchasing *system*.

EFT (Electronic Funds Transfer): This is a *system* that is designed to move financial funds and information between parties in an electronic format. It was originally developed for use in clearing bank operations and the major *networks* handle over US$1 billion worth of transactions per day.

EL: This is an acronym for *Electroluminescent*, which is a material such as phosphorus, that emits light when a voltage is applied to it from an independent source.

Electroluminescent Display: A display device that is used in association mainly with *portable computer systems* and allows a more compact or flat screen to be produced for the unit.

Emulation: The process of using a *computer* or other electronic device to operate on data and code produced for a different *computer* or type of machine, but which will appear to the *end-user* as if it were the original type of device. e.g. a *word processor* may be able to emulate a telex-machine, or a particular type of *computer* may be able to appear to handle *software* as a different type of *computer*.

Emulation Display: This is a *computer* terminal, *workstation, word processor* or *personal computer* that is able to emulate another machine. See *Emulation*.

End-user: The person who uses the *computer* and benefits from its functions and operations. Traditionally with central *mainframe computer systems*, the end-users were not always in direct contact with the *computer* itself, since their tasks such as analysis of sales data were processed by *data processing* personnel. However, with the development of the *personal computer*, the end-user is now more frequently the person actually using the machine.

EPOS: This is an acronym for Electronic Point of Sale and involves *computer systems* that are linked to cash-till units at check out positions in retail stores and shops. The technology includes *scanning* devices using bar-code technology to identify items presented by the purchaser, which are then charged in electronic format. In many *systems*, the billing process by credit card is also linked to the funds transfer of credit card *systems*. In sophisticated *systems*, it is possible for prices to be altered by the *computer* in response to changes in stock levels.

Ethernet: *Local area network* developed by Xerox using a baseband approach.

Expansion Board: A *printed circuit board* that may be inserted into a *computer* to give it extra functionality, which might be to provide more *memory*, a better display capability, more communications *interfaces*, extra *disk* or tape controllers, analog to digital converters.

Extended Industry Standard Architecture (EISA): This is a 32-*bit* expansion *bus* design introduced by a consortium of IBM *PC*-compatible *computer* makers to compete with IBM's proprietary *Micro Channel Bus*. Unlike the *Micro Channel Bus*, the EISA *bus* is downwardly compatible with existing 16-*bit peripherals* such as *disk drives* and display adapter.

Fax Board: An adapter that fits into an expansion slot of a *personal computer*, so that the *personal computer* can perform the key functions of a fax machine at a significantly lower price.

Fiber Optics: These are *communications systems* which make use of optical fibers for transmission of data. The optical fibers themselves consist of thin strands of glass formed into a wire that is capable of transmitting billions of *bits* of information per second. Furthermore, unlike electrical pulses, light pulses are unaffected by random releases of radiation in their environment. Fiber optics are increasingly used for both long-distance *telecommunications* and *local area networks*, as well as within specific areas of *computer systems*.

File: Generally used to describe a grouping of related records, sometimes referred to as a data set.

File Server: This is a unit that manages a set of *disks* and provides storage and archival services to *computers* on a *network* that may not have their own *disks*. In a *local area network* the function of acting as a file server can be performed by a *personal computer* that provides access to *files* for all the other *personal computers* and *workstations* in the *network*.

Flat-panel Display: A thin display screen used in *notebook* and *laptop computers* that uses one of several display technologies, such as electroluminescence, gas plasma displays, liquid crystal displays, or thin film *transistors*. A backlit display makes the display easier to read.

Floppy Disk: Also called a diskette or flexible *disk*, a low cost, random access form of storage for data and *programs*. The *disk* is housed permanently in a protective envelope with holes in it to allow a read/write head in the *disk drive* to come into contact with the *disk's* surface. As the *disk* is rotated in the drive, the head can be moved across its surface under *computer* control, to allow the *computer* to access information stored anywhere on its surface.

Formatter: This is the part of a *disk* read and write system that will set up a *floppy disk* or *hard-disk* to be used by a particular type of *computer*.

Germanium Transistor: A *transistor* made of the material germanium, which is used due to its semiconductivity and ability to strengthen and harden alloys.

Gigabyte: Giga- is a prefix denoting one thousand million or 10 to the power of 9. A gigabyte is therefore one thousand million *bits* of information.

Graphical Animation: This refers to the type of *software program* that is able to generate incremental changes in graphics drawings that are then run at high speed to create the illusion of movement. The technique was developed by film cartoonists, but involved drawing by hand, whereas the *software* solution can handle the changes much more simply and rapidly.

Graphical User Based System: These are *systems* that make use of *graphical user interfaces*.

Graphical User Interface (GUI): This is the method by which *icons* and graphical images are employed to represent functions used on a *computer*. They avoid the user having to enter commands by means of line text and are much simpler to use. Examples of GUIs include the Apple Macintosh and Microsoft *Windows* displays.

Graphics Design: This involves the design of an object by means of *computer* generated images. The two basic types of graphics used on *computers* are known as *object-oriented graphics*, also known as vector graphics, together with *bit*-mapped graphics, which is also known as raster graphics.

Graphics Tablet: This is an *input device* to a *computer*, which allows the user to draw with an electronic pen on an electronically sensitive panel. The images of the drawing are simultaneously displayed on the screen.

Groupware: This is a type of *software* which has been developed to support a specific *application* on a group basis, making use of computing and *communications technology*. The basis of groupware is that it will allow two or more users to interact in a common environment with a common *interface*, usually on a *local area network*. It is designed to permit the use of *programs* within a group of co-workers and is intended to increase the cooperation and joint productivity of the organisation.

Handheld: This refers to electronic machines such as calculators or *computers* that are small enough to be held and operated in the palm of the hand. Sometimes referred to as *palmtops*.

Hard Disk Storage: *Disk drive* using a rigid magnetic *disk* with the read/write heads operating just clear of the surface. Such *systems* are more expensive than a *floppy disk* but offer greater speed and capacity.

Hard Disk Technology: This refers to *computer* technology that makes use of *hard disk storage* devices, either external or internal to the *computer*.

Hardware: The physical equipment which comprises a *computer system* as opposed to the *programs* (*software*), etc. The mechanical, magnetic, electronic and electrical devices which go to make up a *computer*. The electrical circuitry and physical devices that make up a *computer system*.

HDTV: This is an acronym for *High Definition Television*.

High Definition Television (HDTV): This is a television with double the resolution of the US NTSC standard. Its introduction to the market has been delayed by decisions about the standard for transmitting both signals simultaneously.

High Density Storage Medium: This is a *storage device* that makes use of fine grained magnetic particles. It has higher capacity than ordinary double-density devices, but it is more expensive to manufacture.

High Density Transmission Systems: These are *communications* systems that are able to send data in high density streams or bursts and include broad bandwidth *systems*.

High Resolution Screen: This refers to the degree of visual definition that is sufficient to produce well defined characters, even at large type sizes, as well as smoothly defined curves in graphic images on a *computer* screen or *monitor*.

High-end Machine: This can refer to a *computer* or *server* that is at the top of a company's offerings and includes features or capabilities likely to be needed only by the most demanding users or professionals.

High-end Server: This is a *server* which is capable of supporting a large number of *workstations* and *personal computers*, usually in excess of one hundred machines.

High-level Languages: English-like coding schemes which are procedure, problem and user orientated, they must therefore be translated to *machine code* instructions before a *computer* can obey them. The most common high level languages are ALGOL, BASIC, COBOL, FORTRAN and PASCAL.

Hollerith Analyser: This was a machine developed by Herman Hollerith to count the 1890 U.S. census. It represented the first automatic *data processing* machine and made use of a hand punch to record the data in punch cards and then made use of a tabulating machine to count their totals. The company which Hollerith formed to sell his machine on a worldwide basis for accounting purposes, was later merged into the company that was to be renamed International Business Machines, IBM.

Horizontal Software Compatibility: This refers to the ability of different types of *applications software* (which may be produced by different companies) to transfer data easily between one another without any special operations. For example, a suite of *programs* for *word processing*, *spreadsheet* operations and graphics work could transfer data between each other through the use of a multi-finder *operating system*.

IBM Compatible: This refers to a *personal computer* that operates all or almost all of the *software* developed for the IBM *personal computer* (whether in PC, XT, or AT form) and accepts the *expansion boards*, adapters and *peripheral* devices developed for the IBM *systems*.

Icon: A pictorial symbol which appears in a display whose shape indicates its nature.

Information Software: This is *software* that is used to present the user with specific information as opposed to control *software* or *operating system software* that might be transparent or unobserved by the user.

Information Technology (IT): The distribution and use of information by means of *computers* and *telecommunications* products, *systems* and *networks*.

Ink-Jet Printer: A non-impact *printer* that uses a stream of charged ink to 'paint' characters. Ink-jet printers are controlled by digitally-stored information.

Input: Information received by a *computer*, or its *storage devices*, from outside. Data that is submitted to the *computer* for processing.

Input Facilities: See *Input/Output Devices*.

Input/Output (I/O): A general term for the equipment used to communicate with a *computer* and the data involved in the communication.

Input/Output Devices: Devices capable of both transmitting input to a *computer* and of receiving output back from it. Any item of equipment which permits data and instructions to be entered into a *computer's* central *memory*, e.g. Optical Character recognition, keyboards, *terminals*, mice and light pens. Any device capable of receiving information from a central processor. It may be some form of backing storage, or a *peripheral* unit which 'translates' information into another medium, e.g. a *printer* or *VDU*.

Installed Base (IB): This refers to the size of the number of machines, such as *computers* or *printers* that have been installed and are still in use in a particular market segment. They therefore represent the accumulation of previous shipments.

Integrated Circuit (IC): Integrated circuits are the basis of the third generation of *computer* technology and in principle, integrate a number of circuits onto a single '*chip*' of *semiconductor* material, usually silicon (although, more recently, other *semiconductors* such as gallium arsenide are being used in special *applications*). The density of components on a *chip* has increased from the early ones of Small Scale Integration to *Large Scale Integration (LSI)* and then onto *Very Large Scale Integration (VLSI)*, each one being an order of magnitude more dense than the preceding. Its physical form consists of a package between 1 and 5cm in length, and having between 6 and 40 external connections.

Integrated Computer Package: This refers to a *software program* that combines two or more *applications* that are designed to operate in an integrated manner, such as *word processing, spreadsheet* and graphics. For example, Lotus 1,2,3 or Claris Works.

Integrated Program: See *Integrated Computer Package*.

Integrated System: This involves a combination of *hardware* and *software* that is able to operate as if fully compatible. The *end-user* is therefore able to transfer data and *files* between *computers* and between *software* packages with a minimum of effort.

Interface: This normally refers to a shared boundary between two *systems*, or between a *computer* and one of its *peripheral* devices. As such the term is used most frequently to refer to the *hardware* and *software* required to couple together two processing elements in a *computer system*.

Interface Board: An electronic board component used to provide a connection between two parts of a *computer system*, that would otherwise be incompatible.

Interface Card: This is an electronic circuit board, which is able to allow conversion of electronic signals from one type of machine with another, that would not normally be able to communicate with each other. They often work in conjunction with *software interfaces*.

Interface Circuit: An electronic circuit that provides an *interface*.

IT: An acronym for *Information Technology*.

K: A symbol used to denote 1000 (strictly 1024) when referring to specific capabilities of a *computer system*. An abbreviation for kilo, denoting a thousand (10^3). When referring to *storage capacity*, k is generally used to mean about a thousand. For example, a 64k word store actually contains 65,536 words.

Kb: An abbreviation for *Kilobyte*.

Kilobyte (Kb): A measurement of *computer memory*, usually abbreviated to 'K' or 'Kb'. A kilobyte is the closest power of 2 to 1,000. 1K = 1,024 *bytes*.

LAN: An acronym for *Local Area Network*.

Language: A set of rules and representations, used to communicate information with a *computer*, between a *computer* and its user or between *computers*. Low-level languages include assembly language, which uses numbers and *machine code*, which uses mnemonics. In a high-level language, instructions are expressed in more natural language, using words.

Laptop: A small *portable computer* that is light enough to hold on your lap and can be used in transit from internal battery power. The smallest *laptop computers*, which weigh less than six pounds and can fit in a briefcase, are called *notebook computers* and tend to be more expensive than their equivalent desktops.

Large Scale Integration (LSI): This is the fabrication of up to 100,000 discrete *transistor* devices onto one chip in integrated electronics.

Large Scale Integrated Circuit (LSIC): This consists of an electronic *integrated circuit chip*, which contains between 3000 to 100,000 discrete *transistors*.

Laser Printer: A type of non-impact *printer* that uses a laser to produce images on the drum of an electrostatic *printer*/copier, and thus onto paper.

LCD: An acronym for *Liquid Crystal Display*, which is a technology used for displaying data. It operates by making use of the characteristics of certain crystals which are in the liquid phase at room temperature and which darken under the influence of an electrical field. LCDs are used in nearly all calculators and digital watches where the fact that it takes a relatively long while to produce the display is not important, but the extremely low current required is important (so that the batteries need to be changed rarely).

LED: An acronym for *Light Emitting Diode*.

Light Emitting Diode (LED): This is a *diode* which glows when current is applied. LEDs are often used in *computers* (for example, to indicate various fault conditions) and were used in early digital watches. However, although the display was bright, it could not be left on all the time due to the power used and so the use of LEDs in such circumstances has, to a very large extent, been superseded by LCDs.

Local Area Network (LAN): This consists of a system which links together *computers*, electronic mail, *word processors* and other electronic office equipment to form an inter-office, or inter-site *network*. Such *networks* usually also give access to 'external' *networks*, e.g. public telephone and data transmission *networks*, viewdata, information retrieval systems, etc.

Local Language Packages: This refers to *applications* packages such as *word processing*, which have been converted into the native language of a particular country. For example the local language version of a *word processing program* that was originally produced in the United States in American English would need to be converted into French for sale in France and even into English style of English for sale in Britain. The last example would be particularly important to allow for differences in page set-up sizes and spelling dictionaries, where there exist major differences between the US and the UK version of English.

Logarithm: This was developed by John Napier in 1614 to simplify multiplication and division tasks in mathematics. It represents the exponent indicating the power to which a fixed number, known as the base, must be increased in order to obtain a specific number or variable.

Logic Set: A group of logic instructions in the *computer*.

Logic Unit: A unit within the *computer system* responsible for performing logical instructions.

Low-end Machine: This represents a machine at the bottom end of a company's range of product offerings. As such it is usually inexpensive and may either be a lower performance version of more powerful *systems* or alternatively, may represent a basic machine built around obsolete or near-obsolete technology.

LSI: This is an acronym for *Large Scale Integration*.

Luggable Computer: Most of the early "*portable*" types of *personal computer* developed during the early to mid-1980s were usually quite bulky machines often weighing over 15lbs. Although technically transportable from one location to another, with relatively simple set-up facilities, their heavy weight and bulk often led to users and analysts referring to them as luggable.

Mac: This is an abbreviation for the Macintosh family of *computers* developed by Apple Computer Inc.

Machine Code: The code used in machine *language*. The only set of instructions that a *computer* can execute directly; a cycle that designates the proper electrical states in the *computer* as combinations of 0s and 1s. The actual instructions that are executed by a *computer*. Virtually all modern *computers* are binary and so machine code is expressed as a sequence of '1's and '0's, arranged in words.

Magnetic Core: An iron-alloy doughnut shaped ring about the size of a pin head of which *memory* can be composed; an individual core can store one binary digit; a technology used in *second generation computers*, it has now been overtaken by *semiconductor RAM* memories.

Magnetic Media: The various types of media used in secondary storage on which data recording is effected by writing a magnetic pattern onto the magnetizable surface of the medium. The term distinguishes these types of media from others that use different recording techniques, e.g. optical *disks* and *paper tape*.

Mainframe Computer: A term used to denote a large *computer*, distinguishing it from a *minicomputer* or a *microcomputer*. It is increasingly difficult to define exactly what is meant by each of the terms, but a *mainframe* can be characterised by being able to support a large number of users (often hundreds) interactively, having fairly large amounts of main *memory* (some *megabytes*) and backing store (perhaps of the order of *gigabytes*). The cost of a *mainframe computer* ranges from hundreds of thousands to millions of US dollars. Its name derives from the fact that early *mainframes* were built on a large frame or chassis for use in large centralised *data processing* departments.

Management Information System (MIS): This is a *system* providing information for decision making, usually intended for senior management. It usually consists of a formal *network* that extends *computer* use beyond routine transaction processing and reporting and into the integration of *applications* together with the area of management decision making; its goal is to get the correct information to the appropriate manager at the right time. When originally coined, the term was intended to describe comprehensive computerised management information systems.

Mass Storage: This term refers to that class of secondary *storage devices* capable of storing very large volumes of data; although it offers cost advantages over *disk* storage, it has a much slower retrieval time which is measured in seconds. Also referred to as 'backing storage' or 'bulk storage'.

Massive Parallel Computer: A *mainframe* type of *computer* where more than one processor is active amongst a group of processors at any one time. A massive version of this machine involves a large number of processors all being active at the same time.

Mb: An acronym for *megabyte*.

Megabyte (Mb): This is derived from 'mega', meaning 1 million; 1 megabyte = 1,000,000 *bytes*.

Memory: This is the primary storage area of the *computer*, such as *Random Access Memory*. As such it is distinguished from secondary storage, such as *disk drives*.

Memory Board: An electronic circuit board which houses *memory chips* and can be inserted into a *computer* to provide or expand its *memory*.

Memory Pack: This is a solid state secondary *memory* unit that is used for insertion into a calculator or *palmtop personal computer* and can store *applications* or data.

Metal Oxide Semiconductor (MOS): A product of *semiconductor* technology that, although somewhat slower than LSI bipolar, is significantly less expensive.

Micro: Within the *computer industry* it is the term used as an abbreviation for *microcomputer*, which was the name originally used before *personal computers* became more popular to explain the same type of machine. Technically, it represents one millionth of a space or time measure. However, its more general meaning is small or tiny. In comparison to the then existing *mainframe* and *minicomputers*, the *desktop computers* were very much smaller.

Micro Channel Architecture (MCA): The design specification of IBM's proprietary *Micro Channel Bus*. An MCA-compatible *peripheral* is designed to plug directly into a *Micro* Channel *Bus*, but will not work with other *bus architectures*.

Microcomputer: A *computer* which is based on a *microprocessor*. Although the terms microcomputer and *microprocessor* are often used interchangeably, this usage is incorrect since the latter is merely the *central processing unit* whereas a microcomputer is a complete *computer*, including (usually) primary and secondary storage and *I/O* facilities. Since the 1980s the term *personal computer* has been substituted instead to refer to *desktop* or *portable computers*.

Micro Disks: These are 3 1/2 inch *floppy disks* which were originally developed by Sony and are used as a secondary storage medium on *personal computers*.

Microelectronics: The technique of manufacturing many different interconnected electronic *components* in a small physical space which developed from the use of *integrated circuits* in electronic devices.

Microprocessor: A *central processing unit* implemented on a *chip*. It is an integral part of a *microcomputer*, but does not contain the *I/O interfaces* and *memory unit*.

Millions of Instructions Per Second (MIPS): A measure of processing power. A modern large *computer* would be rated at over 10 MIPS or millions of instructions per second. A measure of computing power, particularly in general purpose *mainframe computers*. A measure of machine performance which defines the number of machine instructions that can be executed every second. A *microcomputer* might execute, say, 0.2 MIPS while an extremely powerful '*super computer*' might execute some hundred MIPS.

Mini: This is an abbreviation for *Minicomputer*.

Mini Supercomputer: This is a category of *supercomputer* that is between 25% to 100% faster than a standard *supercomputer*, but costs less. It is not the same as a *super minicomputer*, which is a class of *minicomputer*.

Minicomputer: A category of *computer* that fits between a *microcomputer* and a *mainframe computer*.

Minifloppy Drive: This is a 5 1/4 inch diskette secondary storage unit.

MIPS: This is an acronym for *Millions of Instructions Per Second*.

MIS: This is an acronym for *Management Information System*.

Modem: A contraction of the term 'modular-demodulator', a device which allows digital signals to be transmitted through an analog medium (usually a telephone line) by using the digital signal to modulate a suitable carrier frequency and of course, reversing the process at the receiving end.

Monitor: A form of television which is used as an output device for a *computer*. It differs from a television set in that the tuning circuitry is absent and (usually) the various signals necessary for colour are separated (red, green, blue and sync) rather than being multiplexed together. There are two types of monitor, 'interlaced' and 'non-interlaced', the former referring to ones where the picture is created as it is in a television set scanning lines 1, 3, 5... then a second scan for lines 2,4,6... whereas a non-interlaced monitor scans them 1,2,3... The quality of the latter is higher than the former.

MOS: This is an acronym for *Metal Oxide Semiconductor*.

MOS Field Effect Transistor (FET): This is a *metal oxide semiconductor* device which has three *terminals*, namely, source, gate and drain. Unlike bipolar devices, FETs are unipolar in nature and the gate is insulated from the source and the drain areas, whilst the channel forms when the gate voltage is applied. Unlike bipolar *transistors*, FETs require very little *input* current to the gate, except for a small pulse, which has the effect of charging or discharging the capacitance of the gate.

Motherboard (Backplane): A plastic board on which circuits are printed and sockets are soldered to create *integrated circuits*.

Mouse: A small device which has a roller ball underneath and can be moved around by hand. As the mouse is moved, so the screen cursor moves in approximately the same direction and distance.

MPU: This is an acronym for *microprocessor* unit. See *Microprocessor*.

MS-DOS: This is an acronym for Microsoft *Disk Operating System* which was developed by Microsoft Corporation as IBM's *disk operating system* on their original *PC*, but which is marketed by IBM as *PC-DOS*.

Multi-tasking: Running several *programs* for one user concurrently.

Multi-user: This refers to a *computer system* that can support a number of users at the same time. See *Multiple-user system*.

Multimedia: Multimedia is as yet fairly poorly defined, since it is still an evolving phenomenon. Generally speaking it refers to the mixing of audio and video *systems* based around a *personal computer* to create interactive *programs*. The *personal computer* and surrounding *peripherals*, including cameras, scanners, *optical character recognition systems*, voice synthesisers, etc. go to make up a multimedia system.

Multimedia Storage: This refers to different storage media used in *multimedia*, such as *CD-ROM* or optical *disks*.

Multimedia Techniques: This refers to the processes used in the production of a *multimedia program*, which can include animated graphics, sound recordings, etc.

Multimedia Technology: See *Multimedia*.

Multiple-user System: A *computer system* that enables more than one person to access *programs* and data at the same time. Each user is equipped with a *terminal*. If the system has just one *central processing unit*, a technique called *time-sharing* provides multiple access by cycling the access period to the processing unit amongst users.

Network: The simplest definition is 'a number of interconnected *computers*'. This simple definition conceals a major field of *computer* science which can be considered to have started in the mid-1960s when various experiments were undertaken in order to interconnect different *computers*. Nowadays, it represents the interconnection of a number of locations or devices by communications facilities. Generically, a network is an interconnected group of nodes. Nodes can be *computers* or *peripheral* devices. The *connectors* between the nodes can be telephone lines or some of the more exotic links such as satellites or microwaves.

Notebook Computer: A *portable* or *laptop computer* that weighs approximately 6 pounds or less.

Object-Oriented: See *Object-Oriented Programming*.

Object-Oriented Programming: This involves the use of a non-procedural *programming language* in which *program* elements are conceptualised as objects that can pass information between each other. They are self contained units that include their own data and *programming* code, as such they can be used to build more complex patterns of performance.

OCR: An acronym for *Optical Character Recognition*.

OEM: An acronym for Original Equipment Manufacturer, which refers to the company that actually manufacturers a piece of *hardware*. Another company then adds value to the OEM's product, either by building it into a *system*, or placing their brand-label on the product, then marketing and selling it under their own name.

Off-line: Devices are said to be on-line or off-line. Operations are said to take place on-line or off-line. Simply stated, on-line means under the control of a *computer* and off-line means not under the control of a *computer*.

Office Automation (OA): The term was used extensively during the 1970s to describe the *application* of *computers* to office tasks such as electronic filing systems, *word processing systems*, *computer* graphics systems, electronic mail, *desktop publishing*, decision support *systems*, *database* management *systems* and teleconferencing *systems*.

Open Architecture: A *computer system* in which all the *system* specifications are made public so that other companies can be encouraged to develop add-on products such as *peripherals* and extensions for the *system*.

Open System: This refers to *hardware* and *software computer systems* where the architectural design conforms to non-proprietary standards rather than to the standards of a specific supplier of *hardware* or *software*. In principle, the *hardware* and *software* should then be able to operate in conjunction with any other products that conform to the same open *systems* standard.

Open Systems Interconnect (OSI): An international standard for the organisation of *local area networks (LANs)* established by the International Standards Organization (ISO) and the Institute of Electrical and Electronic Engineers (IEEE).

Operating Memory: The *memory* used in temporary primary *memory* to perform a process.

Operating System (OS): A set (usually large) of *programs* which *interface* between the *applications programs* and the *hardware*. The complexity of operating systems varies from small ones on *personal computers* which perform relatively few functions to highly complex (and large) ones on *mainframes*. The latter are often the result of thousands of man-years of effort, however, as *personal computers* become more powerful, their operating systems are becoming increasingly complex as they are now incorporating an increasing amount of graphical and networking capabilities.

Optical Character Encoders/Decoders: Devices for encoding or decoding the flow of data between optical character recognition products such as *scanners*, electronic cameras and bar-code readers.

Optical Character Recognition (OCR): Devices capable of 'reading' characters on paper and converting the optical images into binary-coded data.

OS: An acronym for *Operating System*.

OS/2: A multi-tasking *operating system* for IBM *PC*-compatible *computers* that provides protection for *programs* running simultaneously and enables the dynamic exchange of data between *applications*.

Output Facilities: See *Input/Output Devices*.

Palmtop Computer: These are *personal computers* which are small enough in size to fit comfortably into a person's hand, whilst operated by the other hand. Early and many subsequent designs of palmtops had or have specialised keyboards or keypads, whilst some carried QWERTY layouts. In effect, they look like large hand-held calculators, except they are more powerful. The most recent generation of these machines are designed for use with a pen based *input* and are known as *Personal Digital Assistants*.

Paper Tape Punch: A data recording medium in which characters are represented by horizontal patterns of holes punched across the width of the tape.

Paper Tape Reader: A device capable of sensing the pattern of holes punched in a tape, and of converting them to appropriate binary-coded signals.

Paper Tape Read-out Printer: See *Paper Tape Reader*.

Parallel Transmission: Processing or transmission of instructions or data simultaneously, as opposed to *serial transmission*.

Pascaline Calculator: This was a calculating machine designed and developed by the French mathematician, Blaise Pascal during the period of 1640 to 1642. Although it could only add and subtract, it gained attention due to the fact that thereafter some 50 further machines were built after its public presentation in 1645. Apparently, some accountants at the time expressed their concern that they might be replaced by this technology.

PC: An abbreviation for *personal computer* but also used as a marketing label by IBM for their early *personal computers*, hence the IBM PC.

PC-DOS: *Disk operating system* for the IBM *PC*.

PDA: An acronym for *Personal Digital Assistant*.

Pen Based Systems: *Personal computers* equipped with pattern recognition circuitry so that they can recognise human handwriting as a form of data *input*.

Pen Based Technology: See *Pen Based Systems*.

Peripheral: This is a device attached to a *computer*, such as a *disk drive, scanner, VDU* or *printer*, which is usually under the control of a central processor.

Personal Assistant: Today's use of the term personal assistant tends to refer to people who are usually responsible for assisting executives or managers in their tasks. These may include filing, taking dictation or audio-typing, producing letters, arranging meetings, acting as a gatekeeper, controlling information flows between their boss and the outside world. Tomorrow's use of this term is likely to grow from the current early versions of *PDAs* or *Personal Digital Assistants*, which are currently mobile compact machines, but which may eventually become a *network* of *systems* to support the individual on a worldwide basis.

Personal Computer: A general-purpose *microcomputer*. Originally a *computer* that can be used by one person alone, but which now may be used by others on a *multiple-user system*.

Personal Digital Assistant (PDA): A small *palmtop* sized *personal computer*, increasingly incorporating *pen based technology*.

Personal Workstation: A *workstation* used by a single user, often referred to as a Single User *Workstation* or SU/WS.

Piracy: The activity of illegal copying of *hardware* or *software* designs for commercial resale in the *personal computer* market.

Planar Process: A process for the production of *semiconductor* materials.

Planar Technique: See *Planar Process*.

Plotter: An *output device* that produces hard-copy graphical images. Most plotters now are able to print in different colours by the use of a set of pens (four or eight) and either the pens are able to move on both axes or they can move along one axis and the paper moves in the other. However, they have been superseded in many instances by colour *laser printers*.

Polysilicon: A combination of more than one type of silicon conducting based materials.

Portability: An attribute of a *program* which can be transferred to another *computer system* and run without modification to the *program* or its data.

Portable: This can refer to the ability of a *software program* or *peripheral* to work with a variety of machines (See *Portability*). It is nowadays most commonly used to refer to a *personal computer* that can be carried easily between one place and another. However, it may not necessarily be usable when a mains supply is not available for power.

Power PC: This refers to a joint project between IBM, Apple Computer and Motorola to develop a next generation *personal computer* based upon a Motorola *microprocessor*.

Power Users: This refers to users of *personal computers* and *workstations* who have a demand for large amounts of *memory* and processing power and are usually highly proficient in the use of a number of different *software application programs*.

Printed Circuit Board (PCB): Most of the connections between *chips* and other electronic *components* in a *computer* are made, not by cables, but by copper tracks etched on a fibreglass board, called a circuit board or a printed circuit board (PCB), on which the *components* are mounted.

Printed Circuit Board Substrata: The plastic board on which the *printed circuit board* is located.

Printer: An output device producing hard-copy on paper. There are many types of *printer* including *dot-matrix*, *daisy wheel*, *ink-jet* and *laser*.

Processing Speed: The speed at which a *microprocessor* can work. This is normally expressed in megahertz. The higher the megahertz number, the faster the processor.

Program: This consists of a list of sequential instructions which have been constructed or written in a *programming language*. It is a term used as synonymous with *software*. A distinction can be made between two types of program. In the case of a procedural program, it gives a precise definition of the procedure that needs to be followed by a *computer system* in order to obtain a set of required results. In contrast, a non-procedural program specifies certain constraints that need to be complied to in the results that are produced. However, such a program does not specify the procedure by which these results should be obtained. Instead, the *computer* itself is required to calculate the procedure which is normally determined by a kind of logic function.

Programming: Programming is the process by which a set of instructions is produced for a *computer* to make it perform specified activity. The activity can be anything from the solution of a mathematical problem to the production of a company payroll.

Programming Language: A *language* used for writing *computer programs*.

PROM: An acronym for Programmable *Read Only Memory*. This is a kind of *read-only memory (ROM)* *chip* that can be programmed by the customer rather than the *chip* manufacturer. It is thus able to reflect design requirements of a *computer* company, since the circuit design is not rigid as in the case of *ROMs*.

Proprietary System: A proprietary system refers to the *hardware* and *software* being designed and patented to a particular company or individual. It is not in the public domain and is usually not compatible with other *systems*, except by special conversion processes. Contrast with *Open Systems*.

RAM: An acronym for *Random Access Memory*.

Random Access Memory (RAM): *Memory* for which the time of access is independent of the data item required. All primary storage such as core and *semiconductor memory* are random access, so that *memory* can be read from, or written to, in a random access fashion.

Read Only Memory (ROM): As implied, a form of storage which can only be read from and not written to. Once information has been entered into this *memory*, it can be read as often as required, but cannot normally be changed. Currently available video *disks* are read-only devices.

Real Time: This involves an immediate response. It is used in *computers* to refer to the process by which a *computer system* responds instantaneously to a command. In business *systems* it is usually applied to high-volume transactions processing and reservations *systems*, whilst in process control of machine tools and manufacturing it is always in real-time operations. In areas such as avionics, on-board aircraft *computers* have to operate in real-time, in order to provide pilots with a reflection of what is happening to the aircraft at any given moment and in order to make immediate responses in areas such as flight-control and performance *systems*.

Register: A dedicated *memory* location within the *central processing unit*, generally having a capacity equivalent to the word size of the *computer* concerned and having specific properties for use during arithmetic and/or logical operations.

RISC: This is an acronym for Reduced Instruction Set Computing, which is a *central processing unit* *(CPU)* in which the number of instructions the processor can execute is reduced to a minimum to increase processing speed.

ROM: See *Read Only Memory*.

Scanner: This is a *peripheral* device that digitises artwork or photographs and can then store the image as a *file*, which can be manipulated or merged into a text or other form of page layout.

Scanning: The process of creating an electronic *file* by means of a *scanner*.

Seamless Environment: This refers to a *computer system* which may be based upon a number of different *systems*, but which appears to the user as one consistent *system*.

Second Generation Computer: A *computer* using *transistors* as its basic *component* technology; faster, smaller, more powerful and more reliable than first generation; higher-level *programming languages* and *operating systems* available.

Semiconductor: Any material which acts as an electrical conductor when the voltage is above a certain level, and as a resistor when it is below it (i.e. it can act as an electronic switch). Semiconductor technology has been able to produce in great quantity electronic *components* that are microscopic in size. They have also been produced very economically and under many different sub-technologies within semiconductor technology. Perhaps the best known semiconductor is silicon which is used in making *chips*, but other semiconductors are used for this purpose (e.g. germanium and gallium arsenide).

Serial Transmission: This involves a method of data communication in which transmission of *bits* of data is accomplished by sending the *bits* one after another, with a start and stop *bit* to mark the beginning and end of the data. The process is cheaper than *parallel transmission* and because of the lower speed can be used on telephone lines.

Server: See *File Server*.

Server Based Networks: See *File Server and Network*.

Shrink-wrapped Software: This refers to the mass produced type of *applications* and *operating systems software programs* which are packaged in "shrink-wrapped" polythene packing for the consumer marketplace.

Silicon Chip: A wafer of silicon providing a *semiconductor* base for a number of electrical circuits.

Silicon Gate Technology: This is a particular gate array used in *semiconductor* technology.

Simulation: This involves the use of *computer applications* to imitate the behaviour of some existing or intended system. Examples of areas where simulation is used include *communications network* design, where simulation can be used to explore overall behaviour, traffic patterns, trunk capacity or aircraft simulation.

Simulation Models: See *Simulation*.

Single Board Systems: This refers to a *printed circuit board* on which are located all the core parts of a *computer*, namely, the *microprocessor, memory, input/output*, together with a clock.

Slide Rule: This is a mechanical hand-held form of calculator with a high degree of accuracy that consists of two strips of material, with the narrow piece sliding along a groove located in the wider piece, which surrounds it on both sides. Each piece is calibrated in logarithmic scales, trigonometric functions and other scientific measures. Originally they were made of wood, but later the material changed to plastic. Some designs are circular in design, such as in an aviation pilot's slide rule. However, the demand for slide rules was dramatically reduced from the 1970s onwards, with the development of electronic hand-held calculators.

Small-systems Computer: This is a *computer* that was used in small businesses based upon low-end *minicomputers*, prior to the development of more powerful *personal computers*.

Software: A collection of *programs* and routines providing instructions to a *computer system*. It is also a synonym for '*computer programs*'. Software is generally divided into *application* software and *systems* software (where the word '*program*' may be used in place of 'software').

Software Developers: These may be individuals or a company involved in developing *software programs*. It is a term often used to describe the suppliers of *software applications programs*. Furthermore, it involves more than simply *programming*, since it includes the design of the *software* objectives and requires a sound understanding of the *application* for which the *software* is being written. For example, an accounting *software* developer would need to have a thorough grasp of accounting procedures and principles as well as being able to design a *software* package that could perform the tasks of book-keeping and other accounting activities and records.

Software House: A company whose primary business is to produce *software* or assist in the production of *software*.

Software Program: See *Software*.

Spreadsheet: This is a *program* to help with management planning and budgeting usually in a columnar and row pad layout.

Stand-alone: The ability of a piece of equipment to operate independently of any other equipment. For example, a *personal computer* or *workstation* that can operate independently is often called a 'stand-alone *system*', or a *printer* that has its own built-in processor and can print material without dependency upon a *computer* processor, once it has received the data.

Storage Capacity: This refers to the amount of data that can be stored in a *storage device*. It is usually measured in *bytes* and may range from a few *kilobytes* up to a number of *gigabytes*.

Storage Device: This is a device that can receive data and then store it for subsequent retrieval. The variation in such devices is widespread and is based upon the type of medium used, which is commonly either magnetic or optical, the *storage capacity* and the speed of access and retrieval. *Semiconductor* devices used in *random access memory* may take only a few nanoseconds to retrieve data, however, the cost of storing data in this medium is much higher than for secondary storage devices, which naturally take a little longer to operate and are usually in the order of milliseconds or even seconds. In effect, the faster the performance, the more expensive the medium.

Storage Disk: This represents a specific secondary storage technology used to store and retrieve data, such as a magnetic *disk*, magnetic tape, or optical *disk*.

SU (Single User): This is a term used to distinguish *personal computers* and *workstations* that are used by a single user and are independent of other *computers* or *networks*. In the early days of the *personal computer industry*, all *personal computers* were single user, since they did not usually incorporate any communications capabilities with external *computers*. However, the growth of *local area networks* and the *downsizing* phenomenon has meant that a large proportion of *personal computers* and *workstations* are now linked together through some form of *communications network*, which means data can be shared between multiple users.

Sub-systems: This refers to the component parts that go to make up a *system*. In the *computer* itself it can refer to the *microprocessor, input/output*, clock and *logic unit*, whilst in a *system* that consisted of a *local area network*, then the sub-system would comprise of the various *personal computers, servers, workstations, printers* and other *system* units within the overall *system*.

Supercomputer: A sophisticated, expensive *computer* designed to execute complex calculations at the maximum speed permitted by state of the art technology. They are used mainly for scientific research, especially for modelling complex, dynamic *systems*, which incorporate a multitude of variables, such as the world's weather, macroeconomics, or the motions of a galaxy's spiral arms.

Super Minicomputer: A medium sized *multi-user computer* whose *systems* and architecture have evolved from the *minicomputers* of a few years ago. Such a machine may in fact be more powerful than a basic *mainframe computer*, however, they hold different development paths.

Supplemental Components: These refer to additional *components* such as packaging, boxes, etc. in addition to the electronic *components* necessary to make-up a *personal computer*.

Switching Devices: These are devices that may be mechanical or electronic in nature and which direct the flow of electrical, electronic or optical signals. In early *computers*, these consisted of electrical vacuum tube valves, which were replaced by *transistors*, which were condensed into *integrated circuits*, then into *large scale integrated circuits*, *very large scale integrated circuits* and then finally the *microprocessor*. In this switching device there are thousands of switching devices within the *silicon chip*. In telecommunications technology, early switching *systems* were electro-mechanical in nature, but here too, electronics has led to *microprocessor* based and optical *systems*.

Switching Theory: This involves the theory of manipulative methods used in switching algebra, which is a specific branch of algebra. It includes Boolean-algebra together with state-diagram methods of description, in addition to minimization methods.

SX: This refers to a specific version of the Intel 386 *microprocessor*, which handles data internally, 32 *bits* at a time, just as the DX does, but it communicates with *RAM* at 16 *bits* at a time. The only advantage of the SX is that it is easier and cheaper to incorporate into older *personal computer* designs.

Systems: These consist of something which may be regarded as an entity in its own right, but at the same time consisting of a set of related parts, organs or *components*. In the field of computing, it can have many meanings, depending on the context in which the term is used. Most frequently, in its simplest form, it refers to a set of *hardware* units comprising of the *computer* itself, a *monitor*, keyboard and *printer*, together with the associated *operating systems software* and *applications programs*. However, an increasing number of cases refer to a *computer* system that is corporate wide, known as the enterprise system, wherein hundreds of *computers* and *peripherals* together with their relevant *software* are linked together in one giant system.

Systems Integration: This involves the task or activity of integrating various different types of *hardware* and *software* into a single *system*.

Systems Integrator: This refers to a person or organisation involved in the process and activity of *systems integration*.

Tabulator: This is a machine that automatically feeds punched cards at the same time as reading data from them. The data is then directly listed and/or totalled for specific sets of card groups.

Tape Back-up Unit: This is a tape-based unit to make high speed copies of secondary data *disks* for security purposes.

Technical Workstation: Although the term *workstation* was used during the 1970s to describe machines such as the Xerox Star, it was not until the 1980s that the *workstation* market really became established. Initially, they consisted of *microprocessor* based *desk-top computers* that were designed for specialised technical tasks such as *computer aided design* or *computer aided engineering*. However, with the development of *local area networks* and more powerful *personal computers*, the term has become somewhat more general and may sometimes be used to describe any *personal computer* or *terminal* used in a working environment. Furthermore, an increasing number of the original *workstation* manufacturers are now marketing their machines for commercial office applications. In this convergence, technical *workstations* is a term used therefore to refer to *workstations* that are used for technical purposes and *applications*.

Telecommunications: This refers to a *system* incorporating the combined use of *computer* and *telecommunications* facilities. It is based around the science of transmitting data over distances. The term is often used to refer to transferring voice or data through links provided by PTTs.

Telecommunications Common Carrier: These are companies that provide *network* operations. They may range from specialised common carriers who own and operate their own *networks* to others who lease transmission capacity from other *network* operators and resell it to business users.

Telecommunications Industry: This refers to those groups of companies involved in the manufacture and/or marketing of *hardware* and *software* products and *systems* for use in the field of *telecommunications*.

Telecommunications Infrastructure: This refers to the overall structure of the *telecommunications industry* in a particular region or country. The more developed this infrastructure, then the more the private and government sectors can develop their *information technology* based services and operations.

Terminal: A device for sending and/or receiving data over a *communications* channel. It usually consists of both a keyboard and a *VDU*. The term is sometimes used to describe a single *workstation*, e.g. of a *word processor*, whether or not it possesses a communications capability.

Toggle Switch: A manually operated switch which can be set to either of two positions.

Tower Personal Computer: This refers to a *personal computer* which is housed in a floor standing cabinet that is taller than it is wide. *Desktop computers* can be made into a tower shape by turning them onto their sides and then mounting them onto a floor mounted base. However, more powerful high-end *personal computers* are now configured and built in a tower design since they are too large to fit onto the desktop.

Transistor: An electronic device made of semi-conducting material which can be used to amplify or switch signals, it represents a technological stage in the development of electronic devices; superior to valve *technology*, but inferior to *integrated circuits (chips)*; the technology of *second-generation computer systems*. The name derives from transfer of electricity across a resistor.

Transparent System: In computing terminology this refers to a hidden *computer* operation or entity that programmers have made invisible so that the *end-user* remains unaware of its existence.

Turnkey System: Jargon used for a *microprocessor system* that is supplied and installed completely ready to use. Just 'turn the key'! The contrast is with a *system* that requires setting-up/*programming* before it can do anything useful.

UCSD-p : An abbreviation for the *operating system*, USCD Pascal which was developed as a *portable system* to run on a variety of *microcomputers* at the University of California and later marketed by

Softtech., Inc. The same technique is applied to other *languages* in the p-system *software*.

UNIX: An *operating system* originally developed by Bell laboratories in 1971 for use on DEC PDP 11 *minicomputers*. It was intended to provide a simple uniform environment in which relatively small numbers of users, with considerable share interests over and above the fact that they were all using the same *computer system*, could collaborate on a shared project. Although it has become very popular and has been implemented on a very wide range of *systems*, there also exists some divergence between a number of competing versions, which has now led to a movement toward an internationally agreed definition of a UNIX standard led by AT&T.

User Base: This is a term used in market data which refers to the demand characteristics of existing users.

User-friendly: A term applied to *computer hardware* or *software* facilities which are designed to be simple for the user to understand and operate. Such facilities are in contrast to the highly technical origins of most *computer systems*, which were developed by technicians for use by technicians.

User Interface: This refers to that part of an *operating system* to which the user has direct access and through which the user performs various tasks on the *computer*. Examples include the use of a mouse with bit-mapped graphics and the use of *windows*.

User Memory Capacity: This refers to the *memory* capacity available on a single user's *personal computer* or *workstation*.

Utilities: This represents the collection of *programs* that forms part of every *computer system* and provides a variety of functions to assist the user in achieving more efficient performance in the use of the *computer* in areas such as *printing*, text retrieval or file searching.

Vacuum Tube Valve: This was the original technology for manufacturing electronic *components*; inferior to *transistor* technology and characteristic of the technology found in first-generation *computer systems*.

Value Added Reseller (VAR): This refers to the type of distribution channel which adds value to *computer hardware* or *software* products. For example, they may offer training or *software* consultancy services.

Valve Technology: This refers to the technology used for electrical machines which made use of *vacuum tube valves*.

VAR: An acronym for *Value Added Reseller*.

VDU Monitor: The term VDU is an acronym for *Visual Display Unit*. Also see *Monitor*.

Video Conferencing: Also referred to as teleconferencing. This involves a number of participants being able to view each other between remote and/or separate locations by means of video cameras and audio monitoring equipment. The *system* requires a high bandwidth of television capacity set up in a *network* that makes use of coaxial cables, optical fibres and microwave and/or satellite transmission. By making use of this technology, company executives can for example hold meetings between Tokyo, London and San Francisco and interact with each other across the screen, in much the same way as television news readers interact with their reporters in the field who are broadcasting "live" in real-time.

Videoboard: These are *printed circuit boards* that facilitate the generation of graphics and text on the display screen of a *personal computer*.

Videophone: This is a telephone *system* that has a built-in camera and display *monitor*, which allows the user to see a moving image of the person at the other end of the line, at the same time as hearing their voice. Although piloted in France and elsewhere during the 1970s, the technology has only recently improved sufficiently to make it a potential commercial product, both in terms of performance and cost. However, the quality and speed of image transmission is still relatively poor and very slow, making use of phased refreshing of the image. One does not therefore receive an image that is near to television standard. However, in time this will undoubtedly become available.

Virtual Reality: This is a form of artificial reality created by the use of *computer systems* which are based upon *computer* art, graphics and *simulation* techniques. In a virtual reality system, the user is projected into three dimensional space and surrounded by images generated by the *computer*. These may include buildings, people or any other object or creature designed into the *software program*. Furthermore, the *system* can be interactive with the user. At this time, virtual reality is in its infancy and based upon *personal computer systems*, with users wearing a glove and helmet with built-in stereoscopic displays of the *computer* generated environment. The glove allows users to point and manipulate illusory objects in their view. Currently, such *systems* are used mainly in the commercial markets as a game, where users can hold a gun or sword and fight with other users and/or *computer* generated persons and creatures. As such these *systems* represent a form of three dimensional video-game. However, the technology of high-performance simulation which is based upon *mainframe* and/or *minicomputer systems* has been used for some time in areas such as the military for training tank operators or in aviation for training pilots. In these larger *systems*, the user sits in a mock-up of the actual tank or aircraft and the *computer* simulates the outside environment in response to the user's actions at the controls of the tank or aircraft. Such *systems* are now so sophisticated, that they are used for most of the training and checking of airline pilots. In time, virtual reality is likely to become a major industry in its own right, with *applications* from entertainment, through architectural design, to *simulation* of virtually every process of activity imaginable.

Visual Display Unit (VDU): This is a device equipped with a *cathode ray tube* for the visual display of information.

Voice Encoder/Decoder: These are electronic devices that convert voice signals to an electronic format for processing by a *computer* or convert electronic signals in a *computer* back to a voice output via a synthesiser and speakers.

Windows: This refers to a rectangular shaped frame that appears on a *computer* screen in which one can view a document, *spreadsheet* or graphical display. In a windowing environment, it is possible to run a number of *applications programs* concurrently with windows open for different documents or *files*. The success of Microsoft's Windows *program* has meant that many *personal computer* users associate the term "windows" with this *program*.

Windows Graphical Interface: This refers to the format of a windowing environment which provides the user with *windows*, pull-down menus, on-screen-fonts and scroll bars.

Windows NT: Microsoft's Windows New Technology.

Word Processing: A system specifically designed for the manipulation of text, both as individual characters and as logically related groups of characters (i.e. words and phrases). The use of *computer systems* to edit and format text.

Word Processor: A *system* designed specifically for *word processing*.

Workstation: These originated as *stand-alone desk-top computers* used for technical *applications*. During the late 1980s they have converged with high-end *personal computers* and now run a number of commercial *applications*. Distinctions between the two types of machine are now difficult to make, however, most *workstations* are based upon *RISC* related technology.

Workstation Network: A *network*, based upon a number of *workstations*.

BIBLIOGRAPHY

Altman, Lawrence Special Report, "Memories, It's a User's Paradise: Cheaper RAMs, Reprogrammable ROMs, CCDs and Bubbles Coming Along", *Electronics,* 20 January, 1977.

Bain, J. S. *Barriers to New Competition*, Harvard University Press, 1956.

Baker, R. H. *Downsizing: How to Get Big Gains from Smaller Computer Systems*, McGraw-Hill, 1992.

Bell, Daniel *The Coming of Post Industrial Society*, Basic Books, New York, 1973 and Harper and Row, New York, 1976, Heinemann, London, 1974.

Blackburn, J. D. *Time-Based Competition: The Next Battle Ground for American Manufacturing*, Business One Irwin, 1991.

Blodgett, J. H. Herman Hollerith, Data Processing Pioneer, unpublished Master's Thesis, Drexel Institute of Technology, 1968.

Bonoma, Thomas V. *The Marketing Edge*, The Free Press, 1985.

Bowden, Lord (ed.), *Faster than Thought*, London, 1953.

Braun, Ernest and MacDonald, Stuart *Revolution in Miniature: History and Impact of Semiconductor Electronics*, Cambridge University Press, 1978.

Business Week, Cover Story. Quote from unknown Tandy Corporation Executive at time of IBM's launch of the Personal Computer, 3 October 1983.

Business Week, "Inside Intel", 1 June 1992.

Business Week, "Microsoft", 24 February 1992.

Business Week, "Savvy Consumers Keep PC Makers Hopping", 2 November 1992.

Capra, Fritjof *The Tao of Physics*, Bantam, 1980.

Caves, R. E. and Porter, M. "From entry barriers to mobility barriers", *Quarterly Journal of Economics*, Vol.91., May 1977.

Cecchini, P., Catinat, M. and Jacquemin, A. *The European Challenge 1992: The Benefits of a Single Market*, Wildwood House, 1988.

Chandler, A. D. "The enduring logic of industrial success", *Harvard Business Review*, March-April 1990.

Cool, K. O. and Schendel, D. E. "Performance differences among strategic group members", *Strategic Management Journal*, 1988.

Dataquest, *Dataquest Personal Computer Industry Report*, 1983.

de Bono, Edward *The Use of Lateral Thinking*, Pelican Books, 1967.

Decision Resources, "The Personal Computer Industry", *Research Letter*, L780901, Arthur D. Little, 7th September, 1978.

Decision Resources, "The Personal Computer Industry - An Update", *Research Letter, Impact Services*, L791002, Arthur D. Little, 12 October 1979.

Decision Resources, "The Outlook for the U.S. Personal Computer Industry", Arthur D. Little, T811201, December 1981.

Dimnet, Ernest *The Art of Thinking*, 1928.

Dosi, G. "Technological Paradigms and Technological Trajectories", *Research Policy*, Vol.11., 1982.

Dostoevsky, F. *The Idiot*, Magarshack, David, translator, 1868.

Dudley, James *1992: Strategies for The Single Market*, Kogan Page, 1989.

Eliot, T. S. *The Four Quartets*.

Ferguson, C. H. "Computers and the Coming of the U.S. Keiretsu", *Harvard Business Review*, July-August 1990.

Fertig, Robert T. *The Software Revolution: Trends, Players, Market Dynamics in Personal Computer Software*, North Holland, 1986.

Fiegenbaum, A. Dynamic aspects of strategic groups and competitive strategy: Concepts and empirical examination in the insurance industry, unpublished doctoral dissertation, University of Illinois at Urbana-Champaign, 1987.

Fiegenbaum, A. and Thomas, H. "Strategic groups and performance: The US insurance industry 1980-1984", *Strategic Management Journal*, Vol.11. 1990.

Forrester, Tom (ed.), *The Microelectronics Revolution*, Blackwells, 1980.

Freiberger, Paul and Swaine, Michael *Fire in the Valley: The Making of the Personal Computer*, Osborne/McGraw-Hill, 1984.

Fylstra, D. H. "Software: The Lever in Personal Computer Sales", *The Rosen Electronics Letter*, 21 July, 1980.

Galbraith, J. R. *Designing Complex Organisations*, Addison-Wesley, 1973.

Ghazanfar, A. Analysis of Competition in the Office Reprographics Industry in the UK. unpublished doctoral thesis, London University, 1984.

Gilder, George *Microscosm, The Quantum Revolution in Economics and Technology*, Simon and Schuster, 1989.

Goldstine, Herman H. *The Computer, from Pascal to von Neumann*, Princeton University Press, 1972.

Hammer, M. "Re-engineering Work: Don't Automate, Obliterate", *Harvard Business Review*, July-August 1990.

Harrigan, K. R. Strategies for Declining Industries, unpublished doctoral dissertation, Harvard Graduate School of Business Administration, 1979.

Hendricks, C. H. *The Rightsizing Remedy: How Managers can respond to the Downsizing Dilemma*, Business One Irwin, 1992.

Hopkins, Gerard Manley *Ecce Homo*.

Hunt, M. S. Competition in the Major Home Appliance Industry 1960-1970, unpublished doctoral thesis, Harvard University, 1972.

International Data Corporation, Japan Personal Computer Market Review and Forecast: 1991-1996, IDC Report, Massachusetts, U.S.A., August 1992.

International Data Corporation, IBM Data and Strategy Book, IDC Report, Massachusetts, U.S.A., 1983.

Irving, Washington *Notoriety, Tales of a Traveller*, 1824.

Jemison, D. B. "The Importance of an Integrative Approach to Strategic Management Research", *Academy of Management Review*, Vol. 6, No. 4, 1981.

Kay, J. (ed.), *"1992: Myths and Realities"*, published by the Centre for Business Strategy Report Series, London Business School, 1989.

Kimberley, Paul *Microprocessors: An Introduction*, McGraw-Hill, 1982.

Kiplinger, Austin H. and Kiplinger, Knight A. *America in the Global '90's*, The Kiplinger Washington Editors, Inc., 1989.

Kogut, B. "Designing Global Strategies: Comparative and Competitive Value-Added Chains", *Sloan Management Review*, Summer 1985.

Kotler, Philip *Marketing Management: Analysis, Planning and Control*, 5th ed., Prentice-Hall, 1984.

Levitt, Theodore *The Marketing Imagination*, The Free Press, 1983.

Lorenz, Christopher *The Design Dimension: Product Strategy and the Challenge of Global Marketing*, Basil Blackwell, 1986.

Mascarenhas, B. "Strategic group dynamics", *Academy of Management Journal*, Vol. 32., 1989.

McCrindle, J. A. "The Origins of Today's Microcomputers", McCrindle, J. A. (ed.), *Microcomputer Handbook*, Blackwell Scientific, 1985.

McGee, J. "Strategic groups: A useful linkage between industry structure and strategic management," Thomas, H. and Gardner, D. M. editors. *Strategic Marketing and Management*, Wiley, 1985.

McGee, J. and Segal-Horn, H. "Strategic Space and Industry dynamics: The implications for international marketing strategy", *Journal of Marketing Management*, Vol. 6, No. 3, 1990.

McGee, J. and Thomas, H. "Strategic Groups: Theory, research and taxonomy", *Strategic Management Journal*, Vol. 7 (2), 1986.

McGee, J. and Thomas, H. in McGee, J. and Thomas, H. (eds.) *Strategic Management Research: A European Perspective*, John Wiley & Sons, 1986.

McGee, J. and Thomas, H. "Making Sense of Complex Industries", in Hood, N. and Vahlne, J. E. (eds.), *Strategies in Global Competition*, Routledge, Kegan Paul, 1988.

McGee, J. and Thomas. H. "*Analysis of sequential entry paths: Entry theory, technological change and industry dynamics*", Unpublished, 1990, (under review).

McGee, J. and Thomas, H. "Strategic Groups and Intra-Industry Competition", *International Review of Strategic Management*, 1992.

Morrow, George. *Business Week*, 3 October, 1983.

Mosely, M. *Irascible Genius, A life of Charles Babbage, Inventor*, London, 1964.

Nelson, R. and Winter, S. *An Evolutionary Theory of Economic Change*, Harvard University Press, 1982.

Noyce, Robert N. "Microelectronics", *Scientific American*, Vol. 237, No. 3.

Noyce, Robert N. "Microelectronics", in Tom Forrester (ed.), *The Microelectronics Revolution*, B. Blackwell, 1980.

Noyce, R. N. and Hoff Jr., M. E. "A History of Microprocessor Development at Intel", *IEEE Micro.*, 8 February, 1981.

Obenzinger, M. M. "The Personal Computer Market: A Profile for Growth", *Industry Review*, Lehman Brothers Kuhn Loeb, January 1983.

Ohmae, K. *Triad Power: The Coming Shape of Global Competition*, The Free Press, 1975.

Oster, S. "Intra-industry structure and the ease of industry change", *Review of Economics and Statistics*, Vol. 64, August 1982.

Parker, J. E. S. *The Economics of Innovation*, Longman, 1978.

Pascal. B. *Pensees*, W. F. Trotter, translator, 1670.

Pavitt, K. "Some Characteristics of Innovative Activities in British Industry", *Omega*, Vol. 11, 1983.

Pavitt, K. "Sectoral Patterns of Technical Change: Towards a Taxonomy and a Theory", *Research Policy*, Vol. 13, 1984.

Pavitt, K. "Technology, Innovation and Strategic Management", in *Strategic Management Research: A European Perspective*, McGee, J. and Thomas, H. (eds.), John Wiley & Sons, 1986.

Pearson, Jamie Parker *Digital at Work: Snapshots from the First Thirty-Five Years*, Digital Press, 1992.

Penrose, E. T. *The Theory of the Growth of the Firm*, Basil Blackwell, 1959.

Pinchot III, Gifford *Intrapreneuring: why you don't have to leave the corporation to become an entrepreneur*, Harper and Row, 1985.

Porter, Michael E. "The Structure within Industries and Company Performance", *Review of Economics and Statistics*, Vol. 61., 1979.

Porter, Michael E. "How Competitive Forces Shape Strategy", *Harvard Business Review*, March-April, 1979.

Porter, Michael E. *Competitive Strategy: Techniques for Analyzing Industries and Competitors*, The Free Press, 1980.

Porter, Michael E. "The Contribution of Industrial Organization to Strategic Management", *Academy of Management Review*, Vol. 6, No. 4, 1981.

Porter, Michael E. *Competitive Advantage, Creating and Sustaining Superior Performance*, The Free Press, 1985.

Prahalad, C. K. and Hamel, G. "The core competence of the corporation", *Harvard Business Review*, May-June 1990.

Rogers, E. M. *Diffusion of Innovations*, The Free Press, 1962.

Scherer, F. M. *Industrial Market Structure and Economic Performance*, Rand-McNally, 1980.

Schumpter, J. A. *Capitalism, Socialism and Democracy*, Harper, 1942.

Senge, P. *The Fifth Discipline: The Art and Practice of the Learning Organisation*, Doubleday/Currency, 1990.

Shakespeare, William *The Tempest*, Act iv, Sc.1.

Shonk, J. H. *Team-Based Organisations: Developing a Successful Team Environment*, Business One Irwin, 1992.

Sideris, George "AMS Brushes off Blows", *Electronics*, 30 August, 1973.

Simmonds, K. "Peaks and Pitfalls of Competitive Marketing", *LBS Journal*, Vol. 10, No.1, presented at the Stockton Lecture at London Business School, January 1985.

Simons, G. L. *Introducing Microcomputers*, The NCC Publications, 1979.

Smith, D. K. and Alexander, R. D. *Fumbling the Future*, William Morrow & Co., 1988.

Smith, P. G. and Reinertsen, D. G. *Developing Products in Half the Time*, New York, Van Nostrand Reinhold, 1991.

Stalk, George "Time - The Next Source of Competitive Advantage", *Harvard Business Review*, July-August 1988.

Stalk, G. and Hout, T. *Competing Against Time: How Time-Based Competition is Reshaping Global Markets*, Free Press, 1990.

Steffens, J. W. Entry Behaviour and Competition in the Evolution of the Personal Computer Industry, (1975-1983), unpublished doctoral thesis, The University of London, 1988.

Steffens, J.W. "The Intelligent Organisation", paper presented at the ITiMA 1993 Conference in Malmo, Sweden, 1993.

Tilton, J. *International Diffusion of Technology: The Case of Semiconductors*, Washington, D. C., The Brookings Institution, 1971.

Time Magazine, "An Easy-Come: Easy-Go World", 5 September, 1983.

Tolstoy, Leo *War and Peace*, Penguin Books edition, 1978.

Torrero, E. A. "Focus on Microprocessors", *Electronic Design*, Vol. 22, No. 18, 1974.

Venture Development Corporation, Report on *The Personal Computer Industry*, 1977.

Venture Development Corporation, "The Personal Computer Industry, II: A Strategic Analysis, 1981-1985", May 1981.

Wilson, Robert W., Ashton, Peter K. and Egan, Thomas P. *Innovation, Competition and Government Policy in the Semiconductor Industry*, Charles River Associates, 1980.

Wolff, Howard "4096-bit RAMS are on the Doorstep", *Electronics*, 12 April 1973.

Yankee Group Report, Boston, 1982.

Yankee Group Report, Boston, 1983.

Young, Stephen and Hamill, James (eds), *Europe and the Multinationals: Issues and Responses for the 1990's*, Edward Elgar, 1992.

INDEX